Happy Birthday! Thank you for
befriending us.
Here is a quotation from the Puritan
John Flavel that will bless your
heart all your days. "The Scripture
teaches us the best way of living,
the noblest way of suffering, and
the most comfortable way of dying."

In Christ,
Jimmy & Mary
09/10/09

RYKEN'S BIBLE HANDBOOK is one of the most accessible reference tools to surface in decades. Tailored to Bible teachers and students alike, this resource provides vital information for understanding every book of the Bible. The authors' years of scholarship and personal daily study of God's Word equip them well to uncover key doctrines and offer tips for application from Genesis to Revelation. **Alistair Begg,** senior pastor, Parkside Church, Cleveland, Ohio, and author of *Pathway to Freedom: How God's Laws Guide Our Lives*

RYKEN'S BIBLE HANDBOOK fulfills the Chinese proverb "Give a man a fish, and you feed him for a day. Teach a man to fish, and you feed him for a lifetime." Readers will learn to analyze and interpret the Bible for themselves, and so feed themselves and the church. Indispensable! **R. Kent Hughes,** senior pastor, College Church, Wheaton, Illinois, and coauthor, with Barbara Hughes, of *Disciplines of a Godly Family*

This book truly delivers on a promise made in its opening pages: "This handbook teaches *how* to study the Bible." Like good tour guides, the authors set us up to anticipate *and participate,* thereby enriching the learning and preserving the joy of personal discovery. They give us a "heads up" on some of the challenges in each book and then suggest ways to approach and meet those challenges. I'm glad to recommend this reference tool. **Jan Howard,** Midwest director, *Neighborhood Bible Studies*

The more I study the Bible, the more I am absolutely convinced that God wrote a Book. No one can refute that it is the preeminent Book in existence. The Bible has traveled more highways, walked more paths, knocked on more doors, and spoken to more people in their mother tongue than any other book. Now with Leland Ryken's masterful help in this practical handbook, you can discover more of the Bible's grandness and get deeper into God's Word for yourself. The more diligently you give yourself to its study, the more convinced you'll be of God's direct involvement in history and in the lives of his people—past and present. **Dr. James MacDonald,** pastor, Harvest Bible Chapel, Arlington Heights, Illinois, and radio Bible teacher on *Walk in the Word*

As a Bible teacher who seeks to help other believers study the Bible, I am always on the lookout for helpful Bible study aids. The new *Ryken's Bible Handbook* is among the best material I have found. I heartily recommend it to all who want to grow in their understanding and application of God's Word. **Jerry Bridges,** Navigators collegiate ministry staff and author of *Growing Your Faith*

RYKEN'S BIBLE HANDBOOK stands out as a well-packed, user-friendly help for studying and teaching the Bible. The handbook does not try to eliminate the hard work of Bible study, as some books on Scripture do, but rather offers resources for it. This is a truly educational treasure trove. All who aim to be discerning biblical Christians will appreciate it enormously. **J. I. Packer,** professor of theology at Regent College and author of *Keep in Step with the Spirit*

Ryken's
BIBLE
handbook

LELAND RYKEN
PHILIP RYKEN
JAMES WILHOIT

Tyndale House Publishers, Inc.
Wheaton, Illinois

Library of Congress Cataloging-in-Publication Data

Ryken, Leland.
  Ryken's Bible handbook / Leland Ryken, Philip Ryken, and James Wilhoit.
    p. cm.
  ISBN-13: 978-0-8423-8401-8 (hardcover)
  ISBN-10: 0-8423-8401-4 (hardcover)
  1. Bible—Criticism, interpretation, etc. I. Title: Bible handbook. II. Ryken, Philip Graham, 1966-. III. Wilhoit, Jim.
IV. Title.
  BS511.3.R94 2005
  220.6′—dc22   2005062273

Printed in Thailand

11 10 09 08 07 06 05
7   6   5   4   3   2   1

contents

introduction

THIS HANDBOOK is a guide that equips readers and teachers of the Bible to conduct explorations of the actual text of the Bible, both individually and in groups. Whereas most handbooks concentrate on either background information or summary of content, this handbook provides tools for analysis. Accordingly, this handbook is filled with "prompts" that lead readers to analyze and interpret the books of the Bible for themselves. Taken one step further, these prompts can easily be translated into discussion questions for a small group Bible study or a personal inductive Bible study.

This handbook is attuned to the literary forms of writing that comprise the Bible. In fact, this book can accurately be called an introduction to the genres (types of writing, such as story, proverb, or genealogy) that make up the Bible, along with guidelines for interpreting each genre. This handbook teaches *how* to study the Bible. Among handbooks it may be unique in being a book of methodology, not simply a summary of biblical content—a handbook devoted to Bible reading and study as *process*, not simply as *product* (where the authors are more concerned with conveying information to their readers).

The distinctive features of this handbook include the following:

- A "fact sheet" presenting at a glance the most important things a reader needs to know about each book of the Bible, including implied purposes, author's perspective, implied audience, things that unify the book, special features of the book, and challenges facing the reader or teacher of the book, with accompanying ways to meet the challenges

- For the longer books of the Bible, a preliminary chart showing the unity and overriding framework of each book in a visual way that is easy to comprehend. (We wish to credit the charts of Irving Jensen as having provided us with the model for how charts can aid a reader's grasp of the unity and organization of a book of the Bible.)

- A host of further helps showing the big patterns in each book of the Bible, along with signposts to how the parts of each book relate to the whole
- Sections tracing clearly the flow of each book from beginning to end, in terms appropriate to the genre (type of writing) of the book
- Highlighting of key events, characters, places, themes, and verses of each book
- Lists of key doctrines in the book, and a section showing how the book contributes to the Bible's story of salvation in Christ
- Suggestions for applying the book
- For each book, a collection of the most helpful insights from published commentary on the book
- One-page articles on the major genres of the Bible (such as story and poetry) and other topics (such as the golden age prophecies of the Old Testament and the religious sects at the time of Jesus)

All Bible handbooks include outlines of the content of the books of the Bible. In regard to the outlines in this book, we have tried to strike a balance between "too much" and "too little." Equally important, you can trust the outlines to be true to the actual contours of the biblical text, as we have avoided smoothing out the complexity of what you will find as you look carefully at the pages of the Bible.

In writing this handbook, we have done our work with a desire to help Christian readers of the Bible to understand the Bible better, and teachers of the Bible to teach it more effectively. We believe the Bible to be God's inspired word to the human race and a guidebook for belief and living. We hope that this handbook will be used by Bible study leaders, students, youth pastors, teachers of children, and anyone else who reads or teaches the Bible. Additionally, this handbook contains enough fresh information to interest preachers and Bible scholars.

The ultimate goal of knowing the Bible is finding salvation through faith in Christ Jesus. As Paul wrote to Timothy, "You have been taught the holy Scriptures from childhood, and they have given you the wisdom to receive the salvation that comes by trusting in Christ Jesus" (2 Timothy 3:15).

Leland Ryken, Philip Ryken, James Wilhoit

part one

THE BIBLE AS A BOOK

THE BIBLE AS A BOOK
God's Revelation to the Human Race

FORMAT. Old Testament: 929 chapters, 23,138 verses; New Testament: 260 chapters, 7,957 verses; Cumulative: 1,189 chapters, 31,095 verses

AUTHORS' PERSPECTIVE. God, the ultimate author, speaks with complete authority and knowledge. God used human authors to write the Bible's individual books, which provide both the human perspective and the divine perspective on life.

PURPOSES OF THE BOOK.
1. A revelatory purpose: The Bible reveals to people the things that God most wants them to know.
2. A salvific (pertaining to salvation) purpose: The Bible is designed to lead people to trust in Jesus Christ for salvation and eternal life.
3. A practical purpose: The Bible shows people how to live and what to avoid.
4. A nurturing purpose: The Bible is a means by which believing readers find refreshment and an infusion of grace.

SPECIAL FEATURES. The divine authority that is evident throughout the Bible; the immense range of subject matter; the large number of types of writing (literary genres); the pervasive religious orientation of the material; a format of two testaments, corresponding to God's old and new covenants with his people; the Bible's unified message across many books from many centuries; the only infallible, inerrant book ever written, and God's only written revelation to humanity

CHALLENGES FACING THE READER OR TEACHER OF THIS BOOK.
1. The immense length and magnitude of the book
2. The ancient strangeness of the Bible's world and customs, when compared to our own

3. The diversity of subject matter and forms of writing
4. The fact that most of the Bible is embodied in distinctly literary forms rather than the utilitarian prose of our daily lives
5. The way in which the Bible's refusal to gloss over human failing convicts us of our own failings
6. The need for spiritual discernment to understand the Bible's spiritual truth

HOW TO MEET THE CHALLENGES.

1. Relinquish the idea that you need to read the Bible through as you read a novel. Instead, read the Bible as you do other anthologies of diverse writings.
2. The Bible requires a "bifocal" approach: First, enter the world of the Bible, and then look *through* that world to your own.
3. Relish the Bible's different forms of expression.
4. Welcome the opportunity to put into practice what you have learned about literature and to learn more about how literature works.
5. Accept the Bible's bad news about human behavior, and pay attention to what the Bible says about God's gracious solution to the problem of human sinfulness.
6. Ask the Holy Spirit to guide you into the truth of God's Word.

FACT SHEET

This great story has within it many complex parts—*fragments of history, law codes, moral systems, stories, poems, prophecies, philosophies, visions, wise sayings, letters—but the main structure or outline is simple. It can be seen as a completed circle which first moves downward from the garden of Eden into the wilderness of human history, and then slowly and painfully back to the starting point, as man proceeds toward Eden restored or the New Jerusalem.*

ALVIN AND HOPE LEE
The Garden and the Wilderness

The Bible as a Whole

	Pentateuch	History	Poetry and Proverbs	Major Prophets	Minor Prophets	Gospels	Church History	Epistles to Churches	Pastoral Epistles to Individuals	General Epistles	Apocalypse

Genesis, Exodus, Leviticus, Numbers, Deuteronomy

Joshua through Esther: Twelve Books

Job, Psalms, Proverbs, Ecclesiastes, Song of Songs

Isaiah, Jeremiah, Lamentations, Ezekiel, Daniel

Hosea through Malachi ("The Book of the Twelve")

Matthew, Mark, Luke, John

Book of Acts

Romans through Colossians (Seven Epistles)

Thessalonians through Philemon (Six Epistles)

Hebrews through Jude (Eight Epistles)

Book of Revelation

The Old Testament: 39 Books

The New Testament: 27 Books

Christ's Saving Work Promised and Foreshadowed

Christ's Life and Saving Work Accomplished

"Long ago God spoke many times and in many ways to our ancestors through the prophets." (Hebrews 1:1)

"Now in these final days, he has spoken to us through his Son." (Hebrews 1:2)

Most people experience the Bible as a collection of individual pieces. This is not totally wrong, inasmuch as the Bible is made up of individual books. The very word *Bible* (*biblia*) means "little books." But the Bible is also *a* book. The purpose of this introductory chapter on the Bible as a book is to delineate ways in which the Bible forms a unity.

The Form of the Book

In its external format, the Bible is an anthology of diverse works by separate authors. At this level, though not in its content, the Bible reminds us of an anthology of English or American literature. Its individual books were written by at least three dozen human authors over a span of nearly two thousand years. Like other anthologies, the Bible is composed of numerous different genres (types of writing, such as narrative and poetry). This comprehensive anthology, which is a book for all seasons and temperaments, covers every aspect of life.

The Bible as a Story

Although the Bible is not a single story, and even though it includes many nonnarrative genres, it is nonetheless helpful to think of the overall pattern of the Bible as a story. If we take a wide-angle view, the Bible is a series of events having a beginning, a middle, and an end. The beginning is literally the beginning—God's creation of the world, as narrated in Genesis 1–2, and humankind's spoiling of that world, as narrated in Genesis 3. The end of the story is literally the end—God's final destruction and banishment of evil and his establishing of eternal bliss for believers in Christ—as narrated in the book of Revelation. The middle of the story consists of God's providential oversight of fallen human history.

- "The Holy Scriptures are our letters from home." *Augustine of Hippo*
- "Think in every line you read that God is speaking to you." *Thomas Watson*
- "The Bible is worth all other books which have ever been printed." *Patrick Henry*

The overall shape of this story is like a *U* in which events begin in perfection, fall into corruption, and painfully wind their way back to the final defeat of evil and the triumph of good. The crucial turning point is the crucifixion and resurrection of Jesus Christ. Because the Cross entails the horrific death of God's Son, it is the lowest point of all, yet paradoxically this proves to be the basis for elevating humanity to salvation, as the Resurrection proves.

While human actions are important in this story, the story of the Bible is primarily the story of God's working out his purposes in history and

How We Got the Bible

The process that produced our English Bibles involved five distinct steps:

Revelation. This expresses the idea of an unveiling of something that is hidden so that it can be known and understood. When we speak of the Bible as revelation, it is a description of God's actively disclosing to people dimensions of his nature, character, glory, attributes, ways, will, values, and plans—in short, of himself as a person—so that humans may know him. Without revelation, there could be no Scripture.

Inspiration. When we speak of the word *inspiration* theologically, we use it in a different sense from what we mean when we say that an artist is inspired. In theology, inspiration refers to the fact that God infused the process of writing Scripture with his presence, so we can say that the words of Scripture are the very words of God. This does not diminish the genuine human element that was involved in the craft of writing the books of Scripture. The Bible is a product of human and divine activity. God guided the writing of the authors without bypassing their experiences, personalities, and literary craft.

Transmission. Several thousand years ago God gave humans a divinely inspired, self-disclosed, revelatory message. But this would be nothing more than an interesting bit of history were it not for the careful transmission of these texts through the centuries. The Bibles we have today are the product of Hebrew scribes and Christian monks who carefully copied the manuscripts and preserved them accurately.

Canon. The word *canon* means "measuring stick." Since the fourth century, Christians have used *canon* as a term for the authoritative list of books of the Bible. It is a measuring stick in that it reflects the standard for determining the authenticity of books to be read in church and used in worship as the Word of God. The canon was not something imposed on the books of the Bible. It was a matter of *recognizing* the books that had risen to the status of an authoritative canon. This process of recognition occurred over several centuries and was never marked by a single up-and-down vote. The formation of the canon was a process of determining a book's historicity and in the case of the New Testament, ascertaining a clear apostolic connection.

Translation. The Bible was written in Hebrew, Aramaic, and Greek. To be of practical use, the Bible needs to be in the language of the people. The oldest and most important translation of the Hebrew Scriptures (into Greek) is what we know as the Septuagint. This translation had its origins in the third century BC in Alexandria, Egypt, and was the Bible used in the earliest churches. The impulse to translate the Bible continued with the famous Latin translations, and it is still going on today as the gospel is carried to every tribe and tongue.

eternity. Not only is God the One in control, but he also has a plan that unfolds as the story progresses. It is a story of providence (oversight and provision for the world); judgment against evil; and redemption from destruction through the person of his Son, Jesus Christ. (For more on the story dimension of the Bible, see "The Story Lines of the Bible," page 9.)

The protagonist, or central character, in the story is the triune God. The unifying plot conflict is the great spiritual battle between good and evil, between God and Satan. God's unfolding plan—centered on the saving work of Jesus Christ—weaves its way through this plot conflict. The setting encompasses total reality, including heaven, earth, and hell.

The Cast of Characters

The leading character, or protagonist, of the Bible is God. He is the One whose presence as Father, Son, and Holy Spirit unifies the story of universal history with its myriad of details. The characterization of God is the central motif, or theme, of the Bible, and it is pursued from beginning to end. Correspondingly, a question that will continually yield analytic insights for individual passages in the Bible is, *What do we learn about the character of God in this passage?*

All other characters and events interact with this divine protagonist. They are ultimately judged according to their relationship with God: He rewards those who seek him and depend on him for salvation, and he punishes those who rebel against him. The cast of characters appears endless. In one way or another, the Bible encompasses all creatures, including ourselves.

A distinctive feature of the Bible is the supernatural world that surrounds and transcends earthly existence. Earthly existence is not self-conained. Events and human experiences keep reaching beyond the earthly and physical realm to the supernatural and spiritual realm. Seemingly mundane events such as the falling of rain or the birth of a child are shown to be part of an unseen spiritual reality, which God calls people to believe in by faith.

Three Impulses That Govern Biblical Writers

One way to organize the material in the Bible is to distinguish among three impulses that governed the writers as they selected their material and three corresponding types of writing. They are as follows:

- The historical impulse: This means that much of the Bible, especially the Old Testament, is firmly rooted in the history of an author's

The Story Lines of the Bible

To speak of *the* story line of the Bible, in the singular, is simplistic and a partial distortion of what we actually find in the Bible. It is more helpful to identify several story lines that unify the Bible as a whole.

The story of salvation history. The main story in the Bible unfolds as follows: God creates a perfect world. Adam and Eve introduce sin into the world. God's judgment stands against human sinfulness, but throughout human history God has had a plan whereby his grace saves those who believe in the atonement of his Son, Jesus Christ. The Bible's story of salvation history is an intricate network of interrelated events and references, all of them centering in the re- demptive work of Jesus in his death and resurrection. (For more on the story of Jesus throughout the Bible, see the article on page 17.)

The story of how God governs history. God performs acts in addition to salvation. In the Bible we read the story of God's acts of creation, acts of providence (provision and control) in the history of nations and individuals, and individual acts of mercy and judgment. Because this story encompasses all creatures and all time, it is sometimes called universal history.

The story of how God intends people to live. Many passages deal with the conduct of life in the everyday world. By positive and negative examples and by means of many different genres, the Bible tells the story of how God intends people to live.

The great conflict. Another unifying thread in the Bible is the great spiritual and moral battle between good and evil. A host of details and characters make up this conflict: God and Satan, angels and demons, God and his rebellious human creatures, good and evil people, inner human impulses toward obedience or disobedience to God. Virtually every story, poem, and proverb in the Bible contributes to the ongoing plot conflict between good and evil.

The drama of the soul's choice. The story of salvation narrates the sovereign work of God in history, but there is a human counterpart in the Bible, consisting of the choices people make. On virtually every page, we observe the choices of characters. Some of these choices represent responses to God while others are responses of people to one another or to their external circumstances. The individual "chapters" in this story are series of actions and mental attitudes in which people choose between good and evil. Life is momentous as we witness characters at the crossroads of life. For the characters of the Bible, there is no neutral ground: They choose either for or against God.

time. The resulting writing is filled with historical facts and figures that require us to look for universal religious and moral principles that apply to our situation today.

- The literary impulse: Literature has two main characteristics: (1) the content of human experience, rendered as concretely as possible in order to capture the very qualities of life as we live it and (2) the embodiment of that content in distinct literary genres, such as story, poetry, vision, and many others.

- The theological impulse: In this type of writing, the primary aim is to express ideas about God and religion in a direct way. Because the Bible is a religious book, many people think that it is entirely theological, but in terms of how the material is presented, this is untrue. The other two types of writing are as much in evidence in the Bible as the theological type is.

These three impulses converge in the Bible. Most passages possess some qualities of all three. Nonetheless, one is usually dominant in a given passage, and individual passages will yield most if they are approached first of all in terms of the kind of material they contain and also the author's intention in the passage.

The Purposes of the Book

The Bible serves multiple purposes. Above all, the Bible exists to lead people to see their need of a savior and to believe in the atoning death and resurrection of Jesus Christ for salvation. Paul told Timothy that it was by "the holy Scriptures" that he was enabled to "receive the salvation that comes by trusting in Christ Jesus" (2 Timothy 3:15), and John said that the purpose of his Gospel was "that you may continue to believe that Jesus is the Messiah, the Son of God, and that by believing in him you will have life" (John 20:31). A second aim is to guide people in daily living: As the psalmist said, "Your word is a lamp to guide my feet and a light for my path" (Psalm 119:105).

Additionally, the Bible informs and illuminates our minds, telling us the religious and moral truths that we need to know to make adequate sense of what we encounter day by day: "The teaching of [God's] word gives light" (Psalm 119:130). Reading the Bible also equips believers to live godly lives. According to 2 Timothy 3:16-17, the Bible "is useful to teach us what is true and to make us realize what is wrong in our lives. It corrects us when we are wrong and teaches us to do what is right. God uses it to prepare and equip his people to do every good work."

Finally, the Bible exists to exalt the triune God. The glorious character and works of the Father, the Son, and the Holy Spirit are continuously lifted up in our praise as we read the Bible. Thus the Bible enables us to achieve the purpose for which we were made, namely, to glorify God and enjoy him forever, as the Westminster Shorter Catechism states.

The Flow of the Book

The story of this massive book is episodic, not a single action such as we find in a novel. Additionally, the narrative sections are continually interrupted by nonnarrative elements. Still, there is an inner sequence to the material, based partly on historical chronology, partly on the progression from the Old Testament to the New, and partly on the literary genres of the Bible.

The broadest structure is found in the two divisions of the Bible: the Old Testament, or Old Covenant, and the New Testament, or New Covenant. The basic principle is that the Old Testament foreshadows its fulfillment in the New Testament. Events and themes in the Old Testament look forward to the New; events and themes in the New Testament look back to the Old.

The percentage of the Old Testament found in the New is larger than most people think. One-third of the New Testament consists of Old Testament allusions or quotations (Andrew E. Hill, *Baker's Handbook of Bible Lists* [Grand Rapids: Baker, 1981], 104). Northrop Frye has expressed the importance of this in this way: "References to the Old Testament in the New . . . extend over every book— not impossibly every passage—in the New Testament. . . . The New Testament, in short, claims to be, among other things, the key to the Old Testament, the explanation of what the Old Testament really means. . . . The general principle of interpretation is traditionally given as 'In the Old Testament the New Testament is concealed; in the New Testament the Old Testament is revealed'" (Northrop Frye, *The Great Code* [New York: Harcourt, 1982], 79).

As we move through the Bible from beginning to end, we can organize blocks of books into the following progressive phases:

- Creation and the Fall (primeval history—the Bible's story of origins)

- "All Sacred Scripture is but one book, and that one book is Christ, because all divine Scripture speaks of Christ, and all divine Scripture is fulfilled in Christ." *Hugh of St. Victor*

- "In the Old Testament, we have Jesus predicted. In the Gospels, we have Jesus revealed. In Acts, we have Jesus preached. In the Epistles, we have Jesus explained. In the Revelation we have Jesus expected." *Alistair Begg*

- Covenant (God's dealings with the patriarchs and the nation of Israel that stemmed from them—patriarchal and early national history)
- Exodus (law and epic as dominant genres)
- Conquest and early settlement in the Promised Land (history and hero stories—Joshua, Judges, Ruth)
- Israelite monarchy (court history, Psalms, and wisdom literature)
- Exile from and return to the land of Israel (prophecy)
- The life of Christ (the Gospels)
- Beginnings of the Christian church (Acts and the Epistles)
- Consummation of history (apocalypse)

The Religious Orientation of the Bible

The Bible is unified by its religious orientation. It is pervaded by a consciousness of God, and it constantly views human experience in a spiritual and moral light. Part of this orientation is the theme of two worlds—a visible earthly sphere and an unseen spiritual world that can be viewed only by faith. Biblical writers take it for granted that life exists simultaneously at these two levels. Their constant appeal is that people order their lives by the unseen spiritual realities that the Bible reveals.

Because human life is thus surrounded with spiritual and supernatural potential, the Bible invests human experience—our own experience—with a sense of ultimacy. All of life is revealed as having spiritual and supernatural importance. There is a constant penetration of the spiritual world into the earthly order and a continuous reaching of the earthly order upward toward the supernatural realm. God is a constant actor in human and earthly affairs. Every event takes on a spiritual and moral significance.

Another aspect of the religious orientation of the Bible is its vivid awareness of values. The sense of right and wrong is highlighted, and for biblical writers the question of what is good and what is evil is a preoccupation. Equally important is the sense of values, based on a conviction that some things matter more than others. Spiritual values hold a position of supremacy, and nothing assumes true value apart from its relationship to God.

Preoccupation with History

One thing that makes the Bible (especially the Old Testament) difficult for modern readers is the extensive attention that the biblical writers give to history. For us, this history is ancient history. The historical books of the Old Testament often read like "straight history," and it is sometimes difficult to see what religious meaning or instruction we can extract from the

Ten Things the Bible Says about Itself

The Bible makes more claims about itself than perhaps any other book. The following are ten claims that human authors of the Bible make regarding this book:

- The Bible is God's Word and is thus more than a human book: "We also thank God constantly for this, that when you received the word of God, which you heard from us, you accepted it not as the word of men but as what it really is, the word of God" (1 Thessalonians 2:13, ESV).
- God used human authors to write the Bible, and these writers wrote under God's direction: "No prophecy was ever produced by the will of man, but men spoke from God as they were carried along by the Holy Spirit" (2 Peter 1:21, ESV).
- The Bible is a guide that enables people to find their way through life: "Your word is a lamp to guide my feet and a light for my path" (Psalm 119:105).
- The Bible teaches the way of salvation: "You have been taught the holy Scriptures from childhood, and they have given you the wisdom to receive the salvation that comes by trusting in Christ Jesus" (2 Timothy 3:15).
- The Bible is necessary to life itself: "Man shall not live by bread alone, but by every word that comes from the mouth of God" (Matthew 4:4, ESV).
- The purpose of the Bible is to equip people for Christian living: "All Scripture is breathed out by God and profitable for teaching, for reproof, for correction, and for training in righteousness, that the man of God may be competent, equipped for every good work" (2 Timothy 3:16-17, ESV).
- The Bible is a living force in a person's life: "The word of God is alive and powerful. It is sharper than the sharpest two-edged sword, cutting between soul and spirit, between joint and marrow. It exposes our innermost thoughts and desires" (Hebrews 4:12).
- The Bible was written by authors who had mastered writing as a craft: "Besides being wise, the Preacher also taught the people knowledge, weighing and studying and arranging many proverbs with great care. The Preacher sought to find words of delight, and uprightly he wrote words of truth" (Ecclesiastes 12:9-10, ESV).
- The Bible is accessible to us: "This command I am giving you today is not too difficult for you to understand, and it is not beyond your reach. It is not kept in heaven, so distant that you must ask, 'Who will go up to heaven and bring it down so we can hear it and obey?' . . . No, the message is very close at hand; it is on your lips and in your heart so that you can obey it" (Deuteronomy 30:11-14).
- The Bible is stable and enduring: "The word of our God stands forever" (Isaiah 40:8); "Heaven and earth will disappear, but my words will never disappear" (Mark 13:31).

material. Combined with national history are other historical genres—the diary, the personal and family journal, biography, and hero story—that seem more accessible to us. Here is a specimen of the type of personal story that is frequently intermingled with national or public history: "A man from Bethlehem in Judah left his home and went to live in the country of Moab, taking his wife and two sons with him. The man's name was Elimelech, and his wife was Naomi. Their two sons were Mahlon and Kilion. . . . When they reached Moab, they settled there. Then Elimelech died, and Naomi was left with her two sons" (Ruth 1:1-3).

Several avenues exist for assimilating the historical parts of the Bible. One is to understand that the Bible is not a fictional book but a history book in which the acts of God really happen. A second avenue is to be aware that the history of the Bible is kept within a moral and spiritual framework, so that in reading it we learn what we need to know about God's dealings with people and nations. What happened in ancient history is what happens throughout history and reaches to our own lives as well. Biblical history thus yields moral and religious lessons. Third, much of the history of the Bible is really salvation or redemptive history—the history of the family and nation through which Christ the Messiah was born.

This history is progressive: It unfolds in successive stages until it reaches its culmination in Christ. There is an obvious movement in God's plan from interacting with a man (Adam) to a family (Abraham) to a nation (Israel) to the world (Jews and Gentiles in Christ).

Unity of Outlook

Despite its variety of authorship and diversity of material, a unifying worldview emerges from the Bible. The Bible is not a theological outline, but its ideas are ultimately unified, producing a unity of faith. God and people are the same throughout the Bible. The physical world is not considered good in one biblical book and bad in another; it is always good as created, even if corrupted by sin. More important, the nature of sin and the plan of salvation by God's grace remain constant. Although salvation is administered in various ways at various times (e.g., the Old Testament sacrificial system), there is only one way of salvation: faith in Jesus Christ. How, then, were people saved before his coming? By believing in the Savior to come. This overriding doctrinal framework is the context within which we should read the Bible's individual parts.

Of course no individual passage of the Bible is likely to cover the whole territory on a given topic. The parts are interdependent, and we must view them as a coherent whole. As we do this, we see paradoxes emerge: The Bible maintains a balance between such poles as the goodness and badness of people, the justice and mercy of God, the friendliness and hostility of the world of nature, and human responsibility and divine sovereignty.

Unifying Stylistic Traits

In a book as comprehensive as the Bible, there are no features of style that are evident in every passage. Yet the writers of the Bible do show certain preferences, including the following:

- A preference for the concrete over the abstract: Writers describe God as a rock or a shepherd, for example, not as deity defined in theological terms such as *omnipresence* or *omniscience.*
- A preference for realism: The writers of the Bible portray life as it really is, including the evil and ugly.
- A preference for simplicity of style: Paradoxically, the writers accompany this with majesty of effect.
- A preference for universal experiences and images rather than exclusive ones: The Bible shows life at its core, such as all people in all places at all times have known it.
- A preference for brevity: Biblical writers prefer brief units over lengthy ones.
- A preference for affective power: The Bible has a unique power to move our affections as we read.

Key Doctrines

Revelation. The Bible itself is a revealed book. In addition, in its pages we read much about Scripture, about God's revelation in nature (natural revelation) and to people, and about Christ as God's revelation of himself in human form.

God (Theology). The triune God's existence, attributes, and actions

The Works of God. Creation, providence, judgment, and salvation

The Person (Anthropology). Men and women are creatures made in God's image, human sinfulness and the moral responsibility of the creature, the renewal of the believer in Christ by the Holy Spirit, the eternal destiny of every person in heaven or hell

Covenant. The divine-human love relationship as demonstrated in a series of binding promises that God made with people

Christ (Christology). The person of Christ (focusing on his incarnation as the God-man) and the work of Christ (focusing on his perfect life, his atoning death, his glorious resurrection, and his triumphant return)

Salvation (Soteriology). How God accomplished redemption through Jesus Christ and applied it to believers through the Holy Spirit. The specific doctrines of salvation include election, justification by faith, adoption, sanctification, and glorification.

The Church (Ecclesiology). The nature and work of the church, including the sacraments of baptism and the Lord's Supper

Last Things (Eschatology). The return of Christ, the final judgment, heaven, and hell

Tips for Reading or Teaching the Bible

Read and analyze books and passages in terms of their literary type, or genre, such as story or poem. Every genre has its own methods of operating and rules of interpretation, and passages begin to fall into place for us when we know and apply these to what we read. (Each of the major genres of the Bible receives a one-page article somewhere in this handbook. See the "Index of Articles" on page 659.)

As you read a book of the Bible or an extended story such as the story of Abraham, a whole "world" takes shape in your mind and imagination. Taking time to describe that world in general terms is a good way to clarify your thinking about what a book or story teaches or embodies. For example, the world of the story of Ruth is a domestic world in which family relationships are crucial.

Ask yourself what a passage reveals about God and people. Virtually every passage in the Bible is a comment about the nature of God and the nature of people. It is nearly always helpful to look for those comments in a specific passage.

The writers of the Bible have a picture of the world and of what is right and wrong in it. Accordingly, we can nearly always ask these questions of a passage: (1) What is the nature of reality (i.e., what really exists)? (2) What constitutes good or right? (3) What constitutes evil or wrong? (4) What is of most value, and what is of least value (the question of values)?

Look on the characters about whom you read as representing people in general. The material in the Bible is both particular and universal. As readers, we look first *at* the experience in a given passage. But we must also look *through* the particulars to universal human experience, including our own. With the Bible, the way to our hometown is through Jerusalem, that is, through the particular lives and places about which we read. As part of the universality of the Bible, the particular lives and places carry a significance larger than themselves.

Jesus throughout the Bible

It was the most amazing sermon ever. Jesus—who had just been raised from the dead—was walking with two of his disciples on the road to Emmaus. As they walked, they talked, and "Jesus took them through the writings of Moses and all the prophets, explaining from all the Scriptures the things concerning himself" (Luke 24:27). This crucial verse proves that the whole Bible, including the Old Testament (or "Moses and all the prophets," as they called it in those days), is about Jesus.

This is most obviously true of the prophecies about the Messiah (which means "Christ"). Such details as the place of his birth (Micah 5:2), the focus of his ministry (e.g., Isaiah 61), the manner of his death (e.g., Psalm 22; Isaiah 53), the certainty of his triumph (Genesis 3:15), the blessings of his covenant (Jeremiah 31:31-34), and the eternity of his kingdom (2 Samuel 7:11-13) are all recorded in the pages of the Old Testament.

Further, many of the people, places, and events of the Old Testament bear witness to Christ. The law displays his righteousness; the sacrifices anticipate his atonement; the Tabernacle is a symbol of his incarnation; the psalms are his praises; and so forth. Similarly, the prophets, priests, and kings of Israel teach us about the prophetic, priestly, and kingly ministry of Jesus Christ (for information about Jesus as prophet, priest, and king, see the articles on pages 351, 71, and 153).

How do we recognize these connections? Primarily by reading what the New Testament says about the Old but also by learning what is truly symbolic in the Old Testament and then considering how each symbol is fulfilled in Christ.

The New Testament also is about Jesus. The four Gospels tell the story of his life, death, and resurrection, showing that he is the Son of God and the Savior of sinners. People usually think that the book of Acts is about the church, and it is. However, the author (Luke) begins by referring to his "first book" (the Gospel of Luke) and describes it as being "about everything Jesus *began* to do and teach" (Acts 1:1, emphasis added). The clear implication is that Jesus had more to do and teach (through his Holy Spirit), and that is the subject matter of the book of Acts.

Acts is followed by letters to the church of Jesus Christ. Each of these epistles gives further teaching about Jesus Christ and what it means to follow him. Finally comes the book of Revelation, which celebrates Jesus' glory and promises his ultimate triumph over sin and Satan.

To summarize, the Bible is about Christ from beginning to end. The Savior expected in the Old Testament is exhibited in the Gospels, explained in the Epistles, and expected again in the book of Revelation. As we read and study the Bible, we enjoy an ongoing encounter with Jesus and his saving work.

Read most Bible passages through a general grid that contains the idea of law and gospel, or warning and promise. Most passages have a stated or implied "bad news" dimension (sin and judgment) accompanied by a stated or implied "good news" aspect (grace and hope).

Relate every aspect of Scripture to its ultimate fulfillment in Christ. Every chapter in this handbook has a section that identifies how each book of the Bible contributes to the Bible's story of salvation in Christ.

Make a distinction between the different ways of reading the Bible. One is *devotional reading,* in which we read mainly to take in God's truth and receive nourishment for our spirits. We might also call this *formative reading* because we seek to be formed by what we read. A second is *analytic reading,* or what we normally call Bible study. We can think of this as *informative reading,* meaning that we desire to learn as much as we can about a passage. This careful study of a passage or book of the Bible takes two forms: a quick reading to grasp the big picture, followed by a slower, more detailed analysis to discern the full richness of the passage or book.

Strike a balance between individual Bible study and Bible study in a group setting with other believers (or unbelievers in an evangelistic or preevangelistic Bible study).

Allow the beauty of the Bible to quiet your spirit. The writer of Ecclesiastes tells us that he "sought to find words of delight" (12:10, ESV). The beauty of the Bible is one of its appeals. As you read, allow it to arouse your love of beauty wherever you find it.

As an extension of this calming of your spirit, you can relish the sense of being restored to right thinking as you read the Bible and bring yourself into line with what the Bible says about how things should be in your own life and in the world.

Frequently Asked Questions

If you have had conversations about the Bible with people who are not Christians or who may simply be unfamiliar with God's Word on any but a very elementary level, you have probably encountered some of the same questions over and over again. It is important to be prepared to answer these, not because having the answers is guaranteed to convince others of the truth of the Scriptures, but because having clear answers to these questions is part of following God's command to "always be prepared to give an answer to everyone who asks you to give the reason for the hope that you have" (1 Peter 3:15, NIV). The following are some of the questions Christians encounter again and again:

How Can I Know for Sure That the Bible Is True?

1. The writers speak with great authority, often claiming that their words are actually God's words; you can trust the authority and reliability of the biblical writers.
2. For centuries, Christian believers have staked their lives on the truth of the Bible, and their lives attest that they made the right choice.
3. At the level of human experiences embodied in the Bible, you can confirm the Bible's truthfulness to reality simply by looking at the world around you and observing the daily news.
4. If you read the Bible with the presupposition that it is true, it will confirm its truthfulness to you.
5. Ancient history and archaeology generally confirm the truth of the Bible.
6. Finally, the best and fullest proof comes from the Holy Spirit: The same Spirit who inspired the Scriptures works in your mind and heart to convince you that the Bible is the Word of God.

What Is the Difference between the Old Testament God
and the New Testament God?
There is no essential difference between the God of the Old Testament and the God of the New Testament. God's character and attributes are the same in both: He is always holy and just, powerful and merciful, loving and kind. People sometimes think that there are more frequent displays of God's anger in the Old Testament or that the New Testament says more about God's love. However, the Old Testament is just as thoroughly a message of grace for sinners as the New Testament is. Furthermore, in the New Testament, God the Father and God the Son remain angry at sin and at people who defy their authority, although it is probably true that the Old Testament contains more *statements* about God's anger. And while it is true that with the coming of Christ, the events in the New Testament lean more in the direction of salvation, it is also true that the New Testament speaks clearly about the final judgment.

Where Should I Start to Read the Bible?
You can read the Bible profitably anywhere within its pages. There is a broad chronology to the Bible (as noted earlier in the Flow of the Book section), but in the final analysis the Bible is such a large anthology of separate pieces that you will not be able to hold it all in your mind at once. In a sense, the Bible is a reference book. What follows are a few generalizations to aid your reading of the Bible:

1. The four Gospels are the place where you can learn most directly about Jesus and his saving work.
2. The book of Psalms, being a collection of lyric poems, gives expression to the emotional side of the Christian life, teaching as well how to pray and worship.
3. The book of Genesis informs you about how the world and basic human institutions such as the family began. In these beginnings you can see many of the foundational principles by which individuals and societies need to live.
4. The Epistles (i.e., letters) explain the doctrinal and ethical principles of the Christian faith and teach what it means to belong to the church of Jesus Christ.
5. The book of Revelation is the most complete—but not the only—repository of information about the end times.

Why Is It Important to Read and Study the Old Testament?

1. Knowing the Old Testament is necessary in order to get a complete picture of God's character and of his saving work in history.
2. The Old Testament is a rich repository of universal human experience; it covers aspects of life that the New Testament does not.
3. The Old Testament contains poems, proverbs, and prophecies that are part of a complete understanding of the Christian faith.
4. What the New Testament teaches about the way of salvation is rooted in the Old Testament.
5. The fact that God revealed himself in the Old Testament proves that it is an important object of study. Jesus said, "I did not come to abolish the law of Moses or the writings of the prophets. . . . I tell you the truth, until heaven and earth disappear, not even the smallest detail of God's law will disappear until its purpose is achieved" (Matthew 5:17-18).

The Main Themes
1. THE CHARACTER OF GOD. The unfolding characterization of God as he interacts with his creatures is the aspect of the Bible that is most continuously present.
2. THE ACTS OF GOD. The God of the Bible is preeminently the God who acts. His mighty works occur in six main arenas: heaven, human history, the nations, the people of God (believers), external nature, and individual human lives. The acts that he performs within

Teaching the Bible

We composed this handbook with teachers of the Bible continuously in mind. It is our hope that small-group leaders, Sunday school teachers, and anyone else who teaches the Bible will use the information and "prompts" as a springboard for analyzing the text when they prepare Bible study lessons.

Effective Bible teaching rests on three principles: First, Bible teaching must focus on the actual text of the Bible and should not allow anything else to obscure the Bible itself. So-called background information *about* the Bible is never a legitimate substitute for looking at the Bible itself. Second, the goal of Bible teaching is to deepen the teachers' and students' friendship with God through Jesus Christ. Third, God has chosen to communicate his truth and beauty in the Bible through human language and ordinary forms of writing (including literary forms such as story and poetry).

One of the most effective ways to teach the Bible is through the inductive method. This method is question based and leads learners through a three-step process of discovering the Bible's meaning. Such a study begins with careful *observation* of the passage, largely through asking the questions who? what? when? where? how? and why? The purpose is to get learners to stare at the text and see for themselves what it says. After observation comes *interpretation* of the text to see what it meant for the first audience and what it means for us today. Finally, the study ends with a focus on *application* of the Scriptures to our own lives.

Here are the primary rules for mastering a text and then serving as a "travel guide" for students:

• Approach and understand the text in keeping with the kind of writing it is. This means asking the questions appropriate to the genre (literary type) of the text. With a story, for example, you look at characters, setting, and plot. For poetry, you ponder the images and figures of speech.

• Determine what unifies the passage you are preparing to teach. Unity is both thematic (one or more ideas that organize the passage) and structural (how the material is organized from beginning to end).

• Remember that you must first journey to the world of the ancient text and enter fully into the spirit of a passage in its original context, then make a return journey to your own time and place, applying the principles to your own situation.

• The task of interpretation is not complete until you have related the passage to the Bible's central message of salvation in Jesus Christ.

• In applying the Bible, remember that coming through the historical particulars of the Bible are the universal experiences of the human race.

these arenas include creation, providence, judgment, and redemption.

3. THE NATURE OF PEOPLE. By means of both direct statements and stories about characters, the Bible gives full treatment to the question of what people are like. A balanced view of the person emerges as the Bible shows that people are capable of both unspeakable evil and, by the grace of God, powerful good.

4. THE NATURE OF THE VISIBLE WORLD. Here, too, we learn many things about the world that God created. Of particular importance is the idea that people's problems do not stem from the outside world; events in that world provide the occasion for people to respond in godly or ungodly ways.

5. THE EXISTENCE OF TWO WORLDS. An important part of the biblical worldview is that reality consists of two spheres: (1) the visible earth and (2) an unseen spiritual world. People inhabit both of these simultaneously.

6. THE DIVINE-HUMAN RELATIONSHIP. God and people are inevitably related, and the Bible explores the nature of God's relationship to people and their relationship to him. Biblical authors write out of a painful awareness that sin has disrupted the relationship but also out of a hopeful awareness that God's grace can restore it.

7. SALVATION BY GRACE. Human beings are not saved by virtue of their own actions. They are saved in spite of their sin, and only through a sacrifice of atonement.

Applying the Bible

There are no magic formulas or gimmicks for applying the Bible to our lives. Some time-tested principles of application include the following:

• As we mentioned earlier in this chapter, the way to our hometowns is through Jerusalem. This means that before we apply the Bible to our own lives, we need to understand a biblical passage in its original context. Do not be impatient with this. Before we can apply Paul's statements about whether or not to eat food offered to idols, we need to understand the facts about the offering of food to idols in the ancient Roman religion. The important principle here is that we need to look *at* the literal details of a text before we look *through* them to our own lives and times.

• Once we have journeyed to the world of the biblical text, we need to make a return trip to our own situations. We need to build bridges between the biblical world and the modern world. Looking for universal human experience in the Bible is a great ally in this regard. So is the knack of seeing the timeless spiritual principles that are embodied in the literary and historical details of the Bible.

- Reading the Bible has a corrective value as we bring our lives and values into line with what we find there. As we read the Bible, we find our way of viewing the world and ourselves refashioned and set right. This is a form of application of the Bible to our lives.

- The Bible's message is two-pronged: The bad news of God's law shows us our sin, but the good news of the gospel shows us that God has grace for sinners. These two messages run right through the Bible, often appearing in the same passages. We apply the bad news about our sin by seeing our need for repentance, forgiveness, and correction; we apply the good news of grace by coming to God in faith, receiving Jesus Christ, and resolving to live the way God directs us to live.

- The Bible is full of examples—both positive and negative—that show us how to live in a way that is pleasing to God. The supreme example is Jesus Christ, whose righteous life and patient endurance in suffering establish the pattern for our own lives in the world.

- Reading the Bible is intended to draw us into worship. On every page we encounter God's attributes and see his saving grace. The proper response is to give him the glory, turning the themes of Scripture into prayer and praise.

PERSPECTIVES
ON THE BIBLE

What a book the Bible is, what a miracle, what strength is given with it to man. It is like a mould cast of the world and man and human nature, everything is there, and a law for everything for all the ages. And what mysteries are solved and revealed. Fyodor Dostoyevsky's fictional character Father Zossima in *The Brothers Karamazov*

The most striking quality of the Bible as a book is its variety. David Norton

The Bible is not "partly true and partly false, but all true, the blessed, holy Word of God." J. Gresham Machen

The symbols of the Bible are simple and universal symbols, such as men and women everywhere can understand: food and drink, hunger and thirst, love and hatred, . . . light and darkness, laughter and tears, birth and death. Roland M. Frye

[The Bible is] the light to our paths, the key of the kingdom of heaven, our comfort in affliction, our shield and sword against Satan, the school of all wisdom, the [mirror] in which we behold God's face, the testimony of his favor, and the only food and nourishment of our souls. Preface to *The Geneva Bible*

There is a sense in which the Bible, since it is after all literature, cannot properly be read except as literature; and the different parts of it as the different sorts of literature they are. C. S. Lewis

The scripture containeth . . . first, the law, to condemn all flesh; secondarily, the gospel, that is to say, promises of mercy for all that repent and acknowledge their sins. William Tyndale

The heavenliness of the matter, the efficacy of the doctrine, the majesty of the style, the consent of all the parts, the scope of the whole (which is, to give all glory to God), the full discovery it makes of the only way of man's salvation, the many other incomparable excellencies, and the entire perfection thereof, are arguments whereby the Bible doth abundantly evidence itself to be the Word of God: yet notwithstanding, our full persuasion and assurance of the infallible truth and divine authority thereof, is the inward work of the Holy Spirit bearing witness by and with the Word in our hearts. From the *Westminster Confession of Faith*

I have found in the Bible words for my inmost thoughts, songs for my joy, utterance for my hidden griefs and pleadings for my shame and feebleness. Samuel Taylor Coleridge

The Scriptures teach us the best way of living, the noblest way of suffering, and the most comfortable way of dying. John Flavel

Scripture is like a river, broad and deep, shallow enough for the lamb to go wading, but deep enough for the elephant to swim. Gregory the Great

The Scripture is the library of the Holy Ghost. Thomas Watson

The word of God will stand a thousand readings; and he who has gone over it most frequently is the surest of finding new wonders there. James Hamilton

part two

THE OLD TESTAMENT

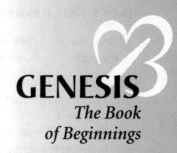

GENESIS
The Book of Beginnings

FACT SHEET

FORMAT. 50 chapters, 1,533 verses

IMPLIED PURPOSES. To record the first events of human history, along with the foundational principles on which God created human life in this world. The second part of the book, the history of the patriarchs, has as its purpose to show God's choice of a family and nation through whom he would bless all people who believe in him.

AUTHOR'S PERSPECTIVE. The author is above all a historian with a penchant for historical figures and facts, and a storyteller who embodies his message in characters and events. The book of Genesis contains almost no direct commands or instructions to the reader, preferring instead to take a narrative approach.

IMPLIED AUDIENCE. The original audience was the believing Jewish community. It is often suggested that the time of the Exodus might have been the time when Moses composed the book, based on the logic that as the nation was being formed, people would naturally have wondered about its prenational origins. But all Christians have an interest in knowing the foundational principles of life and redemption.

WHAT UNIFIES THE BOOK. The story line; the gallery of memorable characters; the theme of the covenant; the character of God; the chronological progression of the history that is recounted; an abundance of universal human experience

SPECIAL FEATURES. A focus on a handful of heroic characters (Adam and Eve, Noah, Abraham, Isaac, Jacob, Joseph); an emphasis on the family as the arena of significant action; repeated attention called to the origins of places, names, and rituals; the ancientness of the world that is portrayed; an abundance of encounters and conversations

CHALLENGES FACING THE READER OR TEACHER OF THIS BOOK.
1. The seeming remoteness from our own situation of the world portrayed
2. The episodic nature of the action
3. Interspersed summaries of historical material (including genealogies) that break up the flow of the action

HOW TO MEET THE CHALLENGES.
1. Build bridges between the ancient world of the text and your own experiences. (How are the characters in the story like people you have known? How are the events the same as things that happen or have happened to you and your family?)
2. Instead of looking for a single line of action, such as you would find in a modern novel, be prepared for relatively self-contained episodes that need to be treated as events in themselves.
3. Accept the sections of concentrated historical facts as establishing the general point that God enters space-time history.

The characterization of God may indeed be said to be the central literary concern of the Bible, and it is pursued from beginning to end, for the principal character, or actor, or protagonist of the Bible is God. Not even the most seemingly insignificant action in the Bible can be understood apart from the emerging characterization of the deity. With this great protagonist and his designs, all other characters and events interact, as history becomes the great arena for God's characteristic and characterizing actions.

ROLAND M. FRYE
The Reader's Bible

Patriarchal History

37–50 Joseph and His Brothers		
36 Generations of Esau	A Single Family Line	
27–35 The Story of Jacob		
25:19–26:35 The Story of Isaac	Four Main Characters: Abraham, Isaac, Jacob, and Joseph	
12–25:18 The Story of Abraham	God Unfolds a Plan to Bless His Covenant People in All Nations	

Primeval History

10–11 Dispersion of the Nations	The Whole Human Race	
6–9 Noah and the Flood	Four Main Events: Creation, Fall, Flood, Tower of Babel	The Human Race Forfeits God's Blessing
4–5 Cain, Abel, Genealogies		
3 The Fall into Sin		
1–2 God's Perfect Creation		God Blesses His Creation

AN OUTLINE OF

GENESIS

It is a natural human impulse to want to know how things began. Stonehenge in England is a prime example. As experts have speculated on its origins, they have multiplied possible explanations for how this ring of stones came to be where it is. Some of the theories are that it was a place of religious worship or a monument to victory or a burial ground or a jousting ring or an astronomical observatory.

The Bible is likewise preoccupied with the origins of things, and this preoccupation starts with the first book of the Bible. This theme extends far beyond an explanation of how the physical universe came into existence. It includes explanations of the origins of human nature, of human life in the world, of domestic relations, of moral good and evil, of the company of believers in God, of proper worship, and of God's plan of redemption.

DID YOU KNOW?
The Hebrew word for *Genesis* means "in the beginning," based on the first word in the book. The word *Genesis* came from the Greek translation of the Hebrew word and means "origin," "beginning," "source," or "generation."

The Form of the Book

Genesis is an anthology, or collection, of stories. This means that narrative is the primary form. But Genesis does not tell a single, ongoing story the way a novel does. Instead it presents cycles of collected stories. Therefore, we need to be prepared for somewhat abrupt transitions when we move from one story to the next. We also need to be prepared for a relatively self-contained quality to many of the episodes that make up the overall narrative. (For more on how to read and analyze stories, see "The Story Lines of the Bible," page 9.)

Only one character is present from the beginning of the book to the end, and that character is God. Virtually every passage in Genesis provides answers to the question What is God like? This question and a secondary one—How do God and people relate to one another—provide a helpful analytic grid for all parts of the book.

The unifying plot of Genesis is God's interaction with the sinfulness of the human race. The history that Genesis tells has a double thrust: the evil of the human race that brings God's judgment upon it, and God's redemptive actions in saving a remnant of believers for himself. It is obvious already in Genesis that *God has a plan* for dealing with human sinfulness. A subplot is the story of characters' trusting God versus trusting what seems sensible or expedient from a human point of view.

Within the overall historical pattern of narrative, Genesis is a collection of hero stories. Such stories are organized around representative characters whom the writer offers as models of the human condition and who, despite failings, are mainly examples to be emulated. (For more on this topic, see the article titled "Hero Stories," page 213.) Because the hero stories of the Bible are historically true, we can also regard them as belonging to the genre of biography.

Key Places and Characters

Chapters 1 through 11 are primeval history: the history of the world in its earliest stages. The settings in this part of the story tend to be cosmic, elemental, unlocalized, and expansive. The rest of the book, which is called patriarchal history, occurs largely in what the book of Genesis calls Canaan and what we know today as Palestine and Israel. But despite this localized center of the action, there is an international flavor to the action, as from time to time the leading characters journey beyond their main place of residence. The action shifts from Canaan to Egypt numerous times.

Genesis combines two approaches to history. One view is that history is made up not chiefly of big public events and characters but of the everyday lives of ordinary people. But along with this emphasis on the commonplace, the history that Genesis tells also includes epoch-making events and "larger than life" figures. The chief human characters in Genesis are some of the most famous people in history: Adam and Eve, Cain and Abel, Noah, Abraham and Sarah, Isaac and Rebekah, Jacob, and Joseph.

FAMOUS COUPLES IN GENESIS
- Adam and Eve
- Abraham and Sarah
- Isaac and Rebekah
- Jacob and Leah
- Jacob and Rachel

Unifying Elements

- The characterization of God and the story of his dealings with people
- The presence of representative figures such as Adam, Eve, and Abraham
- The story of the covenant—God's relationship with his people as formulated in a reciprocal agreement—a binding promise sealed in blood
- The story of God's dealing with wayward humanity and individuals (divine grace contending with the sinfulness of people)
- The narrative ingredients of setting, action (plot), and characters
- The tracing of a single family line

Key Doctrines

The Nature of God. The acts and attributes of God are so extensive in Genesis that it is possible to compile a relatively complete theology of God on the basis of this one book.

The Nature of People. Genesis is the foundational text for what
theologians call anthropology (the nature of people), with people's
creation in God's image a key ingredient.

Creation. Genesis tells of the origin of the creation and then embodies
many principles relating to it, such as its goodness in principle, its now
fallen state, and the world of nature as the environment in which
people sustain their lives.

Sin. Genesis not only tells how sin entered the world but also provides a
veritable anatomy of what sin is and how it works in people's lives.

Judgment. The story of God's dealings with human sinfulness yields a
thorough doctrine of divine judgment.

Grace. The book's continuous counterpoint to divine judgment is God's
mercy to undeserving humanity.

Covenant. The entire book of Genesis can be organized around the
successive covenants (reciprocal relationships) that God establishes
with the human race and with those who believe by faith. (For more on
this idea, see the article titled "Covenant" on page 93.)

Redemption. The story of God's salvation of people who believe in him
begins in the third chapter and then underlies the entire book.

Tips for Reading or Teaching Genesis

**THE EIGHT HEROES
OF GENESIS**
- Adam
- Abel
- Enoch
- Noah
- Abraham
- Isaac
- Jacob
- Joseph

To make sense of Genesis, you need to approach
the individual stories with the usual narrative questions in mind. You cannot do justice to the book
without talking about plot (centered around one or
more conflicts), setting, and characterization as the
basic terms.

The emerging portrait of God must be continuously on your radar screen.

In the whole Bible, no other book contains such
an abundance of recognizable human experi-
ences—experiences such as good and bad choices, sibling rivalry,
intergenerational conflict, and birth and death. Be sure to do justice to
the human side of Genesis.

Genesis is foundational to the whole Bible. Keep a mental list of foundational principles about God, people, the creation, evil, covenants, and
redemption (along with others).

Be on the lookout throughout the book—even in its genealogies—for
ways in which there is a systematic working out of the theme of the conflict
between good and evil, the seed of the woman and the seed of the serpent.

To a modern reader, much about Genesis is mysterious: the preoccupation with genealogies, for example, or the ancient place-names and customs. You do not need to master all of these details in order to glean the main truths of this book.

quick overview of genesis

Primeval History:
1:1–3:24	Creation, life in paradise, and the fall into sin
4:1–11:32	Human history after the Fall: Cain and Abel, Noah and the Flood, the dispersion of the nations at the tower of Babel

Patriarchal History:
12:1–25:18	The story of Abraham and Sarah
25:19–26:35	The story of Isaac and Ishmael
27:1–35:29	The story of Jacob and Esau
36:1–50:26	The story of Joseph and his brothers

The Flow of the Book

The Creation of the Universe (Chapter 1). The book of Genesis offers no biography for God as the ancient myths did for their gods. It simply assumes the existence of God with its majestic opening statement in Genesis 1:1: "In the beginning God created the heavens and the earth." The creation story itself is one of the most patterned passages in the Bible. First, the chart below shows that on the first three days God created three places, or settings, and on the next three he created corresponding appropriate creatures for each setting:

1	light	4	light bearers
2	sky and sea	5	birds and sea creatures
3	dry land and vegetation	6	land animals and man

Second, all six days of creation are composed of a set of repeated formulas and phrases (with variations), as follows:

1. Announcement: "And God said . . ."
2. Command: "Let there be . . ." or some other form of "let."
3. Report: "And it was so."

4. Evaluation: "God saw that it was good."

5. Placement in time: "There was evening and there was morning, the first [etc.] day" (v. 5, ESV).

KEY VERSE

"God saw everything that he had made, and behold, it was very good" (1:31, ESV). The evil that became the daily reality of the human race was not inherent in the universe as God created it; God made everything good in origin and in principle.

Life in Paradise (Chapter 2). Genesis 2 makes no attempt to cover the same territory as Genesis 1. The first chapter deals with the creation of the cosmos; the second chapter deals with God's creation of the Garden of Eden for his human creatures. Genesis 2 is a companion story to Genesis 1, and tracing the contrasts-within-parallels provides a good way of working out the meanings of Genesis 2. The main organizing framework for Genesis 2 is an ever-expanding list of God's provisions for the human race, including physical life (v. 7), an environment that is both beautiful and functional (v. 9), food, work (v. 15), moral choice (vv. 16-17), human companionship and marriage (vv. 20-24), and communion with God.

The Fall into Sin (Chapter 3). Genesis 3 completes the Bible's story of origins by explaining how the presence of sin and suffering came into a world that God had made perfect. The chief meaning of the story is human disobedience against God and God's punishment of that sin. The story patterns that embody this meaning include temptation, crime and punishment, fall from innocence, and initiation into sin and its consequences. Even in this story of tragedy, though, we can see elements of balancing mercy (including the first promise of the gospel, v. 15).

Life outside of Eden (Chapters 4–5). The immediate effects of the Fall are shown working their way outward. The major story in this sequence is the story of Cain and Abel (4:1-16). It is a story of sin, murder, and judgment. To see the relevance of the story—its universal aspects—we need to note the abundance of recognizable human experiences. These include domestic violence, sibling rivalry, murder, a guilty child, lying to a parent (God), lack of self-control, harboring a grudge, giving in to an evil impulse, anger at having gotten caught, an attempted cover-up, trial and sentencing, and more. The story tells not only what *happened* but also how sin *happens*—anytime, anywhere. A good framework for analyzing the story of Cain and Abel is to view it as an exploration of Cain's evil heart.

Narrative as a Form of Writing

Narrative, or story, is the dominant genre (type of writing) in the Bible. The overall structure of the Bible is narrative; that is, it has a beginning, a middle, and an end. In terms of actual content, there are more stories in the Bible than any other genre. Here are the most important things that you need to know about stories, including those in the Bible:

- Stories are composed of events, not ideas.
- It is important to identify the unifying action or actions of a story and not reduce them to an idea. Examples of unifying actions are quest, journey, and rescue. The unifying motif in the story of Abraham's offering of Isaac (Genesis 22) is the test of the hero.
- Dividing a story into successive scenes, or episodes, and naming them accurately is important when analyzing a story. The story of Abraham's offering of Isaac unfolds as follows: the test announced, preparations for the test, taking the test, interruption of the test, and interpreting the test results.
- Stories consist of three main ingredients: plot (action), setting, and character.
- The essence of plot is one or more conflicts that run their course and end in some type of resolution. In the story of Cain's murder of Abel (Genesis 4:1-16), Cain is in conflict with God, with his brother, and with the evil in his own soul (v. 7).
- Settings are important. They serve as appropriate "containers" for the action and characters that operate within them, contribute atmosphere, and embody symbolic meanings that are important to the story. In the story of Lot (Genesis 19), the city of Sodom creates an atmosphere of evil, symbolizes sexual perversion, and contributes to the action by making the rescue of righteous Lot necessary.
- It is important to get to know characters in a story as fully as possible. We know characters by their actions, personal traits and abilities, thoughts and feelings, relationships and roles, responses to events or people, and adherence to universal character types, such as trickster or villain or traveler.
- The meaning of a story comes mainly from the story as a whole, not from its individual parts. A good way to determine the meaning of a story is to operate on the premise that the stories of the Bible are *example stories*. You need to formulate a statement of what a given story is an example *of* and what it says *about* that thing. It is also useful to understand that characters in a story undertake an experiment in living that leads to a certain conclusion, from which we can conclude something about life universally.

The story of Cain's career as a criminal is followed by a panorama of additional people (4:17–5:32). The basic rhythm we need to be ready to handle as we work our way through Genesis is a back-and-forth movement between a focus on individual characters and events and interspersed summaries that cover many people or events. Many of the summaries take the form of genealogies, which in Genesis tell the story of human civilizations as well as families. (For helpful information about genealogies, see "Genealogies in the Bible" on page 177.)

Noah and the Flood (Chapters 6–9). There are many death-rebirth stories in the Bible. This is the first one. The first thing to do with the famous story of the Flood is to get a grip on the chronology of events. The Flood and its aftermath took approximately a year. The sequence of the events mattered a lot to the writer, so take time to work it out. The main plot conflict is God versus the evil earth. The story of judgment against sinful humanity is combined with a rescue story in which a faithful remnant (Noah and his family) is spared. Compiling a portrait of the exemplary qualities of Noah is a good approach to the positive thread in the action. While the story deals with important spiritual principles such as sin and its punishment, it is important to relive the drama of the action, which is told in leisurely detail and is one of the most vivid stories in the Bible. This U-shaped story of death and rebirth speaks to the human need for God's redemption and rescue.

The Dispersion of the Nations (Chapters 10–11). The human race repopulated the earth after Noah's family made a new beginning, but the downward spiral into sin soon began again. The key event was the construction of the ill-fated tower of Babel (11:1-9), which resulted in the dispersal of the human race on the basis of language. One good approach to the story of Babel is to view the tower as having an element of symbolism: It represents people in community against God, a venture in human self-suffiiency, the urge for permanent achievement and security, human aspiration and pride, human inventiveness and technology, and civilization. A good springboard to analyzing this issue is to explore why God disapproves of the grand venture.

The Story of Abraham, Father of Nations and of Believers (12:1–25:18). While the larger story of Abraham is composed of numerous individual stories, we can bring the action into a unity in our thinking if we keep these patterns in mind:

- The story is a quest story in which Abraham and Sarah pursue a quest for a son, for descendants, and for a land—the people-and-place motif, or land-and-seed motif.
- The story is structured as a progressive revelation of the covenant. The covenant is the contract that God enters into with Abraham (and later with the other patriarchs). The contract consists of *promised blessings* (a son, descendants, land, and the promise to be the God of the faithful) and *obligations* (to obey God). Every time God renews the covenant with Abraham, we receive more information about how God will fulfill the covenant.
- The ongoing portrait of the hero helps to unify the action, and it embodies much of the religious meaning of the story as well.
- The story is a travel story, and we can make better sense of what is happening if we keep in view the traits of a travel story—changing locales for the action, adventure, encounters with people and the divine, danger, testing, conflict, suspense, and the growth of the traveler's character.
- The action that unifies the entire story of Abraham is this: It is the story of the hero's quest to find fulfillment of God's covenant promises, and of the struggles, defeats, victories, and discoveries that he experiences in this quest.

The following chart divides the story of Abraham into its successive episodes:

12:1-9	Call of Abraham
12:10-20	Sojourn in Egypt
13	Separation of Abraham and Lot
14	Abraham's Rescue of Lot
15	Renewal of the Covenant
16	Birth of Ishmael

17	Covenant Sign Established
18:1-15	Hospitality to Angelic Visitors
18:16-33	Intercession for Lot
19	Destruction of Sodom and Gomorrah
20	Deception of Abimelech
21:1-7	Birth of Isaac
21:8-21	Expulsion of Ishmael
21:22-34	Discord about a Well
22	Offering of Isaac
23	Death of Sarah
24	Marriage of Isaac
25	Death of Abraham

All of the motifs reach their climax in chapter 22 with Abraham's willingness to offer his son Isaac as a sacrifice.

KEY VERSES
"Because you have obeyed me . . . I will certainly bless you" (22:16-17). Here is the covenant in miniature: God demands obedience, and he promises blessing in return.

The story of Abraham contains an additional motif that encapsulates much of the meaning of the story: Abraham's ongoing inner struggle over whether to act in faith or in expediency (doing what from a human viewpoint seems most immediately advantageous). As we move through the story, we should note the back-and-forth swing between these two ways of behaving.

Although it is customary to divide the stories of the patriarchs into successive units, this obscures the way in which the stories of fathers and sons overlap each other. The following chart shows how the stories overlap:

```
ABRAHAM 12:1 . . . . . 25:18
        ISAAC 21:1 . . . . . . . 28:9
                JACOB 25:19 . . . . . . 49:33
                        JOSEPH 37:1 . . . . . . 50:26
```

The Story of Isaac (25:19–26:35). Isaac is the "forgotten" patriarch. Although the familiar formula of "Abraham, Isaac, and Jacob" treats Isaac as an equal with the other patriarchs, he gets much less space in Genesis than the other patriarchs. Like them, Isaac is the head of a family, or clan. His sphere is that of a domestic figure, enlarged by the fact that he is the recipient of God's covenant. A good exercise is to analyze how the story of Isaac embodies familiar ingredients of Genesis as a whole.

The Story of Jacob: The Triumph of God's Grace over a Scoundrel (Chapters 27–35). Jacob is the most colorful figure in Genesis. His very name (which means "he grabs by the heel" or "he struggles and overcomes") hints at his typical role as the person who generates conflict wherever he goes. He is the least idealized of the patriarchs, though he undergoes a notable conversion when he wrestles with the angel of God. The following will help to unify the story of Jacob and provide a beginning for understanding its meanings:

- The story is above all an extended conflict story. Jacob is the agent of conflict in his interactions with others (especially family members, inasmuch as this is a family story).
- The story has a strong satiric element in it, as Jacob's character flaws are repeatedly laid out to view.
- The story is also organized around the motif of God's mercy contending with frail humanity. Old Testament commentator Derek Kidner claims that this section of Genesis "shows once again the grace of God choosing difficult and unpromising material."
- The unifying pattern is the struggle of Jacob to become a godly character. The turning point comes when he wrestles with the angel of God at the Jabbok River (32:22-32).

KEY VERSES
"I am not worthy of all the unfailing love and faithfulness you have shown to me, your servant. . . . But you promised me, 'I will surely treat you kindly, and I will multiply your descendants'" (32:10-12). In Jacob's prayer to God, we can see not only his own essential experience but also that of the human race: unworthiness through human sinfulness and failure, with only God's covenant mercy as a basis for God's favor.

Like the story of Abraham, the main part of the story of Jacob falls into a series of self-contained episodes that form a circular pattern: early life in the parental home (25:19–28:9), a twenty-year exile in Haran (28:10–30:43), and a return to the land of the hero's origins (31–35). At the beginning of each of these phases of action, an oracle or appearance from God foreshadows the next phase of action—the promise to Rebekah that the younger of her two sons would supplant the older (25:22-23), the dream at Bethel in which Jacob receives the covenant blessing (28:10-22), and the wrestling match with the angel of God where Jacob receives his covenant name, Israel (32:22-32).

The following chart divides the material into its episodes:

25:19-26	Birth of Jacob
25:27-34	The Exchanged Birthright
27	The Stolen Blessing
28	Jacob's Dream at Bethel
29:1-30	Jacob's Marriages
29:31–30:24	Jacob's Children
30:25-43	Jacob's Struggles with Laban
31	Jacob's Flight from Laban
32	Wrestling with the Angel
33	Reunion with Esau
34	Rape of Dinah
35	Return to Bethel

The Story of Joseph and His Brothers: Providence in the Life of a Suffering Servant (Chapters 37–50). Joseph is the most exemplary character among the patriarchs of Genesis. The story is a hero story par excellence. Joseph is the first suffering servant in the Bible—the person who suffers undeservedly for the redemption of others. The main theological theme of his story is divine providence, seen in God's ability to bring good out of the evil that engulfs Joseph in the first half of the story. The story features a boy hero that follows the rags-to-riches archetype.

KEY VERSE

"You meant evil against me, but God meant it for good" (50:20, ESV). This is the providential theme of the story of Joseph—a story of human tragedy that God transforms into a happy ending.

We can see in the chart below that the story of Joseph consists of four cycles in which a similar pattern is repeated.

The story of Joseph is a suspense story that leads us to wonder how the opening predictions that Joseph's family will bow down to him can possibly be fulfilled, given the events of Joseph's life. The story also juxtaposes two lines of action: Throughout most of the story, it appears that Joseph's life is unfolding as a tragedy, but the tragic events turn out to be part of a story with a happy ending.

The Main Themes

1. God is the sovereign creator and director of the world and of the events of history.

2. People are inevitably related to God, and they elicit either God's favor or judgment.
3. Faith is the essential dimension of a person's fostering a relationship with God.
4. The human race is generally inclined to do what is wrong.
5. But there are also many virtuous characters and events that inspire us to emulate those characters.
6. Life presents people with a continuous need to choose either God or something opposed to God (such as self or evil).
7. God has established a covenant with the human race in which he will bless those who believe in him.

	Chapter 37	39:1-18	39:19–41:36	41:37–50:26
Authority Figure	Jacob	Potiphar	The jailer	Pharaoh
Person Who Rises to Prominence	Joseph	Joseph	Joseph	Joseph
People in Subservience	The brothers	The servants	The prisoners	The citizens of Egypt and Joseph's brothers
A Garment That Signals the Transition in the Fortune of Joseph	Joseph's robe (removed)	Joseph's cloak	New clothes (41:14)	Royal clothing (41:42)
A Place of Both Imprisonment and Preservation	The pit	Potiphar's house	Prison	The land of Egypt

Contribution of the Book to the Bible's Story of Salvation in Christ
The fall of the human race into sin (Genesis 3) is what lies behind the Bible's story of salvation history. Sin is what made salvation necessary (Romans 5:12-21 explains the theological significance of Adam's fall in the story of salvation). The story of salvation begins in Genesis 3:15, with its promise that Eve's offspring will bruise the head of the serpent, that is,

Satan. Furthermore, God's covenant with the patriarchs, with its promise that through Abraham's lineage all nations will be blessed, is really a prediction of Christ's atoning work.

Applying the Book

In a book as encyclopedic as Genesis, applications are nearly endless. Here are some starting suggestions: Since the character and acts of God are the central focus of Genesis, an obvious application is that we must accept its portrait of God as the truth and respond to him accordingly, chiefly in faith and obedience. If the question of relating properly to God is the central issue of life, the book of Genesis provides numerous demonstrations of how that can happen.

On the human plane, the book of Genesis, with its gallery of memorable characters and events, provides numerous examples of virtue to follow and vice to avoid. It is a handbook for daily living. Of special importance is the family sphere, where we are shown—mainly through negative examples to avoid imitating—how to order our own families. We will not go wrong if we regard the stories of Genesis as example stories.

The book of Genesis shows that we live out the great spiritual issues in the everyday routines. The book is filled with commonplace events, and the most prevalent sphere of action is domestic, not national. The characters are mainly family members, not rulers of nations. The application here is that we need to believe that everything we do is part of our spiritual and moral lives.

PERSPECTIVES
ON THE BOOK OF GENESIS

Genesis offers the reader a comprehensive introduction to the Bible. Sin emerges as the major problem the human race has to overcome, and God acts through people to defeat sin. Paul R. House

Genesis begins with a garden and ends with a coffin. What a commentary on the results of sin in this world! Warren Wiersbe

Genesis spans more time than any other book in the Bible; in fact, it covers more than all sixty-five other books of the Bible put together.
Bruce Wilkinson and Kenneth Boa

We must not think of these as ordinary . . . people; but, next to Christ and John the Baptist, they were the most outstanding heroes this world has ever produced. . . . Those patriarchs were most holy men endowed with superior gifts, being the heroes, as it were, of the entire world.
Martin Luther

The people throughout the book are normal and familiar, such as we are accustomed to meet in our day-to-day intercourse with our fellow men. . . . Though they are lifelike, alive, and normal, they are not . . . average human types. They eat, sleep, shepherd the flock, till the soil, make love, and generally pursue the interests common to all men. But . . . they . . . represent in their being something greater than themselves.
Solomon Goldman

Genesis, in fact, is in various ways almost nearer the New Testament than the Old, and some of its topics are barely heard again till their implications fully emerge in the gospel. . . . The book of Genesis, like the Old Testament in microcosm, ends by pointing beyond its own story.
Derek Kidner

The theme of Genesis is grace. R. Kent Hughes

How simple are the images of Israel's ancestors! They have almost more shadow than light. . . . The nobleness of these figures consists in the fact that they conquer in the strength of the grace granted to them. . . . Their mistakes are the foils of their greatness for sacred history. Franz Delitzsch

[The author] represents man as devoid of all good . . . and under sentence of eternal death; but he soon adds the history of his restoration, where Christ shines forth with the benefit of redemption. John Calvin

[In the stories of Genesis,] the sublime influence of God . . . reaches so deeply into the everyday that the two realms of the sublime and the everyday are not only actually unseparated but basically inseparable.
Erich Auerbach

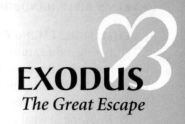

EXODUS
The Great Escape

FORMAT. 40 chapters, 1,213 verses

IMPLIED PURPOSES. To glorify God by telling *the* great story of Israel's salvation. Also, to record the origins of Israel as God's covenant nation.

AUTHOR'S PERSPECTIVE. The author (Moses, according to the New Testament) gives a firsthand account of Israel's escape from Egypt, journey through the wilderness, and encounter with God at Mount Sinai. His approach is both personal (he records his own private experiences with God) and national (he is writing the authorized history of Israel). While he revels in the defeat of Pharaoh and the Egyptians, his goal is to glorify Israel's God.

IMPLIED AUDIENCE. The nation of Israel and the people of God throughout history

WHAT UNIFIES THE BOOK. The strong presence of God as the main actor in the great drama of salvation; the personality of Moses as deliverer, mediator, and lawgiver; the people of Israel, whose salvation is at stake; the covenant, which forms the basis for Israel's renewed relationship with God at Mount Sinai; the Egyptian context, which exercises a strong influence on the Israelites even after they escape; the glory of God in the worship of his people

SPECIAL FEATURES. God's revelation of his divine name; ten terrible plagues on Egypt; the institution of Passover; the crossing of the Red Sea; the Ten Commandments; instructions for building the Tabernacle; *theophanies*—physical manifestations of the invisible God—at the burning bush, on Mount Sinai, and in the Tabernacle

CHALLENGES FACING THE READER OR TEACHER OF THIS BOOK.

1. Losing momentum after chapter 20, when the book turns from narration (the story of Israel's exodus from Egypt) to legislation (God's laws for daily life and worship)
2. Skeptical attacks on the book's historical accuracy
3. Knowing to what extent the miraculous events in Exodus (such as the parting of the Red Sea) may also have had natural causes

HOW TO MEET THE CHALLENGES.

1. Learn how the laws of the covenant and the worship in the Tabernacle fulfill God's purposes for Israel's exodus from Egypt.
2. Remember the divine authority of Scripture and that recent scholarship tends to support Israel's long exile in Egypt.
3. Understand that even when God uses his miraculous saving power, he is still free to employ natural forces such as the wind.

THE MOST COMMON MISCONCEPTION ABOUT THIS BOOK. That most of the material in chapters 21–40 is essentially unrelated to the epic adventure in the first half of the book. In fact, these chapters complete the story by reestablishing the covenant and setting Israel apart as a nation dedicated to the holy worship of God.

FACT SHEET

*E*xodus is about a man, Moses, who sets all against the reality of divine sovereignty and measures all in terms of God's requirements. Exodus is about a nation, Israel, moving from slavery in Egypt into freedom. . . . But ultimately Exodus is about the God of the covenant who has instituted a new relationship between himself and those whom he has called to be his people. It is about how he introduces himself to them, acts on their behalf and shows them the real difference it makes that the LORD is their God, and about the patience he shows as he leads them out of their grumbling, even outright rebellion, until he comes to dwell in their midst.

JOHN L. MACKAY
Exodus

AN OUTLINE OF EXODUS

Persecution	Judgment	Redemption	Providence	Law	Worship (False and True)
1 Growth and Groaning of Israel in Egypt	7–10 The First Nine Plagues	14 Crossing the Red Sea	15:22–18:27 The Journey through the Wilderness	19–20 The Ten Commandments	32 The Golden Calf
2 Birth and Preparation of Moses	11–13 Passover and the Final Plague	15:1-21 The Song of Salvation		21–23 The Book of the Covenant	33–34 The Commandments and the Covenant Renewed
3–4:17 The Call of Moses				24 Covenant Renewal	35–39 The Tabernacle Built according to Plan
4:18–6:30 The First Audience with Pharaoh				25–31 Plans for the Tabernacle and Its Priests	40 The Glory in the Tabernacle
God Present in Compassion	God Present in Justice	God Present in Salvation		God Present in Righteousness	God Present in Glory
God's People Suffering in Slavery		God's Grace Demonstrated in Deliverance		God's People Covenanted in Community	God's Glory Revealed and Revered
Israel in Egypt		From Egypt to God's Mountain		Israel at Mount Sinai	

Exodus is an epic tale of fire, sand, wind, and water. The adventure takes place under the hot desert sun, just beyond the shadow of the great pyramids of Egypt. Two mighty nations, Israel and Egypt, are led by two great men: Moses the liberating hero and Pharaoh the enslaving villain. Almost every scene is a masterpiece: the baby in the basket, the burning bush, the river of blood, the angel of death, the crossing of the sea, the manna in the wilderness, the water from the rock, the thunder on the mountain, the Ten Commandments, the golden calf, the pillar of cloud by day and fire by night.

This story, once heard, is never forgotten. For Jews the narrative defines their very existence, the rescue that made them the people of God. For Christians it is the gospel of the Old Testament, God's first great act of redemption. For people under oppression it is the story that promises the last, best hope of salvation. So we return to Exodus again and again, sensing its significance for our own spiritual pilgrimage.

DID YOU KNOW?
Exodus is the Latin form of the Greek word *exodos*, which means "exit" or "departure." On the Mount of Transfiguration, Moses and Elijah used the same word to describe the saving work that Jesus would do on the cross (see Luke 9:31, ESV).

The Form of the Book

The story of the Exodus is told as an epic adventure that begins in the middle of Israel's trouble, as epics generally do. In keeping with epic conventions, Exodus tells the story of a cosmic confrontation that requires an extended journey and is resolved by a mighty deliverance. It presents Moses as the heroic (although imperfect) national leader who answers God's call to rescue his people. And it records the founding of Israel as the people of God, providing a strong sense of national identity. In this context, the relevance of the second half of the book becomes apparent: God's law is Israel's constitution, and the Tabernacle is the place for national assembly.

Exodus is also part of a longer narrative that runs from Genesis to Deuteronomy (known as the Five Books of Moses or the Pentateuch). Some scholars compare the renewal of the covenant in Exodus (chapters 19, 20, 24, and 34) to ancient ceremonies for ratifying an international treaty. Chapter 20 contains three of the main parts in any covenant treaty between a great lord and one of the vassals under his protection: (1) the preamble, which identifies the parties to the agreement, (2) the prologue, which outlines the history of their relationship, and (3) the stipulations, which explain the parties' reciprocal responsibilities. In this case, God is the great king who sets the legal terms for Israel as a nation he has rescued and now calls into his royal service. Although Exodus does not include the conventional sanctions for violating a treaty, we can find the blessings and curses for keeping or breaking God's covenant elsewhere in the Pentateuch (e.g., Deuteronomy 27–28).

Key Words and Phrases

Key words and phrases in Exodus include the following:

- *deliver:* describes the main action in the story
- *holiness:* used more than 150 times in various forms to describe both God and the things he sets apart for his service, such as the Tabernacle and its priests
- *I am the LORD:* an assertion of God's character as the basis for his actions and authority
- *Pharaoh's heart was hardened:* shows both Pharaoh's culpability for his own sin (e.g., 8:15) and God's sovereignty over Pharaoh's stubborn refusal to let God's people go (e.g., 4:21; cf. Romans 9:14-18)
- *glory:* the goal of Israel's deliverance, as it is for everything that God ever does

> **DID YOU KNOW?**
> When Moses asks for God's name, God replies, "I AM WHO I AM" (3:14). Then God adds the closely related name "Yahweh" (3:15), or "LORD," which comes from the Hebrew verb translated "to be" and means "he who is." These mysterious names testify to God's eternity, self-existence, and self-sufficiency.

The Aim of the Book

Exodus tells the story of Israel's exit from Egypt and establishment as a nation. But the author has an even grander purpose in mind, namely, to magnify the glory of God in saving his people. The great problem at the beginning of the book is the Israelites' inability to go out and glorify God because Pharaoh wants to keep their service all to himself; hence God's explicitly stated reason for rescuing the Israelites: "My great glory will be displayed through Pharaoh and his troops, his chariots, and his charioteers" (14:17). There are visible manifestations and descriptions of the brightness of God's glory throughout the book—at the burning bush (3:1-6), in the song by the sea (15:11), in the wilderness (16:10), and on Mount Sinai (24:16; 33:18-23)—but the climax comes at the very end, when "the cloud covered the Tabernacle, and the glory of the LORD filled the Tabernacle" (40:34).

Key Places and Characters

The places in Exodus have an awe-inspiring quality. Egypt is the prison house of oppression. The burning bush is holy ground. The Red Sea is the place of greatest danger and grandest deliverance. The wilderness is the place of preparation and testing. Sinai is the holy mountain of God's awesome presence, thundering with the voice of his authority. And the Tabernacle is the house of God's glory, where people worship in holiness and awe.

The characters in Exodus are equally memorable, especially the main protagonist and his antagonist. Moses is the great hero: born in obscurity, rising to greatness, liberating his people from slavery, and founding a great nation. But he is also a flawed hero—a man with a criminal record for a capital offense who is slow to answer God's call and sometimes impatient with God's people. Pharaoh is the archetypal villain, seething with all the irrational paranoia, malevolent hatred, and false remorse of an abusive personality.

Two of the main characters in Exodus are actually groups of people, in keeping with the nationalistic emphasis of an epic story. There are the oppressive Egyptians, some of whom come to fear the God of Israel. Then there are the grumbling Israelites, who seem to get delivered almost in spite of themselves, although at least by the end of the story they come to worship God.

There are also a number of lesser characters. Some are members of Moses' family, such as his sister, Miriam, and his father-in-law, Jethro. Others are close colleagues, such as Joshua, the general. But the most important is Aaron, the older brother who serves Moses in the area of public relations but is best remembered for his colossal blunder in making the golden calf (and for his lame excuses: "You know how the people are" and "Out came this calf!"). On a more positive note, Bezalel and Oholiab are the gifted artists who have a special calling from God to make the Tabernacle.

These are all memorable characters. Nevertheless, the real hero of Exodus is the God of Israel. God is busy all the way through the book—hearing the prayers of his people, remembering the promises of his covenant, dictating his demands to Pharaoh, punishing his enemies, rescuing his people, leading them through the wilderness, laying down the law, designing his dwelling place, and finally descending in glory when the Tabernacle is finished.

Key Doctrines
The Sovereignty of God. God rules the world, working in history to reveal his glory.

Revelation. God reveals himself through the things he says and does so that his people can know him as their God.

Salvation. Exodus views salvation in terms of freedom from captivity, redemption from slavery (6:6), adoption as children (4:22-23), the substitution of sacrificial blood, and membership in a worshipping community.

Covenant. First, God rescues his people because he remembers the promises of his covenant (2:24); then, once he has rescued his people, he restores the relationship by renewing the covenant—his everlasting love commitment to Israel, sealed in blood.

Holiness. This describes both the awesome holiness of God and the holiness he requires of his people as a nation set apart for his service. Holiness includes the idea of moral purity, but in Exodus it primarily means that something or someone has been dedicated to God.

Law. Exodus presents the law as a gracious gift from God for the people he has already redeemed out of Egypt. However, as a perfect standard of righteousness, the law given in the Ten Commandments also exposes our sin and shows us our need for a Savior.

Judgment. God justly executes his wrath against people who break his law.

Atonement. Through the offerings made at Passover, on Mount Sinai, and in the Tabernacle, Exodus shows that God forgives sin through the blood of a righteous sacrifice.

Worship. As we learn from God's law (especially the second commandment and the regulations for the priesthood) and from Aaron's misadventure with the golden calf, we are to worship God only in the way he commands.

KEY VERSES

"I am the LORD. I will free you from your oppression and will rescue you from your slavery in Egypt. I will redeem you with a powerful arm and great acts of judgment. I will claim you as my own people, and I will be your God. Then you will know that I am the LORD your God who has freed you from your oppression in Egypt" (6:6-7). God makes his promise of redemption with a view to having a special love relationship with his people.

Tips for Reading or Teaching Exodus

Read Exodus in connection with the other four books of Moses. Looking back, how do the Genesis promises of land and seed (or a people and a place) set the agenda for the plot conflicts of Exodus? What is the connection between the story of Joseph at the end of Genesis and the situation of the Israelites at the beginning of Exodus? Looking forward, how does the end of Exodus prepare us for what Leviticus has to say about the ministry of the priests and the proper use of the Tabernacle? How does it prepare us for the wilderness journey that resumes in the book of Numbers?

The detailed descriptions of the Tabernacle and its furnishings tend to get tedious. This is not surprising: The Tabernacle was meant to be seen, not read. So this is one place where a picture is worth a thousand words. (See the diagram on page 57.) Resources such as David M. Levy's book *The Tabernacle: Shadows of the Messiah* provide detailed drawings of every aspect of the Tabernacle. Better yet, study the plans from Exodus and build your own scale model.

quick overview of exodus

1:1-22	Egypt enslaves Israel and sentences its sons to die.
2:1–4:31	God prepares and persuades Moses to deliver the people of God.
5:1–6:30	Moses has his first meeting with Pharaoh, and things go from bad to worse.
7:1–10:29	God sends nine plagues against Pharaoh and the Egyptians.
11:1–13:22	God sends the last and deadliest plague, from which the Israelites are saved by the blood of the Passover lamb.
14:1–15:21	The Israelites cross the Red Sea and live to sing about it.
15:22–18:27	In spite of the grumbling of God's people, he saves them from starvation, dehydration, and annihilation.
19:1–24:18	God hands down Ten Commandments and renews his covenant with Israel.
25:1–31:18	God gives Moses instructions for building the Tabernacle—the place of his earthly presence.
32:1–34:35	Aaron sets up an alternative worship service, with disastrous results.
35:1–40:38	The people build the Tabernacle God's way, and God fills it with his glory.

The Flow of the Book

The House of Bondage (Chapter 1). Exodus begins where Genesis left off: God is fulfilling his covenant promise to bless the children of Israel, now sojourning in Egypt. But—ominously—there is a new pharaoh in the land, who turns out to be a slave driver and, worse, a genocidal maniac.

Our Hero (2:1–4:17). Quietly, and behind the scenes, God begins to execute his plan of salvation. Through Moses' training in Pharaoh's court, his sympathy with people under oppression, his long years in the wilderness, and even his disastrous attempt to deliver Israel one Egyptian at a time, God is preparing him to lead the children of Israel. Notice how his early experiences serve as the prototype for what would later happen to the Israelites: Born in slavery and under the sentence of death, Moses is delivered through a watery ordeal and goes out into the wilderness, where he meets the living God at Mount Sinai. Also notice the desperate pleas of God's people at the end of chapter 2; the rest of Exodus is the answer to their prayers. Finally, consider what lessons Moses learns about God and about himself as he tries (unsuccessfully) to convince God that he's the wrong man for the job.

> **KEY VERSE**
> "This is what the LORD, the God of the Hebrews, says: Let my people go, so they can worship me" (9:1). God sent this message to Pharaoh by way of Moses. The mention of worship is not a subterfuge, as some have thought, but expresses the whole purpose of the Exodus: that God would receive glory from his people.

Go Down, Moses (4:18–6:30). Moses briefs his brother, Aaron, returns to Egypt, and utters his famous line: "Let my people go." Pharaoh scoffs at Moses and punishes the Israelites by forcing them to make bricks without straw. As the plot conflict intensifies, God repeats his promise of deliverance.

A Plague on Your House (Chapters 7–10). The plagues (from the Latin word *plaga,* meaning "a blow or wound") were God's judgment on the Egyptians for enslaving his people. However, the book of Exodus claims that they were also a judgment on Egypt's *gods* (12:12). The Egyptians depended on different deities to do different things for them: provide food, protect their children, aid them in their passage to the afterlife, etc. Many of Egypt's gods and goddesses were represented by various animals or by the sun, and the plagues seem to target some of these very deities (see the list of "Ten Terrible Plagues" below). It is worth considering what false gods we are tempted to depend on to control our economy, provide our food, or protect our health.

The Deadliest Plague and the First Passover (11:1–13:16). The last and most terrible plague was the death of every firstborn Egyptian son. Unlike the other plagues, this one also struck at the Israelites. But God provided a way for their sons to be kept safe: If they smeared the blood of a spotless lamb

TEN TERRIBLE PLAGUES

1. Blood (against Hapi, Khnum, and the other river gods of the Nile, which was the strength of Egypt's economy)
2. Frogs (against Heqet, the goddess of childbirth, who was represented as a frog)
3. Gnats or Lice (against the earth-god Geb)
4. Flies (against Khep-rer, the beetle-god of resurrection, or Beel-zebub, the demonic "lord of the flies")
5. Livestock (against Apis and other bovine deities, such as Hathor, the goddess of love and beauty)
6. Boils (against Amon Re, Thoth, Sekhmet, and the other gods of healing)
7. Hail (against Nut, the goddess of the sky, and Seth, the protector of crops)
8. Locusts (against Min, Nepri, Anubis, Senehem, and other gods and goddesses of the fields)
9. Darkness (against Aten, Re, and Atum, the supreme deities of the sun, who were associated with Pharaoh)
10. Death (against Osiris and Anubis, the gods of the dead, and against the deity of Pharaoh's firstborn son)

on their doorposts, the angel of death would pass over their houses. This ritual has been preserved in the annual celebration of Passover. Notice how the Israelites were to communicate the significance of these events to the next generation. What did Passover teach the Israelites about their identity as the people of God? How did it prefigure the saving work of Christ?

Crossing the Red Sea (13:17–15:21). Here is the first (but not the only) climax in the book of Exodus. God is the divine warrior who destroys his enemies, judges them for their sins, and with the same mighty act saves his people from certain destruction. The Song of Moses is not superfluous; in a way it is the whole point of the story. The story of salvation is always a musical: God has saved his people for his glory, and now they have a new reason to sing God's praise.

Pilgrims through This Barren Land (15:22–18:27). God continues to guard and guide his people, providing bread from heaven, water from the rock, victory over their enemies, and leaders to help Moses. But the Israelites aren't always happy about it.

On God's Mountain (Chapters 19–24). The people gather at the foot of Mount Sinai and prepare to meet God, who thunders with such holiness that they are not allowed to touch his mountain. He gives them the Ten Commandments (20:1-17), which as we all know, are easier to break than they are to keep. These are followed by a long list of laws usually known as the Book of the Covenant (20:21–23:33). The case laws in these chapters show how to apply the Ten Commandments to real-life situations, especially those that relate to public worship and social responsibility (work relationships, fair business practices, property law, personal injuries, etc.). Most important, rather than to get caught

The Ten Commandments

At first, the Ten Commandments seem relatively simple, and they may even seem simple to keep. After all, most people have never committed a murder, or at least they think they haven't. However, when we understand the full implications of the Ten Commandments, they prove to be more difficult to keep than we ever imagined. Here are some important guidelines for interpreting and applying the Ten Commandments:

- Each commandment is based on the righteous character of God. We are not to have any other gods because he is the only God there is. We must not lie because he is the God of truth, and so forth.
- Each commandment must be read in the context of the whole Bible. For example, when we read the second commandment, which forbids making idols, we must also consider passages such as Ephesians 5:5, which says that even our greed is a form of idolatry.
- Each commandment applies inwardly as well as outwardly. Therefore, as Jesus taught in his Sermon on the Mount, the seventh commandment condemns lust as well as sex outside of marriage (see Matthew 5:28), and anger is tantamount to murder (see Matthew 5:21-22).
- Each commandment should be interpreted both positively and negatively. Where a sin is forbidden, a corresponding duty is required, even if it is not mentioned explicitly. And where a duty is required, the corresponding sin is forbidden. To put it another way, there is a "do" that goes with every "don't," and a "don't" that goes with every "do." For example, the third commandment forbids the misuse of God's name, but more positively, it requires us to honor God's name.
- Each commandment stands for a whole category of sin. So when the ninth commandment tells us not to give false testimony, it is ruling out every kind of mistruth, from little lies to big ones. Although the Ten Commandments generally specify the most egregious form of each kind of sin (murder is the worst manifestation of anger, adultery is the worst kind of sexual sin, etc.), they also include all the lesser instances of the same kind of sin (such as physical violence or pornography, to name two).

To know the full implications of the Ten Commandments is to understand how impossible it is for us to keep them. This is good, because the more we see our sin, the more we know our need for God's grace in Christ, who is the only One who ever could and ever did keep the whole law of God.

up in the particulars, you need to see what kind of covenant relationship God wants his people to have with him and with one another. Consider how the rituals for ratifying the covenant in chapter 24 establish the basic biblical pattern for the public worship of God: Look for a call to worship, the reading of God's Word, a confession of faith, and the sharing of a sacramental meal.

The Blueprints for God's House (Chapters 25–31). While Moses was up on the mountain, God showed him a prototype for his sanctuary, the Tabernacle (see diagram opposite). This was a large tent—not unlike the ones the Israelites lived in—designed to serve as God's dwelling place with his people. At the same time, its fences and protective curtains were designed to preserve a safe distance from the holiness of God, who made his dwelling in the Holy of Holies (which only the high priest could enter, and only on the Day of Atonement).

Each item of furniture in the Tabernacle portrays our need for God. The *altar of burnt offering* shows our need for a sacrifice for our sins. The *bronze basin* shows our need for holy cleansing. The *table of showbread* shows our need for daily provision. The *golden lampstand* shows our need for life and light. The *altar of incense* shows our need for prayer. And the *Ark of the Covenant*—which represents God's throne and was covered with the mercy seat, where the high priest sprinkled blood on the Day of Atonement—shows our need for God's mercy. These chapters also include instructions for the holy garments of the priests who served in the Tabernacle. What did their clothing (chapter 28) and consecration (chapter 29) communicate about their relationship to God, their service at the Tabernacle, and their identification with the Israelites?

Unholy Cow (Chapters 32–34). Meanwhile, back at the camp, Aaron and the Israelites are busy breaking God's laws faster than Moses can bring them down

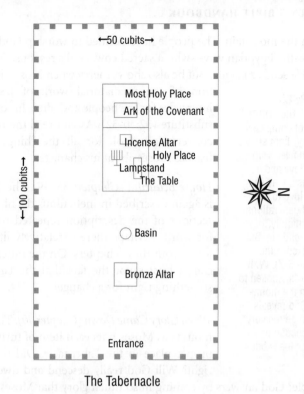

Most Holy Place

Ark of the Covenant

Incense Altar

Holy Place

Lampstand

The Table

←50 cubits→

←100 cubits→

N

Basin

Bronze Altar

Entrance

The Tabernacle

The Ark of the Covenant and the Mercy Seat

from the mountain. The people have decided to worship God their own way—the Egyptian way—with a sacred cow. God's response is appropriate: He sends a plague. But he also shows mercy when Moses, in anticipation of the mediatorial work of Jesus Christ, intercedes for the people and offers his own life as a substitute (32:30-32). As you read the rest of their conversation, look for all the things that God teaches Moses about his character.

KEY VERSES
"Yahweh! The LORD! The God of compassion and mercy! I am slow to anger and filled with unfailing love and faithfulness. I lavish unfailing love to a thousand generations. I forgive iniquity, rebellion, and sin. But I do not excuse the guilty" (34:6-7). With these words, spoken to Moses on the mountaintop, God reveals himself to be the very God we encounter throughout the Exodus.

House Beautiful (Chapters 35–39). The Tabernacle is again described in meticulous detail, with large sections of the description repeated nearly word for word. Perhaps there is relatively little new to learn from these chapters. On the other hand, we can at least savor the fact that the Israelites did something right for a change!

When Glory Came Down (Chapter 40). The suspense mounts as Moses puts each item of furniture in its proper place in the Tabernacle. Did they build it right? Will God really descend and dwell with his people? God answers by coming in so much glory that Moses can't even enter the Tabernacle! Exodus thus ends the way the world will end: with God living with his people in glory.

The Main Themes

1. DELIVERANCE. God delivers his people from slavery so that they can know him as their Savior and serve him as their Lord.
2. COVENANT. God has bound his people to himself with an everlasting promise, sealed in blood.
3. HOLINESS. God is so transcendently holy that he must separate himself from his people, even when he allows them limited access (as he does at the burning bush, the top of Mount Sinai, and the Holy of Holies). The people who serve a holy God must also be holy; therefore, they are separated from the world to observe the righteous requirements of God's law.
4. THE PRESENCE OF GOD. Most of the dramatic moments in Exodus relate in one way or another to the awesome presence of God, as he listens to the prayers of his people in Egypt, meets Moses at the

burning bush, delivers his people from their enemies, meets with his people at the mountain, and dwells in his Tabernacle. God's great promise to his people Israel—the one that distinguishes them from everyone else on earth—is this: "My presence will go with you" (33:14, ESV).

Contribution of the Book to the Bible's Story of Salvation in Christ

The Exodus is about Jesus as much as it is about anything else. When Paul reflected on the water Moses brought from the rock, he said, "that rock was Christ" (1 Corinthians 10:4). The apostle Jude went so far as to say that "Jesus . . . saved a people out of the land of Egypt" (Jude 1:5, ESV).

As the great Old Testament story of salvation, Exodus set the pattern for salvation in Christ. Jesus became the new Moses of a new exodus by going down into Egypt, passing through the waters of baptism, being tested in the wilderness, and then going up the mountain to give God's law (see the Sermon on the Mount, Matthew 5–7). And Jesus did all this for our salvation. By bringing us through the waters of baptism, he has set us free from our bondage to sin. Now he guides us on our pilgrimage through the wilderness, feeding us our daily bread and leading us to the glory of the Promised Land.

Many of the characters, events, and institutions in Exodus typify the person and work of Christ. The prophetic ministry of Moses typifies Jesus as the mediator of a new covenant. The Passover sacrifice typifies Jesus Christ as the Lamb of God whose blood atones for our sin (1 Corinthians 5:7), only this time—in a stunning reversal—God saves us by offering *his* firstborn Son. The Ten Commandments typify the character of Christ, and because we fail to meet their righteous standard, they also show us our need for him. And the high priest typifies the ministry of Christ in making a sacrifice for sin.

Similarly, the Tabernacle preaches the gospel of Jesus Christ. When the apostle John said, "The Word became flesh and dwelt among us" (John 1:14, ESV), the word he used for "dwell" was the Greek word for "tabernacle." In other words, by his incarnation Jesus became the true Tabernacle—God's dwelling place on earth. Furthermore, the articles in the Tabernacle all find their fulfillment in Christ. His sacrifice (*the altar of burnt offering*) enables us to approach the Holy Place, and the water of his baptism (*the bronze basin*) cleanses us from sin. He is the Bread of Life (*the table of showbread*) and the Light of the World (*the golden lampstand*). Since he is our eternal intercessor (*the altar of incense*), his prayers for us continuously rise like sweet incense before God's throne of grace. Best of all, his perfect blood has been sprinkled on the mercy seat (*the Ark of the Covenant*), allowing us to enter the Holy of Holies in heaven (see Hebrews 9:11-12). And all of this is just for starters. What other connections to Christ do you notice as you read and study Exodus?

Applying the Book

After summarizing the events of the Exodus, the apostle Paul wrote, "These things happened to them as examples for us. They were written down to warn us who live at the end of the age" (1 Corinthians 10:11). Paul was referring specifically to sins such as idolatry, envy, and sexual immorality, which were so common among the Israelites. But we can apply the principle more broadly: What happened to Israel in the Exodus helps us know how to live—and how not to live—today.

Like the Israelites, we have been delivered from the Egypt of our sin. Now we are traveling through the wilderness, waiting for the day when we will enter the Promised Land. Thus we can trace the story of the Exodus somewhere in the geography of our own souls. Are we trusting in the blood of the sacrificial Lamb that God has provided for our sins? Are we walking with God by faith through the wilderness of this fallen world? Are we obeying his law for our lives? And are we entering God's house, drawing near to worship him in the beauty of his holiness?

Finally, the book of Exodus teaches us to look to Jesus for our salvation. Like the Israelites, we need a Liberator to save us from our slavery to sin and to destroy our spiritual enemies. We need a Lamb to atone for our sins. We need a Guide to lead us through the wilderness to the Promised Land. We need a Provider to feed us bread from heaven and water from the rock. We need a Lawgiver to teach us how to love and serve the living God. And we need a God whose presence will be with us forever and whose glory defines the very meaning of our existence.

PERSPECTIVES
ON THE BOOK OF EXODUS

Well it's a great story. I think I'm a judge of stories and that's a great story. E. L. Doctorow

Exodus is a book for everyone. . . . It is the picture of our spiritual journey out of the world of bondage to sin and into the freedom of forgiveness and

*the full inheritance we have in Jesus Christ. So, here in Exodus, God calls
us from the anguish of our bondage and . . . bids us to set our feet on a
new way. Though that way may be accompanied, as it were, by . . .
the hardship of wilderness, we too . . . will know His overshadowing
presence.* Maxie D. Dunnam

*The qualities and temper of the episodes . . . properly reflect ancient
Egyptian customs. . . . The biblical author constructed such poignant and
profound pieces as a critique of contemporary Egyptian dogma and
practice and as a demonstration of the truth and power of Yahweh.*
John D. Currid

*[The exodus] cannot possibly be fictional. No nation would be likely to
invent for itself, and faithfully transmit century after century and
millennium after millennium, an inglorious and inconvenient tradition of
this nature.* Nahum Sarna

*The theme of the book of Exodus is quite clear. God enabled one small
group of miserably oppressed people to escape from tyranny. He chose
them for himself, he confronted them, and he revealed himself as the one
true God. He showed them who and what he was. He showed them
what they were like and sent them on their way to begin a new life.*
Godfrey Ashby

*[Exodus] relates how God fulfilled His ancient promise to Abraham by
multiplying his descendants into a great nation, redeeming them from the
land of bondage, and renewing the covenant of grace. At the foot of the
holy mountain He bestows on them the promises of the covenant, and
provides them with a rule of conduct by which they may lead a holy
life, and also with a sanctuary in which they may make offerings for sin
and renew fellowship with Him on the basis of forgiving grace.*
Gleason L. Archer

*The Tabernacle is an external pledge of the permanence of the Covenant of
Grace. The God of deliverance (the Lord) has taken up His abode in the
midst of His people. Yet, they are excluded from immediate access into His
presence by the veil which shut off the most Holy place to all but the high
priest and to him also, save on the Day of Atonement. . . . Thus, the
arrangements of the Tabernacle were typical, preparatory for the one
Sacrifice that has taken away the sins of the world.* Edward J. Young

LEVITICUS

Safeguarding the Covenant Nation

FORMAT. 27 chapters, 859 verses

IMPLIED PURPOSE. To convey God's guidelines for Israel's worship, social and legal life, and aspects of everyday living. Israel was becoming a nation and a society, so we can infer that a purpose of the book was to lay down a kind of spiritual and moral constitution for a nation.

AUTHOR'S PERSPECTIVE. The author objectively records what God told Moses, and he occasionally narrates events with that same objectivity. The author is a master recorder and a person with endless patience for details.

IMPLIED AUDIENCE. The book is a record of what God said to Moses, so in a sense, Moses is the implied audience. Moses was God's intermediary to the nation of Israel, so the covenant people of Israel were also the original audience. God also expects his people today (believers in Christ) to pay attention to his guidelines.

WHAT UNIFIES THE BOOK. The stance of an authoritative God giving rules to his people; the continual rhetorical situation of God's speaking to Moses; the format of rules and regulations, usually phrased as commands

SPECIAL FEATURES. The virtually total replacing of narrative by lists of rules and regulations; particularized references to the details of worship, of the physical body, and of human relations. This book of rules leaves nothing abstract.

CHALLENGES FACING THE READER OR TEACHER OF THIS BOOK.
1. A lack of narrative flow
2. The sheer quantity of rules and regulations

3. The lack of reserve in describing the slaughter of animals, human diseases, bodily functions, and sexual behavior

4. The huge gap between the ceremonial laws by which ancient Israel conducted its religious and civil life and our own practices in these areas

HOW TO MEET THE CHALLENGES.

1. Don't expect the book to tell a story in the usual sense.

2. Do not read the book consecutively but rather intermittently.

3. Accept the facts that the ancient world did not share our squeamishness and reticence about the physical body and that the original audience may have had a stronger sense that our bodies can be offered in holiness to God.

4. Look for underlying principles rather than literal application to build bridges between the ancient world and our own experiences.

THE MOST COMMON MISCONCEPTION ABOUT THIS BOOK. That it is a boring book. It isn't: If a pastor were to read most of these chapters in a worship service, there would be electricity in the air.

*L*eviticus *is a manual for the religious organization of reality. . . . The priestly code prescribes a religious regime of fearful severity, a plenitude of requirements and retributions and rewards, all sanctioned by the sound of God's voice. There is little relief from strictness; the book is almost completely written in the imperative. But there are interesting . . . glimpses of the individuals living within the system. There is the man who comes to the priest and says, "Something like a plague has appeared upon my house"—who discovers that there is decay where he dwells, and panics. . . . And there is the leper who must rend his clothes and cry, "Unclean, unclean."*

LEON WIESELTIER
"Leviticus"

27 Vows			
26 Blessing and Curses			
22:17–25:55 Rituals, Offerings, Festivals, Sabbatical, Jubilee			
21–22:16 Rules for Priests			
20 Serious Crimes			
19 Moral Rules	Holiness Code	Emphasis on a Multitude of General Rules	Pleasing a Holy God
18 Sexual Behavior			
17 Sacrifice and Food			
16 Day of Atonement Initiated	Atonement		
13–15 Diseases and Discharges	Uncleanness and Its Treatment		
12 Uncleanness after Childbirth			
11 Unclean Animals			
10 Judgment on Priests' Misbehavior	Institution of the Priesthood		
9 Inauguration of Priests' Ministry			
8 Ordination of Priests			
6:8–7:38 Instructions to Priests	How the Priests Processed the People's Offerings	Emphasis on Offerings and Sacrifices	Approaching a Holy God
4:1–6:7 Sin and Guilt Offerings	Offerings Brought by the Laity		
3 Peace Offering			
2 Grain Offering			
1 Burnt Offering			

AN OUTLINE OF
LEVITICUS

A famous Puritan once wrote that "in a divine commonwealth, holiness must have the principal honor and encouragement, and a great difference be made between the precious and the vile." Such an attitude has been under attack in our culture for a long time, as people have lost a sense of the sacred and have often tried to see how shocking they can be in blaspheming what has traditionally been considered holy. Even in Christian circles there has been an erosion of the idea that some aspects of life need to be set apart as sacred. The book of Leviticus can be an entry into an older way of thinking about the need to uphold the holiness of God and the things he considers sacred.

The Form of the Book
Although most of the book consists of a listing of rules and regulations, the external framework is narrative, or story. Verse 1 reads, "The Lord called to Moses from the Tabernacle and said to him." This narrative framework is kept alive in our awareness as various links tell us who is speaking to whom in the quoted speech that is about to follow. The narrative framework becomes prominent in chapters 8–10, which tell the story of the beginnings of the priesthood, and briefly reappears in 24:10-23.

Having acknowledged this narrative framework, with its accompanying report of speeches by one person to another, we can say emphatically that the actual content of the book is an unfolding series of rules and regulations, sometimes accompanied by warnings of judgment for disobedience and blessing for obedience. We can profitably look at this book as God's guidebook for his covenant, holy people at the very time when he was forming them as a fledgling nation.

The Title and What It Tells Us
While the Hebrew title for this book simply repeats the opening word of the book (translated "and he [the LORD] called"), the familiar title is based on the Greek translation of the Old Testament, known as the Septuagint. The word *Leviticus* means "that which pertains to the Levites." From this we could easily get the wrong impression that the book is a set of guidelines for the priests of Israel. But only a small part of the book addresses the Levites or pertains specifically to them. Most of the regulations are addressed to the nation—the laity. It is probable that God expected the priests to enforce the rules.

Key Characters
God is the great authority figure in Leviticus. His main activity is speaking his will to Moses. As leader of the nation, Moses is the main human

character. The nation, usually referred to as "the Israelites" or "the people," is a corporate character in the proceedings. Aaron and the Levites are the final distinct group in the cast of characters, and the book consistently portrays them as being special within the broader society.

Unifying Elements

- The continual format of God's speaking to Moses and imparting rules and regulations for the life of his people
- The format of lists
- A social or communal focus, i.e., a whole nation or society is in view.
- A utopian theme (the description of a good society and the religious and communal forms that make the good life possible)
- Continuous attention to minute particulars and physical details
- A prevailing tone of seriousness before the demands of an awe-inspiring God

Key Doctrines

Holiness. The mass of details paints a picture of God's covenant people as set apart from uncleanness and immorality, just as God is set apart from these things.

Covenant. The book of Leviticus is a handbook on how God expects his people to live as part of the binding reciprocal relationship into which they have entered.

Ethics. Many of the rules govern how people are to relate to other people and the community.

Sanctification. It is also possible to see the rules in Leviticus as giving a picture of the process of becoming pure in life and worship, of doing what delights God.

Atonement. Much of the code that this book lays out has to do with blood sacrifice as the means by which God provides sinful humanity access to himself.

Worship. In a broad sense, Leviticus embodies important principles of worship.

CATEGORIES OF THE SACRED IN LEVITICUS

In Leviticus, God stipulates the things that must be set apart as holy. They fall mainly into these categories:

- sacred persons, such as the priests and Levites
- sacred rituals, such as sacrifices and purification rites
- sacred places and objects, such as the Tabernacle and its furnishings
- sacred seasons and times, such as the Sabbath and annual feasts

Tips for Reading or Teaching Leviticus

One thing that can make the book immediately inviting is being aware that it covers a huge swath of human life. Many of the regulations deal with Old Testament worship, but there are additional levels of meaning—civil, moral, personal. The book addresses several modern concerns—sex, hygiene, communicable diseases, regulating a society, structures of authority within a society. The more you ponder the book, the more relevant to modern life it will become in your thinking.

You cannot relish reading or studying this book without paying attention to the specific details, including an abundance of physical details, that constitute the surface of the text. The way to the universal is through the particular, so you need to exercise your imagination in entering the world of the text.

Once you have looked *at* the particulars of the text, you need to look *through* them to the universal principles they embody. As part of this venture, you need to build bridges between the text and modern life—to see analogies between the two worlds.

quick overview of leviticus

1:1–7:38	Offerings that God demands of his people
8:1–10:20	Rules for the priests
11:1–15:33	Rules governing uncleanness and purity
16:1-34	Stipulations regarding the Day of Atonement
17:1–27:34	An ever-expanding list of rules and ceremonies

The Flow of the Book

Manual of Offerings and Sacrifices (Chapters 1–7). Virtually all modern Bible versions accompany this material with headings that divide the laws into categories. This is a great help. Beyond that, you can be analytic by looking for these things: (1) the focus on the act of offering something to God; (2) the categories of rules for individuals, for the whole congregation of Israel, and for the priests; (3) evidences that these offerings are a system of forgiveness that God himself makes possible and, further, that sin and forgiveness are at the heart of the covenant; and (4) hints of the principle stated in 10:10—the need to distinguish between the holy and the ordinary, or common. Note that the conclusion of this section (7:37-38) is a convenient summary of the types of offerings described and commanded.

It is also helpful to realize that 1:1–6:7 outlines the offerings that the people brought for sacrifice, while 6:8–7:38 is an account of how the priests actually presented these offerings.

These offerings together served three complementary functions: The burnt, sin, and guilt offerings served the purpose of atonement. The grain offering was a gift presented to God, and the peace offering emphasized fellowship or communion with God.

THE FIVE MAIN OFFERINGS STIPULATED IN LEVITICUS
- Burnt offering (an animal sacrifice): 1:3-17; 6:8-13
- Meal or grain offering: 2:1-16; 6:14-23
- Peace offering (an animal sacrifice): 3:1-17; 7:11-34
- Sin offering (an animal sacrifice): 4:1–5:13; 6:24-30
- Guilt offering (an animal sacrifice): 5:14–6:7; 7:1-10

Manual for the Priesthood (Chapters 8–10). Next the book moves to stipulations that govern the priestly class. Look for evidences that the priests serve as an intermediary between the people and God. Note a distinction between the consecration or ordination of the priests (chapter 8) and the beginning of their ministry (chapters 9–10). As you read these chapters, be receptive to the excitement of what is happening: This is the beginning of something new, and in chapter 10 you definitely get the picture that Moses and the priests are "feeling their way" and making false moves in the process. Finally, in analyzing the rituals described in Leviticus, it is helpful to operate on the premise that ceremonial rituals are visual enactments of spiritual realities. Ask what spiritual realities the external actions embody.

Manual of Uncleanness and Purity (Chapters 11–15). The only way to deal with this material is to steel yourself for an anatomy of the physical uncleanness and disease to which the human body is subject. These chapters are an ever-expanding picture of human frailty and limitation—a reminder of how the Fall affected the human body. A second level of meaning is the social dimension of these rules governing the health of the community—especially, perhaps, a traveling community living in close proximity. Then think beyond the physical and social/hygienic levels to the spiritual level. The obsession in these chapters with uncleanness and its purification is a picture of the spiritual state of the human race and the individual members of it. Here is a symbolic picture of human sinfulness juxtaposed with God's holiness.

KEY VERSES

"You must distinguish between what is sacred and what is common, between what is ceremonially unclean and what is clean" (10:10).

"Set yourselves apart to be holy, for I am the LORD your God. Keep all my decrees by putting them into practice, for I am the LORD who makes you holy" (20:7-8).

Institution of the Day of Atonement (Chapter 16). At the heart of Old Testament religion was the great Day of Atonement. Here you actually catch a glimpse of God instituting it. Just as the Day of Atonement was preeminent in the Jewish covenant rituals, it also serves as the linchpin of Leviticus, appearing virtually in the middle of the book and holding both parts together. The best way to make this chapter meaningful for yourself is to analyze the underlying principles you see (e.g., blood sacrifice, the idea of substitutionary atonement, etc.). Then reflect on how these principles become fulfilled in the perfect atonement of Christ.

The Holiness Code (Chapters 17–27). To label this section by the conventional title "the holiness code" (a label of modern commentators) is to run the risk of concealing the actual diversity of the material. These chapters are a miscellaneous list of ceremonial, moral, and civil rules (as the chart earlier in this chapter hints). The organization is somewhat miscellaneous, but this does not mean that the rules are unimportant add-ons (which is what is ordinarily implied by the term *miscellaneous*). On the contrary, these wide-ranging rules are treated as having the utmost importance, being the means by which God's covenant people relate to God and the conditions by which they are blessed or cursed.

Attempts to organize the material too neatly make it look more systematic than it is. What you find is a progressive accumulation of separate rules and ceremonies with interspersed warnings about disobedience and promises of blessing for obedience. However, you can look for distinctions such as the following:

- Acts that are prohibited (It is helpful to ponder why God disapproves of these acts.)
- Virtuous acts that are commanded or required (Think about why God approves of these acts.)
- Ceremonies performed by priests and therefore having to do with covenant worship
- Acts that have to do with personal holiness, such as not hating in one's heart (19:17) or not consulting wizards, and those that have a

Jesus as Priest

The priest was one of three officials (the prophet and the king were the others) who provided spiritual leadership for the Old Testament people of God and pointed to God's ultimate salvation in Christ.

The main function of the priest was to offer sacrifices for the sins of God's people. The supreme sacrifice was the one the high priest offered on the Day of Atonement. But as we learn in Leviticus and elsewhere, Israel's priests offered many daily sacrifices: burnt offerings, grain offerings, peace offerings, sin offerings, and guilt offerings, among others. As they made these offerings, the priests interceded for the people, asking God to forgive their sins.

The millions of blood sacrifices conducted before Christ's crucifixion were not enough: "The sacrifices under that system were repeated again and again, year after year, but they were never able to provide perfect cleansing for those who came to worship. . . . For it is not possible for the blood of bulls and goats to take away sins" (Hebrews 10:1, 4). The mere fact that these sacrifices had to be offered again and again was a sign that they were not the final answer for sin. Although they could remind people of their guilt, they could not remove it.

The Old Testament priesthood had other limitations as well. The priests were supposed to make atonement for others, but they were sinners too, so they needed a sacrifice for their own sins. Furthermore, they were all mortal, so when they died, they could not continue to intercede for God's people.

Enter the perfect priest: "a great High Priest who has entered heaven, Jesus the Son of God" (Hebrews 4:14). Jesus has been raised to a priesthood that will never end, and therefore "he lives forever to intercede with God on their behalf" (Hebrews 7:25). Unlike other priests, he is without sin, and therefore he does not need anyone else to make atonement for him (Hebrews 7:26-27). But here's the real shocker: Rather than bring a sacrifice, Jesus *became* one! He offered himself as the sacrificial Lamb of God, bleeding and dying to atone for our sins. Because he is the infinitely precious Son of God, his blood is sufficient to atone for all the sins of his people, now and forever. As the Scripture says, "Our High Priest offered himself to God as a single sacrifice for sins, good for all time" (Hebrews 10:12).

As you read about the Old Testament priests and their ministry, look for hints of the priestly ministry that we need Jesus to perform on our behalf. And as you read what the New Testament says about Christ's sufferings and death, look for ways his atonement both fulfilled and replaced the old system of sacrifice.

THE SEVEN FESTIVALS OF LEVITICUS 23
- Passover
- Unleavened bread
- First fruits (or first harvest)
- Pentecost (or harvest or weeks)
- Trumpets
- Day of Atonement
- Booths (or shelters or tabernacles)

moral/social dimension, such as refraining from adultery or restoring the fortunes of the poor in Years of Jubilee
- The institution of annual feasts, offerings, and ceremonies
- Implied or explicit blessing as a reward for obedience and punishment as a consequence of disobedience (especially in chapter 26)
- Some additional categories including sexual relations, family life, worship, ceremonial cleanness and uncleanness, civil punishments for crimes, religious feasts and days of observance, and property and slave rights

The Main Themes
1. God is holy (sinless), and he wants his covenant people to be holy also.
2. God has given his covenant people guidelines for living in a way that is holy as opposed to sinful.
3. God has shown his people the sinfulness of sin.
4. Because all people sin, God has provided the means of forgiveness and restitution, consisting especially of blood sacrifices and atonement.
5. God is a demanding God. Modern ideas of halfhearted gestures toward an indulgent deity do not square with what God reveals himself to be like.
6. God has prescribed the proper way to worship.
7. Regarding the Old Testament covenant of grace, Leviticus is an extended handbook of the relationship God established in the Old Testament between himself and the nation for whom he provided salvation.
8. The physical dimension of life is important as part of the religious life.

Contribution of the Book to the Bible's Story of Salvation in Christ
The key to seeing Christ in Leviticus lies in a way of interpreting the Bible known as *typology*. In this arrangement, the Old Testament contains "types," that is, models or symbols, that point forward to Christ, who is the ultimate fulfillment of these foreshadowings. Once we have this in view, the entire system of offerings and sacrifices and the Day of Atonement point to what Christ did on the cross.

Applying the Book

Applying the book properly begins with an awareness of three types of laws in the first five books of the Bible: (1) ceremonial laws, (2) civil laws, and (3) moral laws. The ceremonial laws were fulfilled by Christ and were therefore terminated or abolished. Most of the civil laws are no longer practiced, indicating that they are not timeless but rather were limited largely to Old Testament Israel when it lived under the direct government of God. For example, we no longer turn enforcement of hygiene laws over to the religious leaders in our society, and we no longer exact capital punishment for people who commit adultery. The moral laws are permanent expressions of God's righteousness: Murder and adultery are always wrong. We can dispel any doubt we may have on this point by reading the New Testament letter to the Hebrews.

Proper application begins with determining what kind of law a given regulation represents. The timeless moral laws require our obedience. What they command, God still expects us to do. What they forbid, God still expects us to refrain from doing. When we come to ceremonial laws (all of which have ceased to be binding) and to civil laws that were limited to ancient Jewish society, we need to determine *the universal principles* behind the laws. Once we have determined what these principles are, we need to ponder ways in which we need to apply them in our own lives. For example, we no longer bring grain offerings and animal sacrifices to God, but God does expect us to contribute money and time to Christian causes and church work.

A final application is more general. Compared to the laborious system of ceremonial laws in Old Testament religion, it is easy for Christians to think that God's grace is cheap and his demands easy. We should regard the book of Leviticus as a sobering reminder that God demands perfect holiness from his followers, along the lines of Jesus' statement in the Sermon on the Mount that "you are to be perfect, even as your Father in heaven is perfect" (Matthew 5:48).

PERSPECTIVES ON THE BOOK OF LEVITICUS

When Exodus and Leviticus end, [the people of] Israel possess a comprehensive statement of what God expects from them. They know the basics of [the] covenant, as well as its finer points. They have a place to worship, leaders to guide worship, and sacrifices that will cover their sins. Beyond these vital ingredients, they now possess a national identity: they are Yahweh's holy people. Paul R. House

Leviticus is . . . more than a description of past historical events and more than a collection of dated laws. It tells us about God's character and will, which found expression in his dealings with Israel and in the laws he gave them. Gordon J. Wenham

Leviticus locates the individual in the context of the larger community. Human life is lived in the context of the larger community. . . . The primary theological image of Leviticus is the holy God dwelling in the midst of the Israelite community. Leviticus takes the concrete presence of God seriously and seeks to discover what it means to live life in the presence of the holy God. Frank H. Gorman Jr.

The word holy is used 91 times in Leviticus, and words connected with cleansing are used 71 times. References to uncleanness number 128. There's no question what this book is all about. Warren W. Wiersbe

[Leviticus] not only presents the entire religious system of ancient Israel, but it also lays the theological foundation for the New Testament teaching about the atoning work of Jesus Christ. Allen P. Ross

What the layman bringing an offering needs to know (1–6:7); the professional knowledge required for priests presenting these sacrifices (6:8–7:38); tying into the preceding section that deals with the permanent general precepts for sacrifice, a narrative section dealing with a specific occasion of priestly conduct of sacrifices (8–10); a section dealing with cultic cleanness, coherent but divided into numerous subsections (11–15); standing alone, directions for making atonement for the holy place (16); the law of holiness—a miscellaneous section that does fall into discrete content units as the first half of the book does, though each chapter contains in itself a more or less unifying subject (17–27). Summary of Martin Noth's view of the structure of Leviticus

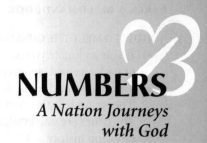

NUMBERS
A Nation Journeys
with God

FORMAT. 36 chapters, 1,288 verses

IMPLIED PURPOSE. To record the events that happened on the journey of the Israelites in the wilderness and the instructions God gave during the journey

AUTHOR'S PERSPECTIVE. The author, a faithful recorder of God's instructions to Moses and a master storyteller of wilderness events, reveals an awareness of what a good society should look like and the ways in which his own nation frequently falls short of that ideal.

IMPLIED AUDIENCE. While some of the instructional passages listing rules and regulations were written for the Israelites undergoing the journey, the bulk of the book was written with posterity in mind. First Corinthians 10:11 says that the events recorded in Numbers "were written down to warn us who live at the end of the age."

WHAT UNIFIES THE BOOK. God as authority figure, lawgiver, judge, and provider; the leadership of Moses; the journey motif; the wilderness setting; the generally bad behavior of the Israelites

SPECIAL FEATURES. Alternating sections of law-giving and narrative; the epic or national scope of the action; vivid stories of God's punishment of people who rebel against legitimate authority; miraculous interventions in the life of the nation; memorable individual images, such as the pillar of fire and cloud, the rod that blossoms, the fiery serpents and brazen serpent, water from a rock, and many more

CHALLENGES FACING THE READER OR TEACHER OF THIS BOOK.
1. The unexpected (by modern readers' standards) interruption of the narrative flow by sections of rules and regulations
2. The need to be interested in history
3. The depressing picture of people who behave badly

HOW TO MEET THE CHALLENGES.

1. If you acclimate yourself to the principle of alternating sections of narrative and law-giving, you will actually find yourself looking forward to the instructional sections.

2. The writer tells the story so well that it is easy to be interested. The issues are universal, and in addition, the story is a chapter in salvation history as God preserves the nation through which he will bless the world.

3. The picture of the Israelites' behavior is a mirror of our own. If we find the spectacle depressing, we need to do something about it and see our own need of God's grace.

The central message of the book . . . may be expressed in words which occur in . . . Romans xi. 22—"Behold therefore the goodness and severity of God." In Numbers we see the severity of God, in the old generation which fell in the wilderness and never entered Canaan. We see the goodness of God, in the new generation which was protected, preserved, and provided for. . . . Closely running up to this central message of the book are two other lessons—two warnings to ourselves; and these also may be expressed in words from the New Testament. The first is a warning against presumption [1 Corinthians 10:1-12]. . . . The second warning is against unbelief [Hebrews 3:12]. . . . The New Testament itself interprets the book of Numbers for us . . . : 1. "Behold the goodness and severity of God." 2. "Let him that thinketh he standeth take heed. . . ." "take heed lest there be in you— unbelief."

J. SIDLOW BAXTER
Explore the Book

34–36 Regulations for Settlement in Canaan — Rules

33 Recap of Campsites on the Journey — Narrative

32 Settling of Tribes East of the Jordan

31 The Battle against Midian — Census and Rules

26–30 Second Census; Varied Regulations — Journey

20–25 Marching, Complaining, Rescue, Moses' Failure, Balaam's Prophecy — Rules

18–19 Duties of Levites; Purification Rituals — Narrative

16–17 Challenges to Aaron's Priesthood — Rules

15 Offerings and Regulations — Journey

10:11–14:45 Marching, Complaining, Rebellion, Judgment, Rescue

9:15–10:10 Final Preparations for Marching — Regulations

7–9:14 Worship Rituals

5–6 General Rules; Laws for Nazirites

3–4 Census and Duties of Levites — Census and Arrangement of Tribes

2 Positioning of Tribes in Camp

1 Census of Warriors

At the Edge of the Promised Land

The Journey in the Wilderness

Preparations for the Journey

AN OUTLINE OF
NUMBERS

Storytellers through the ages have loved to tell stories of traveling groups. It is not hard to see why. When people travel together, they experience life in microcosm. Just think of your own experiences with traveling groups, including family trips. These occasions bring out what is in people. In particular, human nature reveals itself under stress. Numbers is a travel story that reveals bedrock human nature—and God's way of dealing with it. Note also that the journey motif has been the dominant motif for the spiritual life in devotional writing through the centuries.

The Form of the Book
Although Numbers is a long book composed of seemingly innumerable details, it is actually based on a very simple plan. It moves back and forth between sections of instructions and regulations from God to Moses and narrative units that tell a story. Once you get into the rhythm of this, the book is easy to manage.

The specific type of story Numbers tells is known as the travel story—in this case the travels of an entire nation. The story will fall into place if you simply recognize the distinctives of a travel story—journey, change of scene, conflict with the environment and surrounding nations, conflicts within the traveling community, danger, testing, encounters (including encounters with the divine), and quest.

The Story
The underlying story told by means of the alternating sections of law-giving and narrative is not about just any nation. It is the story of God's guidance of his covenant people from the land of bondage to the edge of the Promised Land. In this story it is as important that the people understand their covenant duties as it is that they complete the journey successfully. That is why we find the interspersed sections of instruction. The story is more than a travel story—it is also an initiation into God's design for a covenant nation.

Unifying Elements

- Regular alternating between passages that list rules and regulations and passages of narrative text that advance the journey
- The dominant characters of God and Moses
- The journey motif and conventions of the travel story
- The focus on a nation and its leadership

Key Doctrines

Covenant. The instructional passages teach the obligations of covenant living, and the narrative sections demonstrate God's providential care over his covenant people.

The Nature of God. Both the listing of rules and regulations and the narrative sections embody the attributes of God, especially his holiness.

Sin. In general, the behavior of the Israelites is ignominious, and we understand that sin consists of disobedience to what God commands.

Providence. The narrative sections are a story of God's provision and protection of his people.

Ethics and Sanctification. The sections of instruction carry on the theme begun in Exodus and Leviticus of how God wants people to relate to their fellow humans and to him as a holy God.

Tips for Reading or Teaching Numbers

Do not expect the entire book to tell a story. Only half of the book is narrative.

You need to shift gears when you move from the passages of rules and regulations to the narrative passages, and vice versa. The key activities that the instructional passages require are (1) getting the literal details in view and (2) extracting general moral and spiritual principles from them. The narrative passages require you to apply what you know about how stories work.

Keep the overall story in view: This is an account of how God formed a covenant community and revealed how he wanted the members of such a community to behave toward him and toward one another.

DID YOU KNOW?

• The name *Numbers* derives from a relatively small piece of the total picture, namely, the two census summaries ("numberings"), supplemented by the numbers of items contained in the offerings recorded in chapter 7.

• The hymn "Guide Me, O Thou Great Jehovah" is based on the story told in Numbers.

quick overview of numbers

1:1–10:36	Preparations for the journey through the wilderness
11:1–30:16	The forty-year journey through the wilderness, with interspersed passages of law-giving
31:1–36:13	Final action and law-giving

The Flow of the Book

Preparatory Instructions for the Journey to the Promised Land (1:1–10:10).
If you come to these chapters straight from reading Leviticus, you will
feel on familiar ground. The format of Leviticus continues, consisting of
straight reporting of God's instructions to Moses, interspersed with narrative accounts of the implementing of those instructions. The repeated
formula is along the lines of "the Lord spoke to Moses." In view of the
journey that begins in chapter 10, it is plausible to read the material as being a preparation for the journey, but in fact, the instructions are often
reminiscent of what we find in the book of Leviticus.

While the format is familiar, the situation and content are new and
consist of this sequence: (1) the census of the nation's warriors, chapter
1; (2) the campsite arrangement around the Tent of Meeting, chapter 2;
and (3) the census and duties of the Levites, chapters 3–4. The best way to
read this material is simply to enter into the world it portrays and catch a
sense of the excitement of the venture. Perhaps the general principle is
that God wants society to be orderly, but other lessons are present as well.

The rest of the unit reads like a sequel to Leviticus as God instructs
Moses regarding ceremonial laws and rituals, rules for Nazirites, instructions for sacrifices and worship (along with brief narratives of their imple-
mentation), and instructions for the upcoming march. Your procedure
should be the same as for the book of Leviticus: First get the literal facts
clear in your imagination; then ponder the general principles, such as the
importance of worship, of doing things God's way, of insisting that societies be orderly and law-bound.

Israel on the March (10:11–14:45). Narrative now makes a welcome appearance, and things begin to move. You need to activate all that you
know about how stories work. (For a primer, see "Narrative as a Form of
Writing" on page 35.) Plot, setting, and character are the terms of engagement with the text. This is an epic story—the story of a traveling
community meeting a series of dangers and ordeals. The story also has
the particular virtues of the travel story. The first item on your agenda is
to relive the story as vividly as possible. Look for such standard motifs as
danger, conflict moving to resolution (including conflicts within the
traveling community itself), testing, tragedy, crime and punishment, and
rescue. Then remember that all of these individual stories are in some
sense *example stories*. Analyze what each is an example *of*, and what this,
in turn, tells us about life. The central focus is the picture of what God
and people are like.

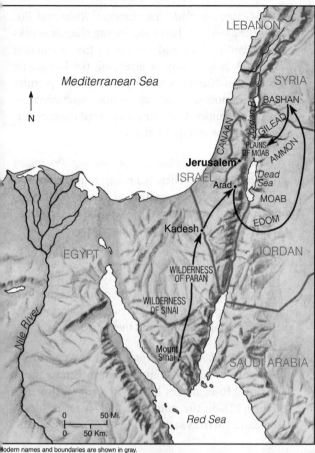

Modern names and boundaries are shown in gray.

they spent most of their desert years. Miriam died here. And it was here that Moses angrily struck the rock, which kept him from entering the Promised Land (20).

4 Arad When the king there heard that Israel was on the move, he attacked, but he was soundly defeated. Moses then led the people southward and eastward around the Dead Sea (21:1–3).

5 Edom The Israelites wanted to travel through Edom, but the king of Edom refused them passage (20:14–22). So they traveled around Edom and became very discouraged. The people complained, and God sent poisonous snakes to punish them. Only by looking at a bronze snake on a pole could those bitten be healed (21:4–9).

6 Ammon Next, King Sihon of the Amorites refused Israel passage. When he attacked, Israel defeated his army and conquered the territory as far as the border of Ammon (21:21–32).

7 Bashan Moses sent spies to Bashan. King Og attacked, but he was also defeated (21:33–35).

8 Plains of Moab The people camped on the plains of Moab, east of the Jordan River across from Jericho. They were on the verge of entering the Promised Land (22:1).

9 Moab King Balak of Moab, terrified of the Israelites, called upon Balaam, a famous sorcerer, to curse Israel from the mountains above where the Israelites camped. But the Lord caused Balaam to bless them instead (22:2–24:25).

10 Gilead The tribes of Reuben and Gad decided to settle in the fertile country of Gilead east of the Jordan River because it was a good land for their sheep. But first they promised to help the other tribes conquer the land west of the Jordan River (32).

1 Mount Sinai Numbers begins at Mount Sinai in the wilderness of Sinai with Moses taking a census of the men eligible for battle. As the battle preparations began, the people also prepared for the spiritual warfare they would face. The Promised Land was full of wicked people who would try to entice the Israelites to sin. God, therefore, taught Moses and the Israelites how to live right (1:1—12:15).

2 Wilderness of Paran After a full year at Mount Sinai, the Israelites broke camp and began their march toward the Promised Land by moving into the wilderness of Paran. From there, one leader from each tribe was sent to spy out the new land. After 40 days they returned, and all but Joshua and Caleb were too afraid to enter. Because of their lack of faith, the Israelites were made to wander in the wilderness for 40 years (12:16—19:22).

3 Kadesh With the years of wandering nearing an end, the Israelites set their sights once again on the Promised Land. Kadesh was the oasis where

PUTTING GOD TO THE TEST

In 14:22, God charges the Israelites with having put him to the test and with disobeying him "these ten times" (ESV). Here are the ten events:

- Complaining after Moses and Aaron told Pharaoh to let Israel go (Exodus 5:20-21)
- The Red Sea crisis (Exodus 14:10-12)
- The bitter waters of Marah (Exodus 15:23-24)
- The lack of food near Elim (Exodus 16:1-3)
- Disobedience regarding the gathering of manna (Exodus 16:19-28)
- The lack of water at Rephidim (Exodus 17:2-3)
- The golden calf incident (Exodus 32)
- Complaining at Taberah (Numbers 11:1-3)
- Craving meat (Numbers 11:4-6)
- The unbelief of ten of the spies (Numbers 13-14)

Law-Giving Interlude: Supplemental Rules and Rituals (Chapter 15). This freestanding chapter breaks the narrative flow and returns to the instruction mode. A helpful way of analyzing the law-giving sections of Numbers is to operate on the premise that ceremonial rituals are visual enactments of spiritual realities. Look for the spiritual realities embodied in the external actions.

Challenge and Vindication of Aaron's Priesthood (Chapters 16–17). There is a return to narrative, and all of the episodes revolve around Aaron's right to the priesthood. Ponder how this inset narrative sequence relates to the bigger design of Numbers.

Law-Giving Interlude: Rules Governing the Priests and Levites (Chapters 18–19). You can assimilate these instructions regarding ceremonial regulations by first grasping the literal details and then thinking about general principles and their application.

On the March Again (Chapters 20–25). As narrative conventions take over, apply what you know about stories. Moses makes his tragic error in this unit (20:10-12). In the middle of this narrative block, the nation arrives at the edge of the Promised Land (22:1).

Interlude: Census and Supplemental Regulations (Chapters 26–30). A helpful grid for analyzing this block of instructions from God to Moses and the Israelites is to ponder what the material says about what matters to God and what, accordingly, should matter to his covenant people.

The Final Leg of the Journey (Chapters 31–33). A sense of narrative closure sets in as the nation on the march engages in battle and a few tribes settle east of the Jordan River. Chapter 33 reinforces the sense that the story is reaching its end by recapping the stages of the journey from Egypt to Canaan, naming each campsite. This is a good point at which to codify your own generalizations about the journey that you have reenacted as you read Numbers.

Final Law-Giving Interlude: Concluding Rules (Chapters 34–36). The format returns to the account of what "the Lord said to Moses," by now familiar from other parts of the Pentateuch. The new wrinkle is that this time the regulations deal with land allotments and settlement in Canaan.

The Main Themes
1. God expects his followers to live according to his rules and in a manner that is different from that of the rest of the world.
2. God has revealed how he wants his covenant people to live, and these commands extend both to how they worship him and to their moral behavior toward fellow humans.
3. People have an innate tendency to disobey what God has stipulated.
4. God holds his people responsible for their sins when they refuse to live by his rules.
5. Despite all the waywardness that followers of God display, God remains faithful to them and continues to guide them in a redemptive direction.

Contribution of the Book to the Bible's Story of Salvation in Christ
There is less overt typology in Numbers than in Leviticus, but we can still interpret many of the regulations as pointing forward to the sacrifice of Christ. New Testament passages that apply details in the story to Christ include John 3:14 (the bronze serpent) and 1 Corinthians 10:4 (the rock). More important than specific details is the overall story. Numbers records how God formed and protected the covenant nation of Israel, from which would come the Messiah. Finally, Balaam's prophecy contains a famous messianic prophecy (24:17).

Applying the Book
We can begin with the narrative aspect. It is a striking story of God's provision and protection in the physical crises of life. What God did for

1 CORINTHIANS 10:1-13 AS A COMMENTARY ON THE STORY TOLD IN NUMBERS
- The events are a warning to us not to crave evil things (v. 6).
- The events were written down for our instruction, or as examples for us (v. 11).
- We should not put God to the test or grumble, as the Israelites did (vv. 9-10).
- We can see evidences of Christ in the story (v. 4).
- Although we are subject to temptation or testing as the Israelites were, we are not doomed to succumb (v. 13).

the Israelites in the wilderness, he can do for us in our wilderness experiences. Beyond that, the individual narrative episodes are example stories that teach us about God, about the world, and about how people should live.

We can apply the sections of rules and regulations in the same way that we could apply similar material elsewhere in the Pentateuch. They teach us about God, about morality, and about worship.

The figure of Moses provides one of the best biblical models of leadership. Except for his famous lapse at the rock, he exemplifies what God is looking for in leaders. Moses is a case study in courage. We can apply the lessons as leaders and followers.

PERSPECTIVES
ON THE BOOK OF NUMBERS

The old generation (1–14), the transition era (15–20), the new generation (21–37). The corresponding movements: Sinai to Kadesh-barnea (1–14), the wilderness wandering (15–20), Kadesh to the Plain of Moab (21–37).
J. Sidlow Baxter's version of the book's structure

Preparation for the journey (1:1–10:10); the journey (10:11–22:1); at the gate to the Promised Land (22:2–36:13). The corresponding scenic shifts: at Sinai, to Moab, at Moab. Irving Jensen's account of the book's structure

In Genesis God elected a people, in Exodus He redeemed them, in Leviticus He sanctified them, and in Numbers He directed them.
Bruce Wilkinson and Kenneth Boa

What then is the essence of religious ritual in the Bible? It is a means of communication between God and man, a drama on a stage watched by human and divine spectators. Old Testament rituals express religious truths visually as opposed to verbally. They are the ancient equivalent of television. Gordon J. Wenham

How faithful is God to promises made to an ungrateful and rebellious people? Does God give people a second chance? What does it mean to be a holy community, and how is that sanctity to be maintained? What kind of

leadership does a journeying people need on its way between promise and fulfillment? How does God provide when the leaders struggle under their burden or even abandon their task? These are some of the important questions addressed in the book of Numbers. Katharine Doob Sakenfeld

The book of Numbers is a study in the contrast between God's faithfulness and human disobedience. R. K. Harrison

God honors faith and punishes unbelief. At the root of all of Israel's sins in the wilderness was unbelief: they did not trust God's Word. . . . Many Christians come to the place of decision (their own Kadesh-Barnea), and they fail to enter into their inheritance by faith! . . . Yes, they are saved, but they fail to fulfill God's purpose for their lives. They will not trust God to overcome the giants, knock down the walls, and give them the inheritance that He has promised. Warren W. Wiersbe

DEUTERONOMY
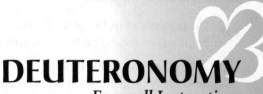
Farewell Instructions to a Nation

FACT SHEET

FORMAT. 34 chapters, 958 verses

IMPLIED PURPOSE. To record what is essentially an extended sermon by Moses. The book arises out of two events: the renewing of the Sinai Covenant on the plains of Moab and the succession of leadership with Moses' pending death and inability to enter the Promised Land.

AUTHOR'S PERSPECTIVE. Moses speaks in his traditional role as authoritative lawgiver. The book is also Moses' farewell discourse as leader of his nation. In addition, Moses speaks as the intermediary of God, who is the ultimate lawgiver in the book.

IMPLIED AUDIENCE. The immediate audience is the generation of Israelites who were born in the wilderness and had not experienced the Exodus and the first giving of the law. They are now poised to do what their parents had not done, namely, enter the Promised Land.

WHAT UNIFIES THE BOOK. The rhetorical form of lists of commands; the implied situation of Moses' delivering farewell discourses to his followers; the idea of the covenant between God and his people; the note of anticipation of entering the Promised Land; preparation for a change in national leadership; God-centeredness, with God as the ultimate being to whom people must relate

SPECIAL FEATURES. Portrayal of God as near; constant calls to remember; memorable summaries of the law in both essence and specific details; emphasis on centralized worship of God in a single sanctuary "at the place he himself will choose"

CHALLENGES FACING THE READER OR TEACHER OF THIS BOOK.
1. The abundance of commands
2. The format of lengthy public oration

3. The presence of technical legal terms
4. Emphasis on issues that faced the Israelites but seem foreign to us

HOW TO MEET THE CHALLENGES.

1. Read the book in small amounts instead of continuously.
2. Imagine yourself present at the solemn delivery of these farewell discourses.
3. Use a study Bible or commentary to help you master the terminology.
4. Determine which commands can still be applied literally, and look for underlying principles in commands that were specific to Israel's time and place.

THE MOST COMMON MISCONCEPTION ABOUT THIS BOOK. That this book merely repeats earlier books of the Pentateuch, in that the title by which we know this book means "second law."

Deuteronomy is a book about a community being prepared for a new life. Though the scene is set more than three thousand years in the past, Deuteronomy is still a book of considerable contemporary relevance. Then, as now, the surrounding world was experiencing a time of change, of political tension and military engagement. But in the midst of world events, a relatively small community was being urged by Moses . . . to commit itself wholeheartedly to the Lord. . . . The book provides a paradigm for the kingdom of God in the modern world; it is a time for renewing commitment within the New Covenant and turning to the future with a view to possessing the promise of God.

PETER CRAIGIE
The Book of Deuteronomy

| | | | Close of Moses' Career as a Leader of His Nation | Last Words from a Leader |

34 Death and Burial of Moses

33 Moses Blesses the Tribes

31:30–32:52 Song of Moses

31:1-29 Arrangement for Joshua to Succeed Moses

Incentives to Obey God's Rules

29–30 Moses' Exhortations to Keep the Covenant

Israel's Covenant Commitment

27–28 Blessings and Curses

21–26 Wide-Ranging Rules, Chiefly Moral

20 Rules for Warfare

19 Criminal Laws

18 Rules for Priests and Prophets

15:19–17:20 Ceremonial Observances

15:1-18 Rules about Slaves

14 Clean and Unclean Animals; Tithe of Produce

12–13 Prohibitions

Specific Rules for Living as God's Covenant People in the Promised Land

Israel's Behavior as God's People

8–11 Mingled History and Rules for Living

7 Instruction to Defeat the Canaanites

5–6 Moses States and Explains the Ten Commandments

Principles for Future Living in the Promised Land

Prospective Stance

4 Moses Exhorts the Nation about the Future

1–3 Moses Rehearses Israel's Past

Learning from the Past

Retrospective Stance

Israel's Identity as God's People

AN OUTLINE OF
DEUTERONOMY

As Moses addresses his nation in the book of Deuteronomy, Israel is in the position of a losing team. They have violated God's laws and directives so blatantly that a whole generation is, in effect, in the penalty box. At the end of Moses' life, as a new generation faces the prospect of entering the land, Moses gives his team what amounts to a pep talk in the form of an extended sermon. The loving, covenant-keeping God is going to give Israel yet another chance. As we discover in the book of Joshua, the people did much better the second time around. The book of Deuteronomy influenced them for good, and it can do the same for us.

The Form of the Book

Deuteronomy is often referred to as a sermon, but in fact it consists of at least three separate addresses or orations by Moses to Israel, delivered on the eve of the nation's entry into Canaan. Unlike Exodus and Numbers, Deuteronomy is not primarily a law book or a history but an exhortation to covenant faithfulness. Many interpreters see the book as structured after Near Eastern vassal treaties (see "Covenant" on page 93). However, the book emphasizes the words of Moses more than the details of the covenant-renewal ceremony that occurs at the end of the book.

The book has the nature of a biblical form known as the farewell discourse. With the nation poised to enter the Promised Land, Moses (who himself was barred from entry as God's judgment against his sin) knows that Israel's future depends on its obedience and commitment to God. In addition to exhorting his listeners, therefore, Moses led the people in a covenant-renewal ceremony recorded in chapters 27–30. As an extension of the farewell to a nation, the book closes with a narrative of Moses' death and his succession by Joshua.

Key Words

- *statutes:* In Deuteronomy, the law is made of decrees and regulations (4:1-2). These terms highlight the multidimensional aspect of the law; it describes not only religious ceremonies but all aspects of life.
- *shema:* This term is used for the central theological statement in Deuteronomy 6:4, which reads: "Hear, O Israel: The LORD our God, the LORD is one" (NIV). In the original Hebrew, the word *shema* is the first word of Israel's confession.
- *remember:* Moses makes it clear that a significant part of his task is to help the people remember God's mighty acts so that they will remain faithful (4:9-14).

Key Doctrines

Covenant Faithfulness. God is shown to be a promise-keeping, trust-worthy God (1:11).

Divine Immanence. God's presence is always near. Moses declares that unlike the unpredictable pagan deities, "the LORD our God is near us whenever we pray to him" (4:7, NIV).

Promise. God gives the Promised Land to Israel, subject to their obedience.

Holiness. God declares his people to be a unique people and calls them to live as a holy nation.

Judgment. As part of accepting the covenant, God's people repeat the blessings for keeping the covenant and the curses for breaking it.

Tips for Reading or Teaching Deuteronomy

Although the book of Deuteronomy is one of the most important books in the Bible, a reader or teacher nonetheless needs to be intentional about finding the relevance of the book for today.

Later Old Testament authors look back to Deuteronomy as a measuring stick by which to assess their culture's moral and spiritual condition. We need to do the same regarding our own culture.

The book of Deuteronomy seems to be mainly concerned with rules and laws, but the actual focus is on the hearts, souls, and attitudes of people.

Another thing that will prevent the book from being only a code of behavior is to remember that the context is the covenant relationship between God and his people.

> **DID YOU KNOW?**
> The title *Deuteronomy* in its English form is based on a Greek word meaning "second law" or "repetition of the law," based on the title found in the Greek translation of the Old Testament (the Septuagint).
>
> The title found in the Hebrew Bible is simply "These Are the Words," the first two words of the book in the Hebrew text.
>
> When in later Israelite history King Josiah found a "book of the law" while repairing the Temple (621 BC), it is likely that the scroll he found contained the book of Deuteronomy; the reforms Josiah instituted resemble the commands found in Deuteronomy.

For all its emphasis on law, the book is also about God's grace; look for evidence of this theme as it is interwoven with the more obvious theme of God's demands for living.

Things to Look For

- The emphasis on remembering and not forgetting God's providential care
- Warnings against being proud upon entering the Promised Land
- Applications of the law to specific life situations

- Preparing the people for a leadership change
- The language of covenant (divine-human contract)

quick overview of deuteronomy

1:1–3:29	Rehearsal of Israel's history, beginning with the Exodus
4:1–11:32	Principles of godly living, including the Ten Commandments
12:1–26:19	Specific rules for living (applications of God's law)
27:1–30:20	Blessings and curses (incentives to obey)
31:1–34:12	Change in leadership established; farewell and death of Moses

The Flow of the Book

History Lesson (Chapters 1–3). In the first part of Deuteronomy, Moses reminds the people of their history. As you read this section, consider why the book begins with this history lesson. What is the persuasive purpose of emphasizing what God has done and how his people have acted? Our modern tendency is to separate generations, but notice ways in which Moses includes the rising generation in the actions of their parents. This reminds them that they are capable of the same disobedience that marked their parents' generation.

KEY VERSE

"What great nation has a god as near to them as the LORD our God is near to us whenever we call on him?" (4:7) An important teaching in Deuteronomy is that the powerful God who delivers is also nearby.

The Ten Commandments and More (Chapters 4–11). As you read this section, consider the problems that plagued the Israelites immediately after the Exodus. Look for ways that this restatement of the basic law code was shaped to emphasize the need for Israel to free itself from its habitual patterns of sinning.

Specific Applications of the Law (Chapters 12–26). The focus of the laws recorded in this section concerns Israel's life in the new land. Two sets of laws are forward looking—regulations concerning the office of the king (17:14-20) and regulations concerning the prophet (18:17-20). Consider how the establishment of these offices represents God's loving accommodation to the realities his people faced. In the best of all worlds, God would have preferred that the people follow him directly, with no need for a king or priest.

Covenant

The importance of covenants in the Bible is illustrated by the fact that we divide the book into two testaments. *Testament* is simply an old term for "covenant." In Scripture, the covenant is one of God's primary acts of self-revelation. God reveals himself as a covenant-making and covenant-keeping God. The key phrase in understanding covenant is God's declaration, "I will always be your God and the God of your descendants after you" (Genesis 17:7). This is the heart of the covenant.

Covenant was a legal or political term that was infused with spiritual meaning. In the ancient Near East, the making of covenants or treaties was part of daily life. There were two basic types of treaties: treaties between equals, which describe the parties in fraternal terms, and vassal treaties, made between a conquering king and a subordinate king (an example is given in Joshua 9–10).

In Genesis, God established a covenant with Adam and Eve at the time of creation. This covenant of works (implied rather than explicitly stated) established the obligations of the creature toward God and outlined consequences for disobeying. God would establish Adam and Eve in a perfect world and meet their needs through divine provision and care. For their part, Adam and Eve were bound to perfect obedience. The next covenant in Genesis is more explicit: the covenant God made with Noah immediately following the Flood, in which God promised never again to destroy the earth with a flood (Genesis 9:8-11).

One of the most dramatic covenant scenes in Scripture is the covenant God established with Abraham (Genesis 15). Here we see why the term *covenant* comes from the Hebrew word meaning "to cut." To prepare for the covenant ceremony, Abraham severed animals into halves. This meant that the covenant was made in blood. It also implied that if either party broke the covenant, they would be liable to the same kind of dismemberment. Typically both parties would pass between the parts of the animals, signifying their joint adherence to the covenant. In this case, God alone passed through the pieces, signifying that he would take full responsibility for both sides of the covenant.

There are many other covenants in Scripture, including the covenant Moses made with God on the mountain (Exodus 24) and God's covenant to establish David's everlasting throne (2 Samuel 7). Standing behind all the other covenants is what the book of Hebrews calls "an eternal covenant [ratified] with [Jesus'] blood" (Hebrews 13:20). This is the covenant God the Father made with God the Son for the salvation of his people.

Blessings and Curses (Chapters 27–30). We have been trained to think of decisions in terms of costs and benefits. As you read this section, look for the incentives Moses offers for keeping the law. Identify the benefits, and take note of the costs that Moses tabulates.

New Covenant, New Leader (Chapters 31–34). In this section, pay attention to the focus on both the nation's and the individual's heart toward God. Moses appeals to the nation as it renews the covenant and to individuals by reminding them that these words are indeed "your very life" (32:47, ESV). Observe how Moses appeals to the corporate and national spiritual identity yet never loses sight of the need for every person to live by what he is saying.

The Main Themes

1. Heart religion is important: "Circumcise your hearts" (10:16, NIV).

2. God is very near, and his commandments can be kept.

3. Make plans to follow God both now and in the future.

4. Doing justice is an essential way to show our respect for God.

KEY VERSE

"Today I have given you the choice between life and death, between blessings and curses" (30:19). This is the message of Deuteronomy in a nutshell: the need for individuals and nations to choose between obeying or disobeying God, with blessing or a curse as the outcome.

Contribution of the Book to the Bible's Story of Salvation in Christ

The life of Moses and his deliverance of Israel symbolize the life and ministry of Christ. We find a prophecy of a new prophet like Moses (18:15-18), and the book closes with a note that this prophet is yet to come (34:10-12). Indeed, the New Testament refers to this prophecy as a reference to Jesus Christ (see Acts 3:22-23; 7:37). The many laws in Deuteronomy reveal the righteousness God requires and has provided for us in Christ. Even the book's curses for covenant disobedience find their place in the gospel: Jesus endured these curses when he suffered and died on the cross.

Applying the Book

A collection of sermons given on the occasion of entering the Promised Land might not look very relevant to our present situation. However, consider how often Jesus quoted this book, including his replies to Satan during his temptations (Matthew 4:4, 7, 10). This book contains one of the most powerful appeals to the spiritual life, with its call to circumcise our hearts and love God. Intimacy with God is balanced by the awesome power of a God who demands obedience and can act to bring deliverance. The most obvious application of the book is to obey the law of God. Blessings follow obedience, which flows from a renewed heart.

PERSPECTIVES
ON THE BOOK OF DEUTERONOMY

The author of Deuteronomy has endowed the book with the typical features of an oration. The rhetorical technique is here fully developed. Moshe Weinfeld

There are only two direct voices which the narrator asks us to attend to in the book: Moses' and God's. Robert Polzin

At first glance, Deuteronomy has the appearance less of a story than of law or preaching. However, it is cast in the form of a narrative, with all the components of plot, scene, character and dramatic tension. The reader of Deuteronomy is drawn into its world. . . . [The Israelites'] immediate situation is outside the land, poised to enter it. In that pause, the possibility of divine blessing spread before them, lies the dramatic power of the book. Israel is in a moment of "decision." . . . This is more than covenant renewal; it is the establishment of a pattern of grace after failure that reaches all the way to the resurrection. J. G. McConville

A rhythmic unity is implanted in [the book of Deuteronomy]—rhythmic unity that turns to exultation. Sweetness of reminiscence and bitterness of rebuke, law and justice, words of confession and words of promise and assurance—a special tenderness bathes it all. Jacob Fichman

Deuteronomy is intended to be at least something in the nature of a "complete course of instruction," an attempt to embrace the sum total of the revelation of Yahweh's will with all that this involved. Gerhard von Rad

The book comes even to the modern reader in much the same way as a challenging sermon, for it is directed towards moving the minds and wills

of the hearers to decision: choose life, that you and your descendants may live (30:19). The work as a whole was evidently intended to give Israel instruction and education in her faith and to press home to her the demands of her faith. J. A. Thompson

Its purpose is to ensure that Israel will walk in obedience and thus live long in the land promised to their forefathers. . . . The reminiscences and exhortations give the book the character of a sermon, all the more impressive because delivered by Moses, the man of God, at the end of his life, to Israel on the verge of crossing the Jordan. . . . Moses speaks like a father who before his death earnestly and in love exhorts, admonishes, and warns his children. Jan Ridderbos

JOSHUA
The Greatest Generation

FORMAT. 24 chapters, 658 verses

FACT SHEET

IMPLIED PURPOSES. To tell the story of how the Promised Land was taken and the land portioned among the tribes, and through this to teach principles of leadership, life, and spiritual warfare to all generations

AUTHOR'S PERSPECTIVE. The story is told with an eye toward drama and giving the big picture. The writer favors generalizations over details so that the broad sweep of conquest and God's deliverance can be told.

IMPLIED AUDIENCE. Future generations seeking to understand Israel's claim to the land and the tribal boundaries

WHAT UNIFIES THE BOOK. The story of conquest; tension with remaining Canaanites; Joshua as leader; a strong narrative element; military strategy; the aspect of divine intervention

SPECIAL FEATURES. Focus on the big picture; suspense concerning whether the tribes will carry out their mandate; the viewing of the conquest of Canaan as a struggle between good and evil (the holy-war motif); an impulse to record geographical facts and figures relating to the division of the land

CHALLENGES FACING THE READER OR TEACHER OF THIS BOOK.
1. Understanding and being interested in military strategy and tactics
2. Accepting the divinely ordained destruction of civilian populations in wartime
3. Dealing with an abundance of unfamiliar geographic references

HOW TO MEET THE CHALLENGES.
1. Learn how ancient warfare was conducted.

2. Recognize God's unqualified intention to have his people occupy the land he had promised to give them and his righteous desire for them to worship him alone rather than any foreign gods.
3. Use an atlas to see the boundaries of the tribes.

THE MOST COMMON MISCONCEPTION ABOUT THIS BOOK. That it is only a history of the conquest. It is far more a theological tract that gives the author's explanation of what happened and why.

_____

The book of Joshua is a literary production designed to create and support the identity of the people it calls "all Israel." They are the people of Yahweh the Divine Warrior. They are the rightful masters of the land of Canaan. They are a people formed by the demands of the law given through Moses. The book seeks to give its readers the courage to meet whatever current challenges are brought on by their identity as Yahweh's people. It also seeks to communicate hope for a future fulfillment of Yahweh's promises. Various literary and rhetorical strategies are used to achieve these purposes: celebrations of the Divine Warrior's victories, narratives about obedience, disobedience, and land grants, verbal maps of claimed territory, sermons urging compliance with the law. . . . The book of Joshua is a witness to the power of a shared story to generate, define, and defend a community.

RICHARD NELSON
Joshua: A Commentary

AN OUTLINE OF
JOSHUA

Chapters			
23–24 Joshua's Last Words and Death			Joshua's Final Acts as Leader
22 Joshua and the Eastern Tribes			
21 Cities Allotted to the Levites		Dividing the Land	Settlement
20 Six Cities of Refuge			
13–19 Parceling of Land to the Tribes			
10–12 Conquest of Assorted Kings	Conquering Canaan		
9 The Gibeonites' Deceit			
8 Conquest of Ai			
7 The Sin of Achan			
6 Conquest of Jericho			
5 Ceremonial Preparations	Preparing for Conquest of Canaan		Conquest
4 Stones of Remembrance			
3 Crossing the Jordan			
2 The Two Spies and Rahab			
1 Joshua Assumes Leadership			

Tell me a story. The phrase captures the universal human impulse to understand our world through telling and hearing stories. The book of Joshua tells a story—the story of God's enabling his people to enter the land. This book is not merely a history but a well-told story designed to drive home the point that obedience to God's law is the sensible way to live.

The Form of the Book

The basic form of the book is narrative, though halfway through it the narrative impulse gives way to recording names and places. The specific type of story we find in this book is battle narrative and military history. This story of conquest has many similarities to ancient epic literature, inasmuch as it deals with the formative moment in a nation's early history. At some moments, moreover, the story becomes a collection of miracle stories, as God enters the action on behalf of the nation of Israel.

A notable feature of this battle story is the way in which we remember the book of Joshua by certain key events and scenes. They include Rahab's hiding of the two spies, Israel's crossing the Jordan River on dry land, the fall of the walls of Jericho, the loss of the initial battle at Ai because of Achan's sin, the successive pictures of families receiving parcels of land as if it were Christmas morning, and Joshua's final summons to Israel to renew its covenant with God.

The history we read in this book is an interpretive history. The author has chosen to emphasize the role of God in the actions that occur, placing this book into the framework of the holy-war motif (God vs. evil nations). Even when we reach the chronicle of how the land was divided, we can see the author pointing out God's deliverance and the blessings that flow from obedience to the covenant.

DID YOU KNOW?
The battles involved with entering the land of Canaan are not ordinary Old Testament battles. Here, Israel is operating uniquely on behalf of God and is called to carry out a complete destruction of the people and their goods. This unique war of holy destruction—which is not the common practice of warfare for ancient Israel—presupposes that God has the sovereign right to execute judgment against Israel's enemies.

Key Characters

- Achan, who disobeys the ban on taking plunder from Jericho, causes Israel to lose the initial battle against Ai, and along with his family is stoned by the Israelites

- Eleazer, Aaron's son, who helps Joshua lead Israel and succeeds him as high priest
- Joshua, Moses' assistant and successor, who leads Israel into the Promised Land and is pictured as a competent and godly leader
- Phinehas, Eleazer's son and Aaron's grandson, who helps negotiate a settlement among tribes to avoid a civil war over a misinterpreted memorial altar
- Rahab, a prostitute from Jericho who shelters two spies and is spared by the Israelites. An ancestor of David and Jesus, Rahab is seen in Scripture as a person of great faith.

Key Doctrines

God's Faithfulness. He fulfills his promise that Abraham's descendants would occupy the land.

God's Jealousy. God is a protective and possessive lover of his people.

Faithful Living. The people achieve a rest in the land that their unfaithful parents did not.

Tips for Reading or Teaching Joshua

Pay attention to the contrast between the two generations: The parents' lack of faith leads them to wander in the wilderness. The generation portrayed in this book shows more faith in carrying out God's commands.

The strong leadership of Joshua and Eleazer can rightly lead to an appreciation of what they did. However, the book is primarily about God's fulfilling his promise.

God sometimes works in unexpected and unconventional ways. The manna stops, Jericho is taken by a marching band, and Ai is captured by a ruse. Deliverance comes ultimately through God's faithfulness.

Allow the drama of the near civil war (22:10-34) to capture you. Consider how heartbreaking this would have been for the leadership.

Unifying Elements

- Joshua as a strong spiritual leader
- Persistent emphasis on conquering and entering the land
- Constant testing of Israel's faithfulness to God
- Battles and military strategy
- Highly edited stories that focus on dramatic or memorable events

The Flow of the Book

Preparing to Enter the Land (Chapters 1–5). Right from the start we see two themes: the place of brilliant human leadership and the importance of divine dependence. Joshua decides to attack Jericho, a move that will divide the land in two. The conquest of Jericho comes about through utter trust in God. According to 1:16-17, this new generation, in contrast to their parents, resolved to obey God. Look for ways in which this generation "got it" in terms of obedience to God.

quick overview of joshua

1:1–5:15	Preparing to enter the land
6:1–12:24	Conquering the land
13:1–21:45	Dividing the land
22:1–24:33	Living in the land

Conquering the Land (Chapters 6–12). Joshua establishes a base of operation in the center of the country and uses it to move south and north. Soon he controls the major cities, and most of the conquest is complete. Throughout this section we see the military brilliance of Joshua, but the clear hero is God, who does whatever is necessary to let his people inherit the land he promised to give them. A governing pattern to look for is the interplay between God's intervention and human creativity and faithfulness (divine-human cooperation).

KEY VERSE

"Choose today whom you will serve. . . . But as for me and my family, we will serve the LORD" (24:15). The need to choose between God and other allegiances pervades the book of Joshua, and Joshua's godly leadership is a constant point of reference.

Dividing the Land (Chapters 13–21). Joshua has taken the major Canaanite cities and military garrisons. The people of the nation now need to disperse throughout the land, conquer the remaining towns, and claim their allotted geography. Caleb typifies the virtuous man of this period, fighting to gain his tribal land at age eighty-five—working to secure an inheritance for his people that he will not directly enjoy. A pattern to notice is the placement of the Levites, who were given cities but not regions of land.

Living in the Land (Chapters 22–24). These chapters round out the life of Joshua as leader of a nation. In successive chapters, notice what is wise in Joshua's dealings with the two and a half tribes east of the Jordan (chapter 22), the nine and a half tribes west of the Jordan (chapter 23), and Joshua's farewell discourse and covenant-renewal ceremony for the entire nation (chapter 24). If these chapters picture a godly commonwealth, what things characterize such a commonwealth?

The Main Themes
1. Israel achieves national greatness because of its faithfulness to the covenant.
2. Joshua embodies that rare blend of sheer brilliance and great humility. He constantly gives thanks to God and honors the memory of Moses.
3. God is faithful to his covenant and promises.
4. The good life in a godly realm. The book of Joshua is a picture of how God intended political entities to conduct their affairs.

Contribution of the Book to the Bible's Story of Salvation in Christ
Christians have long seen Joshua as a forerunner of Christ. In fact, Joshua's Hebrew name, Yeshua, which means "Yahweh is Salvation," is translated in Greek as "Jesus." In the same way that Joshua led Israel into battle, Jesus is our great champion in our ongoing warfare with sin and all the enemies of God. And in the same way that Joshua worked to complete the conquest of the land, Jesus is at work to carry our sanctification to its conclusion.

Applying the Book
From start to finish, Joshua celebrates the fruit of faithfulness to God. The book calls readers to trust God and not follow their fears or resort to expedient behavior. Christians through the centuries have wanted to see in the conquest of the land spiritual lessons concerning our sanctification. The victory is secure by the work of God, but will Israel appropriate what has been given them through faith and obedience? The parallels to our struggle with sin are numerous.

PERSPECTIVES
ON THE BOOK OF JOSHUA

Joshua is a book about a land and a people. Irving Jensen

Joshua is an important book for many reasons . . . for the history it records and for its internal teaching. But what makes the book of Joshua overwhelmingly important is that it stands as a bridge between the Pentateuch (the writings of Moses) and the rest of Scripture.
Francis A. Schaeffer

We see in it much of God, and his providence . . . his faithfulness to his covenant with the patriarchs, his kindness to his people is real notwithstanding their provocations. Matthew Henry

Joshua is . . . the story of how God, to whom the whole world belongs, at one stage in the history of redemption reconquered a portion of the earth from the powers of this world that had claimed it for themselves, defending their claims by force of arms and reliance on their false gods. It tells how God commissioned his people, under his servant Joshua, to take Canaan in his name out of the hands of the idolatrous and dissolute Canaanites. It tells how he aided them in that enterprise and gave them conditional tenancy in his land in fulfillment of the ancient pledge. Arthur Lewis

Between the book's own beginning and end an important transformation takes place. Wandering Israel outside the land becomes settled Israel at rest within it. L. Daniel Hawk

The telling of the Joshua story by the ancient Israelites stirred each successive generation to remember what had happened and to believe that in some way it could happen again. Likewise today, we who are "newcomers" from the nations may appropriate the Joshua story as part of our past and receive encouragement for the present. It tells us of the faithfulness of God to his oppressed people; the struggle for a place to live (land); a successful movement of the disinherited against oppression, injustice, and tyranny; the beginning of a new society based on justice, freedom, and loyalty. E. John Hamlin

The book of Joshua is one of the Bible's greatest testimonies to the mighty acts of God on behalf of Israel. Jerome F. D. Creach

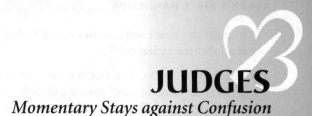

JUDGES
Momentary Stays against Confusion

FORMAT. 21 chapters, 618 verses

IMPLIED PURPOSES. To record the main events in the life of the Isra-elite nation and individuals within it during a generally lawless and morally degenerate era, with a view toward offering pictures of what to avoid and what to follow in our own lives; to show that people need God as their king

AUTHOR'S PERSPECTIVE. The author tells the story in such a way as to show his negative assessment of the general condition of the Israelite nation and his admiration of heroic actions by the good judges along with his belief that God's rule is the only final hope for the human race.

IMPLIED AUDIENCE. The author does not explicitly identify an intended audience, so we are left to infer that he wrote to the Israelite nation in a way that would appeal to its religious conscience—to deter it from evil and prompt it toward the good at a still-early stage of its history. But literary writing such as the kind we find in this book tells us not only what *happened* but also what *happens*, so the wider audience is the human race at all points in history.

WHAT UNIFIES THE BOOK. The portrayal of human depravity; a repeated U-shaped cycle of evil—punishment—crying to God—rescue; literary realism (the portrayal of vice and violence); the genre of hero stories; continual placing of characters and events in specific settings; pictures of the consequences that follow when people do what is right in their own eyes instead of God's

SPECIAL FEATURES. Numerous named characters; realistic portrayal of violence, sex, and immorality; abundance of fighting and mili-tary action; a general aura of lawlessness in the lands portrayed; the impulse to narrate some stories in full-fledged literary manner; skillful characterization

CHALLENGES FACING THE READER OR TEACHER OF THIS BOOK.
1. The sheer abundance of names and individual stories
2. The technique of literary realism, with its vivid portrayal of violence, physical mutilation, and sex

HOW TO MEET THE CHALLENGES.
1. Read the book piecemeal rather than in a short span of time.
2. Brace yourself for the gruesomeness and discomfort that you will meet, confident that the realism tells you something that God thought important for you to experience.

THE MOST COMMON MISCONCEPTIONS ABOUT THIS BOOK. That the book is totally negative and we should think the worst of the characters and events that are presented to us; or opposite to that, that we should think the heroes are totally virtuous

What do these judges have in common? . . . What they have in common . . . is their rich diversity. The book of Judges delights in surprises, in diversity of character and situation, in reversals of expectations. The hand of the Lord falls where it will, often in unexpected places— on a southpaw, on two women, on the youngest son of a poor farmer in a weak clan, on the son of a prostitute, on the son of a barren woman. . . . There is wonder here at the variety of man, at the value of every kind of man. Implicit in Judges is a conviction of the worth of every kind of human gift and human characteristic, a vast democracy of spirit, once this weak and worthless cast is transformed by God's spirit.

KENNETH R. R. GROS LOUIS

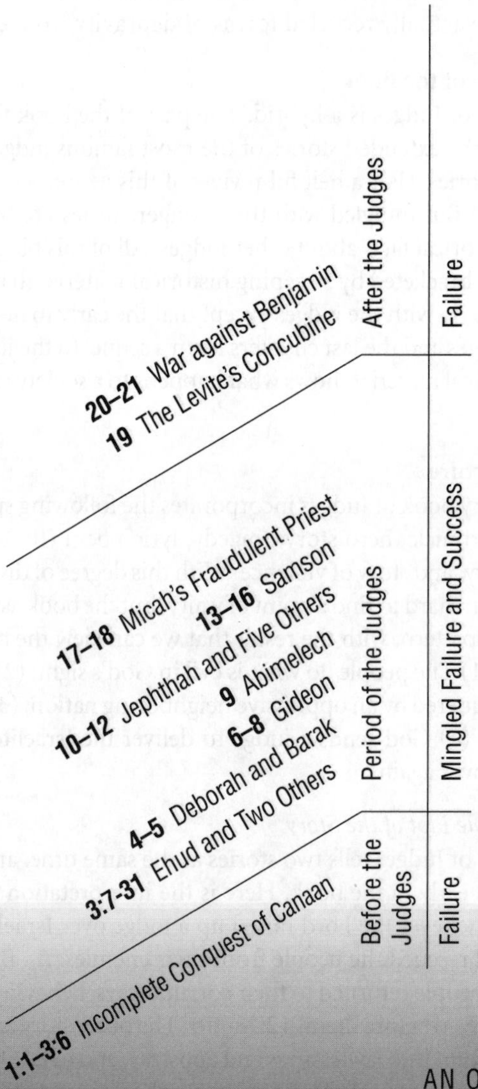

AN OUTLINE OF
JUDGES

Before the Judges	**Period of the Judges**	**After the Judges**
Failure	Mingled Failure and Success	Failure

1:1–3:6 Incomplete Conquest of Canaan

3:7-31 Ehud and Two Others

4–5 Deborah and Barak

6–8 Gideon

9 Abimelech

10–12 Jephthah and Five Others

13–16 Samson

17–18 Micah's Fraudulent Priest

19 The Levite's Concubine

20–21 War against Benjamin

There is a prevailing tendency to think that because the final effect of reading the Bible is uplifting and redemptive, the book itself is a "nice" book. Perhaps we *want* the Bible to be that kind of book. The book of Judges dispels this common misperception. While our own society seems to come up with more and more terrible forms of evil and torture, we learn as we study this book that what we think are modern trends are actually recycled forms of depravity from earlier eras.

The Form of the Book

The book of Judges is a hybrid. The part of the book for which it is best known—the extended stories of the most famous judges—is a collection of hero stories. (For a helpful review of this genre, see "Hero Stories" on page 213.) But mingled with these longer stories are brief units of barebones historical facts about other judges. All of this biographical material, in turn, is bracketed by sweeping historical material that has nothing specifically to do with the judges except that the early material is background to the judges and the last chapters form a sequel to the judges. In addition, the historical material shows what happens to a society that refuses to obey God.

The Structure

The history book of Judges incorporates the following specific genres: historical chronicle, hero story, tragedy, lyric poem (the song of Deborah), battle story, and story of violence. With this degree of diversity in the book, it may seem hard to find a point of unity, but the book as a whole reenacts a common pattern, with the result that we can view the book's structure as cyclical: (1) The people do what is evil in God's sight; (2) God allows them to be conquered by an oppressive neighboring nation; (3) the people cry to God; and (4) God sends a judge to deliver the Israelites. Then the cycle starts all over again.

The Double Plot of the Story

The book of Judges tells two stories at the same time, and the author previews this early in the book. Here is the interpretation the book itself asserts: "Whenever the Lord raised up a judge over Israel, he was with that judge and rescued the people from their enemies. . . . But when the judge died, the people returned to their corrupt ways, behaving worse than those who had lived before them" (2:18-19). The outer story is thus a story of national descent into lawlessness and apostasy, and in fact the book ends with a five-chapter account of how the nation became worse than ever before.

Placed within this outer story, however, is a collection of hero stories that largely celebrate the exploits of heroic judges. Four of these judges are mentioned in the roll call of heroes of faith in Hebrews 11, so we *know* they were heroic.

It is important not to suppress either of the stories that the book of Judges tells. There is an unwarranted attempt in some circles to read everything with suspicion and look for trouble everywhere in the story, including the stories of the judges. On the other hand, we should avoid being so dazzled with the deliverance that God accomplished through heroic leaders that we fail to see the bigger story of the decline of the covenant nation—and the flaws of the heroic judges themselves.

Unifying Elements

- The heroism of the individual judges
- In the part of the book dealing with the judges, the rescue motif
- Conflicts between good and evil, bondage and deliverance, an ordered society and a chaotic society, loyalty to God and disloyalty to him
- The battle motif
- Literary realism, including stories of violence
- Images or examples of evil
- The negative consequences of "doing your own thing"

Key Places and Characters

The main scene of action is the nation of Israel, and that nation is often involved in battles with neighboring nations, placing the action in an international setting. In later Old Testament history, a book dealing with national leaders would have been set at the court, but the book of Judges takes place before Israel had a king, so there is no standard place where the judges perform their heroic feats. The main physical settings in the book are the battlefield and the open field. Balancing that, some of the most vivid and memorable actions take place in confined places: Eglon's chamber; a wine press, where Gideon beats out wheat and is visited by an angel; the city wall, where Abimelech is standing when a woman drops a millstone and crushes his head; Delilah's inner chamber, where the Philistines capture Samson; the threshold of the house where the Levite's concubine suffered abuse and died.

God is the main character, but we learn this mainly from summary statements to the effect that what happens on the human scene is the result of what God did; e.g., "The LORD again raised up a rescuer to save them" (3:15). The most conspicuous human characters are the judges, especially

Ehud, Deborah, Gideon, Jephthah, and Samson. At the end of the book, a violent society assumes a kind of corporate and villainous identity.

Key Doctrines

The Justice and Mercy of God. The double plot highlights that God punishes evil and apostasy but also extends mercy to his people when they turn to him.

Sin. The book is a veritable anthology of ways in which a society can descend into spiritual and moral chaos and the disastrous effects when people do as they please.

Apostasy. The book gives a detailed anatomy of ways in which both individuals and the believing community can fall from the faith (see especially 2:10).

The Person. The book shows that people have an ability to choose what is good, that their bent is to choose what is evil, and that they can rise to heroic heights in the strength of God.

Tips for Reading or Teaching Judges

Do justice to the story qualities of the book, which is a triumph of storytelling, especially in the parts that give extended treatment to individual judges.

There is also an abundance of recognizable human experience to explore.

It is important not to suppress either of the two plots—the triumph of evil in Israelite society and the heroism of some of the judges.

You cannot deal with this book adequately unless you accept literary realism as a form with which God wants us to have some encounter. This book is replete with stories of violence and cruelty, sex and immorality.

Stories require you to make interpretive judgments regarding whether individual actions and characters are good or bad. You cannot avoid the need to make such judgments as you read or teach this book.

quick overview of judges

1:1–3:6	Historical backdrop to the stories of the judges
3:7–16:31	Stories of the judges
17:1–21:25	Spiritual and moral collapse of Israelite society after the judges

The Flow of the Book

Historical Backdrop to the Judges: The Conquest of Canaan Retold (1:1–3:6). The book of Judges eventually becomes an anthology of hero stories, but it starts out as a historical chronicle. The material is extremely diverse, but some unity emerges from the theme of the incomplete conquest of the Promised Land, which is at the same time a failure to take God's rule seriously. Here are the topics covered in this section: conquests in Canaan (1:1-20), a litany of the incomplete conquests of Canaan (1:21-35), an angel's rebuke of Israel for not completing the conquest of Canaan (2:1-5), the death of Joshua (2:6-9), a summary of God's anger at Israel's apostasy (2:11-15), a summary preview of how God raised up judges when Israel turned to him (2:16-19), and another account of how God left unconquered nations of Canaan to test the Israelites (2:20–3:6). While there are doubtless lessons to learn from these negative examples, the primary function of this material is to set the stage for the subsequent stories of the judges and show Israel's need for righteous rule.

Ehud and Two Other Judges (3:7-31). The story of Ehud's assassination of Eglon is one of the best-told hero stories in the Bible. Apply what you know about how stories work. Flanking this masterful drama are summary statements about the judgeships of Othniel and Shamgar. These alert us to the fact that the book of Judges will record the deeds of some judges in summary fashion and others in full literary fashion.

The Victory of Deborah and Barak (Chapters 4–5). Next we have another high point of Israelite military history. Here are specific things that will help you to handle the story correctly: (1) Relive the story as fully as possible, noting the interplay of human courage and ingenuity on the one hand and God's intervention on the other; (2) be sensitive to the mocking flavor of slave literature at the expense of an oppressive foreign nation; and

DID YOU KNOW?
The judges did not "judge." They were charismatic military leaders whose chief function was to deliver the nation from its enemies. Various translations and commentators render the Hebrew word *sophet* as "heroes," "leaders," "chieftains," "deliverers," and "warrior rulers."

Although commentators often speak of a cycle of sin and repentance in the book of Judges, the book never uses the word *repent* for the Israelites' turning to God. Instead the author claims that the people *cried* to God.

Because some of the judges overlapped, no exact chronology is possible, but the period of the judges spanned approximately three hundred years.

(3) make a comparison between prose narrative and lyric poetry as complementary ways of conveying the spirit of an event.

Gideon's Conquest of the Midianites (Chapters 6–8). The story of Gideon is a hero story par excellence, so apply what you know about hero stories. The story of Gideon belongs to the category of stories in which we see the hero gradually develop into a heroic character. In the first half of the story (6:1–7:8), it will be profitable to catalog the things that show Gideon's reluctance or inadequacy along with ways in which God undermines Gideon's confidence about his ability to defeat the Midianites. In the second half of the story (7:9–8:35), God largely drops out of the action as an announced character; notice how virtually every detail shows the human resourcefulness of Gideon as a military leader. Do justice to the human aspect of the story (for example, Gideon begins with what we would consider a classic inferiority complex), and then reflect on the spiritual lessons that are latent in this material.

KEY VERSES

"Once again the Israelites did evil in the LORD's sight, and the LORD gave King Eglon of Moab control over Israel because of their evil. . . . But when the people of Israel cried out to the LORD for help, the LORD again raised up a rescuer to save them" (3:12, 15). Here we can see all the main motifs of the book: the human tendency toward evil, the cycle of doing evil—crying to God—being rescued, and the periodic rise of heroic judges who triumph in God's strength.

Abimelech's Short-Lived Kingship (Chapter 9). This is one of the strangest stories in the Bible. It recounts the attempt of Gideon's son Abimelech to establish himself as king (a position he held for three years). We can analyze this story under the category of "how not to conduct oneself," with the abortive attempt at kingship perhaps showing Israel's need for a king.

Six More Judgeships (Chapters 10–12). Only one of these judges—Jephthah—gets the full treatment. It will be profitable to analyze why the storyteller considered Jephthah to be as important as he obviously did and also why you think the writer of Hebrews celebrates Jephthah as a hero of faith in Hebrews 11.

The Heroism and Tragedy of Samson (Chapters 13–16). Another of the master stories of the Bible, this one is really two stories at the same time: a hero story about a strongman deliverer who has a place in the roll call of heroes in the New Testament book of Hebrews and a tragedy that recounts the self-defeating nature of misplaced trust and spiritual recklessness. We look at the very same events from these two points of view, so that, for example, Samson's marriage to the woman of Timnah is personally tragic (a violation of the spirit of the Nazirite vow) and the occasion for the Israelites to triumph over their enemies the Philistines. A good grid through which to view the story is to look for the things that are heroic about Samson and the things that render him a tragic figure.

After the Judges: Three Gruesome Stories (Chapters 17–21). These five chapters are commonly labeled an appendix, but they take too much space to be treated that way. Early in the book the author states the pattern the book follows: Whenever a "judge died, the people returned to their corrupt ways, behaving worse than those who had lived before them" (2:19). Samson was the last judge in the book of Judges (others follow in 1 Samuel), and the last five chapters illustrate the principle that the nation became even worse than it had previously been.

One of the stories is a story of the idolatry and prostitution of the priesthood (chapters 17–18). The second is the story of the gang rape and murder of a Levite's concubine (chapter 19). The third story is the ensuing punitive battle against the tribe of Benjamin and the strange story of how the men of that tribe seized wives after the battle (chapters 20–21). The first thing you need to do with these detailed stories is to relive them in all their sordid and uncomfortable detail. Then you need to speculate on why God thought it good to include such terrible experiences in the Bible. Finally, you can apply the interpretive grid that the book itself does in its final verse: "In those days Israel had no king; all the people did whatever seemed right in their own eyes" (21:25). These chapters provide an anatomy of the ways in which the human race can mess up when it orders its affairs apart from God and his royal law. What things make up that anatomy?

The Main Themes
1. The certainty of God's judgment against evil and his readiness to deliver those who call on him
2. The evil of apostasy and the importance of practicing the true faith
3. The sinfulness of sin and the innate bent of the human soul to practice it
4. The possibility of choosing heroically for God, and God's willingness to accomplish his providential purposes through the skills of ordinary people

Contribution of the Book to the Bible's Story of Salvation in Christ

The book does not speak directly of Christ. In the stories of heroic rescue through human warriors we can see human manifestations of the ultimate divine rescue performed by Christ the victor. Second, the book gives us vivid pictures of the human depravity that made Christ's atoning sacrifice necessary. Third, the sufficient rule and kingship of Christ stand out in contrast to the limited and merely temporary deliverance of the heroic judges, who fail to achieve the righteous rule that Christ establishes.

Applying the Book

Like the book of Genesis, this book is overflowing with recognizable human experience. A good starting point, therefore, is simply to build bridges between the world of the ancient text and your own world. Once we name the contemporary counterparts to the actions (good and bad) that we see in the book of Judges, it becomes obvious that the book is as up to date as the daily news. What is worthy of condemnation and praise in the book of Judges is worthy of condemnation and praise in our own society as well.

Another avenue to application is to heed the implied warning that the book of Judges sounds for us. Here are some specifics: (1) Societies and individuals who order their affairs in defiance of God's moral law will eventually become a moral nightmare. (2) The propensity of the human heart to drift into evil is an impulse that lies within our own souls and needs to be checked daily. (3) God does not tolerate evil indefinitely.

But the book also offers positive encouragements: (1) God's mercy is available to people who turn to him. (2) God has planted in people the potential for heroism. (3) The stories of the good judges celebrate God's gifts to individuals to accomplish his purposes in the world.

PERSPECTIVES
ON THE BOOK OF JUDGES

The book of Judges is full of paradox. It contains some of the most famous of the Bible's stories and some of the least known. In them there is much that is attractive, perhaps more that is repulsive. Their lessons are at once simple and difficult. They show us man's blackest sin, but we see it by the light of God's most luminous grace. Michael Wilcock

A cursory reading of Judges reveals that it is, in the main, a compilation of independent stories, most of which centre on an individual.
Arthur E. Cundall

The distressing days of the judges; the disastrous sin-factor; the great potential; a low respect for human life. Headings in a commentary on Judges by Leon Wood

I. The Failure of a Second Generation, 1:1–3:6. II. The Salvation of a Long-suffering God, 3:7–16:31. III. The Confusion of a Depraved People, 17–21. An outline of the book from Dale Ralph Davis

Judges lacks the literary unity of other Biblical books; it is more a parade of large and small characters whose very variety may be intended to give insight into God's process of divine selection. Not only does God make a point of going outside the ruling elite to pick His judges . . . but He puts forward a wide range of moral types as well. Phillip Lopate

The dominant, unifying pattern is . . . a theory of history, not only of human history, but of individual histories as well. Someone does wrong [and] is punished for his error. . . . He repents and asks for help . . . ; the help comes; balance or equilibrium is restored; the individual is at peace . . . until he does wrong again and the cycle begins anew.
Kenneth R. R. Gros Louis

RUTH
The Romance of Redemption

FORMAT. 4 chapters, 85 verses

IMPLIED PURPOSES. To tell the story of the love and marriage of an exemplary heroine, to affirm the value of the domestic and commonplace, and to record how God used human love to display his providence and achieve his plan for redemption

AUTHOR'S PERSPECTIVE. The author, perhaps the best storyteller in the Bible, trusts his chosen medium of narrative to speak for itself. He tells the story from a feminine point of view, seen in both his selection of story material and his knowledge of feminine psychology. By means of the story itself rather than editorial comment, the author creates a world that embodies what he most wants to say about God and human values.

IMPLIED AUDIENCE. This book presupposes an audience that is attuned to romantic love, courtship, friendship, feminine experience, nature, farming, family loyalty, the struggle for survival (especially as experienced by the marginalized of society), and (by means of genealogical references late in the book) Jewish and messianic history.

WHAT UNIFIES THE BOOK. The love story; preoccupation with domestic values; a focus on women and their experiences; the captivating figure of Ruth; the outworking of the motif of emptiness vs. fullness

SPECIAL FEATURES. The most complete love story in the Bible; the feminine focus; evocation of a rural farming world; portrayal of two wholly idealized characters (Ruth and Boaz); the most artistically intricate story in the Bible; the only place in the Bible where we see a full-fledged picture of the institution of kinsman-redeemer

CHALLENGES FACING THE READER OR TEACHER OF THIS BOOK.
1. The sheer quantity of artistry and the network of interrelated details in the story
2. The need to decipher some of the cultural customs that occur in the story

HOW TO MEET THE CHALLENGES.
1. Treat each chapter as a story worthy of attention in itself, and take the time to do full justice to the things that are going on in a given chapter.
2. Accept the fact that people in the world of the story did things differently from the way we do them, and pick up the clues from the story itself as to what the customs were (perhaps with help from a study Bible).

THE MOST COMMON MISCONCEPTIONS ABOUT THIS BOOK. That the only thing that matters in the book is that it is a chapter in salvation history and that the wealth of human experience in the book is unimportant

---

The Book of Ruth is a laboratory demonstration that "the greatest of these is love" (1 Corinthians 13:13). . . . What soul-stirring passion of a noble and strong man and a beautiful and queenly woman is portrayed for us. On the human plane, this book tells of the sanctity of domestic life and the holiness of marital love. It lifts marriage to a very high position. It exalts true manhood and virtuous womanhood. . . . Boaz furnishes us with a miniature figure of the Lord Jesus Christ as the Redeemer.

J. VERNON McGEE
Ruth: The Romance of Redemption

1 Background to Romance	**2** Meeting and Courtship	**3** Betrothal	**4** Marriage
Family Loyalty	Hospitality to a Stranger	Romantic Love Triumphant	Married Union and Its Fruits
Ruth Becomes a Widow	Ruth Receives Kindness	Ruth Finds a Husband	Ruth Becomes a Mother

AN OUTLINE OF
RUTH

Washing the dishes, doing the laundry, going to work, experiencing depression over the tragedies of life, helping a friend or family member—does God care about the routines of life, or is he concerned only with "spiritual" experiences?

The book of Ruth provides answers regarding how we should view the everyday events in our lives. It shows that God can redeem the routine. It is true that in the book of Ruth God uses the everyday to advance his plan of salvation for the human race, but the book tells a human story as well as a divine story. The book of Ruth stands as a corrective to an unwarranted disparagement of the earthly and human that we find in some circles. At the same time, it reminds us of God's eternal plan for the redemption of the human race.

The Form of the Book

The book of Ruth is not just a story—it is the Bible's most complete love story. Despite the book's brevity, all of the ingredients of a happy love story, whether in life or literature, are present. They include an eligible and idealized couple who are worthy of each other, background observers (including friends, family members, and the community), a confidant for the lovers, obstacles to love and marriage, and an idealized rural setting. Common characters are a matchmaker and a rival. Key moments in a love story include a memorable first meeting, questioning others about the "eligible other," a report of the first date to a confidant, meetings and secret rendezvous, good-bye scenes, the bestowing of favors, the betrothal, and marriage as the climax.

DID YOU KNOW?
In Hebrew cultures the book of Ruth has traditionally been read at the Feast of Weeks (later called Pentecost), a harvest festival, in tribute to the importance of nature and harvest in this love story.

The book of Ruth is also what is known as an *idyll*—a brief story describing a simple, pleasant aspect of rural and domestic life. The idealized rural world that we enter as we read this book is itself part of the meaning that the book embodies.

Structure and Unity

The book is a quest story in which the goal is to find a home for Ruth (see 1:9 and 3:1) and in which the characters gradually overcome the obstacles to that goal. The resulting pattern is a U-shaped story in which events first descend into potential tragedy and then rise in a happy ending. Each chapter makes a distinctive contribution to the patterns that have been identified (see the chart on page 119).

Domestic and feminine concerns also unify the story. The world that we enter as we read this book is a predominantly feminine world, and we experience the events from a woman's point of view.

The world of the story is the rural world of growing and harvesting crops, and this, too, unifies the story. As we read, we enter an elemental (universal) world at both a natural level (crops and harvest) and a human level (death and birth, grief, friendship, family loyalty, romantic love, marriage, children, community).

Finally, the story is organized as a systematic outworking of a tension between emptiness and fullness, gradually resolved in the direction of fullness. We see this tension at a natural level, a family level, and an individual level.

Key Places and Characters

The land of Moab is symbolic of loss in this story. Bethlehem (literally "house of bread") is the place of the covenant faith into which Ruth is assimilated. As a pastoral (rural) story, the main action in the middle of the story occurs in the fields where the crops are harvested. The climactic event of the couple's engagement occurs in the secrecy of night on the threshing floor, whereas the claiming of Ruth and the wedding occur in the town square in broad daylight.

The central character is Ruth. Next in importance are Naomi and Boaz. The deceased family members of the opening chapter are part of the tragic backdrop to the story. The rival is likewise necessary to the action but not characterized beyond that. The townspeople are a supporting and surrounding cast of characters who create the crowd scenes at the end.

Frequently Asked Question

What is the significance of the *kinsman-redeemer* (Hebrew *goel*)? In the background lies the Levitical command that if a woman's husband died without offspring, it was the duty of the deceased man's brother to marry the widow and produce children through her, supporting them through his own estate. While the story of Ruth and Boaz does not fit the letter of this law (Boaz is not Ruth's brother-in-law), it fits the spirit of the law. Because the word *goel* includes the concept of redeemer, it is natural that commentators have made much of the kinsman-redeemer figure in the story as a foreshadowing of Christ the redeemer.

Key Doctrines

Providence. God uses ordinary events and the tragedies of life to accomplish his redemptive purposes in people's lives.

Redemption. Ruth is one of the few recorded non-Jews in Old Testament times who was successfully assimilated into the believing Jewish community; beyond that, Obed, the son who is born to Ruth and Boaz, is in the messianic line (4:17).

The Ethics of Covenant Living. At least two moral dimensions of the story are important: God's favor toward those who are generous to the marginalized of society, and his benediction on romantic love and marriage.

Fulfilled Womanhood. In the virtuous character of Ruth, we see a picture of one model of womanhood as God desires it.

Tips for Reading or Teaching Ruth

The overall genre of the book is the love story, with the opening chapter serving as the tragic background to the eventual love story. Try to assimilate the book in terms of its adherence to the usual features of a love story.

The book takes place within, and celebrates, the countryside and the farming that occurs there. It is important to do justice to the pastoral (rustic) dimension of the story.

The book of Ruth also celebrates women and domestic values. Look for what the story says about fulfilled womanhood and family relations.

The story is both a human story about ordinary people and a divine story about God's actions. The human level of the action embodies broader principles of God's redemptive activity in history, something highlighted by the fact that Ruth is an ancestress in the messianic line. It is therefore important to explore the tie-ins between the human story and the story of salvation history.

Things to Look For

- Evidences of feminine values, experiences, and psychology
- Examples of heroic and virtuous behavior and character traits
- The ingredients of the genre of the love story
- The world of nature and farming
- Evidences that God's providence permeates the commonplace

The Flow of the Book

The Crucible of Suffering, a Foil to Later Action (Chapter 1). Focus on the downward spiral of the action (an ever-expanding picture of loss), the things that make Ruth heroic, the things that make Naomi unsympathetic, the implied feminine viewpoint, evidences that domestic values are central to the story, and the systematic outworking of the emptiness-versus-fullness motif.

quick overview of ruth

The Harvest as a Symbol of Developing Love (Chapter 2). References to "the beginning of the barley harvest" (1:22) and "the end of the barley harvest" (2:23) frame the action. The progress of the harvest corresponds to the growth of love between Ruth and Boaz. You can analyze (1) what is idealized about the character and behavior of Boaz and Ruth, and (2) the contribution of the action to the evolving romance.

Climax to the Courtship (Chapter 3). The aggressive behavior of the women in this drama is appropriate for a widow needing a kinsman-redeemer, and Boaz's behavior shows his worthy character. In assimilating and teaching the chapter, it is important to do justice to the cleverness and daring of Naomi and Ruth, to the high drama of the action, and to the exemplary behavior of Boaz.

The Celebration of Marriage and Birth (Chapter 4). Here are the things that should guide your analysis of this chapter: (1) Boaz's cleverness at the town gate in winning Ruth as a bride (vv. 1-6); (2) the ways in which the requirements of the marriage are met in a fully legal and public way (vv. 7-12); (3) the way in which the author returns to Naomi (vv. 13-17); and (4) the significance of the genealogical material with which the story closes (vv. 18-22).

KEY VERSE
"May the LORD, the God of Israel, under whose wings you have come to take refuge, reward you fully for what you have done" (2:12). This prayer, uttered by Boaz on behalf of Ruth, sums up much of the book: the role of divine providence in human lives, the picture of human faith and virtue that we see in this story, and God's reward to those who exhibit faith and virtue.

The Main Themes

1. The story exhibits, celebrates, and affirms the importance of the things that God values and that we should value: nature, harvest, the commonplace, and family. The story shows that God values and redeems the routine.

2. The book is a case study in providence—God's directing of events in people's lives to accomplish his purposes.
3. The story is a repository of biblical teaching on romantic love and on the value of the family and domestic issues.
4. The book provides pictures of fulfilled womanhood.

KEY VERSE

"They named him Obed. He became the father of Jesse and the grandfather of David" (4:17). This is more than a patriotic reference to the great king David; it also links the son of Boaz and Ruth to the messianic line from which Jesus was born.

Contribution of the Book to the Bible's Story of Salvation in Christ

The story of God's unfolding plan of salvation occupies the Bible from beginning to end. An important aspect of this plan was the preservation of the messianic line, also known as the Davidic line. At the very end of the book of Ruth, we discover that the story of family loyalty and romantic love that we have been reliving actually involved a family of ancestors of King David, and through him the lineage that produced the earthly father of Jesus. Additionally, the word that is used to identify Boaz as a kinsman-redeemer makes us aware of the ultimate kinsman-redeemer, Christ.

Applying the Book

Applications are abundant. To be followers of God, we need to value the things that God values. The book of Ruth shows many of these: romantic love, family, nature, work, the commonplace, and virtuous living. The characters in the story show that we need to do more than just value these things—we need to live in gratitude for them as God's gifts.

The book also embodies theological realities that we can believe and on which we can base our lives. One of these is providence as it manifests itself in the domestic life of a single family. We can emulate Ruth's pattern of persevering through the personal difficulties of life, and Boaz's example of generosity and love. Second, as a chapter in salvation history, the book of Ruth can prompt us to renewed gratitude for God's great plan of salvation.

PERSPECTIVES
ON THE BOOK OF RUTH

Love song in harvest. Geoffrey T. Bull

A parable of friendship. Gloria Goldreich

The redeeming of Ruth. Alicia Ostriker

How did [Naomi and Ruth] survive their personal tragedies? They remained faithful to one another. They trusted in God. . . . They used their own wits and ingenuity to achieve their desired results. . . . Their success encourages others in distress. That God used Ruth to help produce David shows that even seemingly obscure persons can be used for eternal glory.
Paul R. House

I hold up a picture of the author of Ruth as an artist in full command of a complex and subtle art, which art is exhibited in almost every word of the story. D. F. Rauber

The story of Ruth takes its place as . . . one more bit of Heilsgeschichte *["holy history"], for it clearly aims to trace the background of the great David. In fact, the story could well be described as messianic history, for it serves to trace the plans of God which lay behind the Davidic dynasty.*
Ronald M. Hals

The loveliest complete work on a small scale, handed down to us as an ethical treatise and an idyll. The German poet Goethe

1 SAMUEL
The Heart Approved
by God

FACT SHEET

FORMAT. 31 chapters, 810 verses

IMPLIED PURPOSES. To trace the history of Israel from a loose tribal confederation under the judges to a centralized government under the kings, and by means of that history, to show what God approves and disapproves in leaders (and by extension, in all people)

AUTHOR'S PERSPECTIVE. The author is intimately acquainted with the characters and is deeply sympathetic to David. He interprets the changes in government and leadership from a theological perspective and has a great interest in the character of the leaders.

IMPLIED AUDIENCE. The immediate audience is the people of Israel under the monarchy, who want an explanation of how they got to where they are, namely, by a transition from judgeship to an ill-advised monarchy that contains foreshadowings of a worthy king to follow the failed first king.

WHAT UNIFIES THE BOOK. A strong story line; powerful characters; interpersonal conflict; the motif of testing personal character and integrity; a developing conflict between Saul and David

SPECIAL FEATURES. Preoccupation with leaders as representatives of a nation; a cause-and-effect link between the goodness or badness of leaders and the fortunes of a nation; inclusion of a full-fledged tragedy in the story of Saul's rise and fall

CHALLENGES FACING THE READER OR TEACHER OF THIS BOOK.
1. The strangeness of the world of the story by modern standards (for example, the gold tumors and rats or mice that the Philistines gave as an offering to the Israelites)
2. The need to interpret what is good and bad in the behavior of the leading characters

HOW TO MEET THE CHALLENGES.

1. Accept the premise that customs in the ancient world differed from our own, and having accepted the strangeness of many things, look for what is universal in those details.
2. Keep alert to the mixture of good and bad in the leading characters, who are mixtures of positive and negative behavior.

THE MOST COMMON MISCONCEPTION ABOUT THIS BOOK. That the book is primarily about Samuel. It is equally about Saul and David.

*S*aul is the one great tragic hero of the Bible: not only physically taller than any of his subjects, he is an able ruler and by his standards a fair-minded one. But he seems to do nothing right. . . . Saul becomes a doomed man . . . with intermittent fits of melancholy and of frantic but futile efforts to rid himself of the threat from David. In the Witch of Endor scene he finally turns to the occult powers that he himself had forbidden consultation with, and disaster and death follow. The terrible and inevitable degeneration will remind the modern reader that Shakespeare must have studied the account of Saul with considerable care before writing Macbeth.

NORTHROP FRYE
The Great Code: The Bible and Literature

AN OUTLINE OF
1 SAMUEL

31 Death of Saul

21–30 David's Life as a Fugitive
18–20 Saul's Plot against David
17 David and Goliath
16 David Anointed King

15 Saul's Tragic Choice
11–14 Saul's Early Kingship

10 Saul's Coronation
8–9 Saul's Appointment as King

5–7 Samuel's Judgeship
4 End of Eli's Judgeship
1–3 Birth and Childhood of Samuel

Leadership Change from Eli to Samuel	Leadership Change from Samuel to Saul	Saul's Failure as King	David's Fugitive Life as King in Waiting	Saul's Tragic End
End of the Era of the Judges	Beginning of the Monarchy			
Samuel as Dominant Character	Saul as Dominant Character	Saul as Dominant Character	David as Dominant Character	David as Dominant Character
Dominant Pattern of Decline		Dominant Pattern of Ascent		

Saul was the type of person whose high school class would have voted him most likely to succeed. He was tall and handsome; a good warrior; the father of the loyal and talented Jonathan; and, initially, humble. Yet his success was short lived. Without moralizing, this book shows us that Saul's problems stem from his character and his inability to trust God. David's family, on the other hand, voted David *least* likely to succeed. When Samuel came to David's family to anoint the new king, the young David was not even brought in from the fields as a potential candidate! As Saul's reputation and influence plummeted, David's grew. First Samuel gives us a memorable picture of what God values in a leader.

The Form of the Book
The primary form of 1 Samuel is narrative, or story. More specifically, the book is a collection of hero stories built around three central characters: the prophet Samuel, King Saul, and David, the designated king. (For more on hero stories, see page 213.) The stories of these three commanding figures overlap as we read from beginning to end, and in particular, the story of Saul's tragic decline is played off against the youthful David's ascent in the second half of the book.

Key Characters
The book of 1 Samuel remains in our memories partly as a gallery of striking characters. In the first part of the book, Eli and Hannah are noteworthy. Eli was high priest and judge in Israel for forty years; Samuel grew up under Eli's care during his decline as a deficient father to his own sons. Hannah emerges as the godly mother of Samuel, and we know her particularly through her prayer in chapter 2. Samuel, apparently regarded in Old Testament times as the greatest leader since Moses (Jeremiah 15:1), served as priest, judge, and prophet during the transition from judgeship to monarchy. Saul is a classic abuser: violent, moody, cowardly while at the same time preoccupied with his public image, remorseful without being repentant. Saul's son Jonathan, rejected by his father, befriends his father's rival, David.

Key Doctrines
God's Providence. God is in control of the events in Israel, despite how things look.

Sin. The book clearly portrays the effects of sin as seen in the leadership of Eli and Saul.

The Holy Spirit. The Spirit anoints and empowers people to carry out their God-given tasks.

Prayer. Samuel is a man of prayer. Chapter 8 gives us a glimpse of how God receives Samuel's prayer.

Tips for Reading or Teaching 1 Samuel

The book is organized around the three large personalities who play prominent roles in this time period. As you read, be aware that this is a book of transitions. Israel moves from a loose confederation of tribes to a nation-state, from leadership by a judge who also served as a prophet and priest to a monarchy, and from a nation under the thumb of the Philistines to a country of increasing military prominence. To discern the full riches of this book, you will need to be alert to the transitions that are occurring and to the key role leaders play in the destiny of their nation.

quick overview of 1 samuel

1:1–3:21	First leadership change: from Eli to Samuel
4:1–7:17	Samuel leads Israel.
8:1–10:27	Second leadership change: from Samuel to Saul
11:1–15:35	Saul leads Israel.
16:1–31:13	Third leadership change: from Saul to David

The Flow of the Book

The events of the nation and the behavior of its leaders swing between positive and negative, as the following chart shows:

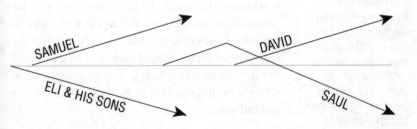

The Judgeship of Samuel (Chapters 1–7). The book begins with a full-fledged hero story that traces the life of Samuel from before his conception to his success as a national leader. The three main sections of this unit are as follows: Samuel's birth (chapter 1); Samuel's call by God (chapters 2–3); and the capture, adventures, and return of the Ark of the Covenant (chapters 4–7). You can give your interaction with this material an analytic focus by tracing the following:

- The traits that make Samuel a heroic character
- The way in which Samuel's ascent and the decline of Eli's family are played off against each other
- The ways in which the sojourns of the Ark are part of a holy-war motif and an index to the religious life of Israel

Israel Becomes a Monarchy (Chapters 8–12). This unit narrates a crucial transition in the history of Israel: the change from rule by judges to rule by a king. Things to note in this regard are the (1) reasons why the change was instituted and (2) evidences in the text that it was a bad decision (refer to Deuteronomy 17:14-20 for helpful background). Note also the extravagant extent to which the author goes to idealize Saul; look for an ever-expanding list of ways in which he was "the most likely to succeed" type. Finally, look carefully at the ways in which Samuel's farewell discourse (chapter 12) places the nation and its king in a position of either-or— either success or failure, either obedience or disobedience.

Saul's Kingship: The Beginning of the End (Chapters 13–15). These chapters show the tragic choices Saul made as king and God's disfavor toward him as a result. Chapter 15 is the heart of Saul's tragedy, but the preceding chapters give us signposts to the tragedy. Your best way to analyze the data is to compile a list of the ingredients that went into Saul's tragic decline: the bad choices he made, the character traits that lay behind those choices, and the ways in which he disregarded God's clear commands. Try to relive the sequence of events as Saul experienced them, and ponder the ways in which Saul is representative of tendencies that you find in yourself and in people around you.

KEY VERSE

"The LORD said to Samuel, 'Don't judge by his appearance or height, for I have rejected him. The LORD doesn't see things the way you see them. People judge by outward appearance, but the LORD looks at the heart'" (16:7). The discrepancy between human standards of value and God's standards is important in 1 Samuel.

Saul's Decline and David's Rise (Chapters 16–24). The next unit tells two stories at the same time, mainly by shuttling from one to the other but occasionally bringing them into intersection with each other. One story is the tragic decline of King Saul. The other is the gradual rise of David as he moves toward becoming king of the nation. We can picture these two lines of action as an *X*, meaning that as the fortunes of Saul decline, those of David ascend. The unit begins with Saul as the established king and David as the teenage, secretly anointed king. As the unit ends, Saul's life—personal, domestic, and civil—is in shambles, and David is getting stronger all the time. Here are specific things that will yield analytic mileage:

- Trace the specific stages of Saul's decline, noting that his collapse occurs at spiritual, psychological, and social levels.
- Trace also the stages of David's ascent. As with Saul, compile a composite portrait of the hero from the specific events in the narrative.
- Observe ways in which the two main characters in this unit are foils to each other—contrasts that heighten the qualities of the other person.
- Pay attention to the ways in which God figures as a named character in the action.

David and His Merry Band (Chapters 25–30). Although Saul makes momentary appearances at this late stage of the story, he recedes into the background as David takes center stage. David here leads the life of a fugitive with a loyal band of followers, in a manner similar to the story of Robin Hood and his followers in English literature. The followers probably numbered around four hundred fighters, plus family. David offers protection for farmers and in return they give him food and goods. He also serves as a mercenary for the Philistines, which almost results in his fighting against Israel. One good exercise to perform while reading this section is to observe the things that make David an idealized and godly man. A second is to read the story for what it is—an adventure story, replete with battlefield action. You can also note the role of minor characters who enter the action, and the lessons you can learn from them.

The Deaths of Saul and Jonathan (Chapter 31). Saul's tragic fall is complete at the end of 1 Samuel. There is much that is sad in this chapter, and you can profitably analyze the ingredients that make Saul's end the tragic event that it is. Three characters dominate the book of 1 Samuel, but the most dominant one is the tragic figure of Saul. There are valuable lessons to learn from looking back and systematizing its main ingredients and lessons.

Prayer in the Bible

The heart of prayer lies in God's desire to enter into relationship with humanity. The Bible records more than six hundred prayers, not counting the Psalms, and offers a compelling invitation to godly men and women to be involved in effective and renewing prayer. God invites us to pray, "Our Father in heaven . . . ."

The redeemed divine-human relationship of mutual love, trust, and commitment provides the context for our prayer. This relationship excludes any attempt to use magic or formulas to control or placate God, setting prayer in Bible times in marked contrast to prayer patterns of many surrounding nations. We see Elijah offering a simple, straightforward prayer clearly rooted in his relationship with God—"I am your servant"—while the priests of Baal vainly seek to win the favor of their deity through frantic prophesying and bloodletting (1 Kings 18:16-38). Similarly, Jesus reminds us that true prayer is a matter of the heart and must be free of show and self-glorification.

The redeemed care passionately about God's reputation and seek to see his name and character vindicated through their prayers. This concern for God's name lifts the prayers of the Bible from a self-oriented wish fulfillment to a God-centered dialogue.

The emphasis on God's reputation brings with it an almost brash boldness. In the prayers recorded in the Bible, this concern is stated negatively: "God, if you fail to do X, the surrounding nations will think you can't act or don't care about us." A good example is the prayer in which Moses asks God, "Why let the Egyptians say, 'Their God rescued them with the evil intention of slaughtering them in the mountains and wiping them from the face of the earth'?" (Exodus 32:12). The petition "May your name be kept holy" also reminds us of the prominence a heartfelt concern for God's reputation should have in our prayers.

The people who pray in the Bible frequently allude to God's character or promises in their prayers. Abraham based his prayer on God's character: "Should not the Judge of all the earth do what is right?" (Genesis 18:25). Moses appealed to previous promises when he prayed, "Remember your servants Abraham, Isaac, and Jacob. You bound yourself with an oath to them" (Exodus 32:13).

Jesus' life is a powerful testimony to the effectiveness of prayers born out of submission and love before the Father. Jesus' prayers were a powerful force for good because he lived with such integrity that what he did and what he prayed said the same things: "While Jesus was here on earth, he offered prayers and pleadings. . . . And God heard his prayers because of his deep reverence for God" (Hebrews 5:7).

Famous Prayers in the Bible

Abraham's intercession for Sodom and Gomorrah (Genesis 18:23-33)

Jacob's prayer in the crisis of meeting Esau after twenty years (Genesis 32:9-12)

Moses talks with God (Exodus 3:1–4:17)

Moses' intercession for his people (Exodus 32:11-13, 31-32)

Hannah's prayer for a child (1 Samuel 1:10-11)

Hannah's prayer of thanksgiving (1 Samuel 2:1-10)

Samuel's prayer for Israel (1 Samuel 7:5-12)

David's prayer in response to receiving the Davidic covenant (2 Samuel 7:18-29)

Solomon's prayer for wisdom (1 Kings 3:6-9)

Solomon's prayer at the dedication of the Temple (1 Kings 8:23-53)

Elijah's prayer on Mount Carmel (1 Kings 18:36-37)

Nehemiah's prayer (Nehemiah 1:5-11)

Job's prayer (Job 42:1-6)

David's prayer for forgiveness (Psalm 51)

Hezekiah's prayer for deliverance (Isaiah 38:10-20)

Jeremiah's prayer of distress in time of persecution (Jeremiah 20:7-18)

Daniel's prayer of confession (Daniel 9:3-19)

Jonah's prayer from the belly of the great fish (Jonah 2:2-9)

Habakkuk's prayer for justice (Habakkuk 1:2-4)

Habakkuk's prayer for deliverance (Habakkuk 3:2-19)

The Lord's Prayer (Matthew 6:9-13; Luke 11:2-4)

Jesus' High Priestly Prayer (John 17)

Jesus' prayer in Gethsemane (Matthew 26:39, 42)

The prayers of the Pharisee and the tax collector (Luke 18:11-13)

The apostles' prayer for divine direction (Acts 1:24-25)

Stephen's prayer for his murderers (Acts 7:60)

The early church's prayer for Paul and Barnabas (Acts 13:1-3)

Paul's prayer for the Corinthians (2 Corinthians 13:7)

Paul's prayer for the Ephesians (Ephesians 3:14-21)

Paul's prayer for the Philippians (Philippians 1:9-11)

Paul's prayer for the Colossians (Colossians 1:9-14)

The last prayer in the Bible (Revelation 22:20)

The Main Themes

1. Leaders set the tone for the nation.
2. The heart of a leader shows in his/her decisions.
3. God desires obedience more than religious show, no matter how splendid.
4. Ultimately, God is the power behind every throne.
5. In times of transition, it is easy to lose a God-centered perspective.

Contribution of the Book to the Bible's Story of Salvation in Christ

Jesus was born of the lineage of David, whom we meet for the first time in this book. Furthermore, in the New Testament, Jesus is presented as prophet, priest, and king, and we see early examples of these in 1 Samuel. We get a glimpse of how political kingship functions, and we begin to see how David exemplifies the character and political qualities that make for a great king. As we read, we see that David is only a pale reflection of Jesus as the perfectly wise, just, and powerful king. In ancient Israel there was a division of power among the offices of prophet, priest, and king. Saul loses his kingship when he takes on the role of priest, but we can trust Jesus to execute all three offices with justice and grace. Jesus is the ultimate "man after [God's] own heart" (1 Samuel 13:14, NIV).

Applying the Book

The story of Saul is the clearest example of a full-fledged literary tragedy that we find in the Bible. It is possible to chart, step by step, the usual phases of dilemma—tragic choice—catastrophe—suffering—perception—death. The book shows how our big choices are the result of a direction set long before.

The book's emphasis on character rather than appearance reflects a truth that every generation must remember. Saul is tall, handsome, and a gifted leader, but he lacks the character to lead the people well over time.

We must appreciate the place of prayer in 1 Samuel. The book opens with Hannah's heartfelt prayer for a child. The prayer of Samuel in chapter 7 teaches us much about prayer and providence, and Samuel's poignant summary of his ministry, "I will certainly not sin against the LORD by ending my prayers for you" (12:23), should be a reminder to all of us about our responsibility to pray.

PERSPECTIVES
ON THE BOOK OF 1 SAMUEL

"Enjoy" is not too strong a word for the deep delight to be had through a sustained effort to enter into the human situations depicted here: the hurts, ambitions, spiritual aspirations and above all the failures. To some extent both Samuel and David failed, and Saul obstinately pursued his own interpretation of his kingly office in such a way as to forfeit the divine favour. Here in these people is real life as we experience it.
Joyce G. Baldwin

More complex than David, and more tortured, Saul lifts us to mountain heights and then drops us into the abyss.   Elie Wiesel

The tragic irony of the Saul story . . . lies in the disparities between the demand on Saul and Saul's capacity to meet it.   Edwin Good

When we look at the Book of [1] Samuel from the human perspective, it is a thoroughly tragic book. Not one of the book's characters escapes tragedy.   Avraham Kariv

Triumph and tragedy are the two words which best describe the content of the books of Samuel.   John Davis

David's story is essentially a story of contrasts. We start with the contrast between David and Goliath, the names themselves serving as a metaphor for the little guy standing up to the bruiser. . . . David's success in this early encounter leads us to the conflict between David and King Saul. Then, just when we think we have left conflict behind, [in 2 Samuel] we enter into the real struggle of this story, that which takes place within David himself . . . when David is forced to reckon with the mixed reality of his own heart.   Richard D. Phillips

2 SAMUEL
*When Good Kings Do
Bad Things*

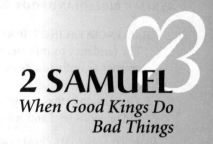

FORMAT. 24 chapters, 695 verses

IMPLIED PURPOSE. To examine godly leadership by tracing the transition from Israel as a loose tribal confederation under the judges to a centralized government under the kings

AUTHOR'S PERSPECTIVE. The author of this court history is intimately acquainted with the characters, and while he is deeply sympathetic to David, he does not hesitate to portray David's failings, primarily by allowing the reader to discern his struggles, victories, and compromises. The author interprets events from a theological perspective and has a great interest in the character of the leaders, as well as in the cause-and-effect link between sin and punishment.

IMPLIED AUDIENCE. The people of Israel under the monarchy who want an explanation about how they ended up where they are, and anyone concerned about godly leadership for the people of God

WHAT UNIFIES THE BOOK. The figure of David, who is the central character from start to finish; the political world in which events occur; warfare as a common action; the double action of David's personal life and public life

SPECIAL FEATURES. A strong story line; powerful characters; interpersonal conflict; the motif of testing personal character and integrity; the tragic structure of David's life as narrated in this book. (Events are prosperous for David until his adultery with Bathsheba and his murder of Uriah in the middle of the book, after which David's life declines.)

CHALLENGES FACING THE READER OR TEACHER OF THIS BOOK.

1. The tendency to misinterpret David's public sins of adultery and murder as unfortunate events rather than as the turning point in the story

2. The tension between appreciating David's leadership at a national and religious level and acknowledging his utter failure at home

HOW TO MEET THE CHALLENGES.

1. Do justice to the pyramid shape of David's life by tracing his ascendancy early in the book and his decline in the last part of the book, with the adultery and murder marking the turning point.

2. Seek to learn from David's real-life struggles without glossing over his mistakes or dismissing them.

F*rom the perspective of the modern historian . . . David's activities in this period seem shrewd, calculated, and consistently effective. His success seems the result of foresight and careful deliberation. This is not, however, the perspective of our narrator, or at least it is not the view of David's actions he means his audience to take. The details he provides about the negotiations between David and the people of Hebron or the elders of Judah, about the fortunes of the Israelite state after the battle of Gilboa, and about the political climate in general in Palestine during this period seem frustratingly incomplete or cryptic to the historian. The reason for this is that the sequence of events is presented, as throughout the story of David's rise to power, not merely as an interplay between circumstances and human deeds, certainly not as a consequence of the ambitious machinations of David, but as the working out of Yahweh's will.*

P. KYLE MCCARTER JR.
Anchor Bible

AN OUTLINE OF
2 SAMUEL

24 David's Census and Punishment
23 David's Mighty Men
22 David's Psalm of Praise
19–21 David's Further Kingship
13–18 David's Conflicts with Absalom
11–12 David and Bathsheba
8–10 David's Successes
7 David's Desire to Build a Temple
6 Ark Brought Back to Jerusalem
5 David Becomes King over All Israel
2–4 David Rules Judah and Battles Israel
1 David's Lament for Saul and Jonathan

David Gradually Consolidates His Political Power	David in Relation to Worship	David's Early Reign	David's Tragic Choice	David Pays the Price for His Sins	Chronicle of David's Mixed Life as King
David Rules Judah Only	David Rules All Israel				
David Rules from Hebron	David Rules from Jerusalem				
Seven and a Half Years	Thirty-three Years				
David's Personal and Public Successes					David's Personal and Public Disappointments

No doubt you have seen an organization brought down by the bad actions of a leader. After the disruption and loss caused by poor management and practices, the leader departs. A new and, we hope, better leader comes along, but the work has just begun. The new leader has to consolidate control. The time of moving from designated leadership to actual leadership can be quite draining. This is the situation we find at the opening of the book of 2 Samuel. David rules part of the nation from a location far in the south of the country, and it takes seven and a half years before he leads the entire nation from a more central capital.

The Form of the Book

The primary form of 2 Samuel is narrative, or story. More specifically, the book is a collection of hero stories built around King David. (For more on hero stories, see page 213.) The stories of this commanding figure dominate the book as we read from beginning to end. Near the middle of the book the hero's sins of adultery, murder, and deceit are reported, and from that point on, David's life takes the downward turn into tragedy. The story of his decline is played off against his youthful ascent, which marks the first half of the book. It is important to grasp that the writer of 2 Samuel (unlike the chronicler in Kings and Chronicles) conceives of David's life as a tragedy, with the turn from prosperity to calamity decisively located in David's acts of adultery and murder in chapter 11. The following diagram shows how we should picture the shape of David's life as interpreted by the writer of 2 Samuel:

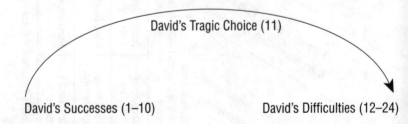

David's Tragic Choice (11)

David's Successes (1–10)　　　　　　David's Difficulties (12–24)

Unifying Elements

- David is the protagonist of this book and appears in all but one of the chapters.
- Contention for the throne is present throughout the book.
- The expansion of the kingdom occurs progressively throughout the

book. David rules a portion of Israel at the beginning, and by the end of the book he rules a formidable and vastly expanded nation.

- "Before the LORD" is a common phrase in this book. The author uses it to express the fact that ultimately all acts are done in the Lord's presence, but not all people recognize this.
- Repentance is a theme throughout 1 and 2 Samuel. People's character is evident both in how they act and in how they respond to sin.

Key Places, Characters, and Objects

- Absalom, David's estranged son, leads a rebellion against his father. The image of David's grieving over his death, "O my son Absalom! O Absalom, my son, my son!" (2 Samuel 19:4) is a haunting picture of an estranged father stricken by his son's death.
- The Ark of the Covenant, a wooden chest overlaid with gold, was part of the sacred furniture of the Tabernacle. The Ark had been captured by the Philistines, but David returns it to the Tabernacle.
- Bathsheba, the wife of Uriah, one of David's most trusted soldiers, has an affair with David and becomes the queen and the mother of Solomon.
- David, the greatest king of Israel, comes from humble origins, maintains a deep love for God during his reign, and is a direct ancestor of Jesus.
- Jerusalem, a Jebusite city, becomes the center of Israel after David captures it and makes it his capital.
- Joab, the military commander of David's forces, plays a crucial role in this book.
- Nathan, the court prophet, serves as a faithful advisor who is willing to speak the truth to David.

DAVID'S ENEMIES David wanted to complete the conquest of Canaan begun by Joshua. He defeated the Jebusites at Jerusalem and the Philistines in the vicinity of Gath. The Ammonites, Arameans, and Moabites became his subjects. He put garrisons in Edom and levied a tax upon them.

Key Doctrines

Covenant. God is seen as a covenant-making and covenant-keeping God. He promises to preserve David's kingdom forever. It is in this covenant that we receive the announcement of the work and lineage of the future Messiah.

Sin. The struggles of Israel's greatest and godliest king show the pervasiveness of sin.

Faithfulness. We see David treating Mephibosheth with great kindness because of the covenant between David and Jonathan. We also see David's lack of faithfulness in responding to the misdeeds of family members, and this tears apart the fabric of the family.

Tips for Reading or Teaching 2 Samuel

The book is filled with political intrigue, but it is subtle and it would be easy to miss. For example, Saul's son Ishbosheth is set up by Abner as a puppet king and later is murdered by his own advisers.

David captures Jerusalem, situated in the middle of Israel's territory but held by the Jebusites. He turns it into the political, cultural, and religious center of the nation. Pay close attention to all that David brings to or establishes in the city.

The theme of confession and repentance runs throughout the book.

Chapter 11 is pivotal to the entire book. It is a hinge that marks the point at which David's life shifts from victory to defeat as God punishes him for his sins and sin produces its inevitable consequences.

quick overview of 2 samuel

1:1–10:19	David's rise
11:1–18:33	David's tragic fall and decline
19:1–24:25	David's last days

The Flow of the Book

David's Rule Secured (Chapters 1–4). Here the story continues without interruption from where 1 Samuel left off. Readers will benefit from looking at the challenges David has to overcome in order to establish his reign:

- Seemingly legitimate heirs to the throne are available in Saul's family.
- At least one is willing to style himself as the heir apparent.
- David was anointed king in private, and Samuel has died, leaving no authoritative witness of this event.

- David has spent time living in another country and working for Israel's enemies.
- Saul was not able to unite the country.
- There are two contenders for the office of high priest.
- After David is publicly anointed king, civil war engulfs the land.

David's Political Successes (Chapters 5–10). The author selects information to highlight how politically astute David was. An example of his political skill is his selection of Jerusalem as the capital. Israel was divided by tribalism, so David took a city that was neutral and turned it into the capital. He also concentrated cultural, religious, social, military, and political resources there. While reading these chapters, ask these questions: For what things does the author commend David? How does this exemplify what the people of God need in a king?

David's Depravity (Chapters 11–12). These two chapters are the turning point in the story. The compactness of the account is striking. In fewer than one hundred words we learn about the adultery, and in fewer than one thousand words we get the entire story of both the adultery and the murderous cover-up. Because of this sparse and unembellished style, readers need to exercise a little imagination to let the story come to life. Be sure to identify the stages that mark David's downward spiral from temptation into sin. Nathan confronts David about his sins and tells him that his dynasty will continue but he will suffer a threefold punishment:

- The sword will not depart from his house; that is, violence will tear his family apart.
- Someone will take David's harem and publicly sleep with his wives because he took his neighbor's wife.
- The child conceived in that affair will die.

As you read the rest of the book, look to see how these punishments are carried out.

David's Struggle for His Throne (Chapters 13–21). Take time to see what is happening here in terms of familiar categories. We get a glimpse of a large, blended family—children from one father and various mothers—all living in a loose extended family. As you read, try to understand the kind of father David has become. How does he respond to family conflict? What does Absalom exploit in his father's governing style?

David's Swan Song (Chapters 22–24). David's worst crisis is over, but his days of glory have also passed. As you read the last chapter, look for the same pattern of positive followed by negative that marked the entire book.

The Main Themes

1. CORRUPTION AS A RESULT OF POWER AND EASE. David had achieved political greatness and peace. It was during this time of prosperity and ease that he committed his tragic sins and lived as a distracted father.

2. THE IMPORTANCE OF CONFESSION AND REPENTANCE. David serves as a contrast to Saul: When David is confronted with his sin, he admits it and grieves over it.

3. THE IMPORTANCE OF THE PLACE OF PUBLIC WORSHIP. The narrative highlights David's self-abandoned worship of God and his recovery of the Ark as well as his desire to build a temple for God.

4. POLITICAL SAVVY. The narrative celebrates the wisdom and resourcefulness of David as a leader.

Contribution of the Book to the Bible's Story of Salvation in Christ

God establishes a covenant with David (chapter 7) in which he assures David multiple times that his dynasty will be everlasting and promises him that a great ruler will come through his family line. The language David heard was veiled, but in light of the gospel, we see this as a clear reference to Christ, the Son of David. The story also points to the need for someone greater than David to rule over Israel—a king after God's own heart who shepherds his family with godliness and resists the temptation to commit adultery, murder, or any other sin.

Applying the Book

The content in this book is as diverse and rich as life itself. We need to let the richness of the material challenge some of our simple views of the virtuous life. The important theme of how prosperity and ease put David in a place to seek pleasure above all else is relevant for all ages. Consider also the disastrous public consequences of the private dysfunction of a family.

PERSPECTIVES
ON THE BOOK OF 2 SAMUEL

Instead of asking David to build God a house, the Lord promises to build David a house. Paul R. House

We find [David] as a sort of Robin Hood of the Bible. We love the stories of his daring courage, his encounter with lions and bears and the giant.
Henrietta Mears

With his ability to exercise proven authority apparently impaired, David lives to see his own sins of murder and adultery replicated in the lives of his sons. V. Philips Long

In the scenic, succinct, and subtle narratives that constitute the books of Samuel, the danger of "overreading," of becoming overly subtle in interpretation, is ever-present, but so is the danger of "underreading."
V. Philips Long

Doctrinally, these books [1 and 2 Samuel] have much to say about the nature of God: about His holiness, His preeminence over all the other gods, His demand to complete obedience on the part of His followers, and His judgment of sin. But they especially contribute the Davidic covenant which, along with the Abrahamic covenant, provides a basis for an ordering of the end times. Specifically God promised David a kingdom forever, a throne forever, and descendants to sit on that throne forever. Such grandiose promises could find satisfactory fulfillment only in David's greater Son, Jesus the Messiah, who will sit on the throne of David in the Holy City forever. Howard F. Vos

David was a man after God's own heart—not because of boasted perfection, but because of confessed imperfections. Henrietta Mears

1 KINGS

A House Divided

FACT SHEET

FORMAT. 22 chapters, 816 verses

IMPLIED PURPOSES. To record the history of Israel from Solomon to the divided kingdom and to document what utter folly it is for kings and nations to turn away from the one true God

AUTHOR'S PERSPECTIVE. The author is both a historian and a theologian. As he surveys the royal history of Israel and Judah, he evaluates everything from the religious point of view. His standard is not political success but spiritual faithfulness to God and the laws of his covenant, as found in Deuteronomy 28 and elsewhere.

IMPLIED AUDIENCE. The remnant of Judah (living in exile in Babylon) and the people of God throughout history who want to know God's plan for a righteous kingdom

WHAT UNIFIES THE BOOK. The succession of kings; the divine standard according to which each king is evaluated; and the repeated narrative formula listing each king's name, kingdom (Israel or Judah), date of accession to the throne, length of reign, religious policies, sources for further information, death, and successor

SPECIAL FEATURES. The rise and folly of Solomon and his glorious kingdom; the construction and dedication of the Temple in Jerusalem; the disaster of the divided kingdom, which permanently separated the ten tribes in the north (Israel, with its capital in Samaria) from the two tribes in the south (Judah, based in Jerusalem); the miraculous ministry of the prophet Elijah and his showdown with the followers of Baal

CHALLENGES FACING THE READER OR TEACHER OF THIS BOOK.
1. Finding spiritual significance in the political history of ancient Israel

2. Relating Kings to Chronicles, which covers much of the same historical territory

HOW TO MEET THE CHALLENGES.
1. Pay attention to the standard used to evaluate each king (e.g., the law of God or the model of another king such as David or Jeroboam) and to the outcome of each king's reign.
2. The biggest difference is tone: Chronicles is more positive in its portrayal of Solomon and the kings of Judah, encouraging people with the fulfillment of God's promises to David. By contrast, Kings fully exposes royal sin as a warning to remain faithful to God.

*W**hat kind of history, then, does 1 and 2 Kings present? One factor dominates the books' opinion of all kings, nations, and events. If the kings serve the Lord and do not worship idols, they are good kings. If they offer sacrifices only in Jerusalem, they are even better. If they destroy idols and bring spiritual renewal, they receive the author's complete approval. Failure in any of these areas leads to national catastrophe. In other words, no factor— economic, military, or otherwise—affects Israel's destiny as much as their relationship to God. This world view causes the author to write a sacred history that warns future generations of Israelites against repeating the same mistakes.*

PAUL R. HOUSE

AN OUTLINE OF 1 KINGS

United Kingdom

Divided Kingdom

1 Solomon Anointed King
2 Solomon Consolidates His Kingship
3 Solomon Asks for Wisdom
4 Solomon's Wealth
5–7 Solomon Builds the Temple
8 Solomon Dedicates the Temple
9 God Speaks to Solomon
10 The Queen of Sheba Sees Solomon's Glory
11 Solomon Foolishly Turns Away from God
12:1-15 Rehoboam's Folly
12:16–13:34 Jeroboam's Rebellion
14:1-2 God's Judgment
14:21–16:34 Decline of Israel and Judah
17 Miracles during the Drought
18 Showdown at Mount Carmel
19 Elijah Runs Away and Meets God
20 Ahab vs. Syria
21 Ahab Commits Murder
22 The End of Ahab

Solomon Becomes King after David	Solomon Gains Wisdom and Wealth	Solomon Builds a Temple, a Palace, a Kingdom

Solomon Follows Other Gods and Comes Under Judgment

The Kingdom Divides

Various Kings Rule

Elijah Prophesies, Prays, and Performs Miracles

Rehoboam and Jeroboam

2 Kings of Judah; 6 Kings of Israel

Ahab and Jezebel

The Reign of King Solomon

Kings of Israel and Judah

Capital City: Jerusalem

Capital Cities: Jerusalem and Samaria

On the eve of an important modern-day election in Israel, *Time* magazine made the following editorial comment: "Sometimes statesmen stumble blindly over an epochal crossroads they do not know is there. Others are given the chance to see the fork in the road ahead and decide deliberately which way to go. Folly is when leaders knowingly choose the wrong path."

First and Second Kings provide ample documentation of the truth of these comments. Each of the kings of Israel and Judah was called to keep covenant with God by defending God's law and promoting his worship. But when confronted with the decision to serve the God of Israel or to follow other gods, not all of them chose wisely, and the consequences were disastrous. We face the same decision every day—are we for God or against him?—and the choice we make is either wisdom or folly.

The Form and Aim of the Book
First and Second Kings are really one book in two parts, divided more for reasons of convenience than for historical or theological significance. The book is written in the form of historical narrative. Like all history, it is selective: It does not tell us everything about the kings of Israel and Judah. In fact, the author frequently tells his readers where they can go for more information (e.g., 14:29). Nor does he devote equal space to everything. Instead, he gives an interpretive history that tells the story of Israel's kings with a specific purpose in mind, namely, to show what happens when political and spiritual leaders choose to worship false gods.

Key Phrases
Key phrases in 1 (and 2) Kings include the following:

- *Did what was evil* (e.g., 11:6) or *did what was pleasing* (e.g., 15:11) *in the LORD's sight.* This summary of each king's relationship to God refers not simply to his actions but also to the attitude of his heart.
- *My father, David* (e.g., 5:3) or *his ancestor David* (e.g., 15:3). Either phrase identifies David as the royal standard for Israel's kings.
- *The high places.* These religious shrines, built on high ground and set up as alternatives to the Temple in Jerusalem, became symbols of Israel's apostasy.
- *The Lord God.* This phrase, used more than five hundred times in 1 and 2 Kings, shows God's rule over Israel, Judah, and the nations.

Key Places and Characters
At the beginning of the book, Jerusalem is the location of the action and the place of God's presence with his people. However, with the division

Jesus as King

Like the prophets and the priests, the kings of Israel were called to provide good spiritual leadership for the people of God. Together these three offices were intended to give people everything they needed: a message from God (the prophets), atonement for sin (the priests), and protection from enemies (the kings).

The Bible views Israel's monarchy both positively and negatively. On the one hand, God gave his people instructions for what kind of king they should choose to rule them (Deuteronomy 17:14-20). Yet when the people finally *did* ask for a king, the prophet Samuel advised them against it (1 Samuel 8).

The rest of Old Testament history—starting with the tragic story of Saul—justifies this ambivalence. Godly kings were a great blessing, but more often than not, instead of protecting their people the kings of Israel and Judah were ungodly men who led their people astray.

Nevertheless, God always promised that one day he would send a righteous king to rule his people forever. This king would come from the royal line of David, for to him it was promised, "The LORD will build a house for you—a dynasty of kings! . . . I will raise up one of your descendants, one of your sons, and I will make his kingdom strong. . . . I will confirm him as king over my house and my kingdom for all time, and his throne will be secure forever" (1 Chronicles 17:10-11,14). Despite the many sins of Israel's kings, God kept his promise and preserved the line of David.

From the very first verse, the New Testament presents Jesus Christ as the true King of Israel, the rightful heir to David's throne. When Jesus began his public ministry, he proclaimed the Kingdom of God, and people gradually started to recognize that he was the sovereign of the Kingdom. This is why the people of Jerusalem gave him a royal welcome on Palm Sunday, saying, "Blessings on the King who comes" (Luke 19:38), and why, ironically, Pontius Pilate put a notice on the cross that read, "This is Jesus, the King of the Jews" (Matthew 27:37). But the real proof of Christ's kingship came with his resurrection from the dead and his exaltation to heaven, where his name is written: "King of all kings and Lord of all lords" (Revelation 19:16).

Kingship is one of the grand themes of the Bible. In the Old Testament kings, we see the inadequacy of all human kings, but in the few good kings we also see glimpses of Christ the King.

of the kingdom, a rivalry emerges between Israel/Samaria (standing for spiritual decadence) and Jerusalem/Judah (standing for the preservation of God's covenant promise). The main characters are as follows:

- David. Even after he dies, it's still his dynasty.
- Solomon. Although he is world renowned for his unrivaled wisdom and his beautiful Temple, his folly becomes Israel's downfall.
- Rehoboam. The foolish young king's oppression divides the monarchy.
- Jeroboam. This king becomes the paradigm for apostasy.
- Jezebel and Ahab. They are the Bonnie and Clyde of Old Testament Israel.
- Elijah. This great prophet was a miracle worker and a man of prayer.

Key Doctrines

Judgment. Sin always has consequences. God rewards kings and nations for obedience and punishes them for disobedience, sometimes using other kings and nations to carry out his judgment.

Prayer. Solomon's prayer of dedication for the Temple (chapter 8) is one of the Bible's best examples of reverent intercession and serves as a guide to prayer for nations and for the people of God. Elijah is one of the Bible's greatest examples of a man of prayer.

Covenant. In spite of the rebellion of God's people, he is faithful to his promises to David and his descendants (e.g., 11:12-13). The covenant binds the people of God and their kings to be faithful in worship and obedient in service.

Worship. The glory of God in Solomon's Temple stands in contrast to man-centered worship at the high places in Samaria. The effectiveness of Elijah's simple prayer at Mount Carmel stands in contrast to the bizarre and futile rituals of the prophets of Baal.

Providence. We see this in the miracles God performed for Elijah and in those Elijah performed for people in need.

quick overview of 1 kings

1:1–11:43	The united kingdom: Israel under King Solomon
12:1–16:34	The divided kingdom: Judah and Israel after Rehoboam and Jeroboam
17:1–22:53	The prophet Elijah: God still at work, in spite of Israel's royal failures

Tips for Reading or Teaching 1 Kings

Strive to keep a balanced view of Solomon. See the wisdom and glory he was given by the grace of God, but don't overlook his foolish mistakes.

Be alert for narrative clues (such as comparisons or outcomes) that provide a standard for evaluating the kings of Israel and Judah in spiritual terms. Also look for a recurring pattern of spiritual formation, deformation, and re-formation.

Read 1 Kings in connection with 2 Kings to see the continuity between Elijah and Elisha and also to see where the apostasy of Israel and Judah finally leads.

The Flow of the Book

The Last Days of King David (1:1–2:11). As David nears death, Adonijah tries to seize the throne. Although the attempt fails, it foreshadows the later division of the kingdom. How does God work through David and other members of the royal court to anoint Solomon as king? David's final charge (especially 2:1-4) deserves special attention because it provides a standard for evaluating Solomon's subsequent actions.

Solomon Asks for Wisdom (2:12–4:34). Solomon takes decisive action to consolidate his power and secure the monarchy. God tests Solomon by offering to give him whatever he asks. Solomon chooses wisely and asks for wisdom. God is pleased with Solomon's request and promises to give him exceptional wisdom, extravagant wealth, and—if he keeps the covenant—extended life. Notice the many ways God fulfills these promises.

Solomon in All His Glory (Chapters 5–10). Solomon's reign is characterized by internal peace, material prosperity, and international prominence. God fulfills his promise to David by enabling Solomon to build God's Temple in Jerusalem. The dedication of the Temple, with Solomon's beautiful prayer and God's descent in a cloud of glory, is one of the high points of Old Testament worship. As the

KEY VERSES

"If you will follow me with integrity and godliness, as David your father did, obeying all my commands, decrees, and regulations, then I will establish the throne of your dynasty over Israel forever. . . . But if you or your descendants abandon me and disobey the commands and decrees I have given you, and if you serve and worship other gods, then I will uproot Israel from this land that I have given them" (9:4-7). With these words to Solomon, God reiterates his covenant promise and gives the royal sons of David a standard to rule by. The rest of Kings confirms the truth of these words by way of positive and negative illustrations.

Queen of Sheba discovers during her famous visit, this is the golden age of Israel, a sign of the greater glory that will be revealed in God's Kingdom to come. However, there are troubling signs that Solomon may be losing his way. Look for signs of spiritual folly, such as the time and money he spends building his own palace (7:1-12).

KEY VERSES

"Since you have not kept my covenant and have disobeyed my decrees, I will surely tear the kingdom away from you. . . . And even so, I will not take away the entire kingdom; I will let [your son] be king of one tribe, for the sake of my servant David and for the sake of Jerusalem, my chosen city" (11:11-13). The divided kingdom, which is God's judgment against Solomon's sin, does not overrule his everlasting promises to David.

Solomon's Folly (Chapter 11). During Solomon's later years, the material prosperity of his kingdom stands in sharp contrast to the spiritual poverty of his soul. The king gives in to the idols of money, sex, and power, thus proving that whatever wisdom he ever possessed came only by trusting in God. Notice the specific temptations that led Solomon astray and the unhappy consequences of his unfaithfulness.

A Royal Failure (12:1-24). Rather than listen to the wise counsel of his elders, Solomon's son Rehoboam inaugurates a harsh regime. The northern tribes rebel and accept the leadership of Jeroboam, and the kingdom is divided into ten tribes in the north (Israel) and two tribes in the south (Judah). This is a decisive moment in Old Testament history because the two kingdoms were never reunited. Humanly speaking, what caused the civil war between Israel and Judah? What indications does the narrative give that the divided kingdom was part of God's sovereign plan?

Jeroboam (12:25-14:20). Although God called him to walk in covenant righteousness (see 11:37-38), Jeroboam becomes the prototypical apostate by setting up golden calves at the high places in Bethel and Dan and saying, "Look, Israel, these are the gods who brought you out of Egypt!" (12:28). This was the sin of Aaron at Mount Sinai: not worshipping different gods altogether but mixing the worship of the true God of Israel with the idolatrous practices of Canaanite religion. The words of the prophets who confront Jeroboam show how God viewed Jeroboam's sin.

The Early Kings of Judah (14:21-15:24). Although 1 Kings mainly deals with Israel, it also mentions four kings of Judah: Rehoboam, Abijam, Asa, and Jehoshaphat (11:41-15:24). These men were descendants of

David, and thus their kingship shows the preservation of the royal line. Asa and Jehoshaphat were both godly men, but because they did not trust God fully, they made unholy alliances with foreign powers.

The Ungodly Kings of Israel (15:25–16:34). The early kings of Israel all perpetuated the apostasy of Jeroboam. In fact, things went from bad to worse, since Omri and his son Ahab did more evil in God's sight than any of their predecessors. As far as God was concerned, none of their accomplishments mattered; faithfulness to his covenant was his only standard.

God's Man Elijah (Chapters 17–22). Ahab was a political success but a spiritual failure. Under the negative influence of his wife, Jezebel, Ahab's great sin was to promote the worship of Baal. This form of spiritual adultery brought trouble to Israel, but God defended his word through the ministry of the prophet Elijah. The conflict in these chapters is not simply between Elijah and Ahab (or Jezebel) but between the true, living God and the false god Baal. Which would Israel choose to serve?

One key to understanding Elijah's ministry is the power of prayer (see James 5:17). Elijah *prayed* that God would punish Israel's idolatry with drought, provide for poor people in desperate need, raise the dead, defeat the prophets of Baal on Mount Carmel, vindicate the ministry of his prophetic word, accept his sacrifice for Israel's sin, and send rain from heaven. He also prayed that God would take his life, but that was only in a moment of weakness, and God still used him for ministry. As you read what happened to Ahab and Jezebel, notice how God vindicated the word that he spoke through his prophet Elijah.

The Main Themes

1. WISDOM AND FOLLY. We see these especially in the life of Solomon but also in the other kings of Israel and Judah.
2. KINGSHIP. The book portrays the good, the bad, and the ugly.
3. PROPHECY. In addition to the prophecies of Elijah, 1 Kings records the words of several lesser prophets (such as Nathan and Micaiah). At a time when kings were Israel's downfall, God preserved his people through the words of his true prophets (as distinguished from false prophets, who also appear in 1 Kings).
4. WORSHIP. True worship is established by Solomon at the Temple and by Elijah at Mount Carmel; false worship is practiced by Jeroboam and Ahab, among others, who reject Temple worship and the God of Israel.

Contribution of the Book to the Bible's Story of Salvation in Christ

The kings and prophets in 1 Kings provide the main lines of connection to Christ, although the Temple also finds its ultimate fulfillment in the body of Christ. The wisdom of Solomon anticipates the incarnation of wisdom in Christ, and the glory of his kingdom anticipates the more glorious Kingdom of Christ. As Jesus said, "Now someone greater than Solomon is here" (Matthew 12:42). However, we see the blessing of Christ's rule more clearly in 1 Kings by way of contrast. The folly of Israel's kings typifies the failure of merely human government and thus shows our need for the perfect rule of Jesus Christ as king. The kings of Judah present Christ primarily through God's preservation of the royal line of David.

The prophets of 1 Kings also bear witness to Christ. As the forerunner of the Christ, John the Baptist was the second coming of Elijah, as promised in the Old Testament (Malachi 4:5-6) and confirmed in the Gospels (Matthew 11:14; Luke 1:17). Like Elijah, John wore unusual clothes, faced opposition from a wicked woman, and baptized his successor in the Jordan River. There are also direct connections between Elijah and Jesus, such as Elijah's later appearance at the Transfiguration and his ministry of God's grace to Gentiles (see Luke 4:25-26).

Applying the Book

Wisdom and folly may be more obvious in the lives of kings and other public officials, but the same categories apply to how we govern our private lives. It is wise for us to walk in humble obedience to God, and it is foolish for us to worship gods such as money, sex, and power. First Kings helps us see the difference. It also warns us about the clear and present danger of going into spiritual decline. No matter how well we begin, we will end badly if we drift away from God the way Solomon did. Finally, 1 Kings provides some excellent models for prayer.

PERSPECTIVES
ON THE BOOK OF 1 KINGS

[1 Kings is the story of a nation's passing] from affluence and influence to poverty and paralysis. G. Campbell Morgan

The author did not merely write history; he sought to drive home moral and spiritual principles. His chief concern was to show that Israel as the people of God, in covenant relationship to Him, were expected to keep His law. They would be blessed for keeping it and punished for failing to do so. Howard F. Vos

The history of Kings does not set out to be a complete and exhaustive portrayal of the period but rather a selection made to illustrate God's overall control of history, even when this is not obvious to observers. The historian does this by a judicious use of his sources and by highlighting the lives of certain individuals. Thus David, king of Judah, is the ideal or model ruler and Jeroboam son of Nebat is typical of those kings of Israel who lead the people into sin. Donald J. Wiseman

First Kings prods us . . . to consider how far anti-biblical practices and values have penetrated the life of the Church and the nation, and to examine ourselves as to how seriously we take the commandments, especially the First and Second. First Kings is especially concerned with those who limp with two different opinions (18:21) and urges them to make a commitment to follow God wholeheartedly. Gene Rice

2 KINGS
*A Pair of
Royal Disasters*

FORMAT. 25 chapters, 719 verses

IMPLIED PURPOSES. To continue recording the history of Israel from the divided kingdom to the Babylonian captivity and to explain how, in accordance with God's righteousness, Israel and Judah both ended up in exile (and thus to show what actions and attitudes tend to bring God's judgment rather than his blessing)

AUTHOR'S PERSPECTIVE. The author is a serious historian with a spiritual agenda. As he finishes telling the tragic tale, begun in 1 Kings, of the decline and fall of Israel and Judah, he proves the truth of an old proverb from Solomon: "Righteousness exalts a nation, but sin is a disgrace to any people" (Proverbs 14:34, NIV). Although the story ends in disaster, the author is not without hope for readers who seek to keep God's covenant—or even for the kingdom of Judah, which still has an heir to David's throne.

IMPLIED AUDIENCE. The remnant of Judah (living in exile in Babylon) and the people of God throughout history

WHAT UNIFIES THE BOOK. The parallel stories of two kingdoms—Israel and Judah—both of which meet a similar fate; the recurring formula used to summarize the reign of each king; the downward spiral of spiritual decline with occasional countermovements of reformation; the testimony of the prophets, who speak for God

SPECIAL FEATURES. The extraordinary ministry of the prophet Elisha; three notable examples of spiritual reformation: Joash, Hezekiah, and Josiah; Israel's captivity by the Assyrians; Judah's captivity by the Babylonians

CHALLENGE FACING THE READER OR TEACHER OF THIS BOOK. The potential to get confused by the ever-expanding list of kings, including many of lesser significance

HOW TO MEET THE CHALLENGE. Focus on the main pattern of spiritual decline without getting lost in the details. Readers who want to master the details should consult a complete chronological chart of the kings of Israel and Judah.

The book of Kings is ultimately answering the question, "In light of God's covenant with Abraham [the land] and with David [an everlasting throne], how did all of this happen to us?" The answer: God has not failed his people; his people, led by their kings, have failed their God.

GORDON D. FEE AND DOUGLAS STUART

Divided Kingdom

- **1** Elijah Prophesies against Ahaziah
- **2** Elijah Taken Up into Heaven
- **3** Moab Rebels against Israel
- **4–8:15** Elisha Performs Miracles
- **8:16-29** Reigns of Jehoram and Ahaziah (Judah)
- **9-10** Jehu's Bloody Reign (Israel)
- **11-12** Joash Repairs the Temple (Judah)
- **13-16** Twelve Kings of Israel and Judah
- **17** Assyrian Captivity of Israel

Continuing Kingdom

- **18–20** Hezekiah's Rescue
- **21** The Worst Kings of Judah
- **22–23:30** Reforms of Josiah
- **23:31–24:20** Last Kings before the Fall of Jerusalem
- **25:1-26** Babylonian Captivity of Judah
- **25:27-30** Epilogue: David's Last Son Survives

Divided Kingdom		Continuing Kingdom
Rulers of Israel	Combined History of Rulers of Israel and Judah	Rulers of Judah
Elisha Succeeds Elijah as Prophet	Various Prophets	
Israel, Judah, and Assyria		Judah and Babylon

AN OUTLINE OF
2 KINGS

How did things ever end up like this? It's a question we ask—or at least ought to ask—whenever we find ourselves in serious difficulty. Often the answer has something to do with our own folly: In the providence of God, we may be in the situation we're in because of the spiritual choices that we have made.

The first readers of 2 Kings found themselves in a similar situation. Living as exiles in Babylon, they sought an explanation for their deportation from Judah. Why were they so far away from home? The answer was that they had turned away from God and were now suffering his judgment against their sin. But the situation was not hopeless—either for them or for us—because God was (and is) still working out his plan.

The Form of the Book
Second Kings is the second part of the unified historical narrative that begins in 1 Kings. Be sure to consult the previous chapter in this handbook on 1 Kings for material that applies to both books. The second half of Kings brings the narrative to a climax with two well-deserved catastrophes: the captivity of Israel by the Assyrians and the captivity of Judah by the Babylonians.

Key Places and Characters
The key places in 2 Kings are Israel and Judah, but Assyria and Babylonia are important as destinations of divine judgment. There are a large number of characters (such as Elijah, Naaman, Jezebel, Jehu, Sennacherib, Isaiah, Manasseh, Zedekiah, and Nebuchadnezzar), but the most impressive figures are the prophet Elisha (who even surpasses his famous teacher, Elijah) and three godly kings—Joash, Hezekiah, and Josiah—who try to reform Judah.

Key Doctrines
Law, Sin, and Judgment. God judges kings and nations by the standard of his law, and he blesses or curses them accordingly. Death and destruction are the wages of sin.
Prophecy. The words of God's prophets always come true, whether prophecies of coming judgment or promises of salvation through the covenant.
Worship. Nothing is more important than worshipping the right God, at the right place, in the right way.

Tips for Reading or Teaching 2 Kings

Review the curses for disobedience in Deuteronomy 28:15-68, a passage that provides crucial background for God's judgment against Israel and Judah.

The broad sweep of the book's history coincides with the ministry of Old Testament prophets such as Isaiah, Micah, Nahum, Zephaniah, Habakkuk, and finally Jeremiah. Reading these prophets in connection with the relevant portions of the history leads to a deeper understanding of Kings.

To see how far Judah has fallen, compare and contrast the ending of 2 Kings with the beginning of 1 Kings. Ask the question again: How did we get here?

quick overview of 2 kings

1:1–17:41	The divided kingdom, ending with Israel's captivity in Assyria
18:1–25:30	The continuing kingdom, ending with Judah's captivity in Babylon

The Flow of the Book

Elisha Succeeds Elijah as Prophet in Israel (1:1–2:12). Having served for many years as Elijah's faithful disciple, Elisha sees his master taken up into heaven in a chariot of fire and inherits a double portion of his spirit. As the narrative continues, look for signs that Elisha is Elijah's true spiritual heir.

God's Man Elisha (2:13–10:36; 13:14-21). Here Elisha gets full coverage. Why do 1 and 2 Kings give so much space to Elijah and Elisha? Partly because the righteousness of their prophetic ministries is such a contrast to the evil of Israel's kings. Notice the ways in which Elisha's ministry seems to surpass Elijah's, particularly in the size and scope of his miracles. Also notice the way in which Elijah's prophecies against the house of Ahab are fulfilled with a vengeance when Jehu becomes king of Israel (chapters 9–10).

Kings of Israel and Judah (Chapters 11–16). The kings of Israel in this section are all evil, walking in the sins of their predecessor Jeroboam and under constant threat from the Assyrians. The situation is somewhat better in Judah, but not much. The outstanding exception is Joash, the boy-king who was rescued from his enemies in infancy and whose great achievement was to rebuild the Temple in Jerusalem. Notice the constant standard 2 Kings uses to evaluate the kings of Israel and Judah: the righteous requirements of the covenant, especially as they pertain to the public worship of God.

The Assyrian Captivity (Chapter 17). The fall of Samaria and the exile of Israel are mentioned rather matter-of-factly. Humanly speaking, the cause of Israel's calamity was Hoshea's treachery, but 2 Kings is much more interested in making a spiritual assessment. Verses 7 through 23 serve as an indictment of Israel and its ungodly kings. What specific sins are mentioned?

KEY VERSES

"The people of Israel persisted in all the evil ways of Jeroboam. They did not turn from these sins until the LORD finally swept them away from his presence, just as all his prophets had warned. So Israel was exiled from their land to Assyria, where they remain to this day" (17:22-23). Here the author summarizes the reason for Israel's exile—Israel's disobedience.

The Last Free Kings of Judah (Chapters 18–23). The action shifts exclusively to Judah, where the question becomes whether the southern kingdom will learn anything from the disaster that has befallen their cousins to the north. Two great kings seek the reformation of Judah. The first is Hezekiah (chapters 18–20), whose kingdom God miraculously rescues from Sennacherib and the Assyrian army and whose health God restores after an apparently fatal illness. The second is Josiah (chapters 22–23), another boy-king, who repairs the Temple, recovers the Book of the Law (Deuteronomy?), reinstates proper worship, renews the covenant, and restores the feast of Passover. How is he a model for the way kings ought to rule? Unfortunately, evil kings come both before and after Josiah, and the sins of Manasseh in particular condemn Judah to exile (see 21:10-16; 23:26).

The Fall of Jerusalem (24:1–25:26). Disaster finally strikes: Nebuchadnezzar and his armies besiege Jerusalem and carry Judah's best and brightest off to Babylon. The writer's restrained account only hints at the terrible suffering of the last days before the city fell. God finally executed the righteous judgment he had threatened for so long. How does this section fulfill the warnings found elsewhere in the book?

Epilogue: Jehoiachin Gets out of Jail (25:27-30). Second Kings ends with the release of Judah's rightful king. Jehoiachin remains in Babylon, where he is alive and well. Although the land has been lost, by the grace of God and the promise of the covenant the royal line has survived, and there is still at least some hope that someday David's kingdom will be restored.

The Main Themes

1. APOSTASY. Under the influence of unrighteous rulers, the people of God have fallen away from the faith of their fathers. God is not impressed with their building campaigns and military victories; he is more concerned with the heart issues of worship and justice.

2. CAPTIVITY. The eventual fall of Samaria and Jerusalem casts the shadow of judgment over the whole book and vindicates the righteousness of God.

3. PROPHECY AND FULFILLMENT. God means what he says, and everything he says comes true. Those who fail to listen to his faithful prophets will be cut off from the land.

4. REFORMATION. Even when God's way is forgotten, his Word is rejected, and his worship is corrupted, righteousness can be restored through the prayer and obedience of godly men and women.

KEY VERSE

"I will also banish Judah from my presence just as I have banished Israel. And I will reject my chosen city of Jerusalem and the Temple where my name was to be honored" (23:27). Having failed to heed God's warning, Judah falls under the same awful judgment as Israel. Happily, although this is the end of 2 Kings, it is not the end of the story.

Contribution of the Book to the Bible's Story of Salvation in Christ

Like its predecessor, 2 Kings reveals our need for the righteous kingship of Jesus Christ and also records the providential preservation of his royal line. Hezekiah and Josiah, both of whom appear in the genealogy of Jesus, may be viewed as ideal kings who help set the pattern for the kingship of Christ (consider the way that Jesus prayed in the face of death, as Hezekiah did, or how, like Josiah, he reformed Temple worship). If John the Baptist was the second coming of Elijah, then Elisha is a type of Christ (although the Gospels only hint at this). His miracles of giving sight to the blind, providing food for the poor, healing lepers, and raising the dead anticipate the greater miracles that Jesus performed in his earthly ministry. Finally, Jesus uses Elisha's outreach to Naaman (a Syrian, and thus a Gentile) as part of the justification for his own mission to people outside of Israel (see Luke 4:27).

Applying the Book

Second Kings teaches us to take God at his word, especially when it comes to the blessings he promises for obedience and the curses he pronounces for disobedience. The judgment that fell on Israel and Judah should remind us that another judgment is coming—the final judgment—and that therefore our spiritual choices have eternal consequences. The people of Judah failed to heed the righteous example of their reforming kings, the true witness of their faithful prophets, or even the cautionary tale of their cousins in Israel. What will it take for us to listen to God and do what he says?

PERSPECTIVES
ON THE BOOK OF 2 KINGS

First and Second Kings are not disinterested, flat historical works. Rather, they emphasize most of Scripture's great theological truths. They stress God's sovereignty over Israel and all other nations. They claim that God created earth and therefore has every right to rule the earth. This rule unfolds in accordance with the Lord's character, which means that mercy, justice, righteousness, and salvation work together when God fashions world events. Paul R. House

The writer of Kings is much concerned to demonstrate that God rules over kings and kingdoms, and that he raises them up and disposes of them as he sees fit. . . . [T]he God who had raised up the Babylonian armies that destroyed Jerusalem could also bring an end to the Babylonian kingdom. Raymond B. Dillard

He is writing from the prophetic standpoint, and his ruling principle is that loyal, faithful obedience to God and His ordinances will insure prosperity while the reverse will be attended with loss, disaster, retribution. Writing from a point of time at which the truth of this principle had been fully confirmed by the ruin of the nation, he can estimate all the successive reigns by its standard, and pronounce judgment on the whole course of the history. The New Analytical Bible

The key to everything is whether a given king has been loyal to the covenant with Yahweh. In Kings this is expressed in . . . his attitude toward the central sanctuary (the Temple in Jerusalem) and whether or

not he advocated syncretism or rival gods altogether, especially Canaanite Baal worship.   Gordon D. Fee and Douglas Stuart

Kings performs its historiographic task from an unabashedly theological perspective. God is the central actor in the plot of Israel's history. God demands the total loyalty of the people and is intolerant of other loyalties and commitments. God rewards virtue and punishes sin. . . . Repentance leads to restoration, but the outcome of repentance still remains in God's hands. God is sovereign over the events of history and nature. God keeps promises, but is not bound by human expectations.   Richard Nelson

1 CHRONICLES
The Story of Israel's Greatest King

FORMAT. 29 chapters, 941 verses

IMPLIED PURPOSES. To record Israelite history with a focus on the kingly figure of David and to impose a distinctly religious perspective on that history. Some commentators believe additionally that the author wrote both to warn and to encourage his original readers.

AUTHOR'S PERSPECTIVE. The author (1) gives an idealized picture of King David's monarchy (omitting negative material such as we find in Samuel and Kings) and (2) presents Israelite history from a religious viewpoint, with emphasis on the Temple.

IMPLIED AUDIENCE. The original audience was the Jews who survived the Exile, but just as the writer offered that audience a history of Israel for its continuing edification, so he offered it to all succeeding generations for their edification.

WHAT UNIFIES THE BOOK. The historical impulse to record and interpret Israelite history; the commanding figure of King David; elaborate attention to the Temple as a building and place of worship

SPECIAL FEATURES. Balance between overview (multiple genealogies) and close-ups (a biography of David and details regarding the Temple); a documentary impulse to record facts and figures, which overrides the narrative impulse to tell a continuous story; the nearly total idealizing treatment of David; repeated use of the formula "all Israel"

CHALLENGES FACING THE READER OR TEACHER OF THIS BOOK.
1. The need to find Israelite history (including genealogies and inventories) interesting and edifying
2. The lack of a narrative flow

HOW TO MEET THE CHALLENGES.

1. Extract religious principles from the particulars, and keep in mind the symbolic importance of both David and Israel as they factor into messianic history.
2. Abandon the quest for a narrative flow, and instead look for the format of documentary records and lists.

The Chronicler seems to treat his historical material as a means to an end rather than as an end in itself. He shows greater interest in the underlying meaning of events than in the events themselves, as illustrated by his special interests. These include . . . frequent speeches and prayers, the repetition of themes, and interest in the basic institutions of society such as the system of worship or the monarchy, and a concern for God's direct intervention in human affairs.

MARTIN J. SELMAN
1 Chronicles: An Introduction and Commentary

1–9 Premonarchal Israelite History

10–12 Beginning of David's Kingship

13 Ark of the Covenant

14 David's Victories

15–16 Ark of the Covenant

17 Davidic Covenant

18–21 Political Events

22–26 Plans for the Temple

27 Political Matters

28–29 End of David's Kingship

God's People	God's Anointed King	The Ark of God's Covenant	God's Covenant with David	Israel's Armies	God's Temple
Genealogies	History of David's Kingship				
Straight History	Interpretive History, with Emphasis on Religious Events but Attention Also to Political Events				
Millennia of Time	Approximately Thirty-three Years				

AN OUTLINE OF
1 CHRONICLES

Cultures and historical eras differ on matters of taste, custom, and ways of viewing the world. A missionary who taught in Africa observed that the interest of native students in the theological wonders of Romans was low but the class came alive when genealogies came under discussion. Instead of being bewildered by the genealogies and lists that greet you in 1 Chronicles, you can profitably try to understand the mind-set that would see religious significance in them (e.g., that God's purposes are achieved by real people in real history). The documentary impulse evident in this book shows that the very hairs of our heads are numbered by a God who cares about individual people.

The Form of the Book

First Chronicles is a compilation of history. At times the author makes moves toward giving us a biography of David, and at times we have hints of a hero story, but the documentary impulse toward recording the facts and figures of history quickly resumes the dominant role. Specific forms of documentary writing include genealogies, inventories, and summaries of events such as David's military victories. We also find speeches, sermons, prayers, and a psalm of praise.

The Story in the History

Even though the book is not structured like a story, an underlying story does emerge. As handled by the chronicler, Israelite history tells a story of how

- the history of Israel from Adam to the beginning of the monarchy shows God's special interest in his chosen people, Israel;
- David is *the* special ruler of Israelite history—the king on whom, in fact, God conferred the covenant promise of an eternal kingdom;
- the Temple plays a central role in Israelite history and in addition has symbolic meanings and importance; and
- the actions of rulers and ordinary citizens have inevitable spiritual importance and consequences.

Key Characters

God is the center of reference—the One to whom all events and characters relate. Next in importance, judging from the way the writer allots his space, is the commanding figure of King David, whose kingship is bracketed by accounts of his predecessor, Saul, and his successor, Solomon. Beyond these individuals, conspicuous place is given to certain groups, including the Levites, the priests, others who assisted at the Temple, and military and civil officials. Finally, even though the chronicler is more interested in leaders than in individual citizens, he does treat "all Israel" as an important corporate character.

Unifying Elements

- The documentary impulse to record facts and figures by means of lists, genealogies, and inventories
- The nation as the subject of the book
- The focus on leaders, including groups such as the Levites and priests
- The kingship of David
- The Temple as the center of the nation's religious life

Key Doctrines

Covenant. The history of Israel is an account of God's dealings with his covenant nation.

The Nature of God. The story of how God interacts with the nation during the era covered in the book is a picture of how he deals with the human race and his people in all eras in history.

Worship. The elaborate details surrounding the Temple as a building and place of worship embody principles of how God must be worshiped.

Obedience. Blessing is shown to be the result of obedience to God's rules for living. Disobedience elicits God's judgment.

Tips for Reading or Teaching 1 Chronicles

Do not get bogged down in the details. Accept them as the medium through which the book communicates religious truth. As one commentator puts it, 1 Chronicles deals with principles.

KEY VERSES

"I will establish [your son's] throne forever. . . . I will confirm him in my house and in my kingdom forever, and his throne shall be established forever" (17:12, 14, ESV). Here are the leading motifs of the book—concern for the kingdom, the idea of covenant (including a new one made with David), and signals that the history recounted in the book points forward to a greater "son of David," namely, the Christ.

In addition to seeing religious significance in the individual parts, read and teach the book with an awareness that the history of David and Israel is a form of messianic history, since this is the line from which Jesus was born.

In addition, ponder the symbolic significance of David as God's king, the covenant nation as God's people, and the Temple as a place for the worship of God.

DID YOU KNOW?

- The Hebrew Scriptures count 1 and 2 Chronicles as a single book called by the Hebrew words meaning "the events of the days." The titles by which we know these two books date back to Jerome in the fourth century and are based on the Greek word *chronikon*, meaning "chronology."

- The writer's extensive attention to the Temple was recorded in its final form after the destruction of that Temple.

The Flow of the Book

Lists of Genealogies (Chapters 1–9). The title of this book lets us know that this is a court history—chronicles of a nation. In case we doubted it, we have nine chapters of genealogies! Lessons you might extract from this material are of a general nature: that God is interested in individuals, that God takes human history seriously, and that the Messiah came from a lineage providentially guided by God. On the latter point, one commentator, H. G. M. Williamson, speaks of how the genealogies "paint a portrait of the people of God . . . as a symbol of both the particularity of [God's] election and the breadth of his grace."

Changing of the Guard from Saul to David (Chapters 10–12). We now have a clue into the direction this particular court chronicle will take: It will focus on the mighty David. These three chapters exist to record the transition from King Saul to King David. In effect, they set the stage for the rest of the book. This is largely straight national history.

David as Religious Leader (Chapters 13–17). What chroniclers choose to include and omit in their biographies is itself an interpretation that influences how we view the subject of the biography. This chronicler generally chooses events that focus on the direction that David provided for the religious life of the nation. Within this umbrella, you can note further things about David as a religious hero.

quick overview of 1 chronicles

1:1–9:44	Genealogy of Israel
10:1–21:30; 27:1–29:30	David's kingship
22:1–26:32	Plans for the Temple and worship

Genealogies in the Bible

Genealogies are lists of ancestors. There are many such lists in the Bible, and it is hard to know how to assimilate and teach lists of names. Here are some useful things to know about the Bible genealogies:

- Ancient cultures had a different mind-set in regard to genealogies. In part, this is an expression of a heightened respect for what we call roots—the origins of a person or family.

- The Bible's genealogies show the importance the ancient world (and some modern cultures) attached to the extended family or clan as an institution.

- Genealogies of the Bible relate to the continuity of generations. This is particularly true for believers, who cherish the way in which "one generation shall commend [God's] works to another" (Psalm 145:4, ESV).

- The genealogies implicitly affirm the importance God places on every individual. Named individuality is important in the Bible. While some genealogies list important figures like clan leaders and political rulers, others include the names of ordinary people; we find lists of people who carried the Tabernacle, came back to the Promised Land, or took their places by the wall.

- The genealogies also show the way in which the religion of the Bible deals with space-time history. It is not a fictional book but a history book.

- Sometimes there is a hidden theological meaning in genealogies of the Bible. For example, some genealogies trace the messianic line—the lineage from which Jesus was born on the human side. Elsewhere genealogies highlight the contrast between the covenant line and the pagan line: The consecutive genealogies of Jacob (Genesis 35:22-26) record the covenant line, and those of Esau (Genesis 36) record the line of pagan hostility toward God. Another example is the contrasting genealogies of descendants of Ham and Shem in Genesis 10–11.

Political Interludes (Chapters 18–20; 27). These chapters record David's military victories and lists of people whom David appointed to military and civil positions.

David's Preparations for the Temple (Chapters 21–26). This, too, is mainly straight history, with little interpretation intermingled. We can read it as a story of priorities—an insight into what David, who was successful in many areas of life, considered most important. At the same time, we can read these chapters as an index to what God considers most important.

David's Last Days (Chapters 28–29). David's final actions round out the picture of a godly ruler. You can profitably analyze the chapters to discern the specific ways in which the writer portrays David's behavior as exemplary.

The Main Themes

1. God directs the history of nations and individuals according to his providential plan.
2. Providence, however, does not negate the ways in which God achieves his purposes through individuals and their choices.
3. The political/national arena has important effects on the lives of individuals; leaders play a key role for good or ill in the lives of citizens.

Contribution of the Book to the Bible's Story of Salvation in Christ

The history of Israel as narrated in this book is a chapter in covenant history and messianic history. Further, in the New Testament, Christ is called the Son of David, suggesting that David was a type, or symbol, of Christ whose role and traits found complete fulfillment in Christ. In the New Testament, Christ is also the metaphoric temple of God, so that we can legitimately see symbolic overtones in the details of the Temple and Temple worship.

Applying the Book

God's dealings with the nation of Israel and its leaders are in principle how he continues to deal with the human race and his covenant people. What pleased and displeased God back then are the same for us today, and we need to live accordingly. For example, in the story of Saul (chapter 10) we see the tragic results of unfaithfulness to God; and in David's error in numbering the people (chapter 21), we see the effects a leader's sins have on a nation. In addition, the importance of worship that comes through the details in chapters 22–26 is something that we can appropriate and practice in our own lives.

PER**SPECTIVES**

ON THE BOOK OF 1 CHRONICLES

[The book is] through and through a theological essay. . . . Chronicles is not only a writing of history; it is a tract. [Furthermore] the Chronicler was a person interacting with texts. Raymond B. Dillard

[The Chronicler was] the first Old Testament theologian. P. R. Ackroyd

As the New Testament teaches, the Chronicler's hopes were realized in Christ. Christ brings to fulfillment and exceeds all of the Chronicler's desires for God's people. Richard L. Pratt

As he speaks to the people of his own time, so he speaks to us. The very objection that "our world is different from the world of the Israelite monarchy" makes us exactly the kind of audience he means to address. J. Alec Motyer

It is not difficult to translate the Chronicler's concerns into contemporary, Christian ones; we stand so close to him in spirit. . . . The Greek sage Dionysius . . . treated history as "philosophy teaching by examples." Similarly the Chronicler saw [history] as a source of spiritual models for his contemporaries to copy or shun. . . . The heartbeat of Chronicles is a concern for spirituality. Leslie Allen

2 CHRONICLES

*A Nation
at Risk*

FORMAT. 36 chapters, 822 verses

IMPLIED PURPOSES. To give a comprehensive history of the last king of the united monarchy and the kings of Judah and to weave into that history a religious view of what makes a nation and a person either blessed or punished by God

AUTHOR'S PERSPECTIVE. The writer is a historian with a discernible philosophy of history. The main ideas are that rulers determine the fate of a nation, that rulers are accountable to God and his law, and that God rewards obedience and punishes disobedience.

IMPLIED AUDIENCE. The book was written for the nation of Judah—so much so that it is a patriotic book like a book of American or British history would be. But the religious and moral principles embodied in that history make the book relevant for all times.

WHAT UNIFIES THE BOOK. The emphasis on kings and their reigns; a simple interpretive grid consistently applied to the kings, who are judged to have done what was either right or wrong in the sight of the Lord; a pervasive concern for worship and the Temple

SPECIAL FEATURES. Mingling of political/military history and religious history; biographical interest ("the lives of the rich and famous" impulse); the importance of court prophets in the action

CHALLENGE FACING THE READER OR TEACHER OF THIS BOOK. The need to see universal, perpetually relevant principles in the history of ancient Israel/Judah

HOW TO MEET THE CHALLENGE. Follow the author's clues regarding the universal religious meanings that he intends for us to extract from the history.

Every culture has an impulse to record its own history. In our day, the newspaper and television news bombard us with the facts, personalities, and happenings of the day or week. We do not question the importance of such news. Even though 2 Chronicles does not record events contemporaneous with the author and his audience, in format 2 Chronicles is the ancient equivalent of the television crew on site with its camera or the author of a news feature sifting through the national archives.

The Form of the Book

The primary form is history, as evidenced by the way in which the writer covers nearly four hundred years in a mere thirty-six chapters. But the relative attention given to many of the kings (especially the good ones) moves the book beyond history to biography. And the even greater attention given to some events moves the book beyond biography to literary narrative, especially heroic narrative. (For relevant information on heroic narrative, see "Hero Stories" on page 213.)

The Story

Behind all the individual stories is the big story of God's oversight of the life of the nation and its rulers. God lays down the ground rules, centered around the covenant idea of obedience versus disobedience, and then he allows individual kings the opportunity to choose. Obedience brings blessing, and disobedience brings judgment. It is as simple as that.

Key Places and Characters

The action takes place, first of all, at a national and international level. The more specific places of action, in order of decreasing prevalence, are the city of Jerusalem, the court, the battlefield, and the Temple.

The chief actor in the national drama is God. Second Chronicles has the feel of old epic literature, where deity constantly initiates action, expresses the divine will, and determines the outcome of human choices. Second in importance are the kings of Judah, with the better ones (Asa, Jehoshaphat, Hezekiah, Josiah) getting the most space. Individual

DID YOU KNOW?
- Among Old Testament writers, the chronicler refers unusually often to other parts of the Hebrew Scriptures.
- Some copies of the Septuagint (the Greek translation of the Hebrew Old Testament) titled 1 and 2 Chronicles "The Things Omitted," to suggest that these two books supplement the history in the books of Samuel and Kings.
- In the arrangement of the Old Testament books in the Hebrew Bible, 2 Chronicles is the last book of the canon.

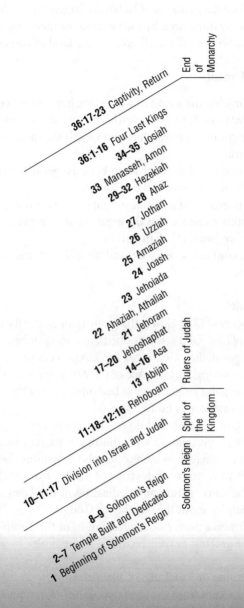

36:17-23 Captivity, Return

36:1-16 Four Last Kings

34-35 Josiah

33 Manasseh, Amon

29-32 Hezekiah

28 Ahaz

27 Jotham

26 Uzziah

25 Amaziah

24 Joash

23 Jehoiada

22 Ahaziah, Athaliah

21 Jehoram

17-20 Jehoshaphat

14-16 Asa

13 Abijah

11:18–12:16 Rehoboam

10–11:17 Division into Israel and Judah

8-9 Solomon's Reign

2-7 Temple Built and Dedicated

1 Beginning of Solomon's Reign

End of Monarchy

Rulers of Judah

Split of the Kingdom

Solomon's Reign

AN OUTLINE OF
2 CHRONICLES

prophets such as Nathan, Micaiah, Elijah, and Isaiah also loom large. Even though the ordinary citizens of Judah are largely a nameless group whose lives are heavily influenced by the behavior of their kings, approximately twenty references to "all Israel" give them a kind of corporate identity.

Unifying Elements

- In 2 Chronicles, the world in which "we live and move and have our being" (Acts 17:28, NIV) is a world of kings and courts.
- There are continual reminders that God is the most powerful and active character.
- There is an up-and-down rhythm between good and bad rulers and between God's blessing and punishment.
- The intermingling of political/military events and religious/spiritual events makes us aware that the great spiritual issues are lived out in the everyday "secular" affairs of life.
- The book contains an ever-expanding gallery of memorable characters.

Key Doctrines

The Sovereignty of God. God is the main actor in the narrated history.

The Justice of God. God rewards obedience and punishes disobedience.

Human Responsibility. God gives the kings every opportunity to know right from wrong, but they make their own spiritual choices.

Sin. There are good kings as well as bad ones, but the book does give us an extensive anatomy of human sinfulness.

Providence. God controls and directs human history.

History. The preoccupation with the moral pattern in Israelite history and the focus on leaders as the ones who determine the destiny of a nation allow us to extract a doctrine of history from the book.

Worship. The construction and dedication of the Temple imply important principles about the worship of God.

Prayer. Solomon's prayer at the dedication of the Temple (chapter 6) is one of the greatest prayers recorded in the Bible.

Tips for Reading or Teaching 2 Chronicles

You need to accept from the start that this book is a political document. It deals with rulers and power structures. Part of the book's meaning concerns government and rule more generally.

While the political history of 2 Chronicles takes an ancient society as its subject, you should operate on the premise that the book tells us not only what *happened* long ago but also what *happens* today. In other words, look for the universal principles that are embodied in the particulars of the text.

When dealing with a historical book of the Bible, including 2 Chronicles, it is always important to extract ideas about what God is like and what people are like.

Things to Look For

- The moral and religious truth of this book is embodied in the kings and their actions. If you interact adequately with the stories of the individual kings, you will easily extract the right religious and moral truth of the book.
- The chronicler lets his interpretation of characters and events show through. Look for the interpretive clues in the text, including the good or bad outcomes of various kings' actions.
- Although a continuous religious thread runs through this history, much of the record concerns the actions that would be recorded in *any* court history from the ancient past. There is no need to suppress this "secular" content.

quick overview of 2 chronicles

1:1–9:31	The reign of Solomon
10:1–13:22	Division of the kingdom into Israel and Judah
14:1–36:23	History of the kings of Judah

The Flow of the Book

Solomon's Kingship (Chapters 1–9). As you work your way through these chapters, note that the way biographers communicate their interpretation of the people about whom they write is through what they choose for inclusion and exclusion. With that in mind, operate first on the premise that the biographer offers Solomon to you as a representative hero from whose experience you are expected to learn something. What do you learn from Solomon's life as recorded here? Second, the narrative of the dedication of the Temple, climaxed by Solomon's prayer, is one of the best stories in the Bible. Relive it as though you were present at the event; then reflect on what you would have learned from being present.

KEY VERSE
"If my people who are called by my name will humble themselves and pray and seek my face and turn from their wicked ways, I will hear from heaven and will forgive their sins and restore their land" (7:14). Here are two emphases in the book: the need for people to submit to God and God's willingness to forgive human sinfulness.

Troubled Political Times in Israel (Chapters 10–11). These chapters are important to the history of Israel and Judah because they mark a turning point for both nations, but they are slight on spiritual edification. Your best strategy is to accept them as important background for the history of the kings of Judah that occupies the rest of the book, and then move on.

The Good, the Bad, and the Ugly (Chapters 12–36). The subject of these chapters is the history of Judah. If you are perplexed by the emphasis on kings in the historical record—or by the specific material included—remind yourself that ancient courts regarded history as important and thus court historians recorded it. Every society has the impulse to record the national events of the time. Just look at what dominates the news in our newspapers and television newscasts.

In addition to this political thread, you will find evidence on virtually every page that the chronicler had a strongly religious view of history. Three ideas make up this interpretive grid:

- What rulers do shows their religious hearts.
- There are moral and spiritual standards by which to judge whether a ruler does the right thing or the wrong thing.
- The destiny of a nation (especially if that nation is God's covenant nation) is determined by the spiritual goodness or badness of its rulers.

It is profitable to pay attention to how this view of history is evident in the accounts of the kings of Judah. In particular, assemble composite portraits of what constitutes good conduct and what constitutes evil conduct, whether in a ruler or in an ordinary citizen. Accept these as *examples* to follow or to avoid.

It will also be helpful if you know that the author of this material followed a formula when deciding how much space to give to a specific king. The chronicler tends to devote lots of space to the good kings, with extensive accounts of what the good kings did, and he tends to record less about the evil kings (leading us to see that ungodly people are ultimately forgotten). God is the overarching and constant character in the story of the succession of kings. Part of the benefit of the account, therefore, is to note the emerging portrait of God and the anatomy of ways in which people relate to God successfully or unsuccessfully.

Some of the events are treated in the form of historical chronicles, with events recorded only in a summary fashion. Sometimes, however, the stories contain enough detail to rank as literary narratives, with a concern to tell us not only *what* happened but *how* it happened. In such cases, you need to apply what you know about how stories work (for a reminder, see the article on page 35).

The Main Themes

1. Leaders play a decisive role in the lives of nations and individuals.
2. In spite of the first theme, however, bad rulers and their decisions do not thwart God's purposes. He achieves his providential and redemptive ends despite human folly.
3. People are responsible to God for their actions.
4. God punishes evil and rewards good.

Contribution of the Book to the Bible's Story of Salvation in Christ

Inasmuch as the history of the kings of Judah ends with the captivity of the nation and the extinction of the monarchy, it is accurate to view the history of the nation ultimately as a history of the failure of God's covenant people (notwithstanding the heroic acts of the good kings). We end the history with a feeling that only God's grace can salvage the wreckage that human sinfulness has caused. In its own way, then, 2 Chronicles is a Christ-shaped vacuum that shows humanity's need for a true savior and king.

KEY VERSE
"The LORD is with you while you are with him. If you seek him, he will be found by you, but if you forsake him, he will forsake you" (15:2, ESV). Here is the plot in miniature, based on the great "if." There are victories and triumphs in this spiritual saga, but in the end the nation and its kings choose wrongly in the great either-or that God puts before them.

Applying the Book

The key to applying 2 Chronicles is to be aware of how narrative embodies its themes. It does so by getting us to feel positively or negatively about the characters and events the storyteller puts before us. The individual kings and events of 2 Chronicles are, at rock bottom, example stories: good examples to approve and negative examples to censure. Some people unjustifiably stigmatize this approach as moralizing, but it is simply the way stories work. Beyond this, we can live in accord with what the book shows us about God's character and actions.

Within such a framework, 2 Chronicles embodies numerous lessons. Solomon's policies of taxation and big spending are a case study in how leaders can engender resentment in their followers. The attempt of Solomon's son to bully a nation carries bad leadership even further. Solomon's religious compromises and decline highlight what can happen to Christians who do not exercise vigilance over their allegiances.

PERSPECTIVES
ON THE BOOK OF 2 CHRONICLES

It is the facts of history from which [the Chronicler] is preaching. He has no need to distort them in order to get his message across. Indeed it would defeat his object were he to do so. . . . The Chronicler does not need to invent in order to edify. He lets the facts speak—some speak more plainly than others—and then tells us what they say; and it is "what took place" that edifies. J. Alec Motyer

The books of Chronicles contain the most consistent teaching in the Bible on the theology of individual retribution, that is, the concept that fidelity to God is rewarded while infidelity is punished. . . . For the Chronicler, punishment followed sin with unerring stroke but at the same time repentance was always possible and this could reverse the punishment or at least modify it. . . . It is chiefly to the individual kings in Israel that this theory is rigorously applied. Celine Mangan

The Chronicler was a theological optimist who wanted to bring fresh hope to his people. . . . To fail to seek the Lord was to become liable to God's judgment . . . whereas seeking God's face afresh was part of the process of restoration (2 Chronicles 7:14). The term [to "seek" God] describes not a searching after God but a whole life orientation towards him. . . . Post-exilic Israelites were being specifically reminded that as well as owing their very existence to God's faithful love, further blessing would follow as they sought him and his ways. Martin J. Selman

May that central message of the Chronicles grip our minds, namely, that response to God is the really decisive factor. It is true both nationally and individually. It was true of old: it is true today. J. Sidlow Baxter

Vocabulary of apostasy, vocabulary of obedience, vocabulary of divine responses. J. A. Thompson, discussing kinds of vocabulary in 2 Chronicles

EZRA
Reestablishing a Covenant Society

FORMAT. 10 chapters, 280 verses

IMPLIED PURPOSES. To record the events of the first and second returns to the land of Israel by a remnant of Jews who survived the Babylonian captivity and to show by means of this history how people in the believing community can conduct their lives in a way that pleases God

AUTHOR'S PERSPECTIVE. The author writes as a member of the Jewish nation, highly interested in the events he records. He is also a master of specific details. The fact that the author includes more priests and Levites than ordinary people in the list of those who had married foreign wives attests to his fairness as a reporter.

IMPLIED AUDIENCE. All Jews and their posterity who were interested in knowing what happened when remnants of Jews returned to their homeland; all covenant people who want to know the bedrock principles on which God's community should live at any time in history

WHAT UNIFIES THE BOOK. The historical/narrative situation of the return of Jews from exile in Babylon; a documentary impulse to record factual data; a focus on religious life in the covenant community; the themes of return and the renewing of the institutions of the covenant community

SPECIAL FEATURES. Historical (documentary) factuality and precision; inclusion of first-person documents, such as the king's decree in 7:11-26, and most notably a section in which Ezra writes in the first-person "I" format (7:27–9:15)

CHALLENGES FACING THE READER OR TEACHER OF THIS BOOK.
1. The need to become interested in historical personages of long ago

189

2. The need to extract significance from a collection of historical facts, including whole sections that consist only of names

3. Knowing how to interpret the wholesale divorces undertaken by the Jewish men who had married foreign women

HOW TO MEET THE CHALLENGES.

1. The story is replete with adventure, discovery, and suspense; it is not hard to become interested in the action.

2. The narrative parts of the Bible embody the universal through the particular. Once you have mastered the literal facts of the situation, you can extract general principles.

3. The wholesale divorces were a onetime event that showed in a graphic way the need to keep separate from evil and to protect the covenant.

t is evident that Ezra-Nehemiah has been composed from a variety of sources—official documents, personal memoirs, letters, and inventories—each written in a different setting, each for a different purpose. . . . The characters of the main actors are drawn with broad strokes. . . . Ezra and Nehemiah are uniformly virtuous: Ezra [is] a model of devotion to the Law (Ezra 7:6). . . . Similarly, . . . the narrator . . . reduces [the surrounding foreign leaders] to a single epithet: "enemies." . . . Between the wicked leaders of the surrounding nations and the righteous leaders of Israel stand the people of Israel. Both collectively and individually they are neither completely wicked nor completely righteous. Sometimes they are one, sometimes the other. . . . We have no doubt how the leaders will act. . . . Not so the people.

DOUGLAS GREEN

				Reforming the Life of the Community

9–10 Ezra's Decisiveness Concerning Intermarriage

Second Return

Reform under Ezra

8 Return of the Remnant

7 Royal Permission for a Remnant to Return

Rebuilding the Temple

Restoration under Zerubbabel

6 Rebuilding Permitted and Completed

4–5 The Rebuilding Halted by Hostile Challenge

3 Rebuilding of the Temple Begun

First Return

2 Lists of Those Who Returned

1 Preparations for the Return

AN OUTLINE OF
EZRA

What would it be like to start a church or school from scratch? Sometimes we get to answer that in real life—with a church plant, a splinter group after a church split, a new Christian school, a new Sunday school class, or a support group. The book of Ezra portrays just such a moment of re-forming a community after it had been carried away into exile for nearly a century and had returned home.

The Form of the Book
The primary form is narrative. But the flow of the story is interrupted by a variety of documentary material—lists of people and supplies, transcripts of official documents, the genealogy of Ezra, and the like. Sometimes the material resembles a story; other times it resembles the daily newspaper or archived material.

DID YOU KNOW?
- The name *Ezra* means "helps" or "God helps."
- Rabbinic tradition, as well as the Jewish historian Josephus, regarded the books of Ezra and Nehemiah as a single composition written by Ezra.
- More than half a century separates the two returns narrated in Ezra.
- Ezra was born in Babylon during the Exile and was in the line of priests traceable back to Aaron.

The Story and Its Key Characters
The overall story is the return of exiles from captivity in Babylon. The Bible records three separate returns: two of them in this book and one in the book of Nehemiah. As the opening verse of Ezra notes, these returns fulfilled prophecies that a remnant would return after seventy years of captivity (relevant passages include Jeremiah 25:11-12; 29:10; and Isaiah 45:1-5, 13).

In this book the lead character in the drama is Ezra. Once he arrives back in Jerusalem, where life had already been restored in the covenant community, he takes charge and sparks begin to fly. Characters of secondary importance include three Persian kings—Cyrus, Darius, and Artaxerxes—all of whom give official permission and financial help for the return of groups of exiles. Additional secondary characters include the following: (1) Zerubbabel, who leads the first return and the rebuilding of the Temple; (2) in the first half of the book, the workers who rebuild the Temple; and (3) in the second half, those ignominious Israelites who have married foreign women.

Unifying Elements
The first unifying element is the story of remnants of Israelites returning in two phases from Babylon, which by now had been

conquered by Persia. Everything revolves around the return and the restoration of Jewish life in the homeland. At every point the book has a documentary feel to it, with lists and the reporting of facts and figures. Permeating the story is a sense of suspense as we wonder if the Temple will be rebuilt, if the Persian kings will continue to look with favor on the project, and how the tiny nation of returnees will respond to Ezra's aggressive remedies against intermarriage.

Key Doctrines

Providence. At numerous points it is obvious that God is directing events to a favorable conclusion for his chosen nation.

Holiness. The second half of the book, especially, emphasizes the need for God's people to be spiritually separate from unbelief.

Covenant. The events recounted highlight the fact that the history being told is the history of God's covenant people.

Things to Look For

- The motif of God's covenant people beginning again, setting up their way of life back in the homeland. What things receive priority? What things are not allowed? Why?
- The writer's preoccupation with documentary reporting
- The prominent role of decisive leaders and authority figures
- The centrality of religious concerns—such as worship, prayer, and heeding God's law—to the life of the believing community

quick overview of ezra

1:1–2:70	Return of a remnant
3:1–6:22	Rebuilding of the Temple
7:1–8:36	Return of a remnant
9:1–10:44	Reforming a backslidden nation

The Flow of the Book

A First Remnant Returns to Jerusalem (Chapters 1–2). The only workable strategy for these two chapters is to view them as the necessary background for the later action. Use your imagination to enter into the spirit of the return of a remnant of exiles from Babylonian captivity to their homeland.

Temple Restoration—Begun, Halted, and Completed (Chapters 3–6). Narrative now takes over, and you can assimilate these chapters by applying what you know about how stories work. Having relived the events in the narrative, you can reflect on the deeper meanings of the rebuilding of the Temple—for the original participants and for anyone who reads the account.

KEY VERSES

"The Temple of God was then dedicated with great joy by the people . . . who had returned from exile" (6:16). The first half of the book deals with the reestablishment of Temple worship.

"O our God, . . . we have forsaken your commandments" (9:10, ESV). The second half of the book deals with the need to return to obeying God's law regarding separation from evil.

A Second Wave of Returning Exiles (Chapters 7–8). Again, enter into the excitement of the events in the narrative. Imagine yourself as one of the returning exiles. Then extract some lessons from the actions that received highest priority when the exiles had completed their journey.

Ezra's Reforms (Chapters 9–10). The focus of the story in these chapters is the need for separation. Whereas the book of Nehemiah focuses on the need to rebuild a physical wall, the book of Ezra focuses on the need to maintain a spiritual and social wall. You can explore the text for ways in which this is worked out, as well as for evidence that the tools by which Ezra erected his spiritual wall were related to the fact that "Ezra was a scribe who was well versed in the Law of Moses" (7:6; see also v. 10). Then reflect on the timeless principles involved in this story of what happened long ago and far away. The rules that Ezra imposed were not ethnic in nature but religious (the trouble with the foreign wives is that they were religious pagans).

Contribution of the Book to the Bible's Story of Salvation in Christ

We need to resist the temptation to try to see Christ prominently in every book of the Old Testament. The book of Ezra records an important chapter in the history of the covenant nation through whom Christ was eventually born. That is a sufficient messianic theme, and there is no need to allegorize to make specific details fit the life of Christ. The New Testament contains no explicit references to the book of Ezra, but it is helpful to remember that the New Testament portrays Jesus as both temple and priest. (See "Jesus as Prophet" on page 351, "Jesus as Priest" on page 71, and "Jesus as King" on page 153.)

Applying the Book

The safest path to application is to view the lives of the returning remnant as a kind of case study in how God's people should live at any point in history. To do this, note what behaviors are held up to approval or disapproval and what values are depicted as preeminent in the believing community. The hero of the story, Ezra himself, embodies much of what is offered to us as exemplary behavior, as seen in his concern for correct worship and his grief over his nation's unholiness.

PERSPECTIVES
ON THE BOOK OF EZRA

The basic theme of Ezra is the spiritual, moral, and social restoration of the returned Remnant in Jerusalem under the leadership of Zerubbabel and Ezra. Israel's worship was revitalized and its people were purified. God's faithfulness is seen in the way He sovereignly protected his people.
Bruce Wilkinson and Kenneth Boa

The theological themes of the book are "God's faithfulness," "Satan's strategy," "separation from sin," and "Christian education (Ezra is a fine example of a great teacher in Israel)." J. Carl Laney

The story recounts how the Jews achieved a "renewed sense of identity." Derek Kidner

Ezra halts the decline of the Jews into heathenism not by decree, but by appealing to the conscience and memory of the nation—by saying to the people of Israel that they must take individual responsibility for their acts and for the consequences of those acts. Jay Neugeboren

The very fact of the Jewish restoration is spiritually eloquent. . . . The covenant still stood, and God did not go back on it. He had cast them out, but He did not cast them off. . . . And as this was true of Israel nationally, so it is true of God's people in Christ individually. J. Sidlow Baxter

[Ezra is] tightly packed with spiritual messages waiting to be extracted. [It communicates] a rich spirituality, [including] the importance of spiritual disciplines such as prayer, fasting, sacrificing, and reading of the Scriptures. . . . There is much we can learn. David M. Howard Jr.

PERSPECTIVES

ON THE BOOK OF EZRA

NEHEMIAH

The Bible's Grand Reconstruction Story

FACT SHEET

FORMAT. 13 chapters, 406 verses

IMPLIED PURPOSES. To record the events surrounding the rebuilding of the wall of Jerusalem by a remnant of returned exiles and the events surrounding the recommitment of the returned exiles to their covenant obligations; by means of this history to show individuals and communities how to live godly lives

AUTHOR'S PERSPECTIVE. The book's "eyewitness account" flavor gives it a sense of immediacy. The author has a high regard for the importance of a society's common people, but he is even more impressed by the way decisive and talented leaders such as Nehemiah and Ezra mobilize a society to do the right things. He therefore holds up heroic leaders for admiration and emulation.

IMPLIED AUDIENCE. Postexilic Jews who traced their continuing covenant life to the survival of the remnant who had returned to Israel and perpetuated the practices of the Jewish faith; beyond that, people of faith who can see eternal principles in the life of a particular believing community at a specific point in history

WHAT UNIFIES THE BOOK. The reestablishment of religious and civil life in Israel's homeland by a remnant who returned after the Exile; the commanding figures of Nehemiah and Ezra; the theme of restoration—of the wall and of covenant worship and obedience

SPECIAL FEATURES. The documentary impulse to record facts and figures; first-person narrative throughout much of the book; vivid portrayal of key events (people working on the wall with tools in one hand and weapons in the other, the reading of the law to the people); Nehemiah's six requests that God "remember" something

CHALLENGES FACING THE READER OR TEACHER OF THIS BOOK.
1. The need to extract significance from mere lists and inventories

2. The remoteness of Nehemiah's world from our own time and place

HOW TO MEET THE CHALLENGES.

1. There are two good approaches to the lists: (1) Imagine yourself at the events in the book, and (2) note the significance of the fact that in biblical religion, as opposed to religions built on fictional stories, God enters the flow of space-time history.

2. Reading narratives requires a two-way journey—first from your own time and place *to* the ancient world and then, by way of bridge building, a return journey to your own world. Nehemiah tells us both what *happened* and what *happens* in believers' lives.

THE MOST COMMON MISCONCEPTIONS ABOUT THIS BOOK.

1. That the story's relevance has long since vanished, so you need to become an expert in ancient history before this book will interest you

2. That the book is primarily a management handbook

—————

The book of Nehemiah: it is a general's diary, a governor's report, a man's plea to be given credit by his God, to be remembered for his good works, a mixture of recordkeeping and plea bargaining, of nationalism and piety, a tale of good management, courage, skullduggery, of moral and physical renewal, a memoir. . . . This is a book [of] matter-of-fact accountings [and] religious assumptions. . . . [Nehemiah] hopes to avoid future punishment by insisting that the people obey God, and . . . he reminds God of His promises of redemption if the people return to His ways. For Nehemiah history was the result of God and man responding to each other as Father and son, as Master and servant.

ANNE ROIPHE
"Nehemiah"

	13 Reforms of Nehemiah
	11–12 Resettling of Jerusalem
	9–10 Covenant-Renewal Ceremony
	8 The Law Read and Explained

Focus on Spiritual Renewal and Rectitude

Activity Centered around God's Law

Religious Life of the Community

Reinstruction, Recommitment, and Reformation of the People

	7 List of Those Who Returned
	3–6 Rebuilding the Wall amidst Conflict Without and Within
	1–2 Planning the Rebuilding

Focus on Work

Activity Centered on the Wall

Civil Life of the Community

Reconstruction of the Wall

AN OUTLINE OF
NEHEMIAH

One of the misconceptions the world, including the Christian world, has foisted on us is that the Bible is mainly a book of theological ideas. To get the practical benefit of these ideas, we have been led to think, we need to search our minds for ways to flesh out theological platitudes. The book of Nehemiah (indeed the whole Bible) shows us otherwise. It puts before us real people engaged in the activities of life—construction projects, defensive armament, leadership and management of people, group dynamics, communal religious activities, and mixed marriages.

The Form of the Book

Although the book of Nehemiah has the same mixture of narrative and documentary material (lists, inventories, genealogies) that Ezra does, Nehemiah has a stronger narrative flair. The rebuilding of the wall becomes a full-fledged conflict story, replete with suspense and heroism, and the covenant-renewal ceremony is one of the grand dramas in the Bible. Still, documentary material continually interrupts the narrative flow, thus showing the historical and bureaucratic impulse of the writer.

An additional thing to note about the story is that it belongs to an important circle of stories (especially important in ancient literature) known as return stories. Like Homer's *Odyssey*, the book of Nehemiah tells the story of people returning to a homeland that is in dire need of rebuilding and reordering.

The Story

The story behind the diverse material of Nehemiah is a sequel to the story we read in Ezra. Ezra tells of two returning remnants; Nehemiah tells the story of a third, which occurred about thirteen years after the second return. Just as the book of Ezra deals with two main events—the effort to rebuild the Temple and a reform movement based on a return to the covenant law—the book of Nehemiah, too, tells about a rebuilding effort (the city wall) and a return to obeying God's covenant rules. The events narrated in Nehemiah cover approximately fifteen years.

Unifying Element

The main unifying element is the world we enter as we assimilate this book. Simply noting the leading ingredients of that world will both unify the story in our thinking and give us reliable signposts to what the book teaches. The list below contains a few ingredients of the world of the story. Instead of considering the list complete, think of some additional ingredients. The world of Nehemiah is characterized by the following:

- The ruined and rebuilt city of Jerusalem is the focal point of the action.
- The Israelites carry out their great actions in a climate of conflict from without and within.
- The felt need for protection, represented by a physical wall but going beyond that, is a preoccupation.
- The ideas of covenant community, covenant living, and communal worship are preeminent.
- Named individuality is important.
- Leadership is held in high esteem and obeyed.
- People's relationship to God is assumed to be the most important thing in life.
- Listening to God's Word is essential to personal and communal living.

This list is only suggestive of how identifying the main features of the world of the story casts light on the unity of the book and its religious meanings.

Key Places and Characters
The most important scene of action is the city of Jerusalem. There is a memorable nighttime scene of a solitary pilgrim riding on horseback through a ruined city. The rebuilding of the wall is the main event of the first half of the book. The central scene of the second half—the renewal of the covenant at a solemn ceremony—occurs in Jerusalem, as does the dedication of the city wall (12:27-47).

The cast of characters is an interesting mix. The lists of names of those who returned to Jerusalem show the important role the common people play in this book and demonstrate as well that God knows all people by name. The scenes of the rebuilding of the wall and the renewal of the covenant reinforce this idea. We also find lists of the names of priests and Levites, and at various points in the action they serve a leadership role. More important yet are the two towering figures Ezra and Nehemiah, who exercise the most initiative in the events and attest to the author's view of the importance of leaders in life.

DID YOU KNOW?
- The name *Nehemiah* means "the comfort of God."
- The careers of Ezra and Nehemiah overlapped.
- The book of Nehemiah has proved effective as a study for religious retreats and seminars.
- In recent years Christians have also used the book as a guidebook for leadership and group dynamics.

In regard to the leaders, it is important to understand that two types of leaders are prominent in this narrative. One category of leaders is governmental, and the other is priestly/prophetic. Both are necessary for an ideal community. Nehemiah, a wall builder, and Ezra, a law reader, bring together the political and religious strands that find ultimate fulfillment in Christ.

Key Doctrines

Covenant. The book of Nehemiah is a handbook for how God's Old Testament people lived under the covenant.

Worship. The restoration of correct worship in Jerusalem is a key to the life of God's covenant people.

Sanctification. The reestablishment of the law is a pattern for how God's followers can lead godly lives.

Providence. God's protection of the fledgling community of returned exiles is a major ingredient in the story.

Tips for Reading or Teaching Nehemiah

Go through the action as if you were one of the returning remnant who experienced the events recorded in the book.

Look for ways in which the key doctrines and themes listed elsewhere in this chapter are embodied in various parts of the book.

Remember that the way to your hometown is through Jerusalem. Reliving the literal details of the story must precede the extraction of universal principles and application of them to your own time and place.

quick overview of nehemiah

1:1–6:19	Rebuilding the wall of Jerusalem
7:1–73	Return of a remnant of exiles
8:1–10:39	Renewal of the covenant
11:1–13:31	Additional details of resettlement and reform

Things to Look For

- The predictable back-and-forth movement between narrative and nonnarrative documentary material such as lists

- The unifying element on pages 200–201 (characteristics of the "world" of). You can get analytic mileage out of it.
- The excitement of the events in the narrative. Having relived the events, you are in a position to extract their religious significance.
- The religious view of life that emerges from this story of a relatively small group of people resettling a ruined homeland
- What the book says about godly leadership and the dynamics of how individuals and groups can thrive under such leadership

The Flow of the Book

Nehemiah's Resolve to Rebuild the Wall of Jerusalem (Chapters 1–2). These chapters are narrative at its most gripping. Your first task is to relive the story, from Nehemiah's tears before the most important political ruler in the world through his traveling about the ruins of Jerusalem on horseback by night. We see in Nehemiah a heroic figure whose courage and vision are examples to us.

The Trouble and Exhilaration of Rebuilding a Wall (Chapters 3–6). The account of the rebuilding of the wall of Jerusalem is a story of conflict, suspense, and heroic endeavor. The excitement of the narrative never wavers, no matter how many times you read it. You can assimilate the story as one of good and evil in conflict and one of human heroism, which in God's strength enabled the underdogs to win.

> **KEY VERSE**
> "We built the wall . . . for the people had a mind to work" (4:6, ESV). Here in kernel form is the first half of the book: a story of human industry in a physical task (the task was completed in fifty-two days, despite opposition).

Reading the Law and Renewing the Covenant (Chapters 8–10). Now we come to one of the truly great stories in the Bible. It takes the form of a drama, complete with stationing of characters in the scene, description of stage props, and direct presentation of speeches. Everything is at the white-hot level of intensity. The spiritual meanings of the events are enshrined in (1) the seriousness with which the participants in the drama take God's law, (2) the sermon that Ezra (not Nehemiah) preaches, and (3) the covenant that the nation endorses. All of these are models for us to follow. The renewal of the covenant is a biblical motif that we can find in Genesis, Exodus, the dedication of the Temple under Solomon, and Jesus at the Last Supper.

Still More Solemn Ceremonies (Chapters 11–12). The utopian feel of the book continues as we see still more glimpses of a good society and the institutional keys that make it possible. You can profitably analyze the chapters by looking for (1) the things that make the life portrayed a good life in a good society and (2) the institutional undergirding that makes that good life possible.

Purging the Wicked Way in the Covenant Community (Chapter 13). Just as the book of Ezra ended with an account of his purging the covenant community of impurity, the book of Nehemiah ends with its hero doing something similar. Here are the questions to answer as you work your way through the chapter: What precise evils raise Nehemiah's ire? Why are these practices offensive to God? What constitutes corrective action in the face of such offenses?

The Main Themes
1. Godly leaders are the key to having a good society.
2. God protects individuals and groups of believers who follow him.
3. God has prescribed how he wants his followers to live. Any failure to do what is right is the result of people's choosing to ignore what God has prescribed.
4. Individuals and believing communities must continually choose to obey God. When they fail to do so, their lives take a downward turn. The book of Nehemiah is a call for daily renewal of one's commitment to God.
5. The godly life always places individuals into relationship with others. It is not possible to live the life of faith in isolation from a community of faith.

Contribution of the Book to the Bible's Story of Salvation in Christ
The Christological implications of this book stem from its emphasis on God's covenant of grace. The book of Nehemiah gives us glimpses into how God's covenant people lived in an earlier phase of salvation history. Christians live in the fulfillment of things that were latent in the Old Testament. Believers in Nehemiah's day were theistic in their thinking and lifestyle; New Testament believers are Christocentric. The literal city of Jerusalem was central to the people in the book of Nehemiah; the physical worship practices that occurred in Jerusalem ceased to be necessary

after Christ's sacrifice (see John 19–21). In short, we can see much in Nehemiah as a foreshadowing of the eventual work of Christ.

Applying the Book

The return of a remnant of Israelites after captivity and their reestablishment of life and worship in their homeland are striking instances of God's mercy toward his covenant people. One application for us is that we are to live in the strength of God's grace, remembering that the people in the book of Nehemiah were not exempt from hard work and the requirements of holy living simply because God was gracious.

The second avenue toward application is to remember how stories work. They put examples of virtue and vice before us to prompt us toward the one and away from the other. The book of Nehemiah is a memorable gallery of exemplary characters, ideals, and actions: pictures of industry, leadership, following God and his leaders, prayer, taking God's law seriously, and taking radical steps to remove sin from the covenant community.

PERSPECTIVES
ON THE BOOK OF NEHEMIAH

Nehemiah is a gem of a book in the spiritual lessons which it teaches us. . . . Lessons and analogies are everywhere in this book. . . . Nehemiah himself is a really first-rank character-study. J. Sidlow Baxter

Titles of books on Nehemiah: Nehemiah the Executive *(Stanley E. Anderson);* Nehemiah the Involved Layman *(Paul A. Stewart);* Excellence in Leadership *(John S. White)*

Quite clearly these two books [Ezra and Nehemiah] are more than a bare chronicle. Here are events to learn from, not only learn about. . . . More than half of [Nehemiah] is a personal record, punctuated with "asides" and frank comments which make it . . . one of the liveliest pieces of writing in the Bible. Derek Kidner

If "Nehemiah's wall" functions to encircle the holy people, it is also a boundary separating clean and unclean, a physical expression of the way Law-keeping was to keep Israel separate from the neighboring peoples.

When Nehemiah shuts the gates to exclude Sabbath breakers from the holy city (13:15-22), two realms on either side of the wall are finally and ideally defined. Inside is all that is holy and clean (Nehemiah 11:1-3; 12:30; 13:22), outside are the wicked (13:17) and profane (13:18).
Douglas Green

As I studied the book I learned, to my amazement, that God has anticipated the problems of those in middle-management. He has also shown us how to handle opposition. . . . He has illustrated for us what we should do when we take over a new job. . . . Most of all, he has demonstrated the importance and practical value of religious convictions in effective administration. Cyril J. Barber, *Nehemiah and the Dynamics of Effective Leadership*

ESTHER
A Star Is Born

FORMAT. 10 chapters, 167 verses

IMPLIED PURPOSES. To tell the story of events surrounding the rescue of the nation of Israel from the threat of extinction while it was in exile in Persia and to celebrate a beautiful and courageous heroine whose name, Esther, means "star." While the story does explain the origin of the Jewish festival of Purim, the more profound and universal purpose of the story is to explain how God's providence can protect his people.

AUTHOR'S PERSPECTIVE. The author shows his bias by the way in which he manages the characterization and action, holding up bad characters to ridicule and celebrating good ones and presenting them sympathetically. The author is a patriot, not an impartial recorder of history. Still, his bias is embodied in the story itself, not in explicit commentary.

IMPLIED AUDIENCE. The original audience of this patriotic and entertaining story is assumed to be Jewish, but the captivating character of Esther makes the story a favorite with all audiences.

WHAT UNIFIES THE BOOK. The presence of an engaging central heroine; the U-shaped pattern of the plot, with events descending into potential tragedy and rising to a happy ending; the villainy of Ahasuerus and Haman; the rescue motif; the hidden providence of God in directing human affairs

SPECIAL FEATURES. Brilliance of storytelling technique (including the presence of suspense, irony, and surprising coincidence); evocative descriptions of places, characters, and events; the absence of God as a named character even though his providence directs events; world making (i.e., the ability of the writer to make the world of his story come alive in the reader's imagination); the foreign and exotic (non-Palestinian) setting of the action

CHALLENGES FACING THE READER OR TEACHER OF THIS BOOK.
1. The leisurely descriptions of places, persons, and dialogues that impede the action
2. Numerous references to Persian customs, especially those that involve the court
3. The cruelty of the Jews' slaughter of their enemies at the end
4. The convergence of so many ingredients of romance stories, making the story seem like a fictional romance rather than a history
5. The absence of God as a named character

HOW TO MEET THE CHALLENGES.
1. Plan to relish not only *what* happened but *how* it happened.
2. Use clues within the text to infer the customs that prevailed in the Persian world of the story.
3. Accept the fact that the Jews fought as they did in self-defense and to defeat monstrous evil.
4. Realize that the presence of literary qualities does not necessarily mean that a story is not factually true.
5. Look for signs that God is present and is guiding events even though the author does not mention him.

That *[God] is unnamed need not entail that he is uninvolved. Indeed, one might suspect that he is responsible for the extraordinary pattern of apparent coincidences that characterizes the narrative and makes possible the deliverance of the Jews from seemingly certain extermination. . . . In fact, the idea that the seeming coincidences of the narrative have been arranged by some higher power . . . is explicit in the text itself [4:13-14].*

JON D. LEVENSON
Esther: A Commentary

8–10 Victory of the Jews

6–7 Esther and Mordecai Thwart Haman's Plot

5 Haman's Plot and Esther's Counterplot

4 Mordecai Pressures Esther to Help Her Nation

3 Why and How Haman Plotted the Destruction of the Jews

2 Esther Becomes Queen

1 Why the Persian King Thought He Needed a New Queen

The Jews Rescued and Victorious

The Jews Threatened

AN OUTLINE OF
ESTHER

Tell me a story. These four words sum up one of the most universal human impulses. The human race, moreover, has generally agreed on the qualities it likes in a story. The ingredients include heroism, villainy, heightened conflict between good and evil, vivid description, characters about whom we care, suspense, intrigue, decisive choice, climax, battles, and poetic justice (goodness is rewarded and evil is punished).

When we judge the book of Esther by these criteria of excellence in storytelling, it is a triumph. It is one of the greatest stories in the Bible, as children perhaps know best. By means of this entertaining story, the author achieves his religious purposes (for example, teaching lessons about right and wrong behavior and about how divine providence guides human events).

The Form of the Book

The book of Esther is a unified narrative. It has a single plot as opposed to a complex or multiple plot. All the material the storyteller includes relates to the rescue of a nation from threatened extinction through the courage of the heroine of the book and through the wise counsel of her cousin.

Even though the plot is single, this central action tells two intertwined stories at the same time. If we view the action as the story of a nation, it is a classic story of rescue. But the book of Esther also tells the rags-to-riches story of the heroine after whom the book is named. The two stories converge in Esther, inasmuch as she is the chief human agent through whom God rescues the nation.

The Structure and Unity

The shape of the story is what literary scholars call a comic plot—a U-shaped story in which events descend into potential tragedy and then undergo a turnaround and march to a happy ending. The detailed descriptions and dialogues are the flesh on this simple, unifying skeleton. Other unifying elements include the following:

- The conflict between Haman and the Jews
- Mordecai and Esther as the most active agents through most of the story

NUMBERS THAT COUNT IN THE STORY OF ESTHER
- 10 banquets or feasts
- 2 fasts
- 3 important man-woman pairings (Ahasuerus and Vashti, Mordecai and Esther, Haman and Zeresh)
- 3 key references to the Persian court chronicles
- 250 appearances of the Hebrew word for "king" or "to rule"
- 37 references to Esther by name
- 0 explicit references to God

- The villainy of Haman
- The world of the story, replete with court etiquette and intrigue; beautiful palaces; banqueting and partying; court figures such as a king, a queen, and courtiers (including Mordecai); battles; and beautiful women

Key Places and Characters

The main settings are the capital city of Susa and within it, the king's court. Specific settings in various phases of the story are the banquet hall in the king's palace, the dormitory (actually a harem) of the candidates for queenship, the palace gate where Mordecai hangs out, the seventy-five-foot gallows, and the dining hall with adjacent garden, where Esther entertains the king and Haman at two famous dinner parties.

Since Esther is the one who manages to save her nation when it is threatened, we should regard her as the lead character. Her cousin Mordecai is almost an equal in the central plot conflict between Haman and the Jews. King Ahasuerus and Queen Vashti are attendant characters, necessary to the action but not part of the central plot conflict (although Ahasuerus symbolizes the decadence of the Persian court).

DID YOU KNOW?
Through the centuries in Jewish circles, when the story of Esther is read at the annual Feast of Purim, it has been the custom to boo and hiss and use noisemakers whenever the name of Haman is mentioned.

Key Doctrines and Themes

Providence. The author embodies this theme in the story itself instead of talking about it, but the chain of events by which the Jewish nation gains deliverance contains so many things human characters could not have planned that providence is the only adequate explanation.

The Sovereignty of God. Although not a named character, we can assume that God is the One who governs the history in the narrative.

The Covenant Promises of God. It is specifically God's covenant nation that is spared through his providential oversight.

Human Heroism. This story shows that God can accomplish his purposes through the agency of heroic believers.

Sin and Judgment. Sinners get what they deserve.

Tips for Reading or Teaching Esther

Relish the leisurely descriptions and dialogues—the "how" of the story and not simply what happened.

Go through the action as the observant companion of Esther and Mordecai, experiencing the events as they experienced them.

The characterization of Ahasuerus and Haman is satiric, as the writer consistently holds them up to exposure. The negative portrayal of the Persian court accounts for much of what is in the book.

Keep abreast of the development of the plot as step-by-step the Jews' situation becomes apparently hopeless and then a way of rescue is discovered.

Look for instances of dramatic irony, a situation in which you as the reader know something that one or more characters in the story do not know. Along with that, enjoy the examples of ironic and humorous reversal of fortune.

quick overview of esther

1:1–2:23	Background to the main action
3:1–7:10	Haman's plot to destroy the Jews, and the Jews' counterplot
8:1–10:3	The Jews' victory over their enemies

The Flow of the Book

Background to the Main Action (Chapters 1–2). The ill-advised demotion of Vashti and the providential promotion of the "slave girl" Esther to the position of queen constitute the backdrop for the rest of the story. It is important to remember that the author's chosen medium is narrative, or story. Your first task is to relive the story as vividly and fully as possible. Once you have done that, the right analytic slant on this material is to start compiling a list of things that are part of the overall providential design permeating the story. Subordinate to that, what early evidences can you see of an anti-Persian bias on the part of the writer?

Haman Hatches His Plot (Chapter 3). The key to the characterization of Ahasuerus and Haman is that the author satirizes them. Find as many evidences as you can in chapter 3 that this pair is the archetypal "bad lot." We naturally wonder what a nice Jewish girl like Esther is doing in a Persian harem. The story is not just about an oppressed minority that finds deliverance but also about a compromised community of faith who, when offered the chance to return to Jerusalem, refused the opportunity.

Hero Stories

Most stories in the Bible are hero stories. The simplest way to define a hero story is to say that it is a story built around the life and exploits of a protagonist (central character), whether male or female. Hero stories spring from a universal impulse—to embody accepted norms of behavior or representative struggles in the story of a character whose experience is regarded as being typical of people in general, though often in a bigger-than-life form. Storytellers who deal with real-life characters select and mold the facts of life to fit the heroic pattern that they present in their stories. Authors have two options: (1) They can choose typical or representative events in the hero's life, or (2) they can focus on the decisive or extraordinary events in the hero's life.

Here are characteristics of literary heroes and heroines:

- They reenact the important experiences and conflicts of the community that produces them. For example, the difficulty that Daniel and his friends face in living a godly lifestyle shows the experience of the exiles living in Persia and, beyond that, of believers in any age.

- They are representative figures in whom people can see their own struggles and triumphs.

- Their actions and characters are largely (but not necessarily wholly) exemplary, meaning that they are models people can look up to and aspire to emulate. It is important not to naively believe that everything a hero does is good.

- Heroes undertake an experiment in living that leads to a certain conclusion. In assimilating and teaching a hero story, the simplest rule to follow is to regard yourself as the observant traveling companion of the central character, learning as much as possible from this protagonist's experiences. Here are further questions that can guide your interaction with hero stories: On the assumption that heroes and heroines represent people generally, what can we deduce about people and life on the basis of a given hero's experience?

- Knowing that there is much about heroes and heroines that is a model for us to follow, be aware that hero stories can teach partly by negative example, that is, by showing us what to avoid. How does the hero or heroine of a given story show us how to live?

- Because hero stories have as their aim to systematize a society's values, what can we say about God's design for people generally and for believers on the basis of a given hero story?

- Finally, heroes in the Bible interact with God. On this basis, what do we learn about how to live in relationship with God?

So this is the story of how God's people realize the dangers inherent in compromising their faith and by God's grace are rescued.

Esther's Great Moment (Chapter 4). Chapter 4 is the pivotal point of the story and the point at which Esther is transformed into a heroic character. You need to look closely at the chapter to see what ingredients go into Esther's transformation and what form the transformation takes.

Esther Confronts and Manipulates the King and Outmaneuvers Her Enemy, Haman (Chapters 5–7). Action takes over at this point. It is important to follow the chain of events in detail. A unifying pattern is Esther's cleverness in carrying out her plan. What is effective about her on-the-spot decisions?

A Nation Is Saved, and Esther and Mordecai Thrive in the Persian Court (Chapters 8–10). The story becomes a classic battle story, and a good approach to the action is to trace the progress of the conflict. The Jews do not simply take matters into their own hands at the end of the story. Their self-defense is necessary because the king cannot change his edict and his only countermeasure is to allow the Jews to defend themselves.

The Main Themes

1. God uses his providence to accomplish his purposes in history. Here are some apparent coincidences that contribute to the rescue of the Jews: the timely vacancy of queenship in the Persian court; the choice of Esther, a Jew, to be the new queen; Mordecai's discovery of the plot on the king's life; Esther's gaining an audience with the king; the king's sleepless night; Haman's early arrival at the palace; Haman's ill-fated pleas for mercy at Esther's feet.

2. Human ingenuity, courage, and heroism are sometimes the agency of God's providence. There is an unwarranted tendency in some Christian circles to disparage what is human. This story refutes that tendency.

Contribution of the Book to the Bible's Story of Salvation in Christ

It is not just any nation that is rescued in this story but the chosen nation through whose lineage Jesus is eventually born. The story of Esther is thus a chapter in salvation history—the history of the line through which God saves the human race when Jesus becomes incarnate and dies for human sins. It is more than a patriotic Jewish story, therefore. The rescue recounted in this book is an event that helped to make salvation possible for the world. Throughout history, the book has also been a source of strength for Christians in times of persecution.

Applying the Book

The way to apply the providential theme is to trust that God will provide what is necessary in our lives as he did for his followers in history. The way to apply the models of heroism is to emulate them and, in particular, become another Esther by choosing the side of God even at the risk of privileged position. Although Esther—an inspiration to us—is not named among the heroes of faith in Hebrews 11, she is there in spirit. Another application is the need to recognize the compromises we make with the world and to take a courageous stand against evil.

PERSPECTIVES
ON THE BOOK OF ESTHER

Starlight. Jill Briscoe's "takeoff" on the fact that the name *Esther* means "star."

The most distinctive feature of style in Esther is the extensive use of elaborative chains of synonyms, the tendency to say precisely the same thing two, three, or four times. Susan Niditch

[Esther is] first introduced to us not as [an] inspiring spiritual or moral [person]. Esther the Favorite is known primarily for her looks. . . . What [is] inspiring . . . was that window of time when [Esther] . . . transcends . . . her role as mere youthful celebrity and rises to the level of hero. Naomi Harris Rosenblatt

The author's feminine bias reveals itself in the way Esther becomes increasingly significant as the story of final victory unravels. The plot is so ordered to emphasize her progressively complex role. From a dependent

orphan, completely submissive to Mordecai's manipulations, she emerges at plot's end as confidently in control of her life—and a nation's.
Wilma McClarty

The distinctive feature in the portrayal of Esther is change. . . . The turning point in Esther's development comes . . . in 4:15-16. It is abrupt and surprising. She resolves to do her duty, and a change immediately comes upon her. Michael V. Fox

What should readers derive from a reading of the Book of Esther? . . . God . . . cares about [his people] when they are in trouble; he cares about them even when they do not know that he is there. . . . By reading the Book of Esther, God's people should come to recognize that there truly is a God behind the seen. Barry C. Davis and A. Boyd Luter

JOB

When Bad Things Happen to Good People

FORMAT. 42 chapters, 1,070 verses

IMPLIED PURPOSES. To depict the experience of human suffering, to explore in the form of drama the question of why the righteous suffer, and to show how people should and should not respond to the experience of undeserved suffering. Perhaps another purpose is to refute the viewpoint, especially prominent in Old Testament times, that there is an automatic correspondence between good behavior and prosperity.

AUTHOR'S PERSPECTIVE. In keeping with the dramatic form in which various characters express their viewpoints, the author maintains an objective stance. He assumes that the reader is on God's side in the events of life, and he gives God the last word.

IMPLIED AUDIENCE. Suffering humanity as it exists at all times and in all places. Secondarily, people who believe that there is an automatic correspondence between good behavior and prosperity

WHAT UNIFIES THE BOOK. The spectacle of human suffering; a religious and philosophical analysis of why the righteous suffer; the debate format; conflict among characters (including Job against God)

SPECIAL FEATURES. Drama as the medium; speeches couched in the form of poetry; unabashed portrayal of angry characters; a pervasive thread of irony in which readers know something that characters in the story do not; a prolonged presentation of rival viewpoints about a single phenomenon (undeserved suffering); symmetrical arrangement of the content (see the chart below); the voice from the whirlwind at the end

CHALLENGES FACING THE READER OR TEACHER OF THIS BOOK.
1. The need to read virtually a whole book composed of poetry

217

2. The presence of long speeches
3. The conflicting philosophical viewpoints that threaten to be confusing through their sheer repetition
4. The need to determine which viewpoint is correct

HOW TO MEET THE CHALLENGES.
1. Resolve to master poetry and to read as slowly and contemplatively as poetry requires.
2. Give up on the idea of a fast-moving story and give yourself to leisurely progress through a book that repeats viewpoints many times.
3. Realize that the speakers keep repeating the same viewpoints, so the book is not as complex as commentators have made it.
4. Realize that the material at the beginning and end of the book gives the correct framework for understanding the book. (We know, for example, that Job suffers not because he is evil but because he is righteous.)

THE MOST COMMON MISCONCEPTIONS ABOUT THIS BOOK. That Job is blameless and exemplary throughout the book and that the book never provides answers about why even good people suffer

The problem of innocent suffering is used as a supremely relevant example to examine the deeper and profounder issue of the whole relationship between God and man. . . . The spiritual pilgrimage of Job is not the end of the journey. That goal we reach when we come into the presence of the Risen Lord. Yet Job has prepared us for this fuller, richer revelation of God's nature and purpose. He has made two great contributions . . . to the living of life. . . . [One is] that suffering may yet be a part of God's purpose. [The second is that] there is a relationship between God and man that does not depend on prosperity. It lies in the abiding presence of God.

EDGAR JONES

Dialogue or Debate

1–2 Prologue

3 Job's Lament

4–14 Cycle 1
- Eliphaz (4–5)
- Job's Reply (6–7)
- Bildad (8)
- Job's Reply (9–10)
- Zophar (11)
- Job's Reply (12–14)

15–21 Cycle 2
- Eliphaz (15)
- Job's Reply (16–17)
- Bildad (18)
- Job's Reply (19)
- Zophar (20)
- Job's Reply (21)

22–27 Cycle 3
- Eliphaz (22)
- Job's Reply (23–24)
- Bildad (25)
- Job's Reply (26–27)

28–31 Job's Concluding Monologue

32–37 Elihu's Speeches

38–42:6 Confrontation between God and Job

42:7-17 Epilogue

AN OUTLINE OF
JOB

If God is good, why is there so much suffering in the world? Why do good people face terrible trials? Why do people who profess faith in God undergo affliction as bad as—or worse than—that endured by people who do not believe in God?

No question has baffled people more than the question of suffering. If you want to engender a lively discussion in a Bible study group, all you need to do is pose the problem of suffering. It lies at the heart of human experience in a fallen world.

Although the Bible speaks to this issue in many places (the frequent note of suffering is a trait that differentiates the Bible from other books), we see the problem posed most starkly and explored at greatest length in the book of Job.

The Form of the Book
The first thing that springs from the pages of the book of Job is that most of the book is written in the form of poetry. When you start to read some of the poetry, you will quickly realize that it is not light poetry but serious poetry. You will not truly enjoy spending time with this book unless you master poetry as a medium. (For a primer on how poetry works, see "Poetry as a Form of Writing" on page 237.)

The second thing that emerges rather quickly is that the form of the book is not narrative or story, although a story underlies the book. The form of the book is predominantly drama and consists of dialogue and speeches. This, too, makes Job a difficult book because in drama the author simply presents what characters say. It is up to the audience to interpret what they hear in the dialogue, with no explicit help from the dramatist. It is important to realize that many of the speeches do not express the truth regarding Job's situation, as God himself confirms in the book's later chapters.

The Structure
The simplest organizational scheme is that the book pictures Job before his suffering, during his suffering, and after his suffering. Of course, that conceals the complexity of the book, but whatever else we say about the structure of the book, everything is built on a simple before-and-after sequence, with the middle carrying the "meat" of the book's argument.

The charts that appear in this chapter provide the next-most-helpful framework. Central to the arrangement of the book of Job is the presence of three cycles of speeches in which Job and his "comforters"

FURTHER PATTERNS IN THE BOOK OF

JOB

	Prose Prologue	Body of the Work in Poetry				Prose Epilogue
	Job Is Patient	Job Is Belligerent but Gradually Mellows			Job Is Silent and Repents	Job Prospers
	The Problem of Undeserved Suffering	The Failure of Human Wisdom to Solve the Problem of Suffering			God's Answer to the Problem of Suffering	
	1–2 Job Is Tested by Satan	**3** Job Despairs	**4–31** Job Is Counseled by "Friends"	**32–37** Job Is Counseled by Elihu	**38–42:6** Job Is Questioned by God	**42:7-17** Job Is Vindicated by God

take turns speaking and responding, in virtually the same order. This threefold cycle is then bracketed by other important material on both sides.

The Middle of the Book

The most difficult part of the book is the middle (chapters 3–37). These chapters are not as complicated as you might think, however. It is true that Job and his "friends" express a range of attitudes toward the problem the book poses, but they keep repeating a few simple ideas. Don't look for more complexity than is actually present. Job's constant themes are that he is innocent (i.e., undeserving of his suffering) and that God is unfair and even sadistic. The friends, likewise, are addicted to a few favorite sermon topics: that God is just, that innocent people do not suffer, that Job's suffering is therefore caused by his sin and is God's hand of discipline on him, and that Job needs to confess his sin and repent. The book of Job is the original model for our saying "With friends like these, who needs enemies?"

What happens in the middle part of Job does not resemble what happens in a theology seminar or a philosophy class but rather in a theater or coffee shop or dormitory. Instead of looking for dispassionate theological or philosophical debate, listen for the voices of people who are angry and are shouting at one another.

Here, then, are the patterns that will enable you to make sense of the middle of the book:

The obtuseness of Job's friends: They do not get the point. Job's friends assume that he is guilty, whereas he knows that he is innocent of the specific charges they make. (On the basis of the prologue, we know this too.) Incidentally, by assuming Job's guilt, his counselors totally miss the question the book actually poses: Why do *the righteous* suffer? The friends are like background static against which Job conducts his journey to understand his suffering. Their constant ignorance actually *elicits* Job's progress in thinking.

The essential pattern that governs Job's behavior in this part of the book is the *quest motif.* Job is on a quest to find an explanation for his suffering. In each of the cycles of speeches, Job is more enlightened as he gradually becomes less angry at God and more humble about the limitation of human knowledge. It is possible to chart Job's progress, although if we charted it, it would be a series of ups and downs.

How to Make Sense of Job's Behavior

A detriment to many people's understanding of Job's behavior is the assumption that because he gives such moving expression to the feelings occasioned by his suffering, he must be expressing the right attitudes throughout the book. There is an easy answer to this misconception, and it comes at the end of the book.

To begin, God's questions from the whirlwind are a rebuke to Job, as the lead-ins and follow-ups make clear (38:1-3; 40:1-2, 6-8). Equally important is the fact that in response to God's rebukes, *Job admits that his behavior has been bad and repents.* First Job stops talking (40:3-5), in acknowledgment that in his accusations against God it was his words that led him into sin. Then Job repents (42:1-6). He admits, "I was talking about things I knew nothing about" (v. 3).

With this awareness, we should view Job's speeches, beginning with his curse against life in chapter 3, as showing how wrong his response to his suffering is after his exemplary behavior in chapters 1–2. The book charts how Job learned from his suffering, but it also exposes how wrong his belligerence toward God was.

Unifying Elements

Partly in review, then, here are the unifying elements that can help make Job a great deal easier to understand than popular misconceptions of the book might have led you to think:

- The central problem, posed at the beginning and repeated to the end, of why *the righteous* suffer
- The obtuseness of Job's friends, who do not understand his innocence and fail to show empathy and really listen once the conversation begins to unfold
- The irony of the friends' orthodoxy in expressing what is generally true: that evil people bring suffering on themselves. The irony is that this orthodox viewpoint (for which there are many proof texts in the Bible) is not true of Job's suffering. Partially correct theology is incorrectly applied.
- Job's quest to make progress in understanding his situation and in his view of God
- The difficulty of fitting "correct" theology to life's situations

Key Characters

We can be grateful that the cast of characters is pretty small. Job is obviously the protagonist. The supernatural backdrop for the action entails a wager between Satan and God, and God emerges as the authority figure to the end of the book. (Satan simply disappears from the action after his defeat.) Job's three friends, or "comforters," are a major presence, and Elihu, who mainly repeats what others have already covered, gets an amazing *six* chapters. Job's family members are hazy background figures.

Key Doctrines

The Sovereignty of God. God remains in control of the action from start to finish. Apart from the premise that God is sovereign, we cannot understand the question of evil that the book of Job poses.

The Problem of Evil and Suffering. The book poses this problem and then explores it theologically.

Theodicy. This is the name given to the branch of theology or philosophy that seeks to reconcile God's goodness and sovereignty on the one hand with the fact of evil and suffering in the world on the other.

The Nature of God. As the characters in the drama express their views, many things emerge about God and his greatness, as do misconceptions regarding God.

Redemption. The book presents an unusual approach to redemption, but it is there—in the pictures we get of Job's righteous life, in his religious stance toward God, in God's implied forgiveness of Job, and in the double measure of blessing God gives Job at the end.

Tips for Reading or Teaching Job

You need not agonize over the arguments that the characters express. Operate on the premise that the characters keep repeating a few simple ideas.

Do not look for progress in the friends or in Elihu. They do not progress in their thinking. Do, however, look for progress in Job's thinking and relating to God.

One way to understand the poetic speeches better is to read them aloud.

Do not at any point automatically assume that the human characters in the drama are speaking the truth—even if there are cross-references in your Bible for the sentiments the characters express. What matters is that in this particular situation of Job's suffering, the human characters largely miss the mark.

The Flow of the Book

Prologue Set in Heaven: God's Wager (Chapters 1–2). Here is one of the most famous scenes in the Bible. What things make it awe inspiring and surprising? The function of the prologue in the overall design of the book is this: It gives readers important pieces of information that the characters in the story do not know. The result is dramatic irony. So the best framework for interpreting these two chapters is to compile a list of the important things we learn and against which we measure what subsequently happens in the book. The following are examples:

- God is allowing but not causing Job's suffering.
- Job is "blameless" (1:1, 8; 2:3), and his suffering cannot be attributed to any sinfulness on his part. In fact, Job is under satanic attack.
- God has not relinquished his providential control over Job's life (1:12; 2:6).
- Job's suffering is a test of his faith.

Given these facts, much of what Job and his counselors are about to say misses the mark. In addition, Job's exemplary response to his suffering in these two chapters sets a standard of which he immediately falls short as we move to the middle section of the book.

quick overview of job

1:1–2:13	Prologue set in heaven
3:1–31:40	Debate between Job and his "comforters"
32:1–37:24	Elihu's pontification
38:1–42:6	The voice from the whirlwind
42:7-17	God's restoration of Job's fortunes

Job's Lament (Chapter 3). Job utters a formal curse against life and expresses a death wish. In other words, he undergoes a fall from his exemplary behavior in chapters 1–2. A good analytic framework is to compile a list of Job's statements that contradict what we already know on the basis of the prologue set in heaven. Also look for evidences that Job needs to undertake a quest for improved understanding.

The First Cycle of Speeches (Chapters 4–14). The best framework for working your way through these speeches is an awareness of the irony that exists, based on what we know from the prologue. The friends represent a pattern that can be called the irony of orthodoxy. That is, they express principles about human suffering that are generally true (sin is punished, God disciplines his followers, innocence does not result in suffering) but, based on what we learned in the prologue, are inaccurate in this particular case.

Job's speeches yield an equally vivid pattern of irony, which we can call the irony of rebellion against God. Look for passages in which Job accuses God of things that we know from the prologue are untrue. For the most blatant examples, see 6:4; 7:11-21; 9:16-24; and 10:20-22.

To summarize the first cycle of speeches, Job's counselors maintain that God is just and Job is guilty of sin. Job insists that he is innocent and God is unjust. Both Job and his counselors are wrong.

KEY VERSE

"Teach me, and I will be silent; make me understand how I have gone astray" (6:24, ESV). Job speaks truer than he knows at this point, but he actually summarizes his entire quest. He *is* eventually silent before God, and he *does* eventually understand his errors of thinking. Here we find the plot of the whole book in miniature.

The Second Cycle of Speeches (Chapters 15–21). It is tempting to think that because the speeches are long, the line of argument must be intricate, and therefore we must look for signs of progress over the first cycle of speeches. We need to resist that fallacy. What we mainly hear is the characters' getting more and more angry at each other but not progressing in their understanding.

The friends keep repeating a few simple ideas, and Job continues to make false statements about his situation and about God. It is possible, though, to see a small amount of progress in Job's thinking. This cycle has more moments in which Job is humble rather than arrogant and is accurate in his statements about God. For key passages of such progress, see 19:23-27 (where Job attains a blessed hope about an afterlife); 21:7-34 (where Job decisively dissociates suffering and sin on the part of the sufferer); and 23:3-12 (where Job expresses new humility and new faith in God's fairness).

The Third Cycle of Speeches (Chapters 22–27). It is futile to look for progress in the thinking of Job's counselors, and Job continues to express some unwarranted bitterness toward God. But the proportion of right thinking on Job's part is higher here than before. So look for (1) still more evidence that the friends do not get the point, (2) further evidence of the irony of rebellion on Job's part, and (3) passages in which Job expresses an appropriate attitude toward himself and toward God.

Two "Set Pieces" to Round Out Job's Dialogue with His Counselors (Chapters 28–31). First, just as Job's formal curse on light/life framed the dialogues on the front side, two formal speeches after the dialogues now complete the bracket, though we can also envision Job as addressing his remarks to his counselors. Chapter 28 is a famous poem that asserts the inability of people to find wisdom and acknowledges that God alone is the source of it. The poem expresses both Job's growing awareness that he cannot solve the problem of suffering through his own reasoning and also his new capacity for transcendence. Look for signs of these two things in the poem.

Second, Job sums up matters by recalling his earlier prosperity (chapter 29), describing his current suffering (chapter 30), and making a great oath of innocence (chapter 31). It is worth pondering how these developments fit into what has preceded. For example, Job decisively confirms that his suffering is not a result of sin on his part.

> **KEY VERSE**
> "Behold, the fear of the Lord, that is wisdom" (28:28, ESV). This statement is the climax of the poem on wisdom, which asserts that people cannot find wisdom and that God alone knows the way to it. This is a turning point in the book of Job, acknowledging that purely human reasoning cannot solve the problem of pain and suffering.

The Speeches of Elihu (Chapters 32–37). Elihu is an angry young man who is irritated at both Job and his counselors. He is long winded and arrogant, and after the smoke has cleared, he has made very little, if any, progress of thought over what Job's friends said. Elihu, too, tells Job to repent. An analysis of Elihu's speeches to see how they repeat territory already covered may perhaps explain why Job does not even respond to them. A minor counterthrust is a passage in which Elihu foreshadows the content of God's later speeches from the whirlwind (36:2–37:24).

The Voice from the Whirlwind—a Theophany (38:1–42:6). We now move to the climax of the book, where the issue of innocent suffering is finally resolved (though not fully answered). There is, of course, something climactic about God's finally speaking after having been silent all along. There is irony in abundance: Job, who had questioned God, is now questioned *by* God, and instead of answering Job's questions and accusations, God asks a series of rhetorical counterquestions. There is also irony in the fact that God's speeches do not even address the question of human suffering.

On the surface, God's science quiz is irrelevant to what has been happening. But the dozens of questions are really an indirect way of bringing

Job to his final understanding and of allowing *us* to infer some answers to the question of innocent suffering. Here are some questions to ask that will aid your analysis of these speeches:

- The speeches show God's awesome and mysterious transcendence—his power and knowledge, which are beyond the earthly. How does this relate to the problem of human suffering?
- Paradoxically, God's statements also show his immanence—his closeness to his creation—and his providence over his creation. How does this data relate to the question of human suffering?
- How do God's speeches, with their emphasis on his wonderful management of the world of nature, constitute a "how much more" line of argument? If God is so thoroughly in control of the natural world and its creatures, can we not trust him even more to care for his human creatures?

KEY VERSE

"I had only heard about you before, but now I have seen you with my own eyes" (42:5). This is the climax of Job's development. Although God has not directly answered Job's questions about why suffering has entered his life, Job has attained a deeper vision of God through his encounter with God in his sufferings.

Job's responses to God's two speeches (40:3-5; 42:1-6) are the other half of the book's solution to the central problem it raises. These passages require careful analysis, with a view toward disclosing what Job learned from his suffering and from his quest to understand it. Specific questions relate to (1) exactly what attitudes Job expresses, (2) why he responds as he does, and (3) how his attitudes relate to the central problem posed in the book. An additional question worth pondering is what Job might say to readers about his suffering after having undergone the process recorded in the book.

Epilogue: Job's Fortunes Restored (42:7-17). The story's happy ending is an example of poetic justice (virtue rewarded and vice punished). You can profitably look for evidences of this (do not overlook the fact that Satan, having been defeated in his wager, has dropped out of the action).

The Main Themes

1. It is beyond human understanding to know fully why God allows human suffering.

2. We can, however, know that God allows but does not inflict undeserved suffering on people, that he does not relinquish his providential control over human destinies, and that suffering can result in growth in wisdom and in a deeper relationship with God.
3. It is foolish and wicked for people to malign the character of God.
4. Human arrogance is inappropriate and repulsive.
5. We can trust God's goodness in the midst of personal suffering.
6. It is important to have experiential knowledge of God as well as "head knowledge."

Contribution of the Book to the Bible's Story of Salvation in Christ

The spectacle of innocent suffering, even though Job himself does not handle it well, is a foreshadowing of the ultimate innocent suffering: that of Jesus in his passion. Beyond that, Job momentarily attains a blessed hope for a bodily resurrection (19:23-27), which a Christian reader naturally assimilates in terms of the New Testament certainty of a physical resurrection based on the resurrection of Jesus from the dead. Finally, believers who live after Christ suffered have a new insight into their own suffering. Scottish novelist and poet George Macdonald said that "the Son of God suffered unto the death, not that men might not suffer, but that their sufferings might be like His." First Peter 4:13 speaks of rejoicing to "share Christ's sufferings" (ESV), with the implication that suffering can conform a Christian to the image of Christ, an understanding that Job did not fully have (see also 2 Corinthians 4:7-18 and Hebrews 12:3-11).

Applying the Book

Much of the application consists of avoiding the bad attitudes and behavior of the characters in the book. We can begin with all of Job's human counselors (including his wife's advice in 2:9). They are a case study in how not to counsel a friend who is suffering. We should not presume to speak for God.

Much of Job's behavior, likewise, is a caution for us when we go through deep waters in our own lives. We should not presume to speak against God on such occasions or to respond with bitterness toward him. Job was overly confident of his ability to solve the mystery of suffering with his own reasoning.

On the positive side, Job's gradual progress throughout the book and the book's conclusion give us models to follow. Job did not have access to the information we receive in the opening prologue, but the point is that we *do* have access to that information, so the book offers us a revelation beyond what Job attained even in his concluding interaction with God.

PERSPECTIVES
ON THE BOOK OF JOB

Magnificent and sublime as no other book of Scripture. Martin Luther

For Western man Job has been the preeminent symbol of innocent suffering. Paul S. Sanders

[Job] discovered not only that God did not abandon the sufferer, but also that suffering and loss had not detached him from God, that it was possible to serve and love God not for the outward things He gave, but for what He was in Himself. G. Buchanan Gray

The Prologue of Job is of the greatest significance for the interpretation of the entire work. . . . The poet uses this framework deliberately and with great artistry to [give] the key to the fuller approach to the solution of the dilemma that the experience of suffering by good men creates.
Edgar Jones

When God speaks to Job from the whirlwind, . . . he reminds Job that there are mysteries in nature beyond his solving, and leaves him to realize that the mystery of suffering is one of these. To Job the supremely important thing is that God has come to him in his suffering.
H. H. Rowley

The book of Job is an astonishing mixture of almost every kind of literature to be found in the Old Testament. Many individual pieces can be isolated and identified as proverbs, riddles, hymns, laments, curses, lyrical nature poems. Francis I. Andersen

These divine answers must be understood as the climax which . . . brings Job's struggles to a conclusion. But it must surprise all who read it that God's answer deals with something completely different from what Job had asked about. . . . God's answer insists upon the absolute marvellousness of his management of the world. . . . God gives the answer by pointing to the glory of his providence that sustains all his creation. Of course this justice of God cannot be comprehended by man; it can only be adored. Gerhard von Rad, on the voice from the whirlwind

The Wager [between God and the devil] was, at its heart, a stark reenactment of God's original question in creation: Will the humans choose for or against me? From God's point of view that has been the central question of history. Philip Yancey

PSALMS
Israel's Hymnal

FORMAT. 150 chapters, 2,461 verses

IMPLIED PURPOSES. To give poetic and lyric expression to the feelings of believers in God; to meditate on the character of God and on the truths that make up biblical faith; to showcase works of literary beauty; to record human responses to God, to nature, to worship, to suffering, and many other human experiences; to provide texts for public and private worship and singing

AUTHORS' PERSPECTIVE. The psalmists write as lyric poets; they are emotionally caught up in the experiences about which they write. Further, lyric poets write to express their responses to something. With that as a given, we can note a difference between predominantly emotional poems, written in the heat of intense feeling, and predominantly meditative (reflective) poems that share a series of thoughts.

IMPLIED AUDIENCE. The believing and worshipping community. Beyond that, we can generalize that this group of people knows about and values the following subjects and experiences: God, worship, nature, everyday life. Further, the audience is assumed to be introspective, interested in the inner life of thought and feeling.

WHAT UNIFIES THE BOOK. Poetry as the medium of expression; an introspective stance; the fact that the poet of a given psalm functions as the reader's representative, saying what the reader, too, wants to say but saying it better; God as the most recurrent subject; a religious frame of reference, even when something from everyday life is the actual subject of a poem

SPECIAL FEATURES. The longest book in the Bible; the self-contained nature of individual poems, which are not episodes or chapters in a single, ongoing sequence; in the Bible as a whole, an unparalleled attention to human feelings; the introspective angle; the preference for concrete imagery and figurative language

CHALLENGES FACING THE READER OR TEACHER OF THIS BOOK.
1. The need to read and interpret poetry
2. The repetitiousness of some parts of Psalms if the book is read sequentially
3. The nonnarrative nature of an anthology of poems

HOW TO MEET THE CHALLENGES.
1. Learn the basics of poetry and its subgenres.
2. Find a way to read especially the first third nonsequentially to avoid getting bogged down in too many lament psalms.
3. Understand that the book of Psalms does not tell a story; it offers meditative experiences on aspects of the religious life.

> I have been accustomed to call this book ... "An Anatomy of all the Parts of the Soul;" for there is not an emotion of which any one can be conscious that is not here represented as in a mirror. Or rather, the Holy Spirit has here drawn to the life all the griefs, sorrows, fears, doubts, hopes, cares, perplexities, in short, all the distracting emotions with which the minds of men are wont to be agitated. ... There is no other book in which there is recorded so many deliverances, nor one in which the evidences and experiences of the fatherly providence and solicitude which God exercises toward us are celebrated with such splendor of diction. ... There is no other book in which we are more perfectly taught the right manner of praising God.
>
> JOHN CALVIN
> *preface to his commentary on the Psalms*

Avoiding the Most Common Mistake in Studying the Book of Psalms

Most Bible handbooks try to treat the book of Psalms like the narrative and expository parts of the Bible. But any attempt to find an ongoing flow to the entire book is virtually useless. The fact that in its original form the book was divided into five separate units provides little help in mastering it. While there are some clusters of related psalms, the book of Psalms as a whole is an anthology of 150 separate poems. In general, these poems are not arranged topically, as some poetry anthologies are. You need to treat each poem as a freestanding unit. There is, therefore, no "outline" for the book of Psalms. The right way to organize the poems is by genre, or type. Correspondingly, what you need in order to master this book is a guide to the main types of poems that make up the book, not an outline.

In light of that, this chapter also lacks a "Flow of the Book" section as well as a chart and an outline. Like everything else in this handbook, we composed this chapter with a single guiding question in mind: What things would a reader of this book of the Bible find most helpful to know in order to read or teach the book well? The material that follows is different in format from other chapters in this handbook and from the approach that you will find in other handbooks, but you can trust it to tell you what you most need to know when handling Psalms.

The Form of the Book

As we have already stated, Psalms is an anthology of poems. The leading genres, each of which is covered in a separate section in this chapter, are listed below:

- lyric poem
- lament psalm
- praise psalm
- worship psalm
- nature poem

In addition, it is useful to know that other classifications of psalms are possible, based not on form but on subject matter, or content. For example, some psalms deal with the king and are called *royal psalms*. The church has traditionally regarded seven psalms as *penitential psalms* because they deal with sin and repentance. Some psalms so obviously foreshadow the life of Christ that they are called *messianic psalms*. Some Bible versions use the label "Song of Ascents" for Psalm 120 through Psalm 134. These are *pilgrim psalms*, sung or recited as the worshippers "went up" to Jerusalem on pilgrimages to the Temple. Psalms that call down God's curse on one's enemies are *imprecatory psalms*. Be aware that these subject-matter classifications cut across the forms in the list above. They are *all* lyric poems, for example, and some are also lament psalms or praise psalms.

Unifying Elements

For all of the book's diversity, there are constant factors that will help to unify our experience of this poetry anthology:

- The organization of the book into individual poems
- The poetic language in which all the psalms are written
- Along with the second element, the verse form of parallelism (stating a truth more than once in similar grammatical form but using different words or images) that is present from start to finish
- Recurrent clusters of topics and experiences: God, human emotions (especially praise and depression), everyday activities, enemies, worship, nature, and the nation (the patriotic impulse). We might think of the psalms as songs of experience.
- The theocentric focus: No matter what subject or human experience makes up the content of a poem, the poem is likely to focus on God sooner or later.

Key Characters

To say that the Psalter does not tell a continuous story does not mean that it lacks a central cast of characters. The character who appears most often is, of course, God, chiefly as the object of praise and worship. There are also numerous references to "the hosts of heaven"—that is, angels—and occasional references to "the gods" of the earth, meaning pagan deities. Among the human characters, David in his role as poet and songwriter is the most important.

The central human character is the ubiquitous figure known so lovingly as "the psalmist."

DID YOU KNOW?
- The title *Psalms* literally means "the book of praises" or "songs of praises."
- The word *Psalter* refers to the book of 150 psalms.
- The Hebrew word *selah*, meaning "to lift up," appears 39 times in the Psalter and was probably a musical notation.
- All but three dozen psalms have some sort of heading or inscription identifying author, genre, or historical context. The scholarly consensus is that these titles are "noncanonical, but reliable early tradition" (Tremper Longman III).

Poetry as a Form of Writing

Poetry is a special use of language, but not an unnatural use. In fact, in most cultures, poetry preceded prose as a form of writing. The fact that approximately one-third of the Bible consists of poetry shows that God wants us to understand and enjoy poetry. Poetry permeates the Bible: In addition to whole books of poetry, the use of imagery, metaphor, and other figures of speech is found in every book of the Bible.

Poetry (as distinct from whole compositions called poems) consists of special resources of language, including the following:

- The basic unit of poetry is the image, broadly defined to mean any word that names an action (such as walking) or a thing. Poets think in images rather than in abstractions.
- Poetry is written in verse form. In the Bible, the verse form is known as parallelism—saying something two or more times in different words and images but similar grammatical form: "The sun will not harm you by day, nor the moon at night" (Psalm 121:6).
- Poets prefer the figurative to the literal. The most frequent figures of speech are image ("he leads me beside peaceful streams" [Psalm 23:2]), metaphor (an implied comparison that does not use the words *like* or *as*, such as "the LORD is my shepherd" [Psalm 23:1]), simile (a comparison using the words *like* or *as*, such as "the LORD is like a father to his children" [Psalm 103:13]), and hyperbole (conscious exaggeration for the sake of emotional effect, as in the statement "you will trample upon lions" [Psalm 91:13]).
- Figurative language requires interpretation. When the poet says that the prosperous wicked "wear pride like a jeweled necklace" (Psalm 73:6), a reader needs to determine the ways in which pride can be like a necklace.

Poems are compositions written in poetic form. Here are some useful things to know about poems:

- They are usually either meditative or emotional in nature. In other words, they present either a series of ideas or a sequence of feelings.
- Poems have something—an idea, a situation, a feeling—that unifies the individual parts. In Psalm 23 the unifying motif is a shepherd's daily provision for his sheep.
- To see how the parts relate to the unifying core, you can use the format of theme and variation. Every individual unit contributes something to the central theme, and it is your task as a reader to interpret how the various units contribute to the whole.
- Poems do not ordinarily tell a story. They are more disjointed than stories, and they consist of reflection or emotions, not events.

This designation refers to the poet of an individual psalm, though the individual poets have so many things in common that "the psalmist" also assumes a kind of corporate identity—a voice that remains constant regardless of who the author of an individual psalm might be. What do we know about this composite figure? We can generalize: The psalmist

- is a master of poetry as a form of expression;
- delights in the artistry of words and poems;
- is introspective, continually looking inward to his own feelings and musings;
- lives in the concrete world of daily experience, not a world of abstract ideas;
- is Godward in his orientation and relates all of life to God; and
- is intimately acquainted with God as a person and with his acts and attributes.

In the next concentric circle, surrounding the central characters of God and the composite poet, is the believing religious community. Its members come from all walks of life: farming, homemaking, warfare, priestly work, parenting, and many others. These people work, worship, cook, raise children, walk in nature, travel, and tend sheep. The people we meet in Psalms could just as well be ourselves and our neighbors.

The Verse Form of Parallelism

You will handle the book of Psalms with a great deal more ease and understanding if you take time to master the verse form in which the entire Psalter is written. It is known as parallelism. This is not of merely scholarly interest but is woven into the very texture of the psalms.

The principle of parallelism is that the poet thinks continuously in terms of pairs or triplets of lines. These constitute the form in which the meaning is embodied. Either the second and third lines *repeat the basic content* of the first line in different words and images, or the second line *completes the thought* of the first line in such a way that the two lines form a unit of thought. Here are the basic types of parallelism:

SYNONYMOUS PARALLELISM. In synonymous parallelism the second line repeats the thought of the first line in similar grammatical form. For example, "The LORD of hosts is with us; / the God of Jacob is our fortress" (46:7, ESV).

More often than not, only part of the first line has a grammatical counterpart in the second line. In the following example, the verb of line one is omitted from line two: "You will not fear the terror of the night, / nor the arrow that flies by day" (91:5, ESV).

ANTITHETIC PARALLELISM. Here the second line repeats the content of the first line in a contrasting way: "The LORD knows the way of the righteous, / but the way of the wicked will perish" (1:6, ESV).

SYNTHETIC ("GROWING" "PROGRESSIVE") PARALLELISM. The second line completes the thought of the first line. Strictly speaking, there is no parallelism of thought but simply a two-line unit: "You prepare a table before me / in the presence of my enemies" (23:5, ESV).

CLIMACTIC PARALLELISM. The second line completes the first, repeating part of the first line and then adding to it: "Ascribe to the LORD, O families of the peoples, / ascribe to the LORD glory and strength!" (96:7, ESV).

The essential principles of parallelism are symmetry and balance. They are evidence of the artistry and beauty of expression that are an important part of the psalms. Another effect of parallelism is meditative: Instead of moving immediately to the next statement, we are forced to ponder an idea a second or third time. Overall, we can say that the effect of parallelism is similar to turning a prism in the light, observing the nuances of a statement.

Key Doctrines

The Nature of God. The psalmists say as much about the acts and attributes of God as any other book in the Bible does, and they tend to say it directly.

Human Nature. The psalms also tell us much about the nature of people, who are portrayed sometimes as deeply flawed but at other times as exemplary in their devotion to God.

Nature and the Physical Creation. Next to early Genesis, the Psalter is the Bible's chief repository of teaching about nature and the physical creation.

Sin and Evil. The lament psalms, especially, provide an anatomy of ways in which people do terrible things in God's world.

Worship. The psalms describe acts of worship and embody attitudes and feelings of worship, reverence, and joy.

Tips for Reading or Teaching Psalms

To handle the book of Psalms correctly, you need to know how poems work. Poetry is language on its best behavior, but it is hardly a foreign language. (For more on poetry as a form of writing, see the article on page 237.) It is important to note that the poetic impulse lies within all of us, as when we speak of the sun rising or of feeling emotionally "low." We also have more contact with poems than we might think, since every song that we sing or hear is a poem. Here are the things about poetry that you always wanted to know but did not know how to ask:

Poems do not ordinarily tell a story.

Poems are not a series of logically structured ideas the way an essay is.

Poems are either meditative/reflective or emotional in content; that is, they present a sequence of thoughts or feelings.

Compared to stories and ordinary expository writing, poems are disjointed in their structure. We need to be ready for rapid shifts without transitions.

Poetry is written in verse form. In the Bible, this verse form is known as parallelism: saying the same thing more than once in different words and images or simply writing in two- or three-line units of similar grammatical makeup.

In poetry, the line is the recurrent unit, not the sentence, as it is in prose.

Poets think in images and concrete realities (light, path, run) rather than in abstractions. Whereas the basic building block in narrative is the scene or episode, in poetry it is, broadly defined, the image.

Poets prefer the figurative to the literal. The most customary figures of speech are metaphor, simile, hyperbole (exaggeration for effect), personification, and apostrophe (addressing someone or something rhetorically).

Figures of speech require interpretation.

Most poems are unified around a central idea, feeling, or situation. You can wrestle a poem into a unity if you set your mind to it.

Poems are structured on the principle of theme and variation.

Poems are also structured on a three-part principle: (1) introduction; (2) development; and (3) concluding note of resolution, or closure.

Lyric Poems

The most important requirement for reading Psalms is the ability to understand and unpack the meanings of the poetic language or idiom in which poets speak. (For a primer on that subject, see the article on page 237.) But the individual psalms are whole and complete compositions that use poetic language. Simply mastering the poetic language will not by itself allow you to master a psalm. The next several pages will outline the main types of poetic discourse you will encounter in the book of Psalms.

The broadest category of poetic composition is called the lyric poem. *All* the psalms, including the subgenres described below, are lyric poems first of all. Here are the most important rules governing lyric poems:

Lyric poems are unified around a central idea, or motif. If you do not discover a lyric poem's unity, the poem will remain nothing more than a collection of fragments. This is not what lyric poets intend. While some lyric poems (including some of the psalms) seem miscellaneous, with ingenuity and a willingness to stare at the poem, perhaps aided by a study Bible, you will be able to formulate an idea of what unifies the poem.

The best framework in which to think about the unity of a poem is that of theme and variation. The theme is the unifying element that governs the whole poem. It might be an idea (the blessedness of the godly person in Psalm 1) or a literary motif (the provisions of a shepherd for his sheep during the course of a typical day in Psalm 23) or an underlying situation (such as the speaker's crisis in a typical lament psalm). The framework of theme and variation is worth its weight in gold when you come to analyze a lyric poem, and it imposes a double obligation on you—to find an umbrella broad enough to cover every unit in the poem and to show how every unit in the poem relates to the unifying theme or motif.

Lyric poems tend to fall into two broad categories based on content. Some lyrics are highly *emotional*, or *affective*, as the poet makes a vivid display of his emotions. Other lyric poems are *meditative*, or *reflective*, as the poet shares a series of thoughts or ideas with the reader. You can profitably identify into which of these categories a given psalm falls and adjust your expectations accordingly.

Finally, lyric poems generally fall into a three-part structure that is remarkably constant. In the *introduction*, the poet puts the central subject or experience to which he is responding before the reader. This is done briefly. In the *development*, the poet elaborates on the announced experience or idea by a series of variations, using one or more of these strategies: repetition, contrast, listing or catalog, and association (branching out from the initial subject or experience to a related one). Lyric poems do not simply end; in the *conclusion* they are rounded off with a note of resolution and closure such as a parting wish, a prayer, or a forward-looking sentiment; e.g., "I will live in the house of the LORD forever" (23:6).

Six Recurrent Motifs in Psalms

- Weeping may tarry for the night, but joy comes with the morning. (30:5, ESV)

- Taste and see that the LORD is good. (34:8)
- He will rescue the poor when they cry to him. (72:12)
- How amazing are the deeds of the LORD! (111:2)
- Out of the depths I cry to you, O LORD! (130:1, ESV)
- I will praise the LORD as long as I live. (146:2)

Lament Psalms

Lament psalms are the most numerous category in the Psalter, composing approximately a third of the book. Lament psalms are identifiable first of all by the fixed form into which the material is cast. Here are the elements of a lament psalm, which can occur in any order and can occur more than once in a given poem:

- the invocation (a cry to God, usually an introductory cry)
- the lament, or complaint (a definition of the crisis, the thing to which the poet is responding, such as slander from enemies or military threat)
- the petition, or supplication
- the statement of confidence in God
- the vow to praise God

Some psalms that fit this pattern are 10; 35; 38; 51; 54; 64; 74; and 77.

The foregoing list of ingredients allows you to see the topical units in a lament psalm. By themselves, they do not provide a procedure for actually interacting with the lament psalms. Here is a list of things that the lament psalmist typically does, that is, a description of his strategy. The lament psalmist

- undertakes a quest to master a terrible crisis and find peace in the midst of it;
- paints a heightened and often figurative picture of the crisis;
- develops a plot conflict between good and evil;
- protests about the situation to God and undertakes a persuasive effort to move God to act; and
- finds a satisfactory solution to his problem in the form of trusting God to act.

The Occasions of Lament Psalms

Lament psalms are occasional poems—poems arising from a specific occasion. Taken as a whole, the lament psalms cover a broad range of threats, including slander from enemies, military threat, drought, disease, doubt, depression, and guilt.

Praise Psalms

The label "psalm of praise" is usually reserved for psalms that praise God specifically, not people. The praise psalm is a fixed form having three main elements:

- the call to praise (which may include as many as three things: a command to praise, the audience to whom the command is directed, and the mode of praise, such as song or shouts or strings)
- the catalog of God's praiseworthy acts and attributes
- rounding off the praise on a note of closure, such as a concluding prayer or wish

The catalog, or list, is the heart of a praise psalm, though occasionally the portrait of God takes its place. This means that a leading task when you master a praise psalm is to divide the catalog into its parts. Here are some helpful tips:

Poets praise God for his acts or his attributes, and usually both occur in a psalm of praise.

Sometimes the poem praises God for onetime acts and other times for repeated or habitual acts.

God's praiseworthy acts occur primarily in three arenas: nature or creation, history, and the personal life of the believer.

The list of actions for which God is praised turns out to be short; the psalmists keep praising God for acts of providence (the preservation of physical life), creation, judgment, and redemption/rescue/deliverance.

Sometimes the poet praises God for specific actions; at other times the acts are very general.

Sometimes the poet praises God for personal blessings and at other times for public or communal or creation-wide actions.

A few of these psalms lack the formal call to praise but in all other essentials are praise psalms. Examples are Psalms 23; 46; and 91.

perSPECTIVES
ON THE PSALMS OF PRAISE

The word *praise* originally meant "to appraise; to set a value on." From this came the meaning "to commend the worth of; to express admiration."

There cannot be such a thing as true life without praise. . . . Exalting is a part of existence. It is so much a part of it, that when one has ceased to exalt God, something else must be exalted. . . . Man must exalt something.
Claus Westermann

All enjoyment spontaneously overflows into praise. . . . Praise almost seems to be inner health made audible. . . . We delight to praise what we enjoy because the praise not merely expresses but completes the enjoyment.
C. S. Lewis

DID YOU KNOW?
The book of Psalms can be viewed as "largely a Temple collection" (C. S. Lewis), meaning that the Temple was the official repository of the poetry anthology that became the book of Psalms (the Temple was the chief poetry library, music plaza, and art exhibit for the Jewish nation).

All Jewish males were required to worship God in the Temple a minimum of three times a year, and we can infer that entire families went when possible.

A concluding note of caution: The foregoing elements of praise psalms deal mainly with the poems' content. By themselves, the elements will not help you master a praise psalm. The praise psalms are poetry first of all, requiring you to do all that poetic discourse demands of you. (For more on poetry as a form of writing, see page 237.)

Worship Psalms

After the lament and praise psalms, the most numerous category of psalms is psalms of worship, also called songs of Zion. The context for understanding these psalms includes these important considerations:

- The collection and performance of the psalms centered around worship in the Temple in Jerusalem.
- God's visible presence resided in the form of a cloud of light known by the Hebrew word *shekinah* ("glory"); this helps to explain references in the psalms to God's living or dwell-

ing in the Temple and why the sense of place is so important in the psalms of worship.

• Pilgrimages (physical journeys) to worship God in the Temple were a regular and required part of Jewish religion (Psalms 120–134 are all pilgrimage psalms).

Many psalms incorporate brief references to worship in the Temple, so it would be easy to build a composite picture of the rituals and emotions that surrounded Old Testament worship. Beyond these psalms with brief portraits of worship, some psalms are devoted entirely to the experience of worship, and these are the songs of Zion. Their differentiating trait is that the content of these psalms is composed of references *to* worship and the sentiments *of* worship. These psalms have no formal structure of their own. Their main strategy is to (1) awaken longing for worship, (2) express the emotions of delight in worshipping God in the Temple, (3) assert the value of worship, and (4) paint brief snapshots of actual worship in the Temple.

Where will we find such worship psalms? The prototypical worship psalm is Psalm 84. Other worship psalms include Psalms 27; 42–43 (a single poem); 48; and 139. In addition, Psalms 120–134 each bear the heading "A song for pilgrims ascending to Jerusalem." Pilgrims sang or recited these psalms as they "went up" to the Temple in Jerusalem. While these are all *pilgrimage poems*, they are not all worship psalms per se. They actually cover an amazing range of subjects as people took stock of their lives on the occasion of a religious retreat from ordinary life. While these songs of ascent are thus an invaluable index to the meditations and emotions of Old Testament worshippers, not all of them fit the definition of a worship psalm. Many are simply generic lyric poems.

Nature Poems

Lament and praise psalms make up well over half the Psalter, and the other big block is the worship psalms. Remaining forms, therefore, must be understood as comprising relatively small numbers. One of the most delightful categories is the nature poem.

As with the worship psalms, not all psalms into which nature finds its way are thoroughgoing nature psalms. After all, nature is the single largest source of imagery and metaphors for the psalmists: "They are like trees planted along the riverbank" (1:3); "The LORD is my rock" (18:2); "As the deer longs for streams of water, / so I long for you, O God" (42:1). Reading the psalms puts us continually in touch with elemental nature, and once we are alert to this, we can be receptive to the effects of nature images.

In addition to these continual short references to nature, there are five nature poems in the Psalter: Psalms 8; 19; 29 (the song of the thunderstorm); 104; and 148. The differentiating feature of nature poems is that they have nature as their subject. Subsidiary traits are the praise of nature (which the psalmists deflect upward to God), vivid word pictures of nature, stimulation of the feelings appropriate to nature, and exaltation of the commonplace. The nature psalms go beyond these general features of nature poetry and assert a thoroughgoing doctrine of origins (creation) and other theological principles that touch on nature.

C. S. LEWIS ON THE NATURE PSALMS

The psalms arose from "a nation of farmers."

The delight that the psalmists express in nature is "a delight which is both utilitarian and poetic."

Unlike pagan nature poetry, which populates every local stream and hill with a deity, the psalmists' doctrine of creation "in one sense empties Nature of divinity."

Because of their doctrine of creation, the psalmists' gusto extends to forces of nature that are either indifferent or actively hostile to people.

The Rest of the Psalter

If the dominant forms in the Psalter are psalms of lament, praise, worship, and nature, what makes up the rest of the Psalter? We need to stress that all of the psalms are lyric poems, so you can do a good job with any psalm by treating it as a generic lyric. Some poems are simply meditative poems, such as Psalm 1 on the godly life and Psalm 119 on God's law. Several psalms deal so thoroughly with the king that they compose a unit called royal psalms (e.g., 21; 72; 101; and 144). Scholars often have a category for psalms of thanksgiving, which express gratitude for a specific blessing from God, but the poems included in that category are mainly praise psalms (e.g., Psalms 18; 66; and 116).

Psalm 45 is an *epithalamion* (a wedding poem). Some psalms rehearse Jewish history (e.g., 78; 105; 106; 135; and 136), and others are prayers (31; 140). Psalm 73 is a psalm of personal testimony. Seven penitential psalms (6; 32; 38; 51; 102; 130; and 143) deal with sin, guilt, and forgiveness. A form known as the *encomium* praises a general character type, using such motifs as a catalog of praiseworthy acts or qualities, the superior nature of the person (often by contrast with its opposite), and the reader's being moved to emulate that person (examples are Psalms 1; 15; 112; and 128).

The Main Themes

1. We should live with God at the center of everything. The psalms embody a theocentric worldview and lifestyle, with a view toward our practicing the same.

2. The Psalms are a many-sided picture of what God is like (his attributes) and what he does (his acts). The Psalter yields a complete theology, though the doctrine of Christology is present only in latent form.

3. Human emotions not only are essential to life and health, they matter to God as well.

4. Earthly life and human endeavors in the ordinary routine are part of God's design for living. We cover nearly the whole range of human activities and callings in the psalms, with the implication that these are the spheres where the great spiritual issues are lived out.

5. Individual and corporate worship of God is central to life. Although not every psalm takes worship as its subject, its approach to all subjects (in other words, all of life) takes place in a context of worship, inasmuch as the Psalter is a collection of poems and songs used in Temple worship.

6. Beauty is important to human life and the religious life. The poetry of the psalms is a form of literary beauty that keeps pressing itself into the foreground. At the level of content, too, the psalms give us many pictures of what is beautiful—in worship, in nature, in God, in human character.

Contribution of the Book to the Bible's Story of Salvation in Christ

The most direct tie-in between the psalms and salvation history exists at the level of messianic prophecy or at the presence of "second meanings" in the psalms that were applied to Christ in the New Testament. We can say of both types of material (explicit prophecy and second meanings) that many passages in the psalms anticipate the coming of the Messiah and were fulfilled in the life of Christ. Some selective examples are Psalms 2; 22; 68:18; and 118:22-23. (J. Sidlow Baxter lists the following as "the principal Messianic psalms": 2; 8; 16; 22; 23; 24; 40; 49; 72; 87; 102; 110; and 118.)

Applying the Book

The most obvious application of the book has to do with the way in which the psalmists give free rein to all their emotions. We can infer that God

DID YOU KNOW?
- New Testament writers refer more often to Psalms than to any other Old Testament book.
- The Psalter is the longest book in the Bible.

created us as emotional beings and that the affective life is important to emotional health and to the religious walk. Perhaps we can call it God's law of introspection, meaning that we need to be honest with and true to our feelings. This does not mean that every emotion displayed in the psalms is something to emulate, just as the narrative parts of the Bible sometimes describe events that they do not prescribe for us to practice. But as J. Sidlow Baxter said, "The first great value of this Book of Psalms is that it provides for our emotions and feelings the same kind of guidance as the other Scriptures provide for our faith and actions." The psalms invite us to make our feelings the allies of our faith and to relate to God by means of them.

A second application is that we should regard all of life as belonging to God. The theocentric focus of the psalms is one of their most refreshing and instructive aspects. The imagery and references in the psalms cover all of life, teaching us the lesson that the spiritual life does not whisk us away to some otherworldly realm that serenely transcends earthly life. But we also learn from the psalms that all of life is intended to reach upward to God and a transcendent realm and that spiritual awareness must permeate all of life. Walter Brueggemann has said that "the Psalms draw our entire life under the rule of God, where everything may be submitted to the God of the gospel."

A third application grows out of the poet's task. The poet is the orator of the emotions, the one who has the words and techniques by which to express the thoughts and feelings that we, too, experience but for which we lack adequate expression. The psalmists are our representatives; they say what we want said but they say it better. The right application is to let the poets' words be our own. As part of this, the psalms can be both sung (verbatim or in paraphrase) and prayed.

A final application is that we can use the psalms as models for individual and corporate worship. They can also provide the very materials by which to worship.

PERSPECTIVES
ON THE BOOK OF PSALMS

The prayer book of the Bible. Dietrich Bonhoeffer

The heart of the Old Testament. Tremper Longman III

Here is poetry which more than vies with that of Milton and Shakespeare, yet it is the poetry of downright reality; and, as "the body is more than the raiment," so here, the reality is greater than the poetry which expresses it.
J. Sidlow Baxter

Although the Psalms are replete with all the precepts which serve to frame our life to every part of holiness, piety, and righteousness, yet they will principally teach and train us to bear the cross. John Calvin

In these busy days, it would be greatly to the spiritual profit of Christians if they were more familiar with the Book of Psalms, in which they would find a complete armory for life's battles, and a perfect supply for life's needs. Here we have both delight and usefulness, consolation and instruction. For every condition there is a psalm, suitable and elevating.
Charles Spurgeon

The Book of Psalms is a vast repository of accurate insights into what it means to be a human being. There are the heights and the depths, the glories and the horrors; hope and despair, joy and desolation. To read the psalms is to explore one's own hidden life and feelings. Chad Walsh

Most emphatically the Psalms must be read as poems; as lyrics, with all the licences and all the formalities, the hyperboles, the emotional rather than logical connections, which are proper to lyric poetry. C. S. Lewis

[In Psalms, we find] poems of orientation, poems of disorientation, and poems of new orientation. [These correspond to] the realities of human life. . . . Human life consists in satisfied seasons of well-being that evoke gratitude for the constancy of blessing. . . . Human life [also] consists in anguished seasons of hurt, alienation, suffering, and death. These evoke rage, resentment, self-pity, and hatred. . . . [Finally,] human life consists in turns of surprise when we are overwhelmed with the new gifts of God, when joy breaks through the despair. Walter Brueggemann

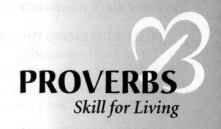

PROVERBS

Skill for Living

FORMAT. 31 chapters, 915 verses

IMPLIED PURPOSE. To lead readers to live a morally and spiritually ordered life by imparting wisdom (skill for living) that covers a wide range of human experience. Right thinking and right acting are the author's goals for his audience.

AUTHORS' PERSPECTIVE. The wise men of ancient cultures were (1) skilled observers of the human condition, (2) teachers, (3) masters of a particular kind of discourse (the proverb), and (4) authority figures who asserted their wisdom without apology or reservation (their proverbs carry their own validation, based on proven standards of human experience).

IMPLIED AUDIENCE. Technically, the recipients of wisdom literature in ancient cultures were young people, but the proverb as a literary form is so universal that the audience of the book of Proverbs is whoever wants to live the good life as defined in religious, moral, and practical terms.

WHAT UNIFIES THE BOOK. The type of thinking and writing known as wisdom literature; the proverb as the basic unit of discourse; the rootedness of the proverbs in everyday experience; wisdom and folly as the constant frame of reference; the stance of the speaker as a wise authority figure who is imparting uncontestable knowledge about life

SPECIAL FEATURES. The smallness of the individual units (the proverb) that make up the book; poetic format, including the verse form of parallelism; focus on individual conduct rather than communal life; preoccupation with everyday "secular" life (virtually no references to religious worship or ceremonies)

CHALLENGES FACING THE READER OR TEACHER OF THIS BOOK.
1. Disjointed organization
2. The need to extract meaning from individual proverbs
3. A sense of monotony if reading the book in large chunks (Chapters 1–9 and 31 are exceptions.)

HOW TO MEET THE CHALLENGES.
1. You can either accept the kaleidoscope of individual units as resembling the nature of everyday life or compose your own proverb clusters as a way of bringing more organization to the material.
2. An individual proverb requires a lot from you, including the need to supply real-life contexts for it. Resolve to "step up to the plate" and spend the amount of time an individual proverb requires.
3. Do not read long sections at one sitting.

Proverbs is written from the context of an ancient semitic society. Most people lived off the land as farmers and shepherds, thus the many references to sheep and cattle (e.g., 27:23ff.), rain (28:3), plowing (20:4), barns (3:10), and property markers (22:28). The Book also includes a number of references to urban life such as market places (20:14), city gates (1:21; 8:3), and royalty (25:6). Most of the proverbs are domestic, dealing with choices people make every day between hard work and laziness, honesty and dishonesty, thrift and prodigality, lending and borrowing, patience and anger, quietness and talkativeness, riches and poverty. They speak of family relationships, business ethics, moral choices, and inner motivation. Generally they are . . . universal in their appeal and application.

ROBERT L. ALDEN
Proverbs

Our era is known as the information age. The availability of data by means of the computer has flooded our lives with facts and figures. There is such an unquestioned assumption that mere information is beneficial that we would do well to ponder T. S. Eliot's two haunting questions: "Where is the wisdom we have lost in knowledge? Where is the knowledge we have lost in information?" The Bible agrees with Eliot's viewpoint. It elevates wisdom over information. The very concepts of wisdom and its opposite, folly, are almost devoid of meaning for us, and yet they were the very essence of reality for the wisdom teachers of the Bible.

The Form of the Book

No matter how hard commentaries and handbooks strive to find a sequential outline for Proverbs, the book remains an anthology of collected proverbs. To master this book, you need to be equipped to do the right things with individual proverbs. The most helpful information we can give you is a procedure for interpreting individual proverbs. (See "Proverb as a Form of Writing" on page 257 and "Wisdom Literature" on page 271.)

A host of specific small genres composes this anthology of proverbs. The entire book is written in the form of Hebrew poetry, which means that you cannot deal adequately with the proverbs unless you apply what you know about the language of poetry and its primary verse form in the Bible (parallelism). (For a reminder of how poetry works, see the article on page 237.) In regard to parallelism, the preferred form in Proverbs is the two-line unit as the main component of meaning.

In addition, you will find the following:

- Comparisons: "Better is a little with the fear of the LORD / than great treasure and trouble with it." (15:16, ESV)
- Contrasts: "The way of a fool is right in his own eyes, / but a wise man listens to advice." (12:15, ESV)
- Analogies: "The fruit of the righteous is a tree of life." (11:30, ESV)
- Brief portraits
- Numerical listings

The two most recurrent forms are the *saying* (an observation stated as a sentence), such as "Hope deferred makes the heart sick" (13:12), and the *exhortation*, or command, such as "Commit your actions to the LORD" (16:3).

Wisdom Literature

While the form of the book is a collection of proverbs, we need to understand that this form was the domain of ancient teachers known as wise men. Proverbial books in the Bible are thus commonly labeled wisdom literature, which is mainly a subject-matter designation. At the level of content, wisdom literature conveys not a systematic philosophy or theology but rather a worldview and a sense of life that gradually build up from specific examples. A good way to analyze the book of Proverbs is to compile your own list of generalizations about the sense of life that permeates the book.

Here are orienting assumptions that underlie the book, but these are in no sense exhaustive:

- There are standards by which we can differentiate good conduct from bad conduct.
- Actions inevitably produce predictable consequences.
- We face constant choices as we live in the world; we must make our choices in an awareness of the sovereignty of God.
- The good life requires strenuous moral effort.
- All of life is momentous.

The Story

A collection of proverbs is not a narrative, but taken together, the proverbs in this book tell a story. The most obvious character is the narrator—the speaker of the proverbs. Even though he sometimes addresses his listener as "my son," you would do well to regard this listener as Everyman, that is, yourself. You are the story's protagonist—the one who must make the great choice between wisdom and folly. In addition, in chapters 1–9 two personified women—Wisdom and Folly—figure prominently in the action.

The plot of the implied story is built around the great choice that every person needs to make between wisdom and folly. The world as portrayed in Proverbs is a cosmic battlefield between right and wrong conduct, between true and false values. The story Proverbs tells is the story of the soul's choice.

Key Characters

A gallery of memorable characters completes the cast of characters—a cast that finally includes dozens of people. The people that we meet in this book are mainly general character types. Some of these we meet repeatedly and finally get to know as fully-painted portraits: the sluggard, the adulterer, Wisdom and Folly as personified women, the drunkard, the virtuous wife. Most of the characters are presented much more briefly. For example, in a typical brief passage (18:8-12) we meet the whisperer (ESV) or gossip, the lazy person, the godly person, the rich man, and the proud person.

Unifying Elements

- The proverb as the basic unit
- Poetry as the form of discourse, coupled with parallelism as the verse form
- The sense of life that characterizes wisdom literature (See above.)
- The sheer diversity of topics, with the focus solidly on life in the everyday world instead of on specific religious practices such as worship and prayer
- An abundance of recognizable human experiences

Key Doctrines

Ethics. Most of the content of Proverbs falls into what we call morality or ethics—rules for living a moral life individually and in relationship to others in the human community.

Wisdom and Folly. It may seem odd to call wisdom and folly a doctrine, but to the ancients the concepts of wisdom and folly summed up much of what people believed about God, people, and the world.

The View of God. Not only does the name of God come up repeatedly, but if we regard God as the source of wisdom, and wisdom itself as reflecting his character, we can learn much about God from the collected proverbs in this book.

The View of the Person. From Proverbs we can also derive a full view of the person, including the individual's capacity for good and evil, wisdom and folly. Above all, the individual is assumed to have the responsibility to choose wisdom and reject folly.

DID YOU KNOW?

- Virtually every culture has used proverbs as a way of summing up its most deeply held values and moral ideals.
- In Old Testament times wise men were one of three categories of religious leaders who derived their authority from God. The other two were the priests and prophets. Jeremiah 18:18 refers to all three groups.
- The Hebrew word *masal*, commonly translated "proverb," actually covers a broad range of literary forms; the word's meaning itself—"likeness, pattern, rule"—is ambiguous.

Sanctification. The book is a call to purity, discretion, patience, and many
other virtues, some of which are seen in people's conduct in their relationships with others and some of which are inner, personal virtues.

Common Grace. Many of the proverbs contain practical wisdom that is
identical to that given by sages in surrounding pagan cultures.

How Scholars Have Defined Wisdom
As We Find It in Wisdom Literature

- "Experiential knowledge" (Gerhard von Rad)
- "The effort to discover order in human life" (Roland E. Murphy)
- "Skill for life" (R. Kent Hughes)
- "Compressed experience" (W. A. L. Elmslie)
- "A quality of mind and spirit that directs all human activity towards
  its proper end" (Dermot Cox)
- "A flash of insight into the repeatable situations of life in the world"
  (Norman Perrin)

Tips for Reading or Teaching Proverbs

From start to finish, your most important need is to be able to relish and
interpret the proverb as a literary form.

Individual proverbs suffer from being placed into an anthology. The
best context for a proverb is the real-life situation where it applies.
Whether you are simply reading through the book or teaching it, the
quality of your experience with the book of Proverbs depends on your
ability to provide a real-life context for individual proverbs, based on
either personal experience or observation. For example, we can find
illustrations of many of the proverbs in what happens on the school
playground.

Even though it is chiefly the first nine chapters that mold individual
proverbs into larger clusters on a common topic, it is relatively easy to
type up your own proverb clusters from the book as a whole. This is well
worth doing, since it enables you to turn a given topic like a prism in the
light and see complementary aspects of a topic such as money or friendship or work or laziness or destructive appetites or anger.

Above all, proverbs are a form of instruction, so read them expecting
to be instructed. Sometimes a proverb gives you a new angle on a topic.
At other times a proverb reminds you of a truth that you know but that
has become dull in your consciousness.

Even though proverbs are often phrased as observations, e.g.,

Proverb as a Form of Writing

A proverb is a concise, memorable statement of a general truth. Within the Bible itself, proverbs are sometimes called sayings. In our own vocabulary, synonyms for *proverb* include *maxim* and *aphorism*. A proverb is an insight into the repeatable situations of life, and its aim is to make an insight permanent by expressing it in a short, memorable saying. Here are some defining traits of proverbs, accompanied by hints for interpreting and teaching them:

- Proverbs are apt and memorable. Analyzing what makes a proverb compelling and arresting can yield preliminary insight into it.
- Proverbs are both simple and profound. You can enjoy the simplicity of a proverb such as "You will always harvest what you plant" (Galatians 6:7). The profundity comes from exploring in how many areas of life the principle is true.
- Proverbs are both specific and general, or universal. In the proverb "Laziness leads to a sagging roof; idleness leads to a leaky house" (Ecclesiastes 10:18), the literal picture is very specific. But the particular picture of a leaking roof is a universal metaphor for any time a lazy person is negligent of duty. We need to let the simple picture come alive in our imaginations and then analyze what the general principle is and think about ways in which it is true in life.
- Proverbs often use figurative language, as in the saying "The way of the righteous is like the first gleam of dawn, which shines ever brighter until the full light of day" (Proverbs 4:18). To interpret such a proverb, we need to give attention to figuring out how "the way of the righteous" resembles the way the light of dawn progresses to "the full light of day."
- Proverbs express experiences and truths that are always up to date and are therefore continually confirmed in our own lives and observations. Accordingly, we need to provide real-life examples or contexts for a given proverb.

Because many biblical proverbs are phrased as observations about life, it is easy to miss their deeper significance. The proverb "A person who strays from home is like a bird that strays from its nest" (Proverbs 27:8) seems on the surface to be no more than an observation about people when they are away from home. But a grid of questions will enable you to probe the deeper meanings of any proverb: (1) What value is affirmed? (2) What virtue is commended? (3) What vice is denounced? The proverb about the person away from home commends the value of wholesome home and family influence; it commends the virtue of not wandering from the moral influences of home and family, and it implicitly warns against the vice of restlessness and moral laxity that can accompany people when they are away from the restraining influence of home and family.

"A gossip goes around telling secrets, but those who are trustworthy can keep a confidence" (11:13), you will find the deeper profundity of individual proverbs if you will apply the grid that these proverbs usually *denounce a vice* and *recommend a virtue or value*. Take time to identify the vices and virtues or values in individual proverbs.

quick overview of proverbs

1:1–9:18	A unified composition constructed around a prolonged contrast between Dame Wisdom and Dame Folly
10:1–31:9	An anthology of individual proverbs and occasional proverb clusters
31:10-31	An encomium praising the ideal wife

The Flow of the Book

The Conflict between Wisdom and Folly for the Human Soul (Chapters 1–9). These chapters are distinctly different from the rest of the book. Even though they are, like the rest of the book, a collection of individual proverbs, they are arranged into clusters, and the material is highly unified and coherent. You will be able to find a unifying plot conflict between Wisdom and Folly, an implied situation of a parent teaching a child, variations on the theme of what constitutes wise conduct, proverb clusters (so that you can deal with longer units that are, in effect, mini-essays on a topic), and controlling image patterns (the path or way, jewel imagery, sexual references, the personification of Wisdom and Folly).

The Great Either-Or (Chapters 10–15). Topically, this collection of proverbs is all over the map. No continuity of thought characterizes them, so do not look for it. But virtually every verse in this six-chapter block uses the technique of antithetic parallelism, in which the two lines (a couplet) express a contrast, generally between wise behavior and foolish behavior or between good and evil. Look for two-line proverbs as the norm.

Collected Proverbs (Chapters 16–27). Again it is futile to look for a sustained flow of thought on a single topic. If you want proverb clusters, you will need to compose your own. Alternately, just allow the diversity of material to raise your consciousness on a wide range of subjects. Most of the proverbs in this unit are not *antithetical* couplets; most are simply two-line units in which the second line completes the thought of the first: "Timely advice is lovely, / like golden apples in a silver basket" (25:11).

This, Not That (Chapters 28–29). Here is another section in which the prevailing rhetorical format is to contrast good and bad, wise and foolish. But the areas of life that are thus set in contrast are miscellaneous and wide ranging.

Collected Proverbs (Chapters 30:1–31:9). Again there is no overall unity of content, but the material in this unit tends to consist of proverb clusters rather than individual proverbs: for example, three things "that amaze me" and four things "that are never satisfied."

Encomium in Praise of the Virtuous Wife (31:10-31). The book of Proverbs ends with a poetic flourish. This chapter is an encomium praising a character type (the virtuous wife and mother). The poem is an acrostic (i.e., an alphabet poem) in which the successive verses begin, in sequence, with the consecutive letters of the Hebrew alphabet. The basic structure of the poem is a catalog of the ideal wife's acts and qualities. You can analyze the portrait by noting the specific acts and qualities for which the wife is praised and the range of spheres in which she acts. The domestic sphere is dominant, as suggested by the way in which references to the wife's relationship to her family form an envelope around the other material.

KEY VERSE
"Fear of the LORD is the foundation of true knowledge" (1:7). Even though most of the proverbs cast the spotlight on everyday life rather than on overtly religious experience, this motto for the book as a whole lets us know that the choices we make in all areas of life are ultimately spiritual and moral in nature. The life of the wise person is a life of faith in God and obedience to him.

The Main Themes

1. There is a standard of conduct that allows us to know the difference between good and bad behavior: Morality is absolute, not relative.
2. In the everyday circumstances of life we continually face the need to choose between wise and foolish behavior.
3. The choices we make have predictable consequences.
4. We can attain the good life if we make the right choices.
5. God is the sovereign ruler and judge of the world.

Contribution of the Book to the Bible's Story of Salvation in Christ

We need to resist simplistic spiritualizing. The fact that Jesus is the wisdom of God (1 Corinthians 1:24) does not mean that Christ is a character in the book of Proverbs. Rather, it means that Jesus was the perfect human, the model for how to put the wisdom of the book of Proverbs into practice. Christ is the ultimate example of the wisdom that Proverbs holds up for emulation. In addition, the moment we dip into Proverbs, we are aware that we are looking into a mirror that exposes our own failings, and in that sense we can read the book as pointing to our need for a Savior.

Applying the Book

The book of Proverbs is the Bible's most sustained collection of specific rules for living. This is true even when a proverb is an observation rather than a command. To apply the book, we need to do these things: (1) ascertain the exact meaning of each proverb, (2) be convinced in our minds that what we read is true, and (3) seek the Holy Spirit's help to practice what we know and believe.

PERSPECTIVES
ON THE BOOK OF PROVERBS

Some descriptors of the message of Proverbs: "a life well managed" (Derek Kidner), "be skillful" (Warren W. Wiersbe), "a seminar on how to live" (Paul R. House), "a mirror held up to life" (Dermot Cox), "an ancient book of timeless advice." (Robert L. Alden)

Proverbs is truly a collection of sayings with no arrangement, outline, order, or progression. When you think about it, however, life is like that. We try to bring order to life, but opportunities, crises, and unexpected intrusions come. . . . Perhaps that is why Proverbs comes to us in the form it does. Robert L. Alden

The sage concerns himself with people as plain, ordinary individuals who live in the world, and with the wisdom and folly of their attitudes and actions in the common things of life. We will therefore find he has much to say on a wide range of very mundane and practical matters like bringing up children, spreading gossip, talking too much, keeping bad company, unscrupulous business practices, and even good table manners. Kenneth T. Aitken

A moral code undergirds [the book of Proverbs], but the real intent is to train a person, to form character, to show what life is really like and how best to cope with it. The favored approach is to seek out comparisons or analogies between the human situation and all else (animals and the rest of creation). Roland E. Murphy

The goal of all wisdom was the formation of character. Instruction, which took place initially in a family setting, focused on individuals rather than society in general. James L. Crenshaw

As we are invited to reflect on the world and on human experience, we can learn lessons which help us to cope better, to manage our affairs, to avoid making damaging mistakes, to foster better relationships; in summary, to live more in line with God's ways. Through this range of proverbs, parables, sayings and riddles, we are brought face to face with a variety of human situations which point us to lessons in prudence, diligence, hard work and justice. . . . Through it all [runs] the [theme] of God's wisdom as the ordering pattern for the good life. David Atkinson

ECCLESIASTES

*Life under the Sun and
above the Sun*

FACT SHEET

FORMAT. 12 chapters, 222 verses

IMPLIED PURPOSES. To make readers feel the futility of life lived by purely earthly values and to lead them to seek satisfaction in God and spiritual values

AUTHOR'S PERSPECTIVE. The author writes as a wise man who looks back over his restless years of wandering, with a view toward encouraging his readers to avoid the dead ends that he wasted his time pursuing.

IMPLIED AUDIENCE. Although the author may have had young people particularly in mind (see 11:9 and 12:1), the human longing to find satisfaction and meaning in life is universal, so the lessons of the book are applicable at every stage of life.

WHAT UNIFIES THE BOOK. Image patterns, such as eating and drinking and chasing after the wind; repeated phrases, especially "under the sun" and "meaningless," or "vanity" (ESV); the motif of searching; the predictable alternation of positive and negative passages; the confessional mode in which the author not only describes the dead ends he pursued but phrases them in such a way as to confess his folly in his varied experiments in living

SPECIAL FEATURES. Despite its brevity, the book covers virtually all of life: work, leisure, entertainment, time, worship, nature, money, death, sleep, eating, drinking, sex, farming, commerce, education, government. In covering all those areas, the book is perhaps the most modern in spirit of any book in the Bible, especially in its portrayal of an acquisitive and hedonistic lifestyle.

CHALLENGES FACING THE READER OR TEACHER OF THIS BOOK.
1. The kaleidoscopic shifting from one topic to another, or the

way in which the book shuttles back and forth between positive and negative attitudes

2. Finding God's perspective on life, which is also the author's final perspective, arrived at after the author pursued alternate perspectives

HOW TO MEET THE CHALLENGES.
1. Follow a reliable outline of the book.
2. Always ask whether a given passage is one of the negative, "under the sun" passages or one of the positive, God-centered passages (which we can assume to be God's perspective as well).

THE MOST COMMON MISCONCEPTION ABOUT THIS BOOK. That it is mainly negative (i.e., a book without hope) and its positive message emerges only at the very end. Actually, the positive note is interspersed throughout the book, and the ending is more mixed than the "positive conclusion" theory would have you believe.

Most people, if they had really learned to look into their own hearts, would know that they do want, and want acutely, something that cannot be had in this world. There are all sorts of things in this world that offer to give it to you, but they never quite keep their promise. The longings which arise in us when we first fall in love, or first think of some foreign country, or first take up some subject that excites us, are longings which no marriage, no travel, no learning, can really satisfy. . . . There was something we grasped at, in that first moment of longing, which just fades away in the reality.

C. S. LEWIS
Mere Christianity

Positive | 12:9-14 Conclusion: The Speaker's Quest Satisfied

Positive | 11:1–12:7 Life above the Sun: Enjoying Life with God at the Center

Negative | 9:11–10:20 Life under the Sun: Observations about Human Folly

Positive | 9:7-10 Living with Zest: An Alternative to the Problems Just Posed

Negative | 6:1–9:6 Life under the Sun: Observations about Life's Disappointments

Positive | 5:18-20 Life above the Sun: The God-Centered Life

Negative | 4:1–5:17 Life under the Sun: How Life Fails to Satisfy

Positive | 3 Two Views of Time: Human and Divine Perspectives

Positive | 2:24-26 Life above the Sun: The God-Centered Life

Negative | 1:4–2:23 Life under the Sun: Cycles, Knowledge, Pleasure, Wealth, Work

Negative | 1:1-3 Introduction: Life Is a Vapor

AN OUTLINE OF
ECCLESIASTES

What can you do when the good life doesn't satisfy? This is the question that the writer of Ecclesiastes asks in the book that has been called the most contemporary book in the Bible. The writer of the book looked for satisfaction and the meaning of life in all the same places that people in our society look for them. He tried money and the things that it can buy. He built an extravagant house. He tried sex and self-indulgence. He tried knowledge and power. He lost himself in both his work and his leisure pursuits.

Ecclesiastes provides an answer to the question of what we can do when the good life doesn't satisfy. Far from being the problem book, as some have claimed, Ecclesiastes expresses the most basic theme of the Bible: Life apart from God and spiritual values is meaningless. Life with God at the center opens the door to enjoying earthly life.

The Form of the Book

As a book of wisdom literature, Ecclesiastes comes to us in the form of collected proverbs. (For a primer on the proverb as a form of writing, see page 271; for information on wisdom literature, see page 257.) To succeed with the book, you need to be able to interpret proverbs. What makes this collection of proverbs relatively easy to read is that it consists largely of proverb clusters, i.e., groups of proverbs on a common theme.

The writer was also a master of poetry. He wrote in the verse form of parallelism, and he spoke naturally in images (words naming actions or things, such as *sun, wind, gardens*), metaphors (implied comparisons, such as "her passion is a trap"), and similes (comparisons that use *like* or *as*, such as "like chasing the wind").

The Story

Although not structured as a story, Ecclesiastes nonetheless tells the story of the author's quest to find meaning and satisfaction in his life. By a series of recollections, reflections, and mood pieces, the writer chronicles his attempts to find satisfaction in all the wrong places. He tells his story in the past tense and from the safe position of someone who eventually found what he was looking for. Above all, this book records one person's search to find the meaning of life.

What's in a Name?

The title by which we know the book derives from the title given to it in the Septuagint (the Greek translation of the Old Testament). It signifies "the preacher."

The name by which the author calls himself is the Hebrew word *Qoheleth*, which literally means "the collector or gatherer." This could refer either to the person who gathers or convenes an assembly or to an author who collects proverbs (see 12:9-12). Acceptable translations include "the preacher," "the teacher," "the philosopher," and "the writer."

Key Words and Phrases

The most important phrase in the book is *under the sun* (or variants such as *under heaven*), which occurs more than thirty times in twelve chapters. The phrase denotes life lived by purely earthly values, without recourse to spiritual and heavenly values.

Another key to the book is the word translated "vanity" or "meaningless." In the original, the word means "vapor" or "breath." Appearing thirty-one times, this word suggests the fleetingness and emptiness of life without God at the center.

Image patterns also recur and help to unify the book. They include eating, drinking, toil, wind, sleep, death, and the cycles of nature.

The Structure

Ecclesiastes is organized as a prolonged contrast between two viewpoints. In terms of the space devoted to it, the major theme is the emptiness of life under the sun. In these passages the author tells the story of his futile quest to find meaning and satisfaction apart from God. These passages do not represent the author's philosophy of life, and they should accordingly not be quoted out of context. We might say that these passages are truthful to life and are therefore normative, representing the author's provisional conclusions about the meaning of life. They are truthful without telling the ultimate Truth.

TEN THINGS THAT DO NOT SATISFY WITHOUT GOD IN ONE'S LIFE
- knowledge (1:12-18)
- pleasure (2:1-11)
- a big house (2:4)
- work and job (2:18-23)
- keeping up with the Joneses (4:4)
- fame or power (4:13-16)
- money (5:10-17)
- children (6:3)
- long life (6:6)
- food (6:7)

Another thing to note about the structure is that it follows the ancient Hebrew way of conducting an argument, which is also increasingly common in our own culture. The author does not argue abstractly but rather gives multiple examples of the truth he claims. He repeats his main points so often that we finally believe the case he makes.

The counterpoint is the glimpses the author gives us of life above the sun, with God at the center of life and with a firm grip on spiritual values. These passages are the writer's final verdict on life.

The book shuttles back and forth between the two types of passages. Most of the negative passages contain the phrase *under the sun*. By contrast, most of the positive passages refer conspicuously to God.

Contrary to a common misconception, the positive affirmation does not come only at the end of the book. In fact, the first God-centered passage occurs early, in 2:24–26. Here is the opening part of that passage: "I decided there is nothing better than to enjoy food and drink and to find satisfaction in work. Then I realized that these pleasures are from the hand of God."

The Aim of the Book

The writer's aim is a persuasive and emotional, or affective, one. He wants us to feel the emptiness of life under the sun and the attractiveness of a God-filled life that leads to contentment with one's earthly lot.

Key Doctrines

The Sovereignty of God. The book portrays God as the creator, judge, and ultimate goal of human existence.

The Nature of People. People are created to find fulfillment in God. They are restless until they find their rest in him.

The Fall. Behind the speaker's futility of life apart from God and his restless search for meaning lies the fall of the human race into sin (see 7:29).

The All-Sufficiency of God. The speaker ultimately finds that the way to find meaning and satisfaction in all areas of life is to live in relationship with God.

Tips for Reading or Teaching Ecclesiastes

Before doing anything else with a given passage, determine whether it is one of the "under the sun" passages or a God-centered alternative to the negative passages. Then interpret the passage in light of that context.

Ecclesiastes has been called the most contemporary book in the Bible. Be sure to draw real-life parallels to the experiences the author records. For example, what forms does the mad urge to acquire possessions (2:4–8) take in your own life? (The picture is as up to date as the latest mail-order catalog.) Another way to say this is that the best confirmation of the truthfulness of this book's proverbs is a long, hard look around you, including the advertisements in the daily news.

The proverb clusters that make up much of this book have the effect of turning a prism in a light, as a central theme is viewed from a variety of angles. Take time to let the theme and its variations sink in. The book of Ecclesiastes is a meditative book; read it in a contemplative way. The format of the proverb lends itself to a meditative approach.

Ecclesiastes is also an affective (related to one's emotions) book, filled with mood pieces. Open yourself up to the moods and feelings it awakens.

quick overview of ecclesiastes

1:1-3	Introduction to the author and major theme
1:4–2:23	Meditations on the futility of life under the sun
2:24–3:22	Positive reflections on life with God at the center and on time
4:1–12:8	Alternating sections asserting that life lived by purely earthly values is empty and that focusing on God can impart meaning and joy to earthly life
12:9-14	Conclusion—the speaker's goal attained

The Flow of the Book

The key to the book's organization is to be aware of the alternating negative and positive passages. A few of the passages are mixed. Here is a guided tour through the book:

Introduction to the Book (1:1-3). The author's forthrightness is one of his most appealing traits. In three short verses he introduces himself, the major theme (life under the sun is meaningless), the key phrase (*under the sun*), and the key word (literally *vapor*, variously translated as "vanity" or "meaningless").

KEY VERSE
"Vapor of vapors" (literal translation of 1:2). The negative theme of Ecclesiastes is highlighted by this metaphor that occurs more than thirty times in the original text of the book.

Life under the Sun, Part 1 (1:4–2:23). The story begins with several mood pieces in which the author describes some of the dead ends where the human race (and he himself) tries to find satisfaction in life. Here are the dead ends:

- The meaningless cycles of life (1:4-11)
- Human knowledge and wisdom (1:12-18)
- Human achievement that will live on after a person's death (2:1-11)
- Wisdom and foolishness (2:12-17)
- Work (2:18-23)

The right way to assimilate these five scenarios is to think about ways in which people in our own culture look for meaning in the same places.

Life above the Sun, Part 1 (2:24-26). Here is the first God-centered passage in the book—the antidote to life under the sun. In this short, snappy passage, the speaker finds meaning in the very same places (eating, drinking, work) where he had earlier declared life to be meaningless. By looking closely at the passage, you can begin to see what things make up the author's solution to the problem of meaninglessness in life.

Two Views of Time (Chapter 3). This chapter falls into two sections: a human view of time, embodied in the world's most famous meditation on time (3:1-8), and God's view of time (3:9-22). Within an awareness that people are subject to the limitations of time, both passages are positive. To get at the heart of this difficult chapter, just note the implied ideas about time.

KEY VERSE

"[God] has planted eternity in the human heart" (3:11). This means that people have a capacity for transcendence—for God and for a spiritual reality that lies above the sun.

Life under the Sun, Part 2 (4:1–5:17). Observe first how the writer keeps the quest motif alive in our awareness by such formulas as "again I observed," "then I observed," "I observed yet another example." Then note the places where he sees life as meaningless (e.g., pictures of oppression, of dissatisfaction in the desire to "get ahead" financially, of the fickleness of fame, of the inability of money to satisfy permanently and at the deepest level). Although the general mood of this section is negative, twice there is a modified or partial solution to the problem posed by life under the sun: Human companionship (4:9-12) and proper worship of God (5:1-7) are alternatives to the negative features of life.

The Human Quest Satisfied, or Life above the Sun, Part 2 (5:18-20). This typical God-centered passage emphasizes the earthly enjoyment that is possible in a life with God at the center. One can profitably analyze what things make this passage different from the preceding "under the sun" passages. By this time it is obvious that the God-centered passages are much briefer than the melancholy "under the sun" sections.

Life under the Sun, Part 3 (6:1–9:6). This section is a virtual recap of life under the sun. You can get a handle on the passage by noting the

Wisdom Literature

Wisdom literature is the name given to books of the Bible—or units within books—made up of proverbs. (For information on the proverb as a form of writing, see the article on page 257.) The term *wisdom writing* refers not so much to the proverbial form of such writing but to the sense of life that emerges from collected proverbs. The two most recurrent forms in which the wisdom writers express their content is (1) the command or exhortation ("Don't fret because of evildoers," Proverbs 24:19) and (2) the observation ("Godliness makes a nation great, but sin is a disgrace to any people," Proverbs 14:34). Here are some identifying features of the sense of life that gradually builds up as we read the wisdom literature of the Bible:

• The wisdom writers are practical in outlook. In fact, wisdom in the Bible is skill for living. These writers are not mainly interested in abstract thought but in ways of behaving. The emphasis in wisdom literature is moral rather than devotional or spiritual.

• Wisdom writers root their observations and commands in everyday human experience. The proverbs of the Bible cover nearly all human activities and professions. Many of the proverbs of the Bible are more secular than religious. Examples include the proverb about cheerful early risers (Proverbs 27:14), the description of the diligent farmer (Proverbs 27:23-27), advice about how to handle one's money (Ecclesiastes 11:1-2), and the observation that "worry weighs a person down" (Proverbs 12:25). Appeals to everyday experience and to nature reinforce the "common experience" atmosphere of wisdom literature, as in "The tongue is a flame of fire" (James 3:6). Wisdom literature thus lets us know that the life of faith does not whisk us away to some spiritual realm removed from everyday life. Instead, it is in the earthly routine that we live out the issues of faith.

• Because the wisdom writers primarily observe life, their utterances are not phrased with the same kind of divine authority that the statements of the prophets have. The prophets speak the voice of God to people. The Bible's wisdom teachers speak a word of testimony and observation to their fellow humans.

• Wisdom writing views life in terms of a great antithesis—a great either-or. As we read, we are continually confronted with such ultimate contrasts as good and evil, wisdom and foolishness. The result is that we feel that life presents us with an endless succession of choices and that character and destiny consist of the choices that we make.

variations on the theme of the inability of earthly life to satisfy human longings. Do not look for a sustained line of argument or story line; instead look for individual proverbs or proverb clusters on the futility of life.

An Alternative to the Problems Surveyed in the Preceding Meditation (9:7-10). These verses contain a zestful command to enjoy earthly life.

KEY VERSE

"Here now is my final conclusion: Fear God and obey his commands, for this is everyone's duty" (12:13). This is the goal of the speaker's quest, the secret end toward which the book of Ecclesiastes has tended from the beginning.

Life under the Sun, Part 4 (9:11–10:20). The news is not *all* bad in this section, but in the wide-angle view that we are taking here, we mainly get more melancholy observations about the inability of life in this world to provide happiness. Continue to note the range of experiences the author covers, along with the reasons, stated or implied, why life comes up empty. Read with an awareness that the form of the book is collected proverbs, not a single line of thought or a story line. If you are perplexed after meditating on individual proverbs, either read on and be content with the overall message of futility or consult a verse-by-verse commentary.

Life above the Sun, Part 3 (11:1–12:8). We now get the climactic affirmation of how to find meaning and satisfaction in life, even though this theme appears in quite different forms, as follows:

- Meditations on being purposeful in an uncertain world (11:1-8): These eight verses are arranged by pairs that balance something negative about life with a command to do something. For example, the first two verses advise that even though the future is uncertain (the negative), we should be generous with our money or, alternately, diversify our investments (the positive).
- A command to young people to enjoy life but to do so with an awareness of God as judge (11:9-10)
- A command to young people to remember God in their youth, before old age gradually makes life a physical burden and ends in death (12:1-8)

Conclusion (12:9-14). Here the writer summarizes how he composed his book (12:9-10), admonishes the reader to pay attention to the truth of what he has written (12:11-12), and offers his final comment on how to find meaning in life (12:13-14). The last two verses are the goal at which the writer arrived in his quest to find a resting place.

The Main Themes

1. Life apart from God and spiritual values is empty and meaningless.
2. Many things in life promise satisfaction, but they never quite keep their promise.
3. Despite that, people naturally pursue happiness in places and ways that cannot meet their deepest human needs.
4. The inevitable result of trying to get more out of life than it has to offer is disillusionment.
5. The corrective to such disillusionment is to look for one's satisfaction in God and heavenly values.
6. Paradoxically, once a person relegates earthly values to the periphery and places ultimate allegiance in God and spiritual values, earthly pursuits turn out to offer meaning and joy after all.

Contribution of the Book to the Bible's Story of Salvation in Christ

As Christian readers contemplate this book's exposé of all human attempts to find satisfaction and meaning in earthly life by itself, they perceive the emptiness of life at ground level as an absence of Christ—a Christ-shaped vacuum, someone has called it. By implication, then, Christian readers assimilate the book as expressing the need for Christ.

Applying the Book

It is easy to apply the message of Ecclesiastes because its themes are so universal. A good starting premise is that people still search for meaning and satisfaction in the same places where the writer of Ecclesiastes searched. We should therefore ask continually what the modern parallels are to the places in which the writer tried to find happiness.

Second, the book brings to our consciousness a whole array of topics and experiences that are very close to our daily lives. As we work our way through Ecclesiastes, we should take time to ponder what our own experiences and attitudes are toward such issues as work, enjoyment, death, unsatisfied longing, and the cycles of life and nature.

Third, one thing that makes the book of Ecclesiastes seem modern is that it falls into the category of protest literature (literature in which the writer expresses a protest against something). It is useful to note the things against which the writer protests, why he protests, and what he sets up as an alternative.

Finally, the God-centered passages in Ecclesiastes constitute an accurate picture of the good life—life as God meant it to be and as it can be. We can therefore keep a list of the ways in which God intends for us to live.

PERSPECTIVES
ON THE BOOK OF ECCLESIASTES

The truest of all books. American novelist Herman Melville

The noblest, the wisest, and the most powerful expression of man's life upon this earth—and also the highest flower of poetry, eloquence, and truth. American novelist Thomas Wolfe

A book of comfort. Martin Luther

The human soul is restless till it rests in God. Augustine of Hippo

The most moving Messianic prophecy in the Old Testament.
H. W. Hertzberg

The book of hope above all others. Jacques Ellul

At bottom we find the axiom of all the wise men of the Bible, that the fear of the Lord is the beginning of wisdom. But . . . his main approach is . . . to see how far a man will get with no such basis. He puts himself—and us—in the shoes of the humanist or secularist. . . . If there is little left after this analysis, it is exactly what the writer intends. . . . He is demolishing to build. Derek Kidner

A Christ-Shaped Vacuum. Robert Short

[The author] writes from concealed premises, and his book is in reality a major work of apologetic. . . . His book is in fact a critique of secularism and of secularized religion. G. S. Hendry

SONG OF SONGS
The Bible's Love Song

FORMAT. 8 chapters, 117 verses

IMPLIED PURPOSES. To express the feelings of romantic love between a man and a woman and to celebrate romantic passion and its culmination in marriage

AUTHOR'S PERSPECTIVE. Probably written by a poet in Solomon's court, the book enters into the spirit of the courtship and wedding of Solomon and his beloved. He ascribes many of the feelings to the lovers themselves so that we feel as though we are directly sharing the feelings of the lovers.

IMPLIED AUDIENCE. The two lovers assume each other as their listener. In effect, we overhear the lovers as they address each other. The poet himself does not address the reader. All we can say is that he assumes that love is a universal experience and an emotion of interest to everyone.

WHAT UNIFIES THE BOOK. The experiences and moods of romantic love; the presence of the two lovers; emotional intensity; pastoral (rustic) imagery; extravagance of poetry; figurative rather than literal discourse

SPECIAL FEATURES. A highly poetic style that is at the opposite pole from ordinary speech; a nearly unrelieved intensity of passionate emotion from start to finish; content arranged as an anthology of separate love poems dealing with a single romance; the presence of specific genres of love poetry, such as the praise of the beloved and the invitation to the beloved to go on a walk

CHALLENGES FACING THE READER OR TEACHER OF THIS BOOK.
1. A highly poetic style that requires an ability to understand and enjoy poetry
2. Frequent comparison of the lovers to objects in nature and life.

This obligates the reader to decide *how* the beloved is like the things to which he or she is compared.

3. The physical attractiveness of the beloved and the passions of both lovers expressed with a frankness, intensity, and intimacy that can easily make us feel uncomfortable

4. The kaleidoscopic structure of the book

HOW TO MEET THE CHALLENGES.

1. Take as much time as necessary to master poetry and to read it slowly and meditatively.

2. Operate on the premise that the comparisons are usually symbolic rather than pictorial.

3. Recognize that the presence of this book in the Bible shows that God intends us to affirm and feel comfortable with the human body and with sexual passion.

4. Either stare at the book until you see how the units are structured, or consult several commentaries to see how they divide the material.

THE MOST COMMON MISCONCEPTION ABOUT THIS BOOK. That its subject is not romantic passion but solely the spiritual relationship between Christ and the church

There are sweet and bittersweet episodes in the Song. There is joy and excitement in the presence of the beloved. . . . The Song celebrates human sexuality as a fact of life, God-given, to be enjoyed within the confines of a permanent, committed relationship. . . . What is celebrated here is total dedication to the beloved other, a permanent obligation gladly assumed. The Song is an extended commentary on the creation story—an expansion of the first recorded love-song in history [Genesis 2:23].

G. LLOYD CARR

"For lo, my love doth in herself contain / All this world's riches that may far be found" (Edmund Spenser). "For thy sweet love remembered such wealth brings / That then I scorn to change my state with kings" (William Shakespeare). "So fold thyself, my dearest, thou, and slip / Into my bosom and be lost in me" (Alfred, Lord Tennyson).

Love poets in all times and places have stated their passions in extravagant terms. The result is intensified romantic feeling expressed in heightened language. One of the best preparations for reading Song of Songs in the spirit in which it is written is to read an anthology of English and American love poetry.

The Form of the Book

Song of Songs is an anthology of love poems. (For reminders on how poetry works, see page 237.) Although this collection of love lyrics is based on a story of courtship and marriage, it is not structured as a story. It is instead organized as a collection of poetic fragments.

Song of Songs is not simply love poetry but something more specific known as *pastoral* love poetry. This means that the poet portrays Solomon and his beloved as a shepherd and shepherdess. (Perhaps the Shulamite girl really was from the farm, but we know that Solomon was not.) Pastoral poetry is a branch of nature poetry, and as we read Song of Songs, we are constantly aware that the action is taking place in a partly imaginary world of ideally ardent lovers in an ideally flowery and fruitful landscape.

Key Places and Characters

Despite the pastoral (rural) setting, the world of the royal court is always breaking through that facade, as in references to a banqueting house and the city of Jerusalem and a royal bower. All we need to know in this regard is that pastoral poetry has usually been written by city poets who use the pastoral imagery as a metaphor for real-life persons, often persons of high standing.

SEVEN THINGS LOVE POETS LOVE TO DO
- portray the emotions of romantic love in a heightened form
- have lovers express their feelings to their beloved
- celebrate the beauty of the beloved, often by listing his or her attractive features
- portray love as unfolding in an idealized natural setting
- compare either the romantic relationship or the beauty of the beloved to things in nature: a woman to a garden, for example, or the delights of being together to sitting in the shade of a tree and eating its fruit
- invite the beloved to the life of mutual love (sometimes expressed metaphorically as going for a walk in nature)
- portray typical moments in a romance: a kiss, a parting, a walk, a wedding

Song of Songs presents three named characters: the central couple in the romance and a group of women called the daughters of Jerusalem. The main action—courtship, wedding, and marriage—is a quest story in which both lovers are in a quest for satisfaction in love. The individual poems express that quest in terms of romantic longing, frustration of the longing by momentary roadblocks (such as physical separation or the need for love to run its course), and satisfaction of the longing in moments of physical presence and union.

THE STRUCTURE OF THE BOOK

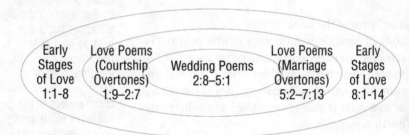

Early Stages of Love 1:1-8

Love Poems (Courtship Overtones) 1:9–2:7

Wedding Poems 2:8–5:1

Love Poems (Marriage Overtones) 5:2–7:13

Early Stages of Love 8:1-14

What You Need to Know about the Chart
- The Song of Solomon is structured in such a way that we move through a series of concentric rings as we progress through the book. After reaching the midpoint, we retread material similar to that presented in the first half, but in reverse order.
- As odd as it may seem by our taste, the last chapter makes us end where we began—at an early stage of the romance.
- Although it seems plausible to interpret the first group of love poems as courtship lyrics and the second group as marriage lyrics, the sentiments are actually very similar. In fact, many of the fragments that appear in the book are universal and could occur at any point in the couple's relationship.

A major hurdle in mastering this book is its kaleidoscopic organization. There is no smooth flow from one poem to the next. Often we are taken right inside the flow of a character's feelings, a technique modern literature calls *stream of consciousness*. Your best strategy is not to worry unduly about divisions but simply to give yourself to the fluid nature of the material.

What about All Those Comparisons?

One of the chief difficulties with Song of Songs for a modern reader is not knowing what to do with the extravagant and unexpected comparisons in the book: The woman is likened to "a mare among Pharaoh's chariots" (1:9, ESV), the man to an apple tree (2:3), and the woman's teeth to a flock of sheep (4:2). Here are the basic principles to follow when assimilating such comparisons:

- The comparisons are not intended as literal comparisons.
- The primary frame of reference is not visual.
- What the beloved has in common with the thing to which he or she is compared is the *quality* of that thing (the woman's teeth share certain *qualities* with twin sheep coming up from the washing—whiteness, wetness, symmetrical arrangement, flawlessness).
- Above all, it is the superlative quality that the lovers share with the things to which they are compared (they are compared to *the best things* in nature).

DID YOU KNOW?
Song of Songs does not mention the name of God, but this does not mean that a divine perspective is missing. The very fact that this collection of love songs appears in the Bible shows that God approves of romantic and sexual passion between a man and a woman.

The most important strategy is just to ask what familiar aspect of romantic love the poet seems to be metaphorically portraying in a given statement. For example, the woman's request to know where her beloved pastures his flocks (1:7) expresses a desire to be with him. The invitation to the beloved to go for a walk in the countryside (2:10-13) is actually an invitation to share the life of mutual love. Entering the garden to satisfy one's appetite (4:16–5:1) is a metaphoric picture of consummating physical love after marriage.

How to Avoid Misreading Song of Songs

There is no evidence that the author of Song of Songs intended his statements as an allegory of the love between Christ and a believer. When preachers or interpreters apply phrases from Song of Songs to the relationship between Christ and the church, what they are actually doing is reaching into the book for metaphors. This is not necessarily wrong, but we should not confuse it with interpreting the book as the writer composed and intended it. Many interpreters have allegorized Song of Songs, either because they do not know how to assimilate love poetry or because they believe that the Bible is more "spiritual" than to endorse physical, sexual love.

Key Doctrines

The Ethics of Romantic Love and Marriage. Song of Songs shows romantic love and wedded sexuality to be good and ennobling, awakening a sense of beauty and enriching those who are in love.

Creation. Although a doctrine of creation is not asserted directly, this collection of love poems that are also nature poems tells us much about the way in which God created people. It implicitly affirms the goodness of the physical world and the human body.

Latent Christology. Although the writer intended the book as a collection of love poems, the fact that the Bible as a whole uses the love relationship as a metaphor for divine-human love allows us to understand something of the love between Christ and the believer from the love between Solomon and his bride.

Tips for Reading or Teaching Song of Songs

The most important thing is to read this anthology of lyrics as love poetry. You and your students need to get over any inhibitions about romantic passion, as well as any feelings that love poetry is silly. Love poetry is one of the largest categories of literature. If you are unacquainted with it, this is your chance to remedy that.

One of the categories of truth that this book expresses is truthfulness to human experience and especially truthfulness to the emotions that make up romantic love. Do not reduce the book to a set of ideas. The first item on your agenda is to relive the emotions that the poet asks you to share.

This book is the very touchstone of poetry. Take the time to refresh your understanding of how poetry works, and then read the book in light of that understanding.

Song of Songs is not an allegory. The fact that others have allegorized it does not make it an allegorical book. The most that we can say in that direction is that there are *analogies* or *parallels* between the human love the couple expresses to each other and divine-human love.

Do not try to read this collection of love lyrics as a story. Its structure is a kaleidoscopic collection of fragments that follow a stream-of-conciousness organization.

The Flow of the Book

Introduction to the Festivities (1:1-8). The purpose of the opening verses is to give us our first signposts to what will follow. If we stare at the verses long enough, we can discern important things about (1) the two lovers, (2) the setting (a fictional rustic setting), (3) the main action (the quest to find satisfaction in love), and (4) the poetic style.

quick overview of song of songs

1:1	Title
1:2-8	Introduction to the couple, the setting, the main action (the quest to find satisfaction in love), and the style of the book
1:9–2:7	The lovers' dialogue
2:8–5:1	Wedding poems
5:2–7:13	Songs of two people in love
8:1-14	Miscellaneous romantic fragments, including the climax toward which the whole book moves (8:6-7, the woman's plea for permanence in love)

Love Poems (1:9–2:7). The background section flows naturally into the courtship that we observe in this section. The main vehicle is a rapid-fire, back-and-forth dialogue between the man and the woman. The main type of truth conveyed is emotional truth, as the lovers express how they feel about each other and their mutual love.

Wedding Poems (2:8–5:1). The technical name for a wedding poem like Song of Songs is *epithalamion* (from the Greek for "on the marriage chamber"). Here it consists of a highly stylized version of common wedding rituals—the pastoral invitation to marriage (metaphorically stated as an invitation to go for a walk in the country), the groom's arrival for the wedding, the superlative beauty of the bride, and references to the sexual consummation of the couple's love.

KEY VERSE
"My beloved is mine, and I am his" (2:16, ESV). For the two lovers in this collection of love poems, the thing that really matters is their mutual possession of each other.

More Songs of Two People in Love (5:2–7:13). With still more sensory imagery and passionate language, we continue to experience the situations and emotions of love: separation, anticipation, reunion, admiration of the beloved. The main business is not to state a series of ideas but to express the experiences and emotions of romantic passion.

Early Experiences of Love (Chapter 8). It seems odd to us, but the sentiments and experiences expressed in the last chapter belong to the early stages of a romance: the wish that the parental home would welcome the beloved (vv. 1-3), impatience in the progress of the romance (v. 4), recollection of a date (v. 5), a request for permanence in love (vv. 6-7), the protection of the maiden's chastity by her older brothers (vv. 8-10).

The Main Themes

1. God wants his creatures to enjoy and celebrate life in this world.
2. Romantic love and human sexuality are good when people pursue them as God intended.
3. Even though the relationship between husband and wife is private in many of its dimensions, marriage occurs in a communal context.
4. The physical world, including nature and human appetites, is good in principle.

KEY VERSES
"Set me as a seal upon your heart, as a seal upon your arm, for love is strong as death. . . . Many waters cannot quench love, neither can floods drown it" (8:6-7, ESV).

This is the climax or moment of epiphany toward which the whole book moves. It expresses the ideal of permanence in romantic love and explains exactly what type of love the individual poems celebrate. Seals were used to claim possession, and they were worn on the hand or around the neck (i.e., to symbolize closeness to the beloved).

Contribution of the Book to the Bible's Story of Salvation in Christ

There is a latent Christology at work in the sense that the Bible as a whole repeatedly uses the analogy of human marriage and sex to portray the relationship between Christ and the believer or the church. Thus many of the individual expressions in the Song of Songs can be applied as showing us dimensions of being united to Christ. In a famous New Testament passage describing godly married love between husband and wife (Ephesians 5:22-33), the author suddenly shifts gears and makes the statement, "I am saying that it refers to Christ and the church" (v. 32, ESV).

Applying the Book

The Song of Songs does not assert ideas; it embodies emotions. We should operate on the presupposition that the romantic emotions the book portrays are normative; that is, they are intended as examples for us to practice in our own lives. The love is romantic, sexual, refined, idealized, and devoted to the beloved. This is God's design for human living.

In addition to praising romantic love, the Song of Songs exalts marriage specifically. It expresses variations on the principle stated in Hebrews 13:4: "Let marriage be held in honor among all, and let the marriage bed be undefiled" (ESV).

There is also an aesthetic application of this book. Beauty is everywhere in the Song of Songs—in the exalted poetry, in the pictures of nature, in the attractiveness the lovers find in each other. The book is even a repository of biblical teaching about the need for recreation.

PerSPECTIVES
ON THE BOOK OF SONG OF SONGS

Those who are in love have a natural inclination to bind themselves by promises. Love songs all over the world are full of vows of eternal constancy. C. S. Lewis

We begin by making the almost trite observation that the Song of Songs is a literary creation. It is a love-song of haunting beauty; it was meant to be sung as a celebration of love, beauty and intimacy. Tom Gledhill

Not only does it speak of the purity of human love; but, by its very inclusion in the canon, it reminds us of a love that is purer than our own. By its very presence in the canon . . . it reminds us that God, who has placed love in the human heart, is Himself pure. Edward J. Young

The Bible would be lacking . . . if one could not find in it expression of the deepest and strongest sentiment of humanity. Richard Niebuhr

The poet is a close observer, both of nature and of lovers.
Michael D. Goulder

The poet was also a close observer of the conventions and fashions of love poetry. Leland Ryken

The Song tells what love and marriage should be. It is a kind of antidote to the way things . . . often . . . are. Robert L. Alden

[In the poet's metaphors describing the physical attractiveness of the beloved,] the focus falls upon the ingenious symbol rather than on the part of the body. Israel Baroway

ISAIAH
A Bible within the Bible

FORMAT. 66 chapters, 1,292 verses

IMPLIED PURPOSE. To proclaim God's messages of indictment, warning, and consolation to the nations, especially God's covenant nation of Judah and the Gentiles who were grafted into it

AUTHOR'S PERSPECTIVE. The author serves as the messenger of what God wanted the nations of Isaiah's day to know about divine purposes. The book of Isaiah is a low-voltage, straightforward account of God's messages. Yet the *poetic effect* of the visions of salvation in chapters 40–66 is rapturous.

IMPLIED AUDIENCE. The nation of Judah before it was carried off to Babylon. The book's messages apply to all people.

WHAT UNIFIES THE BOOK. The prophetic format; a movement from oracles of judgment and warning to oracles of a future salvation; expansiveness (nations as the main characters, and the historical sweep from Isaiah's time to the end of history); the character and acts of God; poetry as the dominant mode

SPECIAL FEATURES. Messianic predictions; eschatological focus; international and cosmic scope; emphasis on the redemptive role of God's suffering servant; the key role of Israel and Zion (a spiritual rather than national entity) in God's redemptive plan for history; poetic brilliance; direct address to nations and groups and forces of nature

CHALLENGES FACING THE READER OR TEACHER OF THIS BOOK.
1. Its massive length
2. Combined with that, lack of a smooth narrative flow and the need to deal instead with a huge collection of brief fragments
3. Difficulty in ascertaining exactly when the futuristic prophecies have been or will be fulfilled

4. The sense of monotony that could set in if one reads straight through the book, which first gives one oracle of judgment after another and then follows that with twenty-seven chapters of oracles of salvation

HOW TO MEET THE CHALLENGES.

1. Read or study it over a period of days and weeks.
2. Rid yourself of narrative expectations and settle into the format of a long collection of separate oracles.
3. Learn to trust your own informed intuitions to differentiate what would be fulfilled in the near future, the intermediate future (the life of Christ), and the eschatological future.
4. Do not feel bound to read the book straight through. Isaiah lends itself to devotional reading, one unit per day.

I t would be best to describe the compositions . . . as "spiritual dramas." . . . But these prophetic dramas are such as no theatre could compass. For their stage they need all space; and the time of their action extends to the end of all things. The speakers include God and the Celestial Hosts; Israel appears, Israel Suffering or Israel Repentant; Sinners in Zion, the Godly in Zion; the Saved and the Doomed, the East and the West, answer one another. . . . But [there are] also elements that are distinctly non-dramatic. The discourse of God, or of some other speaker, will be interrupted by lyric songs, rejoicing over or emphasising what has been said, . . . like the chorales of an oratorio. . . . At times, again, the movement may be carried on by fragments of narrated vision; or critical points may be announced by the author in his own words, like the elaborate "stage directions" of the theatrical drama.

RICHARD G. MOULTON
The Modern Reader's Bible

AN OUTLINE OF
ISAIAH

40–66 Prophecies of a Glorious Future for Zion

36–39 The Story of King Hezekiah

28–35 Mingled Judgment and Salvation

25–27 Prophecies of Deliverance

13–24 Prophecies to the Nations

1–12 Prophecies to Judah

Consolation Dominates

Warning Dominates

Intermediate and Eschatological Future

Present and Immediate/Intermediate Future

The Old Testament prophets were tailor made for our own world. Their skill and bluntness in denouncing what is wrong in the behavior of individuals and nations would have ample material today. Perhaps the daily news allows us to utter our own prophetic oracles of judgment so that we do not need Isaiah to tell us that the world is nearly as bad as it can be. But Isaiah is a "must read" on the subject of *what God intends to do* about the sin that is having a field day in the world.

The Form of the Book

Isaiah is a challenging book in terms of unity and organization. The most important thing to say about the book's form is that it is encyclopedic in nature. Isaiah is a large anthology of prophetic oracles (pronouncements from God). Relieved of the need to find a continuous line of thought, we are free to relish the individual units. The structure is kaleidoscopic, with individual fragments constantly shifting and never in focus for very long.

The book combines prophecy and apocalypse. Briefly then, here is what you need to know about Old Testament prophecy:

The prophets do not first of all *foretell* the future but instead *speak forth* ("forth tell") God's messages to the nations. Much of what the prophets say thus concerns life as it is in the prophet's own time.

When the prophets talk about their own contemporary society, their message falls into three types of material: (1) *description* of what is wrong in society, (2) *denunciation* of what is wrong, and (3) *declaration* that God will judge the evil the prophet has described. If you look carefully at any specific passage in the prophets, you will find one or more of these three things happening.

Taken together, the three types of material just described are called oracles of judgment.

When the prophets take up their warning that God will judge the evil of the nations, their message naturally becomes *predictive of the future.*

Balancing the negative message of judgment, the prophets also announce God's mercy and salvation and his intention to restore his wayward covenant people. These passages are called *oracles of salvation* or *oracles of redemption.*

The oracles of redemption predict future events. In the overwhelming majority of cases, the future restoration is best interpreted either as a highly symbolic or more directly as a literal prediction of the redemptive work of the incarnate Christ, though there is always the possibility of a "near" fulfillment as well. The last third of the book has notable passages of comfort.

Apocalyptic writing is sometimes loosely defined to resemble prophetic writing as defined above. But it is more helpful to reserve the label *apocalyptic* for visions of the distant future that we understand to be eschatological ("end times") in nature. Whenever you read a vision of the future that has the feel of end-times predictions elsewhere in the Bible, you are dealing with apocalyptic writing.

The further thing that you need to know about apocalyptic writing is that the content of these visions is similar to what we find in prophetic writing. Apocalyptic writing, too, denounces evil in the world, and it, too, warns of a coming divine judgment. Like prophetic writing, apocalyptic writing consists of oracles of judgment and oracles of redemption. Furthermore, the phenomenon of messianic prophecy occurs in both prophetic and apocalyptic writing. Prophetic writing predicts Christ's incarnation and earthly ministry, and apocalyptic writing predicts what Christ will do at the end of history.

To sum up, then, prophecy deals with both the present and the immediate and intermediate future. Apocalypse deals with the eschatological end of history—the distant future. Both types of writing consist of oracles of judgment and oracles of salvation. (For more on prophecy and apocalypse as forms of writing, see pages 291 and 633.)

> **HOW THE HEBREW BIBLE WAS ORGANIZED**
>
> The Hebrew Old Testament is divided into three sections: the Law, the Prophets, and the Writings.
>
> - The Prophets fall into two categories: the Former Prophets and the Latter Prophets.
> - The Former Prophets are Joshua, Judges, 1 and 2 Samuel, and 1 and 2 Kings.
> - The Latter Prophets are Isaiah, Jeremiah, Ezekiel, and The Twelve (our Minor Prophets).

Satire and Visionary Writing

We need to add two more literary forms to the mix before you can feel comfortable with prophetic writing such as that in the book of Isaiah. The oracles of judgment take the form of satire: There are objects of attack, there are literary vehicles such as description and brief narratives that embody the attack, and there are implied and stated norms or standards by which God judges evil. (For more on satire as a form of writing, see page 375.)

Both the prophetic and apocalyptic forms make frequent use of visionary techniques. Such writing presents things that are not literally true or perhaps even possible in the real world. The techniques are those of fantasy and symbolism. Here are random examples from the book of Isaiah:

- "The heavens will be black above them; the stars will give no light. The sun will be dark when it rises, and the moon will provide no light" (13:10). This is part of a prediction that the Babylonian army would invade Judah. When the event happened, the sun and moon were not literally dark.
- "How you are fallen from heaven, O shining star, son of the morning! You have been thrown down to the earth, you who destroyed the nations of the world" (14:12). This is a symbolic prediction of the eventual fall of the king of Babylon, who did not literally become a shooting star.
- "Wake up, wake up, O Zion! Clothe yourself with strength. Put on your beautiful clothes, O holy city of Jerusalem" (52:1). There are three bits of fantasy here: (1) A city is personified by being treated as though it were a person, (2) an absent city is addressed as though it were standing in front of the speaker (the technical name for this figure of speech is *apostrophe*), and (3) a city cannot literally clothe itself with a garment.

In visionary writing you always need to be ready to read something that either does not happen in the real world or that is entirely incongruous with what is happening in the prophet's society at that time. This is not to say that the people and nations and events that are presented by means of symbol or fantasy do not really exist and happen. It is only a question of how the writer describes these real situations.

Unifying Elements

- The genre of the anthology of individual prophetic units
- The visionary mode, meaning that much of the book—not all of it— portrays events symbolically and metaphorically, not literally. Remember, this does not mean that the characters and events do not refer to real persons and events. It means only that they are not portrayed literally.
- Two basic kinds of material: oracles of judgment and oracles of redemption
- The kaleidoscopic structure: No matter where you find yourself in the book, you know that you won't be there long.
- The cosmic scope, which encompasses nations and finally the whole earth, with few references to specific individuals. Nearly everywhere you turn in this book, you are dealing with corporate personalities and groups.

Prophecy as a Form of Writing

The biblical prophets primarily speak forth God's message. They use the formula "thus says the Lord" hundreds of times, showing that their message originated with God. While much of what the biblical prophets speak forth is predictive in nature, most of it is not. It is not wrong to loosely *link* prophecy with prediction of the future, but it is wrong to *equate* prophecy with prediction of the future. The following traits characterize the utterances of biblical prophets when they speak God's messages to people and nations:

- The prophets typically begin with the situation in their own nation and world. They are much more focused on the present and immediate future than on the distant future. If we go to prophetic writing expecting to read primarily predictions of the distant future, we will be unequipped to deal with the prophets' contemporary focus.
- As the prophets look at their world, they usually portray various forms of evil. Prophetic writing gives us a detailed picture, or anatomy, of what is wrong with individuals and societies. Much prophetic writing can accurately be called social commentary or social criticism. An example is Amos 2:6: "They sell honorable people for silver and poor people for a pair of sandals."
- In addition to *depicting* evils in their world, biblical prophets *denounce* these evils, warn against them, and predict punishment for the perpetrators. The predictions, moreover, are slanted toward the relatively immediate future, not the end of history ("end times" predictions are called apocalyptic writing). Isaiah 10:12 is a typical prophecy against a contemporary evil: "After the Lord has used the king of Assyria to accomplish his purposes on Mount Zion and in Jerusalem, he will turn against the king of Assyria and punish him—for he is proud and arrogant."
- Biblical prophets also picture and predict a coming restoration of peoples and nations. Sometimes these "golden age" prophecies concern Israel's return from exile, but some of them extend further into the future and become messianic prophecies (predictions of the life and redemptive work of Jesus) or even predictions about the end of history. (For more on the golden age visions in the prophetic books, see the article on page 361.)
- Most prophetic books are collections of individual fragments. Think of them as anthologies of individual pieces of writing.

To sum up, prophetic writing is largely made up of three themes: sin, judgment, and restoration/redemption. Two corresponding forms—oracles of judgment and oracles of salvation—dominate. Prophetic writing can be direct and realistic, but more often it relies on the techniques of visionary writing (see the article on page 325).

- The preponderance of poetry. You always need to be ready to apply what you know about how poetry works.

THE FOUR SERVANT SONGS
Much of the theological meaning of the book is embodied in four famous "songs of the suffering servant." They are found in 42:1-7; 49:1-7; 50:4-9; 52:13–53:12.

Key Places and Characters

The scope of Isaiah is epic in its expansiveness. The prophetic denunciations cover the whole range of Near Eastern nations at the time of Isaiah, and the promises of a future glory encompass the whole earth (Israel and Zion serve as metaphors for the universal people of God). One of the distinctive features of Isaiah is that the list of key places is also the list of key characters. The human characters in this book are the nations of the world.

Of course, the dominant character is God, who permeates the entire book. If you want to know what God is like, the book of Isaiah will provide a sufficient answer.

Key Doctrines

The Nature of God. The book of Isaiah is a one-volume theology book within the Bible. Key aspects of God's character are his judgment against evil and his compassion for the human race.

Sin. The book of Isaiah is also a handbook on sin: what human actions and attitudes make up sin and what God has purposed to do about the problem of sin in his creation.

Judgment. The book of Isaiah is an expansive exploration of why and how God plans to judge the nations and people of the world for their rebellion against him and his moral law.

Salvation. The book of Isaiah contains as many pictures of God's salvation as it does of his judgment.

Atonement. More specifically, the song of the suffering servant found in Isaiah 53 portrays the substitutionary atonement of the Messiah.

Eschatology. The last third of the book is a rich source of pictures of God's acts of salvation, specifically at the end of history and in eternity.

Tips for Reading or Teaching Isaiah

Do not expect an unfolding narrative thread. Isaiah is an encyclopedic work consisting of short individual oracles (pronouncements).

Much of the content of the book is visionary in the sense defined above. Do not go against the grain by resisting the prophet's visionary mode. Just accept the idea that trees will clap their hands and a symbolic flood will cover a whole land (a prediction of military invasion). On the other hand, keep a grip on the fact that these fantastic visions do refer to *events* that did or will really happen.

The prophet's denunciation of the vices of the nations of his time is filled with topical references to a specific past time. Once you have the particulars in view, you need to look *through* them to your own time and place. The vices are universal.

Follow your instincts in picking up on when a given prediction took place or will yet take place. Three main phases exist on the futuristic continuum of Isaiah: the immediate future (ending with the Babylonian captivity), the intermediate future (the coming of Christ), and the distant future (the end times). Some of the generalized pictures of a coming golden age may refer simultaneously to both of Christ's comings.

You need not apologize for finding that the huge blocks of judgment (chapters 1–39, approximately) and of envisioned redemption (chapters 40–66) get repetitive when you read them all at once. One antidote is to find a way to dip into these big blocks over a period of time.

HOW TO MAKE SENSE OF OLD TESTAMENT PROPHECY

Old Testament professor Paul R. House offers the following tips on reading prophecy:

- Approximately 90 percent of Old Testament prophecy deals with everyday matters, and 10 percent with the future.
- Prophecy is thus more a warning against sin than a blueprint for the future.
- Three topics that crisscross prophetic literature and will allow you to follow the argument of any prophetic passage are sin, punishment, and restoration.

quick overview of isaiah

1:1–12:6	Oracles of judgment against Judah
13:1–24:23	Oracles of judgment against surrounding nations
25:1–27:13	Oracles of redemption
28:1–35:10	Collected oracles of judgment and of redemption
36:1–39:8	Narrative interlude: the life of King Hezekiah
40:1–66:24	A rushing torrent of oracles of redemption

The Flow of the Book

Collected Prophecies against Judah: A Sinful Nation and a Coming Messiah (Chapters 1–12). It is important to reemphasize that the book of Isaiah is an encyclopedic work that mingles the ingredients of the whole book in all of its parts. The first twelve chapters are where you need to master the methods the book as a whole requires. Be on the lookout for the following kinds of material, which you will not find in discrete units but instead mingled together:

KEY VERSE

"Woe is me! . . . For I am a man of unclean lips, and I dwell in the midst of a people of unclean lips; for my eyes have seen the King, the LORD of hosts!" (6:5, ESV). Here is the negative theme of Isaiah's prophecy: a terrible awareness of human sinfulness that a holy God must punish.

Oracles of Judgment (e.g., 1:2-9, 10-17, 21-31). When you come to these passages, your best procedure is to apply the questions required by literary satire: What are the specific objects of attack? How do the poetic descriptions embody these objects of attack? By what stated or implied standard does the prophet attack the abuses?

If you stare closely at the text, you will find that sometimes the prophet *describes* the abuses he is attacking (e.g., "The land is filled with idols"), sometimes he *denounces* the abuses (e.g., "Woe to those who . . ."), and sometimes he *predicts God's coming punishment* of the abuses (e.g., "I will break down its walls").

Oracles of Salvation (e.g., 1:18-20; 2:1-4; 9:1-7). From time to time, and without transition, the prophet shifts from passages that condemn evil to passages that predict a coming restoration of the wayward nation. Even within these positive predictions the prophet shuttles back and forth between diverse material: Some of his futuristic prophecies are messianic prophecies that were fulfilled with the coming of Christ ("for a child is born to us"), and some are eschatological/apocalyptic visions of the end of history ("in the last days . . . all the nations will beat their swords into plowshares").

Chapter 6 falls outside the main pattern altogether. It is a narrative account of God's calling Isaiah to be a prophet. The sequence is this: God's confrontation of Isaiah (vv. 1-4), Isaiah's confession (vv. 5-7), and Isaiah's commissioning to the prophetic task (vv. 8-13).

One more analytic framework works well with this block of material. The passage describes sin and outlines three things that God will do with sin: (1) He will appoint a day to punish it, (2) he will send prophetic warnings to the people so they can repent, and (3) he will send the Messiah to save his wayward people.

Canon of the Old Testament

The thirty-nine books of the modern Old Testament were originally divided into only twenty-four, according to the uniform testimony of early Hebrew tradition. Jews divided their Scriptures into three sections: the Law, the Prophets, and the Writings. These are called "the law of Moses," "the prophets," and "the Psalms" in Luke 24:44. The Law contained the Pentateuch in our familiar order, Genesis through Deuteronomy. The eight Prophets were Joshua, Judges, Samuel (1 and 2), Kings (1 and 2), Isaiah, Jeremiah, Ezekiel, and the Minor Prophets (twelve). These were considered one book and were arranged in the same order as our English Bibles. The eleven books of Writings contained three books of poetry (Psalms, Proverbs, Job), the Five Scrolls (Song of Songs, Ruth, Lamentations, Ecclesiastes, and Esther, which were read at the important feasts and arranged in the chronological order of their observance), and three narrative, or historical, books (Daniel, Ezra—Nehemiah, 1 and 2 Chronicles). The following chart shows this organization:

1. The Law
Genesis
Exodus
Leviticus
Numbers
Deuteronomy

2. The Prophets
Former Prophets
Joshua
Judges
Samuel (1 & 2)
Kings (1 & 2)

Latter Prophets
Isaiah
Jeremiah
Ezekiel
The Twelve
  Hosea
  Joel
  Amos
  Obadiah
  Jonah
  Micah
  Nahum
  Habbakuk
  Zephaniah
  Haggai
  Zechariah
  Malachi

3. The Writings
Psalms
Proverbs
Job
Five Scrolls
  Song of Songs
  Ruth
  Lamentations
  Ecclesiastes
  Esther
Daniel
Ezra—Nehemiah
Chronicles (1 & 2)

Oracles of Judgment against the Nations (Chapters 13–24). This unit gives variations on the themes of (1) the evil that people do, (2) God's disapproval of that evil, and (3) God's coming judgment against evil. The scope is international. Do not get bogged down in the historical particulars; look beyond them to the universal ideas. The following simple scheme will suffice: What things displease God? How does God deal with the things that displease him?

Oracles of Salvation (Chapters 25–27). The medium is poetry: images, pictures, metaphors, symbols. They are blueprints of specific future events, so you should not look for esoteric meanings. Your best procedure is to assimilate all of these as pictures of God's salvation in whatever form it might take—anytime, anywhere.

Songs of Judgment and Salvation (Chapters 28–35). By now, the back-and-forth rhythm of prophecy should seem like second nature to you. An ever-shifting series of oracles of judgment dominate this unit; just apply what was suggested earlier. Three times the focus shifts without transition to visions of salvation (30:15-33; 32; 35).

Narrative Interlude: The Strange Case of Hezekiah (Chapters 36–39). In a book that includes nearly every important genre, we now shift gears to narrative, with a lyric poem (Hezekiah's song of thanks for his rescue) tossed in as well. There are memorable events, such as Hezekiah's spreading out the threatening letter before God in the Temple, Hezekiah's prayer, and the angel's killing of 185,000 Assyrian soldiers. About the time this brief narrative seems headed for a happy ending, we finish on a downer, as Hezekiah sets up his nation for eventual sacking by the Babylonians. (To get maximum mileage out of this unit, review and apply the principles in the article on narrative on page 35.)

Oracles of a Future Salvation (Chapters 40–66). A major shift occurs with chapter 40, as judgment recedes from view and the opening verse

announces the keynote: "'Comfort, comfort my people,' says your God."
This unit is an anthology of individual oracles of salvation, and there is
an absolute abundance of famous one-liners and "favorite verses":
"Those who trust in the LORD . . . will run and not
grow weary" (40:31); "The LORD laid on him the
sins of us all" (53:6). Outlines of this material in
handbooks and commentaries attempt to divide
the material into separate sections, but the tidy divisions do not hold up when you look closely at the
actual text. Your best procedure is to treat the individual units as objects of attention in themselves,
keeping in mind the fact that the general movement is a growing crescendo of promises of redemption. The only reliable organizing framework
is to be alert to the following ingredients, *which are
mingled together throughout*:

> **KEY VERSE**
>
> "I am the one who
> helps you, declares the
> LORD; your Redeemer
> is the Holy One of
> Israel" (41:14, ESV).
> This verse epitomizes
> the positive theme of
> Isaiah: The Holy God
> who judges is also the
> redeemer of his
> people.

- Some of the visions *may* refer to the restoration of a remnant of
  Judah after the Babylonian captivity.
- Other visions are messianic in nature, including four famous "servant songs."
- Still other visions (especially many of those in chapters 60–66) are eschatological and apocalyptic in nature and look forward to the end of
  the ages.

At many points, your best way of assimilating the good news Isaiah presents is to accept it as a metaphoric account of God's salvation as it appears anytime, anywhere.

These visions of redemption are addressed to a specific nation, variously called Jacob or Israel or Zion or Jerusalem. Who is in view here?
You can't go wrong if you view these as metaphoric of God's chosen people universally. If you get too nationalistic or geographic in your interpretation, you will tangle your understanding.

The Main Themes

1. When people and nations do what is evil, God will judge them. God
   is a just God who punishes sinners.
2. God is equally a God of salvation. In fact, from eternity he has had a
   plan by which to save people who believe in him.
3. Throughout Old Testament prophecy, including the book of Isaiah,

God gave foreshadowings of Christ, the Messiah, and of how Christ would be the One to save people from their sins by his atoning death.

4. God does not want us to live our lives solely in terms of spiritual salvation and eternal life at the end of human history. He is very concerned about the everyday life we are living right now.

Contribution of the Book to the Bible's Story of Salvation in Christ

The main contribution of the book of Isaiah to salvation history is its treasure trove of messianic prophecies. Some of the prophecies—including those of his virgin birth and his death—deal with Christ's redemptive life; others deal with his coming work at the end of history. A few especially rich messianic chapters are 9, 11, 40, and 53, which talk about such things as the giving of a son who will rule on David's throne forever, an offspring of David on whom the Spirit of the Lord will rest, and a suffering servant who was wounded for our sins. The book of Isaiah is the Gospel of the Old Testament.

Applying the Book

The descriptions and denunciations of sin in the satiric passages directed against evil in the prophet's own nation and the surrounding nations should raise our awareness of what is wrong in our own lives and societies. Further, the warnings the prophet directs by predicting God's imminent and final judgment against people and societies that practice evil should move us to repentance.

The messianic prophecies should lead us to understand and adore who Christ is and what he did and to place our trust in him for salvation from God's judgment. Theologically and apologetically, this allows us to counter a common misconception that the God of the Old Testament is a harsh God of judgment and we need to get to the New Testament before we can find relief from this judgmental God in the story of Christ.

PERSPECTIVES
ON THE BOOK OF ISAIAH

Isaiah is like a miniature Bible. Bruce Wilkinson and Kenneth Boa

The most sublime of all Poets. Hugh Blair

The centerpiece of the story of Israel in the biblical story.
Gordon D. Fee and Douglas Stuart

Five important characters appear in prophecy: God, the prophets, the remnant, the rebels, and the nations. Obviously God is the major character. Yahweh acts as father, king, lover, friend, or judge. . . . The prophets themselves interact with the Lord and convey God's messages to the people. Paul R. House

[The book is structured like] an orchestral score. . . . In an orchestral score one can grasp certain key repeating themes that help unite the work . . . (Zion; the outstretched hand; God's plan of old; the "thorns and briers" motif). . . . The opening chapter [presents] us with a sort of overture, as has been frequently proposed. Christopher R. Seitz

Isaiah has been called the Romans of the Old Testament because, like the Book of Romans, it sets forth God's case against sinners, unveils the wretchedness of the human heart, and reveals the way of salvation for Israel and the world. Herbert M. Wolf

[The prophet Isaiah] made the prophetic message truly relevant to the actual circumstances and problems being faced by all layers of society: the authorities, the spiritual leaders, the common people (esp. the poor), the oppressed farmers, and civilians. S. H. Widyapranawa

Much of what we admire about his prophecy corresponds to the aesthetic concept of the "sublime." Its celestial and terrestrial scope, its inclusiveness of all creation within its range of dialogue, its vision of the power of God to transform a desert into a garden. William F. Gentrup

Those things with which Isaiah reproached his time—idolatry, debauchery, war, prostitution, ignorance—still exist. Isaiah is the undying contemporary of the vices that make themselves servants, and of the crimes that make themselves kings. Victor Hugo

JEREMIAH
*A Prophet for
Post-Christian Times*

FACT SHEET

FORMAT. 52 chapters, 1,364 verses

IMPLIED PURPOSES. To record prophecies of God's judgment against Judah's sin, with promises of ultimate restoration, and to tell the story of Jeremiah's ministry during the last decades before the fall of Jerusalem and the exile to Babylon

AUTHOR'S PERSPECTIVE. Jeremiah writes as a sometimes reluctant and often ostracized prophet—a suffering servant—who grieves for the sins of God's people and the judgment that must surely come and at the same time remains steadfast in the face of persecution because he has quiet confidence in the faithfulness of God.

IMPLIED AUDIENCE. Jeremiah's prophecies are for the people of God (and for the nations) before, during, and after the Babylonian captivity and also for anyone who seeks the courage to stand for God in times of spiritual decline.

WHAT UNIFIES THE BOOK. The weeping prophet—the narrative episodes and occasional prophecies collected in the book over nearly fifty years in Jeremiah's life and ministry; the fall of Jerusalem as the epochal event that dominated Jeremiah's message before it happened, as well as during and after; a constant critique of Judah's ungodly kings, untruthful prophets, and unfaithful people; a heartfelt concern for what happened to Judah, both spiritually and politically, as a nation under God

SPECIAL FEATURES. The dramatic object lessons in which Jeremiah uses visual props to make public prophecies; "confessions" in which the prophet speaks directly and passionately to himself and to God about his sufferings in ministry (10:23-25; 11:18–12:4; 15:10-18; 17:14-18; 18:18-23; 20:7-18)

CHALLENGE FACING THE READER OR TEACHER OF THIS BOOK. Dealing with the disjointed structure of a work that includes both poetic oracles of judgment and autobiographical narratives in prose, that shifts between the first person ("I") and the third person ("Jeremiah"), that is sometimes repetitious, and that tends to take things out of chronological order (e.g., the public reaction to Jeremiah's Temple sermon in chapter 7 recorded in chapter 26)

HOW TO MEET THE CHALLENGE. Recognize that the book is not a direct historical narrative but more like an anthology or a reader: a collection of materials by and about the prophet Jeremiah. One way to approach Jeremiah is first to follow the narrative thread of the prophet's life (mainly chapters 1; 7; 11; 13; 16; 18–20; 26–29; 32; 36–40) and then to read his prophecies.

*F*rom even this cursory survey of the book's contents—memoirs, divine oracles, soliloquies and prayers, a historical appendix, matter dictated by the prophet, reminiscences treasured by others, all assembled with little chronological or logical order, and with considerable repetition—it becomes clear that the book is confusing to read straight through simply because it was not written consecutively.... The book of Jeremiah is in fact a collection, an anthology, of memories, utterances, and events, gathered in stages from different periods in Jeremiah's long ministry and afterward, and arranged, so far as it is arranged at all, with more regard to themes and literary connections than to historical order.

R. E. O. WHITE
The Indomitable Prophet:
A Biographical Commentary on Jeremiah

52 Epilogue: The Fall of Jerusalem Retold
50–51 Prophecy of Destruction for Babylon
46–49 Prediction of Woe to Egypt and Seven Nations
45 God's Message to Jeremiah's Secretary
42–44 Bad News for Those Who Escaped to Egypt
40–41 Jeremiah Released; The Governor Assassinated

Judgment against the Nations

After the Fall

39 The Fall of Jerusalem

Siege and Fall of Jerusalem

The Fall

37–38 Jeremiah in Prison and in a Cistern
36 Jehoiakim Burns Jeremiah's Scroll
34–35 Zedekiah's Treachery; Recabites' Faithfulness
33 Prediction of Jerusalem Restored to David's Son
32 Jeremiah Buys a House in Jerusalem
30–31 Return from Captivity; New Covenant

Book of Consolation

29 Letter of Hope to the Exiles
27–28 Jeremiah Predicts Captivity
26 Jeremiah Tried and Acquitted
24–25 Predictions of Captivity
Prophecies against Judah's Kings and Prophets

Prophecies about the Coming Captivity

21–23 Prophecies against Judah's Kings and Prophets
20 Jeremiah's Dark Night of the Soul
18–19 Jeremiah at the Potter's House
Jeremiah's Prophecies and Dialogues with God

Jeremiah's Experiences as a Prophet

11–17 Jeremiah's Prophecies and Dialogues with God
7–10 Temple Sermon, Predicted Judgment
4:3–6:30 Prediction of Judgment against Judah
2:1–4:2 God Files for Divorce
1 Prologue: Preparation of the Prophet

Jeremiah's First Public Sermons

Before the Fall of Jerusalem

AN OUTLINE OF
JEREMIAH

Jeremiah lived at a time when people had stopped trusting God. Although some of them still met their religious obligations, they did so more out of duty than delight. Their faith in God was primarily a thing of the past, and as a result, public life was increasingly dominated by pagan ideas and practices. In other words, Jeremiah lived at a time much like our own, when true religion is largely a thing of the past. We are living in what might be called post-Christian times. Many people still go to church and call themselves Christians, but the cultural influence of Christianity is on the decline and the gospel is excluded from the public square.

How do we live for Christ in a post-Christian culture? The ministry of Jeremiah gives us some answers. His courage, his passion, his preaching, and even his sufferings show how to live for God when everyone else turns against him. Jeremiah is a prophet for post-Christian times.

The Form of the Book

The story of Jeremiah's life and the history of Jerusalem's overthrow provide a loose narrative framework for the book of Jeremiah. But the book contains a wide range of other biographical, autobiographical, historical, and prophetical material, drawn from a lifetime in ministry. At least some of this material came directly from prophetic oracles, and some of it was dictated to Jeremiah's scribe, Baruch. We also know that major sections of the book had to be rewritten at least once, since King Jehoiakim wickedly consigned the first edition to the flames (see chapter 36). Where the principle of organization is not chronological, it is usually topical. Memorable metaphors and similes characterize the book: "My people . . . have abandoned me—the fountain of living water. And they have dug for themselves cracked cisterns that can hold no water" (2:13). "Does a young woman forget her jewelry? Does a bride hide her wedding dress?" (2:32). "Stand at the crossroads and look" (6:16, NIV). "How can you compete with horses?" (12:5, NIV). "Is not my word like fire . . .?" (23:29, NIV). It is also familiar to many readers for its famous encouragements to boast in the knowledge of God (9:23-24) and to trust in his plans for the future (29:11-13).

Key Words and Phrases

Key words and phrases in Jeremiah include the following:

- *The LORD gave me another message, this is what the LORD says:* phrases for prophetic utterance that demarcate Jeremiah's oracles

- *forsaken, wayward, backsliding:* words that indicate Judah's spiritual decline
- *repent, return:* words that call Judah back to covenant faithfulness
- *heal, restore:* words that express God's ultimate plan to save his people

Key Places and Characters

Virtually the entire book is set in Jerusalem, the city whose destruction was the great tragedy of Jeremiah's generation. Specific locations—the streets of the city, the Temple, the potter's house, the garbage dump outside the city gates—form the backdrop for the prophet's most famous sermons.

The dominant character is Jeremiah, the pariah, or outcast, whose public ministry aroused fierce opposition but whose private life was characterized by intensely intimate encounters with God. The secondary figures start with the last kings of Judah: Josiah, the reformer whose ministry Jeremiah partly commends (2:1–12:17); Jehoiakim, the despot who put the prophet in prison and burned the first copy of his manuscript (13:1–20:18; 25:1–27:11; 36:21-26); and Zedekiah, the Babylonian puppet who threw Jeremiah into a cistern and consulted him for spiritual advice but never followed it (21:1–24:10; 27:12–39:18). The enemies of Jeremiah and Judah include Hananiah and Shemaiah (lying prophets who said the exact opposite of what Jeremiah was saying), Pashhur (the chief of the Temple police who had Jeremiah beaten and put in the stocks), and Nebuchadnezzar (the boastful king of Babylon). On a more positive note, two men are distinguished for their active support of Jeremiah and his ministry: Baruch, the faithful scribe whom God encouraged to be content in his role as a servant, and Ebed-Melech, the Ethiopian who rescued the prophet from the cistern.

Key Doctrines

Sin. The book views sin primarily as unfaithfulness to God and his covenant. A stunning array of vivid word pictures portrays the depravity and deception of the human heart.

Repentance. Even the most wicked people can find forgiveness if they turn to God, but they need to do so before it's too late.

Judgment. Jeremiah contains some of the longest judgment passages in the Bible, which together prove that unfaithfulness to God leads only to condemnation.

The Sovereignty of God. God is the ruler of all nations and the potter who shapes the destiny of his people on the wheel of his providence (see 18:1-10).

Covenant. God's covenant with his people is the perfect standard for exposing their unrighteousness and also the sure promise that guarantees their salvation.

The Word of God. The sharp truth of God's eternal Word stands against the reassuring lies of false prophets. All of its promises of judgment and blessing will come true.

Tips for Reading or Teaching Jeremiah

To get the historical background for Jeremiah's life and ministry, read 2 Kings 22–25 and 2 Chronicles 34–36. For a poetic first-person account of the fall of Jerusalem and its immediate aftermath, read the book's sequel, Lamentations.

A good way to study or teach Jeremiah is to concentrate on the narrative accounts of the prophet's life and ministry.

The poetic and prophetic portions of the book demand a close, careful reading. What visual images come to mind as you study Jeremiah's figurative language?

quick overview of jeremiah

1:1-19	Prologue: the call of the prophet to be God's spokesman to Judah and the nations
2:1–29:32	The book of doom: God's message of judgment against Judah's sin
30:1–33:26	The book of consolation: God's message of hope for his people's future
34:1–45:5	The fate of Jerusalem: the siege and fall of Jerusalem and its aftermath
46:1–51:64	The fate of the nations: prophecies regarding God's dealings with Judah's enemies
52:1-34	Epilogue: a journalistic recounting of the fall of Jerusalem and Judah's journey into exile

The Flow of the Book

Prologue: Jeremiah Called and Commissioned (Chapter 1). God's sovereign call and the prophet's reluctant response can be compared with other call narratives (Moses, Isaiah) in the Bible. (Notice that Jeremiah's call goes all the way back to his mother's womb.) Consider what Jeremiah's call indicates about the kind of message he will bring and the kind of opposition he can expect to experience.

Judah Condemned for Idolatry (Chapters 2–10). Jeremiah's prophecies begin with God's filing divorce papers against his people on the legitimate grounds of spiritual adultery: They have fallen in love with other gods. As God makes his case, look for evidence of his people's infidelity and for information about what kind of judgment God will send if they refuse to repent. As Jeremiah begins his public ministry at the Temple and elsewhere, what are the main themes of his preaching? How does he use poetic images to communicate his message? What picture of the coming judgment begins to emerge?

KEY VERSES

"Look, I have put my words in your mouth! Today I appoint you to stand up against nations and kingdoms. Some you must uproot and tear down, destroy and overthrow. Others you must build up and plant" (1:9-10). God calls Jeremiah to an international ministry of publicly proclaiming God's prophetic word, which will have two results: the overthrow of nations by divine judgment and the establishment of a kingdom by God's grace.

Jeremiah Converses with God and Contends with His Enemies (Chapters 11–20). The threat of captivity as a consequence of idolatry continues, but now Jeremiah begins to illustrate his prophecies with dramatic public demonstrations that usually involve some kind of visual aid. Despite the prophet's boldness, he is struggling to accept the message God has called him to communicate, especially because he is forbidden to intercede for the salvation of his people. As Jeremiah enters into dialogue with God, notice what God's responses reveal about his divine character. In this section Jeremiah also faces increasing opposition from the religious establishment, who (ironically) accuse him of treason for predicting that judgment will fall on Jerusalem. The abuse and imprisonment he suffers precipitate a personal crisis. Notice Jeremiah's conflicting emotions in his lament in chapter 20. This soliloquy gives us a window into the prophet's soul and shows the deep personal price that he has paid for his faithfulness to God's Word. What do Jeremiah's conversations with God teach us about our own communion with Christ?

Jeremiah Critiques Jerusalem's Society (Chapters 21–29). Jeremiah launches into a prophetic attack on the last kings and lying prophets of Jerusalem and reveals the need for a righteous king and a true prophet. Notice that as the city's doom approaches, Jeremiah's prophecies of judgment become more certain and specific while his interactions with the false prophets become more confrontational (they put him on trial for treason, among other things). In chapters 24 through 29 the prophet prepares his people for their eventual exile by telling them to submit to God's will for their captivity. As you read his letter to the captives who have already been carried off to Babylon (29:4-23), consider how its message might also apply to waves of exiles in later deportations. How can Jeremiah's perspective help us live as Christians in a post-Christian culture?

The New Covenant Gives Consolation (Chapters 30–33). Jeremiah moves from sorrow to hope as he looks ahead to Judah's return from Babylon and the reconstruction of Jerusalem. God will renew the covenant his people have broken. Although some of Jeremiah's predictive prophecies have already been fulfilled with Judah's return from exile, others look ahead to the coming of the Messiah and the everlasting city of God. What is Jeremiah's vision of the good life for the people of God? How does his seemingly foolish real estate investment in chapter 32 illustrate the truth of his most hopeful promises?

Jerusalem Collapses (Chapters 34–39). These chapters generally recount Jeremiah's experiences during the last days before the tragic fall of Jerusalem (although chapters 35 and 36 flash back to pertinent events from the reign of Jehoiakim). As the city finally collapses, thus fulfilling Jeremiah's prophecies of doom, the prophet finds himself imprisoned at the bottom of a well. Although the fall of Jerusalem is an unmitigated disaster, it nevertheless vindicates the righteousness of God. It also reveals people's ultimate spiritual commitments. Look for examples of faithfulness to emulate (e.g., the vow-keeping Recabites and the brave servant Ebed-Melech) and unfaithfulness to avoid (e.g., indecisive Zedekiah and foolish Jehoiakim) during distressing times.

The Chaos after the Catastrophe (Chapters 40–45). The tragic events of chapter 39 have left the prophet and the people essentially unchanged.

Jeremiah continues to speak true words from God, warning the remnant of Judah to remain in Jerusalem rather than run off to Egypt. But the people refuse to listen, first resorting to violence and then rebelling against God's clear instructions. The brief interlude in chapter 45 (God's message to Jeremiah's scribe, Baruch) is significant because it shows what one person can do, even when everyone else turns away from God. These are good chapters for self-examination: How am I as stubborn as the Israelites? In what ways do I need to learn the kind of contentment that God commended to Baruch?

The Nations Condemned (Chapters 46–51). Judah is not the only nation accountable to God. As Jeremiah surveys the international scene, he prophesies God's judgment against the surrounding kingdoms, especially Babylon. The language the prophet uses to describe the everlasting destruction of that great city portends the final judgment.

Epilogue: The Fall of Jerusalem Recounted (Chapter 52). The final chapter does not come from Jeremiah himself but from some other historian, who gives the book a proper ending by reporting the destruction of Jerusalem, the humiliation of King Zedekiah, and the desecration of the Temple. This material serves to recap Jeremiah's message and show how his prophecies came true. The book ends on an unexpected note of cautious optimism as King Jehoiachin—who, unlike Zedekiah, accepted Jeremiah's message to submit to the Babylonians—is released from prison and is given a place of safety and dignity in the royal court of Babylon. Where there is life, there is hope—hope that God will restore his kingdom through David's rightful heir. How does this connect with the hope that we have in the gospel?

KEY VERSES

"I will make a new covenant with the people of Israel and Judah. . . . I will put my instructions deep within them, and I will write them on their hearts. I will be their God, and they will be my people" (31:31-33). Jeremiah's thrilling promise of a new covenant looks beyond captivity to a future hope. As far as God's relationship with his people is concerned, the new covenant is substantially the same as the old covenant; the primary difference is that the new covenant will come with a more powerful grace, enabling people to keep it.

The Main Themes

1. The degrading kinds of sin that people commit in a society that turns away from God: child sacrifice, goddess worship, sexual immorality, and public injustice, among others

2. The wickedness of being unfaithful to God—a sin that Jeremiah describes in terms of spiritual adultery

3. The disastrous effects of getting poor spiritual leadership from people who are self-serving (like Judah's kings) and false (like Judah's prophets)

4. The danger of depending on external religion (as the people of Jerusalem did when they trusted the Temple to save them) when what God truly desires is an inward heart of love and service

5. Faithfulness to God in the face of any and all persecution, as Jeremiah demonstrated

KEY VERSES

"People from many nations will pass by the ruins of this city and say to one another, 'Why did the LORD destroy such a great city?' And the answer will be, 'Because they violated their covenant with the LORD their God by worshiping other gods'" (22:8-9). This is Jeremiah's God-centered perspective on the great public events of his time.

Contribution of the Book to the Bible's Story of Salvation in Christ

Jeremiah contains a number of important messianic prophecies. Some of these tend to get overlooked today, but almost all of them appear in the New Testament: a shepherd who will look for the lost sheep of Israel (23:1-4; compare Luke 15:1-7); a righteous branch to rule over Judah (23:5-6); comfort for Rachel and her children (31:15-17; compare Matthew 2:17-18); a new covenant (31:31-34; compare Luke 22:20; Hebrews 8:6-13); and a Lord to be our righteousness (33:15-16; compare 1 Corinthians 1:30). Of equal significance, though, is the whole pattern of Jeremiah's experience as a suffering prophet. He was rejected in his own hometown, wrongly accused of being a false prophet, tried by religious leaders who conspired against him in Jerusalem, beaten, mocked, imprisoned, and—according to tradition—put to death. It is hardly surprising that some people wondered whether Jesus might be the second coming of Jeremiah (see Matthew 16:14) or that Jesus himself was able to trace the pattern of his passion in the experiences of prophets such as Jeremiah (see Luke 24:27).

Applying the Book

When we make the connection between the sins that were prevalent in Jeremiah's day and the sins common to our own culture, Jeremiah turns out to be a pervasively and perhaps surprisingly relevant book. The prophet addressed some of the same issues that confront us in the church (hypocrisy, theological error, and a misplaced confidence in tradition) and in society (corporate corruption, sexual infidelity, and infanticide). And like us, he lived in a country with a strong religious background, so he could call people back to the God they had once claimed to serve. Jeremiah shows us how to speak for God courageously in an increasingly secular culture.

The prophet also serves as a model for practical godliness in times of opposition and persecution. Jeremiah grieved over what was happening to his people, and he sometimes struggled to accept the judgment God was planning to send. From his example we learn how to deal with the same issues in our own lives, honestly weeping over the things that deserve our tears and frankly discussing our difficulties with God in our prayers. Out of the strength of Jeremiah's personal communion with God, he remained faithful for a lifetime without ever losing confidence in God's goodness or hope in God's promises.

PERSPECTIVES
ON THE BOOK OF JEREMIAH

Prophets did not leave off speaking to the people until they were slain. . . . Thus, when Jeremiah was despised, like other teachers and scholars of his age, he could not, though he desired it, withhold his prophecy or cease from reminding the people of the truths which they rejected.
Moses Maimonides

The book of Jeremiah resembles a scrapbook of undated memories and snapshots recalling great moments in a splendid life, over which we pore one by one, with reverence, saying, "Ah, that must have been when. . . ." Jeremiah confronts the earnest reader with a choice: either to read through the book as it is, with all its repetitions and sudden changes, trying to keep the story straight in his mind; or to put the story of Jeremiah into its correct order (so far as possible) and to fit the collected reminiscences of his sayings and deeds into that chronological outline. R. E. O. White

By divine design it was Jeremiah who was called to prophesy in the darkest hours of Judah, when Judah as a nation died. He is known as the "weeping prophet" and "the prophet of the broken heart." But he wept not for his own trials, grievous as they were. It was the sins of his nation and

the fearful destruction these sins were bringing upon them that broke Jeremiah's heart. Irving L. Jensen

The literature of Jeremiah engages in anguished poetic reflection and didactic prose explanation about the cause of Israel's end. . . . Jeremiah's reading is not shaped by power politics but by the categories of Israel's covenantal traditions of faith, which concern the holy purpose and power of Yahweh and the aches and hopes of the faithful community.
Walter Brueggemann

Jeremiah provides us with an extended study of an era like our own, where men have turned away from God and society has become post-Christian.
Francis A. Schaeffer

A prophet's task is to reveal the fault lines hidden beneath the comfortable surface of the worlds we invent for ourselves, the national myths as well as the little lies and delusions of control and security that get us through the day. And Jeremiah does this better than anyone. Kathleen Norris

Jeremiah always holds a fascination to Christian hearts because of the close similarity that exists between his life and that of Jesus Christ. Each of them . . . passed through hours of rejection, desolation, and forsakenness. And in Jeremiah we may see beaten out into detail, experiences which, in our Lord, are but lightly touched on by the evangelists. F. B. Meyer

LAMENTATIONS

A Nation Mourns

FORMAT. 5 chapters, 154 verses

IMPLIED PURPOSES. To lament the fall of Jerusalem and to provide spiritual perspective on a national catastrophe. Where Job deals with the problem of undeserved personal suffering, Lamentations struggles with communal suffering that is fully deserved.

AUTHOR'S PERSPECTIVE. The author (probably Jeremiah, although this is not stated) gives full expression to his anguish after seeing his beloved city destroyed and his people carried off into exile. Although these tragic events vindicate a lifetime of his prophetic warnings, he finds no satisfaction in their fulfillment, only sorrow.

IMPLIED AUDIENCE. Suffering survivors of the siege and sack of Jerusalem, who need help grieving their losses, repenting of their sins, and finding renewed hope in the character of God

WHAT UNIFIES THE BOOK. A mood of almost unremitting sorrow; the dark shadow of the recent disaster that overshadows the book; horrific accounts of death and devastation; the prayers at the end of each lament, which often ask for vengeance against Judah's enemies; the character of God, which both explains why suffering has come and gives hope for the future

SPECIAL FEATURE. Five funeral poems, or elegies, four of which are an acrostic (a literary form in which the first word of each verse or stanza begins with a successive letter of the alphabet in the original language). In this case, the effect is to give full expression to public and private grief by listing Judah's sufferings from *A* to *Z*.

CHALLENGE FACING THE READER OR TEACHER OF THIS BOOK. To fully appreciate the spiritual benefit of lamentation as a spiritual privilege and duty

HOW TO MEET THE CHALLENGE. Study the author's example, and thus learn how to express grief in a godly way.

*J*eremiah, after the city was destroyed and the Temple burnt, bewailed the miserable state of his own nation, not after the manner of heathens, but that he might show that even in so disastrous a state of things, some benefit might be derived from what he says. . . . It is an easy thing to extol in high terms the favor of God in prosperity . . . ; but when things are in a state of despair, and God seems to have forsaken his Church, prophecy still remains in force. . . . When, therefore, he understood that his teaching would not be without fruit, he was thus induced to speak first of God's judgments; secondly, to exhort the people to repentance; thirdly, to encourage them to hope; and lastly, to open the door for prayer to God, so that the people in their extremities might venture to flee to God's mercy; which could not have been done without faith.

JOHN CALVIN
Lamentations

Imagine seeing your hometown suffer a two-year siege at the hands of a brutal army. Imagine watching the people you love—your friends and family—starving for food, being raped by enemy soldiers, and being carried off into exile. Imagine enduring such intense suffering that mothers devour their own children and the living envy the dead. This is what Jeremiah witnessed at the end of his life, and as we hear the cry of his wounded heart, we learn how to identify with God's suffering people and honestly lament our losses in a way that honors God.

Key Words

The key words in Lamentations are decidedly melancholy:

- *weep*
- *woe*
- *afflicted*

The Structure

Lamentations is aptly named, for the book consists of five laments—melancholy dirges that give formal expression to deep feelings of sadness at the time of death:

First Lament: Jerusalem in Her Desolation (Chapter 1). The prophet (vv. 1-11) and the people (vv. 12-22) of Jerusalem weep over the destruction and devastation of their city. Notice how the opening verses set the mood and the scene for the rest of the book. Notice also how the writer personifies the city as a woman who has lost her children and her dignity.

KEY VERSES

"Jerusalem, once so full of people, is now deserted. She who was once great among the nations now sits alone like a widow. . . . For all these things I weep; tears flow down my cheeks. No one is here to comfort me; any who might encourage me are far away. My children have no future, for the enemy has conquered us" (1:1, 16). These verses provide the narrative context of Jerusalem's destruction and capture the melancholy mood that pervades the book.

Second Lament: The Desolation Caused by Divine Judgment (Chapter 2). The writer makes it clear that what the people have suffered is the result of God's sovereign justice. The righteous hand of God has gone against his rebellious people.

Third Lament: Jeremiah Moves from Sorrow to Hope (Chapter 3). The prophet describes his experiences of hunger, homelessness, and imprisonment. Perhaps he is still writing as Judah's representative, but he also seems to refer to his own personal sufferings. The book's major turning point comes in verse 21, as the author confesses his faith and expresses growing confidence in the mercy of God. Look for ways that the second half of this lament gives hope and guidance to the captives in Babylon.

KEY VERSES
"The faithful love of the LORD never ends! His mercies never cease. Great is his faithfulness; his mercies begin afresh each morning" (3:22-23). These familiar verses are usually read out of context. When we see them against the dark backdrop of Jerusalem's suffering, they shine with even more brilliant hope.

Fourth Lament: The Desolation Brought by Judah's Sin (Chapter 4). As the writer vividly relives the horrific conditions during the last days of Jerusalem, he identifies the underlying cause of the disaster: The people had sinned, and thus they deserved their punishment. As the writer records specific sins, notice how he implicates three sources of spiritual leadership: prophets, priests, and kings.

Fifth Lament: A Cry for Mercy (Chapter 5). The last lament reflects the context of captivity, and unlike the previous ones, which seem to have been written in the immediate aftermath of the catastrophe, it may have been written some time after the fall of Jerusalem. This lament is in the form of a prayer for renewal and restoration. The writer makes a desperate plea for God to remember his people and to bless the remnant in their repentance. As you read the final verses, consider what emotional progress (if any) you can observe over the course of the five laments. What is the biblical answer to Jeremiah's final question?

Key Characters
A key character is Jeremiah, the weeping prophet, but even more so the city of Jerusalem, personified as a grieving woman.

Key Doctrines
Sin. The wickedness of human sin
Judgment. The righteousness of God's judgment
Mercy. The hope that springs from the daily faithfulness of God's merciful compassion

Tips for Reading or Teaching Lamentations
To get the full context for Lamentations, read the biblical accounts of the fall of Jerusalem in 2 Kings 25 and Jeremiah 39 and 52, as well as the prophecies of destruction throughout Jeremiah and elsewhere. Lamentations is much more than an appendix to Jeremiah, and to get the full emotional impact, you need to linger over its poetic images of sorrow and suffering.

Contribution of the Book to the Bible's Story of Salvation in Christ

Although Lamentations does not contain any specific messianic prophecies, it anticipates the rejection (1:12), derision (2:15-16), and mockery (3:14) that Jesus suffered on behalf of his people. Taken as a whole, Jeremiah's lamentation for Jerusalem anticipates the tears that Jesus later shed for the same city in its spiritual desolation (see Matthew 23:37-38).

Applying the Book

Because it was written in the raw pain of grief, Lamentations helps give verbal expression to some of our own thoughts and feelings of loss, particularly at times of national tragedy. The book helps us to be honest with God about our emotions and honest with ourselves about the suffering we deserve because of our sin.

DID YOU KNOW?
In the English Bible, Lamentations comes after Jeremiah. This makes good chronological sense. However, the Hebrew Bible places Lamentations with the Writings rather than with the Prophets. This is because the Writings were tied to annual festivals, and Lamentations was read on the anniversary of the fall of Jerusalem.

PERSPECTIVES
ON THE BOOK OF LAMENTATIONS

A desperate recounting of utmost woe. H. L. Ellison

The Lord's stern discipline has awakened within Judah a sense of her own sinfulness, worthlessness, and helplessness. And finally, out of the depths of the bitterness occasioned by divine chastisement, she invokes God's grace and compassion. J. G. S. S. Thomson

Lamentations is a skillfully structured book of five separate poems. Each poem is complete in itself and independent of its predecessor or successor, yet all share a common theme of sorrow over Jerusalem's fall, though from different perspectives. Sometimes the grief is individual; sometimes it is an expression of national grief. The funeral mood was communicated to those who first heard or read Lamentations by the dirgelike meter that characterizes much of the book. F. B. Huey Jr.

In these days of personal, national, and international crises (and disaster) the message of this book is a challenge to repent of sins personal, national, and international, and to commit ourselves afresh to God's steadfast love. Though this love is ever present and outgoing, a holy and just God must surely judge unrepentant sinners. Ross E. Price

EZEKIEL
*Visionary
Genius*

FORMAT. 48 chapters, 1,273 verses

IMPLIED PURPOSES. To denounce sin, to warn of impending judgment against that sin (including the destruction of Jerusalem), and to paint glorious pictures of a future restoration of Israel

AUTHOR'S PERSPECTIVE. The author is a reporter of what God told him to say. We see evidence that Ezekiel was a priest with intimate knowledge of the Temple. A theatrical streak enabled him to enact symbolic parables, and he loved to express truth through symbols. Ezekiel wrote the entire book while in exile in Babylon (1:1-3).

IMPLIED AUDIENCE. Originally Ezekiel's fellow members of the kingdom of Judah, before and after Jerusalem's destruction. Beyond that, the book appeals to anyone who revels in "right-brain discourse," which uses image and vision as its medium.

WHAT UNIFIES THE BOOK. Ezekiel's colorful personality; symbolism; balance between denunciation of evil and prediction of future blessing; the authoritative voice of God ("This message came to me from the LORD"); prophetic/apocalyptic content

SPECIAL FEATURES. Ezekiel's performance of parables; symbolism (dry bones, a divine chariot); God's frequent address of Ezekiel with "You, son of man"; a near obsession with the Temple as a place and symbol; the use of *Jerusalem* to refer to Judah; emphasis on the glory of God; strong autobiographical element

CHALLENGES FACING THE READER OR TEACHER OF THIS BOOK.
1. The length of the book, combined with a dizzying diversity of material
2. The strangeness of much of the content on a surface level
3. The problem of interpretation when we come to the concluding apocalyptic visions

HOW TO MEET THE CHALLENGES.
1. Settle down to live with the book over a period of time; take the book in small chunks, and interact with each unit in terms appropriate to its genre.
2. Try to relish the sheer strangeness of what is happening or being described. Take time to ponder the general meanings (judgment, evil, blessing) that the details embody. The text itself provides interpretations for many of the symbols.
3. View the apocalyptic visions as using a symbolic technique.

THE MOST COMMON MISCONCEPTIONS ABOUT THIS BOOK. That the book is unintelligible and should therefore remain a closed book and that the Temple visions are being fulfilled literally in the modern state of Israel rather than symbolically in Christ and the new Israel (the church)

No prophet was endowed with such vision—no other vision was as extreme. . . . He oscillates between the shame of sin and the grandeur of salvation—for him there is nothing in between. Ezekiel is a man of extremes. His visions move from the ecstasy of the chariot to the terror of the dry bones. . . . Fragmented images, halting sentences, deafening shouts and soft whispers, words and silences are being used to describe what lies beyond description. . . . He speaks to us—to us, too—[about] the frailty of social structures and the irresistible power of dreams. . . . His sermons have the quality and the urgency of eyewitness reporting, [and he is] mindful of every detail. . . . Like all prophets, Ezekiel opened his prophecy with predictions of doom and closed it with words of consolation.

ELIE WIESEL
"Ezekiel"

The Fate of Judah — Present and Imminent Events — Visions of Judgment — Before the Fall of Jerusalem

The Fate of the Nations — Events Somewhat in the Future — After the Fall of Jerusalem

The Future Destiny of Israel — Final Events — Visions of Blessing — After the Fall of Jerusalem

1–3 The Call of the Prophet
4–7 The Coming Siege of Jerusalem
8–11 Visions of the Evil of Jerusalem
12–24 The Coming Doom of Jerusalem
25–32 Judgment of Seven Neighboring Nations
33–39 Israel's Restoration
40–47:12 Visions of a New Temple and Worship
47:13–48:35 Resettling the Promised Land

AN OUTLINE OF
EZEKIEL

Modern cinematic techniques have made fantasy an everyday occurrence. Just consider how many television commercials perform feats of fantasy and disorientation—tricks of sight that violate reality. Moviemakers and composers of television commercials would not engage in such feats if the results were not effective with audiences. We can see forerunners of today's common techniques in the visionary book of Ezekiel.

The Form of the Book

A good starting point for bringing the book into shape is the label of *visionary writing*. Visionary writing makes no pretence of re-creating reality in the world around us. Instead it transports us to a fantastic realm of the imagination. In this visionary world we find a supernatural jeweled chariot that moves to and fro, invested with a spiritual force (chapter 1). Or we find a vision of the elders of the house of Israel worshipping creeping things and loathsome beasts in the Temple in the dark (8:7-13). Almost through the entire book of Ezekiel, you will encounter visions of things that you know are not literally true although they are symbolic of true events.

Closely related to this is the technique of *symbolic reality*. Symbolic reality exists whenever a writer consistently transports us to a world of the imagination where the most important ingredients are symbols. The book of Ezekiel is a collection of great symbols, such as Israel as a vine (15:1-8) and a faithless wife (chapter 16). God's imminent judgment is pictured as a boiling pot (24:1-14), and we know that God's judgment is not *literally* a boiling pot. Egypt is a great cedar that will be felled (chapter 31). Regeneration is a valley with dry bones that come to life (chapter 37). It is a rare chapter in Ezekiel where we do not move in a world of symbolic reality. Two particularly recurrent symbols are Jerusalem as standing for the nation of Judah in the first half of the book and Israel as a symbol for God's people in all ages in the second half of the book.

Of course the genre of prophecy is prominent in the book of Ezekiel. (For a reminder of the chief ingredients of prophecy as a form of writing, see page 291.) Thus we find the common motifs of (1) satiric *description* of evil, (2) *denunciation* of such evil, and (3) *warnings and predictions* that God will judge the evil. Prophecy like this makes continual references to the moral and spiritual conditions of actual societies and is very much rooted in the present and the near future.

In the later stages of the book, prophecy merges into apocalypse, as it does in most Old Testament prophetic books. (For a reminder of what constitutes apocalyptic writing, see page 633.) This means that the subject of the visions is the eschatological end of history.

Finally, it is important not to overlook the obvious: The dominant mode by which the aforementioned genres are expressed is poetry. It is true that Ezekiel generally avoids verse form and instead uses prose. But at the level of content, the book almost continuously uses poetic language. This means that you will need to assimilate and interpret images and figures of speech.

The Structure

The book of Ezekiel is an anthology—a collection of diverse types of writing. This anthology, moreover, mingles various types of writing, usually without transition. You have no alternative but, in effect, to supply your own table of contents as you work your way through the book. In fact, supplying your own descriptive and interpretive titles to the individual units is a good analytic exercise.

A second structural pattern for the book as a whole is the one that underlies virtually all Old Testament prophetic books, namely, the general shift of gravity from evil and its judgment in the first two-thirds of the book to visions of God's restoration of his chosen people in the last third.

Unifying Elements

- The visionary mode (The book more or less continuously consists of imagined characters and events that do not exist in the real world in the form in which they appear in Ezekiel's visions.)
- The technique of symbolic reality (Most of the scenes and actors are symbols.)
- The prophetic and apocalyptic aspects
- The repeated situation of God's speaking to Ezekiel, who becomes a unifying personality in the book
- Satiric put-down of individual and national evil
- The omnipresent prophetic situation of moving between the poles of judgment and restoration

Key Places and Characters

Virtually all the action takes place in what can be called the ancient Near East or Canaan or Palestine or Israel. We are talking about the region that surrounds the eastern half of the Mediterranean Sea. Particularly in the middle of the book, the places of action are the nations that occupied the

DID YOU KNOW?
- The name *Ezekiel* means "God will strengthen" or "God makes strong" or "may God strengthen."
- Ezekiel was both a prophet and a priest (1:3).
- Ezekiel prophesied for a span of approximately two decades.
- Jeremiah began his ministry in Jerusalem about the time that Ezekiel was born there. As a teenager, Ezekiel must have been impressed and influenced by Jeremiah's life and ministry.
- Ezekiel was about the same age as Daniel. Daniel was deported to Babylon in 605 BC, and Ezekiel in the next wave, in 597 BC. Daniel was well established by the time Ezekiel arrived, and Ezekiel refers to Daniel three times (14:14, 20; 28:3).
- More than fifty times we encounter the formula that the people "will know that I am the LORD."

Mediterranean region, providing a national setting for the action. In the first half of the book, the city of Jerusalem is the main setting for the action, though we understand that the capital city represents the whole nation of Judah.

God is the central actor in the book. He is the One whose authoritative voice lies behind the visions and oracles, and he is the One who predicts that he will exercise judgment and restoration. The lead human character is the mediator-prophet Ezekiel, who comes alive in our imaginations as a real person and a unifying personality for the book. The corporate nation of Judah/Israel is the next most prominent character. After that are the nations of the Mediterranean region, sometimes represented by their rulers.

The Story

It may seem out of place to talk about the plot of a nonnarrative prophetic book, but it is helpful to think in these terms. Behind the visions of Ezekiel is the story of a great cosmic battle between good and evil. The protagonist, God, does battle with the evil that is delineated in seemingly endless detail. He predicts that he will defeat evil, and we are given to understand that what he describes as about to happen or already happening (prophecy often portrays future events as already happening) will actually take place.

Along with the battle, then, an important part of the story is its outcome. God wins. Evil loses, in both history and in the age to come. That is the story we can piece together from the prophetic visions.

Key Doctrines

Sin. The first half of the book is an ever-expanding vision of human sinfulness, accompanied by "program notes" that state what God intends to do about human sinfulness.

The Nature of God. The book is about the nature and acts of God from start to finish; a distinc-

Visionary Writing

Visionary writing portrays things that we know do not literally happen in real life but express truth about either this world or the transcendent world (heaven and hell). In this case, the word *vision* implies that the things portrayed are something imagined rather than something you can see or touch. Visionary writing does not reproduce the world in which we live (the literary term for that is *realism*) but rather creates an alternate reality. The standard literary term for such writing is *fantasy*.

Where does such writing occur in the Bible? In many places, but the biggest categories are prophetic writing, as in the book of Ezekiel, and apocalyptic writing, as in the book of Revelation. Despite differences between those two forms of writing, they share the technique of visionary writing, including the following specific features:

- Transformation or reversal of real life. The most common form portrays future events as already occurring, contrary to all that is happening at the time of writing. For example, nations that are currently powerful are pictured as defeated, or a nation or group that is currently persecuted is pictured as restored and prosperous.
- Cosmic or natural forces as characters in the story. In visionary writing, animals, stars, and rivers suddenly replace people as agents in the action that is being envisioned.
- Unearthly agents as characters. In visionary writing, we encounter such otherworldly creatures as two women with wings like a stork's (Zechariah 5:9) and a dragon with seven heads that knocks down a third of the stars (Revelation 12:3-4).
- Unearthly settings and objects. Ezekiel's vision of a divine chariot (Ezekiel 1) and John's account of what he saw when the door of heaven opened to his gaze (Revelation 4) whisk us away to a strange world far removed from anything we experience in this world.
- Unrealistic events. In real life, horses are not red (Revelation 6:4), a branch cannot build a temple (Zechariah 6:12), and a goat's horn cannot reach to the heavens and throw stars to the ground (Daniel 8:8-10), but in visionary writing such events happen routinely.

The element of the unexpected extends from the content of visionary writing to its structure. Visionary writing is usually embodied in the form of visions—brief units following in rapid-fire succession, much as we find in modern film effects. The resulting organization is frequently disjointed and constantly shifting. The material that makes up these units is likewise diverse, consisting of visual descriptions, speeches that the visionary author hears and records, predictions, brief snatches of narrative, direct addresses to characters or to the reader, letters, prayers, hymns, and parables. Dream, not narrative, is the controlling format.

tive touch is the glimpses the book gives of the glory of God, though it would be wrong to reduce the whole book to just this attribute.

Covenant. The book of Ezekiel tells the story of human disregard for God's covenant and God's response to that disregard in the form of judgment and mercy.

Eschatology. Chiefly in the last third of the book, we encounter visions of the end.

Judgment. The usual prophetic theme of God's judgment against sin is evident everywhere.

Salvation. Equally, the book as a whole shows us the certainty and nature of God's salvation.

Tips for Reading or Teaching Ezekiel

Although a story—the cosmic battle between good and evil—underlies the book, you should not look for narrative content or structure. Instead you need to summon what a reading of Isaiah and Jeremiah also requires: patience in settling down to the "long read." Resist the impulse to read for the story line, and resolve to take the time that an anthology of assorted nonnarrative genres requires of you.

Knowing that the book is written in poetic form and, further, that Ezekiel shares with the New Testament book of Revelation the distinction of being the most obvious examples of symbolic reality, you need to (1) do justice to the literal aspect of a symbol such as the chariot of divine glory leaving the Temple (chapter 10) or of a valley of dry bones (37:1-14) and then (2) interpret what the symbol points to.

Resist the potential to get bogged down in the wealth of details such as we find in the vision of the restored Temple and the reparceling of the Promised Land among the twelve tribes (chapters 40–48). Just accept the fact that some of the accumulated detail is a *symbolic richness,* and go for the general meaning, usually a symbolic one (such as the lavishness of God's provision for his people).

Instead of despairing over the mystery and strangeness of some sections of the book, accept them as part of the strange-world motif. The book of Ezekiel exists partly to reveal the mystery of the supernatural. God's thoughts are not our thoughts (Isaiah 55:8), and the disorienting effects of Ezekiel are a way of embodying that principle.

Apply what you know about the genres represented in the book of Ezekiel: visionary writing, prophecy, apocalyptic writing, poetry, and satire.

The Flow of the Book

The Call of Ezekiel to Be a Prophet (Chapters 1–3). Chapter 1 transports you to a strange world—a fantasy world in the sense that what Ezekiel describes could happen only in a vision, which in fact it was. Once you have negotiated the strangeness of the chariot Ezekiel saw, your best approach to this material is to treat it as your initiation into the book as a whole. What do you learn about the prophet and his mission? What do you learn about God? What things characterize the prophet's world? What role does God play in the unfolding series of events and visions?

quick overview of ezekiel

1:1–24:27	The evil and coming judgment of Judah
25:1–32:32	The coming judgment of Judah's neighboring countries
33:1–48:35	Visions of the restoration of a spiritual entity called Israel

Visions of the Coming Siege and Destruction of Jerusalem (Chapters 4–7). In addition to the pictorial aspect of Ezekiel's visions, symbolic actions performed by the prophet are a main part of his message. The only good way to proceed with material such as these visions of what will happen to Jerusalem is to read slowly and let the pictures sink into your imagination. Then ponder what meanings the pictures and symbolic actions imply. In effect, you need to interpret poetry. (For a primer on how poetry works, see the article on page 237.)

The book of Ezekiel follows its own unique, sequential logic here. In this section the prophet simply paints graphic predictive pictures of the terrible fate that will overtake Jerusalem and, by extension, the whole nation. At this point in the book, we do not yet know the reasons for this drastic judgment.

Visions of Jerusalem's Evil (Chapters 8–11). We now get the beginnings of an answer to the mounting question of what could have moved God to such drastic acts of judgment against Jerusalem as those that Ezekiel has predicted. This unit is actually quite mixed in its content, but perhaps the central business is to paint pictures of the sinfulness of Jerusalem. The most helpful grid for dealing with these visions is satire. (For a reminder of what things constitute satire as a form of writing, see the article on page 373.) Assemble a list of the specific sins that Ezekiel holds up to satiric attack and exposure. As we end the unit (chapters 10–11), we largely return to the earlier mode of Ezekiel: visions of God's glory and predictions of a terrible fate that will overtake Jerusalem.

Parabolic Actions, Visions, and Predictions: Variations on the Theme of Jerusalem's Doom (Chapters 12–24). Prophetic discourse is wide-ranging and randomly organized. The only thing that unifies these thirteen chapters is that they focus on the fate of Jerusalem. Under this umbrella, we find a mini-anthology of prophetic forms. There are *symbolic actions,* such as those involving Ezekiel's baggage (12:1-16) and eating and drinking with trembling to signal fear (12:17-20). There is an abundance of *reported symbols,* such as the vine (chapter 15), the two eagles and the cedar (chapter 17), and the boiling pot (chapter 24). We also encounter direct messages of what "the word of the LORD" told Ezekiel to say.

To match this bewildering mixture of *modes of presentation,* the *content* in these chapters is equally varied. We find *descriptions* of Jerusalem's evil and predictions of God's *punishment* of Jerusalem for its evil. Satire not only attacks vice but also lets us know the *norm* or *standard of rightness* by which evil is judged; thus in this unit we find visions of the glory of God and assertions of his justice. And then, true to prophetic form, without transition we encounter visions of God's restoration and blessing (e.g., 16:53-62; 20:40-44).

In short, you need to keep on your guard and resist any suggestion that the section is organized topically and according to an outline. Treat every unit on its own terms. Be true to the nature of the unit, even if it is not clear to you how you suddenly landed on this particular material.

KEY VERSE

"The soul who sins shall die" (18:4, ESV). Here is the bad-news half of the equation in Ezekiel: Sin carries inevitable punishment because God presides over the world in justice.

Small Comfort: Jerusalem's Oppressive Neighbors Will Also Get Their Comeuppance (Chapters 25–32). In this section we see that God's justice is impartial. Judah will be punished, but so will the surrounding pagan nations who had made life so miserable for the Israelites through the centuries. In fact, the satiric visions of indictment and predicted destruction read like a virtual roll call of all the terrible nations that are household names to readers familiar with the Old Testament: Moab, Edom, Philistia, Tyre, Sidon, Egypt, Babylon—they are all here. So are some of their famous kings, such as Nebuchadnezzar and Pharaoh. The chapters read like a gathering of losers, and the fact that there are seven nations lends a symbolic finality to their judgment.

To relish these chapters, read slowly and let each vision or oracle or satiric exposure unfold its meanings in terms of the kind of passage it is. Nearly everywhere, you need to interpret poetry and symbolism, so do not give in to the temptation to take a shortcut around what you are learning about these genres.

Oracles and Visions of Israel's Restoration (Chapters 33–39). The main action of this unit is to paint a picture of national restoration. There are numerous individual "golden age" prophecies here. But the combat motif is also strong and eventually shocking, as Israel's glory will partly be at the expense of its conquest of evil nations, including a symbolic land of Magog and its ruler, Gog.

What are we to make of these golden-age visions? You will not go wrong if you regard them as picturing the timeless experience of God's blessing on people who fear him. For example, a vision of dry bones that come to life (chapter 37:1-14) need not depict any specific future event. The vision is a symbolic, or metaphoric, picture of regeneration: for a New Testament believer, new life in Christ by the Spirit and the Word, and eventual resurrection to eternal life. Some of the visions portray what the incarnate Christ did: for example, the vision of a good shepherd who rescues his sheep and punishes bad shepherds (chapter 34). On the other hand, when we read about Gog and Magog and terrible final battles, it is natural to start thinking in apocalyptic terms and, accordingly, to see these visions as eschatological in nature—an Old Testament foreshadowing of the book of Revelation, with which the book of Ezekiel has numerous specific parallels.

Visions of a Restored Temple (40:1–47:12). If you think that the visions up to this point have been mysterious and often confusing and the interpretive questions severe, you haven't seen anything yet. Chapter after chapter we now read in staggering, specific detail about the resplendent Temple that God showed Ezekiel, along with instructions about worship and offerings that God requires of the people of Israel. The question is what all of this means. In a book that has been symbolic throughout, it hardly seems plausible that God intends us to draw the conclusion that a glorious temple and an elaborate return to Old Testament practices of worship and sacrifice will once again be required. After all, the sacrifice of Christ abolished all of this. We must see the fulfillment of Ezekiel's hopes in Jesus Christ as Israel's once-for-all atonement for sin and in the church as God's new temple.

The safest interpretive route is that of symbolism. In Ezekiel's vision, a river flows from the door of the Temple; Jesus said that from the hearts of those who believe in him "'will flow rivers of living water.' Now this he said about the Spirit, whom those who believed in him were to receive" (John 7:38-39, ESV). Equally symbolic is the New Testament picture of Christians as God's Temple (1 Corinthians 3:16; 2 Corinthians 6:16). Might the Temple of Ezekiel's vision be symbolic of the same thing? A further avenue of interpretation is to regard the Temple as symbolic of an eschatological reality: the glorious saints of God in heaven with the Lamb at the center of their worship.

KEY VERSES

"I will give you a new heart, and I will put a new spirit in you. I will take out your stony, stubborn heart and give you a tender, responsive heart [literally, heart of flesh]. And I will put my Spirit in you so that you will follow my decrees and be careful to obey my regulations" (36:26-27). This is the second half of the equation in Ezekiel: a vision of salvation from sin and the formation of a new creature by God's Holy Spirit.

Resettling Israel All Over Again (47:13–48:35). To complete the symbolic extravaganza, the book ends by supplementing the vision of a restored Temple with a reenactment of the parceling out of the Promised Land to the tribes of Israel. At this point we need to be alert to the fact that apocalyptic writing regularly floods the text with measurements and specifics of location (witness the abundance of measurements that the description of the New Jerusalem receives at the end of Revelation). When in the very last sentence of the book of Ezekiel we read that "the name of the city will be 'The LORD Is There'" (48:35), it is not hard to believe that we are looking at the same eternal kingdom of God that the last book of the Bible portrays in its closing pages. The richness of specific details symbolizes a spiritual perfection, though the earthly imagery paradoxically also reminds us that heaven is a real place, not a vague hope.

The Main Themes

1. God is the ultimate being with whom individuals and nations need to deal. He is the sovereign Lord of history.
2. God judges evil. No one can sin with impunity. People reap what they sow.
3. God is also a God of salvation and restoration. His ultimate restoration will come at the end of history.

Contribution of the Book to the Bible's Story of Salvation in Christ

We need to note at once that there are fewer overt messianic prophecies in

Ezekiel than we would expect in a prophetic book as long as this one. What we can discern, though, are "second meanings" in which we find it natural to see Christ as the ultimate example of certain details in the text: a branch that becomes a majestic cedar on a mountain (17:22-24), a good shepherd who feeds his flock (chapter 34), a coming king ("my servant David") who will rule over Israel (37:24-28). Then, too, the ethical principles embodied in Ezekiel's denunciations are the same as we find in the denunciations made by Jesus in the Gospels. We can view the exhilarating visions of Israel restored and even the long portrayal of a new temple and a new parceling of the Promised Land (in the last nine chapters) as a symbolic picture of what Christ has done and will do as the ultimate Lamb of God and the foundation for the new temple of God's new Israel.

Applying the Book

The application is similar to that for other prophetic books, and we need not apologize for finding the application similar across the board for Old Testament prophecy. The descriptions and put-downs of the unethical behavior of Judah and its neighboring countries exist to raise our own ethical consciousness and prompt us to act morally toward our fellow humans. The same thing applies to the indictments of spiritual misbehavior—as distinct from moral misbehavior—such as setting up metaphoric idols in our hearts (14:4).

Another level of application flows from the exalted pictures the book paints of the glory of God. It is wrong to reduce the book to this theme, but it remains true that Ezekiel has given us some of the most memorable visions of God's glory. The application is to revere this God and live before him in what the Bible calls the fear of the Lord.

Finally, the eschatological parts of the book should awaken our allegiance to and longing for the promised end. Our whole cultural situation conspires against our living with one foot in heaven. The book of Ezekiel can help us to do that.

PERSPECTIVES
ON THE BOOK OF EZEKIEL

All Things Weird and Wonderful. Title of a book on Ezekiel by Stuart Briscoe

The great mystic among the inspired writers. Charles Lee Feinberg

Easily the most bizarre of all the prophets. J. Alec Motyer

[On the book's structure:] The ministry of Ezekiel itself falls into two clear phases: his first five years between his call and the fall of Jerusalem; and the remaining fifteen years after that event. Chapters 1–24 come from the first period and are predominantly oracles of judgment. . . . Chapters 33–48 come from the latter period, and the dominant theme is hope for the future through God's promise of restoration. In between these two major sections are gathered together a selection of the prophecies of Ezekiel against foreign nations. J. Alec Motyer

[On the Temple vision of chapters 40–47:] When the Jews returned from exile and rebuilt the Temple, what they constructed did not resemble Ezekiel's ground plan. . . .We should do what . . . the New Testament does and see how the goal of Ezekiel's Temple finds its fulfillment in Jesus Christ. . . . Christ himself is the new Temple. He is the dwelling of God among humankind, the glory of God made manifest (John 1:14).
Iain M. Duguid

We do not have to look deeply to find the key idea and the focal message of Ezekiel. They confront us on almost every page. With slight variations, that expression, "They shall know that I am Jehovah," occurs no less than seventy times. J. Sidlow Baxter

[The central themes of the book:] "the sovereignty and glory of God," "the utter sinfulness of humans," "the inescapable coming of judgment," "the return of the King and the restoration of the people to their land and a state of blessing." Iain M. Duguid

To [Ezekiel], indeed, everything comes by way of vision and concrete sign.
Victorian poet Francis Thompson

The most salient trait of Ezekiel's style . . . is his extraordinary realistic and visualizing sense. Every idea seems to stand out in concrete form and measure and color, as if [recorded by a] matter-of-fact observer.
John F. Genung

DANIEL

Dare to Be a Daniel

FORMAT. 12 chapters, 357 verses

IMPLIED PURPOSES. To hold up exemplary heroes, chiefly Daniel and his three friends, for admiration and emulation and to record prophetic dreams of future history and the end of the ages

AUTHOR'S PERSPECTIVE. In the narrative half of the book, the author idealizes heroic characters and largely denigrates two pagan kings; in the prophetic half, the author records visions that exalt God and show the fragility of earthly kingdoms.

IMPLIED AUDIENCE. The Jewish community in exile in Babylon. The long-term audience consists of believers in God who want to know how to live in a godless culture and what to expect in the future and at the end of the ages.

WHAT UNIFIES THE BOOK. The unifying personality and heroism of Daniel; dreams and visions; the international context (references to empires and their rulers); continual demonstrations that God is sovereign over earthly history, including kings and kingdoms

SPECIAL FEATURES. Two distinct halves: a narrative half and a visionary/apocalyptic half; masterpieces of storytelling; a gallery of memorable characters; mingling of third-person material (references to what "Daniel" did) and first-person material (where Daniel speaks of himself as "I, Daniel"); action and visions rooted in the time and place of Judah's exile in Babylon and Persia; famous and captivating images (such as the fiery furnace, a disembodied hand that writes on the wall, and a gigantic image of a man composed of various minerals)

CHALLENGES FACING THE READER OR TEACHER OF THIS BOOK.
1. The need to master two entirely different genres in the two halves of the book

333

2. The difficulty of knowing what the strange visions of the second half mean

3. The apparent remoteness of the world of the text from our own time and place

HOW TO MEET THE CHALLENGES.

1. Shift gears from narrative to visionary expectations halfway through a book that is really two books.

2. You can undertake thorough research to see how a range of commentators have handled the prophetic visions, or you can be content with generalized interpretations: that God is sovereign, that earthly empires will fall, that God will bring human history to an end and establish Christ's eternal kingdom.

3. Undertake a two-way journey: first to the world of the text and then back to your own world—as always, the Bible gets at the universal through the particular.

By the use of dreams and visions, signs, symbols and numbers [the book of Daniel declares] the course of history . . . mapping out its course as it proceeds towards its end. In technical language the book is therefore eschatological (Gk. eschaton, end). Like the early chapters of Genesis it is universal in its scope. . . . This is made possible by a series of special visions which reveal to Daniel God's purpose for the world. Such an unveiling of history from a divine standpoint is a salient feature of apocalyptic (Gk. apokalypsis, revelation). . . . Apocalyptic such as we have in the book of Daniel [views] secular world empires in the light of God's purposes for world history.

JOYCE G. BALDWIN
Daniel: An Introduction and Commentary

	Cyrus		
10–12 Vision of the Last Days			
	Darius	Dreams, with Interspersed Narrative	Mainly Predictive of the Future
9 Vision of Seventy Weeks			
	Belshazzar		
8 Vision of the Ram and Goat			
7 Vision of Four Beasts			
	Darius		
6 Daniel in the Lions' Den			
	Belshazzar		
5 Writing on the Wall			
4 Nebuchadnezzar's Insanity	Nebuchadnezzar	Narrative, with Interspersed Dream	Mainly Occurring in Daniel's Present Situation
3 The Fiery Furnace			
2 Nebuchadnezzar's Dream			
1 Daniel and His Three Friends			

AN OUTLINE OF
DANIEL

"Two for the price of one!" The appeal of that advertisement is universal and perennial. The book of Daniel gives us two for the price of one. It takes up two very different questions that are always relevant to Christians. The first is how followers of God can maintain their loyalty to God while living in cultures that are hostile to biblical religion. The second is curiosity about what the future holds and how history will end.

The Form of the Book

The book of Daniel is unique in the Bible in that it falls into two equal halves that belong to different genres. The first half is a textbook example of heroic narrative: stories about representative and exemplary characters. The basic rules of hero stories are stated in the article on page 213 of this book.

The second half is a nearly pure example of prophetic and visionary writing. You can refresh your awareness of prophetic writing, visionary writing, and apocalyptic writing by referring to the articles on pages 291, 325, and 633.

Unifying Elements

- Daniel is the main human character in both halves of the book.
- Virtually everything in the book demonstrates the sovereignty of God over earthly history.
- Supernatural and miraculous events permeate the book.
- Dreams and visions are prevalent in both halves.
- The world of the book is a world of empires and rulers, and royal settings occur frequently.

Key Places and Characters

The most obvious setting for the action in the first half of the book is that of the foreign power in which the Jewish characters move: first Babylon and then its successor, Persia. Most of the action, moreover, takes place in the courts of these foreign powers. In the second half, the main stage of action is a visionary stage: an imaginary place where the chief "stage props" are either symbols (mysterious beasts or a tree that reaches to heaven) or undesignated kingdoms on earth.

The most powerful character and the one who matters most is God. The chief human character is Daniel. The secondary cast of characters includes Daniel's three friends (Shadrach, Meshach, and Abednego) and three world rulers (Nebuchadnezzar, Belshazzar, and Darius). The rulers who populate the visions in the second half are largely unnamed.

Key Doctrines

The Sovereignty of God. God controls events and imposes his will all through the stories and visions of Daniel.

Godliness. In the behavior of Daniel and his three friends, we see what faithfulness to God looks like.

Eschatology. The book of Daniel is a chief repository of biblical teaching about the future and the end.

Tips for Reading or Teaching Daniel

Enter into the spirit of the six stories told in the first half of the book. Their appeal as stories is irresistible, so do justice to them as stories—to the settings, the characters, and the plots.

Because the visions of Daniel have spawned a large volume of commentary and many contradictory views, your best procedure is to go for general meanings of the visions rather than detailed ones. Be content with seeing general themes of God's sovereignty, the mutability of rulers and empires, the certainty of God's eternal kingdom, and the need to trust in God's grand design instead of in temporary earthly securities.

quick overview of daniel

1:1–6:28	Six separate hero stories
7:1–12:13	Four apocalyptic visions

The Flow of the Book

Standing Firm for the Faith at Babylon University (Chapter 1). The best procedure for the first six chapters is to treat them as six separate hero stories. To each of them you can apply the usual questions for hero stories (see the article on page 213). In chapter 1, Daniel and his three friends are a composite hero. Analyze the precise nature of their testing; their heroic qualities and acts; the outcome; and on the basis of those, what the story says about God and godliness.

Daniel, Interpreter of Dreams (Chapter 2). At this point you are still in the narrative part of the book. Instead of getting sidetracked into treating Nebuchadnezzar's dream as prophecy, assimilate it as the storyteller encourages you to: as evidence of Daniel's heroism and as part of the story of Nebuchadnezzar as told in the early chapters of the book. Keep the focus on Nebuchadnezzar and his situation without escaping into charts of history (you will have plenty of this in the second half of the book). As you go through the chapter, it will be helpful to cluster the details around these unifying motifs: (1) the sovereignty of God over human history and over Nebuchadnezzar and (2) the specific things that contribute to the portrait of Daniel as an exemplary hero.

Faith in the Furnace (Chapter 3). This is another self-contained hero story, with Daniel's three friends as the heroes. Pay attention to the narrative qualities first of all (you will not be handling Daniel 1–6 correctly if you are not receptive to the story qualities that make these chapters a favorite with children). These narrative ingredients include an ordeal, a heroic response to the ordeal, and a miraculous rescue. Assemble a portrait of Nebuchadnezzar, as he is important in these early chapters.

KEY VERSE
"The Most High God rules over the kingdoms of the world and appoints anyone he desires to rule over them" (5:21). Here are both halves of the book in a nutshell, with the focus on God's sovereignty and on kingdoms and rulers as the sphere where that sovereignty exerts itself.

A King's Fall and Recovery (Chapter 4). Nebuchadnezzar becomes the unlikely hero of chapter 4. Note also what is heroic about Daniel's actions. Keep in mind that hero stories put the heroes in situations that test them. Physical testing has been the favorite kind of ordeal (hence the large quantity of battle and combat stories), and moral testing has been prominent as well. A smaller circle of stories tests the hero's mental resourcefulness. Stories about heroes who have an ability to interpret dreams are the ancient equivalent of our modern detective stories. But chapter 4 springs a surprise on us: As the story unfolds, Daniel recedes from center stage, and Nebuchadnezzar, insane and then recovered, comes to dominate the action. It is his story that embodies the important themes, so ponder what those themes are (e.g., God's judgment against human pride).

Daniel, Solver of Riddles (Chapter 5). Here is another story that is a favorite with children. Analyze the qualities that make the story so famous and moving. Then think about how the main motifs of the chapter reinforce what has been going on for four chapters—such motifs as persecution, Daniel's heroism, God's sovereignty, the importance of dreams or riddles, miraculous happenings, and God's protection of his people.

Faith in the Lions' Den (Chapter 6). Look for by-now common threads in the action: Daniel's heroism (note the specifics) and its detractors, the response of a pagan king as a main element of the story, and God's control of human events.

Two Prophetic Visions of World Empires (Chapters 7–8). The first six chapters of Daniel are the perfect example of an "easy read," but now the plot begins to thicken. For the second half of Daniel, you need to shift into the mode of prophecy and visionary writing (for information on prophecy, see page 291; for tips on how visionary writing works, see page 325). You have two options for assimilating the visionary half of Daniel: Either you can accept the general level of meaning that God is in control of the history of empires and will bring human history to an end, or you can consult study Bibles and commentaries for pointers on the historical and eschatological particulars of each vision. Whichever you choose, be receptive to the surface level, with its evocative visionary imagery. The visions of chapters 7–8 predict the rise and fall of four ancient empires— Babylon, Persia, Greece, and Rome—all represented in highly symbolic form. It is crucial that you look for the details that are eschatological in nature and that refer to Christ's messianic kingdom.

Daniel's Prayer and Symbolic Vision of Israel's Future (Chapter 9). Daniel's prayer (vv. 3-19) expresses truths that are open to anyone's understanding. The best way to deal with the concluding vision is to accept it as predicting God's victory at the end of history.

Daniel's Vision of the End (Chapters 10–12). Keep in mind your two options: finding a general eschatological meaning or matching the details to specific world empires that are already long gone. Whichever you choose, you need to pick up the messianic thread and the hints of God's glorious termination of human history, such as we read about in the last book of the Bible (for example, international warfare, earthly empires coming to an end, and the resurrection of believers to everlasting life in heaven).

DID YOU KNOW?
- The name *Daniel* means "God is my judge."
- In the original text the book of Daniel exists in two languages: Hebrew in chapters 1 and 8–12, Aramaic in chapters 2–7.
- In the Hebrew Scriptures, the book of Daniel appears not in the section of Prophets but in the Writings.

The Main Themes

1. GOD IS THE SOVEREIGN GOD OF HISTORY. He is the transcendent central character in the history of the universe.
2. GOD INSTRUCTS US PARTLY BY GIVING US EXEMPLARY AND GODLY PEOPLE TO IMITATE. Daniel and his friends are such examples.
3. GOD JUDGES HUMAN SINFULNESS.
4. GOD HAS A PLAN FOR THE FUTURE. It involves the ultimate and final destruction of evil and the triumph of good.

Contribution of the Book to the Bible's Story of Salvation in Christ

The chief messianic element of the book appears in its prophetic visions. Here you will find symbolic details that we can confidently know apply to Christ because they appear elsewhere in the Bible (especially the New Testament). Examples include the vision of the son of man to whom God gives dominion (7:13-14) and the prophecy of a coming ruler who will set up an eternal kingdom (2:44-45).

Applying the Book

The application of the first six chapters flows from their status as a minicollection of hero stories: It is the simple message to be heroic in the ways that Daniel and his three friends were and to avoid the self-destructive behavior and affront to God that Nebuchadnezzar and Belshazzar represented. In the examples of heroism we can see how to live as God's uncompromising followers in a hostile culture.

The application of the visionary second half of the book is to believe that God is in control of history, to flee the wrath to come by placing your faith in Christ as Savior, and to not be bewildered when human history winds its way to a degenerate end before God establishes his eternal Kingdom.

PERSPECTIVES
ON THE BOOK OF DANIEL

We miss the whole purpose of the book . . . if we engage in arithmetical niceties. Sir Robert A. Anderson

Without doubt the principal theological focus of the book is the sovereignty of God. Every page reflects the author's conviction that his God was the Lord of individuals, nations, and all of history. Stephen R. Miller

The two halves each convey a different message on the same theme: the relationship between the kingdom of God and the kingdoms of men. P. R. Davis

[Daniel] was somewhere between the ages of fourteen and nineteen when we pick up the story in Daniel 1. He had been taken from his family, his religious environment, and his support group. He was taken to a foreign country where he was asked to be part of a culture that pressured him to reject his religious roots. Here is a story that offers hope and insight for believers who live and work in environments where they are a minority. Edward G. Dobson

Unlike the prophetic books, Daniel does not emphasize sin, punishment, and restoration, . . . nor does it explain why Israel fell. Instead, Daniel is an apocalyptic book. That is, it stresses the distant future, claims God orders history, and uses symbolic language. Paul R. House

Daniel is to the [Old Testament] what the Book of Revelation is to the [New Testament]. Warren W. Wiersbe

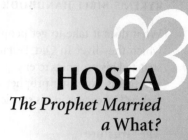

HOSEA
The Prophet Married a What?

FACT SHEET

FORMAT. 14 chapters, 197 verses

IMPLIED PURPOSES. To instill a sense of shame in God's covenant people when they deliberately ignore God's rules for living and are unfaithful to him, and to encourage them to love and obey God in response to his love for them

AUTHOR'S PERSPECTIVE. Hosea writes rather objectively and dispassionately even about his own disappointing marriage to Gomer. He accepts his prophetic role as the servant of God, both in living as a real-life symbol for Israel and in pronouncing messages from God that tended to alienate him from his fellow Israelites.

IMPLIED AUDIENCE. God's covenant people. In the Old Testament this was the nation of Israel, as the book continuously keeps alive in our consciousness. But in the New Testament age the intended audience is Christians, individually and corporately, as the new covenant people of God.

WHAT UNIFIES THE BOOK. The marriage relationship and adultery/prostitution as symbols for how God's people relate to him; the satiric attack on specific sins and attitudes; the format of a divine lawsuit against God's covenant people

SPECIAL FEATURES. The striking story of Hosea's marriage to a prostitute and its restoration, treated as a visible symbol of the book's spiritual message; vivid poetic pictures used as vehicles for portraying moral and spiritual realities (e.g., God's people as an oven or a stubborn heifer or wild grapes); the focus on the theme of the covenant; frank sexual references; anthropomorphism (i.e., portraying God as having human emotions)

FACT SHEET

What does it take to get people to pay attention to the spiritual peril in which they live? In Old Testament prophetic times, God sometimes instructed his prophets to engage in object lessons as a way of teaching spiritual truths. No other prophet was called on to do such a heart-wrenching task as Hosea was in his sordid marriage to a prostitute named Gomer.

The Structure

Part of the book's strategy is to draw parallels between Hosea's marriage to a faithless wife and Israel's faithlessness to God, but this is mainly a background analogy rather than a principle of organization. Most of the book is devoted to God's indictment of his covenant people in passages that are primarily satiric (for information on satire as a form of writing, see page 373). Some outlines of the book tend to claim that the first three chapters deal with Hosea and his wife, Gomer, but this is not exactly true, as this outline shows:

KEY VERSE
"Return, O Israel, to the LORD your God, for your sins have brought you down" (14:1). Like the other prophetic books, Hosea contains two basic themes: how God's people have rejected his commands for living and how, in view of their sinfulness, their only hope is to seek God's grace and forgiveness.

Hosea's Marriage to Gomer (Chapter 1). The names of their children ("Not Loved" and "Not My People") already signal the symbolic nature of the marriage.

God's Charges against Israel (Chapter 2). We leave the marriage behind and listen to God's charges against Israel—whom he portrays as an adulterous wife—and his promise to restore her.

Hosea Reclaims Gomer (Chapter 3). Here we have a brief return to the narrative of Hosea and Gomer, which tells about God's command to Hosea to reclaim his adulterous wife.

An Oracle of Judgment (Chapters 4–7). Hosea communicates God's words of judgment against Israel as a faithless people.

God's Intent to Punish Israel's Faithlessness (Chapters 8–10). An extended account of how God will punish the faithlessness of his people, described previously.

God's Love and Judgment (11:1-11). A mingled portrayal of God's love for Israel specifically and his judgment against her evil.

God's Judgment on Evil Societies (11:12–13:16). God promises judgment and punishment on evil societies for their idolatry and rebellion against God.

God's Future Restoration (Chapter 14). Hosea communicates the prediction of God's restoration of his repentant people.

Key Doctrines and Themes

Covenant. The metaphor of human marriage and its violation in the book of Hosea highlights the covenant nature of the relationship between God and his people. The book views evil not primarily as an ethical issue (as in some of the other prophets) but as a violation of the covenant relationship.

Human Sinfulness. People perversely reject God and resort to spiritual adultery.

The Justice of God. He holds people and nations accountable for their evil and punishes them for it.

The Love of God. God's love for his people does not change, in spite of their adulterous behavior.

DID YOU KNOW?

- The name *Hosea* means "salvation."
- Hosea is the second longest of the twelve Minor Prophets, behind Zechariah.
- Hosea and Amos preached to the northern kingdom of Israel.
- Thirty-two times Hosea uses "the tribe of Ephraim" as his title for Israel because Ephraim was its largest tribe.

Tips for Reading or Teaching Hosea

You can safely view the narrative of the marriage of Hosea and Gomer (Chapters 1 and 3), which follows the paradigm of union—separation—restoration, as a human manifestation of the spiritual message of the book. God relates to Israel in the same way that Hosea relates to Gomer. As the book works out the latter theme, you can compile a list of answers to the following:

- What human acts and attitudes disappoint God?
- According to this book, what can people who reject God expect to receive from him?
- What evidences of God's love and grace do you find in the book?

Contribution of the Book to the Bible's Story of Salvation in Christ

Surprisingly, the book of Hosea lacks the specific messianic prophecies of other Old Testament prophetic books. But because of the marriage metaphor that undergirds the book, it is natural for Christians to assimilate the book through the lens of Christ's love for those who believe in him. After all, Ephesians 5:29, 32 compare Christ's love for the church to the love of a husband for his wife. The prophet Hosea was a foreshadowing of the ultimate spiritual husband, who keeps pursuing his wayward wife.

Applying the Book

Applying the book begins by pondering its central metaphor: a faithless wife. It is a picture of how the human race began its earthly course and one that Christians reenact in their daily lives. Then we need to contemplate ways in which we and the church may be guilty of the same kinds of behavior the book denounces. Reading God's extended lawsuit against Israel should serve as a consciousness-raising function. This, in turn, should lead us to ask for and rest in God's grace and forgiveness in Christ—the ultimate revelation of salvation.

PERSPECTIVES
ON THE BOOK OF HOSEA

The prophet of love. Albert C. Knudson

The prophet of the broken heart. John R. Sampey

The message of Hosea should open the eyes of readers today not only to the awesome nature of God's love for us, but also the terrible harm human sinfulness causes to anyone's personal relationship with God.
Gary V. Smith

Out of [Hosea's relationship to Gomer] he learned the deepest secret of the heart of God, that of its mighty . . . unceasing love, and therefore this prophecy, so tragic and awful in its picture of human sin and divine judgment, thrills to the tireless music of a psalm, and the dominant note is that of love. G. Campbell Morgan

[On the family situation when Gomer walked out on Hosea:] That evening a strange silence pervaded the supper hour. Everyone was conscious of the empty place in the family circle. Suddenly little Lo-ruhamah ["Not Pitied"] looked up into [Hosea's] face. "Where's Mamma tonight?" Ralph Earle

The love of Hosea for Gomer had its source and inspiration in that divine love which it imperfectly reveals. The human relationship is the symbol, the divine relationship the reality. Stephen Winward

For what is the story of Hosea if it is not the story of ourselves as members of that body which is the bride of Christ? We are Gomer and God is

Hosea. He married us when we were unclean. He knew that we would prove unfaithful again and again. He knew that we would forsake him. Still he loved us and purchased us to himself through Christ's atonement. If Hosea's story cannot be real (because "God could not ask a man to marry an unfaithful woman"), then neither is the story of salvation real because that is precisely what Christ has done for us.
James Montgomery Boice

JOEL
Attack of the Killer Locusts

FORMAT. 3 chapters, 73 verses

IMPLIED PURPOSE. To predict terrible woes as acts of God's judgment, with a view toward leading people to repent and thereby share in the promised blessings that the writer depicts in the second half of his prophecy

AUTHOR'S PERSPECTIVE. The author writes with the usual prophetic intensity and as a partisan of God's viewpoint as judge and redeemer of the earth.

IMPLIED AUDIENCE. The original audience was the people of Judah, but the universal audience is all people, especially those who claim to be followers of God.

WHAT UNIFIES THE BOOK. Nature imagery, including references to an invasion of locusts; the genre of prophecy with its twofold rhythm of denunciation and promised restoration. (For more on prophecy as a genre, see page 291.)

SPECIAL FEATURES. Vividness of description; a prophecy occasioned by an invasion of locusts, which the prophet sees as an agent of God's judgment against an evil nation; the Day-of-the-Lord motif; a more equal balance between predicted judgment and predicted blessing than is customary in the Old Testament prophetic books

Tornadoes, hurricanes, forest fires—what is the connection between unfortunate events in the life of a person or nation and bad behavior on the part of the people on whom calamity descends? The prophet Joel does not hesitate to ascribe the cause of calamity to human waywardness, starting with an invasion of locusts, described with technical precision (1:4 lists four stages of a locust's biological development).

The Structure
The book of Joel is structured as four prophetic visions:

A Plague of Locusts (Chapter 1). This vision expands into one of the total blighting of nature.

An Invading Army (2:1-17). This vision of an invasion is accompanied by a call to repentance.

God's Response (2:18-32). This comes in the form of a promise that God will restore prosperity to the land of Judah.

God's Promise of Blessing (Chapter 3). God will rescue Judah from its enemies.

KEY VERSE
"I will give you back what you lost to the swarming locusts, the hopping locusts, the stripping locusts, and the cutting locusts" (2:25). Here is the dual thrust of the book: the loss that people suffer when they turn against God, and God's readiness to restore that loss when people repent of their sin.

Key Doctrines and Themes
Divine Judgment against Sin. This perhaps refers especially to the sin practiced by people who claim to be followers of God.

Redemption. God restores sinners and societies who turn from evil and humble themselves before him.

The Sovereignty of God. The book pictures God as doing whatever he purposes in regard to the fates of nature and nations (the name *Joel* means "Yahweh is God").

Tips for Reading or Teaching Joel
Be receptive to the vivid and moving poetry—of judgment and of blessing. It is more important to experience this poetry than to analyze it.

Be aware that in addition to the usual prophetic themes of the denunciation of the prophet's contemporary society and his call to reform, there is an eschatological and apocalyptic strain in the book, as seen in famous verses about swords being beaten into plowshares (3:10), the weak saying that they are strong (3:10), and the mountains dripping with wine and the hills flowing with milk (3:18).

Although the book is filled with topical references to Joel's day, oper-

Jesus as Prophet

Three offices—prophet, priest, and king—provided spiritual leadership for Old Testament Israel. Each office prepared the way for the person and work of Jesus Christ by showing what kind of Savior God would send his people.

From Moses to Malachi, the Old Testament prophets were called to speak God's word, in some cases confirming it with miracles. Often their ministry involved foretelling the future, as God revealed his promises, although usually the prophets had as much or more to say about the present, as they were given special insight to discern the prevailing sins of their generation. But whether they were speaking out against that day's idolatry or preaching about the judgment to come, they always spoke on God's behalf. As Peter said, "No prophecy in Scripture ever came from the prophet's own understanding, or from human initiative. No, those prophets were moved by the Holy Spirit, and they spoke from God" (2 Peter 1:20-21).

The greatest Old Testament prophet was Moses. However, God promised Moses that one day an even greater prophet would come: "I will raise up a prophet like you from among their fellow Israelites. I will put my words in his mouth, and he will tell the people everything I command him" (Deuteronomy 18:18). This promise applied in a general way to all the prophets after Moses, but it applied supremely to Jesus Christ as God's last and greatest prophet.

The ministry of Jesus Christ was a prophetic ministry. Jesus spoke God's word, often authenticating his message by performing miracles of power. When he went up the mountain and sat down to preach his famous Sermon on the Mount (Matthew 5–7), he was claiming to sit in the place of Moses. As God's true prophet, he said only what the Father told him to say (see John 8:28). He fulfilled the two main callings of a prophet: He addressed the present situation by revealing people's true spiritual condition, and he prophesied about future judgment and glory. Jesus also lived out the sufferings of the prophets. As Stephen said to the Jews at the end of the sermon that led to his martyrdom, "Name one prophet your ancestors didn't persecute! They even killed the ones who predicted the coming of the Righteous One—the Messiah whom you betrayed and murdered" (Acts 7:52).

As you read the Old Testament, pay special attention to what is said by and about the prophets, because by their work and through their sufferings they all bear witness to Christ. Even when they fall into sin or fail to speak the truth, they point to Christ by showing our need for a faithful prophet. As you read the New Testament, remember what the Father said when Jesus appeared on the Mount of Transfiguration with Moses and Elijah: "This is my Son, my Chosen One. Listen to him" (Luke 9:35).

ate on the premise that the principles involved are timeless and universal; the poetic form of the book makes such open-endedness easy to see.

Contribution of the Book to the Bible's Story of Salvation in Christ

First, the eschatological visions of a coming golden age find fulfillment in the messianic age that began when Christ came to earth and will reach its culmination in the age pictured in the book of Revelation. Second, in the apostle Peter's Pentecostal sermon, he interpreted the famous verses about God's pouring his Spirit on all people (2:28-29) as predicting the events of Pentecost (see Acts 2:14-21). Finally, in the dual theme of divine judgment against human sin and the proclamation of mercy, the prophecies of Joel "set forth the very heart of the gospel that found its embodiment in the incarnation of Jesus Christ" (Elizabeth Achtemeier).

Applying the Book

If you simply go with the flow of this prophetic book, it will be obvious what to do: Fear God's judgment against evil, turn from sin, and trust the wonderful promises that are pictured in the golden-age visions of restoration in the second half of the book.

PERSPECTIVES
ON THE BOOK OF JOEL

The book falls into two distinct sections. In the first section (1:2–2:17) the prophet speaks. . . . In the second division (2:18–3:21) Jehovah speaks. Homer Hailey

[Joel 2–3] played a significant part in moulding the language in which the early Church set forth its convictions about what Christ had done and would yet do. C. H. Dodd

[The book] contradicts so much of how we regard ourselves and tells us such unsettling truths: that we are subject to God's judgment every day of our lives and that finally we must stand before God to hear our final judgment; that God can use the very forces of nature itself against us; that our sin corrupts not only ourselves but also the natural world around us; that we are an apostate people, turning to other gods and goddesses.
Elizabeth Achtemeier

Joel refers to three important events, each of which he calls a "day of the Lord." He sees the plague of locusts as an immediate day of the Lord (Joel 1:1-20), the invasion of Judah by Assyria as an imminent day of the Lord (2:1-27), and the final judgment of the world as the ultimate day of the Lord (2:28–3:21). Warren W. Wiersbe

AMOS
Bad News for the Affluent and Complacent

FORMAT. 9 chapters, 146 verses

IMPLIED PURPOSES. To denounce affluent people who oppress the poor of their society, to rebuke the attitudes and lifestyles of people who scorn God's moral commands, and to offer hope for the marginalized and oppressed

AUTHOR'S PERSPECTIVE. The author is highly partisan in that he actively takes the side of the oppressed and is scornful and disrespectful of the affluent and complacent members of society.

IMPLIED AUDIENCE. The original audience was multiple. The bulk of the prophecy is directed against the northern kingdom of Israel, but Judah and the surrounding pagan nations are also included in the section that addresses Israel's neighbors. Beyond the original audience, this book is directed universally to the wealthy and sacrilegious classes of all societies and to those they oppress.

WHAT UNIFIES THE BOOK. The angry voice of the prophet; the predictive element (oracles of judgment and an oracle of salvation at the end); the vivid imagination and poetic style of the author; the shock treatment to which Amos subjects his audience

SPECIAL FEATURES. The angry and unrestrained tone; direct rebuke as the basic mode; the literary skill of the author in small forms such as metaphor, simile, imagery, and epithets (using titles for persons or things, such as addressing the wealthy women of Samaria as "you fat cows living in Samaria" [4:1]); skill at parody (using a common literary form or formula to ridicule, as when the usual priestly exhortation to worship takes the form "Come to Bethel, and transgress" [4:4, ESV]).

CHALLENGES FACING THE READER OR TEACHER OF THIS BOOK.

1. The abundance of references to particular historical situations that prevailed at the time of the author
2. The poetic form of the oracles
3. Knowing how to apply predictions that were directed against ancient nations
4. A disjointed, kaleidoscopic structure

HOW TO MEET THE CHALLENGES.

1. Use hints from the text to read between the lines and reconstruct the original situations.
2. Take time to unpack the images and figurative language.
3. Do not look only *at* the historical particulars but also *through* them to the universal human principles embodied in them.
4. Prepare yourself for the topic to shift every few verses; disorientation and keeping the reader off balance are one of Amos's goals as he attacks people's complacency.

I*n woes and reproaches he depicts his audience so that they may see themselves as deserving the punishment which he announces. . . . The pictures merge into one mural of a basic evil at the centre of the nation's life. . . . His favourite terms for what Yahweh requires of Israel . . . are the word-pair "justice" and "righteousness." . . . The pictures catch Israel primarily in three spheres of public life: the administration of justice in the court, the confident affluent life of the upper classes, and the worship of God in the sanctuaries. . . . Taken as a whole this testimony of Amos says that the crimes of individual Israelites against their fellows had risen to the level of the nation's rebellion against God.*

JAMES LUTHER MAYS
Amos: A Commentary

AN OUTLINE OF
AMOS

1:1-2 Introduction

1:3–2:3 Oracles against the Pagan Nations

2:4-5 Oracle against Judah

Focus on Nations Surrounding Israel

2:6–6:14 Oracles against Israel

7:1–9:10 Five Visions of Judgment

Focus on Israel, the Main Recipient of the Prophecy

9:11-15 Oracle of Salvation

Focus on God's Universal Kingdom of Those Who Believe in His Salvation

Unmitigated Judgment

Hope

Few things are as characteristic of societies and nations in the world to-day as diverse socioeconomic conditions that divide people and nations into categories of haves and have-nots. The problem is not new. As you read the book of Amos, you will catch glimpses of a class-bound society as extreme as any we would find today.

If Amos were living now, we could picture him leading marches and writing letters to the editor of the local newspaper. He speaks as the advocate for the oppressed classes, and he denounces the privileged classes of his society, including the religious establishment and the wealthy.

The Form of the Book
The book of Amos is a prophecy. (See "Prophecy as a Form of Writing" on page 291.) This means that its basic format is a series of oracles (pronouncements) directed at specific groups. In his oracles, Amos makes use of reported sayings from God, direct attack (including the "woe" formula), snatches of description of both the oppressors and the oppressed, proverbs, predictions of judgment (doom songs), and visions. The basic thrust of all these forms is satire. (For a summary of how satire works, see page 375.)

Key Characters
The prophet himself comes alive as a simple country person whose call from God to denounce his nation thrusts him onto the stage of national news. Amos's imagery tends to come from his rural background, with references to sheep, lions, the sky, and the weather. God, the lion who roars in this book, is the great authority figure whose law is the standard by which evil is judged. Both the lifestyles and religious practices of the privileged class are vividly portrayed. Nations are personified as individuals. A final "conglomerate character" is the oppressed of society.

Key Doctrines
Sin. The book is an ever-expanding vision of how sinful the attitudes and lifestyles of individuals and classes of society can become. In the book of Amos, sin is both personal and corporate.
Judgment. In its very form of denunciation, the book shows the reasons for and the vehemence of God's judgment against those who oppress the helpless and misplace their trust in a privileged lifestyle.
Social Ethics. The book of Amos is an ethical treatise that warns against enjoying an affluent and complacent lifestyle at the expense of dis-

enfranchised classes of society. If the book is a handbook on how not to live, by implication it is also a handbook on how to live.

Tips for Reading or Teaching Amos

The bulk of the book of Amos consists of satire. We cannot understand or teach the book well without applying the analytic grid provided for the satiric genre, and the most important thing of all is to identify the objects of attack.

The book is filled with references to specific situations in the society of the author. For these references to have relevance today, we need to build bridges between the world of Amos and what we see going on around us.

The author's purpose in exposing vice is to lead us to a reformation of our lives. Look for glimpses that the book gives of how to live righteous lives.

Things to Look For

- Attacks on specific classes and behaviors
- Angry prophetic tone
- Vivid imagination, as seen in the author's descriptive ability and skill with figurative language
- Implied guidelines on how to live the godly life and avoid a wicked lifestyle

quick overview of amos

1:1-2	Introduction to the author and his prophecy
1:3–2:3	Oracles of judgment against the surrounding nations
3:1–6:14	Oracles of judgment against Israel
7:1–9:10	Five visions of judgment
9:11-15	Salvation promises

The Flow of the Book

Introduction to the Prophet and His Prophecy (1:1-2). Amos presents himself as the plainspoken prophet. Be on the lookout for ways in which this manifests itself throughout the book.

Oracles against the Surrounding Pagan Nations (1:3–2:3). These five oracles against nations that encircle Judah and Israel are among the most stylized passages in the Bible. Each vision follows this pattern: (1) an opening formula ("thus says the LORD" [ESV]); (2) a balanced pair of phrases ("for three transgressions . . . and for four" [ESV]); (3) a set formula for judgment ("I will not revoke the punishment" [ESV]); (4) a statement of charges; and (5) a list of judgments (beginning with the formula "so I will send a fire upon" [ESV]). All the charges brought against these nations involve atrocities in warfare.

Oracle against Judah (2:4-5). Those who profess faith in God are put on the list of evil nations, but the charge is different—rejecting God's law, not the more universal morality of rules governing warfare.

Oracles against Israel (2:6–6:14). The best framework for the individual parts of this section is provided by the literary form known as satire. For each passage or detail, identify (1) the object(s) of attack, (2) the form the attack takes, (3) the implied or stated norm (standard of correctness) by which the attack is conducted, and (4) the tone of the attack.

Five Visions of Judgment against Israel (7:1–9:10). The mode shifts to a series of visions, but the basic framework remains satire.

Oracle of Salvation (9:11-15). Here we get the reversal—the recantation, even—with which virtually all Old Testament prophecies end: God's mercy and blessing remain as a promise and hope to the people. You can profitably ponder how this final golden-age prophecy relates to what has preceded it.

The Main Themes

1. God has a standard of right and wrong conduct, and he holds individuals and nations responsible to obey that standard.
2. God is the sovereign judge of the world.
3. Social justice is part of the godly life. Religious profession must be matched by godly practice toward others.
4. A self-centered and indulgent lifestyle is hateful to God when it is built on the oppression of the helpless. Privilege brings peril, not security.

Golden-Age Prophecies of the Old Testament

"In that day the wolf and the lamb will live together" (Isaiah 11:6). "Foreigners will be your servants. They will feed your flocks and plow your fields and tend your vineyards" (Isaiah 61:5). "The time will come . . . when the grain and grapes will grow faster than they can be harvested" (Amos 9:13).

The Old Testament prophetic books contain many "golden age" prophecies that predict a future state of total bliss and abundance. In fact, most prophetic books move toward a climax that consists of such visions of perfection. The question is, to what do these golden-age prophecies refer? Here are five possibilities, not necessarily exclusive of one another:

- It is possible that the pictures of a coming golden age are metaphoric, or symbolic, pictures of God's favor, either on a specific Old Testament occasion or generally. For example, Zechariah's prediction that "the streets of the city will be filled with boys and girls at play" (8:5) is, if we look at its immediate context, a picture of Jerusalem as it would be resettled after the Babylonian exile, but it might expand beyond that to be a picture of God's blessing on the believing community at any time.

- Some prophecies remained unfulfilled because they were conditional, dependent on the covenant faithfulness of Israel (see 1 Samuel 2:30 and Jeremiah 18:9-10 for texts that directly assert this principle).

- Some golden-age prophecies are symbolic pictures of the coming of Christ in his incarnation and redemptive life. For example, the following prophecy by Isaiah is interpreted in Matthew 4:16 as a messianic prophecy fulfilled by the coming of Christ: "The people who walk in darkness will see a great light. For those who live in a land of deep darkness, a light will shine" (Isaiah 9:2).

- Still other Old Testament golden-age prophecies find their symbolic fulfillment in the New Testament body of believers, known as the church and pictured as a new, spiritual Israel. For example, Acts 15:15-18 applies a graphic picture of the walls of Jerusalem being rebuilt (in Amos 9:11) to the inclusion of Gentiles in the Christian faith.

- Some pictures of a coming golden age are eschatological, or apocalyptic, picturing either a millennium of Christ's perfect rule or the ultimate bliss of heaven. An example is Isaiah 60:21, addressed to a personified Jerusalem: "All your people will be righteous. They will possess their land forever, for I will plant them there with my own hands in order to bring myself glory."

It is often impossible to know which of these possibilities is in view in a given passage, and in fact the various threads often flow together.

Contribution of the Book to the Bible's Story of Salvation in Christ

First, we can filter the pictures of God's judgment against the wicked through the New Testament lens of Christ, who will judge evil at the end of history (see, for example, Matthew 25:31-46 and interspersed pictures of Christ as judge in the book of Revelation). Second, the golden-age prophecy at the end of the book, while having multiple applications, is at one level a messianic prophecy about the blessings that Christ brought to the world. (James so applies it in his comments recorded in Acts 15:13-18.)

Applying the Book

The most obvious applications are ethical: to live with concern for the welfare of the poor and oppressed, to forego personal privilege and self-indulgence, to obey God's commands in all areas of life. Second, we repeatedly see Amos draw a connection between a wicked lifestyle and improper worship practices (2:7-8; 4:1-5; 5:21-27).

Finally, there is a theological message. We must live in an awareness of God as judge (along the lines of the caution in Ecclesiastes 11:9 that "you must give an account to God for everything you do"). And since no one completely measures up to God's standard of right conduct, we must live on the premise that the blessings promised in the concluding oracle of salvation are open to us only on the basis of God's mercy and grace, for which we need to ask.

PERSPECTIVES
ON THE BOOK OF AMOS

Affluence, exploitation and the profit motive were the most notable features of the society which Amos observed and in which he worked. . . . Amos might well have been walking through any of our great cities.
J. Alec Motyer

Amos's dominant emphasis is Yahweh's rejection of Israel's social and religious practices. David Allen Hubbard

Amos was the most severe of all the biblical prophets of judgment.
J. Jeremias

Eight "burdens" (1–2), three sermons (3–6), five visions (7–9).
J. Sidlow Baxter's streamlined version of the content of Amos

The first reformer.   Source unknown

If Amos was a revolutionary, he was also a conservative. He was out not to change the rules but to have them fulfilled. He wanted to go back to a moral order, not to propound a new one.   Howard Moss

Amos's theological methodology is to intertwine the common things of life with the listener's larger theological framework. He sees a theological connection between the things his audience knows about (wars, homes, furniture, banquets, selling grain, sacrifices, the courts, Temples, kings, water, crops, and locusts) and what God is doing in relationship to their lives.   Gary V. Smith

OBADIAH
God's Judgment in Miniature

FORMAT. One chapter, 21 verses

IMPLIED PURPOSE. To prophesy judgment against Edom (descendants of Esau) as a way of encouraging the Israelites who had been the victims of Edom's hostility and looting

AUTHOR'S PERSPECTIVE. The prophet "takes sides" by energetically denouncing Edom and vividly picturing its offenses against God's people, accompanied by a consoling prediction that Israel will one day enjoy a reversal of its fortunes in regard to Edom.

IMPLIED AUDIENCE. The prophet addresses two audiences: the wicked foreign nation of Edom and God's chosen people.

WHAT UNIFIES THE BOOK. The voice of predictive prophecy; military references; conflict among nations (international scope); the common prophetic rhythm of oracles of doom followed by oracles of restoration

SPECIAL FEATURES. The shortest book in the Old Testament; the historical backdrop of Edom's taking advantage of Israel's defeat by an enemy; the Day-of-the-Lord motif

How should Christians respond to the daily news of foreign nations' hostility toward Christians and toward nations that are sympathetic to the Christian faith? The book of Obadiah provides a model.

To understand the historical situation that underlies the book, look for hints within the book itself regarding these historical facts: (1) The Edomites were related to the Israelites (this dates back to the brothers Esau and Jacob). (2) Because of this blood relationship, they should have shown brotherly concern when the Israelites were subjected to military destruction. (3) Instead, the Edomites gloated over the Israelites' misfortune and looted them. To catch the flavor of how offensive the Israelites found this, read Psalm 137.

KEY VERSE
"The day is near when I, the LORD, will judge all godless nations!" (1:15). God is the sovereign judge of the universe, and he can be trusted to oppose what is evil.

The Structure
The book is a series of prophetic predictions, or oracles, that unfold in this order: (1) prediction of Edom's destruction (vv. 1-9), (2) charges against Edom (vv. 10-14), (3) God's judgment against the nations (vv. 15-16), and (4) God's restoration of Israel (vv. 17-21).

Key Doctrines and Themes
The Sovereignty of God. God rules the world, working in history to reveal his glory.

The Justice of God. God holds people and nations accountable for their evil and punishes them for it.

God's Final, Eschatological Defeat of Evil. God wins in the end and establishes his righteous kingdom.

Tips for Reading or Teaching Obadiah
The oracle of judgment against Edom will make more sense to you if you do a little research into the history of that nation (a standard Bible dictionary or concordance will show that there are many references to Edom in the Bible). You can then see universal principles in God's judgment against Edom for its specific atrocities against Israel. Beyond that, a one-chapter book such as Obadiah allows you to get a concentrated picture of what God is like.

Contribution of the Book to the Bible's Story of Salvation in Christ
The biblical context for this prophetic book is the holy war between good

and evil, including between good and evil nations. In its ultimate reaches, this is the story of salvation, which finds its New Testament fulfillment in the work of Christ. Keep the New Testament eschatological prophecies in mind as you read the account of God's judgment against Edom and his restoration of Israel.

Applying the Book

Christians should not apologize for despising the atrocities of evil nations; God also despises these atrocities. We should live our personal and national lives in an awareness of God's judgment against evil and his favor toward what is good. Our ultimate hope is in God's sovereign control of history.

PERSPECTIVES
ON THE BOOK OF OBADIAH

"Obadiah presents a message of hope to God's people. This is done in two different stages," the prediction of judgment against Edom followed by the promise of restoration for Judah. David Baker

It is a compact version of the typical prophetic book, where the opening chapters deal with sin and judgment, and bright Messianic prophecies appear toward the end. Irving Jensen

Look again through these verses of Obadiah, and let Edom picture the "flesh" or Adam-nature. J. Sidlow Baxter

The book teaches that sovereign rule belongs to the Lord. . . . The proclamation of God's dominion raises questions about his goals, his laws, and his motives. John Watts

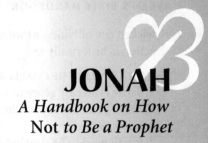

JONAH

A Handbook on How
Not *to Be a Prophet*

FORMAT. 4 chapters, 48 verses

IMPLIED PURPOSE. To tell a story in which two plots unfold together. At a human level the story exposes the bad attitudes of a religious person who has all the right theology but a hard heart. The divine story focuses on God's universal love that extends across national and cultural boundaries.

AUTHOR'S PERSPECTIVE. The viewpoint is satiric, as the writer holds up Jonah, the protagonist, for rebuke. As part of this satiric stance, the story contains a lot of irony and also some humor.

IMPLIED AUDIENCE. The audience is the religious community (in its original setting, pious Jews), which is asked to take an introspective look at itself and resist the impulse to think that because it is God's chosen community, it has an exclusive claim on God.

WHAT UNIFIES THE BOOK. The story line; the central protagonist and his frequently bad attitudes and behavior; evidences that God's salvation is available to all people; the preaching mission of Jonah (including his avoidance of it, his execution of it, and his anger about its effects); the world of elemental nature as the common denominator in the changing settings of the story

SPECIAL FEATURES. The satiric exposure of the protagonist, which is surprising in view of the fact that he is a prophet by calling; pervasive irony; the giantesque motif (i.e., the presence of events that are bigger than life)

CHALLENGES FACING THE READER OR TEACHER OF THIS BOOK.
1. The need to master satire as a form of writing
2. Reconciling what seem to be exaggerations (such as Jonah's surviving in the belly of a fish and the wholesale repentance of the

wicked city of Nineveh) with New Testament indications that the action is historically real

HOW TO MEET THE CHALLENGES.
1. Satire is an easy genre to master (for the basics on satire, see page 375); all you need to do is apply the ingredients of satire to this specific story.
2. If you need to be convinced that the story really happened, read a sampling of evangelical commentaries.

THE MOST COMMON MISCONCEPTIONS ABOUT THIS BOOK. That the events cannot really have happened and that the book cannot be a satire—that somehow we feel a need to find a way to salvage the character of Jonah by the end of the book.

Jonah represents all that the author of the book means to reject. . . . The Book of Jonah is a satire. It portrays the prophet in order to ridicule him. . . . Our attention is directed primarily to the prophet, and his attitude is the focal point of the tale. . . . The attitude of God—and of the author—highlights the attitude of Jonah in order to satirize it.

EDWIN M. GOOD
Irony in the Old Testament

1:3-17 Flight / 1:1-2 Commission	2:10 Rescue / 2:1-9 Jonah's Prayer	3:3-10 Jonah's Preaching Mission / 3:1-2 Recommission	4 Jonah's Complaint
Jonah's Flight	Jonah's Rescue	Jonah's Sermon	Jonah's Resentment about God's Mercy
The Great Sea	The Belly of the Great Fish	The Great City	Outskirts of Nineveh
Most Memorable Scene: The Great Storm at Sea	Most Memorable Scene: Jonah inside the Belly of the Great Fish	Most Memorable Scene: The Wholesale Repentance of Nineveh	Most Memorable Scene: Jonah's Complaint against God as Jonah Sits under His Shriveled Shade Plant

AN OUTLINE OF
JONAH

The story of Jonah has reverberated through the centuries as one of the most vivid narratives in the Bible. It is a favorite with children because it is the story of the big fish. For adults, the picture of Jonah's flight from God is a paradigm of the human condition apart from God. The attempt is perennial, and the story teaches us that no one can run away from God or evade his "missionary plan" to save the nations.

Underneath these obvious meanings of the story is a truly amazing spectacle. A close look at Jonah's words reveals that his theology is orthodox and couched in familiar religious language but he thoroughly disapproves of the very theology he professes. He knows that God is a God of mercy to people of all nations, but that very fact makes him angry.

The Form of the Book

The primary genre of the book is satire (for more on satire as a literary form, see page 375). The four standard ingredients of satire take this form in the book of Jonah:

- The object of satiric attack: the ethnocentrism of Jonah, which leads him to want to keep God's mercy as the exclusive property of the Israelites
- The satiric vehicle: narrative
- The satiric norm: the character of God—especially his mercy—which crosses national and racial barriers
- The satiric tone: light and laughing, as the protagonist is rendered ridiculous

The plot that carries this satiric action is built around two cycles: Jonah's first commissioning as a prophet is followed by his disobedience and repentance. His second commissioning is followed by his obedience and the success of his preaching mission—followed by his anger over the repentance of the Ninevites. The central plot conflicts are Jonah vs. God, Jonah vs. Nineveh, Jonah vs. the world of nature, and Jonah vs. himself (Jonah is repeatedly his own worst enemy).

DID YOU KNOW?
In the Jewish liturgical calendar, the book of Jonah is read at the climactic point of Yom Kippur, the Day of Atonement, the most solemn day of the year, because of the book's emphasis on God's forgiveness of those who repent.

Key Places and Characters

The setting includes both the world of elemental nature (the sea, the belly of the fish, the countryside around Nineveh) and the city of Nineveh itself.

The protagonist in the story is Jonah, and his chief antagonist is God. The cast of characters includes Jonah, God, the pagan sailors, and the entire city of Nineveh (represented mainly by its king). Because all of the action revolves around Jonah, one fruitful approach is to keep asking questions about Jonah—his personality traits, his actions, his motivations, and his refusal to grow as a character and a prophet.

Key Doctrines

The Attributes of God. This book is an extended comment on the mercy of God, with his justice forming a secondary emphasis; divine patience, omnipresence, and sovereign control of creation are also present.

Salvation. The offer of salvation is universal in the sense that it extends to all people and nations.

Human Depravity. Despite the fact that Jonah is a prophet, his behavior and attitudes are pictures of how petty, hateful, and self-centered people—including those who are followers of God—can be.

Repentance. The behavior of the Ninevites as narrated in chapter 3 is a case study in the kind of repentance God requires and accepts.

Tips for Reading or Teaching Jonah

The two lead characters are Jonah and God. If you pay sufficient attention to both, you will have mastered the book of Jonah.

The key to Jonah's characterization is that he is held up to satiric rebuke throughout the story, except for chapter 2.

You can trace step-by-step how Jonah's behavior exhibits how not to be a prophet.

Look for ways in which God's universal mercy is the norm by which Jonah's bad behavior is exposed.

Things to Look For

- The characterizations of Jonah (the ignominious prophet) and God (whose mercy is universal)
- The giantesque motif: Events on an unexpectedly large scale (e.g., the mission of the lone prophet to the capital of the world empire; the fish; the magnitude of Nineveh's repentance and God's mercy; the miraculous plant)
- The satiric impulse to belittle Jonah and his bad attitudes
- Irony based on discrepancy. (For example, Jonah is a prophet who tries to avoid speaking God's message, and although he of all people

should rejoice in God's mercy—especially in light of his deliverance from the fish—he is ill tempered when God spares Nineveh.)

quick overview of jonah

1:1-17   Jonah's commissioning and flight
2:1-10   Jonah's rescue and prayer of gratitude
3:1-10   Jonah's eight-word sermon and its astounding success
4:1-11   Jonah's anger when God spares Nineveh

The Flow of the Book

Jonah's Bad Behavior (Chapter 1). In this handbook on how *not* to be a prophet, nearly everything Jonah does exposes his bad behavior. The action begins with a common scene in prophetic books: the call and commissioning of a prophet. But the action immediately takes a dive as Jonah's first act is to go in exactly the opposite direction from what God has commanded. The first major event is thus an ironic impossibility: No one can flee from the presence of God, as Psalm 139:1-12 makes clear. God's use of the sea to bring Jonah to judgment constitutes a countermovement to Jonah's attempt to evade God. Ironically, the pagan sailors show more sensitivity to God and morality than Jonah does.

KEY VERSE
"Jonah got up and went in the opposite direction to get away from the LORD" (1:3). The action narrated here is the most vivid picture in all the world of a universal human tendency to try to run away from God.

Reversal: Jonah's Repentant Frame of Mind (Chapter 2). Chapter 2 springs a surprise on us: This is the only place in which the story shows Jonah in a godly frame of mind. We shift from narrative to lyric poetry and are thereby taken inside Jonah's thought processes as he exists inside the belly of the great fish. The song of Jonah would be right at home in the Psalter, fitting into the familiar genre of the praise of God for the rescue of the speaker. But this is only a momentary feeling for Jonah and becomes the ironic standard by which we judge his surliness when God extends his mercy to the pagan Ninevites.

Another Reversal: The Repentance of Nineveh (Chapter 3). After God commissions Jonah a second time, Jonah reluctantly but successfully carries

Satire

Satire is the exposure of human vice or folly. It is often accompanied by humor or sarcasm, but these are not necessary ingredients of satire. Three ingredients require attention in a piece of writing that is satiric:

- Satire has one or more objects of attack. If a piece of writing expresses an attack on a person, an institution, or an action, it meets the minimal requirement of being satire. To make sense of a satiric passage, you need to identify the object(s) of attack.
- The attack is embodied in an identifiable literary form, such as story (the book of Jonah and selected parables of Jesus), metaphor (the Pharisees as whitewashed tombs), and direct denunciation ("woe to you"). To do justice to a satiric passage, you need to interact with the form in which it is found.
- There is a stated or implied satiric norm—the standard by which the criticism is being conducted. No analysis of a satiric passage is complete until you have identified the satiric norm. In the book of Amos, the satiric norm is God's law as an expression of his character.

Sometimes the object of attack is obvious. Jesus' parable of the Pharisee who prays a self-congratulatory prayer attacks self-righteous complacency. The book of Jonah attacks ethnocentrism. But other times we need to decipher a "code language" to see what is going on. When Amos declares, "Woe to those who lie on beds of ivory" (6:4, ESV), it is a denunciation of the wealthy and complacent. In Jesus' Good Shepherd discourse, he says, "A hired hand will run when he sees a wolf coming. He will abandon the sheep because they don't belong to him and he isn't their shepherd" (John 10:12). Jesus is using a pastoral metaphor to satirize unreliable and uncommitted religious leaders.

Satire is a major biblical form that can be found in all sections of the Bible. The stories of the Bible frequently hold up character flaws to satiric exposure, as when we repeatedly see Jacob's self-centeredness and competitive nature exposed. The "oracles of judgment" in the prophetic books are satiric in nature inasmuch as they expose specific vices in the lives of individuals or nations. There are passages of satiric rebuke in the Epistles (for example, James 2:14-26 satirizes people who claim to have faith but do not produce good works) and in the discourses of Jesus (for example, the discourse against the Pharisees in Matthew 23). Even the book of Psalms contains satiric pictures of bad behavior or of evil people or fools who deny God or worship idols. Books such as Jonah and Amos are entirely satiric, consisting of objects of attack, forms in which the attack is embodied, and standards by which the attack is conducted.

out his preaching mission to Nineveh. No other eight-word sermon in the history of the world has produced such extravagant results. God's reversal of his threat to destroy Nineveh, after the people repent, demonstrates the chief point of the whole book: that God's mercy is universal, not limited to just one nation.

KEY VERSE
"I knew that you are a merciful and compassionate God, slow to get angry and filled with unfailing love" (4:2). Although Jonah disapproves of God's character as he describes it here, the main meaning of the book rests in its picture of God's readiness to forgive those who repent of their evil.

A Final Surprise: Jonah's Rejection of God's Mercy (Chapter 4). Every phase of the action brings another surprise. We would expect a prophet (especially one whom God had miraculously rescued) to rejoice in God's mercy to the people of Nineveh, but instead, Jonah gets angry and pouts. He even tells us *why* he is angry: He *knew* that God was "a merciful and compassionate God," and he thoroughly disliked it (4:2). Of course, God's character—his compassion extends even to the animals of Nineveh—stands out as a foil to Jonah's attitude of cruelty toward the Ninevites. The last phrase of the book—"and also much cattle" (4:11, ESV)—is a small classic phrase.

The Main Themes

1. God is a God of mercy and compassion to those who repent of their sins and "[turn] from their evil way" (3:10, ESV).
2. The mercy of God transcends national, racial, and cultural boundaries. This is one of the most obvious missionary books in the Old Testament.
3. Ethnocentrism (partiality toward one's own group and disdain for other groups) is sinful, especially when it seeks to claim God as the exclusive property of one's own group.
4. Having the right theology is not enough; one's actions and attitudes must be consistent with correct theology.

Contribution of the Book to the Bible's Story of Salvation in Christ

The New Testament contains two notable references to the book of Jonah: Jesus compared his three days in the grave to Jonah's three days in the belly of the fish (Matthew 12:38-41), and he pointed to the Ninevites as examples of people who repented when they heard the message of judgment (Luke 11:29-32). Furthermore, the story of salvation extended beyond the covenant nation of Israel to the pagan world foreshadows the salvation that Jesus accomplished for the world in his atoning work.

Applying the Book

The book shows what God is like (compassionate and forgiving) and what it takes to please him (repentance, turning from evil). God's patience is evident in how he deals with his recalcitrant prophet. On the other hand, God reaches a point at which he judges sinners. An obvious application is that we must respond to God in terms of his character and requirements.

Each of the main characters or groups of characters shows us how to act. Jonah himself embodies a warning to the believing community, which needs to make sure that it desires the salvation of all people and does not respond with ill-tempered resentment when God extends his grace to other unworthy sinners.

The pagans in the story also are models for us to follow and apply. The sailors who fear God (1:16) and the Ninevites who repent (3:6-9) show us how to respond to God's opportunities to believe in him.

PERSPECTIVES
ON THE BOOK OF JONAH

Jonah is the most beautiful story ever written in so small a compass.
Literary author Charles Reade

In [God's] mind, Nineveh is not a quantity but a quality, not a mere metropolis but an immorality. He takes the symbol of the ancient world's most impressive evil, magnifies and intensifies it by mass, and sends his timorous prophet into the middle of it. Edwin M. Good

The main conflict of the story is that Jonah is a great nationalist, but God is an internationalist. Anonymous Wheaton College student

This element of surprise is a key factor throughout the book.
Leslie C. Allen

Jonah's thoughts and actions are sketched by the author in such a way as to parallel those of the audience to which the book is addressed.
Terence E. Fretheim

Jonah is revealed as a comic character. Donald F. Rauber

The fact that we laugh at Jonah . . . does not minimize the utter seriousness of the book. Roland M. Frye

The book has gripped audiences for hundreds of years; in sermon, folklore, literature, art, and music, Jonah is remembered along with his whale.
Jack M. Sasson

When you run away from the Lord you never get to where you are going, and you always pay your own fare. Donald G. Barnhouse

MICAH

How God Deals with Sinful Humanity

FORMAT. 7 chapters, 105 verses

IMPLIED PURPOSES. To warn all people—but especially God's covenant people—that God does not tolerate sin; to instill an attitude of repentance; and to proclaim the gospel of salvation as the only hope for sinners

AUTHOR'S PERSPECTIVE. Micah writes with prophetic authority, both in his delineation and denunciation of sin and in his predictions of God's intention to save a remnant of the human race. The author assumes that the information the human race most needs is two-pronged: the bad news that the human race is headed for disaster if left to its own inclinations and the good news that God saves people.

IMPLIED AUDIENCE. Primarily God's covenant people, which in the Old Testament were Israel and Judah (Micah's dual audience) and in the New Testament is the Christian church. The book assumes an audience that has a conscience and a desire for salvation and a righteous society.

WHAT UNIFIES THE BOOK. The usual prophetic rhythm between bad news and good news, judgment and salvation; continual references to the covenant people of Israel; the poetic nature of the writing; the format of reported messages from God; intermittent pictures of a future golden age (both messianic and apocalyptic)

SPECIAL FEATURES. Direct address from the prophet, as God's spokesman, to his listeners: "you people of Judah," "O Israel," "you leaders of Israel," "you false prophets," etc.; nature imagery and rural references, in keeping with the prophet's rural origins; ethical focus on social sins, such as oppression of the poor, legal injustice, etc.; messianic and apocalyptic strains in the visions of the future

It is a feature of modern life that forms of violence and evil that shock one generation become commonplace for the next generation. The result is a progressive blunting of sensibilities and a decline of moral standards. One function of prophetic books such as Micah is to call us back to our senses in regard to the sinfulness of sin and the need for God's forgiveness.

KEY VERSE

"No, O people, the LORD has told you what is good, and this is what he requires of you: to do what is right, to love mercy, and to walk humbly with your God" (6:8). This famous verse highlights God's character and the morality to which he holds his covenant people accountable.

The Structure

The basic plan of the book is to alternate between oracles of judgment and oracles of salvation and hope. There are no clear transitions between the two types of material. Micah uses the formula "hear" three times (1:2; 3:1; 6:1 [ESV]), and in each case the first unit is a vision of judgment, followed by a picture of salvation. But these are not three discrete sermons; the material in Micah is actually hetero-geneous. The only reliable scheme is the alternation between judgment and salvation or hope, as follows:

An Oracle of Judgment (1:1–2:11). Descriptions of evil in Israel and Judah are combined with predictions that God will punish it.

God's Promise of Redemption (2:12-13). In this two-verse unit, God promises to redeem a remnant of his covenant people.

An Oracle of Judgment (Chapter 3). The oracle against the leaders of Israel combines the description and prediction of punishment.

An Oracle of Salvation (Chapters 4–5). The prophet portrays the glorious things God will do on behalf of his people "in the latter days," a combined messianic and apocalyptic vision. (Chapter 5:10-15 looks like an oracle of judgment, but it should be interpreted positively as God's purging the nation of evil and protecting it against enemies.)

An Oracle of Judgment (6:1–7:13). The prophet indicts God's wayward people and describes their punishment.

An Oracle concerning God's Mercy (7:14-20). The prophet offers praise to God for his mercy in forgiving sin.

Key Doctrines and Themes

God's Attitude toward Sin. God takes sin very seriously.

God's Attitude toward Justice. God's people must reflect his attitude toward justice by dealing justly with one another and with the oppressed.

God's Sovereign Purpose. God exercises his sovereignty in punishing sinners. It is also God's plan to save sinners by sending a Messiah.
Last Things. God makes an apocalyptic promise of a future golden age.

Tips for Reading or Teaching Micah

You will succeed with Micah if you gear up for an alternation between judgment against present sins and hope for a future salvation. With this as a given, here is what you will see as you spend time looking at the text:

The oracles of judgment follow the rules of satire, so be sure to look for objects of attack (for more on satire, see page 375). Pick up the clues and read between the lines. For example, in the first three chapters you can find references to dispossessing the poor of their houses and farms, leading to homelessness; bribery; and legal injustice against the poor.

The oracles of judgment are composed of two types of material mingled without transitions: the description of evil practices and the prediction/portrayal of God's punishment of those who perpetrate the evil.

> **DID YOU KNOW?**
> • The name *Micah* means "Who is like God?" From the location of Moresheth, some twenty miles southwest of Jerusalem, we know that Micah lived among farmers; we catch glimpses of his rural situation in the specific pictures of oppression against which Micah protests in the first two chapters.

The oracles of salvation shift the focus from the present to the future, and the pictures they paint are more general. Exactly what coming golden age is in view? At certain points you will intuitively assimilate the pictures as pointing to the first coming of Christ, the promised Messiah. At other points the references will strike you as apocalyptic, pointing to the Millennium, or eschaton, at the end of history.

As always, try to build bridges between the details in the text (which on the surface whisk you away to an ancient time and remote place) and your own situation, personally and culturally. Operate on the premise that the particulars of the text preach a timeless message.

Much of the content of the book is embodied in poetry; take the necessary time to unpack the meanings of the images and figures of speech.

Contribution of the Book to the Bible's Story of Salvation in Christ

The main contribution of the book to salvation history is its messianic prophecies of someone who will be a shepherd to his sheep (2:12-13), someone who will judge and establish peace (4:3-4), and someone who will be a ruler from Bethlehem (5:2). Even when pictures of redemption

New Testament era know that the pictures of the weak being made strong (4:7), of a shepherd caring for his flock (5:4), and of God forgiving sin (7:18-20) were ultimately fulfilled in Christ.

Applying the Book
The application of oracles of judgment is always the same: We should let the prophet's indictments be the occasion for our own spiritual introspection, for acts of repentance, for a resolve to resist institutional forms of evil, and for prayers for forgiveness. These oracles teach us that there is no such thing as a "little" sin. The most obvious application of the oracles of salvation is to receive the salvation that God extends in Christ.

PERSPECTIVES
ON THE BOOK OF MICAH

One of the best summaries of true religion to be found in the Bible.
G. Campbell Morgan

The Book of Micah reads like a court document. Micah's prophecies record God's judgment on three groups of plaintiffs: (1) Samaria and Jerusalem; (2) the leaders of Israel and Judah; (3) the people in Israel and Judah. God holds nations, leaders, and individuals responsible for their failure to acknowledge or obey Him. John R. MacArthur

[On how Micah's name ("Who is like God?") corresponds to his message:] Micah added to the Lord's luster by [extolling] his incomparable forgiveness and fidelity (7:18-20), the theme of Micah's book. Bruce K. Waltke

[On 6:6-8, a famous passage ending with a list of "what is good" in God's eyes:] The Mount Everest of the Old Testament, for which alone the Book of Micah deserves immortality. G. Campbell Morgan

Prophetic oracles were not isolated pronouncements concerning only their immediate historical period. . . . They must be understood as incursions of the word of God into an ongoing plan for the world. . . . Micah, perhaps more than any other prophetic book, lets us perceive that. . . . We too live in one era of time included in God's plan for the world. The stream of God's plan flows around us, moving toward a future salvation of the world. Elizabeth Achtemeier

NAHUM
Comeuppance for Nineveh

FORMAT. 3 chapters, 47 verses

IMPLIED PURPOSE. To predict the downfall of Nineveh, capital of Assyria, a downfall that demonstrates God's sovereignty and justice

AUTHOR'S PERSPECTIVE. The prophet enthusiastically throws himself into the spectacle of God's coming destruction of a pagan nation that had destroyed the northern kingdom of Israel and enslaved the southern kingdom of Judah. The author actually taunts the oppressive nation of Assyria.

IMPLIED AUDIENCE. The original audience was Nineveh, which can be representative of any godless and brutal nation at any point in history.

WHAT UNIFIES THE BOOK. Military imagery and battle motifs; the continual denunciation of Assyria's evil and the portrayal of its destruction

SPECIAL FEATURES. One of just a few Old Testament prophetic books devoted to a nation other than Israel and Judah; correlation between the nature of Assyria's offense (cruelty in warfare) and the military imagery used to portray its coming destruction; absence of a concluding oracle of salvation and blessing such as is common to most Old Testament prophetic books

FACT SHEET

FACT SHEET

Modern history has been marred by terrorist dictators and nations that inflict unspeakable cruelties on their victims. Does God know and care about these atrocities? Nineveh was the ancient prototype for terrorism, and the prophecy of Nahum gives us a "God's eye view" of terrorism.

The Structure

The book of Nahum is constructed on a simple two-part plan: an opening vision of God as a divine warrior who is about to rescue Judah (chapter 1), followed by a series of oracles that describe the imminent destruction of Nineveh (chapters 2–3). Although the second part contains recognizable prophetic forms such as taunts, the "woe" formula, and the vivid narrative of destruction, chapters 2 and 3 are both cut from the same cloth and should be treated as a single movement of the book.

Key Doctrines and Themes

The Justice of God. We see this particularly in his judgment against evil.

The Omnipotence of God. He can execute justice even against entire nations.

The Moral Responsibility of Nations. God holds a nation responsible for its terrorism and cruelty against its enemies.

Tips for Reading or Teaching Nahum

Nahum is one of the easier biblical books to understand. Your first task is to relive the pictures of God and of military destruction as vividly as possible, applying all that you know about poetry and figurative language. Once you have looked *at* the contemporary world that Nahum paints, you need to look *through* it and formulate the universal principles embodied in the original situation portrayed in the book.

KEY VERSE
"The LORD will by no means clear the guilty" (1:3, ESV). Here is the message of the book in its essence: God is judge, his verdicts are just, and he is the ultimate cause for the imminent destruction that awaits Nineveh.

Contribution of the Book to the Bible's Story of Salvation in Christ

The implied context of this book is the holy-war motif: Military operations among nations are viewed as part of a spiritual battle between good and evil in which God (often portrayed as a warrior himself) sees to it that the forces of good prevail. Ultimately this holy war comes to center on the atoning work of Christ and his defeat of Satan, the enemy of God's people (see especially the book of Revelation and Ephesians 6).

Applying the Book

Few things are as close to the forefront of the daily news as the spectacle of terrorism and physical cruelty toward people. Correspondingly, few emotions are as deep seated today as the sense of protest and outrage and frequent helplessness in the face of such physical power and oppression. The book of Nahum provides a lens through which to understand these feelings. God, too, is angry at the cruelty of nations and individuals, and his anger provides a model and inspiration for us to resist "the evil that men do" (Shakespeare). Tremper Longman III writes that "as New Testament Christians, we recognize that Jesus Christ empowers the church to fight evil today."

DID YOU KNOW?

- There are twelve Minor Prophets among Old Testament prophetic books.
- In the original Hebrew Bible, the twelve books are treated as a single book known as The Twelve.
- Three of the Minor Prophets—Jonah, Nahum, and Obadiah—prophesied against nations foreign to Israel and Judah.

PERSPECTIVES
ON THE BOOK OF NAHUM

The message of Nahum is not concretely applied to Assyria and Judah until later in the book. The psalm that occurs at the beginning of the book presents a picture of God applicable for all times—he is the Warrior who judges evil. Tremper Longman III

His work must be placed in the first rank of war poetry. John R. MacArthur

The prophet reveals the eternal principle of the omnipotent God that for a nation to survive it must be established upon and directed by principles of righteousness and truth. Homer Hailey

In his brief book, Nahum makes three declarations about God and Nineveh. 1. God is jealous: Nineveh will fall (Nahum 1:1-15). . . . 2. God is judge: How Nineveh will fall (Nahum 2:1-13). . . . 3. God is just: Why Nineveh will fall (Nahum 3:1-19). Warren W. Wiersbe

Nahum excels in superb word-pictures and in the atmosphere of noise and tumult: the scarlet tunics of the fighting men, the flaming of the . . . chariots, the noise of cracking whips and of prancing horses, the corpses piled in heaps, the shaking of the fir trees. Mary Ellen Chase

HABAKKUK

*Living by Faith
When Life Gets Hard*

FACT SHEET

FORMAT. 3 chapters, 56 verses

IMPLIED PURPOSE. To record accurately the author's questions and doubts about God's justice and management of the world, God's reply to those questions and doubts, and the author's expression of faith in God in response to God's revelation

AUTHOR'S PERSPECTIVE. This book is a rarity among the prophetic books of the Bible by virtue of its being, in effect, a first-person account of the author's dialogue with God. The book reads like a personal diary and testimony.

IMPLIED AUDIENCE. The book of Habakkuk is an overheard dialogue between the prophet and God. While the immediate "eavesdroppers" were the people of Judah, the prophet actually talks about issues that are timeless for believers in God.

WHAT UNIFIES THE BOOK. The drama of the speaker's entering into dialogue with God; the question-answer-response format; the poetic nature of the discourse; focus on the question of whether God is trustworthy

SPECIAL FEATURES. The privacy of the situation in the book, as the prophet interacts with God instead of proclaiming an oracle on the street corner; the first-person tone of the book; the book's status as a theodicy—a reconciliation of God's goodness and power with the existence of evil in the world; the famous statement in 3:17-19 that Habakkuk will trust in God even if his external situation becomes disastrous

FACT SHEET

What can believers do when God's promise to be good does not seem to be realized in their external situations in life—when a family member gets cancer or suffers from mental illness, for example? Is God good when a marriage fails or a great injustice occurs in society? Can faith survive in the absence of discernible external blessing? This is the problem that the book of Habakkuk memorably addresses.

KEY VERSES

"Though the fig tree should not blossom, nor fruit be on the vines . . . yet I will rejoice in the LORD" (3:17-18, ESV). Here is the final attitude of the prophet after he has wrestled with the problem of living in a world where violence dominates and his personal situation is in decline: Faith in God is his last, best hope.

The Structure

The book of Habakkuk is organized on a simple plan of dialogue between the prophet and God:

Habakkuk's First Question (1:2-4). Why doesn't God do something about the violence in the prophet's own society?

God's First Answer (1:5-11). God will use the pagan nation of Chaldea, or Babylon, to punish Judah for its violence.

Habakkuk's Second Question (1:12–2:1). Why would God use an even more violent nation than Judah to revel in its own violence?

God's Second Answer (2:2-20). In a fivefold series of "woes," God predicts eventual judgment against Chaldea/Babylon.

Habakkuk's Psalm of Faith (Chapter 3). Habakkuk affirms his confidence in God's strength.

Key Doctrines and Themes

Human Sin. The first two chapters paint detailed pictures of violence.

The Justice and Omnipotence of God. Even though evil gains the ascendancy in human society temporarily, God will have the final word.

The Nature of Faith. Faith takes its stand on God's character and is exercised in the face of much that might bring God's goodness into question.

Justification by Faith. "The righteous will live by their faithfulness to God" (2:4, cited in Romans 1:17 and Galatians 3:11).

The Sufficiency of God to Satisfy. The prophet acknowledges and exalts God's sufficiency, regardless of whatever losses he may suffer (Habakkuk 3:17-19).

Tips for Reading or Teaching Habakkuk

As with every book in the Bible, the surface details of Habakkuk are firmly rooted in a specific place and time in history (see, for example, the references to Chaldea). As always, you need to look through these particulars to the universal experiences that are embodied in a specific moment in history. The underlying issue in the book of Habakkuk is particularly universal since it deals with a problem that every believer confronts sooner or later; namely, what happens to one's personal faith when life falls apart? You should read or teach Habakkuk with an eye on the universal problem it addresses.

DID YOU KNOW?
- The name *Habakkuk* means "to embrace" or "cling" or "clasp" (possibly, by extension, "to wrestle").
- Habakkuk was a contemporary of Daniel and Jeremiah.

Contribution of the Book to the Bible's Story of Salvation in Christ
Habakkuk's hymn (chapter 3) praises God for his greatness, for his conquest of all that opposes him, for his salvation. A Christian reads this litany of God's praiseworthy acts of salvation through the lens of Christ's atoning work; for example, "The righteous shall live by his faith" (2:4, ESV) and "You went out for the salvation of your people" (3:13, ESV).

Applying the Book
The main application comes from (1) universalizing the problems of the violence in society that we observe in chapters 1–2 and (2) making personal the statement of faith the author expresses in chapter 3. We all have our own versions of needing to trust in God's character and salvation when life disintegrates around us.

KEY VERSE
"The righteous will live by their faithfulness to God" (2:4). The New Testament contains three references to this verse: Romans 1:17; Galatians 3:11; and Hebrews 10:38.

PERSPECTIVES
ON THE BOOK OF HABAKKUK

Habakkuk complains, Habakkuk listens, Habakkuk prays.
Irving Jensen's summary of the content

Faith troubled [1–2], faith triumphant [3]; what God is doing [1–2], who God is [3]. Bruce Wilkinson and Kenneth Boa's summary of the content

The Book of Habakkuk . . . comprises two compositions: the oracle of Habakkuk (1:1–2:20) and the psalm of Habakkuk (3:1-19). They belong to different literary genres, but share a common theme: the preservation of loyal trust in God in [the] face of the challenge to faith presented by the bitter experience of foreign invasion and oppression. F. F. Bruce

Title: The Prophet Worshiping. Outline: 1. Prayer: pray for the work of God (3:1-2). 2. Vision: ponder the greatness of God (3:3-15). 3. Faith: affirm the will of God (3:16-19). Conclusion: God doesn't always change the circumstances, but He can change us to meet the circumstances. That's what it means to live by faith. Warren W. Wiersbe's outline for chapter 3

ZEPHANIAH
Variations on the Theme of the Day of the Lord

FACT SHEET

FORMAT. 3 chapters, 53 verses

IMPLIED PURPOSES. To announce the coming judgment of God against the nation of Judah and the surrounding pagan nations and to balance that statement of woe with a concluding prediction of God's restoration of a remnant of his people

AUTHOR'S PERSPECTIVE. The prophet is mainly a reporter of "the word of the LORD that came" to him (1:1, ESV). He himself is dispassionate, but his message comes with the authority that characterizes prophetic utterance.

IMPLIED AUDIENCE. The original audience was the nation of Judah and its neighboring nations. But through its portrayal of a specific and immediate Day of the Lord, the book speaks to later eras about intermediate and ultimate Days of the Lord in which God punishes evil.

WHAT UNIFIES THE BOOK. The predictive nature of the oracles; the Day-of-the-Lord motif; nature imagery; focus on nations; a prevailing tone of warning, balanced at the end with consolation

SPECIAL FEATURES. The usual prophetic pattern in which most of the book predicts divine judgment and then, without transition, pictures a golden age of divine blessing; a corresponding balance between pessimism and optimism; God's speaking in the first-person voice to the nations

FACT SHEET

Partly because of the ability of modern media to inform us about what is happening around the globe, it is easy to get the impression that our own era knows an unprecedented amount of international unrest and bullying. Never have so many nations seemed to deserve punishment for so much misconduct. But the book of Zephaniah alerts us to the fact that the problem of evil on a vast scale is nothing new. In addition it provides a lens by which to view the situation as God does.

The Structure

The structure of Zephaniah is simple and clear in its outline:

An Oracle (Authoritative Expression) of Judgment against Judah (1:1–2:3). This ends with a call to repentance.

An Oracle of Judgment (2:4-15). God will judge surrounding pagan nations.

An Oracle of Judgment (3:1-7). God will judge Jerusalem and, by extension, Judah.

An Oracle of Salvation (3:8-20). In a reversal of all that has preceded, God promises to restore the fortunes of his people.

Key Doctrines and Themes

God's Anger. As Zephaniah expresses it, God is angry at evil, both individual and corporate, and will bring judgment in a coming Day of the Lord.

Repentance. The prophet addresses the possibility that individuals can escape God's Day of Judgment by humbling themselves and turning from their sin before it is too late (2:3).

Redemption. God's plan is to save a remnant from the earth.

Tips for Reading or Teaching Zephaniah

First, the predictions of God's judgment against evil are timeless and perpetually relevant to human history. The nations mentioned in the book of Zephaniah are no longer the national entities in our world, but you can easily substitute updated names, including that of your own nation. It is the *principle* at work that you need to stress. Second, the oracle of salvation at the end is a symbolic picture of what it means to accept God's rule; you can treat the details in the text as a metaphoric picture of ultimate salvation through Christ and the blessings of kingdom living.

Contribution of the Book to the Bible's Story of Salvation in Christ

The ultimate form that God's judgment against evil will take is Christ's conquest as narrated in the Gospels and pictured in Revelation. Also, the picture of salvation with which the book ends ultimately centers on the work of Christ, the true "mighty savior," who gathers outcasts and rejoices over them with singing (3:17).

Applying the Book

To see the relevance of the Old Testament prophetic books, you need to move beyond the historical particulars and identify the universal principles, then apply those principles to analogous nations and situations in your own world. The application is not only national but also personal. Furthermore, the book contains intermittent commands and pictures of godly living that can guide you in your daily life.

KEY VERSE
"Seek the Lord, all who are humble, and follow his commands. Seek to do what is right and to live humbly. Perhaps even yet the Lord will protect you—protect you from his anger on that day of destruction" (2:3). Here are the themes of the book: the coming day of destruction as God punishes evil, the possibility that individuals can escape such punishment by calling on God to save them, and the command to behave antithetically to the evil that God judges.

PERSPECTIVES
ON THE BOOK OF ZEPHANIAH

A message of doom and hope in a shapely, stylish form. It is a coherent, compelling eschatological vision. J. Alec Motyer

He proclaims God's judgment on Jerusalem's ruling classes with a vengeance, but . . . he sees that judgment as performing a positive

function: God's ultimate goal in judgment is the transformation of his people, the creation of a poor and humble people in whose presence the righteous God can live, and this righteous remnant will one day rejoice in God's restoration of the fortunes of Zion. J. J. M. Roberts

As he looks beyond the doom and destruction of a world judgment, the prophet draws a sublime picture of the Messianic age (3:14-20), though he does not mention or describe the Messiah Himself. Homer Hailey

These prophetic voices were principally national in their application. It is nevertheless true . . . that a nation consists of the sum total of the individuals that make it up. Whereas, therefore, the application is first national, it has personal bearing. G. Campbell Morgan

God is represented as searching the streets of this city, like a night-watchman with a lamp. No sinner will be hidden from his eyes or escape his judgment (1:12). It is this figure which led medieval artists to represent Zephaniah himself as the man with the lamp of the Lord. It is a fitting image of the temperament and character, the message and ministry of the prophet. Stephen Winward

HAGGAI
*How to Qualify for
God's Blessing*

FORMAT. 2 chapters, 38 verses

IMPLIED PURPOSE. To record four oracles in which Haggai spurs the returned remnant of exiles from Babylon to get on with rebuilding the Temple, accompanied by assurances of blessing as a reward for obedience to this task

AUTHOR'S PERSPECTIVE. The author of the *book* is a dispassionate recorder of Haggai's oracles and the narrative framework into which they are placed. Haggai, as author of his *oracles*, speaks with customary prophetic boldness and authority as God's spokesman.

IMPLIED AUDIENCE. The original audience was the returned exiles of Judah and more particularly, their leader, Zerubbabel. The more universal audience is God's people in any age who experience deprivation when they procrastinate in doing God's work and who prosper when they actually do it.

WHAT UNIFIES THE BOOK. The format of prophetic oracles; references to the rebuilding of the Temple; the theme of what makes a person and nation eligible or ineligible for God's blessing

SPECIAL FEATURES. Rootedness in a specific situation: the rebuilding of the Temple after the exile; the addressing of the prophecies to the leader, Zerubbabel, not directly to the people; occasional apocalyptic and messianic focus; repeated linking of a society's lack of flourishing to disobedience of God and of its prosperity to obedience

KEY VERSE
"The latter glory of this house shall be greater than the former, says the LORD of hosts. And in this place I will give peace" (2:9, ESV). Here is the focus of the book, which records the specific blessings that came when the returned exiles rebuilt the Temple, but which deals with the more general question of the conditions under which God grants his blessing to people, namely, obedience and worship.

A secular mind-set looks for economic factors to explain the fluctuations in a nation's material prosperity or depression. The same mind-set locates lack of personal flourishing in psychological and environmental factors. The book of Haggai has a different view of why people and nations prosper or flounder.

The Structure

The book of Haggai is simplicity personified. It consists of four oracles embedded in a narrative context: (1) An oracle rebuking the returned exiles for not rebuilding the Temple, followed by a narrative account of the people's obedience to the oracle (chapter 1); (2) an oracle encouraging the people with promises that God's Spirit is among them and that the rebuilt Temple will be glorious (2:1-9); (3) a recollection of the people's past defilement and resultant lack of prosperity as a foil to the new era of obedience that has now begun (2:10-19); and (4) a concluding oracle that predicts generalized apocalyptic destruction of earthly powers and exaltation of Zerubbabel as the representative of God's people (2:20-23).

Key Doctrines and Themes

A Moral and Spiritual View of History. The welfare or misery of people and nations is directly related to their obedience or disobedience to God (1:3-11).

The Supreme Importance of Worship. This includes communal worship (which for the original recipients of the book meant Temple worship).

The Sovereignty of God over human history (2:21-22).

Tips for Reading or Teaching Haggai

While it is not essential to a reader's understanding of Haggai to put it into its fuller historical context, Ezra 1–6 tells the story within which Haggai's prophecy occurred. Although Haggai contains references to specific historical situations, the prophecies themselves are phrased in universal terms that render it easy to grasp the underlying principles. A helpful framework within which to study the book is to view it as giving information about four topics: (1) What are the conditions for receiving

God's blessing? (2) What is the nature of God's blessing? (3) What are the conditions under which people or nations miss out on God's blessing? (4) What is the nature of God's judgment against those who disobey him?

Contribution of the Book to the Bible's Story of Salvation in Christ

In a small way this book is a chapter in messianic history, inasmuch as we find Zerubbabel, the leader to whom the oracles are addressed, in the genealogies of both Joseph (Matthew 1:12) and Mary (Luke 3:27). Beyond that, the apocalyptic visions of what God will do by way of epoch-making acts (2:6-7, 21-22) focus on Christ as the New Testament events unfold (including the future events of which Christ spoke). Christ's body—destroyed by death and raised after three days—is the ultimate temple where God dwells.

DID YOU KNOW?
- The name *Haggai* means "festive."
- Three of the twelve Minor Prophets— Haggai, Zechariah, and Malachi—are known as postexilic prophets.
- Haggai is the second-shortest book in the Old Testament.

Applying the Book

Haggai can be read as a handbook on the conditions that make for blessedness from the hand of God. Obedience and proper worship are the keynotes; you can infer other applications from additional details. The book can also be read as a case study of the need to put first things first and of the blessings that flow from doing so.

PERSPECTIVES
ON THE BOOK OF HAGGAI

Get your priorities right—that is the timeless truth proclaimed by Haggai. Put first things first, and other things also necessary to man will follow as a result. Priority number one in human life is God, for to trust and to love, to revere and to worship, to obey and to serve him, is the chief end of man. For Haggai, the rebuilding of the Temple was the outward and visible sign of the desire and determination of the leaders and people to put God first. Stephen Winward

The assumption that we can enjoy Christian standards and benefits without Christian commitment is prevalent today. . . . [This] book is a tract for our times.   J. Alec Motyer

The completion of the latter Temple (1:1-15), the glory of the latter Temple (2:1-9), the present blessings of obedience (2:10-19), the future blessings through promise (2:20-23).   Bruce Wilkinson and Kenneth Boa's outline for the book

The entire Book of Haggai is an extended commentary on the text of Jesus: "Seek ye first the kingdom of God, and his righteousness; and all these things shall be added unto you" (Matthew 6:33).   Ralph Earle

ZECHARIAH

*An Old Testament
Gospel of Hope*

FORMAT. 14 chapters, 211 verses

IMPLIED PURPOSE. To convey God's prophetic and apocalyptic messages of hope and judgment (chiefly the former) regarding his covenant people, both in the immediate postexilic times and throughout future history

AUTHOR'S PERSPECTIVE. The human author is the prophetic deliverer of messages from God. God is the direct author of the content of this book, and the general drift of his message is to instill hope in his people, with reminders that he will judge evil.

IMPLIED AUDIENCE. The original audience was the remnant who returned from the Babylonian captivity during the era of the rebuilding of the Temple. But very little of the book's content is specific to this situation; the book's symbolic visions are for believers throughout the ages.

WHAT UNIFIES THE BOOK. Visionary mode; symbolism as the main vehicle for expressing the author's content; reasons for hope

SPECIAL FEATURES. A combination of prophecy and apocalypse; highly fantastic details such as are common in dreams; reliance on symbolism to express most of the meaning; many memorable verses; strong futuristic orientation; messianic emphasis

CHALLENGE FACING THE READER OR TEACHER OF THIS BOOK. Knowing to what the visionary and symbolic details refer

HOW TO MEET THE CHALLENGE. Apply what you know about visionary writing and symbolism. (For a reminder, see the article on page 325.) The references are rooted in the immediate situation of the postexilic community, but they also refer to Christ's coming and the end of the ages.

DID YOU KNOW?

- The name *Zechariah* means "God remembers."
- According to Matthew 23:35, Zechariah was murdered in the Temple, between the sanctuary and the altar.
- The book of Zechariah is the longest of the twelve Minor Prophets.
- Except for Isaiah, Zechariah is the most messianic Old Testament prophetic book, both in proportion and in total amount of material.
- The book of Zechariah mentions the city of Jerusalem more than forty times.

The health of any society depends on its images of the future. The book of Zechariah provides a helpful summary of the Bible's images of the future. These numerous messianic prophecies were futuristic for Zechariah's audience, but they can serve as a reminder of the Christian's essential identity today. The apocalyptic visions of the book express the Christian's hope for the future.

The Form of the Book

Like other prophetic books, Zechariah is a collection of individual units. In keeping with the dream format, no narrative continuity emerges. The three main literary forms that you need to apply to Zechariah are the following: prophecy (see the article on page 291), apocalyptic writing (page 633), and visionary writing (page 325). The dominant form is the oracle of salvation, which pictures God's deliverance and blessing. In addition, almost everything in the book is expressed through symbols (starting with a man sitting on a red horse in the midst of myrtle trees in a small valley).

Unifying Elements

- Most paragraphs belong to either the prophetic or the apocalyptic genre.
- Almost as pervasive is the technique of visionary writing, which portrays characters and events that belong to a fantastic world rather than to ordinary reality.
- We move in a world where symbols such as animal horns and the changing of clothes and lampstands convey the meaning.
- The prevailing tone is one of hope.
- Jerusalem and Judah are the recipients of God's intended blessing, which we understand also to represent God's blessings on his universal spiritual kingdom.

Key Doctrines

The Sovereignty of God. There is an unusual emphasis on God's transcendence of the earthly and human, as reinforced by the visionary mode in which the book is embodied.

Apocalyptic/Eschatological Visions — The End Times

Sermon Material — Messages for Contemporary Judah

12–14 Apocalyptic Visions
11 Oracle of Judgment
9–10 Oracle of Redemption
8 Messages of Blessing

7 Messages of Judgment
6:9-15 The Branch

Prophetic Visions — Immediate and Messianic Future

6:1-8 Four Chariots
5:5-11 Woman in Container
5:1-4 Flying Scroll
4 Lampstand, Olive Trees
3 High Priest's Garments
2 Measuring Line
1:18-21 Four Horns
1:7-17 Horsemen's Patrol
1:1-6 Introduction

AN OUTLINE OF
ZECHARIAH

Salvation. The book is filled with symbolic pictures of God's coming redemption: in the restoration of a remnant after the exile and in the return of Christ.

Eschatology. The latter stages of the book portray events that will take place at the end of the ages.

Tips for Reading or Teaching Zechariah

Read or teach in continuous awareness of the literary genres of prophecy, apocalyptic writing, and visionary writing (see the "Form of the Book" section above).

Be prepared to interpret a barrage of symbols: events, characters, and images that stand for something else. For example, the eighth verse of the book tells us that Zechariah saw a man riding on a red horse. A red horse is obviously a symbol, not a literal reality.

At some points the focus of the visions is on present reality during Zechariah's time; at other points, the orientation is futuristic. You will need to differentiate between these two.

Even though much of the book refers to historical particulars during the time of Zechariah or the immediate future, you can extract timeless truths from the historical particulars.

quick overview of zechariah

1:1–6:15	Nine prophetic visions (oracles of blessing)
7:1–8:23	Prophetic messages from God
9:1–14:21	Messianic and apocalyptic visions

Things to Look For

- Abandon all expectations that you will encounter a picture of literal reality around you. Instead, give yourself over to the fantastic nature of what you will encounter: a branch that builds a temple, a sowing of peace rather than grain, the city of Jerusalem being turned into a heavy stone, a flying scroll that devours houses.
- In addition to looking for fantasy instead of realism, be ready to see great symbols communicating most of the meanings of the book: symbols such as a change of priestly garments for the high priest, disembodied eyes as symbols of God's omnipresence, and mysterious living waters flowing out of Jerusalem.

• Look also for a futuristic orientation. At the time the book of Zechariah was being written, virtually everything in it was still futuristic. Many of the prophecies of the first two-thirds of the book have been fulfilled: The rebuilding of the Temple was completed almost immediately, and Christ came five centuries later. The apocalyptic visions of the book's conclusion remain to be fulfilled.

The Flow of the Book

Nine Prophetic Visions (Chapters 1–6). The book opens with a difficult introduction that seems to go in several different directions, but the general import is that the nation must return to the ways of God (1:1-6). Nine visions then appear as a pageant (for a listing, see the chart earlier in this chapter). What follows are tips for mastering the material:

Treat every vision individually, teasing out its meaning on its own terms.

At the level of content, operate on the premise that this is prophecy rather than apocalypse—in other words, that the visions pertain to the present and near future of the remnant that has returned from the Babylonian captivity, not to eschatological events at the end of history. The last vision (6:9-15) is a messianic vision that deals with the intermediate future.

Accept from the start that this is visionary literature in which you enter a "strange world" of the literary imagination—a world in which you encounter red horses and four horns scattered throughout Judah, a flying scroll thirty feet long and fifteen feet wide that destroys houses, and a woman named Wickedness sitting in a cereal container.

Be aware that the technique in use is that of symbolic reality, which means that what you chiefly meet as you read these visions are symbols of great spiritual truths. Your interpretive task is to determine what the symbols stand for.

What about the overall content of the visions? Try to ascertain how the visionary details add up to these main points for the respective visions: Visions 1, 2, 3, and 8 predict God's sovereign protection of his people against their enemies—an oracle of blessing. Vision 4 predicts renewal and purification of the priesthood and, by extension, of all believers. Vision 5 predicts the completion of the rebuilding of the

> **KEY VERSES**
> "Then Jerusalem will be called the Faithful City; the mountain of the LORD of Heaven's Armies will be called the Holy Mountain. . . . And the streets of the city will be filled with boys and girls at play" (8:3-5). We can see here the impulse toward symbolism in the names of the city and the mountain, the visionary and apocalyptic qualities, and the emphasis on God's future blessing.

Temple. Vision 6 predicts that God will judge evil. Vision 7 predicts that God will remove sin from his people. Vision 9, which begins as a symbolic coronation ceremony for the high priest, predicts the coming of the Messiah.

Messages of Judgment and Restoration (Chapters 7–8). An opening question about whether the people should fast (7:1-3) leads to a series of messages from God. The messages in chapter 7 are oracles of judgment, and those in chapter 8 are oracles of salvation, largely apocalyptic in nature. The formula that says, essentially, "a message came from the Lord" or "the word of the Lord says" occurs more than a dozen times in these chapters, lending a fluid quality, not a neat division into four visions.

Messianic and Apocalyptic Oracles (Chapters 9–14). The visionary mode continues, and the book ends the way most Old Testament prophecies end: with visions of God's blessing at some future point in history. The safest approach is to accept the specific details as symbolic pictures of future events. If we operate on that premise, chapters 9–10 are a vision of Christ's coming; chapter 11 is an oracle of judgment against a sinful covenant people, and chapters 12–14 are an apocalyptic vision of God's salvation of his people and his final, eschatological defeat of all forces of evil.

The Main Themes
1. As in all of the prophetic books, a leading theme is the picture of God that emerges from the oracles of judgment and salvation. The focus is on God as both the judge of evil and the source of salvation for those who believe in him.
2. God's ultimate intention is to bless his followers eternally. There is thus a hope for the future.
3. The basis of the promised blessing is the coming of a Messiah who will redeem sinners (for Zechariah's readers, yet to come; for us, already come).

Contribution of the Book to the Bible's Story of Salvation in Christ
Zechariah is filled with messianic prophecies, as the New Testament partly highlights for us. Here are some specimens: God's coming servant as a branch (3:8) who will build a temple (6:12), a jewel that will remove Israel's sins in a single day (3:9), a king who comes to Jerusalem riding on a donkey (9:9), the people of Jerusalem looking on him whom they have

pierced (12:10), and a shepherd who is smitten and whose sheep are scattered (13:7).

Applying the Book

We should note first that this prophetic book lacks the strong ethical emphasis of most Old Testament prophetic books, so that avenue of application is largely closed. The way to apply the messianic prophecies is to believe in the Christ who is here foretold as the best news that could be imagined. According to 1 Peter 1:10-11, the salvation predicted by the prophets "was something even the prophets wanted to know more about when they prophesied about this gracious salvation prepared for [us]. They wondered what time or situation the Spirit of Christ within them was talking about when he told them in advance about Christ's suffering and his great glory afterward." We can be grateful to live in the age of fulfillment. Another main application is to live in hope. The book of Zechariah is a gospel of hope for an age and culture that are notably deficient in images of hope. Finally, interspersed passages in Zechariah emphasize the need for heart repentance as opposed to going through the external motions of the religious life.

PERSPECTIVES
ON THE BOOK OF ZECHARIAH

The prophet of hope. F. B. Meyer

The major Minor Prophet. Bruce Wilkinson and Kenneth Boa

The book, often called the Apocalypse of the Old Testament, makes much use of figurative and symbolical language. . . . The messages of the prophecy are given sometimes in direct prophetic speech, sometimes in the narration of visions, and sometimes in the setting forth of symbolical acts. Charles Lee Feinberg

Chapters 9–14 are the most quoted section of the prophets in the passion narratives of the Gospels and, next to Ezekiel, Zechariah has influenced the author of Revelation more than any other Old Testament writer.
Joyce G. Baldwin

The Book of Zechariah . . . is like some unique masterpiece of music, with simpler movements in the first part, followed by a . . . triumphant finale.
J. Sidlow Baxter

Zechariah's message functions in much the same way as Revelation. . . . His prophecies related both to Zechariah's immediate audience as well as to future generations. John R. MacArthur

MALACHI

*When God's People
Ignore God's Rules*

FACT SHEET

FORMAT. 4 chapters, 55 verses

IMPLIED PURPOSES. To warn God's covenant people about their sinful practices and God's judgment against them, and equally to prompt God's people to live righteously and align themselves with God's grand redemptive plan

AUTHOR'S PERSPECTIVE. As the prophet records God's messages, he throws himself with abandon into his indictment of offenses, with a view toward moving his audience to reform their practices. He also paints such attractive pictures of God's blessings on those who take him seriously that anyone should want to participate in God's program.

IMPLIED AUDIENCE. The original audience was the postexilic covenant people in an era of spiritual malaise and willful flouting of God's commands. These spiritually negligent people were living in the rebuilt Jerusalem nearly a century after the first exiles had returned and perhaps during the era of Nehemiah's reforms, which addressed the very abuses Malachi denounces. Through the original audience, the book speaks to God's people in every era who treat God with indifference or contempt.

WHAT UNIFIES THE BOOK. The major theme of God's indictment of his backsliding people and the minor (in terms of space) counter-thrust of divine blessing on a repentant and believing people; an ever-expanding portrait of a covenant people who have wandered from their covenant responsibilities; continual pictures of the contrast between how covenant people are supposed to live and how they lapse into violating those guidelines

SPECIAL FEATURES. A fluid structure in which the author moves without transition between oracles of judgment and oracles of

407

salvation; repeated use of a three-part format that consists of (1) indictment by God, (2) question by those who have been indicted, and (3) reply by God (e.g., 1:2, 6; 2:17; 3:7-8); use of rhetorical questions in God's speeches of indictment (e.g., 1:6, 8; 2:10, 15); inclusion of such everyday matters as money, marriage, and family; and striking messianic prophecies

Reading the book of Malachi feels rather like eavesdropping on the end of a long family quarrel. In this last book of Prophets, God speaks to Israel through Malachi in the voice . . . of the father who, after so many estrangements and reconciliations, has finally had enough. . . . It is almost as if the Lord of Hosts has grown impatient, grown tired of His children's repeated failure. . . . Unique among the prophetic books, Malachi advances its argument almost entirely through dialectic. God makes a pronouncement, then asks a question. But the question is Israel's question, God's ironic mimicry of Israel's question.

FRANCINE PROSE
"Malachi"

Going to church, paying one's tithes and offerings, resisting the impulse to tell a convenient lie, refusing to capitulate to cultural trends in such matters as divorce—sometimes doing these things seems natural and a privilege, but if one is not vigilant, it is possible to start regarding them as a wearisome burden. The book of Malachi provides an incentive to keep practicing the Christian life as God has outlined it.

The Structure

The organization of the book is not as clear as that of the other Minor Prophets. Here is a scheme that is true to the actual contours of the book: (1) Despite God's showing favor to Israel in bringing judgment on Edom, the priests and their charges have been guilty of a whole litany of evils (chapters 1–2). (2) Malachi predicts the sudden appearance of God's judgment against an apostate people (3:1-5). (3) God accuses his people of neglecting their responsibility to pay his tithe and promises to bless them if they will do so (3:6-12). (4) This back-and-forth section moves between God's judgment against those who ignore his commands and his future blessing on those who honor him (3:13–4:6).

KEY VERSES

"The day of judgment is coming, burning like a furnace. . . . But for you who fear my name, the Sun of Righteousness will rise with healing in his wings" (4:1-2). The book of Malachi keeps shifting back and forth between the fierceness of God's anger against willful disregard for his commands and his promise of a coming redemption.

Key Doctrines and Themes

God's Attitude toward Disobedience. God is angry when his covenant people disregard his commands.

Human Responsibility. God holds his people responsible for their willful evil.

Covenant. Despite the book's brevity, it is a shorthand manual of numerous covenant stipulations that God gave his people in the Pentateuch.

Sin. The book contains vivid pictures of people treating God's rules for worship and daily life with contempt.

Messianic Promise. Numerous individual verses predict the coming of the Messiah and the nature of his person and work.

Tips for Reading or Teaching Malachi

The flow of the book is actually fluid, with the thought shuttling back and forth between indictments from God and, without transition, promises from God to bless his people. Follow the actual contours of the text, not tidy outlines. Be aware that some of God's accusations are specific (e.g., those dealing with divorce and the tithe), but intermingled with those units are charges of a very general nature. Still, since the general format is judgment and blessing, you can profitably compile (1) a running list of offenses that are subject to God's judgment and (2) a portrait of the coming Messiah and the nature of the blessings he will bring.

DID YOU KNOW?
- The name *Malachi* means "my messenger."
- Malachi is chronologically the last Old Testament prophetic book, after which there were four hundred years of silence in scriptural revelation.
- Malachi is a particularly important repository of messianic prophecies.

Contribution of the Book to the Bible's Story of Salvation in Christ

This book contains some of the most famous predictions regarding Christ, some of them rendered even more famous by their appearance in Handel's *Messiah*. They include references to a messenger sent to prepare the way (3:1), Christ's suddenly coming to his Temple (3:1), the question of who can endure the day of his coming and stand when he appears (3:2), a Sun of Righteousness who will rise (4:2), and the Messiah's turning the hearts of fathers to their children and children's hearts to their fathers (4:6).

Applying the Book

The first thing to note is that Christians are the New Testament version of God's covenant people. Malachi's warnings against covenant backsliders are thus also warnings to wayward believers in Christ. The priests in the book of Malachi correspond to Christian pastors and leaders. God's prophecies to Israel are now prophecies to the church. With that as a foundation, the list of indictments against God's people and the pictures of God's judgment against those who are guilty should strike fear into a reader's heart and lead him or her to flee the wrath to come. This book is a veritable manual on God's view of the sinfulness of sin, with emphasis on sins of the heart and neglect of duty by those who profess to be God's people. Equally, the effect of the messianic prophecies should not only instill renewed commitment to Christ but also have the doxological effect of causing readers to offer praise to God.

PER**SPECTIVES**
ON THE BOOK OF MALACHI

Malachi—When People Play Cheap with God.
Heading in *Meet the Minor Prophets* by Ralph Earle

The whole prophecy reveals a calloused people and a sensitive God.
G. Campbell Morgan

Ten times the prophet presents the people as interrupting with an objection by putting the words "ye say" in their mouth. Homer Hailey

Malachi: Questions and Answers.
Heading in *A Guide to the Prophets* by Stephen Winward

His messages against "the sins of the saints" need to be heeded today.
Warren W. Wiersbe

In view of the present sin (1–2); in view of the coming "day" (3–4).
J. Sidlow Baxter's streamlined version of the book's structure

part three

THE NEW TESTAMENT

MATTHEW
Jesus, the Promised Messiah and King

FORMAT. 28 chapters, 1,071 verses

IMPLIED PURPOSES. To present evidence that Jesus is the Messiah who had been promised in the Old Testament and to provide an eyewitness narrative of his life and teachings with a view toward instilling belief in Jesus as Messiah and King

AUTHOR'S PERSPECTIVE. Matthew, a Jew writing to fellow Jews, seeks to provide sufficient reason to believe in Jesus as the Messiah. In pursuit of that purpose, Matthew takes pains to demonstrate that the events of Jesus' life are the fulfillment of Old Testament prophecy. Matthew also writes as a disciple of Jesus who observed most of what he included in his Gospel.

IMPLIED AUDIENCE. The audience is assumed to be Jewish, steeped in a knowledge of the Old Testament. However, Matthew also has as a secondary strategy to persuade Gentiles that Jesus is the Messiah of the whole world (as in the famous great commission).

WHAT UNIFIES THE BOOK. The person and teaching of Jesus; the alternating blocks of narrative and discourse; the story line from Jesus' birth through his earthly ministry to his death and resurrection; the standard ingredients of the Gospel as a genre

SPECIAL FEATURES. Recurrent quotation and citation from the Old Testament; emphasis on Jesus as kingly or royal; messianic preoccupation; orderly arrangement of material, including arrangement in groups of three and seven; apocalyptic (end times) interest; biographical interest (starting with Jesus' birth and ending with his death and resurrection); emphasis on discipleship

CHALLENGES FACING THE READER OR TEACHER OF THIS BOOK.
1. The length of the book (It is the Gospel with the most chapters.)
2. Hostility toward Judaism and its representatives

. . . .

3. Abundance of references to the Old Testament
4. Topical rather than strictly chronological organization of the story

HOW TO MEET THE CHALLENGES.
1. Regard the length of the book as a virtue resulting in a completeness to the treatment of Christ.
2. The writer was himself a Jew, so his hostility to the Jewish establishment was not racial prejudice but theological conviction.
3. Ponder how the Old Testament references apply to Jesus.
4. We tend to take a topical approach every time we report on an event we attend, so with a little adjustment we can take Matthew's alternating narrative and discourse styles in stride.

Probably from the first century to the twentieth, students have memorized the outline of Mathew by counting off the five discourses on the fingers of one hand. . . . Between each of the following discourses, Matthew incorporated stories of Jesus' life . . . : (1) How are citizens of the kingdom to live [5–7]? . . . (2) How are traveling preacher-disciples to conduct themselves on their evangelistic journeys [10]? . . . (3) What were those parables Jesus told [13]? . . . [4] How shall Christians conduct themselves toward each other and as they face persecution [18–20]? . . . [5] How will it all end [24–25]? . . . Note how Matthew even marks each of these discourses with the phrase "When Jesus had finished these sayings" (Matthew 7:28; 11:1; 13:53; 19:1; and 26:1).

SIR WILLIAM RAMSAY
The Layman's Guide to the New Testament

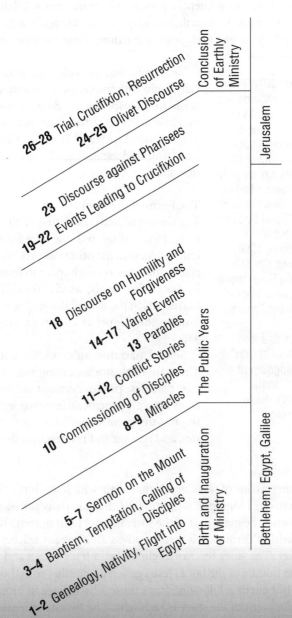

AN OUTLINE OF
MATTHEW

Bethlehem, Egypt, Galilee

1–2 Genealogy, Nativity, Flight into Egypt

3–4 Baptism, Temptation, Calling of Disciples

5–7 Sermon on the Mount

Birth and Inauguration of Ministry

8–9 Miracles

10 Commissioning of Disciples

11–12 Conflict Stories

13 Parables

14–17 Varied Events

18 Discourse on Humility and Forgiveness

The Public Years

19–22 Events Leading to Crucifixion

23 Discourse against Pharisees

24–25 Olivet Discourse

26–28 Trial, Crucifixion, Resurrection

Conclusion of Earthly Ministry

Jerusalem

Jesus is the most influential person in human history. What was he really like when he was on earth, and why were his life and teaching so influential? Whatever one's religious convictions, these questions arouse a natural curiosity.

To satisfy that curiosity, we almost automatically begin with the Gospel of Matthew. Not only is it the first Gospel in the Bible; it was also placed first in all early Christian references to the Gospels. We can therefore read Matthew's Gospel as a gateway to an understanding of Jesus—a grand initiation story.

The Form of the Book

The Gospel of Matthew is first of all a narrative, or story. Plot, setting, and character form the basic elements. As with the other Gospels, though, the storyteller devotes as much space to Jesus' teaching as he does to his deeds, which take their place as actual events in the overall story. (For more information on the Gospel as a form of writing, see page 436.)

Several narrative subtypes fill out the picture. There are birth stories, calling stories, miracle stories, parables, pronouncement stories (which pair an event with a memorable saying by Jesus that interprets the event), conflict stories, encounter stories, and passion and resurrection stories.

The Story

Matthew is one of two Gospels that begin with Jesus' birth, thereby showing a strong biographical impulse. With the nativity stories serving as the prologue, the main part of the story follows Jesus in roughly chronological fashion through his three years as an itinerant teacher and miracle worker. The story reaches its climax with Jesus' death and resurrection. In the middle of the book, Jesus generates conflict with those who reject him but elicits a following from those who believe in him. The general development of the story is highlighted by two statements that come at the beginning of Jesus' public ministry and at the transition point that leads toward the Passion: "Jesus began to preach" (4:17) and "Jesus began to show his disciples that he must . . . be killed" (16:21, ESV).

The Prayer of Jesus

The Lord's Prayer (Matthew 6:9-13) has special importance because it is the only form of prayer given by the direct instruction of Jesus Christ. Here are some of the most important things that you need to know about the Lord's Prayer:

- It is a flexible pattern for prayer. Although it is appropriate to repeat the exact words that Jesus gave his disciples, especially in public worship, the Lord's Prayer is mainly intended to serve as an outline for prayer that we are free to fill in with specifics.
- The main parts of the prayer are the preface ("Our Father in heaven"); the petitions (1) "May your name be kept holy," (2) "May your Kingdom come soon," (3) "May your will be done on earth, as it is in heaven," (4) "Give us today the food we need," (5) "Forgive us our sins, as we have forgiven those who sin against us," and (6) "Don't let us yield to temptation, but rescue us from the evil one"; and the concluding doxology, "For yours is the kingdom and the power and the glory forever. Amen."
- The basic movement of the prayer is from God's glory (as we seek the holy name and heavenly Kingdom of God our Father) to our good (as we request daily provision, daily pardon, and daily protection).
- The prayer is phrased in the plural ("Our Father," "the food we need," "forgive us," "rescue us," etc.). This makes the Lord's Prayer a family prayer in which we do not pray simply for our own daily bread and deliverance from evil but also for the food and safety of all God's children.
- Jesus himself prayed nearly every petition in the Lord's Prayer. He invariably addressed God as his Father, and sometimes as his holy (or "hallowed") Father (e.g., John 17:11). The prayer of his entire life was to do the will of his Father, not his own will (see Matthew 26:39; John 6:38). Jesus prayed for God's blessing when he broke bread (e.g., Matthew 26:26; John 6:11) and for the deliverance of his disciples when Satan tempted them (e.g., Luke 22:31-32; John 17:15). When Jesus died on the cross, he asked his Father to forgive our debts (not his own, of course), and as he did so, he forgave us, his debtors (Luke 23:34). Finally, Jesus prayed for the glory of God's name and Kingdom (see John 17:1).

Although the traditional ending of the prayer ("For yours is the kingdom and the power and the glory forever") does not appear in the earliest New Testament manuscripts, it is thoroughly biblical. Jewish prayers from that time typically ended with some kind of benediction, and the one we use with the Lord's Prayer is drawn from the prayer of David in 1 Chronicles 29:11.

The Structure

The most important principle in regard to the structure of this Gospel is that Matthew the bookkeeper (a tax collector by profession), with his penchant for orderly arrangement, has composed a book that is tightly organized around the principle of alternating between action and discourse, as a later section of this chapter will outline. No strict correspondence can be made between the adjacent sections of narrative and discourse.

EVENTS IN THE LIFE OF JESUS RECORDED ONLY IN MATTHEW
Joseph's dream (1:20-24), journey of the magi (2:1-12), flight into Egypt (2:13-15), slaughter of the innocents (2:16-18), healing of two blind men (9:27-31), healing of a dumb man (9:32-33), repentance of Judas (27:3-10), dream of Pilate's wife (27:19), resurrections in Jerusalem when Jesus arose (27:52-53), bribery of the soldiers (28:11-15), and the great commission (28:19-20)

The second structural principle of Matthew relates to the narrative genre of the book and its cast of characters, which we can view as a series of concentric rings. In the center is Jesus. Immediately around him in frequency of appearance are the disciples. Beyond them are the Jewish leaders, most often referred to as "the Pharisees." In the outermost ring is the general population, sometimes pictured as a nameless crowd and at other times represented by specific characters.

The Aim of the Book

Matthew does not state his aim directly, but we can infer it from the content of his Gospel. He has the biographer's desire to get the facts of Jesus' life and ministry recorded correctly. Within this documentary, he aspires to provide convincing evidence that Jesus is the fulfillment of Old Testament messianic prophecies and that Jesus is the king in the Davidic line about whom the prophets wrote.

Unifying Elements

- The formula "when Jesus had finished these sayings" (ESV) to mark the transition from a block of discourse to a narrative section
- The kingship motif
- The relation of events and teachings of Jesus to Old Testament prophecy
- Repeated formulas, such as "Son of David" as a title for Christ, statements to the effect that "this was done that it might be fulfilled what the prophet said," and "the Kingdom of Heaven is like . . . ."
- The conscious use of formal titles for Christ (for example, Son of David, Lord, Son of Man, Son of God)

- A partly topical arrangement of Jesus' life and teaching
- The Jewish religious leaders' opposition to Jesus

Key Places and Characters

Places assume symbolic meanings in Matthew's Gospel. Bethlehem is the humble place of birth, Egypt the place of refuge, Nazareth the place from which Jesus is regarded as coming, Galilee the place of preaching and ministry, and Jerusalem the place of rejection. Similarly, the desert is the place of John the Baptist's preparatory ministry and Jesus' temptation, the sea a place of danger, the Temple a place of conflict with the religious establishment, the mountain a place of transcendence, and the grave the place of death and its conquest.

The main actors in the drama are Jesus, Mary and Joseph, John the Baptist, the twelve disciples, the Jewish religious leaders, and two political leaders who conduct a trial of Jesus (Caiaphas the high priest and the Roman governor Pontius Pilate).

Key Doctrines

Christology. Matthew has distinctive themes regarding Christ, with emphasis on Christ as the fulfillment of Jewish prophecy and his identity as King.

The Kingdom of God. Numerous discourses and parables of Jesus in this Gospel teach explicitly what it means to enter the Kingdom of God (also called the Kingdom of Heaven).

Salvation. The Gospel of Matthew records the salvific ("bringing salvation") life of Jesus, especially his crucifixion and resurrection, so that we can understand and participate in that salvation.

The Old Testament Law. Especially in the Sermon on the Mount, Jesus gives explicit teaching about himself as the fulfillment of the Old Testament law.

Ethics. Partly (but not wholly) on the strength of the Sermon on the Mount, Matthew's Gospel is a major repository of teaching about what constitutes the moral life (including its dos and don'ts).

OUTLINE OF THE SERMON ON THE MOUNT

- prologue: setting and audience (5:1-2)
- portrait of the ideal Christian (5:3-12)
- Jesus' teaching on being salt and light (5:13-16)
- Jesus' interpretation of the Old Testament law (5:17-48)
- instructions on three religious observances (6:1-18)
- threefold exhortation about choosing right values (6:19-24)
- discourse on not being anxious (6:25-34)
- instruction on three practices (7:1-12)
- three great contrasts (7:13-27)
- epilogue: response of the crowd (7:28-29)

Eschatology. Especially in the Olivet discourse (chapters 24–25), this Gospel contains extended teaching about the last things.

The Devotional Life. Jesus is pictured as a man of prayer, and he teaches about prayer, fasting, and charity.

Tips for Reading or Teaching the Gospel of Matthew

Your best strategy is to focus on the hero of the story, operating on the premise that you are the observant traveling companion of Jesus during his life as an itinerant teacher and miracle worker.

The five sections of discourse (5:1–7:29; 10:1-42; 13:1-58; 18:1-35; 23:1–25:46) are Matthew's compilation of Jesus' teaching on specific topics; explore these sections as systematic expositions of the topics.

Be receptive to Matthew's apologetic aim to prove that Jesus is the prophesied Messiah, and explore the implications of the fact that Jesus is the fulfillment of Old Testament predictions.

Be ready to shift your expectations when you move from a narrative section to a discourse section, and vice versa.

Remember that the way to organize a study of a story is to pay attention to plot, setting, and character.

quick overview of the gospel of matthew

1:1–4:25	Narrative: Jesus' birth and entry into his ministry
5:1–7:29	Discourse: Sermon on the Mount
8:1–9:38	Narrative: a collection of miracle stories
10:1-42	Discourse: teaching about discipleship
11:1–12:50	Narrative: conflict stories
13:1-58	Discourse: a collection of Jesus' parables
14:1–17:27	Narrative: assorted stories
18:1-35	Discourse: teaching about childlike humility and reconciliation/forgiveness
19:1–22:46	Narrative: a kaleidoscope of stories
23:1–25:46	Discourse: denunciation of the Pharisees and the Olivet discourse on the last things
26:1–28:20	Narrative: the trial, crucifixion, and resurrection of Jesus

The Flow of the Book

Nativity Stories (Chapters 1–2). As you ponder Matthew's account of Jesus' genealogy, birth, and infancy, look for clues as to why Matthew

The Last Week of Jesus' Life

Day	Event (All in Jerusalem)	Reference
Sunday	Triumphal Entry (two-mile journey from Bethany, where Jesus stays each night, to Jerusalem)	Mark 11:1-11
Monday	Jesus cleanses the Temple.	Mark 11:15-19
	Religious leaders actively plot to get rid of Jesus.	Mark 14:1-2
Tuesday	Religious leaders question Jesus' authority: "By what authority are you doing all these things?"	Luke 20:1-8
	Jesus is anointed at Bethany.	John 12:2-8
	Judas deserts Jesus and betrays him.	Luke 22:3-6
Thursday PM	Last Supper with the disciples (the Passover meal)	John 13:1-30
Late Thursday & Early Friday	Garden of Gethsemane: Jesus prays and waits for his arrest.	John 17
Early Friday	Confrontation in the garden and Jesus' arrest	Mark 14:43-50
	First trial before Annas, former Jewish high priest; Jesus suffers initial physical abuse.	John 18:12-24
	Jesus appears before Caiaphas, the current Jewish high priest, and the Sanhedrin court and is bloodied by further abuse.	Mark 14:53-65
	Peter denies Jesus.	John 18:15-27
	The Sanhedrin formally condemns Jesus.	Luke 22:66-71
	Jesus is handed over to the Romans, who have authority in capital cases, for a hearing before Roman governor Pilate, who declares, "I find nothing wrong with this man."	Luke 23:1-5
	Hearing before Herod Antipas, who has jurisdiction over Galilee and is interested in meeting Jesus. Jesus refuses to answer Herod's questions and is returned to Pilate.	Luke 23:6-12
	Pilate tries repeatedly to release Jesus, but the Jewish leaders object. On Pilate's orders, Jesus is tortured and beaten beyond recognition (perhaps in an attempt to appease the Jewish leaders, who demand crucifixion). Pilate orders Jesus' execution.	Luke 23:13-25
	Jesus is forced to carry his own cross.	John 19:17-24
12:00 noon–3:00 PM	Jesus' final hours on the cross	Mark 15:33-36
3:00 PM	Death	Mark 15:37
	Jesus' burial	Mark 15:42-47
Sunday	Jesus' resurrection	Luke 24:1-12

selected this particular material and how he intended it to instruct and edify us.

Jesus Initiates His Ministry (Chapters 3–4). Here, too, Matthew has been very selective, so each recorded event and detail must signal something important. What is that significance?

The Sermon on the Mount (Chapters 5–7). After the kaleidoscope of brief events presented up to this point, we now get a leisurely and extended record of Jesus' most famous sermon. Coming early in Jesus' ministry as Matthew chronicles it, we can profitably analyze this sermon as Jesus' inaugural speech for the Kingdom that he has come to establish. What are the key elements in Jesus' plan for his Kingdom? What do we learn about the King of the Kingdom? about the citizens and the obligations of citizenship? What surprises are there? (For example, Jesus says nothing about institutions but locates his plan for the good society in the individual lives and morality of the citizens.)

A Collection of Miracle Stories (Chapters 8–9). The basic ingredients of miracle stories are these: Someone has a need, seeks Jesus' help, and expresses faith or obedience; Jesus performs a miracle; people respond to the miracle and/or to Jesus. With that as a descriptive grid, analyze the individual stories with a view toward discovering what they say about Jesus and about people in their relationship to Jesus. Another good approach is to assume that the miracles of Jesus teach us about the Kingdom of God: its power, its spiritual battles, and other specific teachings that Jesus intersperses with his miracles.

Discourse about the Cost of Discipleship (Chapter 10). The surface action is Jesus' commissioning of the twelve disciples, accompanied by his teaching about how they are to conduct themselves as traveling evangelists. Through these particulars we are given a glimpse of what it means to be a disciple of Jesus—anywhere, anytime. What are the essential principles?

Conflict Stories (Chapters 11–12). To avoid getting lost in this mini-anthology of stories, compile a list of the cast of characters and the specific events. We can view the miscellaneous nature of the material as giving us "a day in the life of Jesus"—a day that doubtless contained the same range of elements that we find in these two chapters. What do we learn about Jesus and his spiritual kingdom in these stories?

Parables (Chapter 13). Although parables are interspersed elsewhere in Matthew's Gospel, the author obviously wanted a block of them together. To get maximum mileage out of these parables, apply the general rules for interpreting parables. (See "Parable as a Literary Form" on page 447.)

Assorted Stories (Chapters 14–17). This is a miscellaneous collection of material, but again we can profitably regard it as allowing us to share what life was like "on the road with Jesus." The best-known events in this block of chapters are the death of John the Baptist, two feedings of multitudes, Jesus' walking on the sea, Peter's great confession, and the Transfiguration. Here are some good pointers for organizing and analyzing the individual units:

> **KEY VERSE**
> "It is enough for the disciple to be like his teacher, and the servant like his master" (10:25, ESV). Matthew says much about the life of the disciple, and in kernel form it means being like Jesus.

- First, assume that each unit has its own point, or purpose. What is that point or purpose?
- We can also trust someone as orderly as Matthew to have selected and expressed the material in such a way that each unit contributes to the bigger issues of his Gospel as a whole. In what ways does each unit function as a building block in the main edifice?
- The question of what a given unit tells or reinforces about Christ and his Kingdom is always relevant.
- For narrative units, asking the usual questions about plot, setting, and character will yield fruit.

Further Lessons about the Life of the Disciple: Discourse on Humility and Forgiveness (Chapter 18). The order of topics in this chapter is (1) the need for disciples to be childlike, (2) the parable of the lost sheep, (3) teaching about reconciliation, and (4) teaching about forgiveness. A good way to approach the chapter is to analyze how these components make up a single coherent discourse.

KEY VERSE
"From that time Jesus began to show his disciples that he must go to Jerusalem and suffer many things . . . and be killed, and on the third day be raised" (16:21, ESV). The story of Matthew's Gospel moves toward the climax of Jesus' passion and resurrection.

Toward Jerusalem: Events Leading up to Jesus' Trial and Execution (Chapters 19–22). There is no need to try to make the material tidier than it is. While the unit consists mainly of stories, there are interspersed elements of teaching, as well as some parables. A new development that is just below the surface is that Jesus is now heading toward his climactic confrontation with the Jewish leaders. A fruitful approach is to scrutinize the material to ascertain what might have made Jesus' behavior and teaching controversial and finally exasperating to people who have the mind-set that, by this point in the story, we know the scribes and Pharisees had. Then we can contemplate (1) how we and our acquaintances might be like those religious leaders and (2) what lessons we need to learn in order to love and obey Jesus in light of his revolutionary teachings. In addition, this section is filled with lessons about living as citizens of the heavenly Kingdom.

Denunciation of the Pharisees (Chapter 23). This is the single most extended piece of satire in the four Gospels. It is relentless in its attack on the Jewish leaders. Things to note are (1) the specific things for which Jesus attacks the scribes and Pharisees, (2) the positive principles of behavior that Jesus commands as an alternative, and (3) application on how to avoid being numbered with the people whom Jesus denounces.

The Eschatological Olivet Discourse (Chapters 24–25). This famous address to Jesus' disciples is the most extended unit of teaching by Jesus about the last days and end of history. The right way to assimilate the address is to see it as an ever-expanding source of information about the end of the age, along with implications for how we should live in order to be ready for eternity.

Jesus' Passion and Resurrection (Chapters 26–28). In all four Gospels, the events surrounding the death of Jesus constitute the largest block of material. Here is what Matthew chose to record:

• Jesus' last Passover supper in the upper room and the events surrounding it (26:1-35)
• Jesus in Gethsemane, ending with his arrest (26:36-56)

- Jesus' trial by Caiaphas and the Sanhedrin and then by Pilate, with separate betrayals by Peter and Judas forming a subplot (26:57–27:26)
- Jesus' crucifixion and burial (27:27-66)
- Jesus' resurrection and the giving of the great commission (chapter 28)

Try to relive these events as fully as possible, and by means of your imagination, participate in the action.

The Main Themes
1. Jesus is the predicted Messiah, the apex and culmination of God's eternal plan for the salvation of the human race.
2. We have a reliable record of who Jesus was and what he did and taught.
3. Imitating Jesus and practicing what he taught and commanded prepares people to live as citizens of God's eternal kingdom.
4. To live as Jesus' disciple is demanding and requires great courage because of the opposition of the world, but the life of discipleship as Jesus delineates it is possible.
5. God's revelation of his truth in the Old and New Testaments is a unified revelation, with the New Testament serving as the culmination of the Old Testament.

> **KEY VERSES**
> "Go and make disciples of all the nations, baptizing them in the name of the Father and the Son and the Holy Spirit. Teach these new disciples to obey all the commands I have given you" (28:19-20). What may appear to be the "Jewish" Gospel is also the universal Gospel: It ends pointing outward to all people.

Contribution of the Book to the Bible's Story of Salvation in Christ
The Gospel of Matthew presents Jesus as the climax of God's eternal plan of redemption—the very Messiah and Son of David about whom the Old Testament weaves an intricate tapestry. Matthew's Gospel gives variations on the themes of the kingship of Christ as God's anointed Savior and on his fulfillment of all that had been foretold through the centuries.

Applying the Book
One application is that of belief. Matthew's Gospel is filled with teaching about Jesus and his message. To apply the material, we need to believe in Jesus as Lord and Savior and in the truthfulness of what he taught. In addition, we need to believe in the accuracy of Matthew's account of Jesus' life and teaching.

A second application is practice. In this Gospel, Jesus provides a thorough outline of how Christians are required to live as his disciples. The application is to live in keeping with what Jesus taught and how he lived. In this regard, we need to note how much ethical teaching this particular Gospel contains, with a frequent emphasis on how costly it can be to follow Jesus.

PERSPECTIVES
ON THE GOSPEL OF MATTHEW

The most important book ever written. Ernest Renan

The most immediately striking characteristic of Matthew's Gospel is what may be loosely termed its "Jewishness." The formula-quotations clearly emphasize . . . that Jesus is the goal of the Old Testament revelation of God. David Hill

It is probable that Matthew's Gospel was primarily addressed to teachers . . . [and] was a manual for such people. . . . The Gospel as a whole was a manual to put into the hands of church leaders to help them in their work. Michael Green

It is a remarkable fact that, among the variations in the order in which the Gospels appear in early lists and texts, the one constant factor is that Matthew always comes first. . . . The early Christians were conscious, in a way few Christians are today, that their faith had its roots in Judaism. R. T. France

[The author] is an earnest and dedicated Christian, and the writing of the Gospel is for him an act of obedience to the risen Christ, who is his Lord. He seeks to honour and serve Christ. Floyd V. Filson

In Mathew all is stylized. People are either good or bad, wise or foolish, obedient or disobedient, merciful or merciless. Michael D. Goulder

Almost all the elements that a modern reader would demand of a biography are lacking. Matthew has two principal interests: the fulfillment of God's purposes in and through Jesus, and how this fulfillment will find expression in the community which Jesus founded. W. F. Albright and C. S. Mann

FORMAT. 16 chapters, 678 verses

IMPLIED PURPOSE. To record a selection of what Jesus did and said during his public years, with a view toward conveying the truth about who Jesus is and the spiritual significance of his life, death, and resurrection

AUTHOR'S PERSPECTIVE. The author himself is an objective reporter, but his selection of material is sufficient to show that he is a believer in Jesus and that he wants his readers to follow Jesus as well. It is possible to detect an incipient apologetic and evangelistic agenda.

IMPLIED AUDIENCE. Scholars have presented evidence that Mark wrote for a Jewish audience, a Greek audience, and a Roman audience, so we should draw the obvious conclusion that Mark wrote for all people, realizing that the need to know Jesus is universal.

WHAT UNIFIES THE BOOK. The presence of Jesus in both word and action; the conflict motif; miracles; the travel motif; the "world" of the story, having recurrent features that become familiar to us as we live with the Gospel; our awareness of a growing crisis that will result in Jesus' death

SPECIAL FEATURES. Fast narrative pace, accentuated by Mark's fondness for the word *immediately*; vividness of descriptive details; portrayal of the disciples as slow to understand and believe; frequent inclusion of how people responded to Jesus (at least twenty-three instances) and similar recording of how Jesus responded to events; a preference for Greek verbs that portray an action in process

CHALLENGE FACING THE READER OR TEACHER OF THIS BOOK. Being the simplest of the four Gospels, this bare-bones account of Jesus'

life is the easiest to read. The main challenge is organizational and consists of the need to discern a unity and pattern to the mosaic of individual units.

HOW TO MEET THE CHALLENGE. Detailed topical outlines may let you down when you look closely at what is actually in the text. Your best option is to view the organization as corresponding to what we know as the genre of a documentary life, which combines "clips" of what someone did and said, where that person went, and how others responded, within a loose chronological framework.

The Gospel of Mark is a historical narrative which sets forth a representative picture of the person and work of the Lord Jesus Christ. It is not primarily a biography. . . . It gives in close succession, probably in general chronological order, a series of episodes in Christ's career with some detail concerning the last week that He spent on earth. . . . It is brief, pictorial, clear-cut, and forceful. Like a snapshot album devoted to one person, it gives a series of characteristic poses of Jesus without attempting close continuity between them. Nevertheless Mark affords a satisfactory understanding of His person and work when the total impression of these individual episodes is put together.

MERRILL C. TENNEY
New Testament Survey

16 Resurrection
14–15 Passion Story
13 Olivet Discourse
11–12 Toward the Crucifixion

Jesus Presses His Claims in Such a Way as to Lead to His Crucifixion

Concentrated Action in Jerusalem

Jesus as Sacrifice

10 Final Glimpse of Jesus' Ministry
8:22–9:50 Jesus with the Disciples
6:1–8:21 Specimens of Jesus' Life
4–5 Parables and Miracle Stories
2–3 Conflict Stories
1 Initiation of Jesus' Ministry

Jesus Reveals Himself in His Public Ministry

Diffused Travel Story That Moves about Galilee

Jesus as Itinerant Teacher and Miracle Worker

AN OUTLINE OF
MARK

Each of the four Gospels presents material and perspectives that differ from the others. Even the same events sometimes seem to be divergent. Which one is the accurate account? Many apparent discrepancies will fall into place if we keep two things in mind: (1) Jesus was an itinerant teacher and miracle worker. Just as a political campaigner today gives varied versions of his talks to different audiences and has similar encounters at many public appearances, so Jesus would have had slightly different versions of similar events. (2) The instant replay of a televised sports event gives us a model for the similar-yet-varied accounts that we find in the Gospels. By the time we have seen the same play from different angles (including even a reverse-angle version), with commentary superimposed, we have exactly what we find in the Gospels—slightly different but equally truthful versions of the same event.

DISTINCTIVES OF MARK'S GOSPEL

- It is the shortest Gospel.
- Proportionately, it has the most miracles.
- Proportionately, it has fewer parables than Matthew or Luke.
- It uses the Greek word meaning "immediately" or "at once" forty-two times, more than the rest of the New Testament combined.
- In keeping with Mark's preference for action, he records only one long discourse by Jesus.

The Form of the Book

On the surface the Gospel of Mark is the most narrative of the four Gospels. After all, it is the most action-oriented and the most streamlined Gospel. And it is surely true that the usual narrative ingredients are the right terms for interacting with the Gospel of Mark, with plot, setting, and characters the essential elements. But when we start to read Mark's account, we find that it is too piecemeal in organization to read like a conventional story. Some scholars offer the mosaic or the collage as the right model by which to assimilate the material.

A more helpful analogy is that of the one-hour television documentary on a famous person's life. What things make up such a documentary? We can expect to find a loosely chronological arrangement of the material, but within that form the arrangement is partly topical. We are given a series of relatively brief units—clips of famous events, snatches of speeches or interviews, and commentary by the narrator and people familiar with the subject of the documentary. There will be crowd scenes and small-group scenes, public scenes and more private scenes. Of course, Mark does not have use of television clips and instead relies on reported narrative. The material, though, is approximately what we find in a documentary life on television. A helpful thing to keep in mind is that a documentary life includes two types of material: (1) typical or representative events, to give the flavor of what happened repeatedly; and (2) crucial, turning-point events that happened once. Documentaries show by their allotment of space what the producers think to be most important, and in this regard we need to note that half of Mark's documentary is devoted to the last week of Jesus' life, with emphasis on his willingly choosing to die on the cross.

Key Places and Characters

There can be little doubt that geography plays a major role in Mark's Gospel, but the symbolism is not quite as clear cut as many commentators claim. Jesus' life as a traveling preacher and miracle worker takes place largely in the towns and countryside of Galilee. The usual claim is that Galilee symbolizes Jesus' success in preaching the gospel. There are, indeed, triumphs of belief, but as you read this material, you are unlikely to think of it as mainly a success story. The Passion story is set in Jerusalem, which without doubt symbolizes rejection and hostility.

The protagonist of the action is Jesus. The central plot conflict is between Jesus and those who reject or oppose him—chiefly the religious establishment but sometimes people from the community and even the obtuse disciples. If the scribes and Pharisees are the villains of the story, the disciples are the loyal confidants of the hero (except during the events surrounding the Crucifixion). The crowds are the final major character. Of course, in a story such as this, "minor" individual characters are important and will repay all the close attention you give them.

Unifying Elements

• The continuous presence of Jesus as the central character
• The travel-story genre, with the usual ingredients of journeying, of changing locations (towns and the natural countryside being the staples), and of encounters with people along the way
• The conflict motif

- Our awareness of progressive danger that will lead to arrest and crucifixion
- The motif of people's responses to what Jesus does and says

Key Doctrines

The Incarnation. Mark shows Christ to be God in human form. You can profitably sift the book for evidence of this and then ponder the implications.

Salvation and Faith. The aim of Jesus' actions and teaching was largely to show people how to be saved and then live as believers.

Ethics. Jesus is first, last, and always the great moral example. To live a morally good life is to live as Jesus did.

Eschatology. Chapter 13 is devoted to teaching about the end times, and numerous interspersed comments by Jesus fill out the picture.

Tips for Reading or Teaching the Gospel of Mark

Knowing that Mark's Gospel is action-oriented, open yourself up to the effect of immediacy that Mark uses as his approach. Mark's Gospel is much celebrated for its vividness of detail; relive the action as vividly as possible.

Do not allow the outlines based on geography or phases in Jesus' ministry to confuse you. Instead, let the "documentary life" genre—with its mosaic of individual episodes, speeches, and encounters—guide your progress through the book.

With individual Gospel units, it is always appropriate to ask what the unit tells you about Jesus and his mission.

quick overview of the gospel of mark

1:1–10:52	Jesus' life as a traveling teacher and miracle worker
11:1–16:20	The last week of Jesus' life, ending with his crucifixion and resurrection

The Flow of the Book

The organization of the Gospel of Mark is very fluid until it reaches the Passion story. There is no consensus among commentaries and handbooks as to how to outline the book. Some outlines divide the ministry of

Jesus into geographical movements, and others into phases of Jesus' disclosure of who he is, but these are of very little help in actually reading the Gospel because the same kaleidoscope of ingredients carries over from one locale or phase of ministry to the next. The following outline is based on kinds of material that we actually encounter in the text, and it largely follows the contours of the chapter divisions.

Initiation into the Ministry of Jesus (Chapter 1). There is a double initiation going on here—Jesus' initiation into his ministry and our initiation into the Gospel of Mark. You can note what you learn about Jesus and his ministry in the series of vignettes that the chapter presents.

Stories of Conflict (Chapters 2–3). Whereas the opening kaleidoscope of stories gives us glimpses of Jesus' success and popularity, these two chapters mainly give us conflict stories in which someone criticizes Jesus for what he has said or done. Questions to ponder as you read include the following: Why do Jesus' opponents object to what he has said or done in a given episode? What do we learn about Jesus in the episode?

Parables and Miracle Stories (Chapters 4–5). This unit consists of four parables and four miracle stories. To master these chapters, you need to apply what you know about parables and miracle stories. (See pages 447 and 437.)

On the Road with Jesus (6:1–8:21). These chapters give us snapshots of Jesus' life during his years as an itinerant teacher and miracle worker. The very randomness of organization captures the sense of what a day in the life of Jesus was like. You can therefore begin by noting the range of material Mark included—rejection of Jesus, the hostility of the religious establishment, the miracles Jesus performed, and belief in Jesus. Then approach each unit in terms of the specific subgenre to which it belongs, such as discourse, miracle story, conflict story, and the like. At every point it is important to ask what the episode reveals about Jesus.

Jesus with His Disciples (8:22–9:50). Read this unit looking for signposts that the action is occurring largely between Jesus and his disciples, thus lending a teaching-learning format to the material. Then put yourself in

KEY VERSE
"The Son of Man came not to be served but to serve, and to give his life as a ransom for many" (10:45, ESV). Here are both the moral and the theological keys to the book: Believers are called to serve others, and Jesus' death is the atonement for human sin.

The Gospel as a New Testament Form

The primary feature of the Gospels is that they inform us about the person and work of Christ, with most of the space given to the three years of his public ministry. The title *Gospel* means "good news" and was taken from the Greek word used to designate the message of salvation in Christ.

The primary form is narrative, or story. It is true that the teaching and discourses of Jesus get as much space as narrative events, but the overall story is the framework within which Jesus' teaching occurs.

The plot of the Gospel narratives is episodic rather than a single continuous action, and the fragmented nature of the material is further highlighted by the characteristic brevity of the units. A host of specific narrative genres (types) appear in the Gospels (see the article on page 437 for an anatomy of the Gospel subtypes). Several patterns unify the Gospels, including the following:

- In the center of everything is the person and work of Jesus.
- In concentric rings around Jesus we find, in order of increasing prominence, (1) the group of followers known as disciples, (2) the religious establishment (often called the Pharisees or the scribes and Pharisees), and (3) ordinary people, sometimes a crowd of onlookers, sometimes specific individuals.
- While the arrangement of material is partly topical (for example, parables of Jesus collected into an extended unit), the organization is loosely chronological, and all of the Gospels devote most of their space to the trial, crucifixion, and resurrection of Jesus.

The Gospels combine three primary ingredients:

- Jesus' teaching and preaching: what Jesus said and taught
- Jesus' actions: what Jesus did
- The responses of people to Jesus: what others did

Furthermore, Jesus' conversations, dialogues, and altercations with opponents constitute a hybrid of the three ingredients above: They are a form of teaching, they are "speech acts" that have the effect of an action, and they involve people's responses to Jesus.

The kaleidoscopic combination of materials reflects the varied nature of Jesus' life during his years as a traveling teacher and miracle worker. Slight differences among the Gospels' highly similar material is partly a matter of the individual writers' selectivity, but it is more likely that as an itinerant, Jesus did similar actions and said similar things many times, much as we find a politician doing during a campaign.

The overall aim of the Gospel writers is persuasion. Their goal in recording and interpreting the events of Jesus' life and his teaching is not simply biographical and historical. The Gospel writers are believers in Jesus who want their readers to believe in the Savior also.

Subtypes within the Gospels

The Gospels are made up largely of the following subtypes:

• Stories surrounding Jesus' birth and childhood: Annunciation stories, Nativity stories, infancy narratives

• Vocation or calling stories, in which someone responds to Jesus' call to follow him or believe in him

• Recognition stories, in which someone recognizes that Jesus is the Messiah, or Savior

• Witness or testimony stories, in which a character testifies about who Jesus is or what he has done

• Conflict or controversy stories, in which Jesus engages in conflict with other characters, usually the religious establishment

• Encounter stories (such as the meeting with the Samaritan woman at the well), in which Jesus confronts a character

• Pronouncement stories, in which an event is paired with a memorable saying or proverb uttered by Jesus, so that both event and saying are remembered together. An example is Mark 2:15-17, where the story of the Pharisees' criticism of Jesus for eating with tax collectors and sinners concludes with Jesus' proverb "Healthy people don't need a doctor—sick people do."

• Miracle stories, which have as many as five ingredients: A need is established; Jesus' help is sought; the person in need or his/her acquaintances express faith or obedience; Jesus performs a miracle; characters respond to the miracle and/or Jesus.

• Parables: stories told by Jesus to teach truth

• Discourses or sermons uttered by Jesus

• Sayings or proverbs stated by Jesus

• Passion stories: stories of events that happened at the end of Jesus' life. Specific types of stories under this general heading include arrival in Jerusalem; Passover/upper room stories; scenes of suffering, arrest, trial; Crucifixion; Resurrection; and post-Resurrection appearances.

Each subtype has its own set of conventions or expectations. If we identify a unit in the Gospels correctly, we can interact with it accurately and do justice to its specificity. Many units combine features of two or more subtypes, but one subtype always dominates.

the position of the disciples and reflect on what you would have learned as you went through this succession of events with Jesus. Many accounts of the book's structure stress Peter's confession near the beginning of this unit (8:27-30) and the Transfiguration that comes just a little after that (9:2-8) as pivotal in the book, but if you look closely at the material in chapters 9–10, you will be hard pressed to see any difference from the preceding material. The real change of direction comes when Jesus marches into Jerusalem as a prelude to the Passion story (chapter 11 and following).

KEY VERSE

"[Jesus] asked them, 'But who do you say I am?' Peter replied, 'You are the Messiah'" (8:29). Peter's great confession highlights the identity motif that is a main theme in the book; here Jesus' identity is climactically proclaimed.

Final Glimpses of Jesus' Life during the Public Years (Chapter 10). This chapter is a good recap of Jesus' life during his public ministry. You can first note its variety: Jesus deals with the hostile Pharisees, blesses little children, interacts with a rich young ruler about the peril of riches, foretells his crucifixion and resurrection, deals with his immature disciples' ambition, and heals a blind man. Then you can reflect on how this range sums up Jesus' ministry during his years on the road.

Events Leading toward the Crucifixion (Chapters 11–12). The types of events and discourses that we find here could have happened at any point in Jesus' public ministry, so you can profitably be conscious of echoes of what has preceded in Mark's Gospel (see "On the Road with Jesus," above). But the placing of the Triumphal Entry right at the beginning of this unit signals that these same familiar activities took place during the final days of Jesus' life. You can therefore ponder how this context affects the way in which you experience and understand the passages.

The Olivet Discourse (Chapter 13). This chapter could be placed with the foregoing ones, but it is a summary of Jesus' eschatological teaching and deserves to be analyzed by itself for what it tells us about the last days. A good analytic framework is to scrutinize the chapter as Jesus' farewell discourse to his disciples.

The Last Days of Jesus' Life: Mark's Passion Story (Chapters 14–15). Every detail in the story of Jesus' arrest, trial, crucifixion, death, and burial is important. You need to reflect on each detail and its spiritual meaning with an awareness that Mark (like the other Gospel writers) records the events and the words that were spoken without intermingling theological interpretation. But *we* come to these events and sayings with the benefit of the Epistles' analysis of the theological meaning of the crucifixion and death of Jesus, so we should read the Gospel accounts in light of that familiar theological commentary. It would be impoverishing, though, to let that knowledge obscure our reliving the events as they happened to the participants who were present at them.

The Resurrection of Jesus (Chapter 16). A good premise for interacting with Mark's somewhat understated story of the Resurrection and Ascension is to think of ways in which this chapter serves as the climax and conclusion to Mark's Gospel. Some ancient manuscripts end the book with verse 8 while others include verses 9 through 20.

The Main Themes
1. We have abundant eyewitness information about who Jesus is and what he has done.
2. The Jesus in whom people are called to believe is known to us by his actions, his teaching (including his parables), and his interactions with people he encountered.
3. Jesus is fully human as well as fully divine.
4. Following Christ requires that we undertake a spiritual journey of obedience and self-denial.
5. Living as Jesus lived will inevitably land a person in conflict with people who reject him.

Contribution of the Book to the Bible's Story of Salvation in Christ
The contribution of this book to the story of Christ lies in its Christology—its teaching about the person and work of Christ. Of special note are the messianic titles *Son of Man* and *Son of God*, which appear, respectively, nearly twenty times and half a dozen times. The title *Messiah*, or *Christ*, appears at least eight times. Jesus himself makes key claims about who he is and what his death will accomplish, including the statement that "the Son of Man came . . . to give his life as a ransom for many" (10:45). Finally, Mark's Gospel has a distinctive emphasis on Jesus as servant.

Applying the Book
Application begins with understanding: who Jesus is, what he did and taught, his atoning death, and his resurrection. Then you need to live out the implications of that understanding. Two obvious areas of such appli-

cation are belief in Jesus as Savior and living out his moral example and commands.

PERSPECTIVES
ON THE GOSPEL OF MARK

Like the other gospels, Mark is not a biography but a topical narrative. Mark juxtaposes Christ's teachings and works to show how they authenticate each other. Bruce Wilkinson and Kenneth Boa

The main purpose of [Saint] Mark was to emphasise the Humanity of Jesus Christ. . . . He showed Himself sensible of the common infirmities of humanity, hunger, weariness, fatigue, and faintness.
Herbert M. Luckock

We have to thank Mark's Gospel for this vivid first-hand impression of Jesus the Man, his looks and gestures, his wonder, grief, and indignation, sitting in the boat teaching, asleep on a pillow in the ship's stern, walking round the Temple taking in the scene, watching the gifts dropping into the Temple box, taking up children in his arms. Percy C. Sands

The Gospel of Mark possesses the quality of action to a higher degree than any of the others. Edgar J. Goodspeed

It is . . . appropriate to label Mark a witness document. . . . It is intended to be neither a formal historical treatise nor a biography of Jesus, but proclamation. . . . The reason that almost half of Mark's sixteen chapters describe the final period of Jesus' ministry is that it is in his suffering, death and resurrection that the revelation of God in Christ is most clearly seen. William L. Lane

[On Mark as "the Gospel for the Romans:"] To [the Roman,] Christ must be presented from the Roman point of view answering to the idea of divine power, action, law and universal dominion. Jesus must appear to him as the man of power, the worker, the conqueror. And this is what is done by the Gospel of Mark, which is the Gospel of power, of action, of conquest over nature, spirits, disease and death. The New Analytical Bible

Jewish Religious Groups in the Time of Christ

The Gospels show Jesus interacting with the major religious movements of his day. Here is what each group believed:

Today the term *Pharisee* sounds pejorative because Jesus often criticized the Pharisees for their hypocrisy—and rightly so. At the time, however, Pharisees had an excellent reputation for theological orthodoxy and spiritual purity. Pharisaism originated as a serious religious movement in the second century before Christ. In addition to the law of Moses (or Torah), the Pharisees accepted oral tradition as a binding authority for daily conduct. Many of their traditions gave practical guidance for outwardly adhering to the Old Testament law, but these traditions became a law unto themselves, and they often missed the heart of true love and obedience for God. The Pharisees believed in physical resurrection and the life to come.

Like the Pharisees, the *Sadducees* emerged sometime in the second century before Christ. Unlike the Pharisees, they denied the authority of oral tradition and adopted a more literal interpretation of the Mosaic law. As we learn from the Gospels, the Sadducees denied the resurrection of the dead, eternal life, and the supernatural reality of angels and demons.

Another group that emerged during the time of Christ was the *Zealots,* who were more political in orientation. Their ultimate goal was the overthrow of the Roman government. The Zealots were fiercely loyal to the Jewish people, language, and traditions. They opposed paying tribute to Caesar on the grounds that they owed their allegiance to God alone. They prophesied great things for the future and worked for the day when Israel would be delivered from Roman domination.

The Gospels also mention several other groups frequently: The *Levites* (members of the tribe of Levi) looked after the Temple in Jerusalem and provided practical assistance in worship. The *priests* were Levites—more specifically, descendants of Aaron—who led public worship and offered sacrifices for the people of God. The *scribes* were skilled in transcribing, interpreting, and teaching God's law. As you read the New Testament, bear in mind that the terms *priest* and *scribe* refer to a man's calling and livelihood whereas the terms *Pharisee* and *Sadducee* refer to theological sects. Generally speaking, though, many priests were Sadducees and most of the scribes were Pharisees.

The *Sanhedrin*, the council of seventy elders in Jerusalem, provided social and spiritual leadership for the Jews. Like the seventy elders who served under Moses, the Sanhedrin sat in judgment over the people of God. The head of the Sanhedrin was usually the high priest. Most (but not all) of its members were scribes and priests; some were private citizens. Although some members of the Sanhedrin were Pharisees, most were Sadducees.

THE GOSPEL OF

LUKE

*The Son of Man Comes
to Seek and to Save*

FORMAT. 24 chapters, 1,151 verses

IMPLIED PURPOSE. To give an orderly account of Christ's life, death, and resurrection so readers may know these things "with certainty"

AUTHOR'S PERSPECTIVE. Luke, a trained physician (see Colossians 4:14), accompanied Paul on some of his missionary journeys. Although not an eyewitness of the events he records, he writes as a careful historian who has conducted thorough research.

IMPLIED AUDIENCE. Theophilus ("lover of God"), whose name may refer to a particular individual, or to any reader who wants to know God. Luke seems to write primarily to Greeks, specifically to those who want to know about Jesus' life and saving work.

WHAT UNIFIES THE BOOK. The story of Jesus as Israel's Messiah and the savior of the world; his relationship with his family, his disciples, the religious leaders, and all the lost people he meets on his way to the cross; the message of salvation especially for the marginalized; the journey motif as Jesus moves toward Jerusalem; the book's beginning and end at Israel's Temple

SPECIAL FEATURES. A full account of Jesus' birth and preparation for public ministry; compassion for those in distress, including sinful and suffering women; medical details of the healing miracles; an emphasis on prayer (eleven of fifteen recorded prayers of Jesus appear here); extensive teaching about money; nearly twenty parables not included in the other Gospels; Jesus' encounter with Zacchaeus (19:1-10); a pervasive note of joy, beginning with "Christmas carols" (chapter 2) and ending with the apostles worshipping the risen Christ and returning to Jerusalem "with great joy" (24:52)

CHALLENGES FACING THE READER OR TEACHER OF THIS BOOK.

1. Understanding to what extent the liberation Christ brings is physical as well as spiritual, social as well as personal
2. Distinguishing the Gospel of Luke from those of Matthew and Mark, which are nearly identical in many places
3. Recognizing the wealth of Old Testament background

HOW TO MEET THE CHALLENGES.

1. Salvation in Christ is both spiritual (forgiveness of sins) and physical (bodily resurrection). Although we must personally trust in Christ, his salvation extends to our social relationships.
2. We can understand Luke's Gospel simply on its own terms; however, to study the overlap between Luke and the other Gospels and to learn more from the significant differences, consult a harmony or synopsis of the Gospels.
3. A Bible with good cross-references will show Luke's quotations and allusions from the Old Testament.

Luke's inspired presentation of Christ is arranged in two great movements: first the "Coming" of the Lord from heaven to earth; and then his "Going" from earth to heaven. . . . Between them they sum up Luke's message of salvation. The pre-existent and eternal Son of God came to our world and became a man like us so that he might secure for us here in this world forgiveness, wholeness, peace with God and the certainty that God's will shall eventually be done on earth even as it is done in heaven. But there is more. By his Going he has taken humanity to the pinnacle of the universe. . . . [A]ll who trust him will one day be brought to share his glory in that exalted realm, and to reign with him at his return.

DAVID GOODING
According to Luke

AN OUTLINE OF
LUKE

1:1-4 Prologue: Luke's Purpose
1:5-4:13 Birth, Boyhood, Baptism, Temptation of Jesus
4:14-6:16 Jesus Begins His Ministry, Calls Disciples
6:17-8:56 Jesus' Teaching and Miracles
9:1-50 Jesus on Discipleship
9:51-10:37 Jesus in Samaria
10:38-13:21 Jesus in Bethany and Judea
13:22-17:10 Journey toward Jerusalem
17:11-19:27 Between Samaria and Galilee; Jericho
19:28-21:38 Triumphal Entry; Teaching in the Temple
22-23:25 Last Supper, Arrest, Trials
23:26-56 Crucifixion and Burial
24:1-49 Resurrection Day
24:50-52 Ascension of Jesus

The Advent of the Son of Man	The Ministry of the Son of Man	The Progress of the Son of Man toward the Cross	The Death of the Son of Man	The Triumph of the Son of Man
"A Prophet Who Did Powerful Miracles" (24:19): Preponderance of Miracles over Teaching	"A Mighty Teacher" (24:19): Preponderance of Teaching (Especially Parables) over Miracles		"The Son of Man Came to . . . Save the Lost" (19:10, ESV)	
Israel	Galilee	Journey to Jerusalem	Jerusalem	
Seeking the Lost			Saving the Lost	

How can I know for sure? It's a question many people ask when they first investigate Christianity. How can I be sure that the Bible is true? How can I know for certain that Jesus died on the cross for my sins and rose from the dead? Sometimes the same questions return later in the Christian life. Even for Christians, there can be times when the gospel suddenly seems implausible, and we wonder whether God is really there after all.

Luke dealt with these kinds of doubts by telling the truth about Jesus Christ. As he says to his readers at the beginning of his Gospel, "I also have decided to write a careful account for you, . . . so you can be certain of the truth of everything you were taught" (1:3-4). Luke wanted people to know what happened, where it happened, and in what order. And as he tells the story of Jesus—the gospel of his sinless life, atoning death, and victorious resurrection—the story itself brings us to a sure and certain knowledge of Jesus Christ.

KEY PHRASE
The phrase *the Son of Man*, which occurs twenty-five times in Luke, emphasizes Christ's deity, not his humanity. In the Old Testament, the Son of Man is the divine Savior who will come to earth in glory and judgment at the end of days.

The Form of the Book
Although it is familiar to Christians, the Gospel is a unique form in world literature. (See "Gospel as a New Testament Form" on page 436.) It is partly a biography of the man Jesus of Nazareth, but it is also a book that invites people to receive Jesus as Savior and Lord. To that end, Luke shows Jesus in action—calling disciples to faith, teaching parables, performing miracles, and enduring suffering. He has shaped these events into the larger story of a journey from Galilee to Jerusalem, with ever-intensifying opposition along the way. The story begins with a leisurely account of the circumstances surrounding Jesus' birth. The main events in the middle of the book are miracle stories and teaching sessions, as well as dialogues Jesus had with his disciples and with leaders in the religious community. But by far the greatest attention is given to the last week of Jesus' life, which culminates in his death on the cross and resurrection from the grave. We are left with the overwhelming impression that what is important about Jesus is not simply his life but especially his death and what happens afterward.

The Aim of the Book
Luke's primary purpose is to help his readers have complete confidence in the truth of what they have heard about Jesus Christ. Apart from Luke's

The Parable as a Literary Form

The parables are stories told by Jesus to embody or teach religious truth. A majority of Jesus' parables teach about the Kingdom of God (also called the Kingdom of Heaven), but a parable such as the Good Samaritan embodies ethical teaching about how we must treat those around us.

Parables belong to the category of folk stories. They take their material from everyday life and are filled with realistic touches. Their characters are universal types such as exist in all places and times. As folk stories, parables repeatedly draw on the rules of popular storytelling—rules such as simplicity of action, conflict between obvious good and obvious evil, suspense, heightened contrasts (called foils), repetition (including threefold repetition), the rule of end stress (what happens last is the key to the meaning of the parable), and archetypes (universal symbols and motifs such as lost and found, master and servant).

In most parables a number of the details in the story have a corresponding "other" meaning, such as the owner of a vineyard symbolizing God and a Prodigal Son symbolizing the rebellious sinner. The right term for such stories is *allegory*, as even the word *parable* hints, since it means "to throw alongside" (to have a double meaning, in other words).

The method for reading and teaching the parables falls naturally into four distinct activities:

- Interacting with the story as a story: with its plot, its setting, and its cast of characters

- Interpreting the allegorical or symbolic meanings where they exist. In the parable of the Prodigal Son, for example, the prodigal symbolizes rebellious humanity, the father who forgives and restores represents God, and the morose older brother pictures the Pharisees.

- Determining the themes (which is not synonymous with interpreting the allegory). The parable of the Prodigal Son, for example, embodies themes such as the tendency of the sinful heart to reject God, the nature of God as loving and forgiving, and the selfishness of religious people who do not share the joy of a sinner's conversion.

- Applying the themes to one's own life

It is untrue that you can find only one theme or "point" in a parable. Most parables embody multiple themes or ideas. The parable of the Prodigal Son, for example, shows the nature of sin as rebellion against God, the nature of God as forgiving, and the disgrace of the holier-than-thou who cannot celebrate the conversion of a sinner.

own ethnicity (he is the only New Testament writer who was not a Jew), there are many indications that Luke is writing primarily for a Gentile audience. He carefully sets the life of Christ in the context of world politics, using technical terms familiar across the Roman world. When he refers to places in Israel, he explains where they are, on the assumption that his readers won't know the territory. He tends to use Greek rather than Hebrew terminology. When he quotes from the Old Testament (which he does more sparingly than Matthew, for example), he does not quote from the original Hebrew but from the Greek translation (commonly known as the Septuagint).

DISTINCTIVE MATERIAL IN LUKE AND WHAT IT TELLS US

The "humanitarian Luke" (his compassion for women and the marginalized members of society and his criticism of the affluent) is partly illustrated by material that we find only in his Gospel: for example, the song of Mary (1:46-55); the announcement of Jesus' birth first to shepherds (2:8-20); the poor in Nazareth who are among the first to hear the Good News (4:16-21); the sinful woman who anoints Jesus' feet (7:36-50); parables of the Good Samaritan (10:30-37), the rich fool (12:16-21), the banquet for outcasts (14:12-14), the Prodigal Son (15:11-32), and the rich man and Lazarus (16:19-31); the conversion of the outcast Zacchaeus (19:1-10).

All of this is in keeping with Luke's special purpose of presenting Jesus as the Savior for everyone. This is true socially: Jesus is for everyone from top to bottom. Luke shows people from every social class—especially the underprivileged and oppressed, who usually get overlooked—coming to Christ. It is also true ethnically: Jesus is for everyone from east to west. Only Luke records the global announcement of the angels: "Peace on earth to those with whom God is pleased" (2:14). Only Luke quotes the song of Simeon, which celebrates Jesus as the Savior "prepared for all people" and "a light to reveal God to the nations" (2:31-32). Only Luke traces the genealogy of Jesus all the way back to Adam, not just to Abraham. He also highlights some of the Gentiles who came to Jesus in faith (the centurion whose servant was sick, the widow of Nain, etc.). Luke wants his readers to be sure that Jesus is the Savior for everyone.

This theme comes to its thrilling conclusion at the end of the Gospel, when Luke quotes Jesus as saying that "this message [about the Messiah] would be proclaimed in the authority of his name to all the nations, beginning in Jerusalem" (24:47). Then the book of Acts—which Luke wrote as the sequel to his Gospel—tells how the disciples took the gospel from Jerusalem to the ends of the earth.

Unifying Elements

The central unifying element in any Gospel is the personality of Jesus Christ—"a man who was a prophet mighty in deed and word before God and all the people" (24:19, ESV). However, as each Gospel writer crafts his narrative, he skillfully weaves in recurring themes that further tie the story together. There are many such themes in the Gospel of Luke: the connection between Jesus and John the Baptist, the training of the Twelve as they gradually learn the cost of discipleship, the passionate commitment of the women who love Jesus, the growing opposition Jesus faces from leaders of the religious establishment, the empowering work of the Holy Spirit in Jesus' ministry, the global reach of the gospel, Jesus' compassion for people who are down and out, the rejoicing that comes to those who put their trust in Christ, the miracles of healing, the parables of the kingdom, the journey to Jerusalem, Jesus on the Sabbath, Jesus at prayer, and Jesus at the Temple. But perhaps the strongest unifying theme is the mission of Jesus: "to seek and save those who are lost" (19:10). Luke shows that in all of Jesus' interactions with all kinds of people who were lost in all kinds of ways, Jesus was seeking to save.

> **DID YOU KNOW?**
> Luke contains four nativity hymns—first sung by Mary, Zechariah, the angels, and Simeon—that are often used in Christian worship. Their titles come from their opening words, as translated into Latin:
> • Magnificat (1:46-55)
> • Benedictus (1:68-79)
> • Gloria in Excelsis (2:14)
> • Nunc Dimittis (2:29-32)

Key Places and Characters

The key places in Luke are Bethlehem (where Jesus was born), Nazareth (where he was raised and later rejected), the towns and villages of Galilee and Judea (where he taught and healed), and Jerusalem (where he went to die). But don't overlook the following: the Temple (where the Gospel both begins and ends—see 1:8ff. and 24:53—and where Jesus had some significant encounters); the cross (where Jesus did his saving work of dying for sin); and the empty tomb (which proves that he is the risen Christ).

Many of the characters in Luke are familiar from the other Gospels. However, some of them deserve special mention. Apart from Christ himself, these include the following:

• John the Baptist, the forerunner who announced the coming of Israel's king
• Zechariah, Elizabeth, Mary, Joseph, Simeon, and Anna—godly, poor Israelites who exemplify the saving faith of the Old Testament people of God

The Parables of Jesus

	Parable	Matthew	Mark	Luke
1	Lamp under a Basket	5:14-16	4:21-22	8:16-17 11:33-36
2	The Wise and Foolish Builders	7:24-27		6:47-49
3	New Cloth on an Old Garment	9:16	2:21	5:36
4	New Wine in Old Wineskins	9:17	2:22	5:37-38
5	The Sower and the Soils	13:3-23	4:2-20	8:4-15
6	The Weeds	13:24-30		
7	The Mustard Seed	13:31-32	4:30-32	13:18-19
8	The Leaven	13:33		13:20-21
9	The Lost Sheep	18:12-14		15:3-7
10	The Hidden Treasure	13:44		
11	The Pearl of Great Price	13:45-46		
12	The Net of Fish	13:47-50		
13	The Householder	13:52		
14	The Wicked Tenants	21:33-34	12:1-12	20:9-19
15	The Wedding Feast	22:2-14		14:16-24
16	The Unforgiving Servant	18:23-25		
17	The Fig Tree	24:32-44	13:28-32	21:29-33
18	The Workers in the Vineyard	20:1-16		
19	The Two Sons	21:28-32		
20	The Moneylender and Two Debtors			7:41-43

- The disciples, who show us how—and how not—to follow Christ
- Many poor people who show us what it means to be lost and need a Savior: the shepherds who hurried to the manger; the grieving widow of Nain; the woman who anointed Jesus with perfume; and all the blind, demon-possessed, leprous, paralyzed, dead, and dying people Jesus healed
- The enemies who put Jesus to death: Judas, Pilate, Herod, and all the scribes and Pharisees who refused to believe that he was the Christ
- Memorable characters from parables that are unique to Luke's Gospel: the Good Samaritan; the rich fool; the Prodigal Son, with his welcoming father and disapproving brother; and the rich man and Lazarus

Key Doctrines

The Incarnation. Luke highlights the humanity of Christ in his long birth narratives, of course, but also in showing the simple poverty of Jesus living as a man among men.

The Holy Spirit. More than any other Gospel, Luke emphasizes the role of the Holy Spirit in empowering the ministry of Jesus Christ.

Salvation. Luke uses the word *save* to refer both to spiritual deliverance from sin and to physical healing from the effects of the Fall; Jesus saves, body and soul.

Forgiveness. In miracles such as the healing of the paralytic (5:17-26), in parables such as the Prodigal Son (15:11-32), and in personal encounters such as those he had with a sinful woman (7:36-50) and a tax collector (19:1-10), Jesus shows the meaning of true forgiveness.

Justification. As Luke tells the stories of the woman at Simon's house (7:36-50), the Pharisee and the tax collector (18:9-14), and the blind man by the side of the road (18:35-43), he explicitly mentions the saving power of faith in Christ.

The Atonement and Resurrection. Luke not only tells the facts about the cross and the empty tomb, but he also explains their meaning: Christ died and rose again so that our sins could be forgiven (24:47).

Tips for Reading or Teaching the Gospel of Luke

Keep Luke's purpose in mind by constantly asking this question: How does this part of the Gospel help me know for sure that Jesus is the Christ?

Each time there is an encounter with Jesus, identify the ways in which someone is "lost." For example, the paralytic whose friends bring him to Jesus needs both spiritual and physical deliverance. Tax collectors such as

Levi and Zacchaeus can hardly be considered poor, yet they are as lost as anyone. In what ways is that so?

Be alert for themes it would be easy to miss in any single passage but that become important by repetition (such as the role of the Holy Spirit in directing the action of the Gospel, the significant healing and teaching Jesus did on the Sabbath, the many times he went off by himself to pray, and his repeated predictions of his suffering and death).

The Gospel of Luke is often compared to the other Gospels, and rightly so. However, it is also the first volume of a two-part work that includes the book of Acts. As you study Luke's Gospel, read Acts to see how themes such as the powerful ministry of the Holy Spirit, the reality of Christ's resurrection, and the preaching of repentance to all nations come to their culmination.

quick overview of the gospel of luke

1:1–4:13	Stories of the birth and early life of Jesus
4:14–9:50	Beginning of Jesus' public ministry of healing and teaching
9:51–19:27	Increasing opposition as Jesus performs miracles and teaches in parables
19:28–24:53	Jesus' crucifixion and resurrection in Jerusalem

The Flow of the Book

Purpose Statement (1:1-4). Luke tells us how and why he wrote his Gospel.

The Coming of the Christ (1:5–4:13). From the beginning, Luke intertwines the story of Jesus with that of John the Baptist. To put this in literary terms, Luke is using John as a *foil*, or contrast, for Jesus. Notice how the comparisons and contrasts created by this technique serve to introduce the person and work of the Christ. John's role as herald serves to announce the coming of the messianic King. What are some other signs that Jesus is the royal Son of David?

Look for early indications that Jesus has come to serve the poor and to save the nations and that his coming will arouse the opposition of his adversaries (including Satan himself). Also look for echoes from the Old Testament. Many elements in the opening chapters give the Gospel an Old Testament feel: the appearance of angels, the miraculous birth of a prophet, and songs that sound as if they come straight from the book of Psalms. Jesus' baptism in the Jordan River and his temptation in the wilderness also have an Old Testament connection: They recapitulate events from the Exodus. Finally, observe how Jesus is being prepared for his ministry and the people are being prepared for Jesus.

KEY VERSES

"The Spirit of the LORD is upon me, for he has anointed me to bring Good News to the poor. He has sent me to proclaim that captives will be released, that the blind will see, that the oppressed will be set free, and that the time of the LORD's favor has come" (4:18-19; compare Isaiah 61:1-2). By reading these words at the synagogue in his own hometown, Jesus is outlining his agenda for ministry and announcing his arrival as Israel's Messiah.

The Ministry of the Son of Man (4:14–9:50). Jesus begins his public ministry in his hometown. There he becomes the proverbial "prophet without honor," largely because he has the audacity to tell people how much they need him and also that God has grace for the Gentiles. Look for examples of God's grace to the Gentiles and to other outsiders.

Most of the material in these chapters is in the form of short stories or teaching segments. From the beginning we see Jesus engaged in two primary activities: preaching and healing. Watch for occasional statements (such as those in 4:15, 42-44; 5:15; 6:17-19; 7:21-22; and 8:1) that summarize these two aspects of his ministry and the effect those statements had on people. Jesus quickly became astoundingly popular, but many of the things he did—such as claiming the authority to forgive sins, eating with sinners, breaking man-made rules for the Sabbath—were destined to bring him into conflict with the Pharisees and other religious leaders. (See "Jewish Religious Groups at the Time of Christ" on page 441.)

Each healing miracle adds something to our understanding of who Jesus is and what he came to do, as he is shown to have power over demons, the devil, disease, and death. Pay attention to the way he treats each person in each story. The teaching Jesus does in these chapters—including the Sermon on the Plain (6:17-49) that parallels Matthew's longer and more famous Sermon on the Mount (Matthew 5–7)—is directed primarily toward the disciples he called to follow him. By the time we get to chapter 9, the disciples are finally ready to confess Jesus as the Christ (9:18-20). Jesus immediately responds by beginning the next phase of the disciples' training, prophesying his Passion (9:21-22, 43-45; compare 18:31-34) and teaching them the full cost of their discipleship.

On the Road with the Son of Man (9:51–15:32). Jesus has turned his face toward the Cross, and now nothing will deter him from fulfilling his mission. So he begins his long, slow journey up to Jerusalem. This is the travel section of the Gospel, and the thread that ties the winding journey together is the progress Jesus makes toward Jerusalem. Along the way he performs several miracles of healing and continues training his disciples, who are serving more and more actively in ministry (see 10:1-24).

Jesus also speaks in more parables. (See "Parable as a Literary Form" on page 447. For a listing of Jesus' parables, see pages 450–451.) Although this form of teaching was introduced in chapter 8, it becomes more prominent in the second half of the Gospel. Especially significant are three parables about seeking the lost that illustrate the theme of Luke's Gospel as a whole: the lost sheep (15:3-7), the lost coin (15:8-10), and the lost son (15:11-32). Jesus uses these parables to identify the reason for the mounting opposition of the Pharisees: They have a completely different attitude toward the lost. Rather than seek to save them, the Pharisees want to exclude them. And this is because the Pharisees have a completely different view of God. Whereas Jesus knows God to be a gracious and forgiving Father, the Pharisees—like the elder brother in the parable of the Prodigal Son—think of him as a harsh taskmaster. The practical application is first to repent, like the Prodigal Son, and then to reach out with the love of his welcoming Father.

> **KEY VERSE**
> "Jesus resolutely set out for Jerusalem" (Luke 9:51). This verse is the pivot of Luke's Gospel, as Jesus goes up to the great city to do his saving work.

The Coming of the Kingdom (16:1–19:27). As Jesus nears Jerusalem, the Kingdom of God becomes a more prominent theme in his teaching, setting the stage for the royal welcome he will receive on his Triumphal Entry. What does Jesus teach about the Kingdom, and how does this differ from the assumptions of his listeners? What does Jesus teach about responsible stewardship, and how does this contrast with the attitude the Pharisees had toward money?

The Death of the Son of Man (19:28–23:56). The climactic events of the Gospel are also the most familiar, so it can be hard to receive them with fresh power. During Jesus' last days he seems to have

> **KEY VERSE**
> "The Son of Man came to seek and to save the lost" (Luke 19:10, ESV). This serves as the theme verse for Luke's Gospel. Jesus seeks the lost throughout his earthly ministry until finally he saves the lost through his crucifixion and resurrection.

spent most of his time teaching at the Temple (19:45–21:38). Luke uses his parable of the evil farmers (20:9-19) to set the stage for the passion of the Christ: Jesus' enemies will stop at nothing, even to the point of killing the Son of God. The end is coming, not just for Jesus but for the whole world, as Jesus teaches in "the little apocalypse" (21:5-36). Jesus also spent his last days with his disciples, instituting the sacrament of the Lord's Supper and giving them their final instructions before his impending death.

THE WEEK THAT CHANGED THE WORLD
- Sunday: The Triumphal Entry (19:28-44)
- Monday: Cleansing the Temple (19:45-46)
- Tuesday: Teaching at the Temple (20:1–21:38)
- Wednesday: The Conspiracy (22:1-6)
- Thursday: The Last Supper (22:7-38)
- Friday: The Trial, Death, and Burial (22:54–23:55)
- Saturday: Resting in the Grave (23:56)
- Sunday: The Resurrection (24:1-53)

When it comes to the trial of Jesus (see 23:4, 13-15) and also to his death (23:47), Luke is careful to show that Jesus was innocent of all charges. This would have been important for a Gentile audience because the Romans reserved crucifixion for the very worst criminals. But the Son of Man was the sinless Son of God. And to the very end he was seeking to save lost sinners, welcoming the thief on the cross into paradise (23:39-43).

The Triumph of the Son of Man (24:1-53). The women who were the last to leave the cross were also the first to see the empty tomb. In the same way that Luke lingered over the subject of the Nativity, he now lingers over the Resurrection, giving a full account of the conversation Jesus had with two disciples on the road to Emmaus and the commission he gave to his disciples afterward. Then the Gospel ends as it began: with great rejoicing in Jesus and the worship of God in his holy Temple (24:52-53).

The Main Themes

1. SALVATION. On the basis of his death on the cross and by the power of his resurrection life, Jesus brings total restoration to both the body and the soul.

2. THE COMPASSION OF CHRIST. Jesus shows love, mercy, and grace to "the poor, the crippled, the lame, and the blind" (Luke 14:13).

3. THE COST OF DISCIPLESHIP. Jesus calls his followers to share in his sufferings for the sake of the gospel.

4. GLOBAL EVANGELISM. The gospel is not just for the Jews but also for the lost sinners of all nations.

Contribution of the Book to the Bible's Story of Salvation in Christ

Like the other Gospels, Luke's Gospel tells the story of the birth, life, death, and resurrection of Jesus Christ. Among the things that Luke emphasizes about Jesus are (1) his identity as the Son of Man and the Great Physician, (2) the initiative he takes in seeking and saving the lost, (3) his concern for all people, especially social outcasts, women, children, and the poor, and (4) his self-understanding as the main subject of Scripture: "Jesus took them through the writings of Moses and all the prophets, explaining from all the Scriptures the things concerning himself" (Luke 24:27; compare 24:44-47).

Applying the Book

The main way to apply the Gospel of Luke is to receive Jesus Christ by faith. This means trusting in his death and resurrection for the forgiveness of sins and beginning to follow him in the difficult way of discipleship. It also means responding to his saving grace with joyous worship, as we see people doing throughout the Gospel.

Luke contains many of Christ's hard sayings, such as "Love your enemies" (6:27), "Offer the other cheek" (6:29), and "Take up your cross" (9:23). Be careful not to dull the sharp edge of these commands by treating them too metaphorically. After all, it is in the same Gospel that Jesus asks us, "Why do you keep calling me 'Lord, Lord!' when you don't do what I say?" (6:46). Another way to apply the Gospel is by embracing the attitude that Jesus has toward the lost and needy. Who are the poor sinners that God is calling you to love? In what practical ways can you serve them?

PERSPECTIVES
ON THE GOSPEL OF LUKE

Luke wished to be taken seriously as a historian. I. Howard Marshall

Luke is a historian of the first rank; not merely are his statements of fact trustworthy; he is possessed of the true historic sense; he seizes the important and critical events and shows their true nature at greater length, while he touches lightly or omits entirely much that was valueless for his purpose. In short, this author should be placed along with the very greatest of historians. Sir William Ramsay

Give honor unto Luke, Evangelist; / For he it was (the aged legends say) / Who first taught Art to fold her hands and pray. Dante Gabriel Rossetti

It is people who interest Luke above all else, and it is through them that he reveals the personality and nature of Jesus. . . . In all his scenes are evident his warm and generous sympathy, his pity and compassion, his sense of human worth. Mary Ellen Chase

The Christ of Luke is the friend of sinners. A. T. Robertson

Zacchaeus is a thoroughly Lucan character, well-off, shady, little, unrespectable—yet responsive to Jesus. He belongs to that suspect fringe of Judaism which plays such a telling part in the book. These, for Luke, are the people whom Jesus not only likes but chooses to stay with and eat with because they are not too encumbered with their piety and virtue to heed the gospel. John Drury

Luke knew how both Gentile and Jew looked down on women. He saw the difference in Jesus. . . . Luke wrote the gospel of womanhood, full of sympathy and tenderness, full of understanding of their tasks and their service. A. T. Robertson

Luke had a special sympathy with the poor man. But that was because of the special circumstances of the poor man, because nobody else had so far shewn him any sympathy at all. [Luke's] real sympathy was with every man. S. C. Carpenter

This Gospel is thoroughly Gentile in its spirit and outlook. . . . Most of us, in the western world, are the kind of people to whom Luke was addressing himself. We have so few material needs, but our spiritual need as Gentiles . . . is even greater than that of Jews. The good news, therefore, is even better for us than for them. And we could hardly have it more attractively presented. Michael Wilcock

Almighty God, who calledst Luke the Physician, whose praise is in the Gospel, to be an Evangelist, and Physician of the soul: May it please thee that, by the wholesome medicines of the doctrine delivered by him, all the diseases of our souls may be healed; through the merits of thy Son Jesus Christ our Lord. Book of Common Prayer (1662)

[On the relationship between Luke and Acts:] In Luke's thought, the end of the story of Jesus is the Church; and, the story of Jesus is the beginning of the Church. C. K. Barrett

THE GOSPEL OF
JOHN
To Believe or Not to Believe—
That Is the Question

FORMAT. 21 chapters, 878 verses

IMPLIED PURPOSE. To record events and discourses from the life of Jesus that will lead a reader or hearer to believe in Jesus as the Savior of the world

AUTHOR'S PERSPECTIVE. John writes as a disciple of Jesus—in fact, as "the disciple Jesus loved" (21:7). John accompanied Jesus on his travels, was an eyewitness of the events, conversations, and speeches that he records, and wants his readers to share his own belief in Jesus.

IMPLIED AUDIENCE. John writes to seekers in all places and all times. His Gospel is sometimes called the cosmic Gospel because it portrays Jesus as the answer to universal human longings. There are so many references to Jewish feasts and rituals that we can also infer that the book presupposes an audience that can relate many of the events and sayings of Jesus to an Old Testament background.

WHAT UNIFIES THE BOOK. The story line; the presence of Jesus as the focus of the action; the prevalence of images and symbols (light, water, bread); memorable statements by Jesus about who he is (e.g., "I am the light of the world")

SPECIAL FEATURES. The matching of events with statements by Jesus that arise from the events; John's poetic temperament (even beginning his Gospel with a poem); arrangement of the central block of material around seven great signs that Jesus performed

CHALLENGES FACING THE READER OR TEACHER OF THIS BOOK.
1. The presence of longer passages than is typical of the other Gospels (long discourses by Jesus and stories and conversations recorded in relative fullness)

459

2. The need to interpret figurative language and symbols (Christ as the Light and the Good Shepherd, for example)

HOW TO MEET THE CHALLENGES.
1. Instead of expecting quick-moving action, resolve to read slowly and meditatively.
2. Take as much time as necessary to absorb long speeches and intricate arguments and to unpack the meanings of the great symbols of the book.

The life of Jesus is told in narratives which are both convincingly factual and artistically significant. . . . Single events possess significance in their own right, leaving pictures printed lastingly on the mind's eye. . . . We see Jesus silhouetted against a world of formalized religion, hypocrisy, envy, evil and suffering. It is a world of death; of spiritual death and of bodily death. To this world he would bring life. His only gospel is life, and life put into words of poetry. . . . His life is framed by light, melting into the divine at either end; his birth is divine, he rises from the dead, and at choice moments he is vividly superhuman, as when the heavens open and God speaks at his baptism and at his transfiguration.

G. WILSON KNIGHT
"The Pioneer of Life: An Essay on the Gospels,"
in The Christian Renaissance

20–21 Resurrection and Appearances to Disciples

18–19 Crucifixion and Burial

13–17 Jesus with His Disciples

5–12 Conflict with Leaders of the Jews

1:19–4:54 Jesus' Initiation into Public Ministry

1:1-18 Prologue

	Victory
	Suffering and Atonement
Teaching	
Jesus with His Disciples	Jesus with Disciples or as Lone Sufferer
	A Few Weeks
	Key Events: Washing of Disciples' Feet; Passover and Upper Room Discourse; High-Priestly Prayer; Jesus' Betrayal, Arrest, Trial, Execution, and Resurrection

| Signs, Discourses, and Conflicts |
| Ministry in the Public Sphere |
| Three Years |
| Key Events: Calling of Disciples; Cleansing of the Temple; Encounters with Nicodemus and the Samaritan Woman; Seven Great Signs (Miracles); the Good Shepherd Discourse |

AN OUTLINE OF

JOHN

"Do you believe this, Martha?" Jesus asks, just after claiming to be "the resurrection and the life" (John 11:25-26). The problem of knowing what to believe is not a modern invention. It has reverberated through the ages.

John's Gospel highlights the question of what to believe—or more properly, *in whom* to believe. Everywhere we turn in this story, we find people either believing in Jesus as Savior or disbelieving in him. John himself tells us at the end of his Gospel that he chose his material "so that you may continue to believe that Jesus is the Messiah, the Son of God, and that by believing in him you will have life" (John 20:31).

We should read John's Gospel in the spirit in which he offers it to us, that is, giving us an adequate reason to believe in Jesus as Savior and Lord. There is an incipient apologetic woven into the book of John. John presents evidence that demands a verdict.

JOHN'S SYMBOLS
John uses symbols to reveal who Jesus is. A symbol requires us first to ponder the literal, physical qualities of an object and then to analyze how these qualities apply to Jesus. The most prominent symbols in John's Gospel are light, darkness, water, bread, shepherd, and vine.

The Form of the Book

Like the other Gospels, the book of John narrates a story. (For a reminder on the ingredients of the Gospel as a genre, see page 436.) The overall story traces the life of Jesus during the years of his public ministry. In effect, we become Jesus' traveling companions during the era of his life when he was an itinerant teacher and miracle worker and then came to the end of his earthly life as a martyr.

Within this master plot we find an assortment of individual stories. Encounter stories and conflict stories are the dominant subtypes. Forces of hostility become increasingly intense as the story unfolds, until Jesus is finally forced to avoid the crowd scenes that dominate the middle of John's Gospel and instead moves about with his inner circle of followers.

The Structure and Unity

The cast of characters helps to unify the story John tells. In the center is Jesus, and there are three corresponding types of material:

- Jesus' actions (what Jesus *did*)
- Jesus' instruction (what Jesus *taught*)
- People's responses to Jesus

Beyond Jesus are the disciples, then the religious leaders, and on the outkirts the crowd of onlookers (sometimes represented by named individuals).

The Miracles of Jesus

Miracles of Jesus	Bible Reference
Jesus turns water into wine	John 2:1-11
Jesus heals a nobleman's son	John 4:46-54
Jesus heals a sick man	John 5:1-9
Jesus heals a man who was born blind	John 9:1-41
Jesus raises Lazarus from the dead	John 11:1-44
Jesus produces a catch of 153 fish	John 21:1-11
Jesus walks on the water	John 6:19-21
Jesus feeds five thousand hungry people	John 6:5-13
Jesus frees a demon-possessed man	Luke 4:33-35
Jesus heals Simon's mother-in-law	Luke 4:38-39
Jesus produces an enormous catch of fish	Luke 5:1-11
Jesus heals a leper	Luke 5:12-13
Jesus heals a paralyzed man	Luke 5:18-25
Jesus restores a withered hand	Luke 6:6-10
Jesus heals a centurion's slave	Luke 7:1-10
Jesus raises a widow's son from the dead	Luke 7:11-15
Jesus calms the storm	Luke 8:22-25
Jesus frees the Gadarene demoniac	Luke 8:27-35
Jesus raises Jairus's daughter from the dead	Luke 8:41-55
Jesus heals the woman with a hemorrhage	Luke 8:43-48
Jesus frees a demon-possessed boy	Luke 9:38-43
Jesus heals a mute, demon-possessed man	Luke 11:14
Jesus heals a crippled woman	Luke 13:11-13
Jesus heals a man with swollen arms and legs	Luke 14:1-4
Jesus heals ten lepers	Luke 17:11-19
Jesus heals a blind man	Luke 18:35-43
Jesus heals a slave's ear	Luke 22:50-51
Jesus heals two blind men	Matthew 9:27-31
Jesus heals a mute, demon-possessed man	Matthew 9:32-33
Jesus heals a demon-possessed Canaanite girl	Matthew 15:21-28
Jesus feeds the four thousand	Matthew 15:32-38
Jesus produces a coin in a fish's mouth	Matthew 17:24-27
Jesus causes a fig tree to wither	Matthew 21:18-22
Jesus heals a deaf and mute man	Mark 7:31-37
Jesus heals a blind man	Mark 8:22-26

The story also has a unifying plot. The central conflict is between belief and unbelief as people respond to Jesus' call to faith in him. In this drama of the soul's choice, we see individuals responding with either faith or rejection.

A third unifying pattern is the pairing of events and discourses throughout the book. As a result, you should draw connections between a discourse of Jesus and the event that has preceded it (and sometimes the event that follows a given discourse). For example, the feeding of the five thousand (chapter 6) appears in the same chapter as Jesus' discourse about being the Bread of Life. The healing of the man born blind (chapter 9) illustrates Jesus' claim in the preceding chapter that he is the Light of the World. His discourse in the following chapter, about good and bad shepherds, is in reference to the fact that the healed man had been expelled from the synagogue.

DID YOU KNOW?
- The emphases of John's Gospel are partly signaled by word patterns (ESV): my Father/the Father (113 times), know/knew (110), believe/believed (110), Jews (62), world (61).
- John omits Christ's parables and instead gives us Christ's great spiritual discourses not included in the other Gospels.

Key Places and Characters

The places where the most important events occur are Jerusalem (the place of rejection and crucifixion), the countryside of Palestine (where people are more likely to accept Jesus than people in Jerusalem are), Samaria, Bethany (home of Mary, Martha, and Lazarus), and Galilee (Jesus' home province).

While John's Gospel gives us a crowded gallery of characters, some stand out. The characters who remain most vividly in our memory are Jesus, John the Baptist, the disciples as a group, Peter and Thomas as individual disciples, Nicodemus, the Samaritan woman, Mary, Martha, Lazarus, Pilate, and Mary Magdalene.

Key Doctrines

The Incarnation. Christ is both human and divine—God in human form.

Salvation and Faith. People can be saved and receive eternal life if they believe in Jesus as Savior and Lord.

Damnation. People who reject Christ's offer of salvation will be condemned eternally.

Resurrection. Jesus has power over death. He raised Lazarus from the dead and was himself resurrected from death.

Christology. God's plan for the ages finds its realization in the person and work of Christ, who is the answer to people's needs and longings.

The Holy Spirit. Jesus' discourse in the upper room includes one of the key New Testament passages on the person and work of the Holy Spirit (16:5-15).

Tips for Teaching or Reading the Gospel of John

John's Gospel is structured as a series or paired events ("signs" performed by Jesus) and discourses that are related to the events; you need to explore the relationships between the respective events and discourses.

John's Gospel communicates much of its meaning by means of the great symbols of the Christian faith (such as light, water, bread); you need to unpack the meanings that are embodied in these symbols.

For every episode and discourse, you should ask what you learn about Jesus and his work.

Things to Look For

- The unifying action of belief versus unbelief
- Number patterns, with the numbers three and seven prominent
- Seven great miracles that John calls "signs"
- Seven famous "I am" statements of self-identification by Jesus
- The linking of events (usually miracles) to speeches by Jesus in which Jesus builds on the corresponding event
- Symbolism (e.g., Jesus as the Good Shepherd and the Light of the World)
- Images that fall into heightened contrasts—light versus darkness, life versus death, that which perishes versus that which is eternal, disease versus health, love versus hate

quick overview of the gospel of john

1:1-18	Prologue praising the incarnate Christ
1:19-4:54	Jesus' initiation of his public ministry
5:1-12:50	Jesus' public ministry, which consists of teaching and miracles and which continually sparks conflict as some believe and others reject Jesus' claims
13:1-17:26	Jesus' instruction of his disciples about servanthood, his imminent departure from them, and the hostility of the world toward his followers
18:1-19:42	The Crucifixion and Jesus' burial
20:1-21:25	Jesus' resurrection and postresurrection appearances

The Flow of the Book

Prologue (1:1-18). John begins his Gospel with a hymn that praises the incarnate Christ. In addition to reading this poem devotionally, we should assume that the passage is intended as an introduction to the whole book that follows. The right question to consider is this: Assuming that this Christ hymn is intended as an introduction to the whole book, what do we learn about Jesus already? For example, we read about Christ's simultaneous deity and humanity, about light and darkness as symbols of spiritual reality, and about Christ's revelation of the Father. Then look for evidences of these things as you continue through the book.

KEY VERSE

"In the beginning the Word already existed. The Word was with God, and the Word was God" (1:1). Right at the outset John asserts the most important thing about Jesus: that he is God.

Initiation into the Public Ministry of Jesus (1:19–4:54). In this phase of the action, Jesus encounters John the Baptist, calls his disciples, performs his first miracles, cleanses the Temple, and calls people—most notably Nicodemus and the woman of Samaria—to belief in him. There is a relative absence of conflict in this phase of the story. Jesus is still establishing himself.

Questions to ponder when reading these chapters include the following:

- How does the unifying plot conflict of belief versus unbelief already enter the story?
- If you were traveling with Jesus during these early days, what conclusions regarding him would you have reached?
- How do miracles and symbols factor into the account?

Opposition to Jesus (Chapters 5–12). The overall story now becomes a conflict story. Numerous conflicts and controversies make up the details. Miracles figure prominently in the material that John chooses for his apologetic purpose, as do speeches by Jesus in which he explains himself. Conversations and debates or altercations are a chief means by which John packages his material, and he presents numerous dramas in miniature. Good interpretations of the material will emerge as you explore the following questions:

- What characters emerge as we move through the individual episodes?
- How do these characters fit the pattern of belief versus unbelief?

- What miracles does Jesus perform, and how do those miracles match the needs of the people for whom he performs them?
- What claims does Jesus make about himself?
- Why do the people who believe in Jesus accept his claims?
- Why do other people reject Jesus?

A Parenthesis in the External Action—Jesus with His Disciples (Chapters 13–17). Before the events of Passion week, Jesus withdraws from the public realm and spends extended time confirming his relationship to his disciples and instructing them (13:1 is a transition verse). Notable events include the washing of the disciples' feet and Jesus' high-priestly prayer for his disciples. Famous discourses in this section include Jesus' prediction of his ascension and his sending the Holy Spirit, his discourse on the true vine, and his farewell discourse to the disciples. Good questions to ponder while reading this section of John's Gospel include the following:

- Assuming that what Jesus teaches his disciples is intended for all followers of Jesus, what are the most important lessons that we can carry away from the events and discourses of this part of John's Gospel?
- Much of Jesus' disclosure to his disciples is predictive in nature, preparing the disciples for life after Jesus' earthly presence. What is there in Jesus' predictions to comfort a believer today, and what is there that might trouble a believer (e.g., predictions that the world will hate those who follow Christ)?
- Elsewhere in John's Gospel, Jesus makes claims about himself to the world at large; here he addresses them to his disciples. How do the claims in the respective sections compare with each other?

> **THE BIBLE'S GREATEST VERSE**
>
> "God loved the world so much that he gave his one and only Son, so that everyone who believes in him will not perish but have eternal life" (John 3:16).
>
> **God:** the greatest lover
> **loved:** the greatest act
> **the world:** the greatest scope
> **so much that:** the greatest result
> **he gave his only Son:** the greatest sacrifice
> **so that:** the greatest effect
> **everyone:** the greatest invitation
> **who believes:** the greatest choice
> **in him:** the greatest object of faith
> **will not perish:** the greatest escape
> **but:** the greatest alternative
> **have eternal life:** the greatest thing imaginable

Seeming Defeat: Jesus' Crucifixion (Chapters 18–19). The teaching element in John's Gospel now recedes from view, and straightforward recording of historical details dominates. Each Gospel writer's account of Passion week

KEY VERSE

"I am the light of the world. Whoever follows me will not walk in darkness, but will have the light of life" (8:12, ESV). This is one of Jesus' seven great "I am" statements in the Gospel of John, and it uses symbolism to highlight the great either-or with which Christ confronts every person.

shares certain details with the other accounts, and each includes material unique to itself. Here is an outline of what John chose to include:

- Jesus' arrest (18:1-14)
- Jesus' trial before Jewish authorities, with Peter's denial of Jesus intermingled (18:15-27)
- Jesus' trial before Pontius Pilate (18:28-40)
- Pilate's handing of Jesus over to the Jewish authorities (19:1-16)
- The crucifixion and death of Jesus at Golgotha (19:17-37)
- The burial of Jesus (19:38-42)

The Gospels mainly record the incidents surrounding Jesus' passion and do not explain the theological significance of the events (it is the Epistles that attach the theological significance of the events). The best way to read this part of John's Gospel is to assume that you are an observer at the events and ponder how you would have assimilated the events you were witnessing.

Seeing Is Believing (Chapters 20–21). After Jesus' resurrection he appears to Mary Magdalene (20:1-18), to ten disciples (20:19-25), to Thomas (20:26-31), and to the disciples on the lakeside (21:1-25). The common thread of these appearances is that they constitute proof of the resurrection of Jesus (as signaled by the statement in 20:8 that when John entered the empty tomb, he "saw and believed").

THE SEVEN GREAT SIGNS

- turning water into wine (2:1-11)
- healing the official's son (4:46-54)
- healing the lame man (5:1-15)
- feeding the five thousand (6:1-15)
- walking on water (6:16-21)
- healing the blind man (9:1-7)
- raising Lazarus from the dead (11:1-44)— the climactic sign

The Main Themes

1. Jesus claims to be the Son of God and the One in whom people must believe for salvation.
2. We can know what Jesus did and taught on the basis of what an eyewitness recorded.
3. Everyone who encounters the claims of Jesus must either accept or reject them. Accepting them leads to eternal life; rejecting them leads to death.
4. Jesus brings truth and life to those who believe.

5. We can know Jesus partly through the great symbols by which he is described—light, bread, water, shepherd, true vine.

6. Jesus is compassionate toward human needs and the One who satisfies our needs and longings.

Contribution of the Book to the Bible's Story of Salvation in Christ

Like the other Gospels, this one tells us basic information about what Jesus taught and did during his public ministry. The things that are distinctive to John's Gospel are (1) the selection of material that serves the apologetic purpose of instilling belief in Jesus as savior, (2) the presentation of Jesus as the Savior of the whole world (the cosmic-Christ theme), and (3) the portrayal of Christ and salvation by means of great symbols of the faith.

KEY VERSE
"These [signs] are written so that you may continue to believe that Jesus is the Messiah, the Son of God, and that by believing in him you will have life by the power of his name" (20:31). This is John's own statement of why he composed his Gospel: that people who read his account will be saved.

Applying the Book

The most obvious lesson to be learned from John's Gospel is the one that John himself claims as his purpose in writing his Gospel. It is the lesson of belief. Jesus is the One in whom people must believe for eternal life. We must also learn the lesson regarding unbelief: Not to believe in Jesus is to perish eternally.

It is not only the once-for-all faith in Jesus as Savior that we need to exercise. In addition, the Gospel of John is a many-sided set of claims that Jesus and others make regarding him; in John's Gospel we also come to know Jesus as a friend and a hero. There is the basis for a complete theology and Christology here, and one of the ways to apply the book is to systematize the main things that we can know about Jesus and his work.

The people with whom Jesus interacts in the pages of this Gospel are a cross section of the world as we know it. People still long, fear, despair, rejoice, and worship. In the gallery of characters that we meet in John's Gospel, we can see ourselves and our acquaintances.

Finally, the Gospel of John is filled with the teaching and commands Jesus gives to his disciples and others. These statements tell us how to live. To apply the Gospel of John, we need to practice what Jesus taught by word and example.

PERSPECTIVES
ON THE GOSPEL OF JOHN

This Gospel meets the spiritual needs of the soul, whether Jew or Gentile. To this end John gives the great discourses on the new birth; Christ the water of life; the bread of life; the light of the world; the way, the truth, the life; the vine; the resurrection and life. Thus the divinity of our Lord appears in His words as well as in His works. The New Analytical Bible

Jesus' life is complementary to his words. By picture-language and by dramatic example his work is done. G. Wilson Knight

The book abounds in clearly drawn portraits of character. . . . The writer delights in little pictorial touches which serve to give a concrete reality to the narrative. E. F. Scott

The outstanding feature from a literary point of view is its particularity of detail. Percy C. Sands

[The Gospel writer] Mark was always hinting at a secret—"the mystery of the Kingdom of God." John has told the secret. C. H. Dodd

The Gospel of belief. Merrill C. Tenney

The most philosophical Gospel. Buckner B. Trawick

The spiritual Gospel. Clement of Alexandria

The most mysterious book in the New Testament. Reynolds Price

All four Gospels preach that Jesus is the Messiah, but each has its own major unifying theme. . . . In John, it is the people's response to Jesus, the decision they make when forced to judge him. Donald Juel

THE ACTS OF THE APOSTLES

The Emergence of
Christ's Church

FORMAT. 28 chapters, 1,007 verses

IMPLIED PURPOSE. To give a careful account of the origin and early development of the Christian church, placing emphasis on the role of the Holy Spirit in giving birth to it and on the faithful ministry of key individuals

AUTHOR'S PERSPECTIVE. The book is as much an interpretation or explanation of the events in the early church as it is a history. The collection of individual stories has the authenticity of eyewitness accounts. The author is sympathetic to the leaders of the early Christian movement, but he always places the accent on God's action in the events that unfold. Also, Luke views his book as extending his Gospel, telling the whole story of Christ in two volumes (see 1:1-2).

IMPLIED AUDIENCE. Like the Gospel of Luke, Acts is dedicated to Theophilus (literally, "lover of God"). But the broader audience is assumed to be followers of the Way who want to know exactly how the Christian movement got started. The audience includes both Jews and Gentiles, and both groups would have had their most pressing questions answered, namely, how the new Christian religion relates to Old Testament Hebraic religion and the conditions under which non-Jews have become part of the Christian church. In keeping with this expansiveness, the readers of this book are assumed to be cosmopolitan in experience, acquainted with the major cities of the Mediterranean region in the first century.

WHAT UNIFIES THE BOOK. The story line; the dominance of Peter in the first half and Paul in the second half; a series of speeches; the journey motif; cycles of preaching leading to converts leading to persecution, and then on to a reenactment of the cycle; the power

471

of the Holy Spirit; the spreading of the church outward from Jerusalem

SPECIAL FEATURES. Speeches placed in a clear context; dramatic personal changes (such as the conversion of Saul and Peter's eating with Gentiles); strong geographical organization, from Jerusalem to all Judea and Samaria and to the ends of the earth; interest in key personalities

CHALLENGES FACING THE READER OR TEACHER OF THIS BOOK.
1. The book presupposes a basic knowledge of the geography of the Mediterranean region.
2. There is a need to understand something of the Jewish religion and its relationship to the predominant Gentile culture.
3. There is a bewildering multiplicity of events.

HOW TO MEET THE CHALLENGES.
1. Read with an atlas or a study Bible with maps nearby.
2. Once alerted to the need to piece together Jewish practices, look for clues in the text.
3. Read the story like an adventure story in which scenes and events keep changing at a lively pace; look for variety rather than a single story line.

The Acts is a book of persons, not things; of personalities, not institutions and church organization. . . . The history of Christianity in Luke's narrative centres in Peter and Paul. . . . The selection of these two, with Stephen as a link between, has given something of a unity to the book. . . . [The book] has all the liveliness of a book of personalities. The very title strikes the personal note. . . . It is the only kind of book that could have been sufficiently readable, coming just after the peerless gospel memoirs.

PERCY C. SANDS
Literary Genius of the New Testament

1-7 The Coming of the Holy Spirit in Power to Found the Church

8-12 Expansion of the Church

13-28 Paul's Three Journeys and Trials

Witness in Jerusalem

Witness to Judea and Samaria

Witness to the Ends of the Earth

The Church Discovers Its Identity

The Church Reaches into the World

Leading Character: Peter. His Pivotal Event for the Action of Acts: The Vision That Convinced Him That Gentiles Were Included in God's Kingdom

Leading Character: Paul. His Pivotal Event for the Action of Acts: His Conversion on the Way to Damascus

AN OUTLINE OF
ACTS

The desire to discover one's roots is deeply embedded in the human psyche, and it extends to institutions as well as individuals. When we discover the origins of people or institutions, we can usually tell a lot about their identity.

The book of Acts records the origins of the Christian church. It is an exciting story in its own right—more exciting than what television dramas or movies ordinarily give us. But beyond that, we should study Acts to discover (1) the nature of the church and its message and (2) guidelines for how Christians should live and witness in the world.

Acts is about the birth and spread of the church through the power of the Spirit. The tension mounts as the fledgling church faces some key tests. Can the Christian movement stay unified? How will it handle ethnic differences? What does it mean for a Gentile to convert to the Way? Will opposition from non-Christians defeat the church? The book of Acts reads like a serial story with weekly installments.

The Form of the Book

The book of Acts tells a story and follows the usual rules of storytelling. Plot, setting, and character are the main ingredients. Instead of a single protagonist, we have two: Peter in the first half and Paul in the second half, with Stephen and Philip as bridges between the two. Viewed in another way, the Holy Spirit is the unifying character throughout the book.

Specific subtypes make up the overall story. Especially in the second half, the story is a travel story, based on a series of journeys. The story is also an adventure story, replete with trials, riots, persecutions, narrow escapes, shipwrecks, and rescues. Many of the scenes, moreover, are constructed like dramas (this is especially true of the speeches and trial scenes).

Key Places and Characters

Places play a key role in Acts, and for the most part they are the great cities of the ancient Greco-Roman world, including Palestine. The action begins in Jerusalem, symbolic of the Jewish religion from which Christianity emerged. The story ends in Rome, capital of the Western world. Between these bookends, the book reads almost like a roll call of leading cities in the Mediterranean region in the first century.

The central character in the action is the Holy Spirit. The leading human characters are Peter, the other disciples as a group, Stephen, Philip, and Paul. The religious and political authorities—Jewish authorities in the first half and various Roman authorities in the second half—play key roles in the action. Numerous memorable minor characters fill out the cast of characters.

Something about the Historical Context

There is an aspect of the political context in Acts that is foreign to the Western world today. It exists in countries where there is a theocracy—a government in which religious leaders have power to punish people who deviate from the official religion. It is true that in the first century Roman authority was supreme at every level, but we infer that when the Jews went to Roman authorities seeking approval for certain desired actions, the Romans were quick to approve since it was viewed as a matter of Jewish religion. The result is something that looks confusing to us: Repeatedly in the book of Acts governmental authorities do not curb the Jewish leaders and their courts (mainly the Sanhedrin) from arresting, imprisoning, trying, and punishing Christians in a manner that we would expect to be reserved for governmental agencies. If occasionally an enraged Jewish mob even killed a Christian (as in the martyrdom of Stephen), Roman authorities apparently turned a blind eye.

An additional way of understanding the situation is to realize that the ancient world did not have our sophisticated Western system of courts that potentially touch all areas of life. A lot of prosecution of crimes occurred at a local tribal or clan level, independent of the state judicial system. If we picture the Jews as renters under Roman owners of a metaphoric apartment building, a lot of what happened in the apartment building was left to its manager.

SYNONYMS FOR "CHRISTIANS" IN ACTS

- believers (1:15)
- disciples (6:1-2, ESV)
- followers of the Way (9:2)
- saints (9:13, ESV)
- brothers and sisters (21:7)
- followers (5:36-37)
- the church (20:17)
- the flock (20:28-29)

Unifying Elements

- Pervasive references to the Holy Spirit
- The dominating presence of Peter and Paul and occasionally other strong leaders
- The geographically outward expansion of the early church
- The journey motif
- A recurring cycle of events
- Christian leaders arising and preaching the gospel
- God performing mighty acts through them

- Listeners being converted and added to the church
- Opponents beginning to persecute Christian leaders
- God intervening to rescue the leaders or otherwise protect the church
- The importance of speeches (including dialogues, sermons, and trial defenses)
- The idea of being a witness

PENTECOST: THE BIRTHDAY OF THE CHURCH

Pentecost is the Greek name for the Old Testament Feast of Weeks (Leviticus 23:15). It falls fifty days after the beginning of Passover (*Pentecost* is Greek for "fifty") and celebrated the end of the grain harvest. Since it was a pilgrimage feast, Jews from all over the Diaspora (dispersion) were in attendance (2:9-11 gives a catalog of places). In Christian liturgy Pentecost marks the birth of the church. In Acts it marks the massive ingathering of converts. The agricultural imagery has a symbolic force: It marks the beginning of a great harvest of souls.

Key Doctrines

The Church (Ecclesiology). Acts records the establishment and early development of the church and is a chief New Testament repository of teaching about the nature of the church, including its offices of elder and deacon.

The Holy Spirit. Acts describes the coming of the Holy Spirit in power at Pentecost (2:2-4) and through narrative provides teaching on the role of the Holy Spirit in ministry and Christian living.

Conversion. Acts repeatedly emphasizes the need for people to turn from their false views and practices and convert to following Christ.

The Gospel. Acts consistently proclaims the message of the Cross and the Resurrection.

Communion of the Saints. Acts is a story of people working on a shared mission with shared possessions.

The Providence of God. The story of Acts demonstrates how God directs events for his purposes.

Tips for Reading or Teaching Acts

Acts conveys its message mainly by narrative means. You need to pay close attention to what happens, where it happens, who does the acting, and what results from the action. The author mainly narrates what happened and does not stop to explain things. You need to infer the principles from the action.

Pay attention to *where* you are. Setting plays a crucial role in Acts. Be sensitive to the radical differences between the three cities found in this book—Jerusalem, the center of Judaism that contains the Temple;

Antioch, a Greek city with a Jewish presence; and Rome, capital of the Roman Empire.

Read the speeches with care. Make sure that you are aware of the audience being addressed, including its prior religious commitments.

Look for the "little" people. This book is organized around two huge personalities (Paul and Peter), but there are lessons to learn from the stories of "little" people such as Dorcas, who is described as "always doing kind things for others and helping the poor" (9:36).

Operate on the premise that the events Luke records are *representative* of types of events that happened repeatedly. For example, Luke gives us a specimen of preaching in the Temple (chapter 3), the working of signs (chapter 3), martyrdom (chapter 7), a Sabbath service in a synagogue (13:13-52), an address to Greek intellectuals (17:16-34), a Christian worship service (20:7-12), and so forth.

The motif of witness is a unifying thread. Note such things as who witnesses, in what circumstance, and by what means. Also observe the content of the witness and its results.

quick overview of acts

1:1-8	Prologue
1:9–8:3	The witness in Jerusalem
8:4–11:18	The witness to Judea and Samaria
11:19–28:31	The witness to the ends of the earth

The Flow of the Book

The book of Acts picks up the story of Jesus' ministry where Luke's Gospel (called "my first book" in Acts 1:1) leaves off, with Jesus' resurrection and appearances to his followers. Acts begins by recording Jesus' ascension (the only full account in the New Testament) and the coming of the Holy Spirit. The book of Acts thus serves as a bridge between the Gospels, which record the life and teachings of Jesus, and the Epistles, which explain the theological and moral meaning of what Jesus did and taught.

The first section of Acts records the ministry of the Holy Spirit in Jerusalem. The following chart summarizes the flow of the action:

1:4-11	Ascension of Jesus
1:12-26	Choosing a new disciple
2:1-47	Pentecost
3:1-26	Lame man healed; Peter's sermon
4:1-31	Witness and persecution of Peter and John
4:32–6:7	Multiple events in life of the early church
6:8–8:3	Martyrdom of Stephen

Jesus' Ascension and Mission Strategy (1:1-8). The first eight verses—the story of the final words and ascension of Jesus—provide an introduction to the entire book. The threefold directive in verse 8—"in Jerusalem and in all Judea and Samaria, and to the end of the earth" (ESV)—is a road map to the action that occurs in Acts. In that same verse, Jesus states that this missionary strategy will happen "when the Holy Spirit has come upon you" (ESV), and this, too, foreshadows what happens in the rest of the book.

KEY VERSE

"Repent and be baptized every one of you in the name of Jesus Christ for the forgiveness of your sins, and you will receive the gift of the Holy Spirit" (2:38, ESV). This is the heart of the gospel that will be repeated again and again in the preaching recorded in Acts.

Jesus' Ascension and the Selection of a Twelfth Disciple (1:9-26). The rest of the opening chapter shows the disciples "feeling their way" now that their Master has departed. You can profitably imagine yourself present at the events and ponder how you would have understood what was happening.

Pentecost (Chapter 2). Starting with the event of Pentecost, things begin to happen at a dizzying pace. Here are the important things to do with chapter 2: (1) Make sure that you have an accurate grasp of everything that happened as narrated in the chapter; (2) analyze (and perhaps outline) the content of Peter's sermon as an evangelistic sermon; and (3) analyze the aftermath of the sermon (vv. 37-47) to see how it, too, constitutes a strategy for evangelism.

The Early Church Discovers Its Identity (Chapters 3–7). As you relive the foundational events of the early church, try to forget about the church life with which you are familiar and instead imagine yourself present at the time of the events that are recorded. What are the unifying patterns? What questions would you have had? How do you think you would have responded to the events? Then ponder what lessons there are for us.

The middle section of Acts records the expansion of the action outward from Jerusalem into Judea and Samaria.

Conversion Stories and Miracles (8:4–12:25). This section of Acts is a mini-anthology of conversion stories, including those of Simon the sorcerer (8:9-24), the Ethiopian eunuch (8:26-39), Saul (9:1-30), those who believed after Peter's miracles of healing (9:32-42), and Cornelius and his family (chapter 10). A key theme is the expansion of the church to include non-Jews, or Gentiles. A helpful grid for looking closely at the conversion stories is to ask (1) who witnesses, (2) what is the content of the witness, (3) who is the recipient of the witness, (4) what is the nature of the conversion or change in the convert's life, and (5) what are the results of the conversion?

KEY VERSES

"Peter replied, 'I see very clearly that God shows no favoritism. In every nation he accepts those who fear him and do what is right'" (10:34-35). This is the keynote of the middle section of Acts: The gospel includes the Gentiles as well as Jews who believe in Christ.

The final movement in the outward spiral of Acts is the ministry to the ends of the earth. Paul's three missionary journeys are the main action. The following chart organizes the concluding phase of Acts:

Paul's First Missionary Journey 13–14	Elymas the magician; preaching in Antioch; attempted stoning at Iconium; attempt to worship Paul and Barnabas at Lystra; further travels
Jerusalem Council 15:1-35	Church leaders meet and decide not to require Gentile converts to adhere to Jewish ceremonial rules
Paul's Second Missionary Journey 15:36–18:21	Macedonian call; Lydia converted; demon driven out of slave girl; escape from prison at Philippi; conflict at Thessalonica and Berea; speech to the aereopagus in Athens; preaching and conflict at Corinth
Paul's Third Missionary Journey 18:22–21:26	Apollos converted; miracles through Paul; riot at Ephsesus; further travels; raising Eutychus from the dead; further travels; farewell meeting with Ephesian elders
Paul's Career as a Prisoner 21:27–28:31	Defense before the Jews; rescue from an execution plot; defenses before Felix, before Festus and Agrippa; journey to Rome, including shipwreck

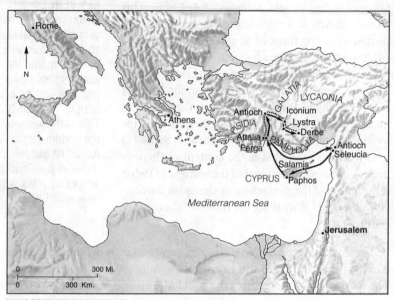

PAUL'S FIRST MISSIONARY JOURNEY (ACTS 13:1—14:28)

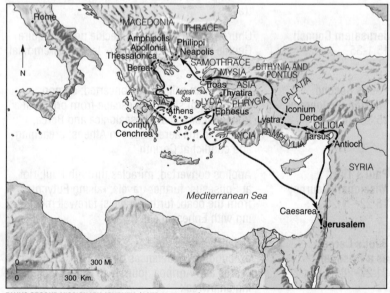

PAUL'S SECOND MISSIONARY JOURNEY (ACTS 15:36—18:22)

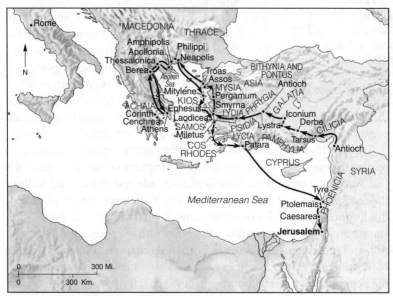

PAUL'S THIRD MISSIONARY JOURNEY (ACTS 18:23—21:16)

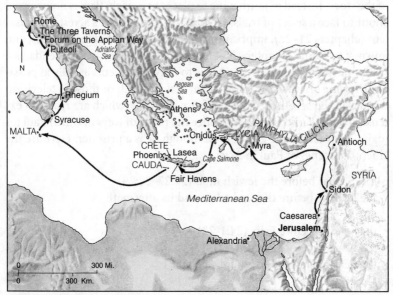

PAUL'S JOURNEY TO ROME (ACTS 21:17—28:31)

The Missionary Journeys of Paul (13:1–21:26). To get a handle on this multi-episode story, accept that it is first a travel story and second an adventure story in which Paul's life is one narrow escape after another. Accordingly, treat each place that Paul visits as a story that deserves your attention as a separate adventure. For each visit, note such things as the specific place that Paul visits, the cast of characters, the main events, the exact nature of Paul's witness, and the results that it evokes.

Chapter 15, which recounts the meeting of the Jerusalem Council to resolve the question of whether Gentile Christians needed to practice the Old Testament ceremonial laws, is an interlude inserted in the middle of the section narrating the journeys of Paul. You might contemplate how this council fits into the bigger picture of what happens in Acts. Other key events in the incorporation of Gentiles into the church are Peter's vision and subsequent preaching to Cornelius (chapter 10), Peter's defense of Gentile conversions (chapter 11), and Paul's turning to the Gentiles at the beginning of his missionary journeys (chapter 13).

Paul's Arrest, Trials, and Defenses (21:27–28:31). Paul's career as a missionary gives way to his career as a prisoner for the gospel in the last phase of the story. Instead of journeying to places to preach, Paul is now moved about to face a series of trials. Highlights include Paul's arrest in Jerusalem (chapters 21–22), imprisonment in Caesarea (chapters 23–26), and journey to Rome (chapters 27–28). The first item on your agenda as a reader or teacher of these chapters is to relive the events as fully as possible, drawing on what you know about real-life trials or those in television dramas. Then scrutinize Paul's defense speeches, which are really an extension of his earlier sermons. Notice the range of ways in which Paul remains a witness of the gospel even though he is a prisoner. Here are the chief trial scenes of Paul in Acts:

- his defense before the Jewish mob (21:27–22:29)
- the hearing before the Sanhedrin and its aftermath (22:30–23:10)
- the hearing before Felix (24:1-23)
- the hearing before Festus (25:1-12)
- the hearing before Festus and Agrippa (25:13–26:32)

The Main Themes

1. The great commission given by Jesus in 1:8 announces the two most prominent themes in the book—the power of the Holy Spirit and the priority of evangelism in the life of the early church.

2. It is the task of Christians to be courageous in sharing the gospel.

3. The task of the church is to preach and teach the gospel of Christ, both informally and in church situations.

4. In the book of Acts God has given foundational principles for how the church—including church offices and leaders—is to be organized and to function.

5. God has given his church a missionary task.

6. God by his Holy Spirit will equip his followers to speak and act Christlike, even in the face of great opposition.

Contribution of the Book to the Bible's Story of Salvation in Christ

The book of Acts is a key chapter in the Bible's story of salvation because it records the beginning of the Christian church. The emergence of the church is the final earthly phase of God's unfolding plan of redemption, as the church now succeeds the nation of Israel as the chief repository of God's salvation in Christ. Beginning here, to be saved by belief in Christ's atoning death and bodily resurrection is to enter the body of believers as it exists in the world.

In addition, the numerous sermons and dialogues in Acts express the content of the gospel of Christ. We learn about the necessity of belief in Christ's atonement, the content of that belief, and the results of embracing the gospel. In this we can see a continuation of the gospel as Jesus preached it during his lifetime.

SPEECHES IN ACTS

Speeches are a major ingredient of Acts. The book records thirty-two speeches, and these, along with their context, account for approximately one-fourth of the book. The speeches as we have them are often too short to be complete speeches and should be thought of as summaries of the actual speeches. Here are specimens of the main types of speeches in Acts:

- evangelistic: Peter to Jewish audiences (2–5), Paul in Athens (17)
- apologetic: Stephen's defense (7), Peter's explanation of why he ate in a Gentile home (11), Paul's defense speeches (22–23, 25)
- exhortative: Paul's farewell speech to the elders at Ephesus (20)
- deliberative (part of a process of deliberation): speeches at the selection of Matthias as a disciple (1:15-26) and at the Jerusalem Council (15)

Applying the Book

The first thing that needs to be said is that while the book of Acts lays down general guidelines and principles for how Christians are to behave individually and as a church, the approach of the book is narrative, with the result that we have no warrant for concluding that every action that is recorded is something that is to be directly and literally followed in later ages of the church. With that caution in place, what follows are some obvious applications, which at many turns challenge contemporary attitudes.

Most obviously, Acts is filled with examples of courageous Christians whom we should strive to imitate.

The world of Acts was as pluralistic, pagan, and multicultural as our society is. We learn from Acts that Christians should not succumb to a relativistic attitude or timidity about preaching the gospel of Christ as the only way of salvation.

For those witnessing in settings where the Scriptures hold no authority, we see the example of Paul as he quotes the Greek poets and seeks to contextualize his presentation of the gospel while holding to a core of essentials that transcend culture.

In a day when Christians are enamored of techniques and models of ministry, we see the power of the Holy Spirit propelling the church forward. The power of the Spirit to change lives and protect the church in times of opposition and persecution is the foundation of the church's work.

Even though Acts does not elevate method over content and a reliance on the Holy Spirit, it is obvious that the leaders of the early Christian movement had strategies for how they went about their task of evangelism. These are worthy of study to ascertain their underlying principles.

In a time when spiritual leadership is seen as a commodity to be guarded by prosperous churches, we see how the early churches sent out the most effective leaders as missionaries to proclaim Christ instead of simply protecting the status quo.

PERSPECTIVES
ON THE BOOK OF ACTS

Acts of the Holy Spirit. Lloyd J. Ogilvie

The Acts of the Exalted Christ by the Holy Spirit in the Church Founded by Him through the Apostles. Richard Gaffin

At first sight as a church history the Acts is very disappointing, because it is so incomplete. There are such great gaps. . . . But the feeling of disappointment is really due to want of ability to appreciate St. Luke's historical method. As he knew that the secret of history lies in personality, so he knew that the true way of writing history is not to compile bare records but to draw living pictures. Richard B. Rackham

We can say his aim is to write an edifying work for Christians, which will at the same time present the case for Christianity to Gentiles.
W. Marxsen

The first thing that strikes a reader who stands back from the Acts enough to view it as a whole is that it is a cyclical book. Michael D. Goulder

Each story has a point of its own. Edgar J. Goodspeed

The selectivity of place . . . is . . . striking. . . . Jerusalem dominates the first part of the book. . . . Toward the end of the book, there is a similar emphasis on Rome. . . . There must be a theological motive for such selectivity. . . . Jerusalem is the world center of the chosen people. . . . Rome is the center of the Gentiles. Albert C. Winn

The book of Acts shows tremendous interest in the idea of witness.
Allison A. Trites

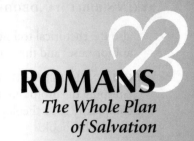

ROMANS
The Whole Plan of Salvation

FACT SHEET

FORMAT. 16 chapters, 433 verses

IMPLIED PURPOSES. To give a full summary of the great doctrines of salvation with their practical implications for the church; to prepare the way for a personal visit to Rome; and to lay the groundwork for a joint missionary enterprise to Spain

AUTHOR'S PERSPECTIVE. Having long been unable to make a missionary visit, Paul introduces himself to the Romans by writing them a complete statement of his mature theology. He writes with a deep spiritual burden for Jews who have not yet come to Christ and also for Gentiles who seek a deeper understanding of the gospel.

IMPLIED AUDIENCE. Christians in the great city of Rome—both Jews and Gentiles—are the immediate audience, but because of its universal scope, the theology of Romans is for everyone.

WHAT UNIFIES THE BOOK. The impressiveness of its sustained theological argument; the theme of righteousness, which God both requires for salvation and provides as a gift through faith in his Son; a dual concern to address the religious traditions and spiritual concerns of both Jews and Gentiles with a view to their unity in the church

SPECIAL FEATURES. The biblical perspective on classic theological questions such as, What about those who have never heard? (They are under God's wrath.) How can guilty sinners be righteous before a holy God? (Christ gives them the gift of his righteousness.) Why do Christians still sin? (The sinful nature is still at war with the Holy Spirit.) Why are some people saved but not others? (God's sovereign and predestinating grace makes it so.) There is also the rhetorical technique known as "diatribe," in which the author raises and then answers objections to his own arguments.

CHALLENGE FACING THE READER OR TEACHER OF THIS BOOK. Grasping the profound doctrine of Paul's most difficult letter. The complexity of its theological argument makes it the Bible's most formidable book.

HOW TO MEET THE CHALLENGE. Mastering the theology of Romans—which is as rewarding as it is difficult—takes a lifetime of careful study. The logic of its main argument is relatively straightforward, as you will see in the "Quick Overview" on page 492. However, each section of the book requires careful, verse-by-verse analysis.

THE MOST COMMON MISCONCEPTION ABOUT THIS BOOK. That the practical material in chapters 12–16 is not closely related to the doctrinal material in chapters 1–11, when in fact this is where the apostle has been intending to go all along

I had greatly longed to understand Paul's letter to the Romans, and nothing stood in the way but that one expression, "the righteousness of God," because I took it to mean that righteousness whereby God is righteous and acts righteously in punishing the unrighteous. . . . Night and day I pondered until . . . I grasped the truth that the righteousness of God is that righteousness whereby, through grace and sheer mercy, he justifies us by faith. Thereupon I felt myself to be reborn and to have gone through open doors into paradise.

MARTIN LUTHER
Luther's Works

AN OUTLINE OF ROMANS

Our Problem

- 1:1-17 Greetings and Thesis: The Gospel of Righteousness by Faith
- 1:18-32 Immoral Gentiles Are Guilty
- 2:1-16 Moral People Are Guilty
- 2:17-3:8 Jews Are Guilty
- 3:9-20 We Are All Guilty

God's Solution

- 3:21-31 Justified by Grace, through Faith
- 4 Example: Abraham Justified by Faith
- 5:1-11 The Benefits of Justification
- 5:12-21 Condemned in Adam, Justified in Christ
- 6 Dead to Sin, Alive to God
- 7 Freedom from Bondage to the Law
- 8:1-17 Life in the Spirit
- 8:18-30 Glory in the Spirit
- 8:31-39 The Inseparable Love of Christ

Our Response

- 9:1-29 Past: God Glorified in Israel's Election
- 9:30-10:21 Present: Israel Set Aside Because of Unbelief
- 11 Future: Israel Restored by Grace
- 12:1-2 Offering Yourself as a Sacrifice
- 12:3-8 Spiritual Gifts
- 12:9-21 Loving Everyone, Including Enemies
- 13:1-7 Church and State
- 13:8-14 The Law of Love
- 14:1-15:13 Stronger and Weaker Christians
- 15:14-33 Paul's Plan for the Future
- 16:1-24 Final Greetings
- 16:25-27 Closing Doxology

Sin	Salvation	Sanctification	Sovereignty	Service
Total Depravity	Justification by Faith	Sanctification through the Spirit	Election by Grace	Reformation of the Church and Society
God's Holiness in Condemning Sin	God's Grace in Justifying Sinners	God's Power in Sanctifying Believers	God's Sovereignty in Saving Jews and Gentiles	God's Glory in Our Obedience
God's Righteousness Revealed in Wrath	God's Righteousness Imputed	God's Righteousness Obeyed	God's Righteousness in Election	God's Righteousness Demonstrated
The Need of Salvation	The Way of Salvation	The Life of Salvation	The Scope of Salvation	The Service of Salvation

Romans is a Bible within the Bible. Every book in the Bible has something essential to contribute to our understanding of the history of salvation and its implications for daily Christian living. But more than any other biblical book, Romans pulls together the plan of salvation and sets it forth in a systematic way. God has spoken to us in stories, poems, proverbs, parables, and historical narratives. But he has also spoken to us in doctrinal propositions that give us a clear understanding of the Christian faith. Romans is the Bible's own systematic theology—the summary of its saving doctrines.

The Form of the Book

Like Paul's other writings, Romans is an epistle—an apostolic letter written to a local church. And like his other letters, it contains greetings and remarks that reflect its interpersonal context. But Romans is also unique. Paul's other letters address a variety of local concerns, and as a result they tend to be loosely organized (the way personal letters often are). By contrast, Romans is tightly structured, and the main line of its doctrinal argument makes little or no explicit reference to local issues. It is much more than a personal letter: It is also a theological treatise for the church universal.

Key Words and Phrases

As a work of systematic theology, Romans uses a good deal of technical vocabulary. Here are some of the most important terms to know:

- *righteousness*, which God both requires in his law and gives by his grace
- *declare* (or *count, reckon, impute*), which is a financial term used to describe the righteousness that is credited to the believer by faith
- *propitiation*, an important theological term used in 3:25 in some translations to describe God's turning aside his own wrath through the sacrifice of his Son
- *law*, which is used in more than one sense: Sometimes it refers to God's righteous standard (especially as revealed in the Old Testament) and sometimes to the principle of good or evil that governs a person's life (also translated "power")
- *faith*, which unites us to Christ and enables us to receive his righteousness
- *sinful nature*, or *flesh*, which refers to fallen human nature in its weakness and depravity

Frequently Asked Question

When Paul writes about his battle with sin in 7:15 ("I want to do what is right, but I don't do it. Instead, I do what I hate"), is he referring to the time before he came to Christ or to his present experience as a Christian? Although some commentators disagree, this passage is best understood as Paul's experience after he became a believer. Thus it helps us understand the ongoing conflict between the Spirit and the sinful nature in the Christian life: "In my mind I really want to obey God's law, but because of my sinful nature I am a slave to sin" (7:25). As Luther explained it, we are at the same time righteous and sinners.

Key Doctrines

Sin and Judgment. Romans justly condemns the universal depravity of humanity (both the original sin we inherit from Adam and the sins we actually commit) and declares its deadly consequence: the wrath of God, both in this life and in the life to come.

Justification by Faith. On the basis of the atoning work that Jesus did on the cross, God imputes the righteousness of Christ to believing sinners, justly declaring them to be righteous in his sight.

The Holy Spirit. The Holy Spirit takes the redemption accomplished by Christ and applies it to the believer.

Sanctification. Romans teaches the theology of sanctification by the life-giving, sin-defeating work of the Holy Spirit and also helps with the practice of sanctification by showing what the sanctified life looks like in the church and in the world.

Adoption. The Holy Spirit makes us children of God, with full access to our Father's affection and a full right to inherit all the blessings he has for us in Christ.

Glorification. The Spirit who sanctifies us will also make us glorious at the final resurrection.

Perseverance. Nothing can ever separate us from the love of God in Christ. Those who belong to Christ are kept forever and will not fall away.

Predestination and Election. God's grace is God's choice, since before the beginning of time.

KEY VERSES

"I am not ashamed of the gospel, for it is the power of God for salvation to everyone who believes, to the Jew first and also to the Greek. For in it the righteousness of God is revealed from faith for faith, as it is written, 'The righteous shall live by faith'" (1:16-17, ESV). Paul's thesis statement for the book introduces its main themes: the power of the gospel for salvation, the unity of Jews and Gentiles in the church, and the gift of God's righteousness in Christ, to be received by faith.

Tips for Reading or Teaching Romans

There are two ways to study Romans: the fast way and the slow way. Ultimately, mastering the book's theology requires careful and disciplined study. However, it is also spiritually beneficial to read through the book more rapidly, missing some of the details but still getting the main flow of the argument.

Since Romans synthesizes so much biblical teaching, it provides a clear lens for seeing the rest of Scripture. On a careful reading, be sure to use a Bible with cross-references and look up all the Old Testament passages mentioned in Romans. Keep in mind that when Paul and the other New Testament writers quote from or allude to something from the Old Testament, they typically have an entire passage in mind—not just a single verse but the verse in its context.

quick overview of romans

1:1–3:20	Lost in Sin. Paul sets forth the world's biggest problem: We are all guilty before God and are therefore under his wrath.
3:21–5:21	Justified by Faith. God has provided the solution in Christ: By virtue of his perfect life and atoning death, sinners who believe in Christ are legally and justly declared righteous before God.
6:1–8:39	Sanctified by the Spirit. Sinners who have been declared righteous actually become righteous by the life-changing work of the Holy Spirit, who sets them free from the dominating power of sin and death.
9:1–11:36	Chosen by God. Salvation does not come by human choice or effort but by the sovereign grace of God, as we can see in his plan for the Jews as well as for the Gentiles.
12:1–16:27	Transformed by Grace. Believers in Christ are called to offer themselves to God as living sacrifices, serving him in the church and the world.

The Flow of the Book

Greeting, Context, and Thesis (1:1–17). Paul, who writes as an apostle of the true gospel of Jesus Christ, expresses his long-standing desire to visit the Romans in person. In the meantime, this letter will have to suffice. His personal remarks come to a climax with a bold statement of his faith, which also serves as the thesis statement for his letter: God offers righteousness as a gift to every believer in Christ (1:16-17). Be alert for the various ways that Paul supports this thesis in the rest of the Epistle.

The Whole World Guilty (1:18–3:20). The main argument of the Epistle starts with a problem of deadly seriousness—sin, and not just sin but the wrath against sin that God's righteousness requires. Then, as well as now, this is a problem for three kinds of people: (1) immoral pagans who do not have the Scriptures yet are still without excuse because God has revealed his law to them in creation, writing it on their hearts (1:18-32); (2) moral people who believe that what they do is good enough for God, especially in comparison with others (2:1-16); and (3) religious people who know God's law but do not fully keep it and whose outward obedience, such as it is, does not come from the heart (2:17–3:8). In short, "All people, whether Jews or Gentiles, are under the power of sin" (3:9). "No one is righteous—not even one" (3:10). "Everyone has sinned; we all fall short of God's glorious standard" (3:23). God's verdict is just: We are all guilty. Consider how the ideas in this part of Romans might be useful in doing personal evangelism with various unbelievers you know.

Justification by Faith in Christ (3:21–5:21). Thankfully, there is a solution, which Paul introduces with the momentous words *but now.* Although we are not righteous, we can be declared righteous by the merits of Jesus Christ, credited to us by faith. Paul asserts this central doctrine of salvation at the end of chapter 3 and proceeds to illustrate it in chapter 4 with the Old Testament example of Abraham. God has always saved people by faith and not by works, and Abraham—who was justified *before* he was circumcised or did anything righteous—proves it: "Abraham believed God, and God counted him as righteous because of his faith" (4:3). The happy results of justifying faith—such as peace with God, access to grace, hope in glory, love for God, and salvation from the wrath to come—are outlined at the beginning of chapter 5. How are these blessings evident in your own life? Paul then summarizes the doctrine of justification by drawing a comparison between Adam and Jesus

KEY VERSES

"God, with undeserved kindness, declares that we are righteous. He did this through Christ Jesus when he freed us from the penalty for our sins. For God presented Jesus as the sacrifice for sin. People are made right with God when they believe that Jesus sacrificed his life, shedding his blood" (3:24-25). This gracious doctrine of justification by faith in Christ is the heart of Romans—and the heart of the gospel.

Christ (5:12-21). As God justly imputed Adam's sin to the entire human race (resulting in condemnation and death), so now God graciously imputes the righteousness of Christ to everyone who has faith in him (bringing justification and life).

Sanctification by the Holy Spirit (Chapters 6–8). One might think that God's gracious declaration of righteousness would lead us further into sin since there is no longer any need for us to do good works to justify ourselves. However, now that we are joined to Jesus Christ by faith, a powerful new force is at work to bring spiritual change. In chapter 6 Paul explains that we are no longer under the dominion of sin. Since we are united to Christ in his death and resurrection, we are dead to the dominion of sin and alive to God in holiness. In chapter 7 he explains that we are no longer in bondage to the law, which held us captive because of our sin. What the law failed to do—that is, produce righteousness—God now does through his Spirit. So in chapter 8 Paul describes the life-transforming work of the Holy Spirit in setting us free from sin and death, giving us new life in Christ, making us the children of God, enabling us to persevere through suffering, helping us to pray, and assuring us of our eternal salvation. Pay special attention to the metaphors Paul uses in these chapters to describes the Spirit's liberating work of grace: death and resurrection, slavery and freedom, and the termination of a marriage vow at death.

DID YOU KNOW?
According to Romans 8:38-39 there are ten things that can never separate us from the love of God: death, life, angels, demons, the present, the future, worldly powers, height, depth, and anything else in all creation.

Election (Chapters 9–11). This section of the letter goes in a new direction as Paul expresses his personal anguish that so many of his fellow Jews have rejected Jesus Christ, refusing to receive his righteousness. This does not imply that God's plan has failed, however, and Paul uses the occasion to address a wider theological issue: Why does God show some people mercy while others are left to die in their sins and ultimately to suffer God's wrath? Paul answers this question by using examples from the Old Testament to show that God chooses some to show his mercy and passes by others to show his justice: In either case, he is glorified in the display of one of his perfect attributes. Paul concludes this section by explaining the reasons for his confident hope that God has not rejected his people forever. A remnant of the Jews will be saved by grace, and in the future they will be gathered into the church.

Epistle as a Form of Writing

Epistles, or letters, are the dominant New Testament genre in terms of space. They are a combination of private correspondence and public address. Generally speaking, the Epistles are not systematic treatises on a single topic. A few of the New Testament Epistles are relatively systematic expositions of doctrine, but most are structured much like the letters that we ourselves write and receive. When the lyric (emotional) impulse takes over, the structure becomes virtually stream-of-consciousness, with thoughts tumbling out of the writer's mind in emotional and not merely logical fashion.

The Epistles are "occasional" letters: They address specific audiences and specific situations. The authors answer questions that have been raised or speak to situations with which the writers are acquainted. You can profitably relate the paragraphs in an epistle to the stated or implied context (occasion) that gave rise to the letter.

In form, many New Testament Epistles consist of five main parts:

- Opening or salutation: names of the sender and addressee and a greeting
- Thanksgiving: including features such as a remembrance of the recipient(s) and a prayer for spiritual welfare
- Body: beginning with introductory formulas and ending with either eschatological or travel material
- Paraenesis, or moral exhortations: For more on this subject, see the article on page 505.
- Closing: final greetings and benediction

Most New Testament Epistles begin with a doctrinal section and then move toward practical application.

In reading an epistle, it is important to follow the actual flow of thought. The only safe rule is to "think paragraph." Be ready for frequent shifts in thought. The structure is often a loose association of ideas rather than a logical, step-by-step line of thought.

The Epistles contain frequent poetic elements. You need to be ready to interpret metaphors ("We are his house, built on the foundation of the apostles and the prophets" [Ephesians 2:20]), rhetorical questions ("If God is for us, who can ever be against us?" [Romans 8:31]), paradox ("When I am weak, then I am strong" [2 Corinthians 12:10]), and addresses to imaginary listeners ("O death, where is your victory?" [1 Corinthians 15:55]). In addition, one reason the Epistles are so familiar to Bible readers is that they have the memorable quality of proverbial writing: "Come close to God, and God will come close to you" (James 4:8).

Putting God's Righteousness into Practice (12:1–15:13). Like most of Paul's letters, Romans has a major section of practical application near the end. Now that we have received God's amazing grace in salvation, the only reasonable response is to turn our lives into a sacrifice of praise, offering ourselves for God's service. These chapters show what righteousness looks like when it governs our relationships to God, to the church as the body of Christ, to our enemies, to the ruling authorities, to society in general, and especially to Christians who are less mature in the faith. Notice that all of these relationships are to be characterized by love.

KEY VERSES

"I appeal to you therefore, brothers, by the mercies of God, to present your bodies as a living sacrifice, holy and acceptable to God, which is your spiritual worship. Do not be conformed to this world, but be transformed by the renewal of your mind" (12:1-2, ESV). These verses make a significant transition from doctrine to practice in the book of Romans. They also show us God's way of changing our lives: The renewal of our minds transforms our actions.

Paul's Future Plans, Farewell Greeting, and Final Doxology (15:14–16:27). The end of chapter 15 gives us more information about Paul's reasons for writing. How does this section provide context for the rest of the letter? Take special notice of what Paul says about his calling in 15:15-16. How does this help to explain what he has written? When we remember that Paul had never been to Rome, chapter 16 contains a surprisingly large number of personal greetings. This shows the strong sense of community that the early church enjoyed across the Roman world.

The Main Themes

1. SIN AND SALVATION. The book of Romans never strays far from the basic issues of the gospel.
2. GRACE. Salvation is God's work from beginning to end, and this is all to his glory; even our sanctification is carried forward by the work of the Holy Spirit.
3. RIGHTEOUSNESS. The righteousness God requires in his law he gives through his Son and works into our lives by the Holy Spirit.
4. FAITH. The righteousness of God becomes ours by grace, through faith.
5. THE GOSPEL. The good news about Jesus Christ is more than simply the way to become a Christian; it is the beginning, middle, and end of the Christian life.

6. THE CHURCH. The unity of Jews and Gentiles is God's eternal plan for his people.

Contribution of the Book to the Bible's Story of Salvation in Christ

The book of Romans gives the Bible's most complete treatment of *soteriology*, or the doctrine of salvation in Christ. It says relatively little about the person of Christ, the details of his life, his present ministry in heaven, or his second coming. Instead, the focus is on everything that Christ accomplished through his death on the cross: redemption, reconciliation, propitiation, adoption, sanctification, glorification, and especially justification.

Applying the Book

The most obvious way to apply the book of Romans is simply to learn what its closing chapters have to say about our various relationships. But the book can also help us at a more fundamental level. The best motivation for a life of fruitful service to God is a deep grasp of God's grace in the gospel. Nowhere is this grace more clearly explained or triumphantly celebrated than in the book of Romans. For this reason it is the theology of Romans—with its emphasis on what God has done for us in Christ—that will help us the most with our Christian practice. This is in keeping with what Romans itself says about God's method for transforming our lives: God changes us by renewing our minds (12:2), and our minds are renewed as we read and meditate on God's Word. What better book to study than Romans?

PERSPECTIVES
ON THE BOOK OF ROMANS

A compendium of Christian doctrine.   Philipp Melanchthon

The quintessence and perfection of saving doctrine.   Thomas Draxe

The most profound book in existence.   Samuel Taylor Coleridge

The Gospel according to Paul.   F. F. Bruce

A thorough study of this epistle is really a theological education in itself.
Griffith Thomas

Christianity has been the most powerful, transforming force in human history—and the book of Romans is the most basic, most comprehensive statement of true Christianity. James Montgomery Boice

No other New Testament writing gives such a systematization of the doctrine of the gospel. . . . All the others address specific problems, special needs, or dubious practices. They address believers with specific teachings and admonitions against the backdrop of what they had already heard in the body of belief. In Rome, however, no one had ever preached the complete gospel. Therefore, the Roman letter can be said to be a unified statement of . . . our situation before God and in the world.
Udo W. Middelman

[In Romans Paul] opens to view the degeneracy of human reprobation. We ask, why? It is upon that degradation that the righteousness of God supervenes, and the glory of the gospel is that in the gospel is made manifest a righteousness of God which meets all the exigencies of our sin at the lowest depths of iniquity and misery. . . . Only a God-righteousness can measure up to the desperateness of our need and make the gospel the power of God unto salvation. John Murray

In the book of Romans God is saying to the readers of the whole world— Jew and Gentile—that though they have failed to attain a righteousness acceptable to a holy God, this righteousness may be received as a gift from Him, through faith, in the person of His righteous Son. Irving L. Jensen

It is worthy not only that every Christian should know it word for word, by heart, but occupy himself with it every day, as the daily bread of the soul. It can never be read or pondered too much, and the more it is dealt with the more precious it becomes, and the better it tastes. Martin Luther

1 CORINTHIANS
The Controversies That (Almost) Killed a Church

FACT SHEET

FORMAT. 16 chapters, 433 verses

IMPLIED PURPOSES. Paul founded the church in Corinth on his second missionary journey (Acts 18). He is writing in response to a report of problems in the church and answers questions posed by church members.

AUTHOR'S PERSPECTIVE. Paul feels a deep personal connection with the church and its leaders. He is fully aware of the situations they are facing and responds with firm love in the face of open rejection of his teaching and pattern of ministry.

IMPLIED AUDIENCE. The letter is addressed to the church in Corinth, and we can infer that Paul expected the leaders in the church to follow through on his directions. Through this first-century church situation, the letter speaks to all believers and churches confronting similar problems and questions.

WHAT UNIFIES THE BOOK. The author's close connection with the church to which he is writing; the format of answering questions that have been raised by church members; tensions between the church and the pagan culture; a strong corrective tone

SPECIAL FEATURES. Instruction on sex, marriage, and celibacy (chapter 7); the institution of the Lord's Supper (11:23-29); the extended analogy between the church and a person's body, used to teach the principle of unity in diversity of gifts (chapter 12); the famous chapter praising the superiority of love (chapter 13); teaching on the spiritual gifts (chapter 14); the gospel of the Resurrection (chapter 15)

CHALLENGES FACING THE READER OR TEACHER OF THIS BOOK.
1. Understanding the situations in the Corinthian church that Paul addresses

2. Seeing the relevance of specific church problems that may seem remote

3. The difficulty of following the line of thought in a letter that often appears disjointed as it moves from one question to the next as well as back and forth between doctrine and correction

HOW TO MEET THE CHALLENGES.

1. Take time to gain an awareness of the occasion for this letter, as signaled by references in the letter.

2. Seek to identify the larger issues at stake when specific issues such as idolatry or ceremonial foods are raised.

3. Take as much time as necessary to master the flow of thought as Paul moves to the next topic.

Perhaps the single greatest theological contribution of our letter to the Christian faith is Paul's understanding of the nature of the church, especially in its local expression. If the gospel itself is at stake in the Corinthians' theology and behavior, so also is its visible expression in the local community of redeemed people. The net result is more teaching on the church here than in any of Paul's letters. . . . If Romans and Galatians make it plain that one is not saved by obedience to the law, 1 Corinthians makes it equally plain that the saved are expected to live out their lives in obedience to the "commandments of God" (7:19) and the "law of Christ" (9:21). If such obedience is not required for entry into faith, it is nonetheless required as the outflow of faith.

GORDON FEE
The First Epistle to the Corinthians

16 Personal Matters

15 The Resurrection
14 Spiritual Gifts
13 Superiority of Love
12 Unity in Diversity
11 Worship and the Lord's Supper
8–10 Food Offered to Idols
7 Sex and Marriage

Paul Answers Questions That Have Been Raised

Difficult Issues in the Church

Counsel

6:12-20 Chastity
6:1-11 Lawsuits
5 Incest

Paul Responds to Reports of Incest and Lawsuits

Immorality in the Church

Correction

3–4 Call to Unity
1:18–2:16 God's Wisdom vs. Human Pride
1:10-17 Reports of Divisions
1:1-9 Salutation

Paul Speaks to Chloe's Report of Divisions in the Church

Divisions in the Church

Concern

AN OUTLINE OF
1 CORINTHIANS

Have you ever experienced the ordeal of controversy and division in a local church? The church in Corinth faced many vexing questions. It was locked in a dispute that featured angry words, charges and counter-charges, and charismatic leaders with their own groups of followers. Some church members sought advice from their church's founder, the apostle Paul. In this letter Paul addresses the concerns they shared and the questions they asked.

The Form of the Book

First Corinthians is a letter occasioned by specific issues facing the Corinthian church. It appears that Paul wrote an earlier letter (see 5:9), which has been lost, in which he warned against associating with self-styled Christians who were remorselessly indulging in sexual immorality. First Corinthians is organized around issues and questions the Corinthians raised. (For information on the epistle as a New Testament genre, see the article on page 495.)

Key Words and Phrases

- *The temple of the Holy Spirit.* Together, the people of God—the followers of Jesus Christ—are "the temple of God" (3:16), and each individual believer is the "temple of the Holy Spirit" (6:19). This teaching about the presence of the Spirit at the personal and corporate level is central to the spirituality of Christian community.
- *The body of Christ.* There was division and confusion among the Corinthians about their roles and relations in the church. Paul uses the analogy of the human body—in which every part plays a vital role in the well-being of one person—when speaking of the diversity of gifts and unity of fellowship in the church.
- *Spiritual gifts.* These special abilities, given by the Holy Spirit for the glory of God and the service of the church, had become badges of personal honor and symbols of spiritual power and had caused divisions in the church.
- *Carnal/spiritual Christians.* Paul writes to at least two different groups in the church that have different spiritual needs. These should not be seen as universal categories (still less as two levels of spiritual achievement) but as specific groups within the Corinthian church, with its unique struggles.

Key Doctrines

Sexuality. Because of the deep spirituality of sexual expression, sexual sins are regarded as being especially harmful to Christians.

Worship. Practical regulations for public worship are grounded in a theology of God and his church.

Resurrection. The resurrection of the body is defended as the foundation for the Christian hope in life after death.

Revelation. Paul sets forth the importance of the Holy Spirit in assisting our understanding of Scripture.

Tips for Reading or Teaching 1 Corinthians

Remember Corinth's location and social milieu. It was a cosmopolitan port city that exhibited a pluralism of religious and spiritual traditions and was known for its loose living. Someone has called Corinth the combined New York City, Los Angeles, and Las Vegas of the ancient world. Look for ways in which the problems that had infiltrated the Corinthian church can be correlated with the surrounding culture.

This letter was occasioned by the questions of people in the church. Pay constant attention to what questions the author is addressing, as well as to how he addresses them.

The author's overriding concern is the health of the church. As you read about topics such as spiritual gifts, look for community application first and personal application only secondarily.

As you read, work from principle to application. Much of what is said here was written to deal with specific problems. Find the universal principle, and then apply it to your own church situation.

quick overview of 1 corinthians

1:1–6:20	Paul deals with various church problems.
7:1–16:24	Paul answers questions raised by people in the church.

The Flow of the Book

The Meaning of the Cross and Paul's Credentials for Ministry (Chapters 1–2). A focus on the Cross and the Resurrection is woven throughout this book, which begins with the Cross and ends with the Resurrection. Paul wants to contrast the Corinthians' pride and divisive spirit with Christ's loving sacrifice. Look for evidence throughout the letter that Paul's aim is persuasive: He wants to convince the Corinthian Christians to correct the inroads that false teaching and wrong practices have made. Observe the specific ways in which Paul seeks to persuade his audience.

Problems in the Church (Chapters 3–6). Paul had received reports concerning divisions, immorality, and lawsuits within the church. He begins by scolding the Corinthians for their spiritual immaturity and then takes on each of the issues raised by church members. Be on the lookout for an implied contrast in Paul's mind between the right path to follow and the wrong path on which the Corinthian Christians have embarked. What hints do you find of two competing kingdoms on a collision course?

KEY VERSE

"I am writing to God's church in Corinth, to you who have been called by God to be his own holy people. He made you holy by means of Christ Jesus, just as he did for all people everywhere who call on the name of our Lord Jesus Christ, their Lord and ours" (1:2). Here is the letter in brief—addressed to the specific issues of the church in Corinth, calling these immature Christians to holy living, and all of this in an awareness that through the particulars of the Corinthian situation we can see the timeless relevance of the issues and Paul's teaching on them.

Paul's Answers to Practical Questions (Chapters 7–10). Chapter 7 begins, "Now regarding the questions you asked in your letter," signaling that this unit will consist of Paul's guidance on topics about which he had been asked for advice. As you read this section, pay attention to the points at which Paul takes up a new question (7:1; 7:25; 8:1; in later sections, 12:1; 16:1; note that the same Greek word appears in all of these verses). The topics covered include marriage and singleness, eating meat offered to idols, and abuses of liberty (in other words, license). Pay attention to Paul's line of thought on each of these topics, and look for universal principles in specific situations that may no longer be current in our culture, such as eating food offered to idols.

Issues concerning Worship and Spiritual Gifts (Chapters 11–14). The Corinthians had also asked questions about worship and church life, and in this unit Paul offers detailed teaching about these aspects of corporate Christian community. The guidance is timeless because such issues as divisions in the church and questions of how to conduct public worship are timeless. Note the specific antidotes that Paul offers for abuses that have surfaced—and still surface—in the church, noting in this regard how the famous chapter on love speaks to issues of diversity and competitiveness in the church.

Teaching about the Resurrection (Chapter 15). Yet another question had focused on the nature of the Resurrection. Look for a twofold division of

Paraenesis in the Epistles

Paraenesis (pronounced para-NEES-us) is a Greek word meaning moral instruction and exhortation. While the word is doubtless a difficult one, no good substitute has emerged. Paraenesis is one of the five standard ingredients in the New Testament Epistles. This section of an epistle consists of lists of vices and virtues, sometimes phrased as rules for living stated negatively as prohibitions and positively as commands. In both cases the imperative form of the verb is often (but not always) used.

Many New Testament Epistles begin with a theological discussion and then move to ethics or practical application. Often the ethical section consists of paraenesis. In Colossians 3:5, for example, the list of vices begins with the formula "Put to death the sinful, earthly things lurking within you." After the negative prohibitions we get the list of commanded virtues, beginning with the statement "Since God chose you to be the holy people he loves, you must clothe yourselves with tenderhearted mercy, kindness, humility, gentleness, and patience" (Colossians 3:12). This, in turn, flows into one of the so-called household lists (Colossians 3:18–4:1). In other epistles you can find paraenesis scattered throughout the letter. For example, 1 Timothy 2 lists rules for worship, chapter 3 for leadership in the church, and chapter 5:3-16 for widows.

A basic division exists between lists of virtues and vices that are a cluster of commands on a given subject and miscellaneous lists of individual rules. First Corinthians 7 is a whole chapter of commands regarding marriage. You can easily analyze such a unified paraenesis on the principle of theme and variations. But it is hard to teach lists of individual vices and virtues such as we find in Romans 1:29-31. With such seemingly miscellaneous lists, you can sometimes discover a pattern in one or more of the following ways:

- the cumulative or intensifying effect of repetition

- clusters according to topics

- correspondence to the context that emerges within a given epistle (for example, the vices listed in 2 Corinthians 12:20-21 reflect the situation in the Corinthian church)

- in contrast to this, lists of vices and virtues that are universal—key sins and virtues as viewed by the Christian faith

- patterning, as when the nine virtues listed in Galatians 5:22-23 fall into groups of three or when the vices and virtues listed in Galatians 5:19-23 "answer" to each other as opposites

the subject: In the first half of the chapter Paul asserts the reliable fact of Christ's resurrection as the basis for the believer's resurrection, and in the second half he corrects wrong ideas about the Resurrection that had occasioned questions from the Corinthian church. This chapter is the key repository of New Testament teaching on the Resurrection. What specific things does it teach about this central doctrine of the Christian faith?

Personal Matters (Chapter 16). The conventions of letter writing take over in this concluding chapter. What picture of the Christian life emerges from this personalia?

The Main Themes

1. The church is the body of Christ.
2. Church discipline is essential to preserve the health and peace of the church.
3. The Cross is the foundational truth to which we always return.
4. God's revelation is our guide for life, but it will always look foolish from the world's perspective.
5. The Holy Spirit should be the power behind our church life.
6. Pride and dissension tear apart the very fabric of the church.

Contribution of the Book to the Bible's Story of Salvation in Christ

Paul vividly portrays the centrality of the Cross and the Resurrection— that is, the gospel (see 15:1-8). Despite its seeming weakness and ineffectiveness, the Cross of Christ is the wisdom and power of God. Paul also interprets the meaning of the Last Supper in terms of Christ's sacrifice in his death (11:23-26). With regard to the Resurrection, Paul tells the Corinthians that if Christ has not been raised from the dead, their "faith is in vain" (15:14, ESV). Even the book's strong emphasis on Christian unity and community is centered on the person and work of Jesus Christ. It is because Christ cannot be divided that his church cannot be divided.

Applying the Book

You need to be aware that application is nearly continuous in this book. One application is the need to set a curb on individualism in the Christian life in realization that the life of faith occurs in a local church.

As one lives in the church, moreover, the focus must not be on "discovering your own spiritual gifts" as much as on honoring and encouraging other people's spiritual gifts.

You can and must live the Christian life in whatever situation you find yourself (married or single, for example, or slave or free).

Churches must guard the integrity of the faith through loving, biblical, church discipline when situations require it.

God wants his followers to grow in love and service that build up the church and send a strong witness to the world.

PERSPECTIVES
ON THE BOOK OF 1 CORINTHIANS

[The Corinthians] were wandering; Paul called them back to the center.
Bruce Barton

No other book is so completely devoted to the topic of Christian community, no other book rivals 1 Corinthians in applicability to our current situation. Lyle Vander Broek

This is certainly the most practical of all Paul's letters. Ray C. Stedman

Paul gives the Corinthians, and us, problem-solving principles that apply in any age, and in any congregation. Lawrence O. Richards

Paul's first letter to the Corinthians might well be entitled "Christian Hot Potatoes" in today's culture. Craig L. Blomberg

The wonderful church at Corinth, the brilliant jewel in the crown of Paul's labor, was failing. Henrietta Mears

His love for that church was therefore of special intensity. It was analogous to that of a father for a promising son beset with temptations, whose character combined great excellencies with great defects. Charles Hodge

The Gospels do not explain the Resurrection; the Resurrection explains the Gospels. Belief in the Resurrection is not an appendage to the Christian faith; it is the Christian faith. John S. White

2 CORINTHIANS
In Defense of
True Christian Ministry

FORMAT. 13 chapters, 257 verses

IMPLIED PURPOSES. To commend its recipients for the spiritual progress they have made, to raise money for needy Christians, and to reassert Paul's apostolic authority in response to recent attacks

AUTHOR'S PERSPECTIVE. Paul writes as someone intimately connected with the church to which he writes, having ministered there for a year and a half. He has witnessed the Corinthians' repentance and the persistence of certain divisive elements in the church.

IMPLIED AUDIENCE. In the first part of this letter to a local church, Paul addresses those who are spiritually receptive; in the second part, he speaks to those who question his leadership.

WHAT UNIFIES THE BOOK. The ever-present emphasis on suffering as the means of revealing God's glory and power; personal appeals; the author's dealing with concrete church and ministry issues; addresses to detractors

SPECIAL FEATURES. References to Paul's suffering; aspects of Paul's life that are recorded in this book alone; abrupt changes in tone; memorable phrases, such as "a thorn in the flesh"

CHALLENGES FACING THE READER OR TEACHER OF THIS BOOK.
1. Identifying and understanding Paul's opponents
2. Appreciating the disjointed nature of this personal letter
3. The emphasis on redemptive suffering, which may be foreign to some readers

HOW TO MEET THE CHALLENGES.
1. Take the time to compose a profile of Paul's antagonists.

2. Welcome the change in subjects and asides as evidence of this being a personal letter.
3. Accept Paul's challenging word about the importance of suffering.

THE MOST COMMON MISCONCEPTION ABOUT THIS BOOK. That this is the second letter that Paul wrote to the Corinthians. It is more likely the fourth (see, for example, 1 Corinthians 5:9).

The call of the Gospel is "come . . . and die" with Christ (4:10–12) in expectation of God's future which, at present veiled from our eyes, is grasped by faith (5:7) and awaited with confidence. This two-beat rhythm (death/life; distress/consolation; affliction/glory; weakness/strength) runs through the epistle and finds its heart in the incarnate (8:9), atoning (5:18-21), and enthroned Lord (4:5) whose "grace" and strength meet every human need (12:10; 13:13), for he "died and was raised" (5:15) and lives by God's power (13:4). Yet his present power is seen in the paradox of the suffering apostle (4:7; 13:4) who "acts out" in his ministry the Gospel he proclaims and embodies (5:20).

RALPH MARTIN
2 Corinthians

AN OUTLINE OF 2 CORINTHIANS

	Paul's Missionary Career					Paul as Future Visitor
	Paul's Current Situation	Paul's Character	Paul as Moral Counselor	Paul as Money Collector	Paul as Boaster	
1:1-7 Salutation						
1:8-11 Paul's Sufferings for Christ						
1:12-2:11 Paul's History with the Corinthians						
2:12-6:10 Paul Explains and Defends His Ministry		Paul's Ministry				
6:11-7:16 Miscellaneous Commands						
8-9 Appeal for Generous Giving			Paul Exhorts His Spiritual Children			
10:1-12 Defense against Charge of Weakness				Paul Defends His Apostolic Credentials		
10:13-12:13 Paul's Apostolic Boast						
12:14-13:10 Concluding Appeals						Paul Lays the Foundation for Future Dealings with the Corinthians
13:11-14 Epistolary Closing						

Imagine a deep friendship that has become so strained that one party questions the sincerity and motives of the other. This is what Paul faced with the Corinthians. His first impulse was to visit his challengers in person, but when this proved impossible, he decided to write a letter instead. The resulting epistle is a tender and personal letter from an apostle to a church he dearly loved.

INFORMATION ABOUT PAUL FOUND ONLY IN 2 CORINTHIANS

- Paul's understanding of his own ministry (chapter 4)
- Collection for the church in Jerusalem (chapter 9)
- Composite summary of a life of suffering for the cause of Christ (11:23-29)
- Paul's vision of heaven (12:1-6)
- Paul's thorn in the flesh (12:7-9)

The Form of the Book

Second Corinthians is a heavily autobiographical letter. There are so many references to its author that perhaps more than any other New Testament Epistle it can be called a personal letter, such as we might write or receive. Because much of the personal material is Paul's reply to detractors, the letter also has the character of an apology—that is, a spirited defense of the author's life and ministry. Further ingredients of the letter flow from what has just been said—self-portraiture, lyric outbursts of emotion, denunciation of opponents and practices, sarcasm, threats, expressions of personal affection. Most New Testament Epistles are "occasional" letters (letters occasioned by specific situations in the author's life), but perhaps 2 Corinthians is the most occasional of all. (For more information about the epistle as a form of writing, see the article on page 495.)

Key Doctrines

Reconciliation. Jesus' sacrifice restores the relationship between God and humankind.

Atonement. The Cross fully pays the penalty for our sin.

Suffering. God shows himself faithful in our trials.

Church Discipline. The church cannot afford to overlook either immorality or false teaching but must respond to it in a godly and courageous way.

Tips for Reading or Teaching 2 Corinthians

Look for personal details about Paul that are found nowhere else.

Observe the evidence of Paul's enormous personal investment in the Corinthians.

Be alert for shifts in tone, which sometimes signal a change of audience.

Pay attention to Paul's purpose in writing about his trials, noting what he establishes by these autobiographical sections.

You face an important decision regarding this book, which is filled with so much autobiography: Either this is primarily a book about one person—Paul—or it is about principles that apply to every Christian's life. You need to choose the second of these approaches. What happened to Paul happens also in your own Christian life.

quick overview of 2 corinthians

1:1–7:16	The nature of Paul's ministry
8:1–9:15	Paul's collection of money
10:1–13:14	Paul's apostolic credentials

The Flow of the Book

Paul's Ministry (Chapters 1–7). This section carries the reader along with a strong story line. We learn about aspects of Paul's life that are not revealed anywhere else. Paul's life as revealed here is a life of extraordinary suffering and endurance as an itinerant missionary. This unit of the epistle is oriented to the past, whereas subsequent sections focus on the present and even a hint of the future as Paul predicts a coming visit. As you read chapters 1–7, look for specific ways in which Paul defends his past ministry in Corinth and builds an understanding of the nature and purpose of Christian ministry in general. What do we learn here about what it means to serve Christ and his gospel?

Discourse on Generous Giving (Chapters 8–9). The subject of this unit of the letter is financial contributions to needy Christians in Jerusalem (see 1 Corinthians 16:1-4 for the likely context). Notice at once how easy it is to "build bridges" between the first-century Christian church and situations in your own home church or Christian organization. The best way to read this unit is to look for

KEY VERSES

"Your lives . . . are a letter from Christ showing the result of our ministry among you. This 'letter' is written not with pen and ink, but with the Spirit of the living God. It is carved not on tablets of stone, but on human hearts" (3:2-3). We see here the two dominant themes of the letter: Paul's vindication of his own ministry and the picture of the Christian life as an inner spiritual reality that bears witness to God in the world.

evidence of how Paul conducts a very delicate persuasive strategy. The hoped-for contribution from the Corinthian church is behind schedule. Paul wants to motivate his readers to dig into their pockets for the sake of Christian behavior. Note how he encourages, coaxes, and convicts.

Paul's Boasting of His Apostleship (Chapters 10–13). A contingent in Corinth continued to oppose Paul's teaching and pastoral directives. To these unrepentant church members Paul now directs his attention. The tone and demeanor change, and Paul writes strong words of warning as he defends his ministry. As you read this section, notice how Paul conducts a persuasive argument designed to move his hearers to a change of mind and heart. Also look for passages of lyric intensity and personal fervor as Paul turns the conventional literary form of the boast (usually uttered by warriors in epic literature) to a defense of his apostolic credentials and his personal integrity.

The Main Themes
1. Christians have a ministry of reconciliation.
2. God's strength is sufficient for any trial, and even in our trials we can demonstrate God's grace.
3. Giving money to Christian causes is an outflow of a changed heart.
4. Correct doctrine is essential. Paul defends his emphasis on sound theology.
5. The unity of the church must be protected and promoted.

Contribution of the Book to the Bible's Story of Salvation in Christ
This letter contains clear language about the work of Christ on the cross (especially 5:14-15) and his ministry of reconciliation (5:18-21). Jesus is shown to be the comforter of the persecuted (1:3-7), the fulfillment of all the promises of God (1:20), the revelation of God's glory and truth (3:12-18; 4:6), the righteous judge (5:10), and the creator of new spiritual life (5:17). The sufferings of Christ are also regarded as the paradigm for the whole Christian life (4:7-12; 12:9-10).

Applying the Book
This letter is filled with clear commands and applications of theology to the Corinthian situation. The challenge for us today is to bridge the gap between our contemporary situations and the ancient world of Corinth. A good starting point is to discern the universal principles behind Paul's applications. For example, what should motivate our giving? What did

Paul see as priorities for our giving? If Paul's own missionary career showed that he was willing to sacrifice all personal preferences for the sake of the gospel, how should we live out the same attitude?

This letter also contains memorable verses that are worthy of focused application: "We have this treasure in jars of clay" (4:7, ESV); "We walk by faith, not by sight" (5:7, ESV); "If anyone is in Christ, he is a new creation" (5:17, ESV); "The one who plants generously will get a generous crop" (9:6); and "My grace is sufficient for you, for my power is made perfect in weakness" (12:9, ESV). These verses challenge us to live out the truth of the gospel in our ministry and our churches.

PERSPECTIVES
ON THE BOOK OF 2 CORINTHIANS

Apologia Pro Vita Sua [Latin phrase meaning "defense of his life," a customary official or unofficial title for certain types of autobiography].
A common designation for 2 Corinthians through the centuries

What an admirable Epistle is the second to the Corinthians, how full of affections. [Paul] joys, and he is sorry, he grieves, and he glories. Never was there such care of a flock expressed, save in the great shepherd of the fold, who first shed tears over Jerusalem, and afterwards blood.
George Herbert

This letter is valuable not only for its insight into Paul's heart, but also as a guide to anyone who seeks to serve others in a godly, loving way.
Lawrence O. Richards

"Theologically driven passion for the purity of God's people." This . . . encapsulates the motivation behind the writing we call "2 Corinthians." At the same time, the letter before us is, without a doubt, the most personal of all Paul's correspondence. As a result, his last letter to the church in Corinth, more than any of his other letters, is "theology of the flesh." Scott J. Hafemann

In the epistle Paul reflected on his ministry and described it as "the ministry of reconciliation." Reconciliation is one of the most

comprehensive words in the New Testament and is fundamental to all facets of Christian ministry. It touches the most significant issues of theology and life and is the very heartbeat and mission of the church. . . . This ministry belongs to the whole church, and all Christians are to be ministers of reconciliation since they are members of the body of Christ. . . . No ministry is nobler than this ministry. French Arrington

Paul's "second" letter to the Corinthians is, without a doubt, one of the strongest witnesses to the fact that everything that Paul says, writes, and teaches is not developed in the neutral realm of a general consideration, but is a part of his work and desire, his dramatic life-struggle itself. Scott J. Hafemann and Hans von Campenhausen

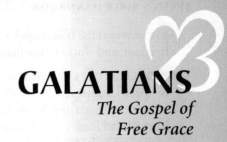

GALATIANS
*The Gospel of
Free Grace*

FORMAT. 6 chapters, 149 verses

IMPLIED PURPOSE. To address a sudden crisis in Galatia (a region in the southern part of Asia Minor), where Jewish-Christian missionaries ("Judaizers") were telling Gentiles that they had to receive the Jewish sign of circumcision in order to fully belong to Christ. In order to combat this legalistic attack on the gospel and to protect the churches he founded from abandoning Christian orthodoxy, the author (Paul) defends the doctrine of justification by faith alone.

AUTHOR'S PERSPECTIVE. Paul is agitated and alarmed, more so than in any of his other letters. He immediately mounts a vigorous defense of his apostolic authority, not because this is important to him personally but because it is connected to the thing that matters to him more than anything else in the world: the free grace of God, which does not come by keeping any law but only by trusting in Christ.

IMPLIED AUDIENCE. Believers in the churches of Asia Minor (modern-day Turkey) who enthusiastically embraced the gospel at first (see Acts 13–14) but were in danger of turning away from it by adding works to faith. Since the instinct to justify ourselves is so deeply ingrained in our sinful natures, we all need to hear the gracious gospel of Galatians.

WHAT UNIFIES THE BOOK. The central and dominating concern to defend God's free grace in the gospel; an urgent tone and invective language, which reveal the author's impatience with his readers and antipathy toward his theological opponents (to the point of cursing them and wishing for their castration); pairs of sharply contrasted opposites (law versus grace, works versus faith, the false

517

gospel versus the true gospel, death versus life, bondage versus freedom, and works of the flesh versus fruit of the Spirit)

SPECIAL FEATURES. Galatians may be the first letter Paul ever wrote. Its special features include a difficult allegory comparing law and promise to Hagar and Sarah, the mothers of Abraham's sons Ishmael and Isaac (4:21-31), and a famous description of the fruit of the Spirit (5:22-23).

CHALLENGE FACING THE READER OR TEACHER OF THIS BOOK. Grasping the nuances of Paul's sophisticated biblical and theological arguments about law, grace, and the gospel

HOW TO MEET THE CHALLENGE. Like Romans, to which it is often compared, Galatians requires careful study; however, the main point is hard to miss: We cannot be justified by performing any works of the law but only by faith in Jesus Christ.

Paul] *had faithfully instructed [the Galatians] in the pure gospel, but false apostles had entered in his absence and corrupted the true seed by false and corrupt dogmas. For they taught that the observance of ceremonies was still necessary. This might seem trivial; but Paul fights for it as a fundamental article of the Christian faith. And rightly so, for it is no light evil to quench the brightness of the gospel, lay a snare for consciences and remove the distinction between the old and new covenants. He saw that these errors were also related to an ungodly and destructive opinion on the deserving of righteousness.*

JOHN CALVIN
Galatians

It is always possible to slip into a performance-based approach to Christianity in which the way we feel about our relationship to God depends on what we do for him rather than on what he has done for us in Christ. Whenever we try to improve our standing with God by observing religious rituals, doing charitable deeds, or performing pious acts of devotion, we are placing a surcharge on God's free grace. We are saying that faith in Christ is fine as far as it goes but we need something more.

Paul wrote his letter to the Galatians to combat this way of thinking. It is a letter for "recovering Pharisees"—for Christians who struggle to leave their old legalism behind. Sometimes we forget to keep living by the grace that saved us when we first came to Christ. Galatians reminds us of the good news that Jesus Christ has done *everything* necessary for our salvation. We cannot earn the grace of God; it only comes free.

The Form of the Book

Galatians is structured more like a rhapsody than a symphony. Its sense of organization does not come from a series of tightly constructed and logically connected movements but from one central theme carried through the work in one energetic burst from beginning to end. We'll look at this in more detail under "The Flow of the Book."

Key Words

The key words in Galatians all cluster around the contrast between true and false theology: *faith* and *works*, *law* and *gospel*, *sinful nature* and *Spirit*. The key word for Paul's opponents was *circumcision*—removal of the foreskin—an Old Testament sacrament that marked a male's entrance into the covenant community. The key word for Paul was *justification*. This legal term means being proclaimed innocent in a court of law. In its biblical sense, to be justified means to be declared righteous before the bar of God's justice.

> **KEY VERSE**
> "We know that a person is made right with God by faith in Jesus Christ, not by obeying the law. And we have believed in Christ Jesus, so that we might be made right with God because of our faith in Christ, not because we have obeyed the law. For no one will ever be made right with God by obeying the law" (2:16). This verse—which encapsulates the message of Galatians—is triply redundant. *Three times* in the space of just one verse, Paul says that we are justified by faith or belief, and *three times* he says that we cannot be justified by doing works of the law.

Key Characters

Paul mentions four important men in Galatians: Peter (Paul's fellow apostle), Barnabas (Paul's first fellow missionary), Titus (one of Paul's young protégés), and Abraham (Paul's prime exhibit of justification by faith under the old covenant). But the most important people—the theological opponents who tried to pervert Paul's gospel of justification by faith alone—are not mentioned by name. Usually called "the Judaizers," these Jewish-Christian legalists taught that Gentiles had to become Jews in order to become Christians. Acts 15:1 summarizes their theology: "Unless you are circumcised as required by the law of Moses, you cannot be saved." The Judaizers did not deny that justification came by faith; however, by adding circumcision to the message of the Cross and by adding law to the gospel, they were denying that justification came by faith *alone*.

Key Doctrines

The main doctrines in the letter, such as justification by faith alone, have already been discussed. But we should make special mention of the *Holy Spirit* (who is received simply by faith in Christ), *redemption* (our rescue from slavery through the payment of a price), *adoption* (with the high privilege of calling God "dear Father"), and *the law* (which is a curse to sinners because no one can keep it, but a blessing to believers because it shows us our need for Christ).

Frequently Asked Questions

Does the visit to Jerusalem that Paul mentions in chapter 2 coincide with the events described in Acts chapter 11 or those in Acts chapter 15? Probably the former but possibly the latter. How can we reconcile Paul's doctrine of justification by faith with the statement by the apostle James, who says, "We are shown to be right with God by what we do, not by faith alone" (James 2:24)? What Paul and James say is complementary, not contradictory. Paul writes to people who want to make good works part of the basis for their justification and tells them that justification is Jesus Christ plus nothing. James writes to people who won't do any good works at all and tells them that they do not have true faith because saving faith always proves its validity by what it does.

Tips for Reading or Teaching Galatians

Galatians is an argumentative letter, so it helps to know as much as we can about the arguments it was written to attack. What did the Judaizers teach? We can learn a good deal about their theological position by paying constant attention to the way Paul refutes it. For example, we can infer from his vigorous defense of his apostolic authority that the Judaizers were attacking his credentials. Similarly, Paul's discussion of the Old Testament suggests that his opponents used Abraham as their prime example of a man who was circumcised to be saved. With this background in mind, Paul's response comes with special force: "The real children of Abraham, then, are those who put their faith in God" (3:7).

quick overview of galatians

1:1–2:21	Autobiography: the personal section of the epistle, in which Paul *defends* the gospel of free grace by asserting his apostolic authority
3:1–4:31	Theology: the doctrinal section of the epistle, in which Paul *explains* the gospel of free grace by giving a series of biblical and theological examples
5:1–6:18	Ethics: the practical section of the epistle, in which Paul *applies* the gospel of free grace by exhorting the Galatians to keep walking in the freedom of the Spirit

The Flow of the Book

Greeting (1:1-5). Right at the beginning, Paul praises God for the two great facts of the gospel he was given by God and upon which everything depends: the crucifixion and the resurrection of Jesus Christ. Although he gives a doxology, his customary words of thanksgiving for the church are conspicuous by their absence. The church is having a crisis, and he moves right on to address it.

How Shocking! (1:6-10). In a state of obvious agitation, the apostle abruptly expresses his amazement and astonishment that the Galatians are turning away from the good news of the gospel. They are following "another gospel"—but in fact, there *isn't* any other gospel. The gospel that comes from God is the only gospel there is, and anyone who says otherwise deserves to be cursed.

Where Paul Got His Gospel (1:11–2:10). In order to defend the one true gospel—the gospel he first preached to the Galatians—Paul argues that it came straight from God. Reading between the lines, we can guess that when the Judaizers came to Galatia preaching another message, they tried to discredit Paul by dismissing him as a second-rate apostle with a secondhand gospel. So in order to defend his gospel, Paul also had to defend his own apostolic authority. He did not derive his gospel from any other apostle, he says, but received it by a direct revelation from Christ. Notice how Paul uses his own experiences and his interactions with the apostles in Jerusalem to make his case. Although his gospel was in full agreement with their gospel, it was independent of their endorsement.

Justification by Faith Alone (2:11-21). On a memorable occasion when Paul rebuked Peter in Antioch (not so much for racism as for his denial of God's free grace), the other apostles needed *him* to correct their gospel! This incident affords Paul the opportunity to move from talking about the source of his gospel to the gospel itself. The essence of this gospel is the doctrine of justification by faith alone: We do not get right with God by keeping his law but by trusting in Jesus Christ. Period. There is nothing else that we need to do to be saved. Paul ends the chapter with a rhetorical question: If we could be saved by doing the good works of God's law, why did Jesus have to die for our sins?

Arguments for the Doctrine of Justification (Chapter 3). In order to bring the Galatians back to their senses, Paul presents a series of arguments that explain why justification comes by faith alone, not by works or even by faith plus works. First he appeals to experience: Did you Galatians receive the Holy Spirit by keeping the law or by trusting in Christ? Then he uses teaching from the Old Testament: Was Abraham declared righteous by his works or only by his faith? Which came first: the law or the promise of the gospel?

Along the way, Paul explains the law's limitation (it can only bring us under God's curse because we are unable to keep it) and the law's function (not to save us but to show us our guilt so that we see our need for the gospel). The climax comes at the end, where Paul explains that we receive the salvation promise of Abraham by faith in Jesus Christ and not by working the law. You might find it useful to divide Paul's argument into separate sections.

An Analogy, an Appeal, and an Allegory (Chapter 4). Paul uses the analogy of minors who have to grow up before receiving their inheritance to explain the purpose of the law and the spiritual blessings we freely inherit by faith. He also makes a personal appeal, reminding the Galatians how he first gave them the gospel. Look for clues about the works they were tempted to add to faith. Also notice Paul's deep feelings for his friends and the contrast he draws between his own motivations and those of his opponents. Paul's last argument is a complex allegory based on connecting Abraham's sons and their mothers to the gospel and the Galatians (see if you can line up the points of comparison). Paul's conclusion is that adding works to faith as the basis for our standing before God leads us only into spiritual slavery.

Faith Working through Love (Chapter 5). Here it becomes clear that the main issue for the Judaizers was circumcision. What matters to God, however, is not circumcision or any other external ritual but faith— "faith expressing itself in love" (5:6). In the second half of chapter 5, Paul guards against a danger that is equal and opposite to legalism: license, or the attitude that once our sins are forgiven, we can sin as much as we please. But as believers in Christ we need to fulfill the law of God's love. We do not exercise our freedom in Christ by following the desires of the old sinful nature (note that half of the sins listed deal

with discord, such as the Judaizers were causing in the church), but by keeping in step with the Spirit, who produces supernatural fruit in our lives.

Conclusion (Chapter 6). After giving a series of practical exhortations, Paul closes by recapitulating the main theme of his letter: the false gospel of requiring circumcision for salvation versus the true gospel of the Cross. He doesn't want anyone to miss out on the freedom that comes through faith in Christ.

The Main Theme
The central theme of Galatians is freedom: the freedom from bondage to works of the law, which comes through faith in Jesus Christ.

Contribution of the Book to the Bible's Story of Salvation in Christ
Galatians defends the pristine gospel of salvation by grace alone, through faith alone, in Christ alone. It also teaches us something significant about the Cross: Since crucifixion was a sign of God's condemnation (see Deuteronomy 21:23), when Jesus was crucified he suffered the curse that we deserve for breaking God's law (Galatians 3:13). Therefore, the Cross is our rescue (1:4), our redemption (4:5), and our "boast" (6:14)—indeed,

it is our life itself: "I have been crucified with Christ. It is no longer I who live, but Christ who lives in me" (2:20, ESV).

Applying the Book

We apply the teachings of Paul in Galatians by heeding his practical exhortations and also by rejecting any form of performance-based Christianity. The danger comes when we take anything in addition to Christ—even good things such as our devotional activities, behavioral standards, theological positions, ministry commitments, and political causes—and make it part of the basis for our standing before God.

PERSPECTIVES
ON THE BOOK OF GALATIANS

The Magna Carta of Christian Liberty. Various sources

The sum of the letter is as follows: the Galatians are going astray because they are adding Judaism to the gospel of faith in Christ. . . . Disturbed by these tendencies, Paul writes this letter . . . in order that they may preserve faith in Christ alone. Marius Victorinus

The argument is this: Paul wants to establish the doctrine of faith, grace, the forgiveness of sins or Christian righteousness, so that we may have a perfect knowledge and know the difference between Christian righteousness and all other kinds of righteousness. Martin Luther

The Epistle to the Galatians is especially distinguished among St. Paul's letters by its unity of purpose. The Galatian apostasy in its double aspect, as a denial of his own authority and a repudiation of the doctrine of grace, is never lost sight of from beginning to end. J. B. Lightfoot

When, from time to time, someone appeared who understood and proclaimed the genuine message of Galatians, he was liable to be denounced as a subversive character—as indeed, Paul was in his own day. But the letter to the Galatians, with its trumpet-call to Christian freedom, has time and again released the true gospel from the bonds in which well-meaning but misguided people have confined it so that it can once more exert its emancipating power in the life of mankind, empowering those who receive it to stand fast in the freedom with which Christ has set them free. F. F. Bruce

Paul in Galatians is not merely firing unrelated salvos at his audience; he has a plan and a direction he intends his series of arguments to tend towards. His words are carefully chosen and the arrangement of the material bears the mark not only of an orderly mind, but of one used to following certain rhetorical patterns of argumentation.
Ben Witherington III

The Galatian converts, who had received this gospel of grace, were now turning away to another gospel, a gospel of works. . . . They did not deny that you must believe in Jesus for salvation, but they stressed that you must be circumcised and keep the law as well. In other words, you must let Moses finish what Christ has begun. Or rather, you yourself must finish, by your obedience to the law, what Christ has begun. John R. W. Stott

EPHESIANS
*The Identity and Conduct
of Those Who Are in Christ*

FORMAT. 6 chapters, 155 verses

IMPLIED PURPOSES. To celebrate the wonders of what God has done for believers in Christ, to heighten believers' awareness of their identity in Christ, and to call Christians to embrace the duties that accompany their exalted status as believers in Christ

AUTHOR'S PERSPECTIVE. Freed from the need to speak to specific situations in the life of a local church, the author writes about Christians generally and with a cosmic viewpoint. A natural teacher, he seeks to enlarge his readers' grasp of what they have entered into as believers in Christ.

IMPLIED AUDIENCE. Since the letter lacks specific references to its audience, Christians of any era can walk into Ephesians and make it their own. The book is for the body of Christ. From the topics covered, we can infer what aspects of Christian thinking and behavior the author thought needed improvement.

WHAT UNIFIES THE BOOK. The ever-expanding list of the riches that believers have in Christ; continual reminders of the duties that accompany being "in Christ"; balance between what Christ has done for believers (their position in him) and what Christians must do in response; a focus on the church, not as an institution, but as the corporate body of believers

SPECIAL FEATURES. A universal and cosmic orientation (seen partly in the absence of local references); the central importance of being "in Christ"; occasional references to the spirit world; reliance on the identity motif (a concern to show Christians who they are in Christ); the lyric quality (exuberant tone); an unusual range of aspects of Christian doctrine and behavior covered in just six chapters (condensed, "packed" writing); famous passages on predestination, marriage, and the Christian in the full armor of God

CHALLENGES FACING THE READER OR TEACHER OF THIS BOOK.
1. The need to follow a sometimes-fluid flow of thought
2. Mastering the interrelated parts in a densely doctrinal book

HOW TO MEET THE CHALLENGES.
1. On a first or second reading, accept that the flow of thought resembles the somewhat loose organization of informal letters.
2. Then ponder and even chart the ways in which the writer echoes and builds upon ideas and motifs introduced earlier.

T*he letter is famous for its advanced doctrine of the Church. . . . It is, however, an error to suggest that teaching about the Church dominates the epistle. . . . The epistle is essentially about Christ . . . and this Christ is one who first of all renews individual human lives and only then welds them into this new kind of community called the Church. In fact, in chapters 1–3 there is far more about the great privileges which the individual Christian receives from God through Christ than about the corporate life of the Church. . . . It is a misunderstanding of this epistle to see the Church as a kind of mystical entity with some kind of ethereal existence apart from the transformed lives of the individuals who compose it. Membership in the Church is not a substitute for a personal apprehension of the privileges of the Christian faith, but is the outcome of that personal faith with its experience of Christ and new life in Christ.*

C. LESLIE MITTON
Ephesians

6:21-24 Concluding Personalia and Benediction — Personal Conclusion

6:10-20 The Christian in Complete Armor — Spiritual Warfare

5:21-6:9 Household Rules — Domestic Duties

4:17-5:20 Rules for Living the Christian Life — Moral Conduct

4:1-16 Unity and Diversity in the Church — Church Unity

3 Paul's Apostolic Calling and Message — Testimony and Prayer

2 The Great Before and After — Transformation

1:3-23 What God Has Done for Believers in Christ — Position and Possession

1:1-2 Salutation — Personal Introduction

The Behavior That Must Characterize Believers

Believers' Walk in Christ

What Christians Must Do

The Position That Believers Have in Christ

Believers' Wealth in Christ

What God Has Done in Christ

AN OUTLINE OF
EPHESIANS

Is the Christian faith primarily personal and individualistic, or is it primarily corporate? When you read the New Testament Epistles, do you most readily think of the statements as applying to "the Christian" or to "the church"? The book of Ephesians provides a good occasion to reach some conclusions about these questions.

Commentaries and handbooks are divided right down the middle about whether Ephesians concerns "the Christian" or "the church." We know that the letter was written to a group of Christians rather than to an individual, but that is true of all of the New Testament Epistles through 2 Thessalonians. Once scholars pin church-oriented headings on the various units, the content seems to fit that framework naturally. But if we begin with the text itself and not with externally imposed headings, we will find only two main units (4:1-16, on the unity of the church, and 5:23-32, on Christ's headship of the church) in which Paul explicitly talks about the church. Paul's comments about Gentiles and Jews being reconciled deal with a theological reality, not merely with factions within a local congregation. In this book we have attempted a compromise by phrasing our discussion in terms of "Christians" (plural) to indicate that Paul's statements apply to the shared experience of individual Christians, with implications for the local church as a corporate body.

The Form of the Book

This book is a "textbook illustration" of the genre of the epistle (for more on the conventions of the New Testament Epistles, see the article on page 495). The five components of the epistolary genre are the opening, consisting of the sender, addressee, and greeting (1:1-2); the thanksgiving, which calls to mind the spiritual riches of the addressee and prayer for spiritual welfare (the rest of chapter 1); the body of the letter (2:1–4:16); paraenesis, or exhortations (4:17–6:20); and the closing, which includes personal references and final wishes (6:21-24). While the form is thus typical, the content lacks a familiar ingredient of New Testament letters: references to the particular situation of the group to which the letter is addressed, including a list of personal greetings.

The Structure and Unity

The structure of the book of Ephesians is somewhat difficult. The book partly has the unity of a letter written in the midst of intense feeling and heightened insight. Within the familiar movement of a letter, you will find your experience of Ephesians unified if you start to keep a mental or written list of key topics to which the author keeps returning. Some of these are the identity that believers have in Christ, the constantly expanding list of things that Christ has done, and characteristics of the life that Christians are enjoined to live now that they have been converted. You will not be threatened by the sheer quantity of details if you keep relating them to the big ideas.

It is useful to know from the start that this book has something of the quality of a Christian manifesto—an authoritative outline of Christian doctrine and ethics. The book of Ephesians is a small-scale book of Romans—a minihandbook of basic Christian theology and morality.

Key Doctrines

Christology. The letter is a major New Testament statement of what Christ did in salvation and of all the blessings that come to believers as a result of those actions.

Election. The believer's salvation is founded on the sovereign and eternal choice of God.

Ecclesiology. The letter makes key statements about the unity and diversity of the universal church, especially if we regard the descriptions and commands as addressed to Christians corporately.

Salvation. This letter is not concerned specifically with justification, as some other epistles are, but with the totality of salvation by grace through faith, including election, adoption, redemption, and glorification.

Sanctification or *Ethics.* The second half of the letter consists mainly of moral commands.

Union with Christ. All the blessings of salvation are located in Christ.

> **DID YOU KNOW?**
> • Ephesians was John Calvin's favorite New Testament Epistle.
> • In the original Greek, the first half of Ephesians is characterized by an exalted style, with formal language and long, drawn-out, stately sentences.
> • There are numerous specific parallels between Ephesians and Colossians.
> • References to the church in this epistle are to the church universal rather than to a specific local church.
> • The phrase *in Christ* appears nine times (ESV), and variants of *in him* appear another nine times.

Tips for Reading or Teaching Ephesians

Be receptive to the exhilaration with which the author writes, especially in the first half. Relish the long sentences and exalted vocabulary, remembering that high thoughts must have high language.

Read or teach in an awareness of the five main elements of a New Testament Epistle (see "The Form of the Book," above).

Keep relating individual statements to your list of big ideas that lend coherence to the letter.

Operate on the premise that the author wrote to Christians who needed to have their vision of their identity and duties expanded. Compile a mental or written list of the specific areas in which the author sought to spur his readers to better thinking and behavior.

quick overview of ephesians

1:1–3:21   The identity that Christians have in Christ
4:1–6:24   How Christians must live on the basis of their position in Christ

The Flow of the Book

Rapturous Celebration of Believers' Riches in Christ (Chapter 1). Technically, the unit follows the sequence of salutation (vv. 1-2), listing of blessings (vv. 3-14), and prayer (vv. 15-23), but the celebratory mood is the same throughout. You can scrutinize the passage for key words, and you can compile a list of blessings that come to those who believe in Christ and things they possess in Christ. More specifically, look for evidence that the emphasis in this letter is Trinitarian, as the work of salvation is treated as an eternal plan carried out by the triune God—Father, Son, and Holy Spirit.

KEY VERSE
"Blessed be the God and Father of our Lord Jesus Christ, who has blessed us in Christ with every spiritual blessing" (1:3, ESV). This exuberant verse introduces the main theme of the first half of Ephesians: Every blessing of salvation is located in Christ.

The Conversion Story of All Christians (Chapter 2). The whole chapter is phrased in terms of before and after, then and now, death and life. You can profitably compile a list of things that characterize the lost and the regenerate, and you can analyze what the chapter says about how the great change from one to the other happens (by grace, through faith, not on the basis of works). Also, look for evidences that Paul has an eye on the implications of his writing for the church as a corporate body, especially in his comments about the joining of Jews and non-Jews together with Christ in the newly emerging Christian community.

533 . . . . EPHESIANS

Paul's Explanation of His Apostolic Role and Message (Chapter 3). At the surface level, conventions of the personal letter take over as we move through these units: direct address to readers (vv. 1-6), recap of Paul's missionary ministry (vv. 7-13), prayer for the readers (vv. 14-19), and benediction (vv. 20-21). But in keeping with the nature of this epistle as a doctrinal manifesto about God's eternal plan of salvation, there is something more going on than a pastor's desires for his readers. In this chapter Paul outlines the specific apostolic calling he received from God to explain and disseminate the doctrines of grace to the Gentiles. Paul's unique apostolic calling was crucial to the emergence of a Christian church that built on but went beyond Old Testament Judaism by the inclusion of Gentiles. This, in turn, was crucial to God's plan for the cosmos.

KEY VERSE
"At one time you were darkness, but now you are light in the Lord. Walk as children of light" (5:8, ESV). Here is the double thrust of the book: the new position that Christians have received by virtue of being in Christ, and an accompanying obligation to live as new people.

Reflections and Instruction regarding the Unity of the Church (4:1-16). Two concepts dominate the passage: diversity and unity. How do these two relate to each other in the church? A good analytic slant on the material is to compile a list of the ways in which the church is unified and the actions required by individual members to fulfill God's calling for the church.

Rules for Living the Christian Life (4:17–5:20). This is the familiar paraenesis of the Epistles. (See "Paraenesis in the Epistles" on page 505 for information about this component of the New Testament Epistles.) Look for evidence that although there are exceptions, the passage consists mainly of prohibitions until you get to verses 15-20 in chapter 5, which state the positive antidote to the vices that are prohibited. Other things for which to look are categories such as personal and relational exhortations, clusters of related sins, the distinction between attitudes and actions, and ways in which all three persons of the Trinity enter the passage.

Household Rules (5:21–6:9). The prevailing individualistic emphasis of the preceding unit now gives way to a thoroughly relational section that covers wives and husbands, children and parents, slaves and masters. Note what is required of each group and ways in which the writer repeatedly links these commands to Christ.

The Christian in Complete Armor (6:10-20). The mode is obviously metaphoric, as various spiritual resources are described as parts of a warrior's armor. You can compile a list of the spiritual qualities and virtues to which Paul gives metaphoric shape (truth, righteousness, etc.). Then note the nature of the battle and the "soldierly" behavior that it requires.

Conclusion (6:21-24). This consists of personalia and greetings.

The Main Themes

1. Personal conversion, sanctification, and participation in the corporate life of the church are important in a Christian's life.
2. The riches that believers have in Christ are both personal and corporate (something to be shared with other believers).
3. God's goal for his church is that its members will be united rather than divided.
4. God has given believers detailed instructions on how to live spiritually and morally.
5. God's equipping of Christians is not meager but abundant.

Contribution of the Book to the Bible's Story of Salvation in Christ

The book has particular "angles" on Christology. It emphasizes the exaltation of Christ and pictures him as a cosmic Savior and Lord: God has "put all things" under the authority of Christ (1:22). Eschatology in this letter is "realized" eschatology; that is, it pictures believers as already seated with Christ "in the heavenly realms" (2:6). The letter makes numerous references to what Christ accomplished by his life, death, and resurrection, securing all the blessings of salvation for everyone who is united to him by faith. Christ is portrayed as the One who gives us life and unites us in love, glorifying himself in the church.

Applying the Book

The goal of the first half of the book is to raise believers' awareness of their identity in Christ. We can help the author achieve that goal by accepting that "in Christ" is, indeed, our identity and position. The goal of the second half is to equip believers with rules for living. We can make that goal a reality by practicing what the author commands us to do. More specific applications abound: We need to live daily in an awareness of our position in Christ; we are saved by grace and need to relinquish thoughts of meriting salvation; we are to avoid ethnic and racial divisions in the church, prizing both our unity and diversity in Christ (2:11-22); the body of Christ must be unified and live in mutual love; by faith we can be victorious in the great spiritual battle that is constantly raging (6:10-20).

PERSPECTIVES
ON THE BOOK OF EPHESIANS

The divinest composition of man. Samuel Taylor Coleridge

The crown of St. Paul's writings. J. Armitage Robinson

The central message of the book: "Be rich." Warren W. Wiersbe

[Outline of the book from a classic eight-volume commentary:] God's Ultimate Purpose (1:1-23); God's Way of Reconciliation (2:1-22); The Unsearchable Riches of Christ (3:1-21); Christian Unity (4:1-16); Darkness and Light (4:17–5:17); Life in the Spirit (5:18–6:9); The Christian Warfare (6:10-13); The Christian Soldier (6:10-24)
D. Martyn Lloyd-Jones

One of our chief evangelical blind spots has been to . . . proclaim individual salvation without moving on to the saved community. . . . Nobody can emerge from a careful reading of Paul's letter to the Ephesians with a privatized gospel. For Ephesians is the gospel of the church.
John R. W. Stott

Before the Church becomes possible there is need for the new quality of individual life in Christ. . . . Basic, therefore, to this new kind of corporate life embodied in the Church is the renewed life of the individual within the new community. C. Leslie Mitton

[The letter is written to believers who] were in need of inner strength, further knowledge of their salvation, greater appreciation of their identity as believers and as members of the Church, increased concern for the Church's unity, and more consistent living in such areas as speech, sexuality, and household relationships.   Andrew T. Lincoln

[Ephesians is matched only by Romans] as a candidate for exercising the most influence on Christian thought and spirituality. Raymond E. Brown

Cosmic reconciliation and unity in Christ are the central message of Paul's Letter to the Ephesians. Peter T. O'Brien

QUOTES

ON THE BOOK OF EPHESIANS

PHILIPPIANS
The Joy of Living in Christ

FORMAT. 4 chapters, 104 verses

IMPLIED PURPOSES. To express thanksgiving for a generous gift of missionary support, provide a personal update, and address practical problems in a local church

AUTHOR'S PERSPECTIVE. Paul writes from a Roman prison cell, which he finds as good a place as any to live for Christ, share the gospel, rejoice in God's provision, and write an exuberant letter of spiritual encouragement to his partners in ministry.

IMPLIED AUDIENCE. Members of the church that Paul started in Philippi—loyal and longstanding supporters of his missionary work—and anyone else who has a mind to follow the life pattern of the crucified and risen Christ

WHAT UNIFIES THE BOOK. An irrepressible mood of joyful thanksgiving; the warm mutual friendship and spiritual partnership between Paul and the Philippians; the humble sacrifice of Christ, which serves as the paradigm for Christian service

SPECIAL FEATURES. A famous hymn about Christ's humiliation and exaltation (2:5-11); an unusually high number of memorable passages that summarize the whole Christian life (e.g., 1:21; 2:12-13; 3:12-14; 4:11-13)

CHALLENGE FACING THE READER OR TEACHER OF THIS BOOK. The difficulty of living out the pattern of Christlike humility the book sets forth

HOW TO MEET THE CHALLENGE. The way to become more like Christ is to know him in the sufferings of his death and the power of his resurrection—a knowledge that the Holy Spirit gives us through the Word, sacraments, and prayer.

FACT SHEET

Missionaries are always looking for at least two kinds of support: spiritual support and financial support. As a result, their letters nearly always contain earnest appeals for prayer and an update about their personal circumstances, including any material needs. Philippians is just this kind of letter. In it, the apostle Paul thanks the Philippians for their support, and as he does, he tells them how his work is progressing and seeks to give them some spiritual encouragement.

The Structure

Paul's thank-you epistle to the Philippians is more experiential and less doctrinal than most of his other letters. It can be loosely organized into the following sections:

Greeting, Thanksgiving, and Prayer (1:1-11). Paul celebrates his long-standing partnership with the Philippians with a heartfelt prayer for God to bless them.

Living and Dying in Christ (1:12-26). Paul rejoices that his imprisonment has actually served to advance the gospel, both inside and outside his prison cell. Apparently under some threat of execution, Paul reflects on the meaning of his life and proclaims, "To me, living means living for Christ, and dying is even better" (1:21).

Having the Mind of Christ (1:27–2:11). Paul exhorts the Philippians to maintain their Christian unity and to remain steadfast as they suffer opposition. In other words, he wants them to have the mind of Christ, who humbled himself to the very death. By way of reminder, Paul traces the great parabola of redemption, in which Christ went from glory to glory by way of the Cross (2:5-11). Paul's hymn on the person and work of Christ—with its high praise for the glories of Christ's deity and astonished reverence at the humility of his humanity—is one of the high points of the New Testament.

Exhortations and Examples (2:12-30). On the basis of Christ's humiliation and exaltation, Paul exhorts the Philippians to put God's saving work into action in their own lives, using himself, Timothy, and Epaphroditus as examples of Christlike service. How do these men exemplify the life of Christ? Notice that what Paul says about his companions provides the context for his letter.

Knowing Christ (3:1–4:1). Here Paul turns more explicitly to theology, warning the Philippians not to put any confidence in their own righteousness but to trust in Christ alone for their salvation. His own testimony is the perfect example: In order to get right with God, Paul had to discount all his spiritual achievements and claim Jesus Christ as his only righteousness. But this does not mean that Christians are not called to obey, and at the end of the chapter Paul exhorts the Philippians to keep working until they reach their eternal reward.

Further Exhortations (4:2-9). Paul promises the Philippians that God will give them peace, provided that they maintain Christian unity, rejoice with thanksgiving, pray instead of worrying, and love the good, the true, and the beautiful.

Giving Thanks for Gifts Received (4:10-23). Paul finally gets around to what must have been the main reason for his letter, namely, to thank the Philippians for their generous gift. He testifies that he has "learned the secret of living in every situation" (4:12), which is to trust Christ for everything he needs. Nevertheless, he is grateful for their help, and while he is unable to reciprocate, at least he can assure them that God will supply all *their* needs too.

> **KEY VERSE**
> "I want to know Christ and experience the mighty power that raised him from the dead. I want to suffer with him, sharing in his death" (3:10). This verse shows the theological and practical thrust of the epistle: The crucifixion and resurrection of Jesus Christ set the pattern for the life that we have in him.

Key Words and Characters

The key words in Philippians are *joy* and *rejoice*, which occur more than a dozen times, and also *mind*, as in having the mind of Christ, which is the basis for personal godliness and Christian unity.

Apart from Paul himself, notable characters include Timothy and Epaphroditus (his exemplary coworkers) and Euodia and Syntyche (squabbling sisters in Christ who represent the trouble that Christians sometimes have getting along with one another).

Key Doctrines and Themes

The Sovereignty of God. This applies especially to the outworking of our salvation (1:6; 2:12-13).

The Humiliation of Christ. Christ humbled himself in both his incarnation and his crucifixion.

The Exaltation of Christ. God has raised Christ to a place of supreme lordship, where he will one day receive universal praise.

Union with Christ. The source of salvation and the pattern for the Christian life is Jesus Christ; to be a Christian is to become "one with" Christ (3:9), knowing him both in his death and in his resurrection (3:10-11).

Justification. Our confidence to stand before God is based not on our own works but on the righteousness of Jesus Christ, which we receive by faith.

The Communion of Saints. Since we are united to Christ, we share his mind and are united to one another in the church.

The Sufficiency of Christ. Jesus Christ is the reason for our joy and the source of true contentment in every situation.

Tips for Reading or Teaching Philippians

Pay constant attention to the two main threads that run all the way through the letter: the rich partnership that Paul has with the Philippians and the sacrificial pattern of the life of Christ and the Christian. For further background on the Philippians, be sure to read the story of how the church got started (see Acts 16).

quick overview of philippians

1:1-30	Paul's thankful prayers and joyful perspective on life and death as he preaches the gospel in a Roman prison
2:1-30	Paul's celebration of Christ's humiliation and exaltation and illustrations of them in the lives of faithful Christians
3:1-21	The supremacy of knowing Christ and striving for his glory rather than putting any confidence in religious accomplishments
4:1-23	Final exhortations, with grateful acknowledgment of the spiritual and financial support that Paul had received from the Philippians

Contribution of the Book to the Bible's Story of Salvation in Christ

The main contribution of Philippians is to apply the gospel of Christ to daily Christian living. Notice that the great hymn to Christ in chapter 2 is introduced to support a practical exhortation: "Don't be selfish; don't try to impress others. Be humble, thinking of others as better than yourselves. . . . You must have the same attitude that Christ Jesus had" (2:3-5).

Applying the Book

The most obvious application, then, is to pattern our lives after Christ's by offering ourselves in humble sacrifice for others. Philippians also helps missionaries and their supporters know what kind of relationship God wants them to have in ministry: a giving, sharing, praying partnership. Finally, no one should miss the secret of contentment that Paul shares in the last chapter: In every circumstance, and even in the face of death, Jesus is enough for us.

PERSPECTIVES
ON THE BOOK OF PHILIPPIANS

[A useful outline of the book:] Christ our life (1:1-26; key verse: 1:20); Christ our pattern (1:27–2:30; key verse: 1:27); Christ our goal (3:1–4:1; key verse: 3:8); Christ our sufficiency (4:2-23; key verse: 4:11)
Irving L. Jensen

Intensely intimate, it lacks formality. Paul sets down his ideas as they come to him, and they are primarily concerned with personal matters— himself, his friends, Timothy and Epaphroditus, and the problems and generosity of the Philippian community. It is a far cry from being a theological treatise. And yet unconsciously he writes theologically, or Christologically, for his mind is saturated with thoughts of Christ, God, man, salvation, Spirit, end times. Gerald F. Hawthorne

[In] one type of ancient letter, the letter of friendship, . . . the writer would share his or her own present thinking (often including reflection on one's circumstances) and inquire about the other's circumstances. Mutuality and goodwill always find expression in such letters, as do the obligations of benefits received and given. That Paul had entered into such an arrangement with the Philippians (alone among all his churches) is explicitly stated in 4:14-16. All kinds of other features of friendship thus appear in Philippians. Gordon D. Fee and Douglas Stuart

Looking at the other epistles, each with its own divine and also deeply human characteristics, we find Philippians more peaceful than Galatians, more personal and affectionate than Ephesians, less anxiously controversial than Colossians, more deliberate and symmetrical than Thessalonians, and of course larger in its applications than the personal messages to Timothy, Titus, and Philemon. H. C. G. Moule

COLOSSIANS
*The Supremacy and
Sufficiency of Christ*

FORMAT. 4 chapters, 95 verses

IMPLIED PURPOSES. To assert that Christ is supreme in all things, to correct specific false doctrines and practices on the basis of the sufficiency of Christ, and to exhort Christians in practical living

AUTHOR'S PERSPECTIVE. Paul writes with intense personal concern for the Christians he addresses and with passion for truth as opposed to error. Further, he speaks as an authoritative teacher of true doctrine and as a debater denouncing an opponent's ideas.

IMPLIED AUDIENCE. Paul writes to Gentile converts (the Colossian church) who are being seduced by religious teachings and practices that distort the gospel by adding to the list of beliefs and practices that constitute genuine Christianity.

WHAT UNIFIES THE BOOK. The conventions of New Testament Epistles; the direct address from Paul to a specific church situation; the theme of the sufficiency of Christ; a continual emphasis on false teaching—what *not* to believe and practice

SPECIAL FEATURES. The subtlety involved in Paul's giving a Christianized version of some of the very terms (such as *mystery* and *knowledge*) and concepts (such as the contrast between the earthly and the heavenly) that were used by the heresy against which he wrote; Christocentric focus; prevalence of the vocabulary of *fullness* and *all*, which in at least one version (ESV) appears twenty-five times

CHALLENGES FACING THE READER OR TEACHER OF THIS BOOK.
1. Piecing together an exact picture of the heresy that Paul denounces
2. Seeing how the entire letter correlates with the main theme of the supremacy of Christ

HOW TO MEET THE CHALLENGES.

1. Get help from commentaries and/or take the time to piece together the false teachings and practices from the hints contained in the letter itself.
2. Make a conscious interpretive effort to relate all of the parts of the letter to the implied theme that Christ is sufficient in all things.

Colossians is one of the most Christ-centered books of the Bible. In it, Paul stresses the supremacy of the person of Christ and the completeness of the salvation He provides in order to combat a growing heresy in the church at Colossae. Christ, the Lord of creation and Head of the body which is His church, is completely sufficient for every spiritual and practical need of the believer. The believer's union with Christ in His death, resurrection, and exaltation is the foundation upon which his earthly life must be built. Relationships inside and outside the home can demonstrate daily the transformation that faith in Jesus Christ makes in the walk of the believer.

BRUCE WILKINSON AND KENNETH BOA
Talk thru the Bible

	Personal Greetings	Christian Fellowship

4:7-18 Concluding Greetings

	Practice	Submission to Christ

3:1–4:6 How to Live as Followers of the Sufficient Christ

	False Doctrine	

2:8-23 Description and Denunciation of False Religion

	True Doctrine	Supremacy of Christ

1:21–2:7 Further Claims about Christ

1:15-20 Christ Hymn

	Personal Greetings	Christian Fellowship

1:1-14 Introduction to the Letter

AN OUTLINE OF
COLOSSIANS

The human impulse to want to do something to earn favor with God is perennial. In paganism and some forms of Christianity, this is seen in physical asceticism (denying or even punishing oneself), doing acts that are viewed as meritorious with God, and performing religious rituals, offerings, and sacrifices. But the impulse can take subtle forms in every Christian's life. The Epistle to the Colossians places this perennial problem of "works salvation" in a first-century setting, when the question of how the Old Testament ceremonies apply to New Testament Christianity was the main struggle of the early church. This epistle provides a lens through which we can come to understand the problem as it exists in our own lives. In answering the question of what it takes to achieve salvation, Colossians warns us against thinking that we need to add anything to Christ's atoning work.

DID YOU KNOW?
Colossians is one of Paul's four "prison epistles." The others are Ephesians, Philippians, and Philemon.

The Form of the Book

Colossians follows the familiar contours of New Testament Epistles. It contains greetings and salutations, a doctrinal half, a practical/ethical half (including lists of dos and don'ts), and closing greetings and instructions. (For a reminder on the conventions of the epistle as a genre, see page 495.)

In addition, Colossians has the form of a debate. Because Paul consistently has a specific heresy in view, the letter emerges as his half of an implied debate. We thus find the familiar ingredients of an announced resolution (that Christ is sufficient), refutation or rebuttal of an opposing viewpoint, and persuasive appeals to both accept and act upon the truth.

Unifying Elements

- The mingling of three types of material—doctrinal, practical/ethical, and personal
- A Christological focus (Paul both explains and praises the person and work of Christ as being sufficient.)
- The impulse to describe and refute specific false doctrines
- The continual addressing of a specific church (the one at Colosse) and its situation
- The use of both the rhetorical form of direct address to an audience and exhortation (a continual series of commands)

Key Doctrines

Christology. In Colossians, the most Christological book in the Bible, Paul asserts and celebrates Christ's humanity, divinity, substitutionary atonement, and exaltation.

Revelation. The battle against heresy is at root an issue of truth versus error, and God's revelation of his truth is the antidote to error.

Creation. The universe as God created it and the incarnation of Christ in physical form are good and therefore not to be denigrated.

Salvation. Christ's atonement is the only sufficient basis of salvation.

Sanctification. The book includes an extended passage of ethical instruction in holy living (in the family and beyond).

Tips for Reading or Teaching Colossians

The first half of the book is an ever-expanding description of a specific heresy that Paul is out to discredit; keep a running list of the specific teachings that make up this false religion. For example, look for places where these wrong ideas are the implied context: (1) the need to be initiated into special forms of religious knowledge, such as might come through visions, for example; (2) the need to observe certain religious ceremonies and rituals; (3) asceticism (denial of physical appetites, which are viewed as bad); and (4) the need for intermediaries, such as angels, between people and God.

Colossians is also a continual account of the person and work of Christ. Keep a running list of things that you learn about Christ and his work.

This letter was occasioned by a specific church situation. Be alert to the references to the Colossian church, and build bridges to your own life and to the contemporary church.

Look for direct and implied references to the concept of *knowledge*: Variants of the word appear thirteen times (ESV), including references to the false views of knowledge that Paul seeks to refute.

quick overview of colossians

1:1-14	Salutation, thanksgiving, and prayer
1:15–2:23	Doctrinal instruction about Christ, Paul's apostolic ministry, and false teaching
3:1–4:18	Practical exhortations about Christian living

The Flow of the Book

Introduction (1:1-14). Epistolary conventions govern the opening of Colossians. We find the familiar salutation (vv. 1-2), thanksgiving (vv. 3-8), and prayer (vv. 9-14). A good avenue to exploring these verses is to operate on the premise that they are pictures of Christian living and then to assemble a composite portrait of such living.

Christ Hymn (1:15-20). This famous Christ hymn falls into two symmetrical halves—one praising Christ's supremacy in the creation (vv. 15-17) and the other praising his supremacy in the church (vv. 18-20). Drawing parallels between the two halves is a helpful exercise. (It will be more apparent if you record the two halves in side-by-side columns and as poetic lines.)

KEY VERSE
"That in everything he might be preeminent" (1:18, ESV). This is the main focus of the whole book: Christ is supreme.

Implications of Christ's Sufficiency (1:21–2:7). Paul next makes practical application of what he has just asserted in the Christ hymn by reminding members of his audience of their own conversion through the sufficiency of Christ (1:21-23), his own ministry as a manifestation of the supremacy of Christ (1:24-29), and his concern that the Colossians continue in the truth regarding the sufficiency of Christ (2:1-7). A good analytic grid is to ask how Paul's assertions in these areas correlate with his main theme of Christ's sufficiency. Also, if we are aware that part of the heresy Paul combats in this letter is the teaching that truly spiritual people are clued in to special spiritual mysteries, we can see already in this section an implied rebuttal of heresy.

Warning against False Doctrine and Practice (2:8-23). We now get a picture of the false doctrines that were threatening the Colossian Christians. The best way to tease out the meaning of the passage is to compose a list of the specific teachings and practices of the false religion that Paul denounces. For example, it is obvious that the false philosophy taught that the physical world is bad and that truly spiritual people have been initiated into some special knowledge.

From Doctrine to Practice (3:1–4:6). In keeping with Paul's custom in his epistles, there is a shift from doctrine to practice. The passage unfolds like this: the foundational principle of Christian living (setting one's sight on Christ) (3:1-4); a list of vices to avoid (3:5-11); and a list of virtues to be practiced, including "household instructions" involving the family relations between husband and wife, parents and children, and masters and servants (3:12–4:6). As you analyze the passage, observe the proportion of commands that are matters of individual behavior versus those that are relational.

Concluding Instructions and Greetings (4:7-18). We can read these details as filling out our acquaintance with Paul and, by way of application, getting a picture of what ought to characterize every Christian's life at some level (for example, note how many partners in ministry Paul names).

The Main Themes
1. Christ is supreme in all things.
2. Because Christ is sufficient for believers, they should avoid thinking that in addition to him and his atonement they need special forms of knowledge or rituals of self-denial.
3. Living the Christian life requires that believers put off sinful behavior and practice the spiritual virtues God has commanded.

Contribution of the Book to the Bible's Story of Salvation in Christ
Colossians is the most explicit and memorable statement in the Bible about the supremacy of Christ in both the created universe and the church. Beyond that, the distinctive contribution of this epistle to the story of salvation history is that Jesus is sufficient to fill all spiritual longings and needs, so that we have no need of anything beyond Christ's atoning work to make our salvation complete.

Applying the Book
One application is to acknowledge that ideas have consequences and that false religious ideas lead to unchristian thinking and living. We should leave the book of Colossians with a renewed commitment to study Christian doctrine. Somewhat more specifically, the particular false doctrines that Paul refutes (false notions about what constitutes spirituality and legalistic practices) still exist in Christian circles. We can profitably think about modern-day parallels to the first-century situation covered in this letter.

Another realization that should settle on us is that if Christ is truly supreme and sufficient, our love for him should be absolute. We need to conclude that if

KEY VERSE
"See to it that no one takes you captive by philosophy and empty deceit, according to human tradition . . . and not according to Christ" (2:8, ESV). This warning against false doctrine is the negative theme of Colossians.

we were as devoted to Christ as we ought to be, our behavior (partly as outlined in the second half of this epistle) would take care of itself somewhat naturally. An additional application is laudatory; that is, reading the book should lead us to praise Christ.

Finally, the lists of exhortations in the second half simply need to be obeyed. The application is to practice what is commanded. (See "Paraenesis in the Epistles" on page 505.)

PERSPECTIVES
ON THE BOOK OF COLOSSIANS

Paul has one main answer to the erroneous teaching, and that is the Person and work of Christ; and so we get the high Christology of the Epistle. Herbert M. Carson

The book of Colossians has remarkable spiritual symmetry. Its purpose is to refute gnostic thought by demonstrating the complete supremacy and adequacy of Christ. In doing this Paul fights fire with fire—the opponents' knowledge is countered by the full knowledge of Christ. R. Kent Hughes

[Colossians] is a warning against all religious syncretism, and a summons to remember the absolute uniqueness of God's revelation in Jesus Christ. William Barclay

In refutation, Paul proceeds positively rather than negatively. . . . He points out the all-sufficiency of what the Colossians have already received, in order to prevent them from seeking anything new. J. Gresham Machen

1 THESSALONIANS
An Exiled Missionary's Letter to a Fledgling Church

FORMAT. 5 chapters, 89 verses

IMPLIED PURPOSES. Paul wants to say in letter form what he cannot say in person because he has been prevented from paying a return visit to Thessalonica. Paul wants to express thanks for a good report of the Thessalonians' progress in the Christian life, to exhort them to live sanctified lives, and to clarify the doctrine of Christ's return.

AUTHOR'S PERSPECTIVE. No Pauline letter expresses more warmth and personal enthusiasm for the recipients than this letter to treasured Christian friends. Additionally, Paul slants his admonitions to live godly lives around the doctrine of Christ's return.

IMPLIED AUDIENCE. The immediate audience was a group of Christians, largely Greek in composition, whose beginnings as a church had been under the missionary teaching of Paul. Christians of all subsequent generations can read the letter as if addressed to them as well, teaching what they, too, need to know about Christ's second coming and the implications of believing that it will happen.

WHAT UNIFIES THE BOOK. Intimacy of tone between the author and recipients of the letter; eschatological orientation, especially regarding the return of Christ; the conventions of an informal letter

SPECIAL FEATURES. Repeated direct address to the recipients: "brothers" or "brethren" (literal English translations) and "brothers and sisters" (NLT); unusually high proportion of references to Paul's relationship to the recipients of the letter so that some scholars legitimately view all of the first three chapters as a personal salutation; the "coming" of Christ as a continuous undertone, coupled with the most explicit New Testament teaching about the Rapture (the event of believers being "caught up" mentioned in 4:17)

Imagine that you were given the opportunity to write an open letter to your church or a church of which you were a former member. What would you choose to write and emphasize? First Thessalonians is in effect an open letter to a church from a former spiritual leader of the group.

The Structure

Here is an outline of the book, accompanied by prompts to aid in your analysis:

Epistolary Opening (Chapter 1). After the expected personal greetings (v. 1), Paul launches into effusive praise of the Thessalonians for their exemplary Christian lives. As an analytic grid, you can profitably mold the things for which Paul praises the Thessalonians into a composite portrait of the ideal Christian. According to this passage of praise, how should Christians live?

Paul's Reflection on His Experiences with the Thessalonian Christians (Chapters 2–3). These two chapters are autobiographical reflection, as Paul takes stock of his past experiences with the recipients of his letter, first recalling his own on-site acquaintance (Chapter 2) and then what he has heard of Timothy's ministry among the Thessalonians (chapter 3). We can infer that Paul founded the Christian group and that Timothy helped to move it toward stability and maturity (3:2-3). Coming through all these particulars is a general picture of how Christians should conduct themselves, both individually and as a church. What things make up the portrait of good Christians and churches? Then consider Paul's behavior as a model of how we should relate to groups of Christians and, by extension, to individual Christians.

Instruction in Christian Living (4:1-12; 5:12-22). Having reflected on the Thessalonian church, in the second half of the letter Paul turns to an instructional mode. Two separated passages follow the outline of a formula found in virtually all of the epistles and known as *paraenesis*—lists of dos and don'ts, virtues and vices. Look for patterns in these two particular lists.

Instruction about Christ's Return (4:13–5:11). This is one of the most extended New Testament passages on the return of Christ. First Paul outlines the sequence of events that will unfold with the second coming of Christ. What is that sequence? Then Paul sketches out how Christians should live in light of the Second Coming. What are the keynotes?

Epistolary Conclusion (5:23-28). Even here we can compile a brief portrait of how Christians should live.

Key Doctrines and Themes

Sanctification. In the sections of commendation and exhortation, the subject is godly living, summed up in the memorable statement that "God's will is for you to be holy" (4:3).

Eschatology. There is specific teaching on Christ's return.

Communion of the Saints. Much of the book outlines how Christians should live and relate to one another (even Paul's stance toward the recipients of his letter is a model of this).

Scripture. This teaching is gleaned from scattered references to the Word of God and the great assertion that the Thessalonians "received the word of God . . . not as the word of men but as what it really is, the word of God" (2:13, ESV).

> **KEY VERSE**
> "Now may the God of peace make you holy in every way, and may your whole spirit and soul and body be kept blameless until our Lord Jesus Christ comes again" (5:23). First Thessalonians has a double thrust: godly living within an awareness of Christ's coming.

Tips for Reading or Teaching 1 Thessalonians

The first three chapters are somewhat unusual in their content, consisting of Paul's feelings toward a specific Christian group and his reminiscence of his experiences with that group. The best analytic grid for this material is to view it as giving you "program notes" about how Christians should live (with Paul's behavior toward the Thessalonians as part of the data that you can explore through this lens).

The commands regarding virtues and vices can be analyzed for underlying patterns.

With the eschatological section, it is important that you let the text speak for itself and not bring externally derived schemes to the text.

Beyond that, you should note that the practical implications of the doctrine of Christ's return get eleven verses while the outline of events itself gets only six verses. Regardless of your views about the end times, the practical teaching is clear.

Contribution of the Book to the Bible's Story of Salvation in Christ

If one looks at the places in the book where Jesus is explicitly named, it will be evident that most of these references concern his second coming (the word for this is *Parousia*, meaning "presence," or "arrival"). While certainly not neglecting the subject of how saved people should live their lives while they wait for the eschaton (end of time), 1 Thessalonians can nevertheless be said to give us a late chapter in salvation history.

Applying the Book

In ways already suggested, 1 Thessalonians can be read as a brief handbook on sanctification. To apply the handbook, we need to adopt the behavior that is outlined. Second, we need to not only believe what Paul says about living in expectation of the return of Christ (4:13-18) but also obey the practical commands for living that he treats as corollaries of believing in Christ's return (5:1-11).

PERSPECTIVES
ON THE BOOK OF 1 THESSALONIANS

Paul writes to the Thessalonians, reminding them [chapters 1–2], informing them how he rejoices over Timothy's report regarding them [chapter 3], instructing them [4:13–5:11], exhorting them [4:1-12 and 5:12-28]. William Hendriksen's outline of the book of 1 Thessalonians

[After the personal reflections (chapters 1–3),] it was natural to move on to exhortation, to write [about] themes that were suggested to him by the news brought by Timothy. These covered three main areas. First, there were questions of general morality. . . . Second, there were problems arising from teaching about the parousia which needed to be clarified. Third, there was need to say something about their life together.
I. Howard Marshall

[If we piece together the things that needed correction among the Thessalonian Christians, we see the understandable] difficulties which a young, very enthusiastic, but as yet imperfectly instructed, church would naturally encounter as it sought to live out its faith. We meet the weak and the faint-hearted, the idlers and the workers, the visionaries and the puzzled. Leon Morris

Looking back: how they were saved [1–3]. Looking on: how they should live [4–5]. J. Sidlow Baxter's outline of the book of 1 Thessalonians

Answers to two questions they have asked: What about those who have died before Christ's return [4:13-18]? When will that return be [5:1-11]?
Sir William Ramsay's outline of the eschatological passage

2 THESSALONIANS
When One Letter Is Not Enough

FACT SHEET

FORMAT. 3 chapters, 47 verses

IMPLIED PURPOSES. To give encouragement and direction to the fledgling church at Thessalonica and to give further instruction on matters that had been raised in the first letter but had not been correctly understood and/or applied, especially regarding the end times

AUTHOR'S PERSPECTIVE. Paul again writes as an exiled missionary with a pastoral and personal concern that the converts at Thessalonica thrive in their Christian lives and "get it right" theologically. The writing, however, is less lavish in personal sentiment and more businesslike than it is in 1 Thessalonians, as though Paul has dashed off a short response.

IMPLIED AUDIENCE. What was said about 1 Thessalonians is true here, too: The immediate audience was a group of Christians, largely Greek in composition, who had formed under the missionary preaching of Paul. But the mistakes Paul corrects in 2 Thessalonians are perennial, so the audience is all Christians who need encouragement, who suffer from misguided apocalyptic fervor, and who have a deficient work ethic.

WHAT UNIFIES THE BOOK. The situation of an apostle addressing a church; a satiric tone as the author puts down bad behavior and bad thinking; a predictable swing between encouragement and reproof

SPECIAL FEATURES. Tough-mindedness in predicting judgment on the ungodly and rebuking wrong thinking and behavior among Christians; eschatological orientation; apocalyptic references, never fully explained, to "the man of lawlessness" who will be revealed in the last days

FACT SHEET

Have you ever written a letter that had only partial effect compared to what you intended? a letter that was misunderstood or needed some added clarification? First Thessalonians was just such a letter. Second Thessalonians offers further instruction and clarification on what Paul addressed in his earlier letter to the church at Thessalonica.

The Structure

As usual with the Epistles, we begin with a salutation (1:1-2) and end with a prayer and benediction (3:16-18). Between these bookends we find a typical informal letter whose structure resembles a letter that we ourselves might write. With a little streamlining, we can divide the material into the following three units:

Paul's Personal Messages to the Thessalonians (1:3-12). We see Paul's thanksgiving for the Thessalonians (vv. 3-4), his assurance that the Thessalonians' antagonists will receive God's punishment (vv. 5-10), and his prayer for the Thessalonians (vv. 11-12).

An Eschatological Passage (Chapter 2). Paul describes what will precede the second coming of Christ (vv. 1-12) and expresses thanks that the Thessalonians have experienced salvation (and thus will be saved from the coming judgment [vv. 13-17]).

Two Commands (3:1-15). Paul tells the Thessalonians to pray (vv. 1-5) and to refrain from idleness (vv. 6-15).

> **DID YOU KNOW?**
> The Puritans made much of 3:10, with its command that if anyone does not work he should not eat. In fact, this was the law in Jamestown, the first permanent English settlement in America.
> While the idleness Paul denounces in 3:6-15 *may* have been occasioned by misguided views that Christ was going to return any day, neither of the Thessalonian letters explicitly draws that connection.

Key Doctrines and Themes

Eschatology. Chapter 2 focuses on what will happen before the second coming of Christ, and 1:5-10 predicts final punishment for the wicked.

Salvation. The letter contains repeated asides in which Paul asserts and expresses gratitude for the Thessalonians' salvation in Christ.

Work. Along with general exhortations to moral living, 3:6-15 is the most extended biblical passage on the subject of work.

Tips for Reading or Teaching 2 Thessalonians

Accept that this is an informal letter with the material loosely arranged, the way our informal letters are. Within the informal organization for the letter, however, notice that each of the three chapters treats a topic at length (1:5-10; 2:1-12; 3:6-15), with shorter elements creating a flow around these "islands" of more-extended teaching.

The line of thought in the longer passages requires careful study and analysis, while the short passages carry their meanings on the surface.

Finally, do not read the end-times passage in 2:1-12 in isolation; compare it to Jesus' Olivet discourse (Matthew 24–25) and similar passages in Revelation. Second Thessalonians simply reinforces familiar eschatological teaching, especially in regard to an unleashing of lawlessness that will precede the end of history.

Contribution of the Book to the Bible's Story of Salvation in Christ

In addition to repeated short passages that talk about salvation in Christ and its effects in the believer's life, this letter, like 1 Thessalonians, fills out a late chapter in salvation history, namely, end-time events (2:1-12), eternal punishment of unbelievers (1:5-10), and glorification of believers (1:10; 2:13-14). Moreover, there are notable passages that celebrate the comfort and peace that Christ gives to his followers.

KEY VERSES
"Now may our Lord Jesus Christ himself, and God our Father . . . comfort your hearts and establish them in every good work and word" (2:16-17, ESV). These verses summarize the three main thrusts of the letter: the *comfort* the Thessalonians can have (chapter 1), a *word* of truth about the end times (chapter 2), and commands to pray and *work* (chapter 3).

Applying the Book

One application stems from the way this book wants us to have correct information about the end times and to think correctly about end-time events (including the eternal destinies of unbelievers and believers). To have correct and precise information is an antidote to the floating vagueness and undue speculation about eschatology that characterize many Christians today. A second application is to put into practice the rules for living that the book outlines, with special emphasis on a biblical work ethic.

PERSPECTIVES
ON THE BOOK OF 2 THESSALONIANS

Patient waiting, watching and working.   J. Sidlow Baxter's overview of the book's structure

[Paul writes] to stop the members of the congregation from supposing that the end of the world is necessarily within the next few days. Various trials must be endured first, he tells them. Therefore, the members of the church should go back to work and to godly living in the world. . . . The Christian is expected to live and do his work each day with that earnestness of purpose which might come with the conviction that any day could be the last before the judgment.   Sir William Ramsay

[On the relationship between 1 and 2 Thessalonians: After sending his first letter, Paul found] that it did not achieve all that he desired. . . . Idleness on the part of some continued, and there were misunderstandings about the parousia which caused others to be troubled in mind. Accordingly, without losing time . . . , Paul set himself the task of putting things in order, and 2 Thessalonians was the result. . . . In this letter he carries on the work he began in the first, encouraging the faint-hearted, rebuking the slackers, dealing again with the return of the Lord.   Leon Morris

[On 1 and 2 Thessalonians:] Practically every major doctrine in the catalogue of faith is represented in these two small epistles. Although they were not written as doctrinal treatises . . . they contain a well-rounded body of theological teaching. . . . Theoretically and practically the Thessalonian letters embody all the essentials of Christian truth.
Merrill C. Tenney

1 TIMOTHY

*A Young Minister Gets Help
from His Mentor*

FORMAT. 6 chapters, 113 verses

IMPLIED PURPOSE. To help a young pastor know what to say and do as he confronts doctrinal deviation and other difficulties in a fledgling congregation

AUTHOR'S PERSPECTIVE. The author writes as an experienced missionary, pastor, and church planter (not to mention, an apostle) who comes to the aid of one of the churches he founded by sharing some valuable lessons he has learned in ministry. He has an equal concern for both the pastor and his people, for creed as well as conduct.

IMPLIED AUDIENCE. Paul writes primarily to Timothy, his "true son in the faith" (1:2) and protégé in pastoral ministry. However, although the letter is personal, it is not private. Paul assumes that the church in Ephesus will also hear the letter and benefit from its instruction. Since it offers basic principles for ministry, 1 Timothy is of perpetual relevance for the church and especially for Christians in positions of spiritual leadership.

WHAT UNIFIES THE BOOK. Paul's personal advice to Timothy as his friend and father in the faith; the apostle's overarching concern to combat false teaching and false teachers; the ethical and theological contrast between good and bad spiritual leadership in God's household, the church

SPECIAL FEATURES. The Bible's most complete summary of a pastor's theology, ministry, and spirituality; lists of spiritual qualifications for officers in the church; advice about caring for people with special needs, including widows and slaves

CHALLENGES FACING THE READER OR TEACHER OF THIS BOOK.
1. Understanding the false doctrines that Timothy faced

561

  2. Interpreting Paul's instructions about the role of women in the church (2:9-15)

HOW TO MEET THE CHALLENGES.

  1. Recognize that these heresies—Gnosticism (the quest for secret religious knowledge), legalism (seeking acceptance from God by keeping the Old Testament laws or other laws), and asceticism (rejecting legitimate physical pleasures on the grounds that they are unspiritual)—are present today.

  2. Recognize that authority of qualified men to teach publicly is part of God's plan for preserving good doctrine and godliness in the church and that in the context of the ancient world, Paul was elevating the place of women by telling them to learn theology.

__O__n the whole there is one guiding thought and purpose: Paul is eagerly desirous and anxious that Timothy may rightly discharge the serious duty imposed upon him, and may perfectly comprehend the difficulties that lie before him, and may know the best means of meeting them. . . . This charge is only temporary, to take Paul's place in his absence; but it may last a long time. . . . The method by which Timothy will best discharge the duty imposed on him is, first, the regulation of the order and manner of public worship; and second, the right organization of the church and of the Christian society which makes up the church on earth.

SIR WILLIAM RAMSAY

The best place to learn Christianity is not in the classroom but in a close relationship with someone who knows Christ. The same principle holds true for Christian ministry: We learn spiritual leadership by watching the life and doctrine of a mature Christian leader. This was the training method that Jesus employed with his disciples and that they in turn passed on to others.

Paul's first letter to Timothy came near the end of their long mentoring relationship in ministry. Timothy had served as the apostle's companion and colleague for nearly twenty years (see Acts 16:1-3), and now he was in charge of his own church at Ephesus. As we listen to Paul's advice about how to handle various problems Timothy is facing in ministry, Paul becomes our mentor as well.

The Structure

The epistle opens with a greeting from an aging apostle to his young son in the faith (1:1-2) and closes with a personal exhortation and general benediction (6:20-21). In the middle he makes a clear statement of his purpose in writing (3:14-16). What follows is a brief outline to aid your reading and analysis of 1 Timothy:

Theology (1:3-20). Paul urges Timothy to fulfill his ministerial calling to defend true doctrine against false teachers within the church.

Liturgy (2:1-15). On the assumption that public worship helps preserve the church from error, Paul commends mission-minded prayer for the men of the church (2:1-8) and modest submission for its women (2:9-15).

Polity (3:1-13). On the assumption that godly leadership is the best defense against doctrinal error, Paul lists the spiritual qualifications for elders (or "overseers," 3:1-7), deacons (or "servants," 3:8-10, 12-13), and perhaps deaconesses (or "wives," 3:11).

Timothy's Training (4:1-16). Paul reiterates Timothy's charge and gives the young pastor personal instructions for his progress in ministry. In both public and private, he is called to counteract false teaching by the godliness of his example: "Keep a close watch on how you live and on your teaching" (4:16).

House Rules (5:1–6:2). Paul gives Timothy instructions for his pastoral relationships with and social responsibilities to young and old, men and women, masters and slaves, and especially widows (5:3-16).

Motives for Ministry (6:3-19). Paul contrasts the pride and greed that motivate false teachers with the righteousness, godliness, and contentment to which Timothy should aspire as a true man of God.

Key Words and Phrases

- *Charge (1:3, 18; 5:21; 6:17 [ESV])*: As an apostle, Paul gives Timothy authoritative commands. Other translations use *command, urge.*
- *Trustworthy saying (1:15; 3:1; 4:9)*: Paul affirms the reliability of these common doctrinal or practical statements from the early church.
- Other key words that highlight major themes in the epistle are *faith* (which occurs nineteen times), *godliness, doctrine, sound,* and *truth.*

Key Doctrines and Themes

Ecclesiology. The letter virtually provides a manual for church organization.

The Fall. Satan's deception of the woman brought sin into the world (2:13-14).

The Incarnation. Christ came in the flesh, lived a righteous life, and is now in heaven (3:16).

Salvation. By the mercy of God, Jesus came to save even the very worst sinners (1:15-16); he is the one, divinely appointed Mediator between unrighteous sinners and a holy God (2:3-6)—the only Savior there is.

The Second Coming. At just the right time, Jesus Christ will return to earth in all the glory of heaven (6:13-16).

KEY VERSES

"I am writing these things to you now . . . so that if I am delayed, you will know how people must conduct themselves in the household of God. This is the church of the living God, which is the pillar and foundation of the truth" (3:14-15). Unable to come and help Timothy in person, Paul has a dual concern with doctrine and life: In order to hold up and hold out the truth, the church must have its house in order.

Tips for Reading or Teaching 1 Timothy

Keep in mind that Timothy received this letter while serving in Ephesus and that other parts of that church's story appear elsewhere in the New Testament. To review its founding, its conflict with paganism, and the relationship of its leaders with the apostle Paul, read Acts 19 and 20:17-38. To learn what happened later on, read Revelation 2:1-7. The theme of false teaching runs through all these passages (notice Paul's prediction in Acts 20:29-30).

As you work through 1 Timothy, ask, What were the personal motivations and core convictions of the false teachers? What effect was their teaching having on the church? How were Paul's practical instructions to Timothy designed to protect the church from these dangers?

Contribution of the Book to the Bible's Story of Salvation in Christ

Paul spends less time talking about Christ here

than he does in his other letters, presumably because Timothy was already well grounded in the gospel. Nevertheless, Paul shares his testimony of the saving grace that Christ showed to him as the worst of sinners (1:12-17) and offers a hymn of praise to Jesus as the incarnate, risen, and ascended Christ (3:16). He also emphasizes that salvation is not the exclusive property of a small group of teachers who have special knowledge; it is offered to everyone who believes in Jesus Christ (4:10), the One who "gave his life to purchase freedom for everyone" (2:6).

quick overview of 1 timothy

1:1-20	Paul's main charge to Timothy: to stop the false teaching of the false teachers
2:1–3:16	Paul's instructions for Timothy: general principles that help promote and preserve sound doctrine
4:1–6:21	More instructions for Timothy: practical advice for a pastor's relationship with different groups of people in the church

Applying the Book

First Timothy is full of practical advice on issues we still face today: doctrinal error, confusion over what constitutes proper worship, a lack of qualified leaders, materialism. Pay special attention to the instructions Paul gives to people who share your situation in life as a man, a woman, a boss, an employee, an elder, a deacon, and/or a pastor. At the same time, recognize that you may also find personal application in Paul's instructions to others. For example, what Paul says about training for godliness applies to every Christian, not just to pastors. Similarly, the qualifications for elders provide a useful checklist for every Christian man. Also pay attention to the guidelines given for the spiritual care of different kinds of people in the church, especially those with special needs, such as widows. Finally, take note of Paul's warnings to the wealthy and his instructions for servant-hearted stewardship.

PERSPECTIVES
ON THE BOOK OF 1 TIMOTHY

Highly relevant to our own times. John Calvin

The congregations of Ephesus were five to eight years old when Paul wrote 1 Timothy. Growing pains were still there, issuing from such important tasks as organizing, teaching, correcting, and unifying. Timothy had a full-time job. Irving L. Jensen

It contains apostolic instruction on the priority of prayer, on gender roles in the conduct of public worship, on the relations between church and state, and on the biblical basis for world evangelization. The apostle goes on to write about local church leadership, the conditions of eligibility for the pastorate, and how young leaders can ensure that their ministry is accepted, and not despised or rejected on account of their youth. Other subjects include the doctrine of creation, and its application to our everyday behavior, the principles governing the church's social work, the remuneration and disciplining of pastors, the superiority of contentment over covetousness, the call to radical holiness, and the dangers and duties of the rich. John R. W. Stott

First and Second Timothy and Titus are called "Pastoral Letters" to distinguish them from other letters of the New Testament written to churches rather than individual pastors. . . . Addressed to particular pastors charged with the care of specific churches, they tend to guide pastoral activity generally. Thomas C. Oden

2 TIMOTHY

Paul's Last Will and Testament

FORMAT. 4 chapters, 83 verses

IMPLIED PURPOSE. To inspire God's servants to persevere in the midst of the sufferings of Christian life and ministry, even unto death

AUTHOR'S PERSPECTIVE. While waiting on death row, Paul writes as a dying apostle who has finished the great fight of the faith and is passing on his last spiritual legacy. Whereas the tone of 1 Timothy was persistently practical, in this letter Paul writes with more personal and passionate affection.

IMPLIED AUDIENCE. Paul writes to Timothy as his beloved son and the minister who will carry the gospel to the coming generation. We can assume that Paul also expected Timothy to share this letter with the Christians in Ephesus and elsewhere.

WHAT UNIFIES THE BOOK. Many reminders of the strong personal connection between Paul and Timothy; the theme of faithful endurance through the trials of ministry, as exemplified by Paul and expected of Timothy

SPECIAL FEATURE. The apostle's final testimony: "I have fought the good fight, I have finished the race, I have kept the faith" (4:7, ESV).

The dying words of a godly person are treasured forever. As an example, consider the famous last words of John Newton, former slave trader and author of "Amazing Grace": "My memory is nearly gone, but I remember two things—that I am a great sinner, and that Christ is a great Saviour."

DID YOU KNOW?
The essential doctrine of the inspiration of Scripture is partly drawn from 2 Timothy 3:16, which says, "All Scripture is inspired." More literally, this verse says that all Scripture is "*ex-spired*." In other words, it is breathed out by God, and thus it comes with his full authority and perfection.

Paul's second letter to Timothy, the last letter he ever wrote, was written from a Roman jail while he awaited execution. It gives us what are nearly the dying words of the apostle—a man who was facing the end of his life and ministry and who had suffered abandonment by most of his friends. As we read the epistle, we draw close to the old apostle so that we can hear the whisper of his last words to the church.

The Structure
After one of his typical salutations (1:1-2), Paul exhorts Timothy to do the following things:

Guard the Good Deposit (Chapter 1). In light of his own sufferings and impending death, Paul exhorts Timothy to be faithful to his calling as a Christian and a minister and especially to safeguard sound doctrine for the church.

Be an Approved Workman (Chapter 2). This chapter lays out a pattern for Christian ministry that reproduces disciples (vv. 1-2), endures hardship (vv. 3-13), sticks to Scripture (vv. 14-18), and pursues holiness (vv. 19-26).

Understand the Last Days (3:1-9). As he describes the terrible times that will precede the second coming of Christ, Paul highlights three ungodly affections: love of self (narcissism), love of money (materialism), and love of pleasure (hedonism).

Continue What You Have Learned (3:10–4:5). At a time of moral decadence and spiritual ignorance, Timothy needs to keep his head squarely on his shoulders and remain true to Paul's godly example, to the Scriptures he has studied all his life, and to his calling as a teacher, preacher, and evangelist.

Come before Winter (4:6-22). As he makes his final greetings, fully preparing to die, Paul asks Timothy to visit him in prison and bring what he needs, especially since almost everyone else has abandoned him.

Key Doctrines and Themes

Scripture. The letter includes Paul's famous manifesto about the inspiration of Scripture and its usefulness for all of life (3:16-17).

Eschatology. Looking beyond the end of his life, Paul describes both the difficult days of the last times (3:1-5) and the glories God is waiting to reveal (1:10-12; 2:10; 4:1, 8, 18).

quick overview of 2 timothy

1:1–2:26	Courageously endure present sufferings for the gospel.
3:1–4:22	Faithfully serve Christ, through suffering, to the very end.

Perseverance. By exhortation as well as example, Paul challenges us to "be ready to suffer . . . for the sake of the Good News" (1:8) until we ourselves have remained faithful and finished the race.

The Church (Ecclesiology). By telling Timothy how to pass on the faith, Paul charts the course for gospel ministry after the age of the apostles.

Contribution of the Book to the Bible's Story of Salvation in Christ

Paul sees his sufferings as somehow connected to Christ's. He is suffering for the gospel (2:8-9) and sharing in the sufferings of Jesus (1:8). This is also the source of Paul's hope in suffering, as his letter places special emphasis on the resurrection of Jesus Christ (1:10; 2:8) and Christ's final role as the righteous judge (4:1, 8). Be sure not to miss the faithful saying (or hymn?) about Christ in 2:11-13.

Tips for Reading or Teaching 2 Timothy

Explore the meanings of the metaphors that Paul uses to describe Timothy's ministry, such as teacher, soldier, athlete, worker, farmer, vessel, and servant.

In Paul's exhortations to Timothy, he frequently appeals to his own life as an example or model for others to follow. Keep a list of what we learn about Paul's life and ministry as the epistle

KEY VERSES

"Timothy, my dear son, be strong through the grace that God gives you in Christ Jesus. You have heard me teach things that have been confirmed by many reliable witnesses. Now teach these truths to other trustworthy people who will be able to pass them on to others" (2:1-2). With these warm personal words, Paul exhorts Timothy to holy boldness and tells him how to safeguard sound theology for the coming generations of the church.

unfolds; then ponder ways in which all Christians might apply the model to their own lives.

Note the ways in which this epistle offers direction for Christians who are enduring hardships and preparing for death.

Applying the Book

The relevance of this epistle lies partly in how the sins and forms of opposition described in the letter correspond to our own cultural situation. Pay attention to these parallels. For example, how does the list of vices in chapter 3 act as a lens through which we can look at our own culture?

From the repeated reminders about being bold or not being ashamed (1:8, 12, 16; 2:15), we can infer that Timothy was by temperament a timid person. What motivations does the epistle offer for us to be bold?

perSPECTIVES
ON THE BOOK OF 2 TIMOTHY

In the first epistle the charge to Timothy as a manager of a great office guides Paul's whole thought, and the personal feeling towards a pupil and friend is submerged. In the second epistle the affection for Timothy dominates Paul's mind, though never to the exclusion of the charge with which Timothy is entrusted. Accordingly, the second epistle is far more personal to Timothy: it shows him far more as a human being in his relation to other human beings, and especially to Paul himself.
Sir William Ramsay

Life looks different when one is immediately facing death. This letter has a special clarity, serenity, and finality. Paul well knew that in all likelihood he was communicating his last words to an old friend, a traveling companion in mission for two decades. The circumstances of radical human limitation (helplessness, imprisonment, death) intensify natural human affections.
Thomas C. Oden

The apostle's overriding preoccupation . . . is with the truth, that it may be faithfully guarded and handed on. The pertinence of this theme . . . is

evident . . . for contemporary culture is being overtaken and submerged by the spirit of postmodernism. . . . The postmodern mind . . . declares that there is no such thing as objective or universal truth; that all so-called "truth" is purely subjective, being culturally conditioned; and that therefore we all have our own truth, which has [as] much right to respect as anybody else's. . . . In contrast to this relativization of truth, it is wonderfully refreshing to read Paul's unambiguous commitment to it.
John R. W. Stott

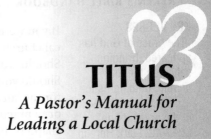

TITUS
A Pastor's Manual for Leading a Local Church

FORMAT. 3 chapters, 46 verses

IMPLIED PURPOSES. To advise a young pastor how to conduct his work in the church and to instruct him regarding the priorities he should set for his ministry

AUTHOR'S PERSPECTIVE. Paul writes with apostolic authority, as evidenced by the way in which he phrases most of his letter in the imperative. To pack in all the instruction he can in a letter that is short even by New Testament epistolary standards, he writes in a curt and businesslike manner. A certain urgency of tone emerges.

IMPLIED AUDIENCE. The stated recipient of this letter is Titus, a young pastor serving a church on the island of Crete, whose citizens were notorious for bad behavior. Although the book of Acts does not mention Titus, his name appears numerous times in the Epistles, where he emerges as Paul's coworker. Beyond the stated recipient, the letter is addressed to all pastors and laypeople. Its advice is timeless and binding for all churches.

WHAT UNIFIES THE BOOK. The rhetorical situation of an apostle in his late years advising a young pastor who had been converted under his ministry; the local church as the implied context for the letter; the blending of theology (right belief) and ethics (right behavior), evident in the very structure of the letter (see below).

SPECIAL FEATURES. The directive stance of the writer, who phrases most of the letter as commands; rooting Christian ethics directly in Christian theology so that the relationship between theology and behavior is not treated as a both-and relationship but rather as a cause-and-effect relationship; condensed content, the effect being like a telephone conversation in which the speaker knows he has only a few minutes available to talk

KEY VERSES

"The grace of God has appeared, bringing salvation for all people, training us to . . . live . . . godly lives in the present age" (2:11-12, ESV). Here in microcosm is the double thrust of the letter: the theology of salvation as the motivation and empowerment to live godly lives in the world. We see the same emphasis in 3:8: "that those who have believed in God may be careful to devote themselves to good works" (ESV).

If you were to write a manual to direct life in a local church, how would you shape the document? Should you compose an organizational chart? Should you write a job description for the pastor? for the laity? Should you give priority to theology or to practical Christian living? In just three short chapters, Paul's letter to Titus provides answers to these questions. Though addressed as a series of directives to the pastor, the letter also outlines what church members should believe and how they should behave.

The Form of the Book

Epistolary conventions form a bookend pattern around the book. At the beginning a rapturous salutation sweeps us into a sense of the wonder of faith in Christ (1:1-4), and at the end we have the customary greetings to friends (personalia) and a concluding benediction (3:12-15). Between these bookends the letter falls into four easily manageable units of thought:

- *1:5-16.* A contrast between good leaders and bad leaders: qualifications for church elders (1:5-9) and denunciation of false teachers, described as the exact opposite of good elders (1:10-16)
- *2:1-15.* A pair of passages that balance ethics and theology: commands for godly living (2:1-10) and a theological basis for godly living (2:11-15)
- *3:1-8.* The cycle repeated: commands for godly living (3:1-3) and a theological basis for godly living (3:4-8)
- *3:9-11.* Advice to a pastor

Despite the diversity of topics, most of the letter is phrased as a series of commands from Paul to Titus, the pastor.

Key Doctrines and Themes

The Glory of Salvation in Christ: For all its brevity, the book of Titus shines with ecstatic statements about what Christ has brought to believers. (One example would be 3:5: "He washed away our sins, giving us a new birth and new life through the Holy Spirit.")

Christology: Titus 2:13 is one of the few direct statements in the New Testament declaring that Jesus is God.

Ethics: Nearly half the letter deals with how elders and laity are supposed to live.

The Need to Practice One's Theology in One's Moral Life: Paul reminds Titus, "You yourself must be an example . . . by doing good works of every kind. Let everything you do reflect the integrity and seriousness of your teaching" (2:7).

Ecclesiology: The entire letter focuses on life in the church.

Conversion: Paul paints a vivid before-and-after picture of the prototypical life of the Christian (3:3-7).

The letter also makes striking, if brief, comments about *Christ's second coming* (2:13) and the *Holy Spirit* (3:4-7, a passage that also asserts *salvation by grace alone*).

> **THREE GREAT REVELATIONS FROM GOD**
> - He has revealed his word (1:3).
> - He has revealed his grace, bringing salvation to all people (2:11).
> - He has revealed his goodness and love, thereby saving us (3:4-5).

Tips for Reading or Teaching Titus

It is hard to know how to read or teach a list of commands, which is what makes up most of Titus. The meaning seems to be all on the surface. Here are some analytic grids that can spare you from finding nothing more to do than quote or paraphrase what is obvious:

You can note a basic division of the behavior that Paul commands into virtues and vices.

You can classify the virtues and vices into categories such as personal, spiritual, relational, and moral.

Beginning with your awareness that the letter deals with church life, you can assemble a composite portrait of a church that practices everything commanded in this letter.

Contribution of the Book to the Bible's Story of Salvation in Christ

The author keeps coming back to descriptions of what Christ has done for believers. There are repeated references to such bedrock doctrines as the redemption that Christ accomplished, his coming again, his mercy, justification by grace, and the power that Christ by the Holy Spirit gives believers to live godly lives. The whole letter teaches about the church that Christ has redeemed and commands.

Applying the Book

This letter is a small handbook on how to live the Christian life in the church. Reading it can raise one's consciousness on that subject and by way of reminder lead one to live as the author commands in the name of Christ. To apply this book requires a pliant and submissive spirit—a desire to be a godly person. Finally, this letter is a manual for church life; to apply it, a person needs to be the kind of church member the letter describes. This application is both individual for church members and corporate for the church as a local body.

PERSPECTIVES
ON THE BOOK OF TITUS

The letter to Titus is much like Paul's two letters to Timothy and was written for much the same purpose—to encourage and strengthen a young pastor whom he had discipled, in whom he had great confidence, and for whom he had great love as a spiritual father. He was passing the baton, as it were, to those young pastors who were ministering in difficult situations. . . . Titus is an evangelistic letter whose ultimate purpose was to prepare the church for more effective witness to unbelievers on Crete.
John MacArthur

[In the pastoral Epistles,] Paul's goal when speaking to certain social groups (men, women, slaves, the affluent), to church leaders (overseers/elders, deacons), to believers in general or to his coworkers is to restore stability to the churches and encourage the Christian life of witness. . . . In general, Paul sought to splice back together the belief and practice dimensions of Christian living that the heretics had separated with their emphasis on special knowledge and their careless disregard for conduct. Consequently, when Paul described genuine Christian living, his focus was very much on the observable life. Philip H. Towner

There is a lack of studied order, some subjects being treated more than once . . . without apparent premeditation. The various brief doctrinal statements are intermixed with personal requests or ecclesiastical advice.
Donald Guthrie

In 1 and 2 Timothy the emphasis is on doctrine: in Titus it is on good works. First Timothy is a charge. Second Timothy is a challenge. The epistle to Titus is a caution—a strong and urgent reminder that sound faith must be accompanied by good works. . . . These three "Pastoral" epistles are really a trinity in unity, exhorting us to "guard" the precious "deposit" of the Gospel. In 1 Timothy we are to protect it. In 2 Timothy we are to proclaim it. In Titus we are to practise it. J. Sidlow Baxter

PHILEMON
The Return of the Slave

FACT SHEET

FORMAT. One chapter, 25 verses

IMPLIED PURPOSES. In its original context, the purpose was to instruct the Christian master of a runaway servant regarding how to receive the servant after he had been converted to faith in Christ. In this historical particular, we are intended to see a more universal principle governing forgiveness and the relationships of Christians to one another in brotherly love.

AUTHOR'S PERSPECTIVE. This is the most personal of Paul's letters and is accordingly simple in style and focus. Given the sensitive nature of the situation that occasioned the letter, this piece of correspondence is a masterpiece of tact and indirect persuasion.

IMPLIED AUDIENCE. The master of a servant; the master is named Philemon, and the servant is Onesimus. The local church and specific people were also part of the original audience (see v. 2).

WHAT UNIFIES THE BOOK. The rhetorical situation of the author's trying to persuade a friend to do something contrary to normal human inclination: to receive a runaway servant as a brother in Christ instead of punishing him

SPECIAL FEATURE. The situation that occasioned the letter, namely, the return of a runaway slave

The human race has always practiced a pecking order in which social and economic gradations are the basis for asserting a hierarchy of power and privilege. But the Christian faith elevates spiritual equality in Christ over social conventions of power and privilege. Paul's letter to Philemon highlights this spiritual equality, even while maintaining the legitimacy of a hierarchy of authority and social roles such as master and servant.

KEY VERSE

"He is no longer like a slave to you. He is more than a slave, for he is a beloved brother" (1:16). We see here the central teaching of this letter: that belief in Christ is a great equalizer—one that takes precedence over the external distinctions that prevail in the world. This does not mean that all external distinctions among roles are denied.

The Structure and Unity

The outline of the book is simple: salutation (vv. 1-3), Paul's praise of Philemon's love and faith (vv. 4-7), Paul's appeal on behalf of the returning servant, Onesimus (vv. 8-22), and final greetings and benediction (vv. 23-25). Permeating this organization is a before-and-after principle that contrasts Onesimus's situation before his conversion to his situation after his conversion. His relationship to his master, Philemon, follows the same contrast. Finally, three key players—Paul, Philemon, and Onesimus, all of whom know each other well—lend unity to the letter.

Key Doctrines and Themes

Forgiveness. Christians need to forgive those who wrong them.

The Equality of Believers in Christ. While hierarchies of authority or social roles do exist and are legitimate, in Christ all believers are on an equal spiritual footing.

Community. As seen in the relationships among the three key characters in this epistle, Christians are to live out their faith in the context of community (i.e., the local church).

How to Read or Teach Philemon

The best analytic lens through which to explore the book is to identify from start to finish how everything that Paul writes shows his persuasive strategy designed to make a winsome case for Philemon's acceptance of Onesimus as a Christian brother.

Contribution of the Book to the Bible's Story of Salvation in Christ

This short letter shows that belief in Christ affects relationships among

Servants and Slaves

While slavery was widely practiced in the ancient Near East, there are some striking differences between the practice of slavery in the Old Testament and that found under Greek and Roman law. Under the Hebrew system the slave always maintained a limited set of rights and was viewed as a person made in God's image. Under the Roman system it was easy to view a slave as a person below the rank of citizen, and thus slaves became simply chattel, or property, of the slave owner.

The practice of slaveholding varied tremendously from region to region and across time. Some forms of slavery were permanent while others were temporary; some were voluntary, others involuntary. It is especially important to know that the slavery described in the Old Testament was never precisely equivalent to the racially-based servitude that became pervasive in the United States. Most New Testament references to "slave" and "servant" are to indentured servants (employees who willingly contracted to work for an employer and gave up some of their personal rights to do so).

In the ancient Near East, people became slaves for a number of reasons: by capture, by purchase, by birth, as restitution, by defaulting on debts, by the free choice of the slave (indentured servanthood), and by abduction. The Bible seems to accept at least some of these forms of slavery as legitimate economic relationships, especially when slaves had the real opportunity to gain their freedom (as was often the case in New Testament times). However, kidnapping people to serve as slaves—which perhaps most closely parallels the kind of slavery later practiced in the Western world—is expressly forbidden in the Scriptures (see Deuteronomy 24:7; 1 Timothy 1:10).

Slavery is often used metaphorically to describe our spiritual bondage to sin (e.g., Romans 7:14). God's remedy for our slavery to sin is redemption, which may be defined as release from captivity through the payment of a price. Notable examples include Israel's exodus from Egypt (Psalm 105), Boaz's redemption of Ruth (Ruth 4:1-12), and Hosea's redemption of Gomer (Hosea 3:1-2). But the supreme redemption is our release from sin through Christ's death on the cross: "The ransom he paid was not mere gold or silver. It was the precious blood of Christ, the sinless, spotless Lamb of God" (1 Peter 1:18-19). The New Testament sometimes contrasts our old slavery to sin with our new sonship to God through faith in Christ (e.g., Galatians 4:7). Somewhat paradoxically, it also describes the Christian life as a new form of servitude: not servile slavery but willing and joyful service to Christ (e.g., Romans 1:1; 1 Corinthians 7:22; 2 Timothy 2:24).

believers and that it takes precedence over (without eliminating) the social roles among Christians.

Applying the Book

The book of Titus offers a picture of how Christians should live in relationship to one another. The keynotes are accepting one another as equal recipients of forgiveness in Christ, giving generously, thinking the best of fellow believers, and seeking the best for fellow believers. The book also teaches that a person's relationship with Christ affects all other relationships.

PERSPECTIVES
ON THE BOOK OF PHILEMON

Of all Paul's letters, Philemon is the most personal in tone: artless, unpretentious, and direct. Harold Lindsell

[Philemon] is dominated with metaphors of social relationship. The world of these metaphors is a large household established as an alternative society. Dictionary of Biblical Imagery

The Epistle to Philemon is a lesson in the art of Christian relationships. Nelson's Illustrated Bible Dictionary

[Philemon is] a delightful little letter, simple and affectionate as the occasion required. J. Gresham Machen

The briefest of Paul's epistles (only 334 words in the Greek text) is a model of courtesy, discretion, and loving concern for the forgiveness of one who would otherwise face the sentence of death. Bruce Wilkinson and Kenneth Boa

HEBREWS
The Dangers of Drifting

FORMAT. 13 chapters, 303 verses

IMPLIED PURPOSE. To warn readers not to relinquish their faith in Christ but instead to endure and grow

AUTHOR'S PERSPECTIVE. Alarmed by the spiritual danger of his readers, the author combines (1) sustained theological argument and (2) direct appeal founded on the person and work of Christ, who serves as a model to imitate.

IMPLIED AUDIENCE. Although the letter names no recipient, there are clues that the author is writing to a group of persecuted believers with whom he has acquaintance. We can infer that they were Jewish converts to Christianity and that they were in danger of drifting from their Christian faith and practice, partly because of persecution and partly because Judaism still held appeal. This book is designed for all Christians who are in danger of becoming lax in their faith and practice.

WHAT UNIFIES THE BOOK. Motifs of comparison (compared with other persons and things, Christ is declared better); Old Testament foreshadowings and New Testament fulfillments; the persuasive stance; a theological orientation (the author talks about issues such as atonement and faith); Christology

SPECIAL FEATURES. Typology (seeing Old Testament events and characters as foreshadowings of Christ's person and work); references to events and texts from the past; emphasis on sacrifice and atonement; the roll call of heroes and heroines of the faith (chapter 11); argument from lesser to greater (Christ being the greater), often drawing an analogy between something in the Old Testament (e.g., sacrifice) and Christ's person or work

FACT SHEET

CHALLENGES FACING THE READER OR TEACHER OF THIS BOOK.

1. The intricate theological arguments
2. The incessant quoting of Old Testament passages and practices
3. Repetition, especially of the theme of the superiority of Christ to Old Testament anticipations
4. The piecemeal organization of the book
5. A method of argumentation that is partly foreign to us

HOW TO MEET THE CHALLENGES.

1. Take time to grasp the individual theological arguments.
2. Have the patience required to see how and why the author quotes the specific Old Testament passages that he does.
3. Read the book unit by unit on repeated occasions.
4. As always, trust what you see in the text, not what tidy outlines say you are supposed to be seeing.
5. In intellectual arguments, ancient Hebrews (1) kept repeating an idea until the listener agreed with it and (2) quoted authorities and cited examples from the past.

Faith . . . is the art of holding on to things your reason has once accepted, in spite of your changing moods. . . . One must train the habit of Faith. . . . If you have once accepted Christianity, then some of its main doctrines [must] be deliberately held before your mind for some time every day. . . . We have to be continually reminded of what we believe. . . . [No belief] will automatically remain alive in the mind. It must be fed. And as a matter of fact, if you examined a hundred people who had lost their faith in Christianity, I wonder how many of them would turn out to have been reasoned out of it by honest argument? Do not most people simply drift away?

C. S. LEWIS
Mere Christianity

AN OUTLINE OF
HEBREWS

13 Rules for Living

12:3-29 The Need to Endure

11:1–12:2 Mighty Acts of Faith

10:19-39 The Need to Endure

8:1–10:18 The New and Better Covenant

7 Christ as Superior Priest

6 Warning against Negligence

4:14–5:14 Christ as Superior Priest

4:1-13 Warning against Rejecting Christ

3 Christ's Superiority to Moses

2 Exhortations to Embrace Christ

1 Christ's Superiority to Angels

Christians in Need of Instruction and the Will to Endure

Heroes of Faith

Christians at Risk

Recipients of the New Covenant

Priests

Christians at Risk

Priests

Moses and the Jews of the Exodus

Prophets and Angels

Christ's Followers

Christ's Sacrifice

Christ's Priesthood

Christ's Person

The Superior Life of Faith

The Superior Covenant

The Superior Savior

Modern advertising is based on convincing us that everything newer is better. The claim is sometimes true, but surely we have all developed a healthy skepticism regarding that claim. The book of Hebrews offers an interesting slant on the matter: It tells us about the most decisive instance on record in which the "newer" was indeed better.

The Form of the Book

The main form is not the letter but the theological treatise or written sermon. The first nine and a half chapters conduct a sustained theological argument about the superiority of Christ over a number of rivals. These chapters read like an essay that has a thesis, a series of subordinate generalizations, and supporting proof (consisting of data and commentary on that data).

Second, the book reads like a sermon. While some have made a case that the first ten chapters are a sermon, sermonic elements become dominant only halfway through chapter 10, with its fervent appeals to maintain the faith and live like worthy followers of Christ. Still, there are appeals scattered throughout the earlier chapters that resemble what a preacher might say to a congregation.

Third, much of the material has the feel of other New Testament Epistles, so it is not wrong to think of Hebrews as a letter. But we need to realize that epistolary conventions appear directly only in the last eight verses of the book. Like other epistles, Hebrews is occasioned by a specific crisis, and it addresses specific issues and questions.

The Aim of the Book and Unifying Elements

The more closely you study Hebrews, the clearer it becomes how thoroughly the book is unified by the author's pastoral concern to dissuade his readers from drifting from their faith. This persuasive element governs almost everything we find in the book, including the theological argument about Christ's superiority and the continual exhortations about how to live.

Within this persuasive aim, the book is strongly unified by elements that are almost continuously present. The fact that the following things are a pervasive presence does not mean, however, that the organization of the book is easy to follow. Here are the unifying factors:

- The Old Testament frame of reference
- The ways in which Christ and his sacrifice are superior to all rivals
- Preoccupation with holding up people from the past as models in one way or another
- The superiority motif (Christ and the Christian life are compared to other things and are declared superior.)

Key Doctrines

Christology. From start to finish, this book rings with the truth of who Christ is and what he has done.

Salvation. Except for the book of Romans, there is no more extended biblical discussion of salvation or redemption than this one, which stresses Christ as high priest and mediator.

Faith. Hebrews 11 is a high point of what the Bible says about faith.

Covenant. The book details how the old covenant was fulfilled and supplanted by the new covenant in Christ.

Scripture or *Revelation.* The book of Hebrews clearly delineates how the Bible is a progressive revelation in which the crucial change was from the Old Testament to the New Testament.

Eschatology. It is possible to collect many individual passages that talk about the life to come.

Perseverance. The general drift of the book is to warn Christians to persist in belief and to avoid apostasy.

Tips for Reading or Teaching Hebrews

Once again you need to be cautious in your use of tidy outlines of Hebrews that you may find in commentaries and handbooks. These outlines tend to make it look as though the line of argument is continuous. But if, for example, you isolate most of chapters 2–4, chapter 6, 10:19-39, and most of chapter 12—in other words, a third of the book—you will see that they are only slightly tied to the ongoing argument about the superiority of Christ and are instead appeals to readers not to abandon their faith but rather to pursue Christ earnestly.

You therefore need to have in mind two organizational schemes—an outline of the type that we provide in this handbook and the idea of a back-and-forth rhythm between theological argument and practical exhortation on the specific topic of not abandoning the faith.

Partly because of the abundance of Old Testament quotations and accompanying commentary on them, the content of this book is dense. You will need to resolve to think carefully and not simply to read for a devotional uplift.

This book is so rooted in the Old Testament that you could use it as a program for reading parts of the Old Testament in conjunction with it.

This book requires that you use imagination to form mental pictures of something like Christ's entering into a Tabernacle in 9:11-14.

quick overview of hebrews

1:1–7:28	The superiority of Christ to all other creatures, particularly Old Testament examples of excellence
8:1–10:18	The superiority of the new covenant in Christ, based on his atonement
10:19–13:25	The life of faith described, exemplified, and commanded

The Flow of the Book

The Superiority of Christ to Prophets and Angels (Chapters 1–2). Here is an analytic grid to guide your interaction with the passage: Analyze how the author (1) shows the superiority of Christ, (2) reminds us that in this unit he is chiefly comparing Christ with angels, (3) intermittently lets us know that he wants us to make practical application of the theology he is outlining, and (4) uses the Old Testament to support his line of argument. Also, isolate places where the author returns to his implied purpose of warning against abandoning the faith.

The Superiority of Christ to Moses, with Warnings Not to Abandon the Faith (3:1–4:13). Here, too, you can look for the ways in which the author uses Old Testament data to prove the superiority of Christ, this time in comparison with one of the greatest heroes of the Hebrew faith. Although the starting point is the comparison between Christ and Moses, that subject gets only six verses, and the rest of the unit is a warning not to fall into unbelief and miss the promised rest of God (as the Hebrews of the Exodus did).

The Superiority of Christ to the Old Testament Priesthood (4:14–7:28). This section and the next require you to apply a common grid: (1) a line

Heresies in the New Testament Church

Probably the greatest danger for the early church was doctrinal error. Nearly every New Testament Epistle deals with the need to defend truth against false theology. As Paul said to the elders of Ephesus: "I know that false teachers, like vicious wolves, will come in among you after I leave, not sparing the flock" (Acts 20:29).

Two major first-century heresies threatened Christian orthodoxy. The first was the legalistic teaching of the *Judaizers*, who wanted to make certain Old Testament rituals an essential part of the Christian faith. In particular they insisted on making the ceremony of circumcision mandatory for Gentiles: "Some men from Judea arrived and began to teach the believers: 'Unless you are circumcised as required by the law of Moses, you cannot be saved'" (Acts 15:1). The best way to learn how the church responded to the Judaizers is to read the report of the Jerusalem Council in Acts 15 or study the book of Galatians. But to summarize, the apostles argued that to add *anything* to the finished work of Jesus Christ is to overthrow God's grace in the gospel. We are justified by faith alone, not by circumcision or any other work in addition to faith.

The other major heresy did not come from Judaism but from pagan philosophy. It was known as *Gnosticism*, a term derived from the Greek word *gnosis*, "knowledge." The Gnostics claimed to possess secret or superior knowledge about spiritual things. Properly speaking, Gnosticism did not reach its peak until the second century, but some Gnostic ideas were common already in the first century. The apostles responded to these ideas by warning the early church against "those who oppose you with their so-called knowledge" (1 Timothy 6:20).

Gnostics drew a sharp distinction between body and spirit, elevating the latter while denigrating the former. As a result, they tended to downplay or even dismiss the incarnation and bodily resurrection of Jesus Christ (as well as the bodily resurrection of believers). They also tended to be suspicious of legitimate physical pleasures, such as eating meat or enjoying sexual intimacy within marriage.

Because it claimed to offer superior knowledge, Gnosticism threatened the doctrine of revelation and the Christian faith in a clear word from God. Because it rejected the physical world, it threatened the doctrine of creation and the Christian hope in the redemption of the body as well as the soul.

of argument that asserts the superiority of Christ to something in the Old Testament, and (2) intermittent practical appeals to the readers to behave in a manner in keeping with what Christ has done.

KEY VERSE

"Since then we have a great high priest who has passed through the heavens, Jesus, the Son of God, let us hold fast our confession" (4:14, ESV). Hebrews has two main themes: the completely sufficient sacrifice and covenant of Christ and how devastating it would be to relinquish one's faith in Christ.

The Superiority of the New Covenant in Christ to the Old Covenant, Mainly in Regard to the Sacrifices under the Two Covenants (8:1–10:18). Apply the twofold grid noted in the paragraph above.

The Life of Faith That Should Characterize Those Who Believe in This Superior Christ (10:19–12:2). Look for the ways in which the author (1) now moves from theology to the practice of it, (2) brings into focus his implied purpose of encouraging endurance in the Christian faith, and (3) balances exhortation in Christian living (10:19-39) with praise of the quality of faith of Old Testament examples (11:1–12:2).

Admonitions Not to Abandon the Faith (12:3-29). You can look for passages in which the author (1) commands and warns his readers to endure and (2) offers reasons for these admonitions (as in 12:22-24, which describes how believers in Christ have come to Mount Zion, filled with spiritual blessings).

General Exhortations in Christian Living (Chapter 13). This is the familiar paraenesis of the Epistles—the miscellaneous list of rules for living, concluded by a benediction and personal greeting. Even here, though, you can look for ways in which the things that the author chose to include echo earlier parts of his letter and his overall purpose of exhorting Christians who were in danger of drifting from the faith.

The Main Themes

1. Christ is a completely sufficient basis for salvation. No religious rites are necessary in addition to the worship of Christ and belief in him.
2. The Old Testament can still teach us about the person and work of Christ, even though its ceremonies have ended.
3. The Bible tells us what we need to know about belief and practice. If we fail in our spiritual lives, it is because we are not holding on to

the supremely sufficient Christ and/or because we do not adequately appreciate the riches that we have in Christ.

4. Faith is every bit as wonderful as the Christian tradition has said it is.

Contribution of the Book to the Bible's Story of Salvation in Christ

This book's contribution to the story line of the Bible is unique. It explores in detail how the once-for-all sacrifice of Christ fulfilled and thus rendered obsolete the Old Testament system of sacrifice. Throughout this handbook we have shown how Old Testament books contain foreshadowings of what Christ would eventually accomplish. The book of Hebrews is the centerpiece of that discussion.

> **EIGHT "BETTER" THINGS IN HEBREWS**
> - a better hope (7:19)
> - a better covenant (7:22; 8:6)
> - better promises (8:6)
> - better sacrifices (9:23)
> - a better possession (10:34, ESV)
> - a better place (11:16)
> - a better life (11:35)
> - a better word (12:24, ESV)

Applying the Book

The book of Hebrews is both theological and practical. On the theological side, it gives us extensive reasons to believe that Christ is all we need for salvation—that in fact, it would be perverse to dabble with any other religion. On the application side we need to believe the truth of Hebrews with our minds and to move from intellectual conviction to personal devotion and commitment to Christ and the faith he established.

A second application is that the book of Hebrews is the most sustained warning in the Bible about the dangers of drifting in one's Christian life. We can apply the book by daily choosing to believe in Christ and follow him.

A third application is to assent to the implied apologetic perspective of the book. We need to know *why* we believe in Christ rather than in someone else, and we need to take seriously the fact that correct theology—correct thinking about God—is foundational for the Christian life.

In addition, there are things that believers need to practice, such as believing in the blood of Christ for redemption, knowing the Bible thoroughly, trusting in Christ's intercession when we pray, confronting Christians who drift from the path or adopt error, and following the examples of heroes of the faith.

PERSPECTIVES
ON THE BOOK OF HEBREWS

*What we call the Letter to the Hebrews is not, in fact, a letter at all. . . .
Even though it has some epistle-like flourishes at the end . . . the main
body of Hebrews bears all the marks of an early Christian sermon. . . .
Early Christian sermons were heavily influenced by the style of preaching
done in the synagogue, and in terms of structure and methods of biblical
interpretation, Hebrews appears to be an example of a sermon that is
rabbinical in design, Christian in content, and heroic in length.*
Thomas G. Long

*The entire theme of the epistle is built around the word "better." . . . The
greatest single value of the book of Hebrews is its teaching on the present
ministry and priesthood of Christ.* Merrill C. Tenney

*The Epistle to the Hebrews is really a homily first delivered orally and then
sent to other communities for their encouragement. . . . We must listen to
it rather than read it. . . . This implies a greater involvement and a
stronger sense of being addressed directly. The urgency of Hebrews
becomes more understandable to us when we realize that its "author" is in
fact a preacher whose aim is to move his community to conversion and to
fidelity.* Juliana Casey

*The progressiveness of the divine revelation . . . is the master thought
of the Epistle. Christ is the culmination of the long succession of lawgiver
and prophets. They existed for his sake; they were a preparation for him.*
J. Gresham Machen

*It is one of the two greatest theological treatises in the New Testament. . . .
The keyword . . . is "better," which occurs thirteen times. . . . The runner-
up idea is that of finality.* J. Sidlow Baxter

*Christ Divine and Human (1–4), The Shadow and the Real (5–10), A
Call to Faith (11–13). The three overlapping ideas in the book are Christ's
supremacy as God's word to man, Christ's supremacy as man's way to
God, the need for faithfulness.* J. H. Davies' headings for the three main
sections in his outline of Hebrews

JAMES
Faith That Works

FORMAT. 5 chapters, 108 verses

IMPLIED PURPOSES. Because of the famous discourse on faith and works in chapter 2, the universal view is that James wrote to persuade Christians that practical Christian living validates the genuineness of their faith. But beyond that discourse, the content of the book as a whole implies that James's purpose was to instill correct thinking and correct behavior, as other New Testament Epistles do.

AUTHOR'S PERSPECTIVE. The author writes in the tradition of the wisdom teachers of the Bible, observing truths and commanding certain behaviors in the form of proverbs. At the level of content, James is most known for his practical bent of mind, as he insists that faith must show itself in action. In arguing this, the author shows an unusual energy and forcefulness in his writing.

IMPLIED AUDIENCE. The opening verse identifies the original audience as converted Jews living outside Palestine. But there are no references to specific places and churches, and the very format of the proverb makes the message universal and timeless.

WHAT UNIFIES THE BOOK. The proverbial style: an abundance of *aphorisms* (concise, memorable sayings); also the emphasis on the practical demonstration of Christian faith

SPECIAL FEATURES. Lack of a continuous line of argument; preference for clusters of proverbs; the persuasive stance of the author, who seems almost continuously to be conducting a debate against an imaginary opponent or rousing moral sleepers to action; an ethical rather than theological focus; a frequent scolding tone

If you were assigned to write an open letter to your church on the need for Christians to practice their faith in observable acts, how would you package your appeal? Would you try to conduct an abstract argument? Would you quote Bible passages? Would you scold your readers? What topics would you include? Would you provide an abundance of real-life examples of faith in action? The book of James lets us know how the brother of Jesus decided to handle the assignment.

The Form of the Book

The letter of James is mainly a collection of proverbs. Some of these are proverb clusters that result in paragraph units, but if you look closely at many of these, you will find that even short paragraphs in this book often lack a unifying subject.

DID YOU KNOW?
- The author of the book, who became a prominent Christian leader, was almost certainly the brother of Jesus.
- Martin Luther, with his strong convictions about salvation by faith alone, disparaged the book of James, with its emphasis on works, as "an epistle full of straw."
- There are approximately sixty imperatives in the 108 verses that make up the book.

Consider the following passage (which most English translations isolate as a paragraph) as a test case of what you will repeatedly find in James: "Understand this, my dear brothers and sisters: You must all be quick to listen, slow to speak, and slow to get angry. Human anger does not produce the righteousness God desires. So get rid of all the filth and evil in your lives, and humbly accept the word God has planted in your hearts, for it has the power to save your souls" (1:19-21). No matter how long you stare at that passage, no single label will cover it (except "Christian living"), though the commentaries and handbooks attempt to convince you that the passage deals with dissension in the church or the need to show faith by deeds or endurance in testing. Our caution is a comment against the commentators, not a comment on the writer of this epistle, who simply aims to be comprehensive.

The rule that you need to follow is, therefore, this: Trust your own eyes as you stare at a passage.

The principle element of the book of James is wisdom literature, consisting primarily of collected proverbs. Some of these are so varied as to shift the subject with every sentence. Elsewhere you will find brief paragraphs that deal with a single subject. And sometimes you will find longer proverb clusters that develop a line of argument. It hardly needs to be said, in addition, that this collection of sayings is not a

5:19-20 Restoring a Believer — Longer Unit | Single-Proverb Unit

5:13-18 Prayer of Faith — One-Verse Unit

5:12 Avoiding Oaths

5:7-11 Exercising Patience

5:1-6 Avoiding Trusting in Riches

4:13-17 Avoiding Presumption against Providence — Three Longer Units

3:13–4:12 True vs. False Wisdom, God vs. the World, Avoiding Judgmentalism — Collection of Short Units

3:1-12 Control of Speech

2:14-26 Faith Proved by Works

2:1-13 Not Showing Favoritism — Three "Essays" in Proverb Form

1:2-27 Testing, Wisdom, Riches, God's Gifts, Control of Tongue, Active Faith, True Religion — Paragraph-Length Units

1:1 Salutation

AN OUTLINE OF

JAMES

genuine letter in the sense that the other Epistles are, nor is it structured like the conventional epistle.

Key Doctrines
Ethics, or *Sanctification.* James is a handbook for practical Christian living.
Faith and Works. Underlying all of the ethical commands of this book, you can infer theological principles.

Tips for Reading or Teaching James
Rather than rely on outlines built around unifying themes, have confidence in the diversity you see in front of you as you stare at a passage.

Apply what you know about wisdom literature and proverbial thinking (take another look at "The Proverb as a Form of Writing" on page 257 and "Wisdom Literature" on page 271).

quick overview of james

No outline for a quick overview of this book is possible. It is a collection of proverbial units of varying lengths. The outline on the previous page shows that there is a pattern of alternating sections of very brief topical units and longer proverb clusters on individual topics. Highlights include warnings against showing favoritism, sections on proving faith by works and on controlling the tongue, and information about the prayer of faith.

The Flow of the Book
A Collection of Proverb Units (Chapter 1). The book of James serves notice immediately that it is wisdom literature, which means that it relies heavily on the proverb as its preferred form. The style is aphoristic right from the start (an aphorism is a concise, memorable saying). Your only reliable guide to the first chapter is to "think paragraph." The subject changes with every paragraph. The favored approach in commentaries is to say that these verses deal with testing and/or patience under testing, but actually only two of the units deal with testing. Here are the topical units: joy in testing (vv. 2-4), confidently asking God for wisdom (vv. 5-8), warning about the transience of riches (vv. 9-11), multiple thoughts on testing (vv. 12-15), God as the source of good gifts (vv. 16-18), miscellaneous proverbs on living the Christian life (vv. 19-21), the need to put Christian truth into practice (vv. 22-25), and tests of true religion (vv. 26-27).

Two Proverb Clusters (2:1-13). Verses 1-7 prohibit showing partiality to rich people at the expense of the poor, and verses 8-13 branch out from that to the more general point that sins such as partiality make one subject to God's judgment because they represent a failure to live up to God's law in principle.

> **KEY VERSE**
> "Faith is dead without good works" (2:26). The big idea of the book is that faith is genuine only if it produces good works. The book itself is then a catalog of those good works.

A Sustained Argument on the Incompleteness of Faith without Works (2:14-26). In contrast to the piecemeal organization of the book thus far, this passage is structured like a speech in a debate and consists of the usual debate ingredients: a proposition, proofs, and rebuttals of the opponent's position. It is important to be aware that James does not contradict Paul's teaching on justification. Paul's answer to the question of what justifies a sinner before God is faith alone, not works. James asks the very different question of what justifies or proves a person's faith before *people*; his answer is good works.

A Proverb Cluster on the Need to Control One's Speech (3:1-12). This is a heavily poetic passage, consisting partly of analogies between the tongue and forces in nature. To understand *what* is being said, you need to interact with *how* it is said, namely, in the form of analogies.

Seven Proverb Clusters (3:13–5:12). Beware: Even though some of these passages begin with what looks like a unifying topic, by the time you reach the end of the unit the individual proverbs tug away from what you thought was an announced topic. With that caution in place, the general drift of the units is this: true versus false wisdom (3:13-18), the need to serve God rather the world (4:1-10), avoiding slander and a judgmental attitude toward fellow Christians (4:11-12), avoiding presumption against God's providence by thinking that we control our lives (4:13-17), warnings against the negatives of a wealthy lifestyle (5:1-6), the need to live patiently until Christ returns (5:7-11), and avoiding oaths (5:12).

The Efficacy of the Prayer of Faith (5:13-18). While the specific example is prayer for the sick, this situation is offered as an example of the broader principle of the prayer of faith.

Concluding Proverb on Restoring a Wandering Believer from Error to Truth (5:19-20). The self-contained nature of this pair of verses underscores the main thing you need to know about this book: It is an example of wisdom literature that relies on the proverb for its main content.

The Main Themes
1. God has given us rules by which to live the Christian life. He has not left us in doubt regarding what constitutes godly living.
2. Faith in Christ must be more than giving intellectual assent to doctrines. We must live out that faith in practical ways in our everyday lives.

Contribution of the Book to the Bible's Story of Salvation in Christ
The book of James does not give direct or detailed teaching about the person and work of Christ. Nevertheless, the book's contribution to the story of salvation in Christ is obvious: It fleshes out in a myriad of ways how saved people are supposed to live. This book gives us a picture of what Christ saved us to.

Applying the Book
Mark Twain once quipped, "It ain't the parts of the Bible that I can't understand that bother me, it is the parts that I do understand." The book of James is a guidebook to applying the Christian faith. It is not necessarily hard to understand; but to apply it, we need to do what it says, and that takes discipline and an abundance of God's grace. Part of the usefulness of this book is that it not only commands certain virtuous actions but also warns against certain attitudes (such as presumption, greed, prejudice, and doubt).

PERSPECTIVES
ON THE BOOK OF JAMES

A coat of many colors. E. W. Bauman

The Epistle of James is a religious and moral tract having the form, but only the form, of a letter. It contains counsels and reflections on a variety of topics relating to personal character and right conduct, but attains a certain unity from the writer's own traits of sincerity, good sense, and piety, which are manifest in every paragraph. . . . The aphorisms . . . are gathered in paragraphs. . . . [The designation of letter] throws no light on . . . the document itself, which shows in its contents nothing whatever of the specific character of a letter. James Hardy Ropes

His book could be described as a New Testament Book of Proverbs. . . . [James typically] announces a major theme or teaching and then follows up the teaching with stories, figures, and parables that illustrate his theme in either a negative or a positive fashion. . . . James' vivid pictures stick with us alongside the teaching themes. Even his word choices are more visual than they are abstract and ideological. Earl F. Palmer

The argument of the epistle is that true Christian faith must express itself in practical goodness. Hence, all the way through, the emphasis is on good works. . . . We may say that the theme of this epistle is the proofs of true faith. J. Sidlow Baxter

Paul deals primarily with the doctrine of justification before God, which comes not at all through works. . . . James, on the other hand, is dealing primarily with justification before men. G. Coleman Luck

Traits of a popular Greek form of satire known as the diatribe that are prevalent in James: imaginary dialogues, including question-and-answer format; rhetorical questions; apostrophe (direct address to people absent as though they were present); personification; metaphors taken from everyday life, including nature; allusions to famous people of the past (stock instances, or well-known representatives of the qualities that are under discussion); harsh addresses to readers; heightened contrasts. James Hardy Ropes

Of all the epistles, that of James is nearer the Sermon on the Mount than any other. It is possible to find in the epistle no less than twenty-two references to the sermon. In some form each of the beatitudes is alluded to. In his style, which is picturesque and powerful, and in his whole manner of thought, James shows what we may call a family resemblance to his divine Brother. . . . It is a book stamped as it were with the mind of Christ. Observe, for example, the frequent use of figures drawn from nature. Frank E. Gaebelein

1 PETER
Living in Alien Territory

FORMAT. 5 chapters, 105 verses

IMPLIED PURPOSES. To instruct believers about living and enduring as Christians in a society that is hostile to their values and lifestyle and to encourage Christians who are suffering for their faith

AUTHOR'S PERSPECTIVE. Peter writes with lyric intensity about life in Christ and with a great sense of apostolic authority as he exhorts and commands Christians regarding their lives in the world.

IMPLIED AUDIENCE. The original audience was Gentile Christians living in northern provinces of Asia Minor, or modern-day Turkey (1:1), who we infer were beginning to undergo suffering for their faith. But the frame of reference is universal, so the letter is really addressed to earnest and suffering Christians of all places and times. There are references in the letter to Christians living as foreigners or exiles, and these references seem to be both literal and metaphoric.

WHAT UNIFIES THE BOOK. Christocentric emphasis; references to suffering; moral earnestness; a predictable back-and-forth rhythm between theological assertions or celebration and moral implications; emphasis on how Christians must relate to others

SPECIAL FEATURES. Exuberance of tone; exalted language; vivid imagery and figurative language (in virtually any paragraph); reliance on the rhetoric of exhortation and commands

Western nations were once predominantly and even monolithically Christian, but Christians today find themselves in a smaller minority with every passing year. Not only that, but hostility directed against Christians is more and more prominent in the media and in academic and public settings. The book of 1 Peter is written for Christians in such situations.

The Structure

With the salutation (1:1-2) and conclusion/benediction (5:12-14) serving as the bookends, the book falls rather naturally into five units:

The Living Hope (1:3-12). Peter gives an emotionally charged description of the living hope that comes to those who are in Christ.

Exhortations to Live a Holy Life (1:13–2:3). On the basis of the account in 1:3-12, readers are urged to live godly, obedient lives.

Riches in Christ (2:4-10). In this unit, Peter offers another description of the riches believers have in Christ as his living building.

The Duties of Christians (2:11–3:12). Here is another section of commands, covering especially the duties of Christians to others: to the outside world (2:11-12), to social institutions (2:13-17), to masters (2:18-25), to husbands (3:1-6) and wives (3:7), and to fellow believers (3:8-12).

Commands for Christian Living (3:13–5:11). Endurance in suffering gets the most space, but there are numerous interspersed commands covering a wide spectrum of Christian living, as well as commands to elders.

It is obvious that the book moves back and forth in a fluid manner between two subjects: the riches that belong to those who are in Christ and the duties that they therefore need to shoulder, within an implied situation of opposition from the surrounding society.

KEY VERSES

"You are coming to Christ, who is the living cornerstone of God's temple. He was rejected by people, but he was chosen by God for great honor. And you are living stones that God is building into his spiritual temple" (2:4-5). First Peter has a double thrust: It repeatedly celebrates the treasures that believers have in Christ, and it spells out the duties—usually phrased as commands—that are required from people who enjoy such riches.

Key Doctrines and Themes

New Life in Christ. First Peter is rapturous about the manifold ways in which believers in Christ are participating in the privileges of being "born again" in Christ (1:3-5).

Redemption. There are numerous references to the redemptive life, death, and resurrection of Christ.

Sanctification. The extended passages of commands to godly living are an ever-expanding picture of the sanctified life.

The Ethics of Kingdom Living. The book contains numerous commands regarding the behavior God expects of Christians.

Suffering. After numerous early references to suffering, the letter eventually becomes a small classic on the subjects of being united with Christ in suffering and the need to respond in the right ways to that suffering.

Eschatology. There are intermittent references to the end of history and coming glory for believers.

Tips for Reading or Teaching 1 Peter

You need to be aware from the beginning that like many New Testament Epistles, the book's organization is loose. Do not try to imitate the tidy alliterative outlines that you find in handbooks and commentaries; instead, do justice to what is actually in the text, no matter how many-sided a given unit is. You are not totally "at sea," though, because throughout the book the general rhythm is a back-and-forth movement between rapturous declarations of the riches of being in Christ and lists of commands that the recipients of these riches need to follow. With that in mind, you will make good sense of the book if you apply the following three questions to the respective types of material:

> **DID YOU KNOW?**
> - First Peter is deeply rooted in the Old Testament; there are proportionately more Old Testament references here than in any other book of the New Testament.
> - An index to the nature of the book is the presence of thirty-four imperatives.
> - The emphases of the book are partly signaled by word patterns (clearer in the original than in English translations): suffering, behavior or way of life, election or calling, save or salvation, hope, and words dealing with a future inheritance or glory.

- What spiritual possessions do Christians have in Christ?
- What duties accompany such great privileges?
- What is it about our new nature that enables us to perform these duties?

Contribution of the Book to the Bible's Story of Salvation in Christ

If we look closely, 1 Peter has a Christological focus. There are repeated references to Christ's redemptive life and his centrality in salvation history, as well as descriptions of what it means to participate in the salvation that Christ secured for those who believe in him. The word *Christ* appears twenty-six times in the book (NLT). Whereas the Gospels tell the story of

Christ's redemptive life, an epistle such as this explores the results and implications of that redemptive life, with an emphasis on suffering.

Applying the Book

[handwritten: directs us to believe]   *[handwritten: requires it]*

There are two sides to this book—a theological side and a practical side. The theology of the book asks to be believed. The practical side asks for its commands to be lived out in our daily lives. While the practical commands extend to many areas of life, they come to focus on advice for how to behave when undergoing suffering. In fact, the book covers so many virtues and vices that we can read it as a summary of how to live the Christian life.

PERSPECTIVES
ON THE BOOK OF 1 PETER

The most condensed New Testament résumé of the Christian faith and of the conduct that it inspires. Ceslas Spicq

The apostle is a witness, not just to what Jesus did and said while he was in [Peter's] fishing-boat or in his house, but to the meaning of Christ's life, death, resurrection, and ascension. Edmund Clowney

Most outlines of New Testament books are more precise and organized than careful study seems to justify. . . . I heartily urge that students of 1 Peter struggle with its structure themselves. Scot McKnight

In only 105 verses, Peter ranges over a wide field of Christian theology and ethics. Here is the great doctrine of redemption. . . . Here are repeated calls to holiness and to humble trust in God for each day's needs. . . . Here also is profound comfort in sorrow. . . . And here is Jesus. . . . The glory of Christ shines forth from this letter into the hearts of all who read it.
Wayne Grudem

The prominent feature of the epistle is its elaboration of the theme of Christian suffering. D. Edmond Hiebert

The chief value of the epistle is that it shows Christians how to live out their redemption in a hostile world. Salvation may involve suffering, but it brings a hope also, as the grace of God is amplified in the individual life.
Merrill C. Tenney

2 PETER
Let Me Remind You

FACT SHEET

FORMAT. 3 chapters, 61 verses

IMPLIED PURPOSES. To encourage endurance in the Christian faith and development of Christian character, to warn against false teachers, and to strengthen conviction regarding biblical prophecy about the end times

AUTHOR'S PERSPECTIVE. Taking a cue from 1:13-14, scholars regard this epistle as falling into the genre of the farewell discourse from a spiritual mentor (such as Jesus' upper room discourse and as found in the books of Deuteronomy and 2 Timothy). The author claims to be reminding his audience of familiar Christian doctrine.

IMPLIED AUDIENCE. No audience is stipulated in the opening salutation. We can therefore read 2 Peter as an open letter to all Christians: "you who share the same precious faith we have" (1:1).

WHAT UNIFIES THE BOOK. Urgency of tone; an implied conflict between truth and error, with readers put in the position of needing to choose one and reject the other; exuberance of language and exaltation of sentiment

FACT SHEET

SPECIAL FEATURES. A high proportion of "favorite verses," such as the assertion that "his divine power has granted to us all things that pertain to life and godliness" (1:3, ESV) and the command to "make your calling and election sure" (1:10, ESV); vivid imagery, so that much of the letter is called poetic prose; a passion for truth as opposed to error; eschatological fervor

In our own information age, it is easy to get the impression that every new piece of information is somehow better or more important than established truth. Yet as eighteenth-century author Samuel Johnson noted, we need to be *reminded* more often than we need to be *informed*. The author of 2 Peter agreed with that sentiment. In the two places where he states his purpose in writing this letter (1:12-13 and 3:1-2), he uses variants of the word *remind* no fewer than five times.

The Structure

Following the epistolary salutation (1:1-2), this letter has a firm three-part structure, following the chapter divisions in our Bibles:

Peter's Call to Christians' "Higher Selves" (Chapter 1). In this preliminary foundational passage Peter mingles celebratory comments about what Christians have in Christ with commands about living godly lives (vv. 3-11), states his intention for the letter (vv. 12-15), and asserts the reliability of his apostolic teaching (vv. 16-21).

False Teachers (Chapter 2). Peter's condemnation of false teachers includes an assertion that false teachers are present in the church (vv. 1-3), the certainty that God will punish such teachers (vv. 4-10), and a description/denunciation of the false teachers (vv. 11-22, one of the fireworks passages in the Bible, full of vivid description).

Eschatological Discussion (Chapter 3). One of the great eschatological passages in the Bible, chapter 3 is organized like a debate, with a proposition (that Christ *will* return), a refutation of the contrary position (that Christ will not return), and Peter's offer of proof.

Tips for Reading or Teaching 2 Peter

This epistle contains numerous familiar and moving verses that deserve to be contemplated and celebrated. Be sure to let their truth sink in.

Peter himself states that his purpose is not to impart new information but to call his readers to remember what has already been revealed. You should therefore compile a list of familiar truths from the Bible, perhaps letting your mind recall parallel passages.

KEY VERSE

"We have . . . the prophetic word, to which you will do well to pay attention as to a lamp shining in a dark place, until the day dawns and the morning star rises in your hearts" (1:19, ESV). Here is the book in microcosm, with emphasis on the reliable truth of the Bible's revelation, the need to cling to this truth as a way of avoiding error, and the eschatological focus on the return of Christ (chapter 3).

Peter's descriptions of false teachers are particularly vivid. It is important to apply what you know about poetry, "unpacking" the connotations and emotional meanings of the specific images.

The last chapter is a small classic on eschatology, including what is familiarly called Christ's second coming. Take time to systematize all that the chapter says about eschatology.

The Main Themes
1. God's revelation of truth in the Bible is reliable and trustworthy.
2. It is essential that Christians reject false teachers and teaching that deviate from what the prophets and apostles have written.
3. Christians must never doubt that Christ will return and that biblical prophecies of the end (including the final dissolution of the physical world) will come true.
4. This eschatological hope must lead to godly living.

DID YOU KNOW?
When 2 Peter describes false teachers, it attributes to them a dozen of the same qualities and actions that the Epistle of Jude does. These parallels, moreover, appear in the same order in the two books. This has led to speculation that Jude is a condensed version of 2 Peter or that 2 Peter is an expanded version of Jude.

Contribution of the Book to the Bible's Story of Salvation in Christ
Along with the customary assertion and celebration of the riches of salvation in Christ that virtually all New Testament Epistles contain, 2 Peter focuses more particularly on the eschatological doctrine of the return of Christ.

Applying the Book
The key to applying the book lies in the author's repeated references to the need to remember. This book is a call to remember and practice the essentials of the Christian faith. The book is filled with commands that we are expected to obey. The two largest areas of obedience that this epistle impresses on us are the need to use the Bible as a guideline for recognizing and rejecting theological error (chapter 2) and the need to hold firm and not waver in our conviction that what the Bible reveals about the return of Christ and the consummation of history will really happen (chapter 3).

PER**SPECTIVES**
ON THE BOOK OF 2 PETER

The occasion for the writing of II Peter apparently was the information conveyed to the apostle of an outbreak of heresy among the churches addressed. After he had written I Peter, intended to strengthen them amid their sufferings from without, he learned that an even more serious danger had arisen in the presence of heretical teachers within the bounds of the churches. It was this latter danger that called forth this epistle.
D. Edmond Hiebert

The letter itself consists of a "Be zealous," a "Beware," and a "Be prepared." Archibald Hunter

The majesty of the Spirit of Christ exhibits itself in every part of the epistle. John Calvin

The true knowledge (chapter 1), the false teachers (chapter 2), the sure promise (chapter 3). J. Sidlow Baxter's outline of the book of 2 Peter

[Second] Peter belongs to the genre of ancient Jewish literature known to modern scholars as the "farewell speech" or "testament." . . . Such testaments had two main types of content: (1) Ethical admonitions. . . . (2) Revelations of the future. Richard J. Bauckham

The keynote of II Peter is knowledge. . . . The words know *or* knowledge, *in their varied forms, occur sixteen times in the epistle.*
D. Edmond Hiebert

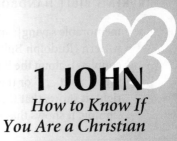

1 JOHN
How to Know If You Are a Christian

FACT SHEET

FORMAT. 5 chapters, 105 verses

IMPLIED PURPOSES. To offer doctrinal and moral touchstones by which Christians can know if their profession of faith is genuine and active; to encourage Christians to live up to God's high standards in their spiritual and moral lives

AUTHOR'S PERSPECTIVE. John's relationship to his readers is decidedly warm and intimate. He calls them "children" and "beloved" or "friends" and uses the pronouns *we* and *us*. First John is a family letter—or perhaps even a grandfatherly letter—to the early church.

IMPLIED AUDIENCE. John assumes an audience composed of Christians. We might infer that John believes that audience is looking for two things: how to know when faith is genuine and how to exhibit love in their lives. Further, 2:19, 26 hint at a church split, and on the basis of this some infer that John writes to a shaken church in which members wondered about whether they were on the right track in their beliefs and Christian walk.

WHAT UNIFIES THE BOOK. Fluid structure (paragraph-by-paragraph movement from one topic to another); a set of recurring topics (the things that authenticate a Christian's profession of faith, love for God and fellow believers, what constitutes correct thinking about Christ); a continuous tone of urgency that the readers will live and believe correctly; an implied context of false teaching that John wishes to discredit

SPECIAL FEATURES. The tone of warm intimacy and informality; reliance on certain evocative images such as light and darkness and walking and abiding, which lend a somewhat mystical tone to this letter (this book is a rich source of famous and favorite Bible verses, hinting at an aphoristic flair [an aphorism is a concise, memorable saying]; antithesis and contrast as a favorite rhetorical pattern (Rudolph Bultmann counted twenty-six antithetical couplets), along the lines of "if we say . . . but . . ." and "he who says . . . but . . ." or the juxtaposition of "when people do what is right, it shows that they are righteous" and "when people keep on sinning, it shows that they belong to the devil" (3:7-8)

*J*ohn] supplies tests by which every body can be sorted into one or other of two categories. According to their relation to his tests, they either have God or have not, know God or do not, have been born of God or have not, have life or abide in death, walk in the darkness or in the light, are children of God or children of the devil. . . . The certainty of Christian people is twofold—objective (that the Christain religion is true) and subjective (that they themselves have been born of God and possess eternal life.

JOHN R. W. STOTT
The Letters of John

Statistics have repeatedly shown how many Americans claim to be Christians, even born-again Christians. When we compare the statistics with the prevailingly secular state of society, however, we are naturally confused. Are there ways to test the reliability of people's claims to be Christians? There are, and 1 John lays them out in plain view.

The Structure

None of the Epistles has proven to be so elusive in its structure as 1 John. There is no consensus on the book's structure. We have provided no outline of the book in this guide. This does not mean that the book is chaotic or difficult to read. It is a delightful and easy book to read, but the structure is fluid. This epistle is built on the model of the informal essay—a fireside chat with John on the Christian life.

The best organizing framework for the heterogeneous material that you will find in 1 John is the following list of topics and motifs that appear and reappear:

KEY VERSE

"I have written this to you who believe in the name of the Son of God, so that you may know you have eternal life" (5:13). John's stated purpose in writing is borne out by the book, which (1) is a family letter for believers and (2) is filled with descriptions and commands that offer a many-sided portrait of the true Christian, by which we can know that we have salvation in Christ.

- *Christology.* This letter repeatedly asserts bedrock doctrine about the person and work of Christ, including his incarnation and the forgiveness of sins.
- *Walking in the light.* God is light (1:5), and Christians must accordingly walk in the light (1:7, ESV).
- *Love.* Above all, 1 John is a small classic on the subject of love—love of God and love of believers.
- *Tests of true Christianity.* The book presents a series of tests by which we can know whether or not we and others are genuine Christians (chapter 2, for example, lists these tests: obeying God's commandments, loving fellow believers, not loving the world, confessing that Jesus is the Christ).

These topics weave in and out. The key strategy is to "think paragraph" as you move through the book. The topics shift with nearly every paragraph, though we keep encountering echoes of earlier passages.

Key Doctrines and Themes

Christology. The person and work of Christ

Ethics, or *Sanctification.* The way God expects Christians to behave toward others, with love emerging as the keynote

Sin, Confession, Repentance, and *Forgiveness.* This epistle contains key
passages that teach about the universality of sin and the forgiveness
that God offers when people confess their sins and turn from them.

The Holy Spirit. Although the total quantity of the letter that speaks of the
Holy Spirit is small, these references are nonetheless a leading New
Testament repository of teaching on the Holy Spirit.

Tips for Reading or Teaching 1 John

Your starting premise must be that this letter is loosely organized, with
the result that you need to "think paragraph" as you read or teach
the book.

Second, you need to be continuously alert to the unifying themes and
motifs that we noted above; they will help to organize your experience of
the book, even though John does not treat individual topics all in one
place but disperses them throughout the letter.

Third, as you read John's commands and tests of true faith, you can
safely infer that John is attempting to counter false teaching that has
arisen on the matters about which he writes.

Finally, be receptive to the practical bent of the author. He does not
simply assert Christian doctrine, for example, but phrases it in terms of
how one can know if he or she is a genuine Christian. As with ethics, the
letter is filled with encouragement to behave in a certain way if we want
to be true followers of the light.

Contribution of the Book to the Bible's Story of Salvation in Christ

There is no more explicit assertion of the Incarnation than the opening
paragraph of this epistle. After that, John gives us repeated information
about life in Christ and what it means to have correct doctrine regarding
Christ. In fact, this epistle is a brief primer on bedrock belief in Christ.

Applying the Book

The grounds of certainty that John offers those who claim to be followers
of Christ fall into two categories: One is believing the right things about
Christ, where the application is simply to believe what John prescribes. A
key command is to "test the spirits" (4:1, ESV), which is a call to intellectual discernment. The second proof is moral; here the application is to
practice what John asserts, especially in the area of love. The word *world*

appears seventeen (NLT) or eighteen (ESV) times and stands as a warning against adhering to the values and morality of a fallen society.

perSPECTIVES
ON THE BOOK OF 1 JOHN

John's epistle gives us "the three cardinal tests" by which we may judge whether we possess eternal life or not. The first is theological and is Christological in nature and concerns correct thinking about Christ, especially his incarnation. The second test is moral, whether we are practising righteousness and keeping the commands of God. . . . The third test is social, whether we love one another. John R. W. Stott's summary of the outline of the book's content that Robert Law claimed in *The Tests of Life* (1885)

The primary concerns are three: the Incarnation; love for the brothers and sisters . . . and the relationship between sin and being God's children. Gordon D. Fee and Douglas Stuart

[On the absence of normal epistolary elements:] There is no address and no greeting at the beginning. No conclusion ends the document. . . . No personal comments suggest that the author is writing a personal letter. No names appear anywhere. . . . Some prefer to call it a sermon or an address. Perhaps it is a pamphlet, a brochure, or an encyclical. Gary M. Burge

[First] John is symphonic rather than logical in its plan; it is constructed like a piece of music. . . . John selects a theme which he maintains through the book, and upon which he introduces a series of variations. Merrill C. Tenney

This little classic of devotion and theology has been treasured by Christians for its profound understanding and beautiful summary of Christian theology: "God is love," and the equally concise formulation of Christian ethics: "Love one another." It presents in their inseparable relation and in fugue-like manner the three themes of love: God's love for man, and man's for God, and brother's for brother. . . . This succinct statement of the positive meaning of Christianity is, however, accompanied by an equally emphatic negation. The counterpart of loyalty to Christ and the brothers is the rejection of cultural society. . . . The injunction to Christians is, "Do not love the world or the things in the world." Richard Niebuhr

2 JOHN
Life in the
Local Church

FORMAT. One chapter, 13 verses

IMPLIED PURPOSES. To warn first-century Christians about false teachers who might arrive in their city and to provide a standard by which to judge what is false in the message of these teachers

AUTHOR'S PERSPECTIVE. The author calls himself "the elder" (v. 1) and writes in an earnest spirit and with apostolic authority about the difference between true Christianity and its counterfeits.

IMPLIED AUDIENCE. Identified as "the chosen lady and . . . her children" (v. 1), the audience is otherwise unidentified and may be a local congregation, individual Christians, or the church universal.

WHAT UNIFIES THE BOOK. A passion to protect true Christianity from false doctrine (the word *truth* appears five times in the first four verses) and to warn Christians against teachers who might seduce them to error

SPECIAL FEATURES. One of the two shortest letters in the New Testament; calling the church a lady

New religious teachers arise continually, especially in the television age. As a result, Christians continually need to make sense of how to respond to the latest message or celebrity. This epistle deals with the problem in a first-century context.

KEY VERSE
"Anyone who remains in the teaching of Christ has a relationship with both the Father and the Son" (1:9). Here is the ultimate reward for embracing truth and rejecting error.

The Structure

Despite its brevity, the letter develops several distinct ideas: salutation (vv. 1-3), a command for Christians to love one another (vv. 4-6), a warning against religious teachers who deny the incarnation of Christ (v. 7), admonition to maintain commitment to the truth and avoid error (vv. 8-9), instructions to avoid extending encouragement to traveling teachers who deny the Incarnation (vv. 10-11), and concluding greetings (vv. 12-13).

Key Doctrines and Themes

The Importance of Truth and Love in the Christian Life. Love for one another and the truth are to be defining characteristics of Christians' lives.

The Incarnation of Christ. Jesus became fully human with a real physical body.

The Need to Embrace True Doctrine and Reject False Doctrine. Christians must hold unwaveringly to the truth and not encourage or support those who do not.

Tips for Reading or Teaching 2 John

Develop a list of what John commands Christians to do and to avoid. Also pay attention to word patterns such as *truth*, *love*, and the terms applied to false teachers.

Contribution of the Book to the Bible's Story of Salvation in Christ

Second John shows that Christ is the truth and that the Incarnation is the central element of Christology.

Applying the Book

Live out the commands to love and embrace the truth that is in Christ.

PERSPECTIVES
ON THE BOOK OF 2 JOHN

Since, in the early days, the Christian movement spread and maintained itself by constant interchange of visits from members of one community to another . . . a decision had to be taken about visitors who wished to make a radical change in the community's convictions. Kenneth Grayston

The practical purpose of the Epistle . . . concerns both the inner life of the local fellowship (4-6) and the doctrinal danger which threatens it from without (7-11). John R. W. Stott

ON THE BOOK OF 2 JOHN

...

3 JOHN
A Home Away from Home

FORMAT. One chapter, 15 verses

IMPLIED PURPOSE. To call Christians to extend hospitality to other believers (especially itinerant Christian workers) who are passing through their region

AUTHOR'S PERSPECTIVE. Calling himself "the elder," he is a person attuned to the practical side of everyday life, such as the need for travelers (especially Christians) to have a place to stay.

IMPLIED AUDIENCE. The stated audience is a specific person named Gaius, but he is actually our representative as John exhorts both Gaius and us to acts of hospitality.

WHAT UNIFIES THE BOOK. The theme of hospitality as it is commanded and as people who refuse to fulfill its obligations are denounced; the vocabulary of the arrival and welcoming of visitors

SPECIAL FEATURE. By word count in the original, this is the shortest book in the New Testament.

With the ready availability of motels, contemporary Americans find it hard to understand the ancient world's obsession with the need to provide housing for travelers. Third John can revitalize our commitment to the ancient ideal of hospitality as a means of safety, provision, and fellowship.

The Structure

The short letters of 2 and 3 John actually resemble Greco-Roman letters more closely than the longer New Testament Epistles. The structure is this: opening greetings to Gaius (vv. 1-4), praise of the ideal of Christian hospitality (vv. 5-8), a rebuke of Diotrephes and his bad behavior (vv. 9-10), praise of the exemplary behavior of Demetrius (vv. 11-12), and concluding remarks (vv. 13-15).

Key Doctrines and Themes

The Importance of Following the Truth. The word *truth* appears five times.
Communion of the Saints. John asserts the ethical virtue of extending hospitality to fellow believers.

KEY VERSE
"Dear friend, you are being faithful to God when you care for the traveling teachers who pass through, even though they are strangers to you" (1:5). This verse describes and commends the key virtue of hospitality.

Tips for Reading or Teaching 3 John

Look for evidence of the teachings listed above; in addition, glean as much knowledge as you can about the four actors of the letter: the elder who wrote it; Gaius, to whom it was written; Diotrephes, against whom John writes; and Demetrius, who carried the letter.

Contribution of the Book to the Bible's Story of Salvation in Christ

The letter gives a glimpse into one virtue that grows out of life in Christ.

Applying the Book

The letter issues three commands: follow the truth, extend hospitality, and imitate, or do, what is good rather than evil.

ON THE BOOK OF 3 JOHN

In the early church the Christian home was the place of the open door and the loving welcome. William Barclay

The basic theme of this letter is the contrast between the truth and servanthood of Gaius and the error and selfishness of Diotrephes. Bruce Wilkinson and Kenneth Boa

Like all the books of the New Testament, it has a message for the entire Church. The devout reader rises from the perusal of it with a more steadfast devotion to the truth and a warmer glow of Christian love. J. Gresham Machen

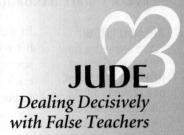

JUDE
*Dealing Decisively
with False Teachers*

FORMAT. One chapter, 25 verses

IMPLIED PURPOSES. To denounce false teachers who have gained entry into the church and to exhort believers to persevere in maintaining the truth of the gospel

AUTHOR'S PERSPECTIVE. The author writes in the white heat of anger as he attacks his opponents more vehemently than anything else we find in the New Testament except for Jesus' denunciation of the Jewish leaders in Matthew 23.

IMPLIED AUDIENCE. Christians in general rather than a specific church

WHAT UNIFIES THE BOOK. Energetic tone (both in the description of the false teachers and the famous benediction with which the letter ends); horror at the threat of apostasy

SPECIAL FEATURES. Vividness of language and imagery; the portrait technique in the section that describes the false teachers; use of satire as a technique (for information on satire as a literary form, see page 375); references to unsavory Old Testament characters

In a day of doctrinaire tolerance for all views and behaviors, Christians today might well wonder how strongly they should oppose people who espouse error. The Epistle of Jude shows when and how to respond to false teachers in the church.

The Structure

Salutation (vv. 1-2); the occasion of the letter, namely, the entry of false teachers into the church (vv. 3-4); three Old Testament examples of God's judgment (vv. 5-7); description and denunciation of the false teachers (vv. 8-16); exhortations to Christians to resist heresy and live a Christlike life (vv. 17-23); benediction (vv. 24-25)

Key Doctrines

Faith. Its reliability as taught by Christ and the apostles

Truth. The need to defend the truth and resist falsehood

Judgment. The certainty of God's judgment against apostates

Tips for Reading or Teaching Jude

Assemble a list of the traits of the false teachers and their doom.

Unpack the meanings of the allusions to Old Testament villains such as Balaam and Korah and of the images and figures of speech (clouds without rain and fruitless trees).

Compile a list of the virtues that Jude commands to the Christian readers of the letter.

Contribution of the Book to the Bible's Story of Salvation in Christ

This letter leads believers to a renewed commitment to faith in the gospel that Jesus taught and that the New Testament writers explain, and it contains a vivid picture of what followers of Christ have been delivered from.

Applying the Book

Renew commitment to the truth of the New Testament, and resolve to resist false religious teaching, even if it comes from within the institutional church or is disseminated by popular Christian media.

ON THE BOOK OF JUDE

The doxology which forms its two closing verses has been used for centuries in the liturgies of many denominations. Sir William Ramsay

The difficult and neglected letter. Archibald Hunter

Jude the Unobscure. Anonymous take-off on the title of Thomas Hardy's novel *Jude the Obscure*

Acts of the Apostates. S. Maxwell Coder

This little letter is a strong challenge to its readers to oppose resolutely all teachings and habits of life that profess to be Christian but deny the essence of the faith. This letter speaks to the modern world as to every previous age. In our century it is the fashion to be tolerant of anything that calls itself Christian. . . . Jude reminds us that there are limits. Donald A. Carson, Douglas Moo, Leon Morris, *An Introduction to the New Testament*

REVELATION
All's Well That Ends Well

FACT SHEET

FORMAT. 22 chapters, 404 verses

IMPLIED PURPOSE. To inform all believers, beginning in the first century AD, regarding "the events that must soon take place" (1:1), that is, in the "latter days" that began with the coming of Jesus in his incarnation

AUTHOR'S PERSPECTIVE. The author writes as a prophet (1:3) who records the visions that he saw. He is the intermediary between God, who is the origin of the visions, and his readers (1:1, 10-11). He writes as a first-person narrator—"I saw"—but he is an observer rather than a participant in the visions: He "faithfully reported everything he saw" (1:2). The author's perspective is that of a visionary who goes on a guided tour of heaven and the future.

IMPLIED AUDIENCE. The visions of the book are given to believers, who constitute the church (1:1, 3). These believers (including us today) are pictured as living through hostile and dangerous times and therefore need assurances of ultimate victory.

WHAT UNIFIES THE BOOK. The visionary mode; a cosmic conflict between good and evil; Christ as the conquering hero; the "strange world" motif; repeated patterns of sevenfold events

SPECIAL FEATURES. Visions as the medium of expression; symbolism as the basic "language" of the book (this is the book of the Bible that uses symbolism most extensively); apocalyptic genre (see the Form of the Book below); a high degree of patterning, all centered around the number seven; portrayals of life in heaven; descriptions of the very "last things" (the ultimate end-times book in the Bible)

CHALLENGES FACING THE READER OR TEACHER OF THIS BOOK.
1. The need to interpret visionary writing, including the element of strangeness, and to interpret poetry, especially symbolism
2. The sheer quantity of details

HOW TO MEET THE CHALLENGES.
1. Learn the conventions and "rules" for interpreting visionary writing (including apocalyptic writing) and poetry (including symbolism).
2. Develop an awareness that every individual section of the book is easily manageable because it is always part of a sevenfold pattern.

THE MOST COMMON MISCONCEPTIONS ABOUT THIS BOOK.
1. That because it is such a strange book, the ordinary reader cannot hope to understand it and only experts hold the key to interpretation of the book
2. That the book portrays events that lie only in the future rather than events that are going on right now

*A*pocalyptic writings are characterized by the use of symbols and highly figurative language. Among writers of this type of literature . . . an empire was symbolized by a wild beast . . . ; men were spoken of under the figure of animals. . . . Symbolic writing . . . does not paint pictures. It is not pictographic but ideographic. . . . The skull and crossbones on the bottle of medicine is a symbol of poison, not a picture. . . . The fish, the lamb, and the lion are all symbols of Christ, but never to be taken as pictures of him. . . . The book of Revelation has very few pictures, but it is full of symbols. . . . The meaning of the greater part of the symbolism of Revelation is quite clear to the modern reader.

DONALD W. RICHARDSON
The Revelation of Jesus Christ: An Interpretation

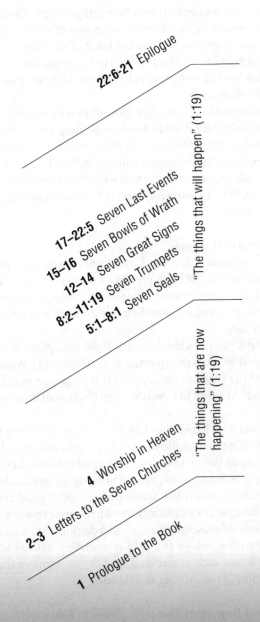

AN OUTLINE OF
REVELATION

In any story, we need to know how things began. The story of the Bible as a whole begins by answering the question of origins. But we also need to know how a story ends. The last book of the Bible brings closure to the grand story of the Bible. It is the closing act of the biblical drama. In effect, this book allows us to peek at the last chapter of human history to see how the story ends.

In addition to this impulse to want to see a story reach closure, people instinctively feel a need to know something about the future. Without a knowledge of how history will end, Christians would feel insecure and perplexed as they see human culture decline. The book of Revelation tells us enough about the future that we can be confident of ultimate victory in Christ. We can profitably look at Revelation as giving Christians a reason for hope.

The Form of the Book

Several important literary forms converge in the book of Revelation. Most obviously, the book presents a series of visions. Instead of telling a single linear story, these visions are arranged in the form of a pageant, with visions rapidly succeeding one another and never staying in focus for very long.

Second, the individual units will fall into place easily if we apply the usual grid of narrative questions, as follows: (1) Where does the event happen? (2) Who are the agents? (3) What action occurs? (4) What is the outcome? Any unit in Revelation can be charted in terms of this narrative grid.

The book of Revelation falls into a type of writing known as apocalypse. While the ingredients of this genre do not provide an analytic grid (as narrative does), knowing the ingredients will help you know what you are looking at as you read. These ingredients include: dualism (the world viewed as divided clearly into forces of good and evil); visionary mode; futuristic orientation; focus on the appearance and work of the divine Messiah; presence of angels and demons; animals as characters and symbols; numerology (the use of numbers with symbolic meanings); cosmic forces such as sea, land, and sky as actors in the drama; and denunciation of the existing social order.

The Most Important Thing You Need to Know
about the Book of Revelation

The basic medium of expression in the book of Revelation is symbolism. This means that instead of portraying characters and events directly and literally, the author pictures them indirectly by means of symbols. Jesus is portrayed as a lamb, a lion, and a warrior on a horse, for example. Churches are portrayed as lamps on lampstands.

To highlight the nonliteral mode of Revelation, the author uses fantasy, which is always characteristic of apocalyptic writing (see above). Only in a fantastic imagination do we find horses that are red (6:4) or a red dragon with seven heads and ten horns (12:3). The right way to assimilate this kind of writing is to accept the strangeness of the world portrayed and abandon a literal way of thinking in favor of reading symbolically.

To say that *the mode* is symbolic is not to deny that *the characters and events* are real. What is at stake is *how the characters and events are portrayed.* The symbols speak of realities—beings who really exist and events that really do happen.

The Time Frame

The author tells us that his visions concern "the events that must soon take place" (1:1). John wrote that statement two thousand years ago, and there is good reason to believe that some of his prophecies were fulfilled already in the first century AD. The point is that we should not assume that everything in Revelation is still futuristic. Surely most of what John portrays has happened in some form throughout history, including our own day. This is not to deny that the events that Revelation portrays as recurring on an ever-escalating scale will reach a climax at the end of history.

It is a safe premise that the symbolic mode of Revelation makes it always relevant and perpetually up to date. To cite an obvious example, the visions of the cataclysmic decline of the elemental forces of nature look more familiar with every passing year as our planet's ecological crisis grows. To believe that the predictions of Revelation will be ultimately fulfilled at a coming end of history should not prevent us from seeing how much of the book is being fulfilled before our eyes.

How Do We Know What the Symbols Refer To?

The best rule of thumb for interpreting the symbols and visions of Revelation is to relate them to common teachings of the Bible and to obvious events in our own world. In particular, Jesus' outline of coming events in his Olivet discourse (Matthew 24–25) provides a blueprint for the visions of Revelation. Jesus outlined this sequence of events that will happen at "the close of the age" (Matthew 24:3, ESV):

1. False teachers, wars, famine, and earthquakes (24:5-8)
2. Persecution of Christians (24:9-22)
3. False christs and false prophets (24:23-28, ESV)
4. Natural disasters, the appearance of Christ, the harvesting of Christ's "chosen ones" (24:29-31)
5. The final judgment (24:32–25:46). We repeatedly cover this same material in the visions of Revelation.

A safe question to keep asking of a given vision is this: Of what familiar doctrine or event in salvation history is this a symbolic version? Examples are the sovereignty of God, God's judgment against evil, God's salvation of believers, the existence of heaven and hell, the great battle between good and evil, and so forth. We do not need to look for mysterious and hidden levels of meaning. The very word *apocalypse* comes from the Greek verb *apokalyptein*, which means "to unveil" or "uncover." The purpose of the visions of Revelation is not to confuse us but to confirm our understanding of the Bible and events in the daily news.

For example, chapter 12 begins with a vision of a woman (Israel) giving birth to a son (Christ), whom the red dragon (Satan) tries to destroy at birth but who is miraculously protected and snatched up to heaven (the ascension of Christ after his incarnate life on earth). This passage is an interpretive key to the whole book because we know the referents (the realities to which the symbols point). The details of the vision are not a literal portrayal of the earthly life and ascension of Jesus, but the details call those circumstances to mind.

We can take a similar approach with the pageant of four horse visions (6:1-8). The symbolism paints a picture of warfare, famine, destruction, and death. To what do these refer? They are a visionary and symbolic version of what Jesus predicted directly in Matthew 24:7: "Nation will rise against nation, and kingdom against kingdom, and there will be famines and earthquakes in various places" (ESV). The sealing of believers (chapter 7) is a symbolic account of how God will eternally save all who believe in him.

What you need when interpreting the symbolic visions of Revelation is a keen eye for the obvious. The things to which the details refer are for the

Apocalyptic Writing

The Greek word *apocalypse* means "unveiling" or "revelation." What is chiefly unveiled in apocalyptic writing is the end of history and the eternity that will follow it. In other words, apocalyptic writing is eschatological (dealing with the end times).

At the same time, apocalyptic writing like the books of Daniel and Revelation also portray principles that are valid throughout history: the spiritual conflict between good and evil and God's sovereign control of history and nature. Apocalyptic writing tends overwhelmingly to be visionary in nature (see the article on visionary writing on page 325). The most important differentiating features of apocalyptic writing are the following:

- Dualism: The universe is clearly divided into good and evil.
- Spiritism: Angels and demons are leading characters.
- Messianic focus: The protagonist is Christ, the Messiah.
- Animal symbolism: Animals such as the lion, lamb, and dragon are among the cast of characters, and they symbolize beings such as Christ and Satan.
- Color symbolism: Colors (e.g., red, white, and black) have obvious symbolic meanings.
- Number symbolism: Examples are seven, ten, and twelve as symbolizing completeness, perfection, or immensity, and six and one-half the sinister quality of falling short of those good qualities.
- Cataclysmic imagery: In keeping with the dual emphasis of apocalyptic writing on God's judgment against sin and eschatology, apocalyptic writing is filled with images of the end that picture the cataclysmic destruction of all earthly existence (the stars fall from heaven, earthquakes occur, and finally the whole earth is burned up).
- Cosmic stage of action: The action encompasses the entire earth and universe. Heaven above and hell beneath fill out the setting for the action.
- Renewal of the place of corporate worship, usually pictured as a restored temple.
- A balance between warning to the unrepentant and comfort to God's followers.

Because the method of portrayal is symbolic and visionary, many of the details in apocalyptic writing are open ended, meaning that they are always being fulfilled and will be fulfilled in an ultimate way at the end of history. The Babylon of the book of Revelation, for example, was the Roman Empire to John's original audience, but it has taken many forms since then. Because the specifics are pictured in indefinite terms, Christians in every era have reason to believe that the end of history could occur in their own lifetimes.

most part familiar—God's judgment of evil, his saving of those who believe, the decline of the earthly order of things. You are best advised to keep relating the symbols to familiar doctrines, events in salvation history, and happenings in the world around you.

The Structure

The basic premise is that everything in Revelation, except for the prologue and epilogue, is part of a sevenfold pattern (see the overview on page 636). This at once makes the book manageable, despite the multiplicity of details.

Second, the book is structured like a pageant—a succession of visions and brief snapshots. There is no single thread of action. In fact, the visions are cyclic and repetitive rather than sequential, though there is an expanding scope as the destruction moves from a fourth of the earth (6:8) to a third of the earth (chapter 8) to the whole earth (chapter 16).

Finally, within each of the sevenfold units there is a general movement from fallen earthly history, associated with evil and calamity, to the final consummation of history, in its two aspects of the punishment of evil and the glorification of believers in heaven. You can be looking for this general rhythm in all of the units.

Unifying Elements

- Plot conflict between good and evil
- Christ as the triumphant hero
- Clusters of images and events: images of battle, worship, evil, judgment, redemption, elemental nature, cataclysm, splendor, heaven
- The arrangement of events into patterns of seven
- The pageant-of-visions format

Key Places and Characters

The setting of Revelation is cosmic, encompassing heaven, earth, and hell. References to earth are often to the whole earth, not just a localized part of it. Once we get beyond the cities named in the seven letters (chapters 2–3), the main settings of earthly action are a symbolic city of Babylon (the human race in community against God) and elemental nature (water, earth, sky, etc.). The single most memorable place is the concluding picture of the heavenly city of God—the new Jerusalem.

Christ is the central character, as even the opening phrase indicates ("the revelation of Jesus Christ," ESV). His great antagonist is Satan. The remaining cast of characters consists of groups—angels, Satan's hosts, crowds of believers and unbelievers. There are many crowd scenes in Revelation, with attention to stationing of characters in a setting and even to costuming. In keeping with the visionary genre of the book, natural forces (such as the sun and stars) and fantastic animals (such as the dragon and the beasts from the sea and the earth) are also major characters.

Key Doctrines

The Sovereignty of God. God controls all creatures and events.

Christology. Revelation specifically exalts, enthrones, and celebrates Christ as lamb, king, and warrior.

Satan. This book gives us the Bible's most extended picture of how Satan operates.

Sin. Revelation shows us the ultimate scope of sin in human history.

Judgment. The book presents repeated evidence that God will judge all evil.

Redemption and *Glorification.* This is also the biblical book that gives the most extended descriptions of believers' complete salvation and glorification in heaven.

Worship. The book contains numerous pictures of heavenly worship.

Eschatology. Revelation is the Bible's most complete and systematic account of the last things.

KEY VERSE

"Behold, I stand at the door and knock. If anyone hears my voice and opens the door, I will come in to him and eat with him, and he with me" (3:20, ESV). Coming at the end of the letters to the seven churches, this famous verse encapsulates the practical nature of apocalyptic writing, which aims to lead people to place their trust in Christ as their only hope against the judgments that would otherwise engulf them.

Tips for Reading or Teaching Revelation

For each individual unit in the sequence of visions, apply the narrative grid of who (the characters), where (the setting), what (the action), and outcome. You can make initial sense of every passage in Revelation with this fourfold grid.

A symbol requires two levels of interaction. The first is the literal, or surface, level, which requires you to get an accurate mental register of the details of action or description. Second, you need to identify the referent—the thing to which the symbols really point. Go for familiar referents: what you know about God, about events in salvation history, about doctrines such as judgment and redemption, and about conditions as you read or see them in the daily news.

No matter where you are in the book, you are somewhere in a unit of seven main events. To render this even more manageable, be aware that the cycles repeat similar material, moving from decline on earth to final judgment against evil and glorification of believers in heaven. You can depend on this rhythm at any point in the book.

Keep relating the visionary details to Jesus' statements about the end times in the Gospels, especially in the Olivet discourse (see "How Do We Know What the Symbols Refer To?" on pages 631–634).

quick overview of revelation

1:1-20	Prologue
2:1–4:11	Letters to the seven churches, followed by heavenly worship
5:1–8:1	Seven seals
8:2–11:19	Seven trumpets
12:1–14:20	Seven great signs
15:1–16:21	Seven bowls of wrath
17:1–22:5	Seven last events
22:6-21	Epilogue

The Flow of the Book

Prologue (Chapter 1). This chapter gives us a fourfold introduction to the book: We are introduced to the theme and source (vv. 1-3), given an epistolary salutation reminiscent of the New Testament Epistles (vv. 4-8), and meet the narrator (vv. 9-11) and the hero (vv. 12-20). It will pay dividends to spend as much time as it takes to decipher exactly what we learn about each of these things. The concluding vision of Christ is our introduction to the symbolic mode of the book, so take time to interpret what individual details such as the long robe and white hair symbolize about Christ.

The Letters to the Seven Churches (Chapters 2–3). Organizationally, the letters themselves fall into a sevenfold pattern (with slight deviations in the order in which the ingredients appear): (1) a greeting: "to the angel of the church in _____"; (2) a title for Christ taken from the vision of him in chapter 1; (3) a commendation of the church; (4) a criticism; (5) a warning; (6) an exhortation to be attentive: "He who has an ear, let him hear" (ESV); and (7) a promise, beginning with the formula "to all who are victorious." You should first reconstruct the situation in the original receiving churches and then look *through* those particulars to the universal principles as they exist in your own life and situation.

Heavenly Worship (Chapter 4). Chapter 4 is a "swing" chapter that can be related to either the preceding unit or the unit that follows it. The letters to the churches have ended with brief visions of the heavenly destination of those who persevere. Now we get a complete picture of that destination. Alternately or simultaneously, we can view the scene of heavenly ritual as a transition to the more celestial and futuristic scenes that will follow (verse 1 speaks of a voice saying to John, "Come up here, and I will show you what must happen after this").

The Seven Seals (5:1–8:1). The sequence begins with the *prelude*, in which the Lamb opens the scroll of the future (Chapter 5). Following the prelude is the account of the opening of each seal:

- The first four seals: four horse visions (6:1-8)
- The fifth seal: consolation of the martyrs under the altar (6:9-11)
- The sixth seal: cataclysmic destruction of the earth (6:12-17)
- The *interlude*: God's sealing of believers (chapter 7)
- The seventh seal: *prelude* to the coming terrors (8:1)

Again, the best plan is to go for the obvious meanings, based on other eschatological passages of the Bible, with their motifs of coming terror and hardship on earth as events decline, the end of earthly history, and God's ultimate salvation of believers in heaven.

The Seven Trumpets (8:2–11:19). At this point it is important to awaken your awareness that the book of Revelation is structured on a repetitive principle of cycles that cover similar territory. In addition, you should continue to go for what is obvious—that as history winds down and the human race continues to operate in self-destructive fashion, there will be cataclysmic upheaval in nature; that God's judgment against evil is certain both in time and eternity; and that Christ will ultimately redeem his followers in heaven.

The sequence of this unit is almost identical to that of the seven seals: a prelude (8:2-6), four visions that form a related cluster (the elemental forces of nature disrupted, 8:7-13), the plague of destructive locusts (9:1-12), destructive troops of cavalry (9:13-21), interlude in the form of a story about two witnesses who are miraculously protected by God (11:1–11:14), and a picture of believers glorified in heaven (11:15-19). The general movement has once again been from the fallen earthly order, associated with evil and terror, to the consummation of history in the dual form of the destruction of evil and the glorification of Christians in heaven.

Seven Great Signs (Chapters 12–14). This sevenfold unit does not advertise its organization the way most of the other units do, so here is an outline:

- the dragon's war against the Son, the woman, and the woman's other offspring (chapter 12)
- the beast from the sea (13:1-10)
- the beast from the earth (13:11-18)
- the Lamb on Mount Zion (14:1-5)
- angelic messages of judgment (14:6-13)
- the harvesting of the earth (14:14-16)
- reaping and judgment of the wicked (14:17-20)

KEY VERSES

"There was war in heaven. Michael and his angels fought against the dragon and his angels. And the dragon lost the battle, and he and his angels were forced out of heaven" (12:7-8). This is the great plot conflict of the book of Revelation—and the resolution of that conflict.

These chapters form what one scholar calls a complete apocalypse, moving from the incarnation of Christ through fallen history to the eschaton (millennium). Chapter 12 is a flashback that explains why the dragon conducts such a vehement battle throughout the visions of Revelation. Like the other passages, this unit will fall into place if you simply relate the details to Jesus' apocalyptic discourses in the Gospels (especially Matthew 24–25).

The Seven Bowls of Wrath (Chapters 15–16). Things are moving toward a climax, as signaled by the fact that these plagues are "the seven last plagues, which would bring God's wrath to completion" (15:1), but in essence we retread familiar territory in this cycle of visions. The sequence is by now familiar: prelude set in heaven (chapter 15); a cluster of five visions involving the elemental forces of nature (16:1-11); a multifaceted vision involving nature, demonic spirits, and assembly for battle (16:12-16); and a final vision of cosmic cataclysm (16:17-21). If the details seem strange, just recall that all these motifs are familiar in biblical pictures of the end.

The Seven Last Events of Final Judgment and Consummation (17:1–22:5).
This is the second section that does not advertise itself as a sevenfold unit,
so here is an outline to clarify the organization:

- the judgment of Babylon (chapters 17–18)
- the wedding feast of the Lamb (19:1-10)
- Christ's defeat of the beast and the false
  prophet (19:11-21)
- the binding of Satan and the millennial reign
  of Christ (20:1-6)
- the loosing of Satan and his defeat (20:7-10)
- the final judgment (20:11-15)
- the description of the new heaven and new
  earth (21:1–22:5)

These are symbolic pictures of true realities. You
can read the details in a spirit of celebration if you
are a believer in Christ.

> **KEY VERSE**
> "After this, I heard
> what sounded like a
> vast crowd in heaven
> shouting, 'Praise the
> LORD! Salvation and
> glory and power
> belong to our God'"
> (19:1). This is the
> victory song of the
> whole Bible,
> celebrating the most
> important fact in the
> whole universe.

Epilogue (22:6-21). We now back off from the tremendous visions of the
book and are made to ponder the urgency of what has preceded, as well as
an invitation to come home.

The Main Themes

1. The fact of spiritual conflict between good and evil and the way in
   which all people align themselves either for Christ or against him
2. The absolute sovereignty of God
3. The judgment of God against all forms of evil
4. The combined pessimism and optimism with which we should
   regard our moment in history and our future—pessimism about
   the way in which the earthly order will get progressively worse and
   optimism about the certainty of final victory for Christ and his
   followers
5. The existence of a heavenly reality that transcends the struggles of
   life and awaits all who believe in Christ

Contribution of the Book to the Bible's Story of Salvation in Christ

The book of Revelation concludes the Bible's story of salvation history.
Furthermore, it is a thoroughly Christocentric story, with Christ as the
exalted One who defeats Satan and wins heaven for his followers. Within
that broad umbrella, this book contains numerous specific pictures of re-

demption, all based on the premise that believers have "defeated [Satan] by the blood of the Lamb" (12:11).

Applying the Book

Most obviously, the book of Revelation conveys important information about the present and future that we simply need to believe and live in an awareness of. In the middle of Jesus' eschatological discourse known as the Olivet discourse, he told his disciples, "See, I have warned you about this ahead of time" (Matthew 24:25), with the implication that the information he imparted about the end times could help his followers make sense of what was happening and not be overwhelmed by events. The book of Revelation can serve the same purpose. It can be a ballast against the false information and speculation that circulate about the end times.

Second, the book of Revelation is filled with information and pictures that can help Christians to endure patiently in the midst of tribulation and persecution. As 13:10 puts it, "God's holy people must endure persecution patiently and remain faithful." Victory in Christ is assured, so we must live out the rest of life with that goal in view.

Another application is what is called doxological ("having the effect of moving one to praise"). There is a lyrical undertow to the book, and the notes of celebration and praise for what God has done are continually breaking through the descriptions of events. As we read, we can allow these to draw us to worship.

PERSPECTIVES
ON THE BOOK OF REVELATION

Revelation is your science fiction thriller of the Bible.
Anonymous Wheaton College student

Much that is contained in the Apocalypse is best perceived by the ear and the imagination, as the visions of Revelation unfold in the mind's eye. Those who remember the great days of radio drama will immediately appreciate this. M. Eugene Boring

We must always begin with the situation of the church to which it was written. . . . [This church] looked and longed for the promised

consummation when God's will would be perfectly done throughout the whole earth. And nothing happened. . . . To a church perplexed by such problems Revelation was written. We must not think of it as a kind of intellectual puzzle . . . sent to a relaxed church with time on its hands and an inclination for solving mysteries. It was sent to a little, persecuted, frustrated church. . . . John writes to meet the need of that church.
Leon Morris

The primary purpose of the book is to describe the consummation of God's redemptive purpose and the end of the age. George Eldon Ladd

The basic compositional device is simple repetition—one vision set after another. . . . The method of repetition, however, has been modified in two very important respects. In the first place, a common stock of symbols links the separate visions, and the repeated appearance of these symbols gives both unity and cumulative effect to the whole. . . . The other technique by which the author achieves an interwoven texture is his use of numerical structure. Seven, the symbol of divine perfection, is the basic and recurring number. William A. Beardslee

Though the descriptions seem so specific, yet it is impossible to visualize them. . . . In spite of the fact that the imagery is material, the effect is wholly immaterial and ideal. J. H. Gardiner

The purpose of symbols is that they should be immediately understood, the purpose of expounding them is to restore and build up such an understanding. Austin Farrar

Here in the final culmination, man and society are perfectly established in community with and under God. This perfection is conveyed through rich and luxuriant symbols of dimensions, design, and decoration. . . . The quality of its richness is set in sharp contrast . . . with the stark simplicity of the opening verses of the Bible. . . . With this vision of the establishment of faithful men within a community of the life everlasting under God, the Biblical epic comes to its incomparable close. Roland M. Frye

Revelation was written that men might enter the city of God.
G. R. Beasley-Murray

the one year bible reading plan

January 1
Genesis 1:1–2:25
Matthew 1:1–2:12
Psalm 1:1-6
Proverbs 1:1-6
January 2
Genesis 3:1–4:26
Matthew 2:13–3:6
Psalm 2:1-12
Proverbs 1:7-9
January 3
Genesis 5:1–7:24
Matthew 3:7–4:11
Psalm 3:1-8
Proverbs 1:10-19
January 4
Genesis 8:1–10:32
Matthew 4:12-25
Psalm 4:1-8
Proverbs 1:20-23
January 5
Genesis 11:1–13:4
Matthew 5:1-26
Psalm 5:1-12
Proverbs 1:24-28
January 6
Genesis 13:5–15:21
Matthew 5:27-48
Psalm 6:1-10
Proverbs 1:29-33
January 7
Genesis 16:1–18:15
Matthew 6:1-24
Psalm 7:1-17
Proverbs 2:1-5

January 8
Genesis 18:16–19:38
Matthew 6:25–7:14
Psalm 8:1-9
Proverbs 2:6-15
January 9
Genesis 20:1–22:24
Matthew 7:15-29
Psalm 9:1-12
Proverbs 2:16-22
January 10
Genesis 23:1–24:51
Matthew 8:1-17
Psalm 9:13-20
Proverbs 3:1-6
January 11
Genesis 24:52–26:16
Matthew 8:18-34
Psalm 10:1-15
Proverbs 3:7-8
January 12
Genesis 26:17–
   27:46
Matthew 9:1-17
Psalm 10:16-18
Proverbs 3:9-10
January 13
Genesis 28:1–29:35
Matthew 9:18-38
Psalm 11:1-7
Proverbs 3:11-12
January 14
Genesis 30:1–31:16
Matthew 10:1-23

Psalm 12:1-8
Proverbs 3:13-15
January 15
Genesis 31:17–32:12
Matthew 10:24–11:6
Psalm 13:1-6
Proverbs 3:16-18
January 16
Genesis 32:13–34:31
Matthew 11:7-30
Psalm 14:1-7
Proverbs 3:19-20
January 17
Genesis 35:1–36:43
Matthew 12:1-21
Psalm 15:1-5
Proverbs 3:21-26
January 18
Genesis 37:1–38:30
Matthew 12:22-45
Psalm 16:1-11
Proverbs 3:27-32
January 19
Genesis 39:1–41:16
Matthew
   12:46–13:23
Psalm 17:1-15
Proverbs 3:33-35
January 20
Genesis 41:17–42:17
Matthew 13:24-46
Psalm 18:1-15
Proverbs 4:1-6
January 21
Genesis 42:18–43:34

Matthew
13:47–14:12
Psalm 18:16-36
Proverbs 4:7-10
January 22
Genesis 44:1–45:28
Matthew 14:13-36
Psalm 18:37-50
Proverbs 4:11-13
January 23
Genesis 46:1–47:31
Matthew 15:1-28
Psalm 19:1-14
Proverbs 4:14-19
January 24
Genesis 48:1–49:33
Matthew
15:29–16:12
Psalm 20:1-9
Proverbs 4:20-27
January 25
Genesis 50:1—
Exodus 2:10
Matthew 16:13–17:9
Psalm 21:1-13
Proverbs 5:1-6
January 26
Exodus 2:11–3:22
Matthew 17:10-27
Psalm 22:1-18
Proverbs 5:7-14
January 27
Exodus 4:1–5:21
Matthew 18:1-20
Psalm 22:19-31
Proverbs 5:15-21
January 28
Exodus 5:22–7:25
Matthew
18:21–19:12
Psalm 23:1-6
Proverbs 5:22-23
January 29
Exodus 8:1–9:35
Matthew 19:13-30

Psalm 24:1-10
Proverbs 6:1-5
January 30
Exodus 10:1–12:13
Matthew 20:1-28
Psalm 25:1-15
Proverbs 6:6-11
January 31
Exodus 12:14–13:16
Matthew
20:29–21:22
Psalm 25:16-22
Proverbs 6:12-15

February 1
Exodus 13:17–15:18
Matthew 21:23-46
Psalm 26:1-12
Proverbs 6:16-19
February 2
Exodus 15:19–17:7
Matthew 22:1-33
Psalm 27:1-6
Proverbs 6:20-26
February 3
Exodus 17:8–19:15
Matthew
22:34–23:12
Psalm 27:7-14
Proverbs 6:27-35
February 4
Exodus 19:16–21:21
Matthew 23:13-39
Psalm 28:1-9
Proverbs 7:1-5
February 5
Exodus 21:22–23:13
Matthew 24:1-28
Psalm 29:1-11
Proverbs 7:6-23
February 6
Exodus 23:14–
25:40
Matthew 24:29-51
Psalm 30:1-12
Proverbs 7:24-27

February 7
Exodus 26:1–27:21
Matthew 25:1-30
Psalm 31:1-8
Proverbs 8:1-11
February 8
Exodus 28:1-43
Matthew
25:31–26:13
Psalm 31:9-18
Proverbs 8:12-13
February 9
Exodus 29:1–30:10
Matthew 26:14-46
Psalm 31:19-24
Proverbs 8:14-26
February 10
Exodus 30:11–31:18
Matthew 26:47-68
Psalm 32:1-11
Proverbs 8:27-32
February 11
Exodus 32:1–33:23
Matthew
26:69–27:14
Psalm 33:1-11
Proverbs 8:33-36
February 12
Exodus 34:1–35:9
Matthew 27:15-31
Psalm 33:12-22
Proverbs 9:1-6
February 13
Exodus 35:10–36:38
Matthew 27:32-66
Psalm 34:1-10
Proverbs 9:7-8
February 14
Exodus 37:1–38:31
Matthew 28:1-20
Psalm 34:11-22
Proverbs 9:9-10
February 15
Exodus 39:1–40:38
Mark 1:1-28

Psalm 35:1-16
Proverbs 9:11-12

February 16
Leviticus 1:1–3:17
Mark 1:29–2:12
Psalm 35:17-28
Proverbs 9:13-18

February 17
Leviticus 4:1–5:19
Mark 2:13–3:6
Psalm 36:1-12
Proverbs 10:1-2

February 18
Leviticus 6:1–7:27
Mark 3:7-30
Psalm 37:1-11
Proverbs 10:3-4

February 19
Leviticus 7:28–9:6
Mark 3:31–4:25
Psalm 37:12-29
Proverbs 10:5

February 20
Leviticus 9:7–10:20
Mark 4:26–5:20
Psalm 37:30-40
Proverbs 10:6-7

February 21
Leviticus 11:1–12:8
Mark 5:21-43
Psalm 38:1-22
Proverbs 10:8-9

February 22
Leviticus 13:1-29
Mark 6:1-29
Psalm 39:1-13
Proverbs 10:10

February 23
Leviticus 14:1-57
Mark 6:30-56
Psalm 40:1-10
Proverbs 10:11-12

February 24
Leviticus 15:1–16:28
Mark 7:1-23

Psalm 40:11-17
Proverbs 10:13-14

February 25
Leviticus
16:29–18:30
Mark 7:24–8:10
Psalm 41:1-13
Proverbs 10:15-16

February 26
Leviticus 19:1–20:21
Mark 8:11-38
Psalm 42:1-11
Proverbs 10:17

February 27
Leviticus
20:22–22:16
Mark 9:1-29
Psalm 43:1-5
Proverbs 10:18

February 28
Leviticus
22:17–23:44
Mark 9:30–10:12
Psalm 44:1-8
Proverbs 10:19

March 1
Leviticus 24:1–25:46
Mark 10:13-31
Psalm 44:9-26
Proverbs 10:20-21

March 2
Leviticus
25:47–27:13
Mark 10:32-52
Psalm 45:1-17
Proverbs 10:22

March 3
Leviticus 27:14—
Numbers 1:54
Mark 11:1-26
Psalm 46:1-11
Proverbs 10:23

March 4
Numbers 2:1–3:51
Mark 11:27–12:17

Psalm 47:1-9
Proverbs 10:24-25

March 5
Numbers 4:1–5:31
Mark 12:18-37
Psalm 48:1-14
Proverbs 10:26

March 6
Numbers 6:1–7:89
Mark 12:38–13:13
Psalm 49:1-20
Proverbs 10:27-28

March 7
Numbers 8:1–9:23
Mark 13:14-37
Psalm 50:1-23
Proverbs 10:29-30

March 8
Numbers 10:1–11:23
Mark 14:1-21
Psalm 51:1-19
Proverbs 10:31-32

March 9
Numbers
11:24–13:33
Mark 14:22-52
Psalm 52:1-9
Proverbs 11:1-3

March 10
Numbers 14:1–15:16
Mark 14:53-72
Psalm 53:1-6
Proverbs 11:4

March 11
Numbers
15:17–16:40
Mark 15:1-47
Psalm 54:1-7
Proverbs 11:5-6

March 12
Numbers
16:41–18:32
Mark 16:1-20
Psalm 55:1-23
Proverbs 11:7

March 13
Numbers 19:1–20:29
Luke 1:1-25
Psalm 56:1-13
Proverbs 11:8

March 14
Numbers 21:1–
22:20
Luke 1:26-56
Psalm 57:1-11
Proverbs 11:9-11

March 15
Numbers
22:21–23:30
Luke 1:57-80
Psalm 58:1-11
Proverbs 11:12-13

March 16
Numbers 24:1–
25:18
Luke 2:1-35
Psalm 59:1-17
Proverbs 11:14

March 17
Numbers 26:1-51
Luke 2:36-52
Psalm 60:1-12
Proverbs 11:15

March 18
Numbers
26:52–28:15
Luke 3:1-22
Psalm 61:1-8
Proverbs 11:16-17

March 19
Numbers
28:16–29:40
Luke 3:23-38
Psalm 62:1-12
Proverbs 11:18-19

March 20
Numbers 30:1–31:54
Luke 4:1-30
Psalm 63:1-11
Proverbs 11:20-21

March 21
Numbers 32:1–33:39
Luke 4:31–5:11
Psalm 64:1-10
Proverbs 11:22

March 22
Numbers
33:40–35:34
Luke 5:12-28
Psalm 65:1-13
Proverbs 11:23

March 23
Numbers 36:1—
Deuteronomy
1:46
Luke 5:29–6:11
Psalm 66:1-20
Proverbs 11:24-26

March 24
Deuteronomy
2:1–3:29
Luke 6:12-38
Psalm 67:1-7
Proverbs 11:27

March 25
Deuteronomy 4:1-49
Luke 6:39–7:10
Psalm 68:1-18
Proverbs 11:28

March 26
Deuteronomy
5:1–6:25
Luke 7:11-35
Psalm 68:19-35
Proverbs 11:29-31

March 27
Deuteronomy
7:1–8:20
Luke 7:36–8:3
Psalm 69:1-18
Proverbs 12:1

March 28
Deuteronomy
9:1–10:22
Luke 8:4-21

Psalm 69:19-36
Proverbs 12:2-3

March 29
Deuteronomy
11:1–12:32
Luke 8:22-39
Psalm 70:1-5
Proverbs 12:4

March 30
Deuteronomy
13:1–15:23
Luke 8:40–9:6
Psalm 71:1-24
Proverbs 12:5-7

March 31
Deuteronomy
16:1–17:20
Luke 9:7-27
Psalm 72:1-20
Proverbs 12:8-9

April 1
Deuteronomy
18:1–20:20
Luke 9:28-50
Psalm 73:1-28
Proverbs 12:10

April 2
Deuteronomy
21:1–22:30
Luke 9:51–10:12
Psalm 74:1-23
Proverbs 12:11

April 3
Deuteronomy
23:1–25:19
Luke 10:13-37
Psalm 75:1-10
Proverbs 12:12-14

April 4
Deuteronomy
26:1–27:26
Luke 10:38–11:13
Psalm 76:1-12
Proverbs 12:15-17

April 5
Deuteronomy
28:1-68
Luke 11:14-36
Psalm 77:1-20
Proverbs 12:18

April 6
Deuteronomy
29:1–30:20
Luke 11:37–12:7
Psalm 78:1-31
Proverbs 12:19-20

April 7
Deuteronomy
31:1–32:27
Luke 12:8-34
Psalm 78:32-55
Proverbs 12:21-23

April 8
Deuteronomy
32:28-52
Luke 12:35-59
Psalm 78:56-64
Proverbs 12:24

April 9
Deuteronomy
33:1-29
Luke 13:1-21
Psalm 78:65-72
Proverbs 12:25

April 10
Deuteronomy
34:1—Joshua 2:24
Luke 13:22–14:6
Psalm 79:1-13
Proverbs 12:26

April 11
Joshua 3:1–4:24
Luke 14:7-35
Psalm 80:1-19
Proverbs 12:27-28

April 12
Joshua 5:1–7:15
Luke 15:1-32

Psalm 81:1-16
Proverbs 13:1

April 13
Joshua 7:16–9:2
Luke 16:1-18
Psalm 82:1-8
Proverbs 13:2-3

April 14
Joshua 9:3–10:43
Luke 16:19–17:10
Psalm 83:1-18
Proverbs 13:4

April 15
Joshua 11:1–12:24
Luke 17:11-37
Psalm 84:1-12
Proverbs 13:5-6

April 16
Joshua 13:1–14:15
Luke 18:1-17
Psalm 85:1-13
Proverbs 13:7-8

April 17
Joshua 15:1-63
Luke 18:18-43
Psalm 86:1-17
Proverbs 13:9-10

April 18
Joshua 16:1–18:28
Luke 19:1-27
Psalm 87:1-7
Proverbs 13:11

April 19
Joshua 19:1–20:9
Luke 19:28-48
Psalm 88:1-18
Proverbs 13:12-14

April 20
Joshua 21:1–22:20
Luke 20:1-26
Psalm 89:1-13
Proverbs 13:15-16

April 21
Joshua 22:21–23:16
Luke 20:27-47

Psalm 89:14-37
Proverbs 13:17-19

April 22
Joshua 24:1-33
Luke 21:1-28
Psalm 89:38-52
Proverbs 13:20-23

April 23
Judges 1:1–2:9
Luke 21:29–22:13
Psalms 90:1–91:16
Proverbs 13:24-25

April 24
Judges 2:10–3:31
Luke 22:14-34
Psalms 92:1–93:5
Proverbs 14:1-2

April 25
Judges 4:1–5:31
Luke 22:35-53
Psalm 94:1-23
Proverbs 14:3-4

April 26
Judges 6:1-40
Luke 22:54–23:12
Psalms 95:1–96:13
Proverbs 14:5-6

April 27
Judges 7:1–8:17
Luke 23:13-43
Psalms 97:1–98:9
Proverbs 14:7-8

April 28
Judges 8:18–9:21
Luke 23:44–24:12
Psalm 99:1-9
Proverbs 14:9-10

April 29
Judges 9:22–10:18
Luke 24:13-53
Psalm 100:1-5
Proverbs 14:11-12

April 30
Judges 11:1–12:15
John 1:1-28

Psalm 101:1-8
Proverbs 14:13-14

May 1
Judges 13:1–14:20
John 1:29-51
Psalm 102:1-28
Proverbs 14:15-16
May 2
Judges 15:1–16:31
John 2:1-25
Psalm 103:1-22
Proverbs 14:17-19
May 3
Judges 17:1–18:31
John 3:1-21
Psalm 104:1-23
Proverbs 14:20-21
May 4
Judges 19:1–20:48
John 3:22–4:3
Psalm 104:24-35
Proverbs 14:22-24
May 5
Judges 21:1—Ruth 1:22
John 4:4-42
Psalm 105: 1-15
Proverbs 14:25
May 6
Ruth 2:1–4:22
John 4:43-54
Psalm 105:16-36
Proverbs 14:26-27
May 7
1 Samuel 1:1–2:21
John 5:1-23
Psalm 105:37-45
Proverbs 14:28-29
May 8
1 Samuel 2:22–4:22
John 5:24-47
Psalm 106:1-12
Proverbs 14:30-31

May 9
1 Samuel 5:1–7:17
John 6:1-21
Psalm 106:13-31
Proverbs 14:32-33
May 10
1 Samuel 8:1–9:27
John 6:22-42
Psalm 106:32-48
Proverbs 14:34-35
May 11
1 Samuel 10:1–11:15
John 6:43-71
Psalm 107:1-43
Proverbs 15:1-3
May 12
1 Samuel 12:1–13:23
John 7:1-30
Psalm 108:1-13
Proverbs 15:4
May 13
1 Samuel 14:1-52
John 7:31-53
Psalm 109:1-31
Proverbs 15:5-7
May 14
1 Samuel 15:1–16:23
John 8:1-20
Psalm 110:1-7
Proverbs 15:8-10
May 15
1 Samuel 17:1–18:4
John 8:21-30
Psalm 111:1-10
Proverbs 15:11
May 16
1 Samuel 18:5–19:24
John 8:31-59
Psalm 112:1-10
Proverbs 15:12-14
May 17
1 Samuel 20:1–21:15
John 9:1-41
Psalms 113:1–114:8
Proverbs 15:15-17

May 18
1 Samuel 22:1–23:29
John 10:1-21
Psalm 115:1-18
Proverbs 15:18-19
May 19
1 Samuel 24:1–25:44
John 10:22-42
Psalm 116:1-19
Proverbs 15:20-21
May 20
1 Samuel 26:1–28:25
John 11:1-54
Psalm 117:1-2
Proverbs 15:22-23
May 21
1 Samuel 29:1–31:13
John 11:55–12:19
Psalm 118:1-18
Proverbs 15:24-26
May 22
2 Samuel 1:1–2:11
John 12:20-50
Psalm 118:19-29
Proverbs 15:27-28
May 23
2 Samuel 2:12–3:39
John 13:1-30
Psalm 119:1-16
Proverbs 15:29-30
May 24
2 Samuel 4:1–6:23
John 13:31–14:14
Psalm 119:17-32
Proverbs 15:31-32
May 25
2 Samuel 7:1–8:18
John 14:15-31
Psalm 119:33-48
Proverbs 15:33
May 26
2 Samuel 9:1–11:27
John 15:1-27
Psalm 119:49-64
Proverbs 16:1-3

May 27
2 Samuel 12:1-31
John 16:1-33
Psalm 119:65-80
Proverbs 16:4-5

May 28
2 Samuel 13:1-39
John 17:1-26
Psalm 119:81-96
Proverbs 16:6-7

May 29
2 Samuel 14:1–15:22
John 18:1-24
Psalm 119:97-112
Proverbs 16:8-9

May 30
2 Samuel
15:23–16:23
John 18:25–19:22
Psalm 119:113-128
Proverbs 16:10-11

May 31
2 Samuel 17:1-29
John 19:23-42
Psalm 119:129-152
Proverbs 16:12-13

June 1
2 Samuel 18:1–19:10
John 20:10-31
Psalm 119:153-176
Proverbs 16:14-15

June 2
2 Samuel
19:11–20:13
John 21:1-25
Psalm 120:1-7
Proverbs 16:16-17

June 3
2 Samuel
20:14–21:22
Acts 1:1-26
Psalm 121:1-8
Proverbs 16:18

June 4
2 Samuel 22:1–23:23
Acts 2:1-47
Psalm 122:1-9
Proverbs 16:19-20

June 5
2 Samuel
23:24–24:25
Acts 3:1-26
Psalm 123:1-4
Proverbs 16:21-23

June 6
1 Kings 1:1-53
Acts 4:1-37
Psalm 124:1-8
Proverbs 16:24

June 7
1 Kings 2:1–3:2
Acts 5:1-42
Psalm 125:1-5
Proverbs 16:25

June 8
1 Kings 3:3–4:34
Acts 6:1-15
Psalm 126:1-6
Proverbs 16:26-27

June 9
1 Kings 5:1–6:38
Acts 7:1-29
Psalm 127:1-5
Proverbs 16:28-30

June 10
1 Kings 7:1-51
Acts 7:30-50
Psalm 128:1-6
Proverbs 16:31-33

June 11
1 Kings 8:1-66
Acts 7:51–8:13
Psalm 129:1-8
Proverbs 17:1

June 12
1 Kings 9:1–10:29
Acts 8:14-40
Psalm 130:1-8

Proverbs 17:2-3

June 13
1 Kings 11:1–12:19
Acts 9:1-25
Psalm 131:1-3
Proverbs 17:4-5

June 14
1 Kings 12:20–13:34
Acts 9:26-43
Psalm 132:1-18
Proverbs 17:6

June 15
1 Kings 14:1–15:24
Acts 10:1-23
Psalm 133:1-3
Proverbs 17:7-8

June 16
1 Kings 15:25–
17:24
Acts 10:24-48
Psalm 134:1-3
Proverbs 17:9-11

June 17
1 Kings 18:1-46
Acts 11:1-30
Psalm 135:1-21
Proverbs 17:12-13

June 18
1 Kings 19:1-21
Acts 12:1-23
Psalm 136:1-26
Proverbs 17:14-15

June 19
1 Kings 20:1–21:29
Acts 12:24–13:15
Psalm 137:1-9
Proverbs 17:16

June 20
1 Kings 22:1-53
Acts 13:16-41
Psalm 138:1-8
Proverbs 17:17-18

June 21
2 Kings 1:1–2:25
Acts 13:42–14:7

Psalm 139:1-24
Proverbs 17:19-21

June 22
2 Kings 3:1–4:17
Acts 14:8-28
Psalm 140:1-13
Proverbs 17:22

June 23
2 Kings 4:18–5:27
Acts 15:1-35
Psalm 141:1-10
Proverbs 17:23

June 24
2 Kings 6:1–7:20
Acts 15:36–16:15
Psalm 142:1-7
Proverbs 17:24-25

June 25
2 Kings 8:1–9:13
Acts 16:16-40
Psalm 143:1-12
Proverbs 17:26

June 26
2 Kings 9:14–10:31
Acts 17:1-34
Psalm 144:1-15
Proverbs 17:27-28

June 27
2 Kings 10:32–12:21
Acts 18:1-22
Psalm 145:1-21
Proverbs 18:1

June 28
2 Kings 13:1–14:29
Acts 18:23–19:12
Psalm 146:1-10
Proverbs 18:2-3

June 29
2 Kings 15:1–16:20
Acts 19:13-41
Psalm 147:1-20
Proverbs 18:4-5

June 30
2 Kings 17:1–18:12
Acts 20:1-38

Psalm 148:1-14
Proverbs 18:6-7

July 1
2 Kings 18:13–19:37
Acts 21:1-17
Psalm 149:1-9
Proverbs 18:8

July 2
2 Kings 20:1–22:2
Acts 21:18-36
Psalm 150:1-6
Proverbs 18:9-10

July 3
2 Kings 22:3–23:30
Acts 21:37–22:16
Psalm 1:1-6
Proverbs 18:11-12

July 4
2 Kings 23:31–25:30
Acts 22:17–23:10
Psalm 2:1-12
Proverbs 18:13

July 5
1 Chronicles
1:1–2:17
Acts 23:11-35
Psalm 3:1-8
Proverbs 18:14-15

July 6
1 Chronicles
2:18–4:4
Acts 24:1-27
Psalm 4:1-8
Proverbs 18:16-18

July 7
1 Chronicles
4:5–5:17
Acts 25:1-27
Psalm 5:1-12
Proverbs 18:19

July 8
1 Chronicles
5:18–6:81
Acts 26:1-32

Psalm 6:1-10
Proverbs 18:20-21

July 9
1 Chronicles
7:1–8:40
Acts 27:1-20
Psalm 7:1-17
Proverbs 18:22

July 10
1 Chronicles
9:1–10:14
Acts 27:21-44
Psalm 8:1-9
Proverbs 18:23-24

July 11
1 Chronicles
11:1–12:18
Acts 28:1-31
Psalm 9:1-12
Proverbs 19:1-3

July 12
1 Chronicles
12:19–14:17
Romans 1:1-17
Psalm 9:13-20
Proverbs 19:4-5

July 13
1 Chronicles
15:1–16:36
Romans 1:18-32
Psalm 10:1-15
Proverbs 19:6-7

July 14
1 Chronicles
16:37–18:17
Romans 2:1-24
Psalm 10:16-18
Proverbs 19:8-9

July 15
1 Chronicles
19:1–21:30
Romans 2:25–3:8
Psalm 11:1-7
Proverbs 19:10-12

July 16
   1 Chronicles
      22:1–23:32
   Romans 3:9-31
   Psalm 12:1-8
   Proverbs 19:13-14
July 17
   1 Chronicles
      24:1–26:11
   Romans 4:1-12
   Psalm 13:1-6
   Proverbs 19:15-16
July 18
   1 Chronicles
      26:12–27:34
   Romans 4:13–5:5
   Psalm 14:1-7
   Proverbs 19:17
July 19
   1 Chronicles
      28:1–29:30
   Romans 5:6-21
   Psalm 15:1-5
   Proverbs 19:18-19
July 20
   2 Chronicles
      1:1–3:17
   Romans 6:1-23
   Psalm 16:1-11
   Proverbs 19:20-21
July 21
   2 Chronicles
      4:1–6:11
   Romans 7:1-13
   Psalm 17:1-15
   Proverbs 19:22-23
July 22
   2 Chronicles
      6:12–8:10
   Romans 7:14–8:8
   Psalm 18:1-15
   Proverbs 19:24-25
July 23
   2 Chronicles
      8:11–10:19

Romans 8:9-25
   Psalm 18:16-36
   Proverbs 19:26
July 24
   2 Chronicles
      11:1–13:22
   Romans 8:26-39
   Psalm 18:37-50
   Proverbs 19:27-29
July 25
   2 Chronicles
      14:1–16:14
   Romans 9:1-24
   Psalm 19:1-14
   Proverbs 20:1
July 26
   2 Chronicles
      17:1–18:34
   Romans 9:25–10:13
   Psalm 20:1-9
   Proverbs 20:2-3
July 27
   2 Chronicles
      19:1–20:37
   Romans 10:14–11:12
   Psalm 21:1-13
   Proverbs 20:4-6
July 28
   2 Chronicles
      21:1–23:21
   Romans 11:13-36
   Psalm 22:1-18
   Proverbs 20:7
July 29
   2 Chronicles
      24:21–25:28
   Romans 12:1-21
   Psalm 22:19-31
   Proverbs 20:8-10
July 30
   2 Chronicles
      26:1–28:27
   Romans 13:1-14
   Psalm 23:1-6
   Proverbs 20:11

July 31
   2 Chronicles 29:1-36
   Romans 14:1-23
   Psalm 24:1-10
   Proverbs 20:12

August 1
   2 Chronicles
      30:1–31:21
   Romans 15:1-22
   Psalm 25:1-15
   Proverbs 20:13-15
August 2
   2 Chronicles
      32:1–33:13
   Romans 15:23–16:9
   Psalm 25:16-22
   Proverbs 20:16-18
August 3
   2 Chronicles
      33:14–34:33
   Romans 16:10-27
   Psalm 26:1-12
   Proverbs 20:19
August 4
   2 Chronicles
      35:1–36:23
   1 Corinthians 1:1-17
   Psalm 27:1-6
   Proverbs 20:20-21
August 5
   Ezra 1:1–2:70
   1 Corinthians
      1:18–2:5
   Psalm 27:7-14
   Proverbs 20:22-23
August 6
   Ezra 3:1–4:23
   1 Corinthians
      2:6–3:4
   Psalm 28:1-9
   Proverbs 20:24-25
August 7
   Ezra 4:24–6:22
   1 Corinthians 3:5-23
   Psalm 29:1-11

Proverbs 20:26-27

August 8
Ezra 7:1–8:20
l Corinthians 4:1-21
Psalm 30:1-12
Proverbs 20:28-30

August 9
Ezra 8:21–9:15
1 Corinthians 5:1-13
Psalm 31:1-8
Proverbs 21:1-2

August 10
Ezra 10:1-44
1 Corinthians 6:1-20
Psalm 31:9-18
Proverbs 21:3

August 11
Nehemiah 1:1–3:14
1 Corinthians 7:1-24
Psalm 31:19-24
Proverbs 21:4

August 12
Nehemiah 3:15–5:13
1 Corinthians 7:25-40
Psalm 32:1-11
Proverbs 21:5-7

August 13
Nehemiah 5:14–7:73a
1 Corinthians 8:1-13
Psalm 33:1-11
Proverbs 21:8-10

August 14
Nehemiah 7:73b–9:21
1 Corinthians 9:1-18
Psalm 33:12-22
Proverbs 21:11-12

August 15
Nehemiah 9:22–10:39
1 Corinthians 9:19–10:13
Psalm 34:1-10

Proverbs 21:13

August 16
Nehemiah 11:1–12:26
1 Corinthians 10:14-33
Psalm 34:11-22
Proverbs 21:14-16

August 17
Nehemiah 12:27–13:31
1 Corinthians 11:1-16
Psalm 35:1-16
Proverbs 21:17-18

August 18
Esther 1:1–3:15
1 Corinthians 11:17-34
Psalm 35:17-28
Proverbs 21:19-20

August 19
Esther 4:1–7:10
1 Corinthians 12:1-26
Psalm 36:1-12
Proverbs 21:21-22

August 20
Esther 8:1–10:3
1 Corinthians 12:27–13:13
Psalm 37:1-11
Proverbs 21:23-24

August 21
Job 1:1–3:26
1 Corinthians 14:1-17
Psalm 37:12-29
Proverbs 21:25-26

August 22
Job 4:1–7:21
1 Corinthians 14:18-40
Psalm 37:30-40
Proverbs 21:27

August 23
Job 8:1–11:20
1 Corinthians 15:1-28
Psalm 38:1-22
Proverbs 21:28-29

August 24
Job 12:1–15:35
1 Corinthians 15:29-58
Psalm 39:1-13
Proverbs 21:30-31

August 25
Job 16:1–19:29
1 Corinthians 16:1-24
Psalm 40:1-10
Proverbs 22:1

August 26
Job 20:1–22:30
2 Corinthians 1:1-11
Psalm 40:11-17
Proverbs 22:2-4

August 27
Job 23:1–27:23
2 Corinthians 1:12–2:11
Psalm 41:1-13
Proverbs 22:5-6

August 28
Job 28:1–30:31
2 Corinthians 2:12-17
Psalm 42:1-11
Proverbs 22:7

August 29
Job 31:1–33:33
2 Corinthians 3:1-18
Psalm 43:1-5
Proverbs 22:8-9

August 30
Job 34:1–36:33
2 Corinthians 4:1-12

Psalm 44:1-8
Proverbs 22:10-12

August 31
Job 37:1–39:30
2 Corinthians
4:13–5:10
Psalm 44:9-26
Proverbs 22:13

September 1
Job 40:1–42:17
2 Corinthians
5:11-21
Psalm 45:1-17
Proverbs 22:14

September 2
Ecclesiastes 1:1–
3:22
2 Corinthians 6:1-13
Psalm 46:1-11
Proverbs 22:15

September 3
Ecclesiastes 4:1–6:12
2 Corinthians
6:14–7:7
Psalm 47:1-9
Proverbs 22:16

September 4
Ecclesiastes 7:1–9:18
2 Corinthians 7:8-16
Psalm 48:1-14
Proverbs 22:17-19

September 5
Ecclesiastes
10:1–12:14
2 Corinthians 8:1-15
Psalm 49:1-20
Proverbs 22:20-21

September 6
Song of Songs
1:1–4:16
2 Corinthians
8:16-24
Psalm 50:1-23
Proverbs 22:22-23

September 7
Song of Songs
5:1–8:14
2 Corinthians 9:1-15
Psalm 51:1-19
Proverbs 22:24-25

September 8
Isaiah 1:1–2:22
2 Corinthians
10:1-18
Psalm 52:1-9
Proverbs 22:26-27

September 9
Isaiah 3:1–5:30
2 Corinthians
11:1-15
Psalm 53:1-6
Proverbs 22:28-29

September 10
Isaiah 6:1–7:25
2 Corinthians
11:16-33
Psalm 54:1-7
Proverbs 23:1-3

September 11
Isaiah 8:1–9:21
2 Corinthians
12:1-10
Psalm 55:1-23
Proverbs 23:4-5

September 12
Isaiah 10:1–11:16
2 Corinthians
12:11-21
Psalm 56:1-13
Proverbs 23:6-8

September 13
Isaiah 12:1–14:32
2 Corinthians
13:1-13
Psalm 57:1-11
Proverbs 23:9-11

September 14
Isaiah 15:1–18:7
Galatians 1:1-24

Psalm 58:1-11
Proverbs 23:12

September 15
Isaiah 19:1–21:17
Galatians 2:1-16
Psalm 59:1-17
Proverbs 23:13-14

September 16
Isaiah 22:1–24:23
Galatians 2:17–3:9
Psalm 60:1-12
Proverbs 23:15-16

September 17
Isaiah 25:1–28:13
Galatians 3:10-22
Psalm 61:1-8
Proverbs 23:17-18

September 18
Isaiah 28:14–30:11
Galatians 3:23–4:31
Psalm 62:1-12
Proverbs 23:19-21

September 19
Isaiah 30:12–33:9
Galatians 5:1-12
Psalm 63:1-11
Proverbs 23:22

September 20
Isaiah 33:10–36:22
Galatians 5:13-25
Psalm 64:1-10
Proverbs 23:24

September 21
Isaiah 37:1–38:22
Galatians 6:1-18
Psalm 65:1-13
Proverbs 23:24

September 22
Isaiah 39:1–41:16
Ephesians 1:1-23
Psalm 66:1-20
Proverbs 23:25-28

September 23
Isaiah 41:17–43:13
Ephesians 2:1-22

Psalm 67:1-7
Proverbs 23:29-35
September 24
Isaiah 43:14—45:10
Ephesians 3:1-21
Psalm 68:1-18
Proverbs 24:1-2
September 25
Isaiah 45:11—48:11
Ephesians 4:1-16
Psalm 68:19-35
Proverbs 24:3-4
September 26
Isaiah 48:12—50:11
Ephesians 4:17-32
Psalm 69:1-18
Proverbs 24:5-6
September 27
Isaiah 51:1—53:12
Ephesians 5:1-33
Psalm 69:19-36
Proverbs 24:7
September 28
Isaiah 54:1—57:14
Ephesians 6:1-24
Psalm 70:1-5
Proverbs 24:8
September 29
Isaiah 57:15—59:21
Philippians 1:1-26
Psalm 71:1-24
Proverbs 24:9-10
September 30
Isaiah 60:1—62:5
Philippians
  1:27—2:18
Psalm 72:1-20
Proverbs 24:11-12

October 1
Isaiah 62:6—65:25
Philippians
  2:19—3:3
Psalm 73:1-28
Proverbs 24:13-14

October 2
Isaiah 66:1-24
Philippians 3:4-21
Psalm 74:1-23
Proverbs 24:15-16
October 3
Jeremiah 1:1—2:30
Philippians 4:1-23
Psalm 75:1-10
Proverbs 24:17-20
October 4
Jeremiah 2:31—4:18
Colossians 1:1-17
Psalm 76:1-12
Proverbs 24:21-22
October 5
Jeremiah 4:19—6:15
Colossians 1:18—2:7
Psalm 77:1-20
Proverbs 24:23-25
October 6
Jeremiah 6:16—8:7
Colossians 2:8-23
Psalm 78:1-31
Proverbs 24:26
October 7
Jeremiah 8:8—9:26
Colossians 3:1-17
Psalm 78:32-55
Proverbs 24:27
October 8
Jeremiah 10:1—11:23
Colossians 3:18—4:18
Psalm 78:56-72
Proverbs 24:28-29
October 9
Jeremiah 12:1—14:10
1 Thessalonians
  1:1—2:8
Psalm 79:1-13
Proverbs 24:30-34
October 10
Jeremiah
  14:11—16:15

1 Thessalonians
  2:9—3:13
Psalm 80:1-9
Proverbs 25:1-5
October 11
Jeremiah
  16:16—18:23
1 Thessalonians
  4:1—5:3
Psalm 81:1-16
Proverbs 25:6-8
October 12
Jeremiah 19:1—21:14
1 Thessalonians
  5:4-28
Psalm 82:1-8
Proverbs 25:9-10
October 13
Jeremiah 22:1—23:20
2 Thessalonians
  1:1-12
Psalm 83:1-18
Proverbs 25:11-14
October 14
Jeremiah
  23:21—25:38
2 Thessalonians
  2:1-17
Psalm 84:1-12
Proverbs 25:15
October 15
Jeremiah 26:1—27:22
2 Thessalonians
  3:1-18
Psalm 85:1-13
Proverbs 25:16
October 16
Jeremiah 28:1—29:32
1 Timothy 1:1-20
Psalm 86:1-17
Proverbs 25:17
October 17
Jeremiah 30:1—31:26
1 Timothy 2:1-15
Psalm 87:1-7

655 . . . . THE ONE YEAR BIBLE READING PLAN

Proverbs 25:18-19

October 18
Jeremiah
31:27–32:44
1 Timothy 3:1-16
Psalm 88:1-18
Proverbs 25:20-22

October 19
Jeremiah 33:1–34:22
1 Timothy 4:1-16
Psalm 89:1-13
Proverbs 25:23-24

October 20
Jeremiah 35:1–36:32
1 Timothy 5:1-25
Psalm 89:14-37
Proverbs 25:25-27

October 21
Jeremiah 37:1–38:28
1 Timothy 6:1-21
Psalm 89:38-52
Proverbs 25:28

October 22
Jeremiah 39:1–41:18
2 Timothy 1:1-18
Psalms 90:1–91:16
Proverbs 26:1-2

October 23
Jeremiah 42:1–44:23
2 Timothy 2:1-21
Psalms 92:1–93:5
Proverbs 26:3-5

October 24
Jeremiah 44:24–47:7
2 Timothy 2:22–3:17
Psalm 94:1-23
Proverbs 26:6-8

October 25
Jeremiah 48:1–49:22
2 Timothy 4:1-22
Psalms 95:1–96:13
Proverbs 26:9-12

October 26
Jeremiah
49:23–50:46

Titus 1:1-16
Psalms 97:1–98:9
Proverbs 26:13-16

October 27
Jeremiah 51:1-53
Titus 2:1-15
Psalm 99:1-9
Proverbs 26:17

October 28
Jeremiah
51:54–52:34
Titus 3:1-15
Psalm 100:1-5
Proverbs 26:18-19

October 29
Lamentations
1:1–2:22
Philemon 1:1-25
Psalm 101:1-8
Proverbs 26:20

October 30
Lamentations 3:1-66
Hebrews 1:1-14
Psalm 102:1-28
Proverbs 26:21-22

October 31
Lamentations
4:1–5:22
Hebrews 2:1-18
Psalm 103:1-22
Proverbs 26:23

November 1
Ezekiel 1:1–3:15
Hebrews 3:1-19
Psalm 104:1-23
Proverbs 26:24-26

November 2
Ezekiel 3:16–6:14
Hebrews 4:1-16
Psalm 104:24-35
Proverbs 26:27

November 3
Ezekiel 7:1–9:11
Hebrews 5:1-14
Psalm 105:1-15

Proverbs 26:28

November 4
Ezekiel 10:1–11:25
Hebrews 6:1-20
Psalm 105:16-36
Proverbs 27:1-2

November 5
Ezekiel 12:1–14:11
Hebrews 7:1-17
Psalm 105:37-45
Proverbs 27:3

November 6
Ezekiel 14:12–16:41
Hebrews 7:18-28
Psalm 106:1-12
Proverbs 27:4-6

November 7
Ezekiel 16:42–17:24
Hebrews 8:1-13
Psalm 106:13-31
Proverbs 27:7-9

November 8
Ezekiel 18:1–19:14
Hebrews 9:1-10
Psalm 106:32-48
Proverbs 27:10

November 9
Ezekiel 20:1-49
Hebrews 9:11-28
Psalm 107:1-43
Proverbs 27:11

November 10
Ezekiel 21:1–22:31
Hebrews 10:1-17
Psalm 108:1-13
Proverbs 27:12

November 11
Ezekiel 23:1-49
Hebrews 10:18-39
Psalm 109:1-31
Proverbs 27:13

November 12
Ezekiel 24:1–26:21
Hebrews 11:1-16
Psalm 110:1-7

Proverbs 27:14
November 13
Ezekiel 27:1–28:26
Hebrews 11:17-31
Psalm 111:1-10
Proverbs 27:15-16
November 14
Ezekiel 29:1–30:26
Hebrews
11:32–12:13
Psalm 112:1-10
Proverbs 27:17
November 15
Ezekiel 31:1–32:32
Hebrews 12:14-29
Psalms 113:1–114:8
Proverbs 27:18-20
November 16
Ezekiel 33:1–34:31
Hebrews 13:1-25
Psalm 115:1-18
Proverbs 27:21-22
November 17
Ezekiel 35:1–36:28
James 1:1-18
Psalm 116:1-19
Proverbs 27:23-27
November 18
Ezekiel 37:1–38:23
James 1:19–2:17
Psalm 117:1-2
Proverbs 28:1
November 19
Ezekiel 39:1–40:27
James 2:18–3:18
Psalm 118:1-18
Proverbs 28:2
November 20
Ezekiel 40:28–41:26
James 4:1-17
Psalm 118:19-20
Proverbs 28:3-5
November 21
Ezekiel 42:1–43:27
James 5:1-20

Psalm 119:1-16
Proverbs 28:6-7
November 22
Ezekiel 44:1–45:12
1 Peter 1:1-12
Psalm 119:17-32
Proverbs 28:8-10
November 23
Ezekiel 45:13–46:24
1 Peter 1:13–2:10
Psalm 119:33-48
Proverbs 28:11
November 24
Ezekiel 47:1–48:35
1 Peter 2:11–3:7
Psalm 119:49-64
Proverbs 28:12-13
November 25
Daniel 1:1–2:23
1 Peter 3:8–4:6
Psalm 119:65-80
Proverbs 28:14
November 26
Daniel 2:24–3:30
1 Peter 4:7–5:14
Psalm 119:81-96
Proverbs 28:15-16
November 27
Daniel 4:1-37
2 Peter 1:1-21
Psalm 119:97-112
Proverbs 28:17-18
November 28
Daniel 5:1-31
2 Peter 2:1-22
Psalm 119:113-128
Proverbs 28:19-20
November 29
Daniel 6:1-28
2 Peter 3:1-18
Psalm 119:129-152
Proverbs 28:21-22
November 30
Daniel 7:1-28
1 John 1:1-10

Psalm 119:153-176
Proverbs 28:23-24
December 1
Daniel 8:1-27
1 John 2:1-17
Psalm 120:1-7
Proverbs 28:25-26
December 2
Daniel 9:1–11:1
1 John 2:18–3:6
Psalm 121:1-8
Proverbs 28:27-28
December 3
Daniel 11:2-35
1 John 3:7-24
Psalm 122:1-9
Proverbs 29:1
December 4
Daniel 11:36–12:13
1 John 4:1-21
Psalm 123:1-4
Proverbs 29:2-4
December 5
Hosea 1:1–3:5
1 John 5:1-21
Psalm 124:1-8
Proverbs 29:5-8
December 6
Hosea 4:1–5:15
2 John 1:1-13
Psalm 125:1-5
Proverbs 29:9-11
December 7
Hosea 6:1–9:17
3 John 1:1-15
Psalm 126:1-6
Proverbs 29:12-14
December 8
Hosea 10:1–14:9
Jude 1:1-25
Psalm 127:1-5
Proverbs 29:15-17
December 9
Joel 1:1–3:21
Revelation 1:1-20

Psalm 128:1-6
Proverbs 29:18
December 10
Amos 1:1–3:15
Revelation 2:1-17
Psalm 129:1-8
Proverbs 29:19-20
December 11
Amos 4:1–6:14
Revelation 2:18–3:6
Psalm 130:1-8
Proverbs 29:21-22
December 12
Amos 7:1–9:15
Revelation 3:7-22
Psalm 131:1-3
Proverbs 29:23
December 13
Obadiah 1:1-21
Revelation 4:1-11
Psalm 132:1-18
Proverbs 29:24-25
December 14
Jonah 1:1–4:11
Revelation 5:1-14
Psalm 133:1-3
Proverbs 29:26-27
December 15
Micah 1:1–4:13
Revelation 6:1-17
Psalm 134:1-3
Proverbs 30:1-4
December 16
Micah 5:1–7:20
Revelation 7:1-17
Psalm 135:1-21
Proverbs 30:5-6
December 17
Nahum 1:1–3:19

Revelation 8:1-13
Psalm 136:1-26
Proverbs 30:7-9
December 18
Habakkuk 1:1–3:19
Revelation 9:1-21
Psalm 137:1-9
Proverbs 30:10
December 19
Zephaniah 1:1–3:20
Revelation 10:1-11
Psalm 138:1-8
Proverbs 30:11-14
December 20
Haggai 1:1–2:23
Revelation 11:1-19
Psalm 139:1-24
Proverbs 30:15-16
December 21
Zechariah 1:1-21
Revelation 12:1-17
Psalm 140:1-13
Proverbs 30:17
December 22
Zechariah 2:1–3:10
Revelation 12:18–13:18
Psalm 141:1-10
Proverbs 30:18-20
December 23
Zechariah 4:1–5:11
Revelation 14:1-20
Psalm 142:1-7
Proverbs 30:21-23
December 24
Zechariah 6:1–7:14
Revelation 15:1-8

Psalm 143:1-12
Proverbs 30:24-28
December 25
Zechariah 8:1-23
Revelation 16:1-21
Psalm 144:1-15
Proverbs 30:29-31
December 26
Zechariah 9:1-17
Revelation 17:1-18
Psalm 145:1-21
Proverbs 30:32
December 27
Zechariah 10:1–11:17
Revelation 18:1-24
Psalm 146:1-10
Proverbs 30:33
December 28
Zechariah 12:1–13:9
Revelation 19:1-21
Psalm 147:1-20
Proverbs 31:1-7
December 29
Zechariah 14:1-21
Revelation 20:1-15
Psalm 148:1-4
Proverbs 31:8-9
December 30
Malachi 1:1–2:17
Revelation 21:1-27
Psalm 149:1-9
Proverbs 31:10-24
December 31
Malachi 3:1–4:6
Revelation 22:1-21
Psalm 150:1-6
Proverbs 31:25-31

index of articles

Additional Popular Reference Books from Tyndale House Publishers

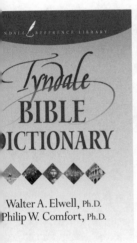

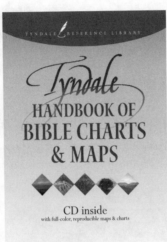

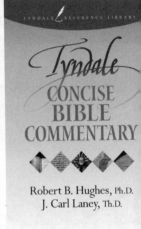

Tyndale Bible Dictionary

edited by
Walter A. Elwell and
Philip W. Comfort

ISBN 0-8423-7089-7

Tyndale Handbook of Bible Charts and Maps

by Neil S. Wilson and
Linda K. Taylor

ISBN 0-8423-3552-8

Tyndale Concise Bible Commentary

by Robert B. Hughes
and J. Carl Laney

ISBN 0-8423-5444-1

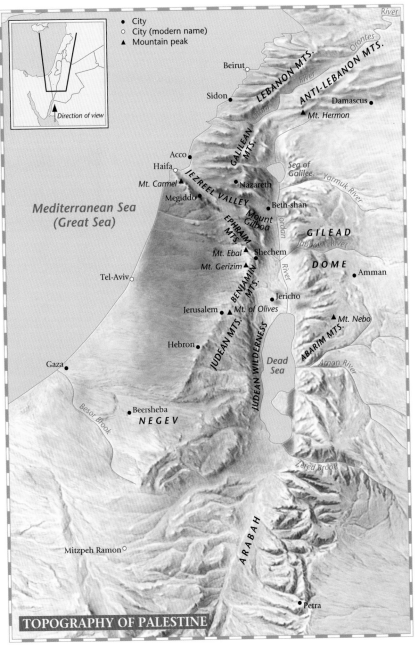

- ● City
- ○ City (modern name)
- ▲ Mountain peak

Direction of view

River

Beirut

LEBANON MTS.

ANTI-LEBANON MTS.

Orontes River

Sidon

Damascus

▲ *Mt. Hermon*

GALILEAN MTS.

Acco

Haifa

Sea of Galilee

Mt. Carmel ▲

Nazareth

JEZREEL VALLEY

Yarmuk River

Megiddo

Beth-shan

Mediterranean Sea (Great Sea)

Mount Gilboa

Jordan River

GILEAD

EPHRAIM MTS.

Mt. Ebal ▲ *Shechem*

DOME

Mt. Gerizim ▲

Jabbok River

Tel-Aviv

BENJAMIN MTS.

Amman

Jericho

Jerusalem ▲ ▲ *Mt. of Olives*

Mt. Nebo ▲

JUDEAN MTS.

JUDEAN WILDERNESS

ABARIM MTS.

Hebron

Dead Sea

Gaza

Arnon River

Besor Brook

Beersheba

NEGEV

Zered Brook

A R A B A H

Mitzpeh Ramon ○

Petra

TOPOGRAPHY OF PALESTINE

Copyright © 1996 Tyndale House Publishers, Inc.

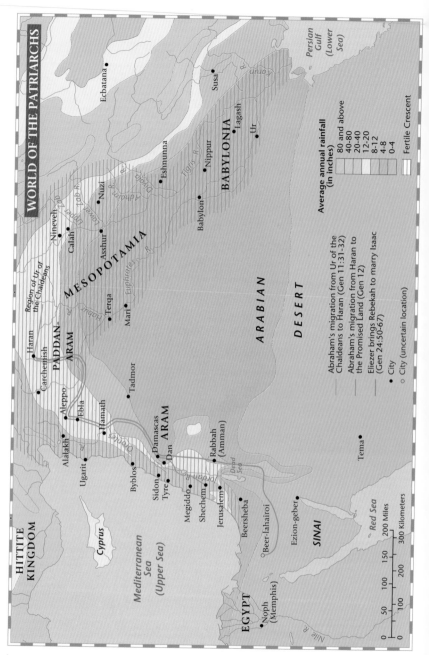

WORLD OF THE PATRIARCHS

HITTITE KINGDOM

Mediterranean Sea (Upper Sea)

Cyprus

Ugarit

Byblos

Sidon
Tyre
Dan
Megiddo
Shechem
Jerusalem
Beersheba
Beer-lahairoi

EGYPT

Noph (Memphis)

Nile R.

Red Sea

SINAI

Ezion-geber

Tema

ARABIAN DESERT

Alalakh
Aleppo
Ebla
Hamath
Damascus
Tadmor
Rabbah (Amman)
Dead Sea
Jordan R.
Orontes R.

PADDAN-ARAM

Haran
Carchemish

Region of Ur of the Chaldeans

MESOPOTAMIA

Nineveh
Calah
Asshur

Terqa
Mari

Euphrates R.
Habur R.

Nuzi

Upper Zab R.
Lower Zab R.
Adhaim R.
Diyala R.
Tigris R.

Eshnunna

Babylon

BABYLONIA

Nippur
Lagash
Ur

Susa

Ecbatana

Zagros Mts.

Persian Gulf (Lower Sea)

Average annual rainfall (in inches)

- 80 and above
- 40-80
- 20-40
- 12-20
- 8-12
- 4-8
- 0-4
- Fertile Crescent

— — Abraham's migration from Ur of the Chaldeans to Haran (Gen 11:31-32)

——— Abraham's migration from Haran to the Promised Land (Gen 12)

— — Eliezer brings Rebekah to marry Isaac (Gen 24:50-67)

● City

○ City (uncertain location)

0   50   100   150   200 Miles
0   100   200   300 Kilometers

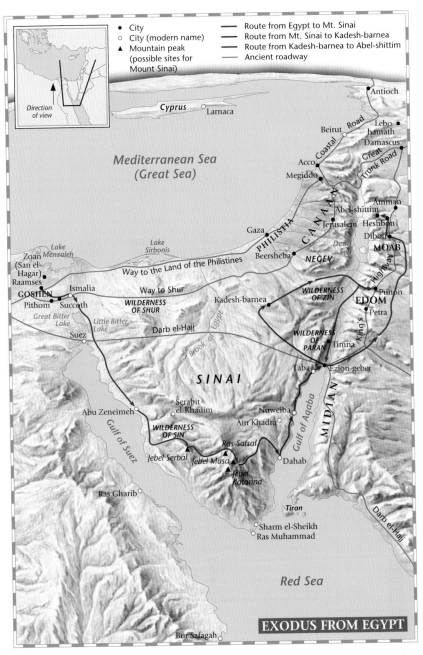

Legend
- • City
- ○ City (modern name)
- ▲ Mountain peak (possible sites for Mount Sinai)
- — Route from Egypt to Mt. Sinai
- — Route from Mt. Sinai to Kadesh-barnea
- — Route from Kadesh-barnea to Abel-shittim
- — Ancient roadway

Direction of view

Antioch

Cyprus   ○ Larnaca

Beirut   Coastal Road   Lebo-hamath
Damascus

Acco   Great Trunk Road

**Mediterranean Sea
(Great Sea)**

Megiddo

Amman

Abel-shittim   Heshbon

CANAAN   Jerusalem   Dibon

Gaza   PHILISTIA   Dead Sea   **MOAB**

Lake Menzaleh   Lake Sirbonis   Beersheba   NEGEV

Zoan (San el-Hagar)   Way to the Land of the Philistines

Raamses

GOSHEN   Ismalia   Way to Shur   Kadesh-barnea   WILDERNESS OF ZIN   Punon   **EDOM**

Pithom   Succoth   WILDERNESS OF SHUR   Petra

Great Bitter Lake   Little Bitter Lake   Darb el-Hajj   WILDERNESS OF PARAN   King's Highway

Suez   Brook of Egypt   Timna

S I N A I   Taba   Ezion-geber

Serabit el-Khadim   Nuweiba

Abu Zeneimeh   Ain Khadra   Gulf of Aqaba   **MIDIAN**

WILDERNESS OF SIN

Jebel Serbal   Ras Safsaf   Dahab

Jebel Musa   ▲

Jebel Katarina   ▲

Ras Gharib   Tiran   Darb el-Hajj

Sharm el-Sheikh
Ras Muhammad

Red Sea

EXODUS FROM EGYPT

Bur Safagah

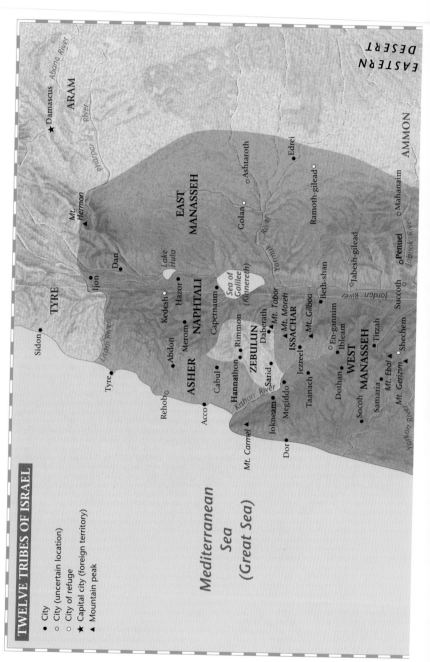

TWELVE TRIBES OF ISRAEL

- • City
- ○ City (uncertain location)
- ○ City of refuge
- ★ Capital city (foreign territory)
- ▲ Mountain peak

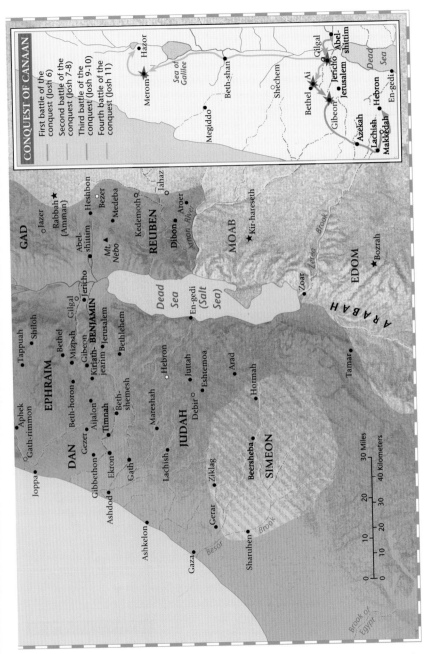

CONQUEST OF CANAAN

First battle of the conquest (Josh 6)

Second battle of the conquest (Josh 7-8)

Third battle of the conquest (Josh 9-10)

Fourth battle of the conquest (Josh 11)

Hazor

Merom

Sea of Galilee

Beth-shan

Shechem

Megiddo

Bethel • Ai

Gilgal

Jericho Abel-
shittim

Gibeon Jerusalem

Azekah

Lachish. Hebron En-gedi

Makkedah

Dead Sea

GAD

Jazer

Rabbah (Amman)

Abel-
shittim • Heshbon

Bezer

Mt.
Nebo • Medeba

Jahaz

Kedemoth

Kir-hareseth

REUBEN

Dibon • Aroer

Arnon River

MOAB

Jaded Brook

Zoar

Bozrah

EDOM

ARABAH

Dead Sea (Salt Sea)

En-gedi

EPHRAIM

Tappuah • Shiloh

Bethel

Mizpah Gilgal

Jericho

Beth-horon Gibeon BENJAMIN

Aphek Kiriath- Jerusalem

Gath-rimmon jearim Bethlehem

DAN Aijalon Beth- Hebron

Gezer Timnah shemesh

Gibbethon Ekron Mareshah Juttah

Joppa Gath Debir Eshtemoa

Ashdod Lachish JUDAH Arad

Gerar Ziklag Hormah

Ashkelon Beersheba

SIMEON

Gaza Sharuhen

Besor Brook

Tamar

Brook of Egypt

0   10   20   30 Miles

0 10 20 30 40 Kilometers

Copyright © 1996 Tyndale House Publishers, Inc.

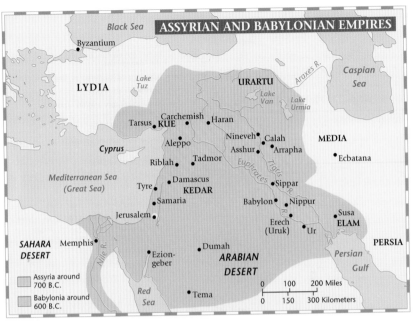

ASSYRIAN AND BABYLONIAN EMPIRES

Black Sea

Byzantium

LYDIA

Lake Tuz

URARTU

Araxes R.

Lake Van

Lake Urmia

Caspian Sea

Carchemish

Tarsus • KUE • Haran

Nineveh • Calah

Asshur • Arrapha

MEDIA

Aleppo

Cyprus

Ecbatana •

Riblah • Tadmor

Euphrates

Tigris R.

Mediterranean Sea
(Great Sea)

Tyre • Damascus

KEDAR

Sippar •

Samaria

Babylon • Nippur

Jerusalem •

Erech
(Uruk) • Ur

Susa •

ELAM

SAHARA
DESERT

Memphis •

Dumah •

ARABIAN
DESERT

PERSIA

Persian
Gulf

Ezion-
geber •

Nile R.

Assyria around
700 B.C.

Babylonia around
600 B.C.

Red
Sea

Tema •

0   100   200 Miles

0   150   300 Kilometers

GREEK EMPIRE

Danube R.

MACEDONIA

THRACE

Black Sea

Sinope •

CAUCASUS MTS.

Pella •

Athens •

HELLAS

Sparta •

ASIA

Ephesus •

Lake Tuz

ARMENIA

Lake Van

Araxes R.

Lake Urmia

Crete

Cyprus

Tarsus • Carchemish

Aleppo • Haran

Gaugamela •

Arbela •

MEDIA

Ecbatana •

Tadmor •

Euphrates

Tigris R.

Mediterranean Sea
(Great Sea)

Tyre • Damascus

Opis •

BABYLONIA

Cyrene •

LIBYA

Jerusalem •

NABATEA

Babylon •

Alexandria •

EGYPT Ezion-
Memphis • geber •

Erech
(Uruk) • Ur

Susa •

Extent of Alexandrian
empire

Ptolemaic realm

Seleucid realm

Antigonid realm

Minor Hellenistic provinces

SAHARA
DESERT

Nile R.

Red
Sea

Thebes •

ARABIAN
DESERT

Persian
Gulf

0   200   400 Miles

0   250   500 Kilometers

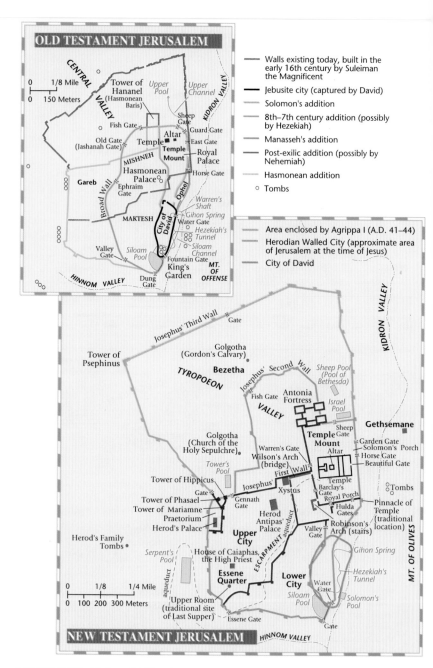

OLD TESTAMENT JERUSALEM

Walls existing today, built in the early 16th century by Suleiman the Magnificent

Jebusite city (captured by David)

Solomon's addition

8th–7th century addition (possibly by Hezekiah)

Manasseh's addition

Post-exilic addition (possibly by Nehemiah)

Hasmonean addition

○ Tombs

0 · 1/8 Mile
0 · 150 Meters

CENTRAL VALLEY

Tower of Hananel (Hasmonean Baris)

Upper Pool

Upper Channel

KIDRON VALLEY

Fish Gate

Sheep Gate

Guard Gate

Old Gate (Jashanah Gate)

Altar

Temple

East Gate

Temple Mount

Royal Palace

MISHNEH

Hasmonean Palace

Horse Gate

Gareb

Ephraim Gate

Broad Wall

Ophel

Warren's Shaft

MAKTESH

Gihon Spring

Water Gate

Hezekiah's Tunnel

Siloam Channel

City of David

Valley Gate

Siloam Pool

Fountain Gate

King's Garden

MT. OF OFFENSE

HINNOM VALLEY

Dung Gate

Area enclosed by Agrippa I (A.D. 41–44)

Herodian Walled City (approximate area of Jerusalem at the time of Jesus)

City of David

Josephus' Third Wall

Gate

Tower of Psephinus

Golgotha (Gordon's Calvary)

KIDRON VALLEY

BEZETHA

TYROPOEON

Josephus' Second Wall

Sheep Pool (Pool of Bethesda)

Fish Gate

Antonia Fortress

Israel Pool

VALLEY

Golgotha (Church of the Holy Sepulchre)

Sheep Gate

Gethsemane

Temple Mount

Garden Gate

Solomon's Porch

Warren's Gate

Altar

Horse Gate

Wilson's Arch (bridge)

Beautiful Gate

Tower's Pool

First Wall

Temple

Tower of Hippicus

Josephus'

Xystus

Royal Porch

Barclay's Gate

Pinnacle of Temple (traditional location)

Tower of Phasael

Gate

Gennath Gate

Hulda Gates

Tombs

Tower of Mariamne

Herod Antipas' Palace

Robinson's Arch (stairs)

Praetorium

Herod's Palace

Upper City

Valley Gate

Herod's Family Tombs

Serpent's Pool

House of Caiaphas, the High Priest

Gihon Spring

Essene Quarter

Lower City

Water Gate

Hezekiah's Tunnel

MT. OF OLIVES

ESCARPMENT aqueduct

Upper Room (traditional site of Last Supper)

Siloam Pool

Solomon's Pool

0 · 1/8 · 1/4 Mile
0 · 100 200 300 Meters

Essene Gate

Gate

NEW TESTAMENT JERUSALEM

HINNOM VALLEY

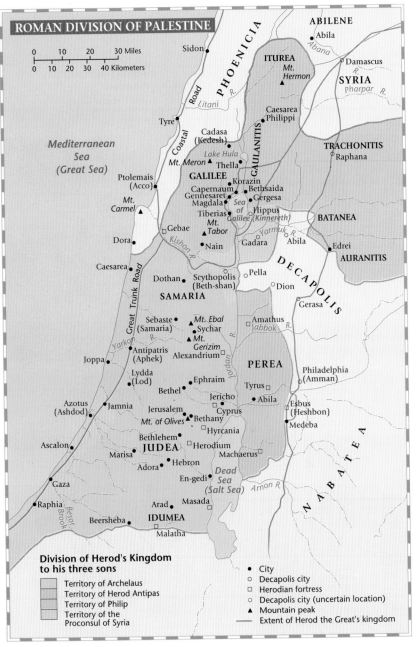

ROMAN DIVISION OF PALESTINE

ABILENE
• Abila

Abana R.

0   10   20   30 Miles
0   10   20   30   40 Kilometers

Sidon •

PHOENICIA

ITUREA
Mt. Hermon ▲

Damascus

SYRIA

Pharpar R.

Tyre •

Coastal Road

Litani R.

Caesarea • Philippi

Cadasa (Kedesh) •

GAULANITIS

TRACHONITIS
Raphana

Mt. Meron ▲

Lake Hula

Thella •

GALILEE

Ptolemais (Acco) •

Korazin •
Capernaum •   • Bethsaida
Gennesaret •   Gergesa •
Magdala •   Sea of
Tiberias •   Galilee (Kinnereth)   Hippus ○

BATANEA

Mt. Carmel ▲

Mediterranean Sea (Great Sea)

Gebae •
Mt. Tabor ▲

Dora •

Nain •

Gadara •   Abila •

Yarmuk R.

Edrei •

AURANITIS

Kishon R.

DECAPOLIS

Caesarea •

Dothan •
Scythopolis (Beth-shan) •

Pella ○

SAMARIA

Dion ○

Gerasa ○

Sebaste (Samaria) •
Mt. Ebal ▲
Sychar •
Mt. Gerizim ▲
Alexandrium □

Amathus □
Jabbok R.

Joppa •

Antipatris (Aphek) •

Yarkon R.

PEREA

Philadelphia (Amman) •

Lydda (Lod) •
Bethel •

Ephraim •

Tyrus □

Azotus (Ashdod) •
Jamnia •

Jericho □
Cyprus □

Abila •

Jerusalem •
Mt. of Olives •   Bethany •

Esbus (Heshbon) □

Hyrcania □

Medeba •

Ascalon •

Bethlehem •
Marisa •
Adora •   Hebron •

Herodium □
Machaerus □

JUDEA

Dead Sea (Salt Sea)

Gaza •

En-gedi •

Arnon R.

NABATEA

Raphia •

Besor Brook

Arad •   Masada □

Beersheba •   **IDUMEA**

Malatha •

Jordan R.

Division of Herod's Kingdom to his three sons

Territory of Archelaus
Territory of Herod Antipas
Territory of Philip
Territory of the Proconsul of Syria

• City
○ Decapolis city
□ Herodian fortress
○ Decapolis city (uncertain location)
▲ Mountain peak
— Extent of Herod the Great's kingdom

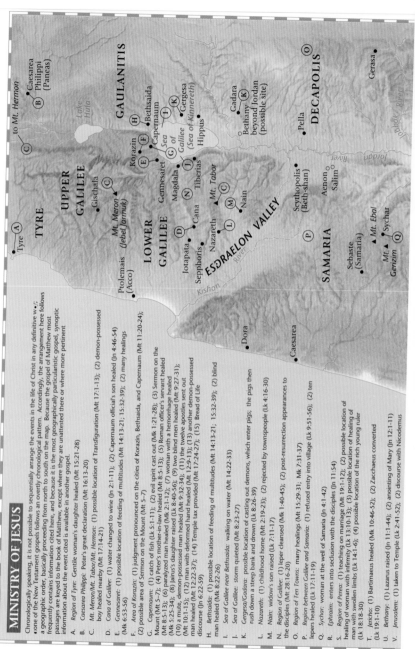

MINISTRY OF JESUS

Chronologically speaking, it is not possible to sequentially arrange the events in the life of Christ in any definitive way; none of the New Testament gospels follows an overtly chronological pattern. Accordingly, the arrangement here follows a geographic order, basically proceeding from north to south on the map. Because the gospel of Matthew most frequently contains information cited here, and because it is the most geographically particularistic gospel, synoptic passages are keyed to the book of Matthew, except where they are unattested there or where more pertinent information about the event cited is available in another gospel.

A. *Region of Tyre:* Gentile woman's daughter healed (Mt 15:21-28)

B. *Caesarea Philippi:* Peter's great declaration (Mt 16:13-20)

C. *Mt. Meron/Mt. Tabor/Mt. Hermon:* (1) possible location of Transfiguration (Mt 17:1-13); (2) demon-possessed boy healed nearby (Mt 17:14-21)

D. *Cana of Galilee:* (1) water changed to wine (Jn 2:1-11); (2) Capernaum official's son healed (Jn 4:46-54)

E. *Gennesaret:* (1) possible location of feeding of multitudes (Mt 14:13-21; 15:32-39); (2) many healings (Mk 6:53-56)

F. *Area of Korazin:* (1) judgment pronounced on the cities of Korazin, Bethsaida, and Capernaum (Mt 11:20-24); (2) possible area of Sermon on the Mount (Mt 5-7)

G. *Capernaum:* (1) catch of fish (Lk 5:1-11); (2) evil spirit cast out (Mk 1:21-28); (3) Sermon on the Mount (Mt 5-7); (4) Peter's mother-in-law healed (Mk 8:5-13); (5) Roman officer's servant healed (Mt 8:5-13); (6) paralyzed man healed (Mk 2:1-12); (7) woman with a hemorrhage healed (Mt 9:20-22); (8) Jairus's daughter raised (Lk 8:40-56); (9) two blind men healed (Mt 9:27-31); (10) a mute, demon-possessed man healed (Mt 9:32-34); (11) the twelve apostles sent out (Mt 10:1-15); (12) man with deformed hand healed (Mt 12:9-13); (13) another demon-possessed man healed (Mt 12:22-37); (14) Temple tax provided (Mt 17:24-27); (15) Bread of Life discourse (Jn 6:22-59)

H. *Bethsaida:* (1) possible location of feeding of multitudes (Mt 14:13-21; 15:32-39); (2) blind man healed (Mk 8:22-26)

I. *Sea of Galilee near Bethsaida:* walking on water (Mt 14:22-33)

J. *Sea of Galilee:* storm quieted (Mt 8:23-27)

K. *Gergesa/Gadara:* possible location of casting out demons, which enter pigs; the pigs then rush down a steep bank and drown (Lk 8:26-39)

L. *Nazareth:* (1) childhood home (Mt 2:19-23); (2) rejected by townspeople (Lk 4:16-30)

M. *Nain:* widow's son raised (Lk 7:11-17)

N. *Region of Galilee:* (1) leper cleansed (Mk 1:40-45); (2) post-resurrection appearances to the disciples (Mt 28:16-20)

O. *Region of Ten Towns:* many healings (Mt 15:29-31; Mk 7:31-37)

P. *Region between Galilee and Samaria:* (1) refused entry into village (Lk 9:51-56); (2) ten lepers healed (Lk 17:11-19)

Q. *Sychar:* woman at the well of Samaria (Jn 4:1-42)

R. *Ephraim:* enters into seclusion with the disciples (Jn 11:54)

S. *Region of Perea:* (1) teaching on marriage (Mt 19:1-12); (2) possible location of healing of woman with infirmity (Lk 13:10-13); (3) possible location of healing of man with swollen limbs (Lk 14:1-6); (4) possible location of the rich young ruler (Lk 18:18-30)

T. *Jericho:* (1) Bartimaeus healed (Mk 10:46-52); (2) Zacchaeus converted (Lk 19:1-10)

U. *Bethany:* (1) Lazarus raised (Jn 11:1-44); (2) anointing of Mary (Jn 12:1-11)

V. *Jerusalem:* (1) taken to Temple (Lk 2:41-52); (2) discourse with Nicodemus

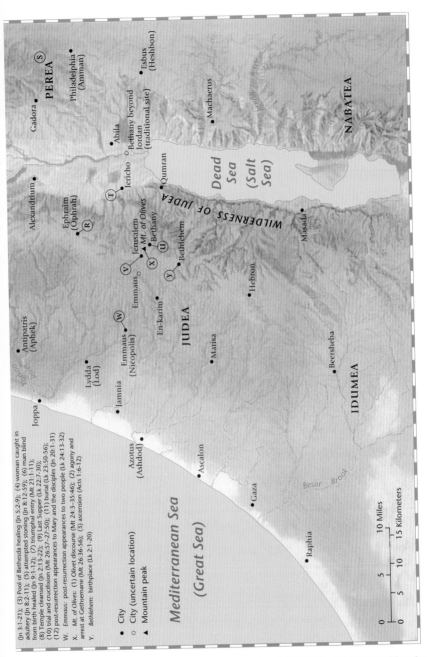

(Jn 3:1-21); (3) Pool of Bethesda healing (Jn 5:2-9); (4) woman caught in adultery (Jn 8:2-11); (5) attempted stoning (Jn 8:12-59); (6) man blind from birth healed (Jn 9:1-12); (7) triumphal entry (Mt 21:1-11); (8) Temple cleansed (Jn 2:13-22); (9) Last Supper (Lk 22:7-30); (10) trial and crucifixion (Mt 26:57-27:50); (11) burial (Lk 23:50-56); (12) post-resurrection appearances to Mary and the disciples (Jn 20:1-31)

W. *Emmaus:* post-resurrection appearances to two people (Lk 24:13-32)

X. *Mt. of Olives:* (1) Olivet discourse (Mt 24:3-35:46); (2) agony and arrest at Gethsemane (Mt 26:36-56); (3) ascension (Acts 1:6-12)

Y. *Bethlehem:* birthplace (Lk 2:1-20)

- City
○ City (uncertain location)
▲ Mountain peak

Mediterranean Sea
(Great Sea)

PEREA

Gadora

Philadelphia (Amman)

Esbus (Heshbon)

Abila

Bethany beyond Jordan (traditional site)

Machaerus

Jericho

Qumran

Dead Sea (Salt Sea)

NABATEA

Alexandrium

Ephraim (Ophrah)

WILDERNESS OF JUDEA

Jerusalem

Mt. of Olives

Bethany

Bethlehem

Masada

Antipatris (Aphek)

Emmaus

En-karim

Hebron

JUDEA

Joppa

Lydda (Lod)

Jamnia

Emmaus (Nicopolis)

Marisa

Beersheba

Azotus (Ashdod)

Ascalon

Besor Brook

Gaza

IDUMEA

Raphia

10 Miles

15 Kilometers

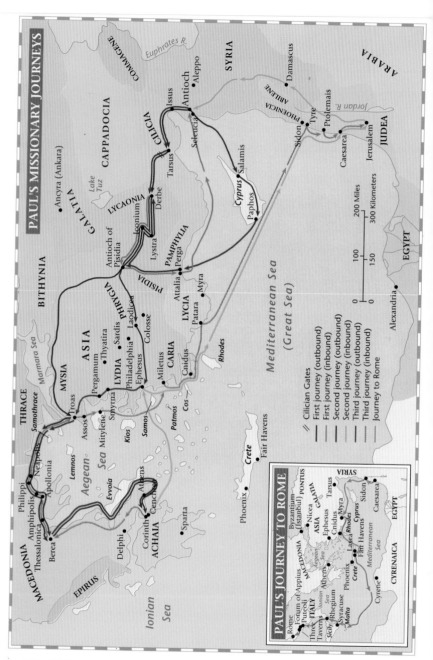

PAUL'S MISSIONARY JOURNEYS

COMMAGENE
Euphrates R.
SYRIA
Aleppo
Damascus
Antioch
Issus
ABILENE
CILICIA
Seleucia
ARABIA
Tarsus
CAPPADOCIA
Ancyra (Ankara)
Lake Tuz
GALATIA
Cyprus Salamis
PHOENICIA
Sidon
Tyre
Ptolemais
LYCAONIA
Derbe
Paphos
Caesarea
JUDEA
Jerusalem
Iconium
Antioch of Pisidia
Lystra
PAMPHYLIA
Perga
BITHYNIA
PISIDIA
Attalia
Myra
LYCIA
Patara
Jordan R.

Mediterranean Sea
(Great Sea)

Alexandria
EGYPT

0   100   200 Miles
0   150   300 Kilometers

MYSIA
Pergamum
Thyatira
ASIA
Sardis
PHRYGIA
LYDIA
Philadelphia
Laodicea
Colosse
Smyrna
Ephesus
CARIA
Miletus
Cnidus
Rhodes

THRACE
Samothrace
Troas
Assos
Mitylene
Kios
Patmos
Samos
Cos

Lemnos
Neapolis
Apollonia
Philippi
MACEDONIA
Amphipolis
Thessalonica
Berea
Aegean Sea
Evvoia
Athens
Corinth Cenchrea
ACHAIA
Sparta
Delphi
EPIRUS

Ionian Sea

Crete
Fair Havens
Phoenix

// Cilician Gates
— First journey (outbound)
— First journey (inbound)
— Second journey (outbound)
— Second journey (inbound)
— Third journey (outbound)
— Third journey (inbound)
— Journey to Rome

PAUL'S JOURNEY TO ROME

Rome
Forum of Appius
Three Taverns
Puteoli
ITALY
Rhegium
Sicily
Syracuse
Malta
Ionian Sea
Byzantium (Istanbul)
PONTUS
Nicea
GALATIA
MACEDONIA
ASIA
Tarsus
SYRIA
Athens
Ephesus
Cnidus
Rhodes
Cyprus
Sidon
Myra
Phoenix
Lasea Fair Havens
Crete
Caesarea
Mediterranean Sea
CYRENAICA
Cyrene
EGYPT

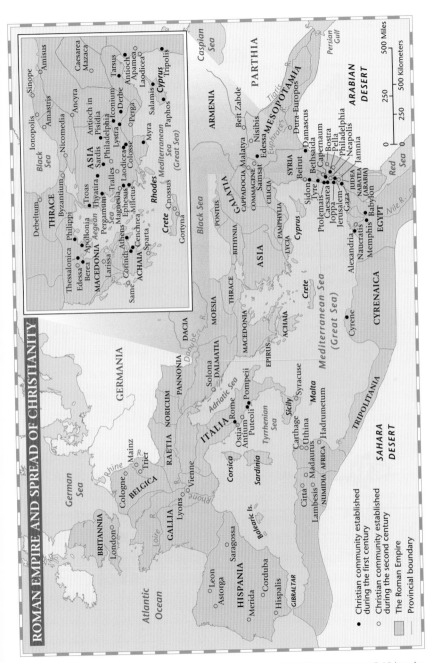

ROMAN EMPIRE AND SPREAD OF CHRISTIANITY

Legend:
- ● Christian community established during the first century
- ○ Christian community established during the second century
- The Roman Empire
- Provincial boundary

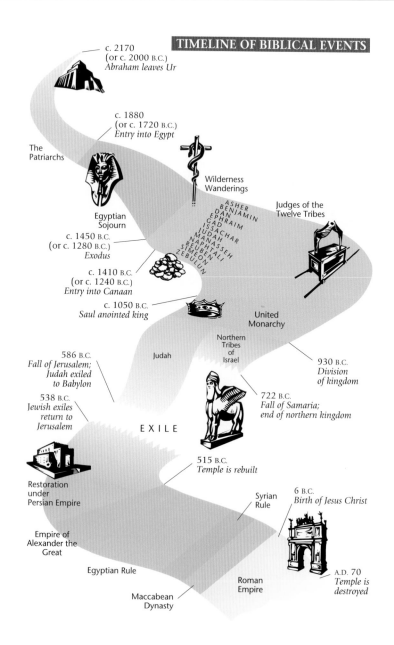

TIMELINE OF BIBLICAL EVENTS

c. 2170
(or c. 2000 B.C.)
Abraham leaves Ur

c. 1880
(or c. 1720 B.C.)
Entry into Egypt

The
Patriarchs

Wilderness
Wanderings

Judges of the
Twelve Tribes

Egyptian
Sojourn

c. 1450 B.C.
(or c. 1280 B.C.)
Exodus

ASHER
BENJAMIN
DAN
EPHRAIM
GAD
ISSACHAR
JUDAH
MANASSEH
NAPHTALI
REUBEN
SIMEON
ZEBULUN

c. 1410 B.C.
(or c. 1240 B.C.)
Entry into Canaan

c. 1050 B.C.
Saul anointed king

United
Monarchy

Northern
Tribes
of
Israel

586 B.C.
*Fall of Jerusalem;
Judah exiled
to Babylon*

Judah

930 B.C.
*Division
of kingdom*

538 B.C.
*Jewish exiles
return to
Jerusalem*

722 B.C.
*Fall of Samaria;
end of northern kingdom*

E X I L E

Restoration
under
Persian Empire

515 B.C.
Temple is rebuilt

Syrian
Rule

6 B.C.
Birth of Jesus Christ

Empire of
Alexander the
Great

Egyptian Rule

Roman
Empire

A.D. 70
*Temple is
destroyed*

Maccabean
Dynasty

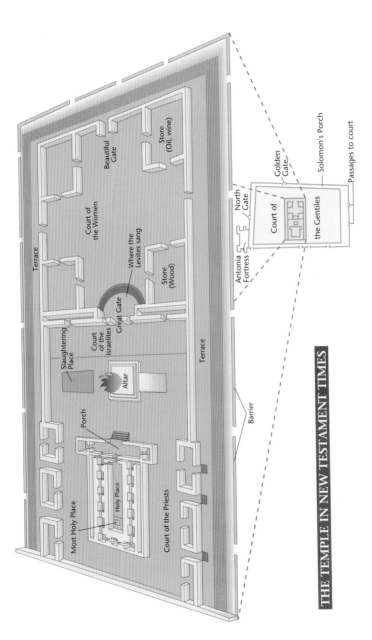

Most Holy Place

Porch

Holy Place

Court of the Priests

Slaughtering Place

Altar

Court of the Israelites

Great Gate

Where the Levites sang

Court of the Women

Beautiful Gate

Store (Oil, wine)

Store (Wood)

Terrace

Terrace

Barrier

Antonia Fortress

North Gate

Golden Gate

Solomon's Porch

Court of the Gentiles

Passages to court

Copyright © 1996 Tyndale House Publishers, Inc.

THE TEMPLE IN NEW TESTAMENT TIMES

ISRAEL AND THE MIDDLE EAST TODAY

ROMANIA Odessa UKRAINE
Bucharest
Sofia
BULGARIA
Istanbul
Black Sea
RUSSIA
KAZAKSTAN
UZBEKISTAN
GEORGIA
Caspian
Sea
AZERBAIJAN
GREECE
Ankara
ARMENIA
Mt. Ararat
Baku
TURKMENISTAN
Halys R.
Oxus R.
Izmir
(Smyrna)
TURKEY
Tabriz
Tehran
Maimana
AFGHANISTAN
Aleppo Mosul
CYPRUS SYRIA
LEBANON Beirut
Damascus
Baghdad
IRAN
PAKISTAN
Mediterranean
Sea
Jerusalem Amman
IRAQ
Alexandria
Cairo
JORDAN
Basra
Shiraz
SINAI
Kuwait
Bandar
Abbas
KUWAIT City
SAHARA
DESERT
Nile R.
EGYPT
SAUDI ARABIA
Persian Gulf
Doha QATAR
Arabian
Sea
Aswan
Red
Sea
Medina
Riyadh

SUDAN
Khartoum
ERITREA
0   200   400 Miles
0 200 400 600 Kilometers
ETHIOPIA

LEBANON Mt. Hermon
Tyre
Kiryat Shemona
SYRIA
GOLAN
HEIGHTS
Mediterranean
Sea
Acco Safed
Haifa Tiberias
Sea of Galilee
Megiddo Nazareth
Netanya
Jenin Beth-shan
Tulkarm
Nablus
Tel Aviv WEST BANK
Ramallah
Jerusalem
Jericho
Qumran
Gaza
Khan Yunis
Hebron
GAZA
STRIP Beersheba
En-gedi
Dead Sea
El-Arish
Dimona
ISRAEL
JORDAN
Mizpe Ramon
Petra
EGYPT
Jordan R.
Amman

SINAI
Eilat Red Sea

AL   SC
GA
FL
Atlantic
Ocean
Gulf of
Mexico

Note the comparative size of
Israel to the state of Florida